New Threats and Countermeasures in Digital Crime and Cyber Terrorism

Maurice Dawson
University of Missouri–St. Louis, USA

Marwan Omar
Nawroz University, Iraq

A volume in the Advances in Digital Crime,
Forensics, and Cyber Terrorism (ADCFCT) Book
Series

Managing Director:	Lindsay Johnston
Managing Editor:	Austin DeMarco
Director of Intellectual Property & Contracts:	Jan Travers
Acquisitions Editor:	Kayla Wolfe
Production Editor:	Christina Henning
Development Editor:	Brandon Carbaugh
Cover Design:	Jason Mull

Published in the United States of America by
Information Science Reference (an imprint of IGI Global)
701 E. Chocolate Avenue
Hershey PA, USA 17033
Tel: 717-533-8845
Fax: 717-533-8661
E-mail: cust@igi-global.com
Web site: http://www.igi-global.com

Library of Congress Cataloging-in-Publication Data

New threats and countermeasures in digital crime and cyber terrorism / Maurice Dawson and Marwan Omar, editors.
     pages cm
  Includes bibliographical references and index.
  ISBN 978-1-4666-8345-7 (hardcover) -- ISBN 978-1-4666-8346-4 (ebook) 1. Computer crimes--Prevention. 2. Cyberterrorism--Prevention. 3. Computer security. I. Dawson, Maurice, 1982- II. Omar, Marwan, 1982-
  HV6773.N4745 2015
  005.8--dc23
                               2015006753

This book is published in the IGI Global book series Advances in Digital Crime, Forensics, and Cyber Terrorism (ADCF-CT) (ISSN: 2327-0381; eISSN: 2327-0373)

British Cataloguing in Publication Data
A Cataloguing in Publication record for this book is available from the British Library.

For electronic access to this publication, please contact: eresources@igi-global.com.

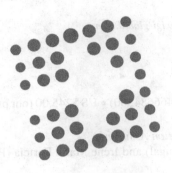

Advances in Digital Crime, Forensics, and Cyber Terrorism (ADCFCT) Book Series

ISSN: 2327-0381
EISSN: 2327-0373

MISSION

The digital revolution has allowed for greater global connectivity and has improved the way we share and present information. With this new ease of communication and access also come many new challenges and threats as cyber crime and digital perpetrators are constantly developing new ways to attack systems and gain access to private information.

The **Advances in Digital Crime, Forensics, and Cyber Terrorism (ADCFCT) Book Series** seeks to publish the latest research in diverse fields pertaining to crime, warfare, terrorism and forensics in the digital sphere. By advancing research available in these fields, the **ADCFCT** aims to present researchers, academicians, and students with the most current available knowledge and assist security and law enforcement professionals with a better understanding of the current tools, applications, and methodologies being implemented and discussed in the field.

COVERAGE

- Digital Surveillance
- Encryption
- Data Protection
- Information warfare
- Cyber warfare
- Telecommunications Fraud
- Identity Theft
- Database Forensics
- Global Threat Intelligence
- Malware

IGI Global is currently accepting manuscripts for publication within this series. To submit a proposal for a volume in this series, please contact our Acquisition Editors at Acquisitions@igi-global.com or visit: http://www.igi-global.com/publish/.

Titles in this Series

For a list of additional titles in this series, please visit: www.igi-global.com

Cybersecurity Policies and Strategies for Cyberwarfare Prevention
Jean-Loup Richet (University of Nantes, France)
Information Science Reference • copyright 2015 • 393pp • H/C (ISBN: 9781466684560) • US $245.00 (our price)

Handbook of Research on Digital Crime, Cyberspace Security, and Information Assurance
Maria Manuela Cruz-Cunha (Polytechnic Institute of Cavado and Ave, Portugal) and Irene Maria Portela (Polytechnic Institute of Cávado and Ave, Portugal)
Information Science Reference • copyright 2015 • 602pp • H/C (ISBN: 9781466663244) • US $385.00 (our price)

The Psychology of Cyber Crime Concepts and Principles
Gráinne Kirwan (Dun Laoghaire Institute of Art, Design and Technology, Ireland) and Andrew Power (Dun Laoghaire Institute of Art, Design and Technology, Ireland)
Information Science Reference • copyright 2012 • 372pp • H/C (ISBN: 9781613503508) • US $195.00 (our price)

Cyber Crime and the Victimization of Women Laws, Rights and Regulations
Debarati Halder (Centre for Cyber Victim Counselling (CCVC), India) and K. Jaishankar (Manonmaniam Sundaranar University, India)
Information Science Reference • copyright 2012 • 264pp • H/C (ISBN: 9781609608309) • US $195.00 (our price)

Digital Forensics for the Health Sciences Applications in Practice and Research
Andriani Daskalaki (Max Planck Institute for Molecular Genetics, Germany)
Medical Information Science Reference • copyright 2011 • 418pp • H/C (ISBN: 9781609604837) • US $245.00 (our price)

Cyber Security, Cyber Crime and Cyber Forensics Applications and Perspectives
Raghu Santanam (Arizona State University, USA) M. Sethumadhavan (Amrita University, India) and Mohit Virendra (Brocade Communications Systems, USA)
Information Science Reference • copyright 2011 • 296pp • H/C (ISBN: 9781609601232) • US $180.00 (our price)

Handbook of Research on Computational Forensics, Digital Crime, and Investigation Methods and Solutions
Chang-Tsun Li (University of Warwick, UK)
Information Science Reference • copyright 2010 • 620pp • H/C (ISBN: 9781605668369) • US $295.00 (our price)

Homeland Security Preparedness and Information Systems Strategies for Managing Public Policy
Christopher G. Reddick (University of Texas at San Antonio, USA)
Information Science Reference • copyright 2010 • 274pp • H/C (ISBN: 9781605668345) • US $180.00 (our price)

www.igi-global.com

701 E. Chocolate Ave., Hershey, PA 17033
Order online at www.igi-global.com or call 717-533-8845 x100
To place a standing order for titles released in this series, contact: cust@igi-global.com
Mon-Fri 8:00 am - 5:00 pm (est) or fax 24 hours a day 717-533-8661

Editorial Advisory Board

Table of Contents

Detailed Table of Contents

Cyber security is becoming the cornerstone of national security policies in many countries around the world as it is an interest to many stakeholders, including utilities, regulators, energy markets, government entities, and even those that wish to exploit the cyber infrastructure. Cyber warfare is quickly becoming the method of warfare and the tool of military strategists. Additionally, it is has become a tool for governments to aid or exploit for their own personal benefits. For cyber terrorists there has been an overwhelmingly abundance of new tools and technologies available that have allowed criminal acts to occur virtually anywhere in the world. This chapter discusses emerging laws, policies, processes, and tools that are changing the landscape of cyber security. This chapter provides an overview of the research to follow which will provide an in depth review of mobile security, mobile networks, insider threats, and various special topics in cyber security.

Mobile devices are becoming a method to provide an efficient and convenient way to access, find and share information; however, the availability of this information has caused an increase in cyber attacks. Currently, cyber threats range from Trojans and viruses to botnets and toolkits. Presently, 96% of mobile devices do not have pre-installed security software while approximately 65% of the vulnerabilities are found within the application layer. This lack in security and policy driven systems is an opportunity for malicious cyber attackers to hack into the various popular devices. Traditional security software found in desktop computing platforms, such as firewalls, antivirus, and encryption, is widely used by the general public in mobile devices. Moreover, mobile devices are even more vulnerable than personal desktop computers because more people are using mobile devices to do personal tasks. This review attempts to display the importance of developing a national security policy created for mobile devices in order to protect sensitive and confidential data.

Chapter 3

Lukáš Aron, Brno University of Technology, Czech Republic

This chapter contains basic introduction into security models of modern operating system like Android, iOS or Windows Phone. There are described the methods of attacks to the mobile devices. Such attacks consist of application based threats and vulnerabilities, network based attacks and internet browser vulnerabilities. The following section contains description of defensive strategies and steps for securing the device. There is also section about securing mobile device for enterprise environment. At the end of this chapter are discussed recommendations for security practices for mobile devices.

Chapter 4

Rasha Salah El-Din, University of York, UK
Paul Cairns, University of York, UK
John Clark, University of York, UK

Phishing is the use of electronic media, like emails and mobile text messages, to fraudulently elicit private information or obtain money under false pretence. Though there is considerable interest in phishing as a security problem, there is little previous research from the human factors perspective and in particular very little empirical support for what makes mobile phishing effective or successful and therefore how best to defend people from it. This chapter describes some of the research conducted from the field of traditional phishing that already embraces the effect of human factors on phishing vulnerability. The limited amount of research exploiting mobile phishing is discussed; including a review of our previous work involving evaluating mobile users' strategies for managing mobile phishing attacks. By reflecting on how these subjects investigate the threat of phishing, this chapter aims to show that empirical research on mobile phishing is scarce and falling behind in terms of identifying underlying psychological processes and inspire future research in this area.

Chapter 5

Arif Sari, European University of Lefke, Cyprus

The purpose of this chapter is to investigate and expose methods and techniques developed to provide security in wireless ad hoc networks. Researchers have proposed variety of solutions for security problems of Wireless Mobile Ad-Hoc Networks (MANET) against Distributed Denial of Service (DDoS) attacks. Due to the wireless nature of the channels and specific characteristics of MANETs, the attacks cannot be defeated through conventional security mechanisms. An adversary can easily override its medium access control protocol (MAC) and continually transfer packages on the network channel and the access point node(s) cannot assign authorization access to shared medium. These attacks cause a significant decrease on overall network throughput, packet transmission rates and delay in the MAC layer since other nodes back-off from the communication. In this chapter the proposed methods are applied for preventing and mitigating different wireless ad hoc network attacks are investigated and effectiveness and efficiency of these mechanisms are exposed.

Chapter 6

Privacy and security are two items being woven into the fabric of American law concerning mobile devices. This chapter will review and analyze the associated laws and policies that are currently in place or have been proposed to ensure proper execution of security measures for mobile and other devices while still protecting individual privacy. This chapter will address the fact that as the American society significantly uses mobile devices, it is imperative to understand the legal actions surrounding these technologies to include their associated uses. This chapter will also address the fact that with 9/11 in the not so distant past, cyber security has become a forefront subject in the battle against global terrorism. Furthermore, this chapter will examine how mobile devices are not like the devices of the past as the computing power is on par with that of some desktops and the fact that these devices have the ability to execute malicious applications. In addition, this chapter will discuss the reality, significance, legal and practical affects of the fact that suspicious programs are being executed offensively and security based attacks can be performed as well with the use of programs such as Kali Linux running on Android.

Smartphone Malware continues to be a serious threat in today's world. Recent research studies investigate the impacts of new malware variant. Historically traditional anti-malware analyses rely on the signatures of predefined malware samples. However, this technique is not resistant against the obfuscation techniques (e.g. polymorphic and metamorphic). While the permission system proposed by Google, requires smartphone users to pay attention to the permission description during the installation time. Nevertheless, normal users cannot comprehend the semantics of Android permissions. This chapter surveys various approaches used in Smartphone malware detection and Investigates weaknesses of existing countermeasures such as signature-based and anomaly-based detection.

In a collaborative environment such as MANET, nodes reliability evaluation is vital. Trust Management can be used to ensure such healthy collaboration it offers a formal and unified framework for trust specification and interpretation. Establishing trustworthy relationships is generally done by maintaining a reputation for each node computed based on direct observations or neighbors' observations exchanged using recommendations. Unfortunately, for malicious reason, such method may be faked by cheaters: several nodes collude in order to rate each other with the maximum value and decrease other nodes' reputations by giving negative recommendations. The main contribution of this chapter is then, the proposition of a trust based environment for MANET and securing it against collusion attack in order to enhance the network QoS. This is achieved using three steps: (1) the definition of a formal trust based environment (2) the addition of a process handling collusion attack and (3) the extension of the whole proposition by a delegation process allowing nodes functionalities sharing.

Chapter 9

Malicious insiders are posing unique security challenges to organizations due to their knowledge, capabilities, and authorized access to information systems. Data theft and IT sabotage are two of the most recurring themes among crimes committed by malicious insiders. This paper aims to investigate the scale and scope of malicious insider risks and explore the impact of such threats on business operations. Organizations need to implement a multi layered defensive approaches to combat insider risks; safeguarding sensitive business information from malicious insiders require firstly, an effective security policy that communicates consequences of stealing or leaking confidential information in an unauthorized manner. Secondly, logging and monitoring employee activity is essential in detecting and controlling system vulnerabilities to malicious insiders. Thirdly, conducting periodic and consistent insider vulnerability assessments is critical to identifying any gaps in security controls and preventing insiders from exploiting them. And lastly, but certainly not least, taking extra caution with privileged users is important to proactively protecting information infrastructure from insider risks.

Chapter 10

Authorship Analysis is the process of examining documents to determine the stylistic details underlying the document and hence inferring about the characteristics of the author of document in order to attribute the authorship to a particular author or to confirm the authenticity of a claimed authorship. The popularity of online communications has paved way to the promotion of numerous fraudulent acts. These illegal activities can be curbed to an extent by identifying the source of the postings, which is made possible by finding the real authors of online documents.Applicability of authorship analysis in the field of forensic linguistics also gathers great importance today. The automation of, process aimed at analyzing the authorship of forensic documents, eases the linguists of the high manual effort spent in analyzing documents and is also advantageous in terms of its accuracy. Here we discuss about the existing methods that have been used so far to deal with automation of authorship analysis and the challenges faced by them.

Chapter 11

Since time immemorial, the legal systems of Great Britain have often been spoken of highly as pinnacles of democracy. However, the split between criminal law and tort law have often caused problems where the police has often focused on the prosecution of people in poverty and where only the wealthy can afford to use the system. This chapter discusses the extent and limitations of existing measures to tackle computer-related crime, particularly with regards to the abusive kind of Internet Trolling, namely "flame trolling." The chapter recommends further research to establish whether it should be the case that in a society based on dualism that criminal and civil cases should be held at the same time, and that in both instances those being accused of an offence or tort should be allowed to bring a counter-claim. It is discussed that in such a system the cases that would be brought are where there is a clear victim who had no part in the offence against them, such as murder, rape, theft and burglary, which are usually carefully planned and orchestrated acts.

Chapter 12
    Ria Perkins, Aston University, UK

This chapter introduces Native Language Identification (NLID) and considers the casework applications with regard to authorship analysis of online material. It presents findings from research identifying which linguistic features were the best indicators of native (L1) Persian speakers blogging in English, and analyses how these features cope at distinguishing between native influences from languages that are linguistically and culturally related. The first chapter section outlines the area of Native Language Identification, and demonstrates its potential for application through a discussion of relevant case history. The next section discusses a development of methodology for identifying influence from L1 Persian in an anonymous blog author, and presents findings. The third part discusses the application of these features to casework situations as well as how the features identified can form an easily applicable model and demonstrates the application of this to casework. The research presented in this chapter can be considered a case study for the wider potential application of NLID.

Chapter 13
    Darrell Norman Burrell, Florida Institute of Technology, USA
    Darryl Williams, Walden University, USA
    Taara Bhat, George Mason University, USA
    Clishia Taylor, National Graduate School of Quality Management, USA

According to the Ponemon (2012) Third Annual Benchmark Study on Patient Privacy & Data Security, 94 percent of healthcare organizations surveyed suffered at least one data breach; 45 percent experienced more than five in the past two years. Data breaches cost the U.S. healthcare industry an average of $7 billion annually (Ponemon, 2012). Electronic health records are becoming more pervasive at hospitals and clinics in the United States. Meanwhile, healthcare organizations are taking small steps toward meaningful exchange and secure data security of patient information. This has created a need for new expertise in health data security from a newly degreed and young in information security professionals from the "Millennial Generation". This chapter explores the attraction, recruitment, and retention of younger-generation professionals with critical and emerging health information security skills.

Sharon L. Burton, American Meridian University, USA
Rondalynne McClintock, Claremont Graduate University, USA
Darrell N. Burrell, Florida Institute of Technology, USA
Kim L. Brown-Jackson, National Graduate School of Quality Management, USA
Dustin Bessette, National Graduate School of Quality Management, USA
Shanel Lu, National Graduate School of Quality Management, USA

Learning management systems (LMSs) are significant in offering highly collaborative, widely accessible, and manageable learning solutions. It is feasible that learning solutions stakeholders pursue an in-depth understanding of the LMS and the vulnerabilities surrounding technology-enabled learning and teaching. The over 300 types of active LMSs, proprietary or open source, are not off limits to hackers. Past research shows that hackers compromise technology systems to ascertain personal identifiable information and interfere with the integrities of post-secondary institutions. Stakeholders must understand how to safeguard the LMS. To address LMS cybercrime concerns, this text reviews vulnerability information on over 12 LMS features. After reading this text, stakeholders will gain increased insight into their works to thwart security related LMS incidents. This text can support stakeholders' knowledge in actions to take prior to the LMS reaching unacceptable vulnerability levels. Researchers and practitioners will benefit from this text's perspective on the LMS and mitigating risk.

Darrell Norman Burrell, Florida Institute of Technology, USA
Aikyna Finch, Strayer University, USA
Janet Simmons, The National Graduate School of Quality Management, USA
Sharon L. Burton, Florida Institute of Technology, USA

This text is an on-going study to provide current information regarding developing underrepresented student populations through STEM specific Charter schools to fulfill pipeline shortages. Current findings show that African Americans are underrepresented in high paying Science, Technology, Engineering, and Mathematics (STEM) fields, especially in cybersecurity. The U.S. pipeline of minority students studying STEM falls short in producing the next generation of cybersecurity professionals; thus, a salient need exists to design, pilot, and test a program to grow the minority student pipeline in the cybersecurity field. The charter school movement is one of the fastest growing education reforms with the ability to make a dramatic impact in the U.S. and internationally. Because charter schools often organize around a mission, theme, or curricular and enjoy freedoms, in organizational structure, mission, and academic program, with all held to high standards, this text proposes cybersecurity charter schools to fill technology voids. This organizational structure, mission, and academic programming, will enable students to become immersed in hands-on, real world applications allowing for experiential learning, which can develop students with cybersecurity expertise, technical knowledge, and skills, and competencies needed to take and pass cybersecurity and information security related certification assessments.

Chapter 16

Dustin Bessette, National Graduate School of Quality Management, USA
Jane A. LeClair, National Cybersecurity Institute at Excelsior College, USA
Randall E. Sylvertooth, National Cybersecurity Institute at Excelsior College, USA
Sharon L. Burton, Florida Institute of Technology, USA

As a region that is rapidly developing its technology base, Sub-Saharan Africa is experiencing many of the issues associated with the benefits of cyber technology as well as its many negative sides. This paper discusses mobile and internet technologies currently being utilized in Sub-Saharan Africa as well as some of the major cybersecurity concerns threatening networks in the region that are associated with the new economic growth on the African continent. Such topics will include a viable increased awareness of news, historical events, and recent gatherings of information on this main topic.

Foreword

Further, North Korea's attack on SPE [Sony Pictures Entertainment] reaffirms that cyber threats pose one of the gravest national security dangers to the United States, the FBI said. Though the FBI has seen a wide variety and increasing number of cyber intrusions, the destructive nature of this attack, coupled with its coercive nature, sets it apart. – https://krebsonsecurity.com/2014/12/fbi-north-korea-to-blame-for-sony-hack/

The research and insights contained within this text could not be more timely or important at a time where the U.S. has seen one of its most brazen cyber attacks in recent history. It has now been proven that terrorist groups, Nation-States, and even individuals can hold major corporations hostage with nothing more than a cheap laptop, the wherewithal and an Internet connection. Cyber terrorism will continue to be one of the governments and law enforcements top priorities. More devices then ever are being connected to mobile networks, while more and more zero-day attacks and vulnerabilities are being designed, shared and made easily accessible to take advantage of vulnerabilities in these networks. The black market is now a vast and complex set of anonymous nodes, servers, and front-end store fronts where attacks, code, stolen information, and everything illegal in-between is being exchanged. Hidden in the deep Internet, goods and services are traded, sold, and purchased with nearly untraceable currency with the advent of Bitcoin. Newly developed malware that could be used to bring down major infrastructure (i.e. Stuxnet) is being traded for freshly stolen Amazon credentials and lifted credit cards as the ink dries on these very pages. Without major cyber security research and innovation, a major cyber attack equivalent to 9/11 is all but inevitable.

The authors' ability to provide new concepts and techniques that can be shared with academia, industry, governments and corporations will enhance cyber security programs and processes as well as lead to innovation in the cyber security field. As data continues to exponentially grow and become one of the most valued commodities of the 21st century, the information contained within these chapters are of utmost value as we continue to attempt to defend and protect our data. All chapters were subjected to a rigorous peer-review process. The first section of the book tackles security in mobile computing. Some of the topics covered include mobile phishing, wireless and ad-hoc networks, privacy, and Smartphone malware. The second portion of the book covers cyber security techniques and cases. Highlights from these chapters include Smartphone malware analysis techniques, and QoS enhancement in mobile ad-hoc networks. The third and final section of the book discusses leadership, communication, and education in cyber security. Topics from this chapter range from learning management systems security, the innovation and promise of STEM oriented cyber security education, and insider threats.

Providing the process for the communication and dissemination of the data within these chapters is vital to the security of every network. The internationally recognized experts, authors and editors have compiled an impressive and comprehensive set of cyber security topics and information on the most important subject of our time.

America's economic prosperity, national security, and our individual liberties depend on our commitment to securing cyberspace and maintaining an open, interoperable, secure, and reliable Internet. Our critical infrastructure continues to be at risk from threats in cyberspace, and our economy is harmed by the theft of our intellectual property. Although the threats are serious and they constantly evolve, I believe that if we address them effectively, we can ensure that the Internet remains an engine for economic growth and a platform for the free exchange of ideas. – President Obama – http://www.whitehouse.gov/issues/foreign-policy/cybersecurity

Ronnie S. Kurlander
Global Technology Solutions, USA & T. Rowe Price, USA

Preface

This book explores multiple aspects of cyber terrorism and cyber crime in today's society. This book provides insights on the negatives uses of technology with comprehensive review of the associated vulnerabilities and mitigations. In the recent events of cyber warfare most notable are the Flame computer virus, expansion of the National Security Agency (NSA) monitoring programs, and suspected attack on Sony for a movie poking fun at North Korea. As governments scramble for cyber security resources whether technological or people it evident that cyber security is the new war being fought.

Our intention in editing this book was to provide new concepts and techniques that are deployed in secure computing, mobile computing, training, and laws. This book is to provide frontier research to include cases that are applicable to modern events. Since the book covers case study-based research findings, it can be quite relevant researchers, university academics, secure computing professionals, and probing university students. In addition, it will help those researchers who have interest in this field to keep insight into different concepts and their importance for applications in real life. This has been done to make the edited book more flexible and to stimulate further interest in topics.

This book is comprised of three sections.

1. Security in Mobile Computing
2. Cyber Security Techniques and Cases
3. Leadership, Communication, and Education in Cyber Security.

ORGANIZATION OF THIS BOOK

In this book, we present 16 chapters aimed at emphasizing threat and countermeasures that are applicable in today's society. For coherency, we have ordered the chapters in terms of similarity of topic. The topic covered range from threats in mobile devices to developing leaders in cyber security.

Chapter 1, "A Brief Review of New Threats and Countermeasures in Digital Crime and Cyber Terrorism", presents the some of the concepts contained within the book. Further discussed are emerging laws, policies, processes, and tools that are changing the landscape of cyber security. This chapter provides an overview of the research to follow which will provide an in depth review of mobile security, mobile networks, insider threats, and various special topics in cyber security.

Chapter 2, " Mobile Devices: The Case for Cyber Security Hardened Systems", discusses how mobile devices are the preferred device for web browsing, emailing, using social media and making purchases. Due to their size, mobile devices are easily carried in people's pockets, purses or briefcases. Unfortunately, the popularity of mobile devices is a breeding ground for cyber attackers. Operating systems on mobile devices do not contain security software to protect data.

Chapter 3, " Security Threats on Mobile Devices", contains basic introduction into security models of modern operating system like Android, iOS or Windows Phone. There are described the methods of attacks to the mobile devices. Such attacks consist of application based threats and vulnerabilities, network based attacks and internet browser vulnerabilities. Another section in this chapters contains a description of defensive strategies and steps for securing the device. There is also section about securing mobile device for enterprise environment.

Chapter 4, "The Human Factors in Mobile Phishing", presents the use of electronic media, like emails and mobile text messages, to fraudulently elicit private information or obtain money under false pretence.

Chapter 5, " Security Issues in Mobile Wireless Ad Hoc Networks: A Comparative Survey of Methods and Techniques to Provide Security in Wireless Ad Networks", investigates and exposes methods and techniques developed to provide security in wireless ad hoc networks. are investigated and effectiveness and efficiency of these mechanisms are exposed.

Chapter 6, "Legal Issues: Security and Privacy with Mobile Devices", raises the issues of privacy and security being woven into the fabric of American law concerning mobile devices. It is essential to fully understand associated laws and policies to ensure proper execution while upholding the law. As the American society significantly uses mobile devices it is imperative to understand the legal actions surrounding these technologies to include their associated uses. With 9/11 in the not so distant past, cyber security has become a forefront subject in the battle against global terrorism. Mobile devices are not like the devices of the past as the computing power is on par with that of some desktops to include these devices have the ability to execute malicious applications.

Chapter 7, "Survey in Smartphone Malware Analysis Techniques", surveys various approaches used in Mobile malware detection and Investigates weaknesses of existing countermeasures such as signature-based and anomaly-based detection.

Chapter 8, "Trust Management in Mobile Ad hoc Networks for QoS Enhancing", is the proposition of a trust based environment for MANET and securing it against collusion attack in order to enhance the network QoS. This is achieved using three steps: (1) the definition of a formal trust based environment (2) the addition of a process handling collusion attack and (3) the extension of the whole proposition by a delegation process allowing nodes functionalities sharing.

Chapter 9, "Insider Threats: Detecting and Controlling Malicious Insiders", presents how malicious insiders are posing unique security challenges to organizations due to their knowledge, capabilities, and authorized access to information systems. This chapter investigates the scale and scope of malicious insider risks and explore the impact of such threats on business operations.

Chapter 10, "Authorship Analysis: Techniques and Challenges", discussed the process of examining documents to determine the stylistic details underlying the document and hence inferring about the characteristics of the author of document in order to attribute the authorship to a particular author or to confirm the authenticity of a claimed authorship. The authors discuss the existing methods that have been used so far to deal with automation of authorship analysis and the challenges faced by them

Chapter 11, "The Need for a Dualist Application of Public and Private Law in Great Britain Following the Use of "Flame Trolling" During the 2011 UK Riots: A Review and Model", recommends further research to establish whether it should be the case that in a society based on dualism that criminal and civil cases should be held at the same time, and that in both instances those being accused of an offence or tort should be allowed to bring a counter-claim. It is discussed that in such a system the cases that would be brought are where there is a clear victim who had no part in the offence against them, such as murder, rape, theft and burglary, which are usually carefully planned and orchestrated acts.

Chapter 12, "Native Language Identification (NLID) for Forensic Authorship Analysis of Weblogs", presents introduces NLID and considers the casework applications with regard to authorship analysis of online material. It presents findings from research identifying which linguistic features were the best indicators of native (L1) Persian speakers blogging in English, and analyses how these features cope at distinguishing between native influences from languages that are linguistically and culturally related.

Chapter 13, "Leadership Approaches for Managing Healthcare Information Security Millennial Employees: Health Information Security Leadership Approaches", presents

Chapter 14 "Learning Management Systems: Understand and Secure Your Educational Technology" presents background data concerning breaches and the lack of associated talent to support these cyber attacks. This chapters explores how to achieve this among millennial employees.

Chapter 15, "The Innovation and Promise of STEM Oriented Cyber Security Charter Schools in Urban Minority Communities: Cyber Terrorism Workforce Development", provides insight on how the US pipeline of minority students studying STEM falls short in producing the next generation of cybersecurity professionals.

Chapter 16, "Communication, Technology & Cyber Crime in Sub-Saharan African", discusses mobile and internet technologies currently being utilized in Sub-Saharan Africa as well as some of the major cybersecurity concerns threatening networks in the region that are associated with the new economic growth on the African continent. This is important as this region is rapidly developing its technology base. Sub-Saharan Africa is experiencing many of the issues associated with the benefits of cyber technology as well as its many negative sides.

Maurice Dawson
University of Missouri – St. Louis, USA

Marwan Omar
Nawroz University, Iraq

Chapter 1
A Brief Review of New Threats and Countermeasures in Digital Crime and Cyber Terrorism

Maurice Dawson
University of Missouri – St. Louis, USA

ABSTRACT

Cyber security is becoming the cornerstone of national security policies in many countries around the world as it is an interest to many stakeholders, including utilities, regulators, energy markets, government entities, and even those that wish to exploit the cyber infrastructure. Cyber warfare is quickly becoming the method of warfare and the tool of military strategists. Additionally, it is has become a tool for governments to aid or exploit for their own personal benefits. For cyber terrorists there has been an overwhelmingly abundance of new tools and technologies available that have allowed criminal acts to occur virtually anywhere in the world. This chapter discusses emerging laws, policies, processes, and tools that are changing the landscape of cyber security. This chapter provides an overview of the research to follow which will provide an in depth review of mobile security, mobile networks, insider threats, and various special topics in cyber security.

INTRODUCTION

Cyber security has become an important subject of national, international, economic, and societal importance that affects multiple nations (Walker, 2012). Since the early 90s users have exploited vulnerabilities to gain unauthorized access to networks for malicious purposes. In recent years the number of attacks on United States (U.S.) networks has continued to grow at an exponential rate. This includes malicious embedded code, exploitation of backdoors, and more. These attacks can be initiated from anywhere in the world from behind a computer with a masked Internet Protocol (IP) address. This type of warfare, cyber warfare, changes the landscape of war itself (Beidleman, 2009). This type of warfare removes the need to have a physically capable military and requires the demand for a force that has a strong technical capacity e.g. computer science skills. The U.S. and other countries have come to understand that this is an issue and has developed policies to handle this in an effort to mitigate the threats (Dawson, Omar, & Abramson, 2015).

DOI: 10.4018/978-1-4666-8345-7.ch001

In Estonia and Georgia there were direct attacks on government cyber infrastructure (Beildleman, 2009). The attacks in Estonia rendered the government's digital infrastructure useless (Dawson, Omar, & Abramson, 2015). The government and other associated entities heavily relied upon this e-government infrastructure. These attacks help lead to the rapid development of cyber defense organizations throughout Europe which has raised the profile of cyber attacks to include awareness to the potential severity of attacks (Dawson, Omar, & Abramson, 2015).

MOBILE NETWORKS

Mobile networks are found in large cities in America to villages in West Africa. Thus the importance of security in mobile networking is essential to maintaining security and privacy for everyday citizens. Mobile devices have become the preferred device for web browsing, emailing, using social media and making purchases (Wright et al, 2012). Many individuals rely on their mobile devices for texting, checking email, making online purchases, and even remote controlling their home alarm system. Thus attackers have developed malware to specifically target these platforms. Understanding the Human Computer Interaction (HCI) and behavioral issues with mobile devices is a start in understanding human pitfalls in security.

DIGITAL CURRENCY

Digital currency has become a new commerce that is growly quickly and gaining the attention of large financial institutions. This crypto currency has been termed "memory" in monetary economics literature (Luther & Olson, 2013). Bitcoin is a peer to peer electronic cash system in which no one controls and there are not an associated printed currency(Nakamoto, 2008). Bitcoin allows for anonymity to occur in this peer to peer electronic currency systems (Reid & Harrigan, 2013). Some argue that the main benefits are lost if a trusted third party is necessary to prevent the action of double spending (Nakamoto, 2008). The technical infrastructure of this decentralized digital currency relies on several cryptographic technologies.

Luther and Olson state that the principle finding of the money and memory literature is that both devices are capable of facilitating exchange (Luther & Olson, 2013). What is missing from the literature is data concerning the use of Bitcoin for illicit activities. However some researchers attempt to assess potential damages and threats to national security, banking industry, child pornography, drug trade, financial fraud, and more. In relation to cyber warfare Bitcoin could pose as an enabler for plausible deniability of foreign governments and institutions for involvement in cyber attacks (Hilse, 2013). Further cyber criminals could store stolen digital funds on any device that can be used as storage (Hilse, 2013). This could pose a threat as laundered, stolen, or self generated funds can be taken anywhere on a storage device such as a micro Secure Digital (SD) that can hold up to 64 Giga Bytes (GB). This could pose an issue in terms of search and seizure of assets as many police forces have inadequate training and personnel to pull off such measures of cyber forensics on a large scale.

In recent year researchers tackle what they have coined the dark side of cyber finance (Bronk, Monk, & Villasenor, 2012). The key theme to take away is that government and industry will need to be able to react quickly and adapt as the criminals and terrorists to meet the threat (Bronk, Monk, & Villasenor, 2012). In a world where monetary funds are difficult to track down through foreign bank accounts digital currency has added yet another lawyer of difficult that allows illicit funds to hide in plain sight. Therefore the only limitations placed the criminals their imagination and skill of individuals who come up with new innovative ways to use technology.

CYBER ESPIONAGE AND SECRECY

Cyber espionage or cyber spying is yet another method of cyber warfare. This method allows for the ability to obtain secrets without the permission of the data owner. The rise in cyber espionage is yet another reason governments must improve cyber security infrastructure. Nakashima details that the U.S. was the target of a massive cyber espionage campaign (Nakashima, 2013). During the Obama Administration the U.S. expanded its cyber reach and infrastructure. However this expanded reach has received negative reviews due to Wikileaks and Edward Snowden.

WikiLeaks and FinSpy

WikiLeaks is an international, online, non profit, journalistic organization that has published classified and sensitive information. This organization claimed to have a database or more than 1 million documents archived from 2006-2010. The servers that were pointing to the website were being shut down on by one (Benkler, 2011). The site contains a sectioned labeled SpyFiles. This section on the site contains SpyFiles with 2 releases in 2011, 1 in 2013, and a release September 2014. The recent release provides insight on FinFisher which is a German company that produces and sells exploitation tools that can take data from multiple Operating Systems (OSs) such as OS X, WIndows, Linux, Android, iOS, Blackberry, Symbian, and WIndows Mobile devices. FinSpy appears to be a malicious trojan designed to intercept and record a variety of information from an infected computer and applications. This software application has been found in Ethiopia aimed at political dissidents (Hankey & Clunaigh, 2013). Even more alarming is that this malicious application has been found within the hands of 25 governments that have questionable records on human rights (Pelroth, 2013). The application has been used to spy own their own citizens. Even Egyptian government members had been given a proposal by the Gamma Group to purchase this Trojan. More troubling is how this application is running on multiple servers with little oversight.

Edward Snowden

Edward Snowden actions will have people regarding him as a patriot or traitor (Goldfarb et al., 2015). Snowden's leak displayed just how big the reach was of the Intelligence Community (IC) into the American public. Snowden's use of a Linux distribution, Tails, that was originally developed as a research project by the U.S. Navy Research Laboratory (NRL) displays the ability to evade detection.

Cyber Weapons: Stuxnet Worm and Flame Malware

During the fall of 2010 many headlines declared that Stuxnet was the game-changer in terms of cyber warfare (Denning, 2012). This malicious worm was complex and designed to target only a specific system. This worm had the ability to detect location, system type, and more. And this worm only attacked the system if it met specific parameters that were designed in the code. Stuxnet tampered directly with software in a programmable logic controller (PLC) that controlled the centrifuges at Natanz. This tampering ultimately caused a disruption in the Iranian nuclear program.

Flame was yet another highly sophisticated malicious program being used as a cyber weapon in various countries. This program was discovered by Kaspersky and it was the largest weapon to date uncovered of its type. Flame was designed to carry out espionage by stealing information about systems, stored files, contact data, and audio conversations (Munro, 2012). Flame conducted as series of attacks against Iran's oil industry. Attacking a nation's critical infrastructure and resources are military strategic tactics that have known been successfully conducted via thousands of line of code.

OPEN SOURCE INTELLIGENCE (OSINT) AND OPEN SOURCE SOFTWARE (OSS)

Open Source Intelligence (OSINT), which is one of several sub-intelligence collection disciplines, is intelligence collected from publicly available sources. Publicly available sources can be but are not limited to newspapers, magazines, industry newsletters, online forums, social media, and web queries. OSINT is the opposite of what is known to many as covert intelligence or intelligence gathered through classified means. However OSINT does not mean the information in the publicly available domain does not have a classified value. It only means that we all have access to it but the associated labels of combined information still remains secret or tied to another unknown data classification per the associated agency.

Open Source Software (OSS) can be defined as software that is made available in source code form. This is important as this source code may fall under the General Public License (GPL) which is a widely used free software license that is managed under the GNU Not Linux (GNU) Project (Dawson et al, 2014). There are currently thousands of active projects on sites such as SourceForge that provide access to innovative tools that make OSINT techniques relatively painless. Chinese and Australian researchers have reviewed the many OSS applications available for data mining and published an extensive review discussing findings (Chen, et al, 2007). These researchers note issues such as usability, maintainability, and stability as an issue (Chen et al, 2007). However OSS applications such as the R programming language, also identified as GNU S, has become one of the most powerful tools among statisticians in industry and academia. Table 1 below provides a review of power software applications that can be used in a variation of cyber related activities.

LAWS AND POLICIES TO COMBAT TERRORISM

The events of 9/11 not only changed policies with the U.S. but also policies with other countries in how they treat and combat terrorism. The United Nations (U.N.) altered Article 51 of the U.N. charter. This article allows members of the U.N. to take necessary measures to protect themselves against an armed attack to ensure international peace and security. However this article raises important issues under international law regarding the use of force (Murphy, 2002). The United Kingdom (U.K.) has the Prevention of Terrorism Act 2005 and the Counter-Terrorism Act 2008 which was issued by Parliament. The first act was created to detain individuals who were suspected in acts of terrorism. This act was intended to replace the Anti-terrorism, Crime and Security Act 200 I as it was deemed unlawful. These acts seem to mirror the same ones, created in the U.S., to monitor potential terrorists and terrorists. The U.K. also shared their information with the U.S. for coordinating individual that may be of risk.

Table 1. BI and OSS tools

Software Application	Description and Potential Use
Python Programming Language	Python is a general purpose, high level programming language that allows developers to write programs in fewer lines. Python has a community based development model which includes almost of all its alternative implementations. In the cyber security community this language is used extensively and especially in tasks of exploitation.
Ruby Programming Language	Ruby is a cross platform language that is licensed by Ruby, GPLv2, and BSD license. This language was developed to match behaviors familiar from other languages.
R Programming Language	R is a free software programming language and environment for statistical computing and graphics. R is powerful and feeds multiple statistical Graphical User Interfaces (GUIs). This language uses a command line interface.
R Studio	RStudio is an open source and enterprise software application for the R statistical computing environment. This application is available for Mac, Windows, and multiple Linux distributions regardless of package manager.
RKward	RKward is an open source GUI and Integrated Development Environment (IDE) for the R statistical computing environment. RKward was originally designed for the K Desktop Environment (KDE) but is found operating in multiple environments.
KaliLinux	Described as the rebirth of BackTrack Linux, this is a Debian Linux distribution for digital forensics, penetration testing, and offensive security. This OS contains many preinstalled programs such as port scanners, packet analyzers, password crackers, and tools to escalate privileges.
Tails	Tails, a Debian Linux based distribution, was originally developed as a research project by the U.S. Navy Research Laboratory (NRL) displays the ability to evade detection. This OS is aimed at preserving privacy and anonymity.It can be booted as a liveUSB or LiveDVD leaving no digital footprint.
RapidMiner	RapidMiner is a program that supports all steps for data mining, text mining, and business analytics.

In the U.S., the methods for national security were enhanced to ensure no threats occur on U.S. soil. These changes include enhanced security in all ports of entry. The signing of the Homeland Security Act of 2002 (HS Act) (Public Law 07-296) created an organization that received funding and lots of resources for monitoring the security posture of this country. Additional changes include enhanced monitoring of citizens and residents within the country to prevent terrorist activities by the mention of keywords e.g. bomb, terrorism, explosive, or Al Qaeda. The USA Patriot was signed into law by President George W. Bush in 2001 after September 11, 2001 (Bullock, Haddow, Coppola, & Yeletaysi, 2009). This act was created in response to the event of 9/11 which provided government agencies increased abilities. These increased abilities provided the government rights to search various communications such as email, telephone records, medical records, and more of those who were thoughts of terrorist acts (Bullock, Haddow, Coppola, & Yeletaysi, 2009). This allowed law enforcement to have the upper hand in being proactive to stopping potential acts against U.S. soil. In the 2011 year, President Obama signed an extension on the USA Patriot Act. This act has received criticism from the public due to the potential to be misused or abused by those in power. This act has allowed government agencies to impede on constitutional rights. The Protecting Cyberspace as a National Asset Act of 2010 was an act that also amends Title 11 of the Homeland Security Act of 2002. This act enhanced security and resiliency of the cyber and communication infrastructure within the U.S. This act is important as the President declared that any cyber aggressions would be considered an act of war. This is also important as Estonia's entire digital infrastructure was taken down by hackers who supported the former Soviet rule. This type of attack could be damaging to the infrastructure in the U.S. causing loss of power for days or more which could result in death.

REFERENCES

Benkler, Y. (2011). Free Irresponsible Press: Wikileaks and the Battle over the Soul of the Networked Fourth Estate. *Harvard Civil Rights-Civil Liberties Law Review*, *46*, 311.

Bronk, C., Monk, C., & Villasenor, J. (2012). The Dark Side of Cyber Finance. *Survival*, *54*(2), 129–142. doi:10.1080/00396338.2012.672794

Bullock, J., Haddow, G., Coppola, D., & Yeletaysi, S. (2009). *Introduction to homeland security: Principles of all-hazards response* (3rd ed.). Burlington, MA: Elsevier Inc.

Chen, X., Ye, Y., Williams, G., & Xu, X. (2007). A survey of open source data mining systems. In *Emerging Technologies in Knowledge Discovery and Data Mining* (pp. 3–14). Springer Berlin Heidelberg. doi:10.1007/978-3-540-77018-3_2

Dawson, M., Al Saeed, I., Wright, J., & Onyegbula, F. (2014). Open Source Software to Enhance the STEM Learning Environment. In V. Wang (Ed.), *Handbook of Research on Education and Technology in a Changing Society* (pp. 569–580). Hershey, PA: Information Science Reference; doi:10.4018/978-1-4666-6046-5.ch042

Dawson, M., Omar, M., & Abramson, J. (2015). Understanding the Methods behind Cyber Terrorism. In M. Khosrow-Pour (Ed.), *Encyclopedia of Information Science and Technology* (3rd ed., pp. 1539–1549). Hershey, PA: Information Science Reference; doi:10.4018/978-1-4666-5888-2.ch147

Denning, D. E. (2012). Stuxnet: What has changed? *Future Internet*, *4*(3), 672–687. doi:10.3390/fi4030672

Goldfarb, R., Wasserman, E., Cole, D., Carter, H., Blanton, T., Mills, J., & Siegel, B. (2015). *After Snowden: Privacy, Secrecy, and Security in the Information Age*. Macmillan.

Hankey, S., & Clunaigh, D. Ó. (2013). Rethinking Risk and Security of Human Rights Defenders in the Digital Age. *Journal of Human Rights Practice*, *5*(3), 535–547. doi:10.1093/jhuman/hut023

Harris, S., & Meyers, M. (2002). *CISSP*. McGraw-Hill/Osborne.

Hilse, L. (2013). *Threat-Assessment: Bitcoin: Danger to the United States' National Security and her Economic & Commercial Interests*. Lars Hilse.

Janczewski, L., & Colarik, A. (2007). *Cyber Warfare and Cyber Terrorism*. Hershey, PA: IGI Global; doi:10.4018/978-1-59140-991-5

Luther, W. J., & Olson, J. (2013). *Bitcoin is Memory*. Available at SSRN 2275730.

Munro, K. (2012). Deconstructing Flame: The limitations of traditional defences. *Computer Fraud & Security*, *2012*(10), 8–11. doi:10.1016/S1361-3723(12)70102-1

Murphy, S. D. (2002). Terrorism and the Concept of Armed Attack in Article 51 of the UN Charter. *Harvard International Law Journal*, *43*, 41.

Nakamoto, S. (2008). Bitcoin: A peer-to-peer electronic cash system. *Consulted*, *1*(2012), 28.

Nakashima, E. (2013). US Target of Massive Cyber-Espionage Campaign. *Washington Post*.

Perloth, N. (2013). Researchers Find 25 Countries Using Surveillance Software. *New York Times*, Bits blog. 10 December. Retrieved from http://bits.blogs.nytimes.com/2013/03/13/researchers-find-25-countries-using-surveillance-software

Reid, F., & Harrigan, M. (2013). *An analysis of anonymity in the bitcoin system* (pp. 197–223). Springer New York. doi:10.1007/978-1-4614-4139-7_10

Wright, J., Dawson, M. E. Jr, & Omar, M. (2012). Cyber Security and Mobile Threats: The Need For Antivirus Applications For Smart Phones. *Journal of Information Systems Technology and Planning*, 5(14), 40–60.

KEY TERMS AND DEFINITIONS

Authentication: Security measure designed to establish the validity of a transmission, message, or originator, or a means of verifying an individual's authorization to receive specific categories of information (Harris, 2002).

Availability: Timely, reliable access to data and information services for authorized users (Harris, 2002).

Bitcoin: Bitcoin is a peer to peer electronic cash system that no one controls and there are not printed currency (Nakamoto, 2008).

Confidentiality: Assurance that information is not disclosed to unauthorized individuals, processes, or devices (Harris, 2002).

Cyber Terrorism: Attacks with the use of the Internet for terrorist activities, including acts of deliberate, large-scale disruption of computer networks, especially of personal computers attached to the Internet, by the means of tools such as computer viruses, worms, Trojans, and zombies (Janczewski & Colarik, 2008).

Integrity: Quality of an IS reflecting the logical correctness and reliability of the OS; the logical completeness of the hardware and software implementing the protection mechanisms; and the consistency of the data structures and occurrence of the stored data. Note that, in a formal security mode, integrity is interpreted more narrowly to mean protection against unauthorized modification or destruction of information (Harris, 2002).

Non-Repudiation: Assurance the sender of data is provided with proof of delivery and the recipient is provided with proof of the sender's identity, so neither can later deny having processed the data (Harris, 2002).

Open Source Intelligence: Intelligence collected from publicly available sources.

Chapter 2
Mobile Devices:
The Case for Cyber Security Hardened Systems

Maurice Dawson
University of Missouri – St. Louis, USA

Jorja Wright
Florida Institute of Technology, USA

Marwan Omar
Nawroz University, Iraq

ABSTRACT

Mobile devices are becoming a method to provide an efficient and convenient way to access, find and share information; however, the availability of this information has caused an increase in cyber attacks. Currently, cyber threats range from Trojans and viruses to botnets and toolkits. Presently, 96% of mobile devices do not have pre-installed security software while approximately 65% of the vulnerabilities are found within the application layer. This lack in security and policy driven systems is an opportunity for malicious cyber attackers to hack into the various popular devices. Traditional security software found in desktop computing platforms, such as firewalls, antivirus, and encryption, is widely used by the general public in mobile devices. Moreover, mobile devices are even more vulnerable than personal desktop computers because more people are using mobile devices to do personal tasks. This review attempts to display the importance of developing a national security policy created for mobile devices in order to protect sensitive and confidential data.

INTRODUCTION

Currently, mobile devices are the preferred device for web browsing, emailing, using social media and making purchases. Due to their size, mobile devices are easily carried in people's pockets, purses or briefcases. Unfortunately, the popularity of mobile devices is a breeding ground for cyber attackers. Operating systems on mobile devices do not contain security software to protect data. For example,

DOI: 10.4018/978-1-4666-8345-7.ch002

traditional security software found in personal computers (PCs), such as firewalls, antivirus, and encryption, is not currently available in mobile devices (Ruggiero, 2011). In addition to this, mobile phone operating systems are not frequently updated like their PC counterparts. Cyber attackers can use this gap in security to their advantage. An example of this gap in security is seen in the 2011 Valentine's Day attack. Cyber-attackers dispersed a mobile picture-sharing application that covertly sent premium-rate text messages from a user's mobile phone (Ruggiero, 2011). Thus, this example illustrates the importance of having a security policy for mobile phones.

Social Networking and Electronic Commerce (E-Commerce) Applications

Many people rely on their mobile devices to do numerous activities, like sending emails, storing contact information, passwords and other sensitive data. In addition to this, mobile devices are the device of choice when it comes to social networking; thus, mobile applications for social networking sites (Facebook, Twitter, Google+) are another loophole for cyber attackers to gain personal data from unsuspecting users (Ruggiero, 2011). Social networking sites are host to a surplus of personal data. That is why malicious applications that use social networking sites to steal data yield severe consequences. Recently, M-Commerce or "mobile e-commerce" has gained popularity in our society. Many smartphone users can now conduct monetary transactions, such as buying goods and applications (apps), redeeming coupons and tickets, banking and processing point-of-sale payments (Ruggiero, 2011). Again, all of these smartphone functions are convenient for the user but advantageous for malicious cyber attackers. Ultimately, there is a niche in technology for cyber security software that is specifically designed for the mobile operating system.

Hypothetical Consequences of Cyber Attacks on Smartphones

The consequences of a cyber attack on a smartphone can be just as detrimental, or even more detrimental than an attack on a PC. According to Patrick Traynor, a researcher and assistant professor at the Georgia Tech School of Computer Science, mobile apps rely on the browser to operate (Traynor, Ahamad, Alperovitch, Conti, & Davis, 2012). As a result of this, more Web-based attacks on mobile devices will increase throughout the year. Traynor also states that IT professionals, computer scientists and engineers still need to explore the variations between mobile and traditional desktop browsers to fully understand how to prevent cyber attacks (Traynor, Ahamad, Alperovitch, Conti, & Davis, 2012).

Challenges with a Mobile Browser

One cyber security challenge for mobile devices is the screen size. For example, web address bars (which appear once the user clicks on the browser app) disappear after a few seconds on a smartphone because of the small screen size (Traynor, Ahamad, Alperovitch, Conti, & Davis, 2012). This is usually the first-line of defense for cyber security. Checking the Uniform Resource Locator (URL) of a website is the first way users can insure that they are at a legitimate website. Moreover, SSL certificates for a website are usually more difficult to find on a mobile phone browser (Traynor, Ahamad, Alperovitch, Conti, & Davis, 2012). This adds another gap in security for mobile devices. Furthermore, the touch-screen attribute of mobile phones can be cause for concern when dealing with cyber attackers. Traynor states that the way elements are placed on a page and users' actions are all opportunities to implant an attack. An illustration of this is seen when an attacker creates an attractive display content (i.e. an advertisement for an app or a link to a social media app) in which the malicious link is carefully hidden underneath a legitimate image. Unfortunately, once the user clicks the image they can be redirected to the malicious content via the link (Traynor, Ahamad, Alperovitch, Conti, & Davis, 2012).

Common Mobile Device OS: iOS and Linux

Apple debuted iOS, or iPhone OS, in 2007, with the inception of the iPhone to the cell phone market (Barrera & Van Oorschot, 2011). Presently, the iOS platform not only runs on iPhone but also iPod Touch and iPad (Barrera & Van Oorschot, 2011). Apple developers specifically write apps to run on all iOS devices. Apple's iOS popularity stems from an easy user interface, including "onscreen interactive menus, 2D and 3D graphics, location services, and core OS functionality such as threads and network sockets" (Barrera & Van Oorschot, 2011).

Apple utilizes various techniques to ensure that the security and quality of their applications are not compromised by malicious cyber attackers. Unlike Android's OS, iOS prevents third-party apps from accessing external data by utilizing a "sandbox mechanism" (Barrera & Van Oorschot, 2011). This mechanism employs policy files that restrict access to certain device features and data (Barrera & Van Oorschot, 2011). App developers use registered Application Programming Interface (APIs) to restrict apps from accessing protected resources (Barrera & Van Oorschot, 2011). Finally, Apple approves every iOS app developers create. The approval process has not been published by Apple, however it is believed that "the company employs both automated and manual verification of submitted apps" (Barrera & Van Oorschot, 2011). Once Apple approves a potential app, Apple "digitally signs it and releases it" to the App Store (Barrera & Van Oorschot, 2011). Ultimately, Apple has the final say pertaining to which apps are available for download in the App Store – "apps that Apple hasn't digitally signed can't run on the device" (Barrera & Van Oorschot, 2011).

Linux is a Unix like Operating System (OS) that is built on the Linux kernel developed by Linus Torvalds with thousands of software engineers. As of 2012 there are over two hundred active Linux distributions. The majority of the kernel and associated packages are free and OSS. This type of software provides a license which allows users the right to use, copy, study, change, and improve the software as the source code is made available. Providing source code allows developers or engineers to understand the inner workings of development. Imagine being able to study Mac or Windows by viewing all the source code to replicate similar developments. This exercise is great for a developer to learn low level coding techniques, design, integration, and implementation. This is also a great method for penetration testing with the ability to test all available back doors within the software.

In terms of associated cost the majority of Linux distributions are free. However some distributions require a cost for updates or assistance that related to specific needs such as OS modifications for server hosting. In software, there is a packet management system that automates the process of installing, configuring, upgrading, and removing software packages from an OS. In the Linux OS builds the most common packet management systems are Debian, Red Hat Package Manager (RPM), Knoppix, and netpkg. The most popular Linux distributions for mobile use are Android IOS and Ubuntu.

Malware Attacks on Smartphone OS

Along with this, malware that targets smartphone operating systems is constantly evolving. An example of this is seen with "Zeus-in-the-Mobile" (ZitMo), a specific form of malware common to the Android operating system. ZitMo targeted Android users' bank apps; it attempted to bypass the banking two-factor authentication, steal credentials and gain access to users' bank accounts, and ultimately money (Traynor, Ahamad, Alperovitch, Conti, & Davis, 2012). This is just one form of cyber attacks that IT professionals are trying to prevent from occurring.

Lastly, it is believed that mobile devices will be the new vector for targeting network and critical systems (Traynor, Ahamad, Alperovitch, Conti, & Davis, 2012). According to the report, mobile devices are an excellent way to spread malware because phones are great storage devices. A hypothetical example of a wsoncyber attack against a company's network is seen when malware is implanted in a smartphone. For example, a clever cyber attacker can write code to remotely control wireless connectivity technology and plant malware on the mobile phone. If that same phone is connected to a corporate network, i.e. the user is charging the phone on the company's computer; the malware can now attack the company's network. IT professionals want to prevent attacks like that from occurring because the economic consequences of such an event would be catastrophic. Ultimately, it is imperative that a national security standard is created for mobile devices in order to protect personal data.

The Android Platform

According to Shabtai et al. (2010), Android is an open-source application execution environment that includes an operating system, application framework, and core applications. Android was designed and released originally by Android Inc. to provide a user-friendly, open, and easy-to-use mobile-based development environment. This open-source mobile development framework is user-centric because it provides a variety of developments, tools, and features. However, this open-development feature also poses challenges to securing sensitive user data and protecting users from malicious attacks, such as phishing applications that are usually sent to users to trick them into providing their financial information and credentials while accessing malicious websites that look the same as the legitimate banking sites.

The Android operating system was first released in October, 2008 by T-Mobile 1G, and soon major telecommunications companies (such as T-Mobile) in both the U.S. and Europe adopted it because of its rich capabilities exemplified by core applications (i.e., email, web browsing, and MMS), entertainment features, and services, such as camera and Bluetooth. This has also led to Android's popularity amongst developers due to the open-source nature of Android, which offers the capability of developing and programming rich applications at the lowest level of Android's operating system. Since its initial release in 2008, Android has undergone many releases, the last being Android 2.2; this latest version of the Android platform brings many new and existing features and technologies to make both users and developers productive. Some of the new services and applications included in the new version aim at increasing speed (CPU is about 2-5 times faster), performance, and browsing (using version 8 engine that provides 2-3 times faster java script heavy page load). This new version also offers improved security features by allowing users to unlock their device using a password policy and the ability to wipe data from devices in case of theft or loss.

The Android Security Model

Android is a multi-process system where each application (and parts of the system) runs its own process. The standard Linux facilities enforce security between applications and the system at the process level; those applications are assigned by users and group IDs. Applications are restricted in what they can perform by a permission mechanism, called permission labels, that uses an access control to control what applications can be performed. This permission mechanism is fine-grained in that it even controls what operations a particular process can perform (Shabtai et al., 2010). The permission labels are part of a security policy that is used to restrict access to each component within an application. Android uses security policies to determine whether to grant or deny permissions to applications installed on Android OS.

Those security policies suffer from shortcomings in that they cannot specify to which application rights or permissions are given because they rely on users and the operating system to make that guess. They are therefore taking the risk of permitting applications with malicious intentions to access confidential data on the phone. Ongtang, McLaughlin, Enck, and McDaniel (2009) best described this security shortcoming by their hypothetical example of "PayPal service built on Android. Applications such as browsers, email clients, software marketplaces, music players, etc. use the PayPal service to purchase goods. The PayPal service in this case is an application that asserts permissions that must be granted to the other applications that use its interfaces" (Ontang, McLaughlin, Enck, & McDaniel, 2009). In this hypothetical scenario, it is unknown whether the PayPal application is legitimate or not because there is no way to determine whether this is the actual PayPal service application or another malicious program. Again, Android lacks security measures to determine and enforce how, when, where, and to whom permissions are granted.

Android's Permissions

Android uses permission mechanisms to determine what users are allowed to do in applications; this is achieved via the manifest permission that grants permissions to applications independently, which in turn, allows applications to run independently from each other as well as from the operating system. This could be a good security feature since the operations run by one application cannot interfere or otherwise impact operations within other applications. For example, users sending email messages will not be allowed (by default) to perform any operation within an application (such as reading a file from another application) that could adversely impact the email application (Developers, n.d). Applications achieve that using the "sandbox" concept, where each application is given the basic functions needed to run its own process; however, if the sandbox does not provide the needed functions to run a process, then the application can interfere with the operations of another process and request the needed functions to run a process. This capability of allowing applications to request permissions outside of their sandbox capabilities could be harmful to Android mobile devices because it opens a window of opportunity for malware to exploit the privilege of accessing sensitive data on Android handsets and thus install malicious software (Vennon, 2010).

METHODOLOGY

This is a conceptual paper; thus the main scope of this paper is to illustrate the importance of security software for smartphone operating systems. Case studies in scholarly journals and reports were used in the construction of this paper. Most sources contain qualitative information, describing predictions of various cyber attacks on mobile devices that may occur by the end of 2012. Quantitative methods were also used to assess the statistical increase in cyber attacks.

RESEARCH RESULTS

The current smartphone statistics are quite daunting due to the widespread lack of security software for mobile devices. The result of this void in security software is vulnerable mobile devices and tablets that are easily susceptible to cyber attacks. According to Andy Favell, editor of the website "MobiThinking," in 2010, 96% of mobile devices and tablets do not contain security software (Favell, 2011). Moreover, the article states that over 2000 various types of mobile malware have been identified in the past two years (Favell, 2011). For example, Hydraq and Stuxnet, specific cyber attacks, "leveraged zero-day vulnerabilities to break into computer systems... Stuxnet alone exploited four different zero-day vulnerabilities to attack its targets" (Symantec, Inc., 2011). Moreover, many enterprises experienced a multitude of targeted attacks against their collection of corporate data in 2010 (Symantec, Inc., 2011).

Figure 1 depicts the current status of security for the majority of today's mobile devices. This is an alarming statistic because, as mentioned earlier, mobile devices are the most popular way to communicate in our society. Malware is increasing at an exponential rate, and consumers' nonchalant attitudes towards mobile security provide the perfect opportunity for cyber attackers to create and spread malware quickly. This breach in cyber security puts businesses at risk also. According to Favell, when consumers use smart devices for work purposes, the devices can access and/or store company emails and sensitive information (2011). This scenario is detrimental to the success and welfare of any company; hopefully, the fact that in 2010 only 4% of all mobile devices contained security software will alert consumers and businesses of the importance of having a secured smart device (Favell, 2011).

Figure 1. The current status of security for the majority of today's mobile devices

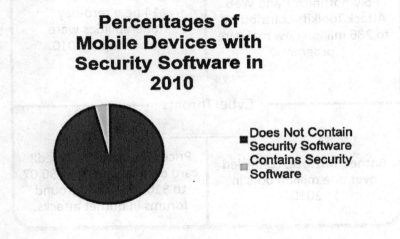

Table 1. Malware programs commonly used to hack into smartphones

Type	Definition	Examples
Trojan	Programs that pose as legitimate applications (Symantec, Inc., 2011).	Android.Pjapps Trojan, Rogue apps, Hydraq
Virus	Software program that can replicate itself and damage files and other programs on host computer.	Stuxnet
Botnet	A network of infected private computers controlled by cyber attackers who sell sensitive data to the highest bidder. Social media applications on mobile devices are now a new avenue for botnets to control devices (Trend Micro, 2009).	Opt-in botnets, Aurora botnet, Rustock
Toolkit	Software programs that can be used to assist with the launch of widespread attacks on networked computers or mobile devices; exploits Java vulnerabilities (Symantec, Inc., 2011).	Phoenix toolkit
Malvertising	Authentic looking advertisements that are linked to false sites (Rao, 2011).	Malicious Ad on social network apps, such as TweetMeme
Worms	Malware programs that self-replicate and is spread over the air (via mobile networks) (Favell, 2011).	iPhoneOS.Ikee.B; iPhoneOS.Ikee

Table 1 illustrates the various malware programs that now infect mobile devices. Originally, trojans, viruses, botnets and toolkits were common infections of personal computers; now, mobile devices are plagued with these various malware programs. In 2010, Favell stated that 2,500 different mobile malware programs exist (Favell, 2011). The majority of existing malware programs target Android apps because Android is the most popular OS, and it is easier for app developers to distribute apps through GooglePlay (Android's App Market) due to Android's lenient verification process (Favell, 2011). In 2009, iPhoneOS.Ikee.B and iPhoneOS.Ikee infected "jailbroken" Apple devices. "Jailbreaking" means to remove Apple's restrictions; this grants the user freedom to use the phone as he/she pleases (Favell, 2011). Now, consumers must be aware of the various malware programs that are prevalent; consumers must also be vigilant to protect their data while using their device.

Figure 2. Illustrates various cyberthreats in 2010
(Symantec, 2011).

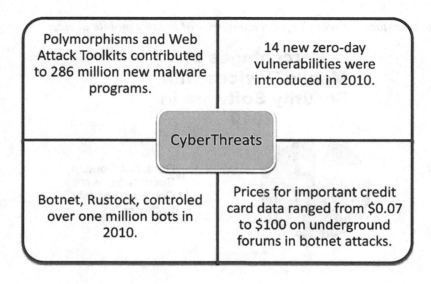

Figure 3. 42% increase in mobile vulnerabilities
(Symantec, 2011)

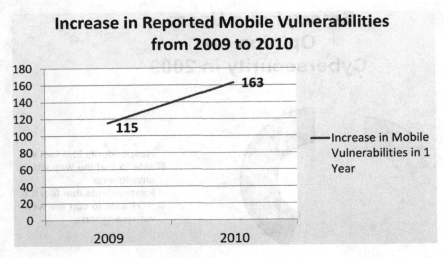

Cyber threats are increasing at an alarming rate. According to Symantec, polymorphisms and toolkits have contributed to the increase in malware programs in 2010. Also, over 200 million malicious programs were created during 2010 (Symantec, Inc., 2011). Moreover, cyber criminals are exploiting the gaps in security with the Android OS. In fact, many zero-day exploits have increased since the inception of the Android Market. Unfortunately, with zero-day vulnerabilities, the attack happens the same day; hence, IT specialists cannot distribute software updates in a timely manner to block such attacks (Symantec, Inc., 2011). Other harmful malware programs, botnets, have wreak havoc on many smartphone OS. The botnet, Rustock, controlled over a million bots at one point in 2010; Grum and Cutwail, other botnet attacks, controlled hundreds of thousands bots (Symantec, Inc., 2011). Lastly, cyber threats that steal bank and credit card information has greatly increased in the past four years. Symantec's Internet Security Threat Report states that black market forums pay top dollars for personal credit card data. The majority of this information is stolen through extensive botnet attacks (2011).

Above is a numerical depiction of the increase in mobile cyber attacks in one year. From 2009 to 2010 there was a 42% increase in the number of mobile vulnerabilities (Symantec, Inc., 2011). Cyber criminals are capitalizing on the popularity of mobile devices; thus, this trend is an indication that will not falter without an intervention. Furthermore, most reported mobile vulnerabilities occurred in the form of Trojan Horse programs that acted as legitimate applications (Symantec, Inc., 2011). While many cyber attackers created some of the most pertinent malware from scratch, "in many cases, they [cyber attackers] infected users by inserting malicious logic into existing legitimate applications" (Symantec, Inc., 2011). Next, the hacker will distribute these malicious apps through public app stores, such as Google Play or Apple's App Store. Pjapps Trojan is a recent example of a malicious app distributed through public app stores (Symantec, Inc., 2011).

Trend Micro, an international leader in data security, surveyed 1,000 smartphone and iPhone owners that were over the age of 18. The data revealed that nearly half (56 percent) of the respondents believe it is safe, if not safer, to browse the Internet from their mobile device as opposed to a PC (Trend Micro, 2009). Contrasting with this, 44 percent of respondents do not feel it is safe to surf the web using a

Figure 4. Percentage of smartphone users that perceive it is safer to surf the Internet via mobile browser (Smartphone Users, 2009).

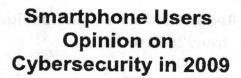

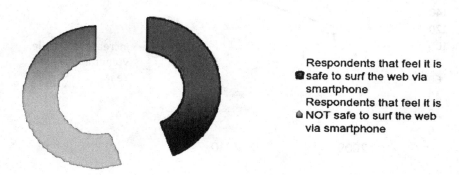

Respondents that feel it is ● safe to surf the web via smartphone

Respondents that feel it is ▲ NOT safe to surf the web via smartphone

smartphone (Trend Micro, 2009). Moreover, according to the survey, only 23% of the respondents use security software that is installed on their smartphone (Trend Micro, 2009). In addition to this, another 20% of respondents "don't think installing security software program[s] on their phones would be very effective (Trend Micro, 2009)." The same respondents feel that there is limited risk when using a mobile web browser. As stated earlier, this false mentality of a safe mobile browser environment has created many opportunities for cyber criminals to steal personal data. Contrasting with this, the majority of the survey respondents are aware of mobile Web threats, and nearly half of them have been infected by some form of malware (Trend Micro, 2009).

spam emails are another prevalent form of cyber threats. As illustrated in Figure 5, out of the 1,000 respondents, 450 (45%) of them received spam emails in the past 3 months (Trend Micro, 2009). 170 (17%) respondents believe there is an increase in the amount of spam emails they have received (Trend Micro, 2009). 500 (50%) of respondents open email attachments on their smartphone; and 390 (39%) respondents click on URL links in emails they received on their phone (Trend Micro, 2009). These statistics can be projected onto the general smartphone user community. In fact, it can be assumed that nearly half of all smartphone users receive spam emails quite often throughout the year, and half of all smartphone users carelessly open email attachments on their phone. Since spam has become a common nuisance in the email environment; it is obvious it would be a nuisance for mobile devices.

Thus, the lack of installed security software coupled with the laissez-faire attitude of today's smartphone users, leads to advantageous loopholes for malicious cyber attackers. 20% of smartphone users do not think installing security software to their phone will reduce their chances of malware attacks (Trend Micro, 2009). Another 20% of users have encountered phishing scams when surfing the internet on their mobile browser (Trend Micro, 2009). Phishing scams lure users into supplying ID information, bank account numbers, usernames and passwords by replying to false email messages (Trend Micro, 2009). Lastly, Apple aficionados must take necessary precautions when using the Safari web browser on their iPhone. Apple's claim to fame is their stylish hardware, iOS Operating System (OS) and sleek

Figure 5. Percentage of smartphone survey respondents that received spam in 2009
(Smartphone Users, 2009).

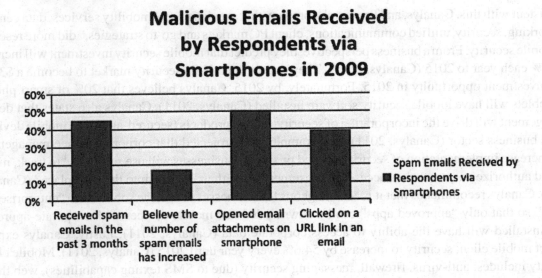

functionality. Unfortunately, the traits that make Apple popular are also the same traits that make the iPhone susceptible to cyber attacks (Trend Micro, 2009). A recent example of this is seen in a reported SMS vulnerability for the iPhone, in which hackers have the ability to control the device if the user is on a malicious site or connecting to the internet through unsecured 3G or Wifi connections (Trend Micro, 2009).

ANALYSIS AND DISCUSSION

Various security services project that cyber attacks on mobile devices will increase exponentially by 2015. This is obvious based on the fact that the majority of mobile devices have no security software at all. Lookout Mobile Security company analyzed the current data on smartphone cyber attacks and released their malware predictions for 2011 (Rao, 2011). Lookout offers various security services for many smartphone operating systems, such as Android, Windows Mobile, Blackberry and iOS (Rao, 2011). Unfortunately, Android users, internationally, had a 36% chance of clicking an unsafe link in 2011 (Rao, 2011).

Lookout also identified the first U.S. mobile malware that steals money from Android smartphone users – GGTracker; and RuFraud, which steals money from Eastern European Android smartphone users (Rao, 2011). Lookout believes that malware creators will furtively combine thousands of mobile devices into extensive botnet-like networks, such as DroidDream, to spread spam, steal personal data and install more malware (Rao, 2011). Moreover, Lookout has predicted the likelihood that smartphone users will click on unsafe links (Rao, 2011). They predict the increase in "malvertising" – malware advertising, advertisements that link back to counterfeit websites – will continue to increase by the end of this year.

Predictions of the Mobile Security Market

Consistent with this, Canalys, an IT research company that specializes in "mobility services, data centers, networking, security, unified communications, client PC markets and go-to strategies," did more research on mobile security. From a business perspective, they predict that mobile security investment will increase by 44% each year to 2015 (Canalys, 2011). They expect the mobile security market to become a $3 billion investment opportunity in 2015. Fortunately, by 2015, Canalys believes that 20% of smart phones and tablets will have mobile security software installed (Canalys, 2011). Canalys also states that device management will drive the incorporation of security-related products (secured-approved mobile devices) in the business sector (Canalys, 2011). For example, it is projected that corporate device management will increase implementation of security-related products. Businesses will use solutions "to track, monitor and authorize corporate data access, as consumers bring their devices into the workplace" (Canalys, 2011). Canalys recommends that it is advantageous for businesses to link the solutions to "enterprise app stores" so that only "approved apps" can be downloaded and mobile devices with corporate-approved apps installed will have the ability to access corporate data (Canalys, 2011). Lastly, Canalys experts predict mobile client security to increase by 54.6% every year until 2015 (Canalys, 2011). Mobile client security includes: anti-virus, firewall, messaging security (due to SMS texting capabilities), web threat security, VPN functionality and encryption (Canalys, 2011).

Presently, the U.S. and Canada are the leaders of mobile security implementation due to their need to adhere with data compliance policies (Canalys, 2011). Nevertheless, the Western European market is expected to grow as globalization, "enterprise mobility and consumerization trends" increase (Canalys, 2011). From 2013 to 2015, mobile security investment will sharply increase in developing countries such as Latin America, Asia, Africa and the Middle East, due to the instant popularity of the price-sensitive operating system, Android (Canalys, 2011). Unfortunately, as the steady growth of Android OS increases so does the volume of mobile malware threats because more consumers can download compromised applications (Canalys, 2011).

Corporations, Cyber Security, and Mobile Devices

Currently, corporations around the world are trying to manage a growing mobile workforce, in which employees are using multiple devices and operating systems (Canalys, 2011). This increase in data consumption exponentially increases the amount of vectors open to cyber attacks and leaves corporate data more vulnerable due to tangible loss of devices (Canalys, 2011). Ultimately, to counteract the era of cyber crimes, enterprises must have a holistic approach to mobile security – every layer of security must be analyzed in order to protect sensitive data. Lastly, Canalys urges service providers to provide security from a "network perspective, regardless of device or operating system type" (Canalys, 2011). Protecting the network of service providers is a key element in providing top notch security for the plethora of mobile devices that are currently on the market.

LIMITATIONS

It is a daunting task to establish a national cyber security standard to counteract the multitude of cyber attacks that exist today. There are quite a few limitations that must be addressed in order to move forward.

Legitimate Applications that Can Be Used to Retrieve Information

Presently, there is valid spy software available for various mobile devices. An example of this is Flexi-iSpy, a legitimate commercial spyware program that cost over $300 (United States Computer Emergency Readiness Team, 2010). FlexiSpy can:

- Listen to actual phone calls as they happen;
- Secretly read Short Message Service (SMS) texts, call logs, and emails;
- Listen to the phone surroundings (use as remote bugging device);
- View phone GPS location;
- Forward all email events to another inbox;
- Remotely control all phone functions via SMS;
- Accept or reject communication based on predetermined lists; and
- Evade detection during operation (United States Computer Emergency Readiness Team, 2010).

The creators of FlexiSpy claim that this application can help protect young children (that have a cell phone) or catch unfaithful spouses. However, the dangers of this software outweigh the positives once it is in the hands of a malicious cyber attacker. This example demonstrates the need for a federal implemented cyber security act to dictate the types of applications that can be available to the general public. For parents, FlexiSpy has wonderful attributes in terms of monitoring the whereabouts of underage children, but these same attributes can be abused by a cyber attacker to gain extremely personal data of a smartphone user.

Another example of a legitimate application that can be exploited by malicious cyber hackers is mobile e-commerce apps (M-commerce). M-commerce involves using a mobile device "to research product information, compare prices, make purchases, and communicate with customer support" (United States Computer Emergency Readiness Team, 2010). In addition to this, merchants can use mobile devices for checking prices, inquiring inventory and processing payments (United States Computer Emergency Readiness Team, 2010). Currently, vendors now have the ability to process credit card payments with a new device called "Square" (United States Computer Emergency Readiness Team, 2010). Square is a third-party smartphone attachment that is plugged into a smartphone's headphone jack and is used for swiping credit cards (United States Computer Emergency Readiness Team, 2010). Square subscribers register their device online through the company's website. This way, subscribers can manage their payment processes through their accounts. Unfortunately, Square can be used for malicious cyber activities, such as "skimming" and "carding" (United States Computer Emergency Readiness Team, 2010). According to the article entitled, "Cyber Threats to Mobile Devices," "Skimming is the theft of credit card information using card readers, or skimmers, to record and store victims' data" (2010). Also, carding is a process used to assess "the validity of stolen credit card numbers" (United States Computer Emergency Readiness Team, 2010). Both processes can be done in conjunction with other legitimate transactions, and can be exploited by cyber attackers to gain sensitive financial data.

A third example of a legitimate application that can be used for malicious activity are advertisement libraries, or ad libraries (Grace, Zhou, Jiang, & Sadeghi, 2012). Many app developers incorporate ad libraries into their legitimate applications for monetary compensation. For example, on the Android Market (now known as Google Play), over 60% of the apps are free to download (Grace, Zhou, Jiang, & Sadeghi, 2012). In order for app developers to be compensated for their product, they use ad libraries, which "communicate[s] with the ad network's servers to request ads for display and might additionally send analytics information about the users of the app" (Grace, Zhou, Jiang, & Sadeghi, 2012). Next, the ad network pays the app developer continuously, based on data that measure "how much exposure each individual app gives to the network and its advertisers" (Grace, Zhou, Jiang, & Sadeghi, 2012). Unfortunately, the Computer Science Department of North Carolina State University revealed that there are many privacy and security issues in some of the most prevalent ad libraries. Granted some of these ad libraries collect information for legitimate purposes, such as a user's location for targeted advertising, a few ad libraries collect personal, sensitive data, such as a user's call logs, account information or cell number (Grace, Zhou, Jiang, & Sadeghi, 2012). Consequently, malicious cyber attackers can use this information to infer the actual identity of the user, and enable greater comprehensive tracking of the user's habits (Grace, Zhou, Jiang, & Sadeghi, 2012). A specific example of an ad library embedded into a popular smartphone app is the game *Angry Birds*, created by Rovio. The company Rovio employed the services from a third-party advertising network to capitalize Angry Birds on the Android Market (Grace, Zhou, Jiang, & Sadeghi, 2012). AdMob is the most popular ad library used by Angry Birds; it sends user's information such as game scores to Google (Grace, Zhou, Jiang, & Sadeghi, 2012). This business arrangement is not uncommon for smartphone app developers. Unfortunately, ad libraries in legitimate applications can be loopholes for cyber attackers to exploit and abuse personal user information. One study discovered that some ad libraries "download additional code at runtime from remote servers and execute it in the context of running the app" (Grace, Zhou, Jiang, & Sadeghi, 2012). It is evident that these results garner the need for additional methods for regulating the behavior of ad libraries on Android apps.

When discussing legitimate applications we should also not forget how easy it is to create malware applications. With the aid of rootkit tools, and freely available malicious code it is easy to create a malware program. Figure 6 displays a simple script that can email as an executable file that will delete targeted files that are necessary for the OS to function. This script took less than four minutes to create.

Figure 6. Example of an executable file

Malware Social Network Exploitation

As stated earlier, the popularity of social networking applications can be a limitation in the fight against cyber threats. The wealth of personal data that social media applications inspire cybercriminals to create malware targeted for these applications. Twitter and Facebook are the main sources of communication and information for today's generation of smartphone users. Unfortunately, accepting shared information on these websites can compromise the security of a user's device. This issue is heightened on Twitter because users are limited to 140 characters when sharing updates or links. So on Twitter, Uniform Resource Locators, or URLs, are shortened severely in order to adhere to the 140 character rule. This is unfortunate because shortened URLs make it more difficult for a user to know if the link is legitimate or malicious. In brief, sharing links via Twitter is an opportunistic way for cyber attackers to lure innocent users into clicking fraudulent links.

Android Malware

Hackers first started to design malware for mobile devices in early 2004 when the Cabir worm came to the scene. Despite the fact that Cabir was only a "proof of concept" attack form and did not cause any serious damage to affected mobile devices, it brought hackers' attention to mobile devices. Android, as a smartphone, is no exception when it comes to mobile malware attacks. Some of the first Android malware was devised by a group of security researchers as an attempt to bring attention to possible malware attacks on the Android platform because Android offers an integrated set of services and functionalities, such as internet access. The researchers were able to create the first Android running malware by exploiting undocumented Android Java functions and using them to create native Linux applications. Specifically, this malware was embodied in a valid, benign, Android application that a user would install. Once the benign application is installed, the malware would propagate the Linux system and execute its malicious payload, thereby wreaking havoc on Android devices. This was an indication of the possible vulnerabilities and risks associated with Android devices (Schmidt, Bye, Clausen et al., 2009).

The most dangerous Android malware is the one that exploits security flaws within the operating system (Linux) to gain root-level access with root privilege. One of the first security flaws was discovered in Android in November of 2008 when security experts found a bug that would allow users and potential attackers to run command-line instructions with root privilege; moreover, the bug, if exploited, would make the Android platform read and interpret actions based on the input text. For example, if an Android user input a simple text message, such as "Hello," it could be interpreted by the operating system as "reboot," which surprisingly reboots the Android device (ZDNet, 2010). This security shortcoming and many other vulnerabilities were discovered in Android over the last two years and have thus continuously raised pressing concerns about the credibility and effectiveness of security controls deployed in Android. Most of those vulnerabilities stem from Android's open-source nature, which allows development of third-party applications without any kind of centralized control or any security oversight.

As a case in point, we can highlight malware risks targeting Android smartphone users. Android smartphone users tend to download and install apps frequently, as all kinds of apps dominate the marketplace; apps usually require access to certain areas of the phone to function, and they ask users to grant permissions at installation time. Many apps tend to request permissions more than they really need to be fully functional. Also, many apps are seemingly benign to users and do not seem to pose any threats to confidential information. Therefore, Android users normally get distracted by enjoying all the features and added functionality offered by apps and do not give adequate attention to the security aspects of those apps. To make matters worse, hackers target popular apps, modify their source code, and then upload them again to the Android Market after injecting their malicious piece. Unfortunately, Google is not proactive in this area in that it does not remove potentially malicious apps until they receive complaints or until apps have already caused disruption and compromised sensitive data. Therefore, the researcher strongly believes that the greatest security risk lies at the heart of Android apps, where attackers are most capable of passing their malicious apps to end users through the Market and gain unauthorized access to confidential data to achieve financial gains. Furthermore, hackers are known to use attack strategies that tend to send expensive SMS messages and dial prime rate numbers as a quick and efficient way to gain money illegally.

Incorporating Pre-Existing Government Guidance

The Department of Defense (DoD) has addressed software security through governance issued under the Office of Management and Budget (OMB) Circular A-130. The focus of Information Technology security was further derived by DoD Directive 8500.2. It specifically states that all Information Assurance (IA) and IA-enabled IT products incorporated into DoD Information Systems (IS) shall be configured in accordance with DoD-approved security configuration guidelines. On April 26, 2010, the DoD released the third version of the Application Security and Development Security Technical Implementation Guide (STIG) provided by the Defense Information Systems Agency (DISA). This document provides DoD guidelines and requirements for integrating security throughout the software development lifecycle. The STIGs are accompanied by the NSA Guides which provide the configuration guidance for locking down a system. There are guides for multiple Oss to include those for mobile platforms.

In terms of development for mobile devices the commercial sector should employ those who have professional certifications such as International Information Systems Security Certification Consortium (ISC)2 Certified Secure Software Lifecycle Professional (CSSLP). The guidance that drives this requirement and those similar is the DOD 5870.01M Information Assurance Workforce Improvement Program. Organizations employing IA technically competent software developers should help mitigate the overall risk. This could be a requirement that could be levied not just upon the mobile phone developer but also the application developer.

The Common Criteria (CC), an internationally approved set of security standards, provides a clear and reliable evaluation of the security capabilities of Information Technology (IT) products (CCEVS, 2008). By providing an independent assessment of a product's ability to meet security standards, the CC gives customers more confidence in the security of products and leads to more informed decisions (CCEVS, 2008). Security-conscious customers, such as the U.S. Federal Government, are increasingly requiring CC certification as a determining factor in purchasing decisions (CCEVS, 2008). Since the requirements for certification are clearly established, vendors can target very specific security needs while providing broad product offerings. The international scope of the CC, currently adopted by fourteen nations, allows users from other countries to purchase IT products with the same level of confidence, since certification is recognized across all complying nations. Evaluating a product with respect to security requires identification of the customer's security needs and an assessment of the capabilities of the product. The CC aids customers in both of these processes through two key components: protection profiles and evaluation assurance levels (CCEVS, 2008). Utilizing guidance such as the CC could allow organizations to appropriately measure the security of their product. The problem is the cost that surrounds commercial companies meeting rigorous standards but this product certification process could replicated at a more cost efficient manner.

Lastly, another limitation for creating a cyber security environment for mobile devices is due in part to a lack of national cyber security policies. The internet is a brand new frontier with no physical or political boundries (Brechbuhl, Bruce, Dynes, & Johnson, 2010). Furthermore, cyber security is a concern of everybody – common smartphone users, business and government officials; also, security issues have normally been the government's responsibility. Contrasting with this, the sectors that are best equipped at dealing with cyber security issues is private or semiprivate enterprises that operate the information and communication technology (ICT) infrastructure, in other words the internet (Brechbuhl, Bruce, Dynes, & Johnson, 2010). Finally, the creation of a national policy is difficult because we currently "lack a feasible policy framework that systematically arrays the issues and specifies parameters that constrain this development" (Harknett & Stever, 2011). Ultimately, cyber security threats are versatile and constantly changing, we must develop programs to match and counteract the transient attributes of cyber security attacks.

Issues with Android Phones and Other Mobile Devices

Smartphones are becoming a more integrated and prevalent part of people's daily lives due to their highly powerful computational capabilities, such as email applications, online banking, online shopping, and bill paying. With this fast adoption of smartphones, imminent security threats arise while communicating sensitive personally identifiable information (PII), such as bank account numbers and credit card numbers used when handling and performing those advanced tasks (Wong, 2005; Brown, 2009). Traditional attacks (worms, viruses, and Trojan horses) caused privacy violations and disruptions of critical software applications (e.g., deleting lists of contact numbers and personal data). Malware attacks on smartphones were generally "proof of concept" attempts to break through the phone's system and cause damage (Omar & Dawson, 2013). However, the new generation of smartphone malware attacks has increased in sophistication and is designed to cause severe financial losses (caused by identity theft) and disruption of critical software applications (Bose, 2008). Because smartphones are becoming more diverse in providing general purpose services (i.e., instant messaging and music), the effect of malware could be extended to include draining batteries, incurring additional charges, and bringing down network capabilities and services (Xie, Zhang, Chaugule, Jaeger, & Zhu, 2009).

Smartphones are rapidly becoming enriched with confidential and sensitive personal information, such as bank account information and credit card numbers, because of the functionality and powerful computational capabilities built into those mobile devices. Cyber criminals, in turn, launch attacks especially designed to target smartphones, exploiting vulnerabilities and deficiencies in current defense strategies built into smartphones' operating systems. Bhattacharya (2008) indicated that because of skill and resource constraints, businesses are ill-prepared to combat emerging cyber threats; this claim is true for smartphones as well, given the fact that those mobile devices are even less equipped with necessary protections, such as antivirus and malware protection software. Some services and features, such as Bluetooth and SMS, create attack vectors unique to smartphones and thus expand the attack surface. For example, in December, 2004, A Trojan horse was disguised in a video game and was intended to be a "proof of concept," which signaled the risks associated with smartphones that could potentially compromise the integrity and confidentiality of personal information contained in smartphones (Rash, 2004). Attackers can easily take advantage of those services provided by smartphones and subvert their primary purpose because they can use Bluetooth and SMS services to launch attacks by installing software that can disable virus protection and spread via Bluetooth unbeknownst to smartphone users.

With the development of innovative features and services for smartphones, security measures deployed are currently not commensurate because those services and features, such as MMS and Bluetooth, are driven by market and user demands, meaning that companies are more inclined to provide more entertainment features than security solutions. In turn, this further increases vulnerabilities and opens doors for hackers to deploy attacks on smartphones. Furthermore, Mulliner & Miller (2009) argue that the operating systems of smartphones allow the installation of third-party software applications, coupled with the increase in processing power as well as the storage capacity. Scenarios like this pose worse security challenges because hackers could exploit those vulnerabilities, which are further compounded by users' lack of security awareness. Smartphone attackers are becoming more adept in designing and launching attacks by applying attack techniques already implemented on desktop and laptop computers; smartphones' enhanced features, such as music players and video games, produce easy-to exploit targets by sending seemingly benign files via music or video game applications to users and luring them into downloading such files. Becher, Freiling, and Leider (2007) indicated that attackers could exploit such vulnerabilities to spread worms autonomously into smartphones. Therefore, hackers usually use a combination of technical expertise along with some social engineering techniques to trap users into accepting and downloading benign applications, which are used later to execute malicious code and affect critical applications running on smartphones.

Attack Vectors and Infection Mechanisms

- **Bluetooth:** This is a wireless communication protocol used for short-range (about 10 meters) transmissions at 2.4 G.H. Bluetooth is one of the most widely used and preferred attack techniques for infecting smartphones because by pairing Bluetooth-enabled devices, hackers are able to access infected phones' critical applications and files, such as email, contact lists, pictures, and any other private data stored in the smartphone. Bluetooth-enabled smartphones are prone to various kinds of attacks due to security implementation flaws that exist in current security specifications. For example, Wong (2005) reveals that when two Bluetooth-enabled devices communicate after establishing a trusted relationship, all the credential information is left on both devices, even after the session is ended. This implementation hole allows potential hackers to have full access to the device, without the owner's knowledge or consent, based on the previously established trust relationship; attackers then can access confidential data stored on smartphones and manipulate it. The only way smartphone users would be able to detect such security flaws is to observe the Bluetooth icon indicating an established Bluetooth connection; otherwise, attackers will have unauthorized access to the victim's smartphone. This security shortcoming, along with other security flaws found in Bluetooth security architecture, such as device-based authentication rather than user-based authentication, make smartphones vulnerable to direct attacks and threaten privacy and critical personal information.
- **MMS/SMS:** Multimedia message service and short message service are both communication protocols that have become widely used and adopted by smartphone users as the standard for fast and convenient communications. Although it might seem unrealistic to think that hackers would ever be interested in targeting MMS/SMS, recent studies have shown that MMS/SMS can contain confidential information that is exposed to attacks due to lack of security services not provided by the cellular network. SMS suffers from exploitable vulnerabilities, such as lack of mutual authentication methods and non-repudiation. An SMS that is sent from a sender to a receiver cannot be

mutually authenticated by both parties, which opens doors for hackers to exploit. Also, senders who send SMS cannot be held accountable for their sent SMS because there is no mechanism that could be implemented to ensure the sender's true identity. The weak security implementation of SMS can also be used as attack mechanisms by hackers, where an arbitrary computer can be used to inject SMSs into the network, thus exposing smartphones to risks. In addition, SMSs are susceptible to man-in-the middle attacks while they are being transmitted over the air. Therefore, attackers are increasingly relying on MMS/SMS as an effective attack vector (Lockefeer, 2010).

- **File Injection and Downloadable Applications:** Malware authors constantly develop new and innovative ways for attacking smartphones; sending benign files that contain malicious code and downloadable applications have proven to be a successful attack mechanism adopted by hackers. What makes such attack vectors effective is the fact that they come in the form of legitimate applications, luring smartphone users to disclose their private and financial information. For instance, in January, 2010, a group of malicious writers calling themselves "09Droid" developed an application that specifically targeted Google Android phones and mobile banking institutions. The application contained the phrase "happy banking" on the summary statement that each application uses to advertise itself to potential users. The attack tempted users to purchase the mobile banking application from the Android Market in order to log on to their mobile banking accounts. While doing so, users would have to reveal their account numbers and passwords, which would then be sent to the authors of the malicious program (Morrison, 2010). This kind of well-crafted attack underscores the powerful capabilities of emerging attacks and the attackers; they target banking institutions and credit unions and use their logos to lure naive smartphone owners into giving their confidential information to applications that look exactly the same as the legitimate ones.

CONCLUSION AND SUGGESTIONS

Fortunately, there are possible solutions to the rampant cyber security problem with mobile devices. Once our society acknowledges that cyber security threats are detrimental not only to one smartphone user, but to the society as a whole; then the inception of a solution can begin. The value of data is steadily increasing, possibly even more so than actual money. It is imperative to establish a culture of cyber security because this issue is multifaceted and technology is constantly evolving.

Cyber Security Is Multidimensional: Collaboration Is Imperative for Its Success

Security concerns are not exclusive to "economists, political scientist, lawyers, business policy or management experts, or computer specialist" (Brechbuhl, Bruce, Dynes, & Johnson, 2010). In order to establish a policy of cyber security, it will take a collaborative effort from a variety of officials in various disciplines in society. Each official brings a specific set of knowledge to the issue of cyber security, and has a potential role in establishing the different set of functions that are needed to create a general intra-and international cyber security standard (Brechbuhl, Bruce, Dynes, & Johnson, 2010). Ultimately, a decentralized approach is the best way to make cyber security an interconnected, coordinating mechanism that benefits the society as a whole (Brechbuhl, Bruce, Dynes, & Johnson, 2010).

Cell Phone Attributes as Security Features

CTO Dan Schutzer of BITS, the technology policy division of the Financial Services Roundtable, states that mobile devices and other mobile devices are equipped with biometric security measures (Traynor, Ahamad, Alperovitch, Conti, & Davis, 2012). Biometric is the statistical analysis of biological data using technology. Schutzer suggests that the cameras that are installed in mobile phones can be used for facial recognition or iris detection (Traynor, Ahamad, Alperovitch, Conti, & Davis, 2012). This is actually a great idea because, thanks to DNA, biologically everyone is different. Thus, the authenticated user of a smartphone will be the only person that can unlock his/her phone. Moreover, Shutzer proposes that the microphones installed in mobile devices can be used for voice recognition (Traynor, Ahamad, Alperovitch, Conti, & Davis, 2012). This is another way to secure and lock a cell phone; and only the authorized user of the phone will be able to unlock the device. In brief, using biometric measures to secure mobile devices is one way to prevent theft

CONCLUSION

Lastly, IT companies are seeing the niche in the market for security software specifically designed for mobile operating systems. Recently, a few companies have presented different mobile security software that consumers can purchase. Bullguard Mobile Security, Kaspersky Mobile Security, ESET Mobile Security, and Lookout Premium are mobile security software currently available for purchase (2012 Best Mobile Security Software Comparisons and Reviews, 2012). The programs range in prices from $19.99 to $39.99. These programs are a start; however, it is up to consumers to purchase them to secure their data. As mentioned earlier, cyber security is a multifaceted issue that must be dealt with accordingly. Ultimately, creating a national standard of cyber security is the best way to counteract the increase in cyber attacks.

REFERENCES

Barrera, D., & Van Oorschot, P. (2011). Secure Software Installation on Smartphones. *IEEE Security and Privacy*, 9(3), 42–48. doi:10.1109/MSP.2010.202

Becher, M., Freiling, F., & Leider, B. (2007, June). On the effort to create smartphone worms in Windows Mobile. *Proceedings of the 2007 IEEE workshop on Information Assurance*. United States Military Academy. West Point, NY. Retrieved from http://pi1.informatik.uni-mannheim.de/filepool/publications/on-the-effort-to-create-smartphone-worms-in-windows-mobile.pdf

2012 Best Mobile Security Software Comparisons and Reviews. (2012). Retrieved April 17, 2012, from Top Ten Reviews: http://mobile-security-software-review.toptenreviews.com/

Bhattacharya, D. (2008) *Leardership styles and information security in small businesses: An empirical investigation* (Doctoral dissertation, University of Phoenix). Retrieved from www.phoenix.edu/apololibrary

Bose, A. (2008). *Propagation, detection and containment of mobile malware*. (Doctoral dissertation, University of Michigan). Retrieved from www.phoenix.edu/apololibrary

Brechbuhl, H., Bruce, R., Dynes, S., & Johnson, E. (2010, January). Protecting Critical Information Infrastructure: Developing Cybersecurity Policy. *Information Technology for Development, 16*(1), 83–91. doi:10.1002/itdj.20096

Brown, B. (2009). *Beyond Downadup: Security expert worries about smart phone, TinyURL threats: Malware writers just waiting for financial incentive to strike, F-Secure exec warns.* Retrieved from http://business.highbeam.com/409220/article-1G1-214585913/beyond-downadup-security-expert-worries-smart-phone

Canalys. (2011, October 04). *Mobile Security Investment to Climb 44% Each Year Through 2015.* Retrieved April 22, 2012, from Canalys: http://www.canalys.com/newsroom/mobile-security-investment-climb-44-each-year-through-2015

CCEVS. (2008). National Security Agency, Common Criteria Evaluation and Validation Scheme. *Common criteria evaluation and validation scheme -- organization, management, and concept of operations (Version 2.0).* Retrieved from National Information Assurance Partnership: http://www.niap-ccevs.org/policy/ccevs/scheme-pub-1.pdf

Eeten, M., & Bauer, J. (2009, December). Emerging Threats to Internet Security: Incentives, Externalities and Policy Implications. *Journal of Contingencies and Crisis Management, 17*(4), 221–232. doi:10.1111/j.1468-5973.2009.00592.x

Favell, A. (Ed.). (2011, November 2). *96 Percent of Smartphones and Tablets Lack Necessary Security Software. Why It Matters to Your Business - A Lot.* Retrieved April 22, 2012, from MobiThinking: http://mobithinking.com/blog/mobile-security-business-implications

Goth, G. (2009). U.S. Unveils Cybersecurity Plan. *Government Policy, 52*(8), 23.

Grace, M., Zhou, W., Jiang, X., & Sadeghi, A.-R. (2012). Unsafe Exposure Analysis of Mobile In-App Advertisements. *Association for Computing Machinery - Security and Privacy in Wireless and Mobile Networks, 5,* 101-112. doi:10.1145/2185448.2185464

Harknett, R., & Stever, J. (2011). In N. Roberts (Ed.), *The New Policy World of Cybersecurity* (pp. 455–460). Public Administration Review.

Harris, S., & Meyers, M. (2002). *CISSP.* McGraw-Hill/Osborne.

Janczewski, L., & Colarik, A. (2007). *Cyber Warfare and Cyber Terrorism.* Hershey, PA: IGI Global; doi:10.4018/978-1-59140-991-5

Kaplan, J., Sharma, S., & Weinberg, A. (2011). Cybersecurity: A Senior Executive's Guide. *The McKinsey Quarterly,* 4.

Lockefeer, L. (2010). *Encrypted SMS, an analysis of the theoretical necessities and implementation possibilities.* Retrieved from http://www.cs.ru.nl

MacWillson, A. (2011, May 9). *Rethinking Cybersecurity in a Mobile World.* Retrieved March 9, 2012, from Security Week: Internet and Enterprise Security News, Insights & Analysis: http://www.security-week.com/rethinking-cybersecurity-mobile-world

Mulliner, C., & Miller, C. (2009). Injecting SMS messages into smartphones for security analysis. *Proceedings of the 3rd USENIX Workshop on Offensive Technologies Montreal, Canada*. Retrieved from www.usenix.org

Ontang, M., McLaughlin, S., Enck, W., & McDaniel, P. (2009). *Semantically rich application-centric security in Android*. Retrieved from Proceedings of teh 25th Annual Computer Security Applciations Conference (ACSAC '09): http://dl.acm.org

Rao, L. (2011, December 13). *Lookout's 2012 Mobile Security Threat Predictions: SMS Fraud, Botnets And Malvertising*. Retrieved April 22, 2012, from Tech Crunch: http://techcrunch.com/2011/12/13/lookouts-2012-mobile-security-threat-predictions-sms-fraud-botnets-and-malvertising/

Rash, W. (2004). *Latest skulls Trojan foretells risky smartphone future*. Retrieved from www.eweek.com

Ruggiero, P. a. (2011). *Cyber Threats to Mobile Phones*. Pittsburgh: United States Computer Emergency Readiness Team.

Schmidt, A.-D., Bye, R., Schmidt, H.-G., Clausen, J., & Kiraz, O. (2009). *Static analysis of executables for collaborative malware detecion on Android*. Retrieved from www.dai-labor.de

Shabtai, A., Fledel, Y., Kanonov, U., Elovici, Y., Dolev, S., & Glezer, C. (2010, March/April). Android: A comprehensive security assessment. *IEEE Security and Privacy, 8*(2), 35–44. doi:10.1109/MSP.2010.2

Symantec, Inc. (2011, April 5). Retrieved April 17, 2012, from Symantec Report Finds Cyber Threats Skyrocket in Volume and Sophistication: http://www.symantec.com/about/news/release/article.jsp?prid=20110404_03

Traynor, P., Ahamad, M., Alperovitch, D., Conti, G., & Davis, J. (2012). *Emerging Cyber Threats Report 2012*. Atlanta: Georgia Tech Information Security Center.

Trend Micro. (2009, August 17). *Smartphone Users: Not Smart Enough About Security*. Retrieved April 17, 2012, from Trend Micro: http://newsroom.trendmicro.com/index.php?s=43&news_item=738&type=archived&year=2009

United States Computer Emergency Readiness Team. (2010, April 15). Cyber Threats to Mobile Devices. (TIP - 10-105-01), 1-16.

Vennon, T. (2010). *Android malware*. Retrieved from http://threatcenter.smobilesystems.com/

Wong, L. (2005). *Potential Bluetooth vulnerabilities in smartphones*. Retrieved from http://citeseerx.ist.psu.edu

Xie, L., Zhang, X., Chaugule, A., Jaeger, T., & Zhu, S. (2009). *Designing system-level defenses against cellphone malware*. Retrieved from www.cse.psu.edu

ZDNet. (2010). *Google fixes android root-access flaw*. Retrieved from ZDNet: www.zdnetasia.com

KEY TERMS AND DEFINITIONS

Authentication: Security measure designed to establish the validity of a transmission, message, or originator, or a means of verifying an individual's authorization to receive specific categories of information (Harris, 2002).

Availability: Timely, reliable access to data and information services for authorized users (Harris, 2002).

Confidentiality: Assurance that information is not disclosed to unauthorized individuals, processes, or devices (Harris, 2002).

Cyber Terrorism: Attacks with the use of the Internet for terrorist activities, including acts of deliberate, large-scale disruption of computer networks, especially of personal computers attached to the Internet, by the means of tools such as computer viruses, worms, Trojans, and zombies (Janczewski & Colarik, 2008).

Integrity: Quality of an IS reflecting the logical correctness and reliability of the OS; the logical completeness of the hardware and software implementing the protection mechanisms; and the consistency of the data structures and occurrence of the stored data. Note that, in a formal security mode, integrity is interpreted more narrowly to mean protection against unauthorized modification or destruction of information (Harris, 2002).

MMS/SMS: Multimedia message service and short message service are both communication protocols that have become widely used and adopted by smartphone users as the standard for fast and convenient communications.

Non-Repudiation: Assurance the sender of data is provided with proof of delivery and the recipient is provided with proof of the sender's identity, so neither can later deny having processed the data (Harris, 2002).

Rootkit: Malicious software designed to hide the existence of programs or processes from the normal methods of detection and enable privileged access to a computer.

Trojan: Malicious non-self-replicating malware program when executed carries out actions determined by the developer of the program. Trojans act as an backdoor providing unauthorized access to the infected computer.

Chapter 3
Security Threats on Mobile Devices

Lukáš Aron
Brno University of Technology, Czech Republic

ABSTRACT

This chapter contains basic introduction into security models of modern operating system like Android, iOS or Windows Phone. There are described the methods of attacks to the mobile devices. Such attacks consist of application based threats and vulnerabilities, network based attacks and internet browser vulnerabilities. The following section contains description of defensive strategies and steps for securing the device. There is also section about securing mobile device for enterprise environment. At the end of this chapter are discussed recommendations for security practices for mobile devices.

INTRODUCTION

Development on mobile devices development has been enormous over past 20 years and its results are all around us. It has been a long time since mobile phones were used only for making a call or writing short text messages. Technologically advanced societies are trying to speed up and simplify any process that can be automated and to provide user an easy access to it. These processes may be implemented as applications on mobile devices and are aimed on helping people to finish daily tasks easily or more quickly. Such mobile devices could be smart phones, tablets, notebooks or similar devices which man can easily carry along with him. Recent years have witnessed an explosive growth in smartphone sales and adoption.

The software on these mobile devices consists of an operating system and applications that are installed on the device. The most widespread operating system is Android (Burnette, 2009; Tesfay,

DOI: 10.4018/978-1-4666-8345-7.ch003

Booth & Andersson, 2012) from Google, which will be the model example for the further explanation, mainly because of its popularity and open source properties, but the principles can be applied to every other platform being used. The paper is going to introduce and explain the principles of mobile threats appearing through all platforms of mobile operating systems. There are also covered topics like securing Android for enterprise environment or recommendation security practices for mobile devices. The introduction into security on mobile devices begins with security models of mobile platforms Android, iOS and Windows Phone, which are explained in the first part of this chapter.

The next section of this paper is being aimed on the basic information about application-based mobile threats, and types of these threats in detail. Mobile threats are endangering the safety of individuals, companies, and if measures are not taken, than the cybercrime can have an impact on the security of the whole society. First, we have to ask the question: Why do threats and attacks on mobile devices exist? The answer is simple since the motivation could be the same as for the attacks on desktop machines.

Primary target of these attacks could be the secret information, whose gain could lead to stealing user's money, but attacker could be able to get an access to the computational power of the device, which could be also used for committing more cybercrime. The reason for emphasizing the security of mobile devices has its roots in this: while only experienced users were working with these devices 20 years ago, nowadays users that do not have any IT education and even small children are using modern technologies.

All security rules which were previously applied to personal or business computers or other non-mobile devices are now being applied to mobile devices. These rules are usually stricter, because owner of the device is also the main user (usually the only user) and may transmit sensitive information outside a secure area (e.g. home or office). It is necessary to refuse an access to this device by unauthorized users.

The simplest type of attack is to steal the device. The owner of the mobile device is generally the only user and that is the reason why there is not great emphasis on the physical security. This could be dangerous if the stolen device is the workstation of the user and the security threat to the whole company when the device is connected into corporate network. These problems related to networks and enterprise environment are covered after the section about application-based mobile threats.

There are a lot of types of security threats on mobile devices, but the weakest point is always non-expert user. In this chapter are discussed these threats that the user cannot control or can be deceived by the attacker. There are also cover defensive strategies and steps what to do for protecting the mobile devices as much as it possible. There are also recommendation security practices for mobile devices in the almost last part of this chapter.

The first section of this chapter is introduction into security models. Such models of modern mobile operating systems and compare them. The second part is targeted to application-based mobile threats and there are covered the most discussed security threats like malware, spyware, and privacy leak threats. After section about application-based mobile threats follow the section with caption defensive strategies. These strategies are steps for protection the mobile device. Different types of mobile threats which come from classical computers are browsers threats. These types of threats are well known from desktops and mobile devices are usually connected to the internet through internet browser which has almost the same vulnerabilities like the desktop one.

Next section is targeted to enterprise environment and how to secure this segment and follows the recommendations and security practices for mobile devices. The last part deals with conclusion about the mobile security in these days and to the near future.

Security Models

In this part of the chapter are descriptions of security models or architectures of Android (Li-ping, 2012), iOS operating system and Windows Phone. Such security models or architectures are unique for each mobile platform, but they have a lot in common. For example all platforms enable creating applications by the third party developers. The differences are discussed in the following text.

Android Security Model

Android is an application execution platform for mobile devices comprised out of an operating system, core libraries, development framework and basic applications. Android operating system is built on top of a Linux kernel. The Linux kernel is responsible for executing core system services such as: memory access, process management, access to physical devices through drivers, network management and security. Atop the Linux kernel is the Dalvik virtual machine (Oh, Kim, Choi & Moon, 2012) or new one Art virtual machine along with basic system libraries. The Dalvik/Art VM is a register based execution engine used to run Android applications.

The Art virtual machine has been introduced in 2014 as successor of Dalvik. It is still in beta mode. Main differences between these implementation is that Dalvik is just-in-time compilation technique. The code is interpreted on demand as the application require. In contrast the Art virtual machine is working in ahead-of-time-compilation technique. That means, after downloading application the code is compiled into native code of the device. More information can be found in (Oh, Kim, Choi & Moon, 2012).

In order to access lower level system services, the Android provides an API through afore mentioned C/C++ system libraries. In addition to the basic system libraries, the development framework provides access the top level services, like content providers, location manager or telephony manager. This means that it is possible to develop applications which use the same system resources as the basic set of applications, like built-in web browser or mail client. However, such a rich development framework presents security issues since it is necessary to prevent applications from stealing private data, maliciously disrupting other applications or the operating system itself. In order to address the security issues, Android platform implements a permission based security model.

The model is based on application isolation in a sandbox environment. This means that each application executes in its own environment and is unable to influence or modify execution of any other application.

Application sandboxing is performed at the Linux kernel level. In order to achieve isolation, Android utilizes standard Linux access control mechanisms. Each Android application package (.apk) is on installation assigned a unique Linux user ID. This approach allows the Android to enforce standard Linux file access rights. Since each file is associated with its owner's user ID, applications cannot access files that belong to other applications without being granted appropriate permissions. Each file can be assigned read, write and execute access permission. Since the root user owns system files, applications are not able to act maliciously by accessing or modifying critical system components.

On the other hand, to achieve memory isolation, each application is running in its own process, i.e. each application has its own memory space assigned. Additional security is achieved by utilizing memory management unit (MMU), a hardware component used to translate between virtual and physical address spaces. This way an application cannot compromise system security by running native code in privileged mode, i.e. the application is unable to modify the memory segment assigned to the operating system.

The presented isolation model provides a secure environment for application execution. However, restrictions enforced by the model also reduce the overall application functionality. For example, useful functionalities could be achieved by accessing critical systems like: access to network services, camera or location services. Furthermore, exchange of data and functionalities between applications enhanced the capabilities of the development framework. The shared user ID and permissions are two mechanisms, introduced by the Android, which can be used to lift the restrictions enforced by the isolation model.

The mechanism must provide sufficient flexibility to the application developers but also preserve the overall system security. Two applications can share data and application components, i.e. activities, content providers, services and broadcast receivers. For example, an application could run and activity belonging to other application or access its files.

The shared user ID allows applications to share data and application components. In order to be assigned a shared user ID the two applications must be signed with the same digital certificate. In effect, the developers can bypass the isolation model restrictions by signing applications with the same private key. However, since there is not a central certification authority, the developers are responsible to keep their private keys secure. By sharing the user ID, applications gain the ability to run in the same process. The alternative to the shared user ID approach is to use the Android permissions. In addition to sharing data and components, the permissions are used to gain access to critical system modules. Each android application can request and define a set of permissions. This means that each application can expose a subset of its functionalities to other applications if they have been granted the corresponding permissions. In addition, each application can request a set of permissions to access other applications or system libraries. Permissions are granted by the operating system at installation and cannot be changed afterwards. There are four types of permissions: normal, dangerous, signature and signature-or-system. Normal permissions give access to isolated application-level functionalities. These functionalities have little impact on system or user security and are therefore granted without an explicit user's approval.

However, the user can review which permissions are requested prior to application installation. An example of a normal level permission is access to the phone's vibration hardware. Since it is an isolated functionality, i.e. user's privacy or other applications cannot be compromised, it is not considered a major security risk. On the other hand, dangerous permissions proved access to private data and critical systems. For example, by obtaining a dangerous permission, an application can use telephony services, network access, records about the location or gain other private user data. Since dangerous permissions present a high security risk, the user is promoted to confirm them before installation.

Signature permission can be granted to the application signed with the same certificate as application declaring the permission. The signature permission is in effect a refinement of the shared user ID approach and provides more control in sharing application data and components. On the other hand, signature or system permission extends the signature permission by granting to the applications installed in the Android system image. However, caution is required since both the signature and signature or system permissions will grant access rights without asking for the user's explicit approval. The source of this section is (Enck, Octeau, McDaniel & Chaudhuri, 2011).

iOS Security Model

Unlike the Android security architecture, iOS security model (Hoog & Strzempka 2011) provides different philosophy for achieving mobile devices security and user's protection. The iOS application platform empowers developers to create new applications and to contribute to the application store. However, each application submitted by a third party developer is sent to the revision process. During the revision process the application code is analyzed by professional developers who make sure that the application is safe before it is released to the application store. However, such an application, when installed, gets all the permissions on a mobile device. Application might access local camera, 3G/4G, Wi/Fi or GPS module without user's knowledge. While Android lets each user handle its own security on their own responsibility, the iOS platform makes developers to write safe code using iOS secure API and prevents malicious applications from getting into the app store.

The iOS security APIs (Halbronn & Sigwald, 2010) are located in the Core Services layer of the operating system and are based on services in the Core OS – kernel layer of the operating system. Application that needs to execute a network task, may use secure networking functions through the CFNetwork API, which is also located in the Core Services layer.

The iOS security implementation includes a deamon called the Security Server that implements several security protocols, such as access to keychain items and root certificate trust management. The security Server has no public API. Instead, applications use the Keychain Services API and the Certificate, Key, and Trust services API, which in turn communicate with the Security Server. Keychain Services API is used to store passwords, keys, certificates, and other secret data. Its implementation therefore requires both cryptographic functions (to encrypt and decrypt secrets) and data storage functions (to store the secrets and related data in files). To achieve these aims, Keychain Services uses the Common Crypto dynamic library. CFNetwork is a high-level API that can be used by applications to create and maintain secure data streams and to add authentication information to a message. CFNetwork calls underlying security services to set up a secure connection. The Certificate, Key, and Trust Services API include functions to create, manage, and read certificates, add certificates to a keychain, create encryption keys, encrypt and decrypt data, sign data and verify signatures and manage trust policies.

To carry out all these services, the API calls the Common Crypto dynamic library and other Core OS-level services. Randomization Services provides cryptographically secure pseudorandom numbers. Such pseudorandom numbers are generated by a computer algorithm (and are therefore not truly random), but the algorithm is not discernible from the sequence. To generate these numbers, Randomization Services calls a random number generator in the Core OS layer. In case that the developers use the presented API properly and do not integrate malicious activities into the application, the application will be accepted into the App store.

Windows Phone Security Model

The Windows Phone security model is the foundation for protecting the confidentiality, integrity, and availability of data and communications. This section provides details about the innovative security architecture of Windows Phone.

The Windows Phone security model is based on the principles of isolation and least privilege, and introduces the "chamber" concept. Each chamber provides a security boundary and, through configuration, an isolation boundary within which a process can run. Each chamber is defined and implemented using a policy system. The security policy of a specific chamber defines what operating system capabilities the processes in that chamber can access.

There are four chamber types. Three of the chamber types have fixed permission sets, and the fourth chamber type is capabilities-driven. Apps that are designated to run in the fourth chamber type have capability requirements that are honored at installation and at run-time. The four chamber types are as follows:

1. **The Trusted Computing Base (TCB):** Chamber has the greatest privileges. It allows processes to have unrestricted access to most of the Windows Phone resources. The TCB chamber can modify policy and enforce the security model. The kernel and kernel-mode drivers run in the TCB chamber. Minimizing the amount of software that runs in the TCB is essential for minimizing the Windows Phone attack surface. Only Microsoft can add signed software components to the TCB chamber.

2. **The Elevated Rights Chamber (ERC):** Can access all resources except security policy. The ERC is intended for services and user-mode drivers that provide functionality intended for use by other phone apps. The ERC is less privileged than the TCB chamber. Only Microsoft can add signed software components to the ERC chamber.

3. **The Standard Rights Chamber (SRC):** Is the default chamber for pre-installed apps. All apps that do not provide device-wide services run in the SRC. Microsoft Outlook Mobile 2010 is an example of an app that runs in the SRC.

4. **The Least Privileged Chamber (LPC):** Is the default chamber for all non-Microsoft apps that are available through the Windows Phone Marketplace. LPCs are configured using capabilities as described in the following section.

A capability is a resource for which user privacy, security, cost, or business concerns exist with regard to usage on Windows Phone. Examples of capabilities include geographical location information, camera, microphone, networking, and sensors. The LPC defines a minimal set of access rights by default. However, the LPC is dynamic and can be expanded using capabilities. Capabilities are granted during app installation, and their privileges cannot be elevated at run time. The capabilities–based least privilege model is advantageous for the reasons like attack surface reduction and user consent and control.

Developers use the capability detection tool that is distributed with the Windows Phone Developer Tools to create the capability list for their app. The capability list is included in the app manifest in the app package (WMAppManifest.xml).

Every app on Windows Phone runs in its own isolated chamber that is defined by the declared capabilities that the app needs to function. A basic set of permissions is granted to all apps, including access to isolated storage. There are no communication channels between apps on the phone other than through the cloud. Apps are isolated from each other and cannot access memory used or data stored by other applications, including the keyboard cache.

In addition, Windows Phone does not allow apps to run in the background at any given time, which prevents hidden apps or spyware apps from preying on users. The moment a user switches to a different app on Windows Phone, the previously used app is put into a dormant state and its application state preserved. This approach ensures that an app cannot use critical resources or communicate with Internet–based services while the user is not using the app.

Measures that help mitigate common risks associated with smartphones, such as exposure of confidential data to unauthorized users, build on the robust security architecture of Windows Phone. In addition, policy management that complements these measures is simplified by the integration of Windows Phone with existing Microsoft infrastructure.

Summary

This part of the chapter was introduction into modern operating systems and their security models. There were descriptions of the most popular mobile operating systems – Android, iOS and Windows Phone. They are using different approach for securing user's data. Android promoted the power and the responsibility of security for applications to developers. Developer of the application should use the recommendations which are written on the official website of the Android operating system. This approach has strong and also weak sites in comparing to iOS or Windows Phone. The weakest point is that, the developers have the absolute power for the application security and user with no experience has very small chance to defend or protect the device. For example user wants some application and do not care about permissions what they confirmed, because without approval these permissions, application will not be installed. In contrast the strongest point is the same approach, but from the another point of view. The user has the power to deny installation the application, because he deny to using current application with these permissions. For example user does not want to allow the access to the contact list or messages for specific application and has the power to stop the installation process.

Another concept has the iOS, each application submitted by a third party developer is sent to the revision process. That is strong protection before malicious application, but the user has no power to deny specific permission.

Each platform has own ways for protecting user's. Despite the protection they are provided, there are still possible security threats and malicious software which is the main problem of the present security on mobile devices. In the next part are described malicious applications and application-based threats.

APPLICATION-BASED MOBILE THREATS

The typical user today downloads or buys software and installs it without thinking much about its functionality. A few lines of description and some reviews might be enough to persuade the user to try it. Except for well-known software (written by software companies such as Microsoft, Google or Apple) or through the open-source community, it can be difficult to verify the authenticity of available software or vouch for its functionality. Shareware/trial-ware/free software is available for personal computers (PCs) and is now available for mobile devices, as well, and only requires one click to install it. Hundreds of software applications pop up every day in the marketplace from seasoned to newbie developers.

The problem is compounded for mobile devices, especially Android. With no rigorous security review (or gate) on multiple Android marketplaces, there are many opportunities for malicious software to be installed on a device. The only gate seems to be during the install process, when the user is asked to approve requested permissions. After that, the user's trust in an application is complete. Users, therefore, don't understand the full implications of the utilities and software that they install on their devices. Given the complexity and interdependencies of software installed, it can become confusing even for seasoned professionals to figure out if a software package is trustworthy. At these times, the need for reverse engineering becomes crucial.

Application-based threats or malicious applications are software codes designed to disrupt regular operations and collect sensitive and unauthorized information from a system or a user. Malware can include viruses, worms, Trojans, spyware, key loggers, adware, rootkits, and other malicious code (Li, Gu & Luo, 2012). The following behavior can typically be classified as malware:

1. **Disrupting Regular Operations:** This type of software is typically designed to prevent systems from being used as desired. Behavior can include gobbling up all system resources (e.g., disk space, memory, CPU cycles), placing large amounts of traffic on the network to consume the bandwidth, and so forth.

2. **Collecting Sensitive Information without Consent:** This type of malicious code tries to steal valuable (sensitive) information – for example, key loggers. Such a key logger tracks the user's keys and provides them to the attacker. When the user inputs sensitive information (e.g. SSN, credit card numbers, and passwords), these can all potentially be logged and sent to an attacker.

3. **Performing Operations on the System without the User's Consent:** This type of software performs operations on systems applications, which it is not intended to do – for example, a wallpaper application trying to read sensitive files from a banking application or modifying files so that other applications are impacted.

Identifying Android Malware

The content of this part is to identify behavior that can be classified as malware on Android devices. The question here is, how do we detect suspicious applications on Android and analyze them? There are a few steps of methodology identifying malware with source code of current application. There is a methodology called reverse engineering (Franke, Elsemann, Kowalewski, & Weise, 2011), but that methodology is not legal. If the user has source code of the application there are steps that the user should follow for identifying the malicious software on the mobile device:

1. **Source/Functionality:** This is the first step in identifying a potentially suspicious application. If it is available on a non-standard source (e.g., a website instead of the official Android Market), it is prudent to analyze the functionality of the application. In many cases, it might be too late if the user already installed it on a mobile device. In any case, it is important to note the supposed functionality of an application, which can be analyzed through steps 2 to 4.

2. **Permissions:** Now that user has analyzed and user understands the expected behavior of the application, it is time to review the permissions requested by the application. They should align with the permissions needed to perform expected operations. If an application is asking for more permissions that it should for providing functionality, it is a candidate for further evaluation.

3. **Data:** Based on the permissions requested, it is possible to draw a matrix of data elements that it can have access to. Does it align with the expected behavior? Would the application have access to data not needed for its operations?

4. **Connectivity:** The final step is analyzing the application code itself. The reviewer needs to determine if the application is opening sockets (and to which servers), ascertain what type of data is being transmitted (and if secured), and see if it is using any advertising libraries, and so forth.

The attackers usually do not have access to original source code without reverse engineering. The easiest way for modifying application is to get the source code and add some malicious behavior. This approach is widely used, but there is another type of adding malicious behavior, which can be done without access to source code of the mobile application. This technique is not generally used by a typical user or developer. A person using the techniques covered here is probably attempting one of the following (which is unethical if not illegal):

1. **To Add Malicious Behavior:** It should be noted that doing this is illegal. Malicious users can potentially download an Android application (apk), decompile it, add malicious behavior to it, re-package the application, and put it back on the Web on secondary Android markets. Since Android applications are available from multiple markets, some users might be lured to install these modified malicious applications and thus be victimized.

2. **To Eliminate Malicious Behavior:** The techniques listed here can be used to analyze suspicious applications, and, if illegal/malicious behavior is detected, to modify them and remove the illegal/malicious behavior. Analyzing an application for malicious behavior is fine and necessary for security and forensics purposes. However, if there is indeed such behavior detected, users should just remove the application and do a clean install from a reliable source.

3. **To Bypass Intended Functionality:** A third potential use of the techniques listed here could be to bypass the intended functionality of an application. Many applications require a registration code or serial key before being used or they can only be used for a specified trial period or show ads when being used. A user of these techniques could edit small code and bypass these mechanisms.

All discussed areas around Malware infection has been real problem for privacy protection on mobile devices. Let me discuss two typical examples of Application based threats.

User would like to have some application which can help him/her with something. But it is not free and the fee for application is not low, but there are lot of possibilities to get the application free from different markets. Problem is not necessary in price, the current application can be for example not available for the current device in Google Play store or another reason for searching somewhere else.

This user can download the application and through the installation process apply for the permissions that are required for complete installation. However the application is for free, usually there are few things which may be dangerous. Current user has to apply required permissions which are usually different according to original application (now the user has to apply more rules than it is necessary). Application has required behavior and some bad behavior in addition, which is hidden to user. This hidden part of the application can steal user`s contacts, messages or get the user`s location and the whole content of device can be controlled by this application or by someone from remote machine. This application can do almost everything to spying the user or totally blocked the current device.

Second example has something in common with previous example. In this scenario we have application on Google Play market and the application has correct behavior, but the permissions which the user has to apply during installation process are inadequate of the manner current application. For example the user would like to have a new music player. However during installation the required permissions need the access to phone calls or sms messages. This can lead to another leakage of information or spying from developer side. Imagine that the user installs this kind of application and use it. That application can read the whole content of all messages which are sent to this device include confirmation messages from banks, emails or enterprise application.

DEFENSIVE STRATEGIES

In this section are covered five main strategies to prevent reverse engineering of an application or to minimize information leakage during the reverse engineering process. Defensive strategies are derived from (Misra & Dubey, 2013)

Perform Code Obfuscation

Code obfuscation is the deliberate act of making source code or machine code difficult to read or understand by humans and thus making it a bit more difficult to debug and reverse engineer only from executable files. Companies use this technique to make it harder for someone to steal their IP or to prevent tampering.

Most Android applications are written in Java. Since Java code gets compiled into byte code (running on a VM) in a class file, it is comparatively easier to reverse engineer it or to decompile it than binary executable files from C/C++. Consequently, we cannot rely only on code obfuscation for protecting intellectual property or user's privacy. We need to assume that it is possible for someone to decompile the apk package and more or less get access to the source code. Instead of relying completely on code obfuscation, we suggest relying on "Server Side Processing", where possible (covered in the following section).

One of the freely available Java obfuscators that can be used with Android is ProGuard (Hoog, 2011). ProGuard shrinks and obfuscates Java class files. It is capable of detecting and removing unused classes, fields, methods, and so forth. It can also rename these variables to shorter (and perhaps meaningless) names. Thus, the resulting apk package files will require more time to decipher. ProGuard has been integrated into the Android-built system. It runs only when an application is built in the release mode (and not in the debug mode). ProGuard might not be one of the best obfuscators out there for Java. However, it is something that one should definitely use in the absence of other options.

Perform Server Side Processing

Depending on the type of application, it might be possible to perform sensitive operations and data processing on the server side. For example, for an application that pulls data from the server to load locally (e.g., Twitter, Facebook), much of the application logic is performed on the server end. Once the application authenticates successfully and the validity of the user is verified, the application can rely on the server side for much of the processing. Thus, even if compiled binary is reverse engineered, much of the logic would be out of reach, as it will be on server side.

Perform Iterative Hashing and Use Salt

Hash functions can be susceptible to collision. In addition, it might be possible to brute force hash for weaker hash functions. Hash functions make it very difficult to brute force (unless user is a government agency with enormous computing power) while providing reasonably high collision resistance.

The SHA-2 family fits this category. A stronger hash can be obtained by using salt.

In cryptography, a salt consists of random bits and is usually one of the inputs to the hash function (which is one way and thus collision resistant). The other input is the secret (PIN, passcode, or password). This makes brute force attacks more difficult, as more time/space is needed. The same is true for rainbow tables. Rainbow tables are a set of tables that provide precomputed password hashes, thus making it easier to obtain plaintext passwords. They are an example of space-time or time-memory trade off (i.e., increasing memory reduces computation time).

In addition, it is recommended to use iterative hashing for sensitive data. This means simply taking the hash of data and hashing it again and so on. If this is done a sufficient number of times, the resultant hash can be fairly strong against brute force attacks in case an attacker can guess or capture the hash value.

Choose the Right Location for Sensitive Information

The location of sensitive information (and access to it) matters as much as the techniques described above. If we store strong hashes at a publicly accessible location (e.g., values.xml or on an SD card or local file system with public read attributes to it), then we make it a bit easier for an attacker. Android provides a great way to restrict access - data can only be explicitly made available through permissions wherein, by default, only the UID of the app itself can access it.

An ideal place for storing sensitive information would be in the database or in preferences, where other applications don't have access to it.

Cryptography

In the iterative hashing section were discussed how to make a user's passwords or sensitive information stronger through the use of cryptography (hashing and salt). Cryptography can also be used to protect a user's data. There are two main ways of doing this for Android:

1. Every application can store data in an encrypted manner (e.g., the user's contact information can be encrypted and then stored in a sqlite3 database).
2. Use disk encryption, wherein everything written to the disk is encrypted or decrypted on the fly.

System administrators prefer full-disk encryption, so as not to rely on developers to implement encryption capabilities in their Apps. The best tips for defense of this type of mobile threat can be found at the beginning of the chain - user. The mobile platform is not secure, because of the developers are humans. But through the ages of evolving mobile operating systems of each kind we have some recommendation for users of these platforms. First of all user should install application only from provider of operating system or manufacturer store. These application should be controlled for malware infection. However this control process is not perfect, the user has to be careful in installation process. The best protection against malware infection can be reading the permissions which are required during installation process even the application is on protected market. Defending example against the application that can read the SMS messages and the user still needs it can be the next few recommendations. The first of all user should see the application manager and check if all applications which can read SMS messages are turned off or should turn them off. The only exception should be original application for receiving SMS messages. Then the user can do some banking stuff or another processes which are related to sending confirmation SMS messages to the current device. This is only for basic protection, because the application for sniffing SMS messages can be type of service, which is usually running in background mode or waiting for SMS event (specific event when SMS message arrives on device) and then this application can still read the SMS message. In this point there is nothing in normal user phone mode (without rooting device) that can protect the access to the messages when the permissions was approved.

Summary

Access Control (relying on the OS to prevent access to critical files), cryptography (relying on encryption as well as hashing to protect confidential data [e.g., tokens] and to verify the integrity of an application), and code obfuscation (making it difficult to decipher class files) are the main strategies that one should leverage to prevent the reverse engineering of applications. In this part of the chapter, were discussed best practices to prevent reverse engineering as well as the potential leaking of sensitive information through it.

BROWSER SECURITY

Mobile devices has access to the internet network and this is usually provides by internet browser which is well known from classical PC. Such browser has only few differences from the PC, for example less consumption of energy or power of the device and also worse performance. This part describes HTML and browser security on mobile devices. There are covered different types of attacks possible, as well as browser vulnerabilities.

Mobile HTML Security

The increasing adoption of mobile devices and their use as a means to access information on the Web has led to the evolution of websites. Initially, mobile browsers had to access information through traditional (desktop-focused) websites. Today most of these websites also support Wireless Application Protocol (WAP) technology or have an equivalent mobile HTML (trimmed-down sites for mobile devices).

WAP specification defines a protocol suite that enables the viewing of information on mobile devices. The WAP protocol suite is composed of the following layers: Wireless Datagram Protocol (WDP), Wireless Transport Layer Security (WTLS), Wireless Transaction Protocol (WTP), Wireless Session Protocol (WSP), and Wireless Application Environment (WAE). The protocol suite operates over any wireless network.

In a typical Internet or WWW model, there is a client that makes a request to a server. The server processes the request and sends a response (or content) back to the client. This is more or less same in the WAP model, as well. However, there is a gateway or proxy that sits between the client and the server that adapts the requests and responses (encodes or decodes) for mobile devices. WAP 2.0 (Tull, 2002) provides support for richer content and end-end security than WAP 1.0.

WAP 1.0 did not provide end-end support for SSL/TLS. In WAP 1.0, communications between a mobile device and WAP gateway could be encrypted using WTLS. However, these communications would terminate at the proxy/gateway server. Communications between the gateway and application/ HTTP server would use TLS/SSL. This exposed WAP 1.0 communications to MITM (Man-In-The-Middle) attacks. In addition, all kinds of sensitive information would be available on the WAP gateway (in plaintext). This meant that a compromise of the WAP gateway/proxy could result in a severe security breach. WAP 2.0 remediates this issue by providing end-end support for SSL/TLS.

WAP and Mobile HTML sites are also susceptible to typical Web application attacks, including Cross-Site Scripting, SQL Injection, Cross-Site Request Forgery, and Phishing. Mobile browsers are fully functional browsers with functionality that rivals desktop versions. They include support for cookies, scripts, flash, and so forth. This means that users of mobile devices are exposed to attacks similar to those on desktop/laptop computers. A good source for detailed information on these attacks is the Open Web Application Security Project (OWASP, 2015).

Cross-Site Scripting

Cross-Site Scripting (XSS) (Backes, Gerling & Styp-Rekowsky, 2011) allows the injection of client-side script into web pages and can be used by attackers to bypass access controls. XSS attacks can result in attackers obtaining the user's session information (such as cookies). They can then use this information to bypass access controls. At the heart of XSS attacks is the fact that untrusted user input is not thoroughly vetted and is used without sanitization/escaping. In the case of XSS, user input is not sanitized for and is then either displayed back to the browser (reflected XSS) or stored (persistent XSS) and viewed later.

Mobile sites are as prone to XSS attacks as their regular counterparts, as mobile HTML sites might have even less controls around validating/sanitizing user input. Treating mobile HTML sites like regular websites and performing proper validation of user input can prevent a site from being vulnerable to XSS attacks.

SQL Injection

SQL injection (Clarke, 2012; Johari & Sharma, 2012; Bhavani, 2013) allows the injection of an SQL query from a client into an application. A successful SQL query (or attack) can provide attackers with sensitive information and enable them to bypass access controls, run administrative commands, and query/update/delete databases.

At the heart of SQL injection attacks is the fact that untrusted user input is directly used in crafting SQL queries without validation. These SQL queries are then executed against the backend database.

Similar to XSS, mobile HTML and WAP sites are prone to SQL injection attacks. Mobile sites might have the same flaws as their desktop counterparts, or, even worse, they might not be performing the validation of user input when accepting inputs through mobile sites. Using parameterized queries or stored procedures can prevent SQL injection attacks.

Cross-Site Request Forgery

A Cross-Site Request Forgery (CSRF, XSRF) (Bhavani, 2013) attack results in unwanted (unauthorized) commands from a user already authenticated to a website. The website trusts an authenticated user and, therefore, commands coming from him, as well. In CSRF, the website is the victim of the trust in the user, whereas in XSS, the user is the victim of the trust in the server/website.

It is typical for a user to be authenticated to multiple websites on a mobile device. Thus, CSRF attacks are possible, just as they are on desktop or laptop computers. In addition, small interface and UI layouts can disguise CSRF attacks (e.g., an e-mail with a URL link) and trick the user into performing unwanted operations on a website.

Phishing

Phishing attacks target unsuspecting users and trick them into providing sensitive information (e.g., SSN, passwords, credit card numbers, etc.). Through social engineering, attackers trick users to go to legitimate-looking websites and perform certain activities. Users trusting the source for this request (e.g., typically in an e-mail) performs the recommended operation and, in turn, provides an attacker with sensitive data.

As an example, a user gets an e-mail that seems legitimate and looks like it came from his bank. It is requesting the user to change his password due to a recent security breach at the bank. For his convenience, the user is provided with a URL to change his password. On clicking the link, the user is taken a website that looks like the bank's website. The user performs the password-reset operation and, in turn, provides the current password to the attacker.

Such attacks are even more difficult for users to recognize on mobile devices. Due to small UI real estate, users cannot really read the entire URL that they are viewing. If they are being redirected to a website, they would not be able to tell it easily on a mobile device.

Differences between legitimate and fake websites are not easy to distinguish on a small UI screen of mobile devices. If URLs are disguised (e.g., tiny URL) or if these are URLs that are sent through a Short Message Service (SMS) message (tiny URL via SMS), it is even more difficult to distinguish between legitimate and fake requests. Many users (even ones who are aware of such attacks) can be tricked into going through with an attack. As mentioned in the previous chapter, Quick Response (QR) codes can also be used for such attacks.

Browser Vulnerabilities

As of the writing of this chapter, there are ~200+ Common Vulnerabilities and Exposures (CVEs) related to the Android platform (search cve.mitre.org for "android"). Of these, many are related to browsers (either built-in browsers or downloadable browsers, such as Firefox). There are a few examples of browser related vulnerabilities which are connected to Android or iOS. The following information are derived from (Luo, Hao, Du, Wang & Yin, 2011; Enck, Ongtang & McDaniel, 2009)

1. **CVE 2008-7298:** The Android browser in Android cannot properly restrict modifications to cookies established in HTTPS sessions, which allows man-in-the-middle attackers to overwrite or delete arbitrary cookies via a Set-Cookie header in an HTTP response. This is due to the lack of the HTTP Strict Transport Security (HSTS) enforcement

2. **CVE 2010-1807:** WebKit in Apple Safari 4.x before 4.1.2 and 5.x before 5.0.2; Android before 2.2; and webkitgtk before 1.2.6. Does not properly validate floating-point data, which allows remote attackers to execute arbitrary code or cause a denial of service (application crash) via a crafted HTML document, related to nonstandard NaN representation

3. **CVE 2010-4804:** The Android browser in Android before 2.3.4 allows remote attackers to obtain SD card contents via crafted content://URIs, related to (1) BrowserActivity.java and (2) BrowserSettings. java in com/android/browser

4. **CVE 2011-2357:** Cross-application scripting vulnerability in the Browser URL loading functionality in Android 2.3.4 and 3.1 allows local applications to bypass the sandbox and execute arbitrary Javascript in arbitrary domains by (1) causing the MAX_TAB number of tabs to be opened, then

loading a URI to the targeted domain into the current tab, or (2) making two startActivity function calls beginning with the targeted domain's URI followed by the malicious Javascript while the UI focus is still associated with the targeted domain

5. **CVE 2012-3979:** Mozilla Firefox before 15.0 on Android does not properly implement unspecified callers of the android_log_print function, which allows remote attackers to execute arbitrary code via a crafted web page that calls the JavaScript dump function

Drive-By Downloads

Drive-by downloads have been an issue with computers for some time. However, they are starting to migrate to mobile devices. A drive-by download is basically malware that gets downloaded and often installed when a user visits an infected website.

Recently, we saw the first drive-by download malware for Android (named "NonCompatible"). When visiting an infected website, the browser could download this malware file. However, it cannot install itself without user intervention. In addition, installation from non-trusted sources needs to be enabled for the user to install this malware. An attacker can disguise such a download by renaming it as a popular Android application or updates to Android itself.

Users are willing to install such files without much thought and, thus, end up infecting their devices with malware. As long as "side loading" and installation of applications from "non-trusted" sources is disabled, such malware should not be able to impact Android devices.

SECURING ANDROID FOR THE ENTERPRISE ENVIRONMENT

This part of the chapter contains security concerns for deploying Android and Android applications in an enterprise environment (Wei, Gomez, Neamtiu & Faloutsos, 2012). At first there is review of security considerations for mobile devices, in general, as well as Android devices, in particular. Then move on to cover monitoring and compliance/audit considerations. This part is derived from (Kodeswaran et. All, 2012).

Android in Enterprise

From an enterprise perspective, there are different ways of looking at Android in the environment, with the main being the following three: deploying Android devices, developing Android applications, and the implications of allowing Android applications in the environment.

The deployment of Android devices and applications is primarily an IT function, whereas developing secure Android applications is part of either development/engineering teams or IT-development teams.

Security Concerns for Android in Enterprise

Today's mobile devices, including Android mobile devices like phones and tablets, are evolving at a rapid rate in terms of hardware and software features. Our assessment of threats, as well as security controls, has not kept up with the evolution of these features. These devices need more protection due to the features available on them, as well as the proliferation of threats to them. Before such devices can be deployed in an enterprise (or applications developed), it is essential that is carefully considered threats to mobile devices, as well as to enterprise resources arising from mobile devices (and users). This can be done using a threat model. In threat modeling, we analyze assets to protect, threats to these assets, and resulting vulnerabilities.

Lack of Physical Control of Device

Mobile devices are physically under the control of end users (not system administrators or security professionals). The fact that a device is with the user pretty much all the time increases the risk of compromise to an enterprise's resources. From shoulder surfing to the actual loss of the physical device, threats arise from the lack of physical control of these devices. Mobile devices are more likely to be lost, stolen, or are temporarily not within the user's immediate reach or view. Enterprise security should assume that once stolen or lost, these devices could fall into malicious hands, and thus security controls to prevent disclosure of sensitive data must be designed with this assumption.

Considering the worst-case scenario in which a lost or a stolen device falls into malicious hands, the best way to prevent further damage will be to encrypt the mobile device (if the storing of sensitive data is allowed) or not allowing devices to access sensitive information (not really possible with Android smartphones). To prevent shoulder surfing, it might be prudent to use privacy screens (yes, there are ones for phones). In addition, a screen lock (requiring a password/PIN) should be a requirement for using these devices, if access to enterprise resources is desired. The best practice would be to authenticate to a different application each time one uses it, although this is tedious, and, most likely, users will not adhere to this (imagine logging into the Facebook application on an Android device every time one uses it).

Use of "User-Owned" Untrusted Devices

Many enterprises are following a BYOD (bring your own device) model (Ballagas, Rohs, Sheridan, & Borchers, (2004). This essentially means that users will bring their own mobile device (which they purchase) and use it to access company resources. This poses a risk because these devices are untrusted (and not approved) by enterprise security, and one has to rely on end users for due diligence. Thus, the assumption that all devices are essentially untrusted is not far-fetched.

Security policies need to be enforced even if these devices are owned by the users. In addition, these devices and applications on them need to be monitored. Other solutions include providing enterprise devices (which have a hardened OS and preapproved applications and security policies) or allowing user-owned devices, with sensitive resources being accessed through well-protected sandboxed applications.

Connecting to "Unapproved and Untrusted Networks"

Mobile devices have multiple ways to connect: cellular connectivity, wireless, Bluetooth connections, Near Field Communication (NFC), and so forth. An enterprise should assume that any or all of these means of connectivity are going to be employed by the end user. These connectivity options enable many types of attacks: sniffing, man-in-the-middle, eavesdropping, and so forth.

An example of such an attack would be the end user connecting to any available (and open) Wi-Fi network and thus allowing an attacker to eavesdrop on communications (if not protected).

Making sure communications are authenticated before proceeding and then encrypted can effectively mitigate risk from this threat.

Use of Untrusted Applications

This essentially replicates the problem on desktop/laptop computers. End users are free to install any application they choose to download. Even if the device is owned and approved by an enterprise, users are likely to install their own applications (unless prevented by the security policy for the device). For Android, a user can download applications from dozens of application markets or just download an application off the Internet.

There are several options for mitigating this threat. An enterprise can either prohibit use of third-party applications through security policy enforcement or through acceptable use policy guidelines. It can create a whitelist of applications that users are allowed to install and use if they would like to access company resources through their Android devices. Although this might prevent them from installing an application (e.g., Facebook), they might still be able to use this application through other means (e.g., browser interface). The most effective mitigating step here is educating the end user, along with policy enforcement. The monitoring of devices is another step that can be taken.

Connections with "Untrusted" Systems

Mobile devices synchronize data to/from multiple devices and sources. They can be used to sync e-mails, calendars, pictures, music, movies, and so forth. Sources/destinations can be the enterprise's desktops/laptops, personal desktops/laptops, websites, and increasingly, these days, cloud-based services. Thus, one can assume any data on the device might be at risk.

If the device is owned by the enterprise, security policies on the device itself can be enforced to prevent it from backing up or synchronizing to unauthorized sources. If the user owns the device, awareness and monitoring (and maybe sandbox applications) are the way to go.

Unknown Content

There can be a lot of untrusted content on mobile devices (e.g., attachments, downloads, Quick Response (QR) codes, etc.). Many of these will be from questionable or unknown sources and can pose risks to user and enterprise data. Take, for example, QR codes. There can be malicious URLs or downloads hidden throughout these codes, but the user might not be aware of these, thus falling victim to an attack.

Installing security software (anti-virus) might mitigate some risk. Disabling the camera is another option to prevent attacks such as those on QR codes. Awareness, however, is the most effective solution here.

Use of GPS (Location-Related Services)

Increasingly, mobile devices are being used as a navigation device as well as to find "information" based on location. Many applications increasingly rely on location data provided through GPS capabilities in mobile devices. From Facebook to yelp, the user's location is being used to facilitate user experience. This has a downside, aside from privacy implications. Location information can be used to launch targeted attacks or associate users' activities based on their location data.

Disabling the GPS is one way to mitigate the risk. However, this is not possible for BYOD (Miller, Voas & Hurlburt, 2012) devices. Another possibility is to educate users on the implications of using location data. Policies preventing some applications (e.g., social media applications) to use location information can also be implemented through policy enforcement.

Lack of Control of Patching Applications and OS

This is an especially acute problem in BYOD environments. Users can bring their own devices and may not patch or update their OS/applications for security fixes that become available, thus exposing enterprise resources to security risks. Think of all the different Android versions (from 2.2.21 to 4.x) in your environment today and the potential security risks for each of them. Users probably have not upgraded or kept up-to-date with security fixes for Android itself. In addition, many users don't install application updates.

Monitoring the devices and trying to ascertain information about the respective versions of their OS/applications can provide information that can be used to flag out insecure OS/applications. Users can then be forced to either upgrade or risk losing access to enterprise resources.

End-User Awareness

Any strategy for securing mobile devices or enterprise resources being accessed through mobile devices must include end-user training. Users should be made aware of the risks (listed above) and understand why security controls are necessary. Adhering to these controls should be part of acceptable-use policy, and users should be required to review this at least annually. In addition, annual security-awareness training and a follow-up quiz might imbibe some of these best practices in their minds. Secure awareness should be complemented by warning users when they are about to perform an unwarranted action (e.g., access unwanted site, download malicious code, etc.).

RECOMMENDED SECURITY PRACTICES FOR MOBILE DEVICES

In the previous section were reviewed common threats to mobile devices and some of the mitigation steps one can take. In this section is covered in detail how to configure (harden) an Android device to mitigate the risks. These recommendation come from (Six, 2011; Burns, 2008; Chang, Tan, Li & Zhu, 2010). Security practices for mobile devices can be divided into four main categories:

1. **Policies and Restrictions on Functionality:** Restrict the user and applications from accessing various hardware features (e.g., camera, GPS), push configurations for wireless, Virtual Private Network (VPN), send logs/violations to remote server, provide a whitelist of applications that can be used, and prevent rooted devices from accessing enterprise resources and networks.
2. **Protecting Data:** This includes encrypting local and external storage, enabling VPN communications to access protected resources, and using strong cryptography for communications. This also should include a remote wipe functionality in the case of a lost or stolen device.

3. **Access Controls:** This includes authentication for using the device (e.g., PIN, SIM password) and per-application passwords. A PIN/Passcode should be required after the device has been idle for few minutes (the recommendation is 2–5 minutes).

4. **Applications:** This includes application-specific controls, including approved sources/markets from which applications can be installed, updates to applications, allowing only trusted applications (digitally signed from trusted sources) to be installed, and preventing services to backup/restore from public cloud-based applications.

Out of the box, Android does not come with all desired configuration settings (from a security viewpoint). This is especially true for an enterprise environment. Android security settings have improved with each major release and are fairly easy to configure. Desired configuration changes can be applied either locally or can be pushed to devices by Exchange ActiveSync mail policies. Depending on the device manufacturer, a device might have additional (manufacturer or third-party) tools to enhance security.

Unauthorized Device Access

As mentioned earlier in the chapter, lack of physical control of mobile devices is one of the main concerns for a user and for an enterprise. The risk arising out of this can be mitigated to a certain extent through the following configuration changes:

Setting up a Screen Lock and SIM Lock

After enabling this setting, a user is required to enter either a PIN or a password to access a device. There is an option to use patterns, although it is not recommend it. Recommendation for a strong password is an 8-digit PIN. Once "Screen Lock" is enabled, the automatic timeout value should be updated as well.

Turning on the "SIM card lock" makes it mandatory to enter this code to access "phone" functionality. Without this code, one would not be able to make calls or send SMS messages.

Remote Wipe

System administrators can enable the "Remote Wipe" function through Exchange ActiveSync mail policies. If a user is connected to the corporate Exchange server, it is critical to enable this feature in case the device is lost or stolen. There are other settings that can be pushed as well (e.g., password complexity). These are covered later in this chapter.

Remote Wipe essentially wipes out all data from the phone and restores it to factory state. This includes all e-mail data, application settings, and so forth. However, it does not delete information on external SD storage.

Other Settings

In addition to the above settings, it is strongly recommended to disable the "Make passwords visible" option. This will prevent shoulder surfing attacks, as characters won't be repeated back on screen if the user is typing a password or PIN.

It is also recommended to disable "Allow installation of apps from unknown sources." It was mentioned before, there are secondary application stores apart from Google Play, and it is prudent to not trust applications from these sources before ascertaining their authenticity. Disabling this option will prevent applications from being installed from other sources.

As a rule of thumb, it is recommended to turn off services that are not being used. A user should turn off "Bluetooth," "NFC," and "Location features" unless using them actively, as well as the "Network notification" feature from the Wi-Fi settings screen. This will make the user choose a connection rather than connecting to any available network. Discourage backing up of data to "Gmail or Google" accounts or Dropbox. Create a whitelist of applications and educate users on the list so they do not install applications outside of the approved list.

A new feature of Android 4.2 enhances protection against malicious applications. Android 4.2 has a feature that, if enabled, verifies an application being installed with Google. Depending on the risk of the application, Android warns users that it is potentially harmful to proceed with the installation. Note that some data is sent to Google to enable this process to take place (log, URL, device ID, OS, etc.).

Another useful feature might be to enable "Always on VPN." This prevents applications from connecting to the network unless VPN is on. Another recommendation is to turn off the USB debugging feature from phones. USB debugging allows a user to connect the phone to an adb shell. This can lead to the enumeration of information on the device. Browser is one of the most commonly used applications on Android devices. Browser security and privacy settings should be fine-tuned (e.g., disable location access).

Android 3.0 and later have the capability to perform full-disk encryption (this does not include the SD card). Turning this feature on encrypts all data on the phone. In case the phone is lost or stolen, data cannot be recovered because it is encrypted. The caveat here is that the screen lock password has to be the same as encryption password. Once the phone is encrypted, during boot time you will be required to enter this password to decrypt the phone.

CONCLUSION

This chapter has described an overview of mobile security threats and possible vulnerabilities. There are modern operating systems with strong security background which are provided to the users. There is nothing more important than the safety of the user's data. In these days there are a lot of known vulnerabilities in these operating systems, applications, internet browsers and specific teams and developers working on issues trying to fix known problems. However, there is the weakest point at this security and that point is always the user of the current device. There is not necessary that the attacker is a developer or technical educated person, it could be anyone who knows something personal and can deceive the user.

For discussed platforms (Android and iOS) exist the additional adjustments which break the basic security model. This is usual called the "rooting" the device. It is because the operation systems are based on Linux or Unix kernel and the administrator or superpower user is called root. Another name for the same unlocking device could be jail-break. This adjustment can bring some more power to the user for settings or installing application from the other sources than is usual, but there are always the risk. The risk is always related to the security of the current mobile device.

The number of daily activated mobile devices rapidly grows and lot of people using these devices every day. These users mainly go to the internet and the use these devices more than classical computers or notebook. From this point of view this is interesting segment for attackers. They know that users have the personal and private data on these devices. The bank segment is trying to move the payment from computers into the mobile devices with using the NFC technology. This will be discussed topic about the security.

REFERENCES

Backes, M., Gerling, S., & von Styp-Rekowsky, P. (2011). *A Local Cross-Site Scripting Attack against Android Phones.* Retrieved April 4, 2015, from https://www.infsec.cs.uni-saarland.de/projects/android-vuln/android_xss.pdf

Ballagas, R., Rohs, M., Sheridan, J. G., & Borchers, J. (2004, September). BYOD: Bring your own device. In *Proceedings of the Workshop on Ubiquitous Display Environments, Ubicomp* (Vol. 2004*)*.

Bhavani, A. B. (2013). Cross-site Scripting Attacks on Android WebView. *arXiv preprint arXiv:1304.7451.*

Burnette, E. (2009). *Hello, Android: introducing Google's mobile development platform.* Pragmatic Bookshelf.

Burns, J. (2008). *Developing secure mobile applications for android.*

Chang, G., Tan, C., Li, G., & Zhu, C. (2010). Developing mobile applications on the Android platform. In *Mobile multimedia processing* (pp. 264–286). Springer Berlin Heidelberg. doi:10.1007/978-3-642-12349-8_15

Clarke, J. (Ed.). (2012). *SQL injection attacks and defense.* Elsevier.

Enck, W., Octeau, D., McDaniel, P., & Chaudhuri, S. (2011, August). A Study of Android Application Security. In USENIX security symposium (Vol. 2, p. 2).

Enck, W., Ongtang, M., & McDaniel, P. D. (2009). Understanding Android Security. *IEEE Security and Privacy*, *7*(1), 50–57. doi:10.1109/MSP.2009.26

Franke, D., Elsemann, C., Kowalewski, S., & Weise, C. (2011, October). Reverse engineering of mobile application lifecycles. In *Reverse Engineering (WCRE), 2011 18th Working Conference on* (pp. 283-292). IEEE. doi:10.1109/WCRE.2011.42

Halbronn, C., & Sigwald, J. (2010). iPhone security model & vulnerabilities. In Proceedings of Hack in the box sec-conference. Kuala Lumpur, Malaysia.

Hoog, A. (2011). *Android forensics: investigation, analysis and mobile security for Google Android.* Elsevier.

Hoog, A., & Strzempka, K. (2011). iPhone and iOS Forensics: Investigation, Analysis and Mobile Security for Apple iPhone, iPad and iOS Devices. Elsevier.

Johari, R., & Sharma, P. (2012, May). A survey on web application vulnerabilities (SQLIA, XSS) exploitation and security engine for SQL injection. In *Communication Systems and Network Technologies (CSNT), 2012 International Conference on* (pp. 453-458). IEEE.

Kodeswaran, P., Nandakumar, V., Kapoor, S., Kamaraju, P., Joshi, A., & Mukherjea, S. (2012, July). Securing enterprise data on smartphones using run time information flow control. In *Mobile Data Management (MDM), 2012 IEEE 13th International Conference on* (pp. 300-305). IEEE. doi:10.1109/MDM.2012.50

Li, J., Gu, D., & Luo, Y. (2012, June). Android malware forensics: reconstruction of malicious events. In *Distributed Computing Systems Workshops (ICDCSW), 2012 32nd International Conference on* (pp. 552-558). IEEE. doi:10.1109/ICDCSW.2012.33

Li-ping, D. I. N. G. (2012). Analysis the Security of Android. *Netinfo Security, 3*, 011.

Luo, T., Hao, H., Du, W., Wang, Y., & Yin, H. (2011, December). Attacks on WebView in the Android system. In *Proceedings of the 27th Annual Computer Security Applications Conference* (pp. 343-352). ACM. doi:10.1145/2076732.2076781

Miller, K. W., Voas, J., & Hurlburt, G. F. (2012). BYOD: security and privacy considerations. *It Professional, 14*(5), 0053-55.

Misra, A., & Dubey, A. (2013). *Android security: attacks and defenses*. CRC Press. doi:10.1201/b14672

Oh, H. S., Kim, B. J., Choi, H. K., & Moon, S. M. (2012, October). Evaluation of Android Dalvik virtual machine. In *Proceedings of the 10th International Workshop on Java Technologies for Real-time and Embedded Systems* (pp. 115-124). ACM. doi:10.1145/2388936.2388956

Owasp, T. (2010). *The Ten Most Critical Web Application Security Risks*. Retrieved April 4, 2015, from https://www.owasp.org

Six, J. (2011). *Application Security for the Android Platform: Processes, Permissions, and Other Safeguards*. O' Reilly Media, Inc.

Tesfay, W. B., Booth, T., & Andersson, K. (2012, June). Reputation Based Security Model for Android Applications. In *Trust, Security and Privacy in Computing and Communications (TrustCom), 2012 IEEE 11th International Conference on* (pp. 896-901). IEEE. doi:10.1109/TrustCom.2012.236

Tull, C. (2002). *WAP 2.0 Development*. Que Publishing.

Wei, X., Gomez, L., Neamtiu, I., & Faloutsos, M. (2012, April). Malicious android applications in the enterprise: What do they do and how do we fix it? In *Data Engineering Workshops (ICDEW), 2012 IEEE 28th International Conference on* (pp. 251-254). IEEE.

KEY-TERMS AND DEFINITIONS

BYOD: BYOD, or bring your own device, is a phrase that has become widely adopted to refer to employees who bring their own computing devices – such as smartphones, laptops and PDAs – to the workplace for use and connectivity on the secure corporate network.

Cryptography: The art of protecting information by transforming it (encrypting it) into an unreadable format, called cipher text. Only those who possess a secret key can decipher (or decrypt) the message into plain text. Encrypted messages can sometimes be broken by cryptanalysis, also called codebreaking, although modern cryptography techniques are virtually unbreakable.

Malware: Malware is short for "malicious software". Malware is a term for any software that gets installed on computer and performs unwanted tasks, often for some third party's benefit. Malware programs can range from being simple annoyances (pop-up advertising) to causing serious computer invasion and damage (e.g., stealing passwords and data or infecting other machines on the network).

Mobile Operating System: A mobile operating system, also called a mobile OS, is an operating system that is specifically designed to run on mobile devices such as mobile phones, smartphones, PDAs, tablet computers and other handheld devices. The mobile operating system is the software platform on top of which other programs, called application programs, can run on mobile devices.

Obfuscation: Obfuscation, in general, describes a practice that is used to intentionally make something more difficult to understand. In a programming context, it means to make code harder to understand or read, generally for privacy or security purposes. A tool called an obfuscator is sometimes used to convert a straight-forward program into one that works the same way but is much harder to understand.

Security Model: A computer security model is a scheme for specifying and enforcing security policies. A security model may be founded upon a formal model of access rights, a model of computation, a model of distributed computing, or no particular theoretical grounding at all. We can divide security model into two categories – positive and negative. A positive security model (also known as whitelist) is one that defines what is allowed, and rejects everything else. This should be contrasted with a negative (or blacklist) security model, which defines what is disallowed, while implicitly allowing everything else.

Security Threat: In computer security a threat is a possible danger in the system. There are common threats categories like virus threat, spyware threat, phishing threat etc.

Virtual Machine: A virtual machine is an operating system OS or application environment that is installed on software which imitates dedicated hardware. The end user has the same experience on a virtual machine as they would have on dedicated hardware.

Chapter 4
The Human Factor in Mobile Phishing

Rasha Salah El-Din
University of York, UK

Paul Cairns
University of York, UK

John Clark
University of York, UK

ABSTRACT

Phishing is the use of electronic media, like emails and mobile text messages, to fraudulently elicit private information or obtain money under false pretence. Though there is considerable interest in phishing as a security problem, there is little previous research from the human factors perspective and in particular very little empirical support for what makes mobile phishing effective or successful and therefore how best to defend people from it. This chapter describes some of the research conducted from the field of traditional phishing that already embraces the effect of human factors on phishing vulnerability. The limited amount of research exploiting mobile phishing is discussed; including a review of our previous work involving evaluating mobile users' strategies for managing mobile phishing attacks. By reflecting on how these subjects investigate the threat of phishing, this chapter aims to show that empirical research on mobile phishing is scarce and falling behind in terms of identifying underlying psychological processes and inspire future research in this area.

INTRODUCING PHISHING

According to Oxford English Dictionary, Phishing is the fraudulent practice of sending emails purporting to be from reputable companies in order to induce individuals to reveal personal information, such as passwords and credit card numbers, online (Oxford Dictionaries, 2014). The word phishing itself originated from the word 'fishing' in a reference to catching something by bait. Same way the fisherman lures a fish with a fake worm to a hook, the 'phisher' lures his victims with an impersonated communication (such as email or website) to a trap to catch their sensitive information.

DOI: 10.4018/978-1-4666-8345-7.ch004

In the literature, there are several definitions for phishing to the extent that there is no consensus over one certain definition. For instance, according to definition adopted by the Anti-Phishing Working Group (APWG), phishing is "a form of online identity theft that employs both social engineering and technical subterfuge to steal consumers' personal identity data and financial account credentials" (Anti-Phishing Working Group,2007). Jakobsson, the renowned phishing expert and co-author of the book 'Phishing and Countermeasures…' defines phishing as "a form of social engineering in which an attacker, also known as a phisher, attempts to fraudulently, retrieve legitimate users' confidential or sensitive credentials by mimicking electronic communications from a trustworthy or public organization in an automated fashion" (Jakobsson & Myers, 2006). The homeland Security defined phishing as "online identity theft in which information is obtained from an individual" (Dunham, 2008).

Although the available research involves many definitions for phishing, most of these definitions do not rigorously identify the phishing attack channel (Dunham, 2008) as the medium may diverge according to the setup of the attack. Therefore, one may find phishing in several forms: email, phone calls or mobile phishing. Even in the latter alone, there are many channels where mobile phishing attacks can be launched through. Examples of mobile-targeted attacks include Bluejacking (via Bluetooth), Smishing (via short message services) or Vishing (via mobile phone call).

INTRODUCING MOBILE PHISHING

The small size, high connectivity and mobility provided by mobile phones empowered them to be one of the most widely used devices all over the world. Yet, these factors made mobile phones subject to different security threats. A recent study by Informa Telecoms (Informa Telecoms, 2009) had put mobile malware, such as ComWar and Capir, and phishing on top of mobile security threats. Ying, Dinglong, Haiyi, and Rau (2007) have summarized possible security attacks to mobile phones as follows:

1. Virus attacks via either SMS, Bluetooth or Computers.
2. Spam messages either via advertising or fraud.
3. Data loss due to loss or theft of mobile devices.
4. Eavesdropping.
5. Internet scam in case of accessing the internet by mobiles.

In fact both mobile and fixed communications face similar threats: Masquerade, eavesdropping, authorization violation, loss or modification of transmitted information or sabotage (Schiller, 2003). What makes these issues need further investigation for the mobile context is the vast spread of mobile phones usage in business. More enterprises' employees rely on their mobile devices in general and on their cellular phones in particular, for running business operations. Yet, few numbers of these organizations really protect these devices. According to Muir (Muir, 2003), less than 10% of mobile devices used by major organizations, have serious protection for stored data.

Despite similarities of threats, traditional security solutions do not necessarily work for mobile environments (Jakobsson, 2011). Instead, both the mobile environment and the mobile users need to be studied for the development of suitable solutions that can address the mobile platform needs. We will discuss briefly these differences both the technical and the behavioral ones.

For the technical differences, some of the significant ones include the small screen, the small keypad, process limitations and power restrictions. These differences are likely to affect security. For instance, the small key pad of the mobile handset makes text entry time-consuming and error-prone. It also encourages mobile users to use short passwords and PINs rather than using strong passwords. The small screen means that webpage address bars are often automatically hidden to make room for other contents; a vulnerability a phisher can take advantage of (Jakobsson, 2011). Regarding battery power limitations, they often obstruct users from using Anti-Virus products. Accordingly, the limited battery resources of the mobile phones affect malware detection (Jakobsson, 2011).

As for the behavioral differences, in terms of security, mobile users do not give their mobile phones same attention and care they give their traditional computing devices. Our previous research has consistently shown that mobile users do not understand the threats associated with their smart phone. Instead, they treat it as merely a telephone device. Another behavioral aspect is the fact that mobile phones are more strongly associated with social activities than computers are (Jakobsson, 2011). In one of the few attempts to study human aspects of mobile phishing, the authors of this chapter have conducted a phishing lab study investigating postgraduate students' ability to detect mobile phishing messages (El-Din, Cairns, & Clark, 2014). It was found that the message pretending to be sent from a friend was the least detected by the participants. Some of them were really keen not to miss a call that may be important. Also, the employment of familiar names, such as Paul or John, in the phishing messages caused the recruits to trust the message. "I recognize the names, I'll call back", "I'll call Mr.Paul Clark", they said. Also the mobile users' lack of knowledge of premium rate numbers was another reason they fell for the mobile phishing messages. "I'll call and ask", "I'll call back to find how true is the text", they said. This implies that individuals may be vulnerable to phishing attacks that use new deceit techniques.

Phishing on mobile phones can take several forms such as Vishing and Smishing. Vishing is the criminal practice of using social engineering over the telephone system seeking confidential information. Such as user names, passwords and banking details. It stands for Voice Phishing. Smishing uses mobile short message service to mount phishing attacks. It stands for SMS Phishing. Both Vishing and Smishing can be performed via context-aware phishing which is called 'spear phishing'. Spear phishing can be defined as an attack that targets specific group at specific time (Dunham, 2004). Here, we stress on the time aspect as an important factor of the phishing process. In fact, we regard three contexts, in specific, of high importance to the phishing response anticipated by the phishing message receivers. These contexts are time, space and technology.

As for the time context, actually, the relationship of a phishing attack to the time of its delivery and to the time of its interpretation determines whether the attack would work as expected or not (Dunham, 2004). Imagine an email asking you to follow a link for electronic voting when there is no election taking place at that time. The message would certainly lose its credibility. Conversely, if a phishing message, asking the user to click a link for car accident insurance claim, hits a person who has just had a car accident, the probability that she would trust the message is extremely high.

The second context of importance to the attacker is the technological context. This context is related to the device on which the victim receives the phishing message. Certainly, the type of technology used by the victims is highly correlated with the way they interact with it, in terms of security. For example, one of the reasons why computer users might be deceived by phishing is their lack of understanding of the way computers work (Jakobsson, 2007). This certainly applies to all kinds of technologies which the users may not feel confident in using, and smart phones are not an exception.

The third context is the space one. The spatial context denotes the physical surroundings where the victim is existed at the time of the phishing attack. In principle, that refers to the place at which the victim receives the phishing message but comprehensively, it implies the situation as a whole; the overall atmosphere around the victim, the location, the activity performed, noise and even weather. A perfect example of how the location affects users' response to phishing is a Bluetooth phishing scenario. Imagine a bank client who has just finished a transaction in his bank X. the minute he steps outside the bank, he receives, on his Bluetooth-enabled phone, a file named 'Bank X contact.sis'. The client thought the file was sent by his bank, most probably something that has to do with the transaction he has just finished few minutes ago. The truth is that the file was sent by a phisher sitting back in his car outside the bank snarfing for clients using Bluetooth devices. The file was actually a Trojan (Dunham, 2004). Another example of special context is sitting in a café and connecting to the available wireless networks. One of them is named after the café itself while in fact it has nothing to do with it.

You can go on and think of more scenarios where these contexts apply. You can even come up with more contexts that mobile phones easily enable for the comfort of mobile users, but, sadly have been used by cyber criminals.

These settings and more make it essential to study mobile security in general and mobile phishing in particular. In the next sections, we will discuss the need for such field of study and view some research in the area of phishing.

THE NEED TO STUDY MOBILE PHISHING

Mobile phishing has been described as 'The problem on the horizon' in the monthly security report of Trend Micro (Micro trend, 2013). It has also been regarded as an emerging threat that targets mobile customers (Boodaei, 2013; Bortinik, 2011) especially that mobile users do not expect to be hacked via their mobile phones, which make them more prone to these attacks. Recent studies that examined users' perception of phishing concluded that: "Emails are very phishy, web pages a bit, phone calls are not" (Jakobsson, 2007) and that phishing attacks can be more convincing on phones than in a desktop browser (Felt, Finifter, Chin, Hanna, & Wagner, 2011). Another factor that may increase mobile phishing problem is the way most service providers communicate with their customers currently. For instance, when communicating with a financial institution nowadays, users are prompted to speak to an automated phone message and to dial-in identifying information such as their bank account details, date of birth and postal code in order to speak to customer support agent. That, in itself, trains users to give out their credentials via phone calls (Jakobsson, 2007). Such method of communication is likely to increase the phisher's credibility specially that users expressed that, in emergencies they would not expect an email, they would expect a phone or a text from what ever service providers trying to contact them (Jakobsson, 2007).

Despite all of the above, we find human interaction with mobile phishing almost missing from the literature. Very few studies have investigated Vishing or SMishing attacks from the human perspective. Via conducting a multi-method set of four studies, our research is trying to contribute to an understanding of both users' perception and behavior towards mobile security in general and SMishing and particular.

Figure 1.

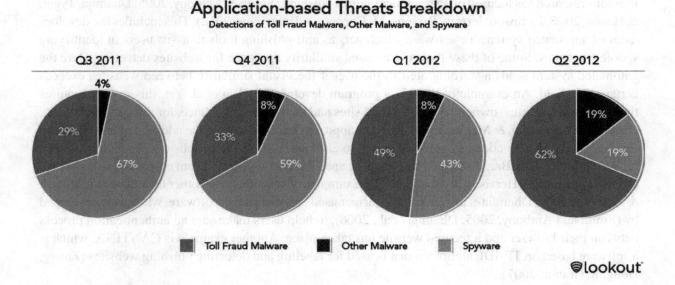

Application-based Threats Breakdown
Detections of Toll Fraud Malware, Other Malware, and Spyware

| Q3 2011 | Q4 2011 | Q1 2012 | Q2 2012 |

■ Toll Fraud Malware   ■ Other Malware   ■ Spyware

☁lookout

THE NEED TO STUDY SMISHING IN PARTICULAR

Among the different forms of mobile phishing, SMishing is of unique characteristics which make it very attractive to spammers. These include the success of the mobile messaging channels and the high level of trust associated with texting. Not only is mobile texting very easy to use, but also the level of trust between the mobile operators and their subscribers, in regards to texting, is unprecedented. According to IAB/DMA survey conducted in the UK in September 2010, 63% of mobile users said they were happy to receive both text and multimedia messages from their operators. This trust meant that almost all messages received by mobile users are opened and read. The numbers are also easily dialed and clicked. Adding to these, the very cheap cost of sending text message spam and the several billing plans increases the risk of mobile messaging abuse. Worse that this is that attackers are currently moving beyond simple spam messages to fraudulent scams, phishing and mobile spyware.

Figure 1 shows mobile threats trend in 2012. It shows a notable rise in the prevalence of mobile Toll Fraud Malware. This is a malware designed to make a premium rate number without the knowledge of the mobile user. It can take the form of either 'Auto-diallers' or 'dialler programs'. Auto-diallers take two forms. The first form is software that automatically dials a phone number that automatically plays a pre-recorded message. The message, known as 'voice broadcasting', usually asks the mobile user to press certain buttons in the keypad. In some cases, the phone call is answered by a live person. The second form of Autodiallers is software that automatically makes many short duration calls to premium rate numbers, usually international without the consent of the mobile user who bears the cost of the call.

INTRODUCING NON-HUMAN FACTORS AFFECTING PHISHING

Previous research has focused on the technical side of phishing (Smith & Anthony, 2005; Dhamija, Tygar, & Hearst, 2006; Pattinson, Jerram, Parsons, McCormac, & Butavicius, 2012). This includes the development of automated systems or software which acts as anti-phishing tools to assist users in identifying spoofed websites. Some of these tools use a visual similarity approach for websites detection. Here the automated system sends a warning alert to the user if the visual similarity between websites exceeds certain threshold. An example of these is a program developed by Liu et al. Yet, this system requires the legitimate websites' owners to register their sites and keywords, in advance, for the system (Wright, Chakraborty, Basoglu, & Marett, 2010). Another approach has investigated the addition of anti-phishing tool bars that could be added to users' browsers to alert users of phishing websites. An example is the browser add-on, TrustBar, developed by Herzberg and Gbara to alert users from un-trusted websites via logos and warnings (Herzberg & Gbara, 2004). Examples of tools that used other techniques are (Smith & Anthony, 2005; Dhamija et al., 2006). The former used "trusted paths" software, which was developed by (Smith and Anthony, 2005; Dhamija et al., 2006), to help users make sure an authentication process between their browser and a secured website has taken place. Another example is CANTINA, which is a software based on TF-IDF algorithm that is used for labeling and detecting phishing websites (Zhang, Hong, & Cranor, 2007).

A number of studies have emerged to evaluate these automated systems (Wu, Miller, & Garfinkel, 2006; Anti Phishing Working Group 2007; Dhamija et al., 2006; Cranor, Egelman, Hong, & Zhang, 2007; Sheng et al., 2007; Zhang et al., 2007). The main purpose was checking their usefulness in real world application. Wu et al. evaluated three anti-phishing tool bars. Their findings indicated that the toolbars were of help to only %35 of the users visiting phishing websites. The reason was that some users ignored the toolbars warnings while others did not notice them at all. However, this result changed when the authors tested pop-up warnings instead, in a follow up study. The pop-up warnings blocked access to the phishing websites unless the users countermand them. Yet, the users were not good in interpreting the security warnings. Accordingly, the authors concluded that it is very hard for individuals to distinguish between phishing and authentic websites. Similar conclusion was suggested by (Anti Phishing Working Group, 2007; Dhamija et al., 2006) who tested the ability of 22 users to detect phishing website from 20 websites in the first study of this sort. They found that anti-phishing browsing cues in place were unsuccessful in alerting the participants. 68% proceeded even when they were presented with fraudulent certificates pop-up warnings. 23% of the participants ignored the status bars, address bars and all other security indicators. Good phishing websites tricked 90% of the recruits (Dhamija et al. 2006).

Consequently, another branch of researchers focused on Training (Sheng et al., 2007; Jagatic et al., 2007; Kumaraguru et al., 2007). Their main goal was educating users on how to detect and avoid phishing attacks. Different approaches have been applied. These included printed materials, such as books and booklets (Jakobsson, 2007), online materials (HSBC 2012; ebay, 2012; Vodafone, 2012; On guard online, 2012), embedded training (Kumaraguru et al., 2007) (where users are trained during their normal daily jobs via emails and pop-up messages) and contextual training (Jagatic et al., 2007) (where simulated phishing attack is designed and targeting the trainees without their knowledge via field experiments).

Very few studies conducted contextual training (Jagatic et al., 2007; Alseadoon et al., 2012; Mohebzada et al., 2012). Not only this sort of studies is ethically complicated but also most of them lack demographic and background information about the participants.

Traditional training, such as books and web-based material, was regarded to have limited effect (Kirlappos & Sasse, 2012; Jakobsson, 2007). Recently, other untraditional methods, such as computer games (Kumaraguru et al., 2007), mobile games (Love, 2005) and comics (Srikwan & Jakobsson, 2008) have been introduced as innovative training approaches.

The effectiveness of training was also evaluated by many studies either via the use of phishing IQ-Tests (Srikwan & Jakobsson, 2008; Halevi & Nasir, 2013; Sheng et al., 2007) or via field experiments (Jagatic et al., 2007). Research was divided on the effectiveness of phishing training. While some studies stressed on the importance of continually reminding the users about the threat of phishing via training and security awareness sessions (Pattinson et al. 2012; Kumaraguru et al. 2007), other studies (Görling, 2006; Sheng et al., 2007) posed doubts about the usefulness of security education. Some, such as Görling, suggested that security education is limited and cannot be a general solution to security problems (Mohebzada et al., 2012). Yet, this opinion was not supported by any practical studies of his; rather he formed this attitude based on a review for recent research in security education. For example, he referred to Adams & Sasse study (Adam & Sasse, 1999) to bring up discussion about weak passwords and their resulting problems and how such studies motivated research on user education and security awareness. Yet, he believes these movements had short term effect. He demonstrated this judgment by discussing the results of Dhamija's phishing IQ-test study mentioned earlier (Dhamija et al., 2006). He regards it as a proof of how hard and time consuming for non expert computer users it is to apply the training they get to scrutinize the websites they visit for phishing indicators. He also based his opinion on the fact that the study found no correlation between phishing vulnerability and factors like education, age or gender. What Görling has missed is that Dhamija study was not measuring the effect of phishing-tailored training in specific. Instead, users' general level of education and weekly hours spent on computers were the variables tested in the study in regards to 'Education'. Accordingly, we can not generalize the results of the study or even relate it to either security training in general or phishing training in particular. It is also worth mentioning that Görling objection is not on security education in itself, but rather on treating it as the default way to address security problems, as users themselves may not be interested in getting educated. He argues that user education alone can never protect users to a large degree. Instead, he calls for borrowing knowledge from other disciplines especially those concerned with behavior such as HCI and Safety research. Same suggestion was adopted by Brostoff and Sasse (Brostoff & Sasse, 2002).

Evaluating the same approach, Sheng et al. studies about phishing training have found positive feedback. Yet, at the same time, the training resulted in users becoming more suspicious of genuine stimuli, as most participants mistakenly rated them as phishing ones during the process of detecting phishing emails and websites (Sheng et al., 2007).

Regarding mobile phishing, research was mainly restricted to technical aspects of websites and operating systems. Felt and Wagner conducted a study over 85 web site and 100 mobile applications. The study suggested that phishing risk on mobile platform was greater than expected.

While the technical literature on phishing is rapidly increasing, little is known, comparatively, about the behavioral and psychological nature of such attacks. Recently, more research efforts are directed to this area. In the next section, we discuss some of these efforts.

INTRODUCING HUMAN FACTORS AFFECTING PHISHING

Recently, more research has been undertaken to determine how, why and in what situations individuals fall for phishing. The first step starts by investigating the phishing techniques the attackers use and then study individuals' response to these techniques.

The most commonly-used approach is called the bait-hook technique. Here the attacker sends unsolicited emails purported to be from a legitimate entity. These emails represent the 'Bait' side that direct the users to a bogus website that looks like a legitimate website and where the users are asked to enter their confidential information (Wright et al., 2010). These websites are the 'Hook' side. It's believed that the 'Bait' depends on exploiting certain human vulnerabilities some of which are the desire to obtain gain, avoid loss, or help others. Examples of which are phishing attacks that deceive the victims by presenting a false offer of a fake prize, asking the victims to donate for a phony cause or impersonating a legitimate entity or figure such as the victims' managers or IT-Support in order to encourage them to provide personal information such as user names passwords. For that, attackers depend on triggering emotions such as greed, fear, heroism or obeying authorities (Halevi & Nasir, 2013). Some of these techniques have been borrowed from sales and marketing and proved to be effective. An example of marketing techniques used employed by hackers is adding the sense of urgency to the phishing message to persuade the victim that the attacker is offering a scarce opportunity that needs an immediate response (Adam & Sasse, 1999).

These findings guided research on phishing cues (Jakobsson, 2007; Dhamija et al., 2006; Vishwanath et al., 2011; Downs et al., 2007). Phishing cues refer to the visual deception signs of the phishing stimuli that can give users an indicator that the stimuli are not authentic. It has been found that respondents' decision to trust a certain message or website depends on visual cues and language errors. The use of logos and grammar mistakes greatly affected users' ability to classify stimuli. Users ignored security indicators and concentrated more on the visual representation of the websites (Dhamija, 2006). Most studies in this field agreed that spelling and design matter (Jakobsson, 2007; Down et al., 2006). They suggest that users do look carefully at URLs (Jakobsson, 2007) those of the web pages and those obtained by mouse-over in emails. However, despite that people were good at detecting IP addresses for authentic pages, they were not suspicious of well-formed forged addresses such as www.chase-alters.com.

Pursuing the same general approach, a group of researchers argue that individual differences affect individuals' vulnerability to phishing. They argue that if for every phishing message some users are 'detectors' while others are 'victims', then there must be individual factors of the users themselves that are responsible for such division (Alseadoon et al., 2012). Accordingly, a branch of research focused on the demographics differences such as age and gender (Dhamija et al., 2006; Jagatic et al., 2007; Sheng et al., 2007; Kumaraguru et al. 2007). Another branch focused on personality traits (Alseadoon et al., 2012; Halevi et al. 2013; Moody et al. 2011).

Yet, again, there was no consensus among phishing scholars in regards to the individual differences effect on phishing vulnerability. While some have concluded that young age groups (18-25 years old) are more vulnerable (Jagatic et al., 2007; Kumaraguru et al., 2007), others' research have concluded totally the opposite, that young people are more alert and good at detecting phishing (Mohebzada et al., 2012). Same applied on gender. Female were found more susceptible then male in some studies (Sheng et al., 2007; Jagatic et al., 2007) whereas male and female were found to be equally deceived by phishing in other studies (Mohebzada et al., 2012). Men were found to be more vulnerable to some attacks more than female, as the field experiment of Mohebzada revealed that 60.9% of male fall for their simulated phishing attack compared to 39.1% of females (Adam & Sasse, 1999). In their two large scaled phishing experiment over around 10,000 university members, they also concluded that there is no correlation between demographics and susceptibly to phishing.

The effect of Personality on phishing vulnerability was recently getting the attention of researchers. In a study conducted by Exeter University, socially-isolated participants tended to be more vulnerable to phishing. Some viewed the monetary scams a gamble they need to take in order to win the prize (University of Exeter, 2012). They attributed their participants' behavior to a lack of emotional control. Similar traits were studied by Halevi et al. (Halevi et al., 2013). They have studied the effect of personality traits on both face book activity and phishing vulnerability of100 students of a psychology class. They used the short form personality questionnaire "NEO-IP FFM" to get quick personality measurements of their participants. The form was filled online with other information about the recruits such as their age, work experience, online activity and their emails as well. These emails were used in the experimental part of the study. Here an email was sent to the students. The email offered an Apple product to the first students to click a link in the email. The link opened a page that has login button. Students clicking this button were considered vulnerable for phishing attacks. The personality results were compared to both the phishing experiment results and to the students' Facebook activity they provided in a survey about type of data they post on their face book accounts. The study suggested that females who scored high on Neuroticism were more vulnerable to phishing scams as well as to face book addiction. Yet, no correlation to any personality traits was found. The study justifies that as women are more likely to express their emotions specially fear, which was investigated by questions that measured the recruits personality. The author has to disagree with that as NEO-IP has been tested and validated so as gender and age factors will not affect its result. Regarding Facebook activity, the study found a correlation between high activity and phishing vulnerability. So people who spend more hours on the Internet and are used to express themselves there are more likely to respond to phishing attacks. The study also found no correlation between people's computer expertise and their ability to detect phishing emails. Accordingly the study suggested that field experiment is more helpful than surveys and IQ-tests in understanding individual's phishing susceptibility.

Chuchuen and Chavarasuth (2010) compared individual personality traits to different phishing strategies. The study used DISC personality model that classifies individual personality into four quadrants: Dominance, Influence, Steadiness and Conscientiousness. The study found that Influential people are more likely to fall for link manipulation attacks while people who are of 'steady' personality were more to fall for spear phishing attacks (Chuchuen & Chanvarasuth, 2010).

One of the studies that relate phishing to personality was that of Parrish et al. (Parrish et al., 2010). Based on the Big Five personality framework, the study suggested a number of traits that affect individuals' susceptibility to phishing attacks. However, no central explanatory mechanism was ever described. The researchers did propose predictions for a correlation between the dependent and independent variables. Yet, these predictions were only based on their interpretations of previous literature. But this, by itself, does not qualify as a model or a theory. Simply aggregating the definitions of the traits does not give each proposed relationship the strength that their connectedness can provide. The traits were identified and classified but there was no analysis, correlational or experimental research done that act as explicatory glue that connects them together. Accordingly, our efforts fell short of a model because we could not pin down the best causal explanation of why conscientiousness, for example, may be the personality trait most negatively correlated with phishing vulnerability, as they stated. Or why giving away sensitive information can be roughly equated with extraversion. The research supports the hypothesis that extraversion leads to increased vulnerability based on two contradictory research results of Workman (2008) in opposition to Weirich and Sasse (Downs, 2006) about the relation between sociability and passwords disclosure.

CONCLUSION

The field of HCISec (Human Computer Interaction in regards to Information Security) has been falling short in incorporating human factors in mobile phishing. Empirical research on this area is scarce and descriptive. However, as demonstrated by this chapter, other areas have investigated phishing in general and mobile phishing in particular from technical perspective. This chapter has, hopefully, shown that existing literature provides essential context and theoretical background for future research in the area of mobile phishing from human computer interaction perspective.

REFERENCES

Adams, A., & Sasse, M. A. (1999). Users are not the enemy. *Communications of the ACM, 42*(12), 40–46. doi:10.1145/322796.322806

Alseadoon, I., Chan, T., Foo, E., & Gonzales Nieto, J. (2012, January). Who is more susceptible to phishing emails? A Saudi Arabian study. In *Proceedings of the 23rd Australasian Conference on Information Systems 2012* (pp. 1-11). ACIS.

Anti-Phishing Working Group. (2007). *Phishing Activity Trends Report*. Retrieved December 2014, from docs.apwg.org/reports/apwg_report_dec_2007.pdf

Boodaei, M. (2011, January). *Mobile Users Three Times More Vulnerable to Phishing Attacks*. Trusteer. Retrieved January 2015, from http://www.trusteer.com/blog/mobile-users-three-times-more-vulnerable-phishing-attacks

Bortinik, S. (2013, January). *Why Do Phishing Attacks Work Better On Mobile Phones?* Retrieved January 2015, from http://www.welivesecurity.com/2011/01/20/why-do-phishing-attacks-work-better-on-mobile-phones/

Brostoff, S., & Sasse, M. A. (2001, September). Safe and sound: a safety-critical approach to security. In *Proceedings of the 2001 workshop on New security paradigms* (pp. 41-50). ACM., 2002. doi:10.1145/508171.508178

Chuchuen, C., & Chanvarasuth, P. (2010). The Relationships Between Phishing Techniques And The User Personality Model. *ICLT 2010 - 2nd International Conference on Logistics and Transport*, Queenstown NZ.

Cranor, L. F., Egelman, S., Hong, J. I., & Zhang, Y. (2007, December). Phinding Phish: An Evaluation of Anti-Phishing Toolbars. In NDSS.

Dhamija, R., Tygar, J. D., & Hearst, M. (2006, April). Why phishing works. In *Proceedings of the SIGCHI conference on Human Factors in computing systems* (pp. 581-590). ACM.

Downs, J. S., Holbrook, M., & Cranor, L. F. (2007, October). Behavioral response to phishing risk. In *Proceedings of the anti-phishing working groups 2nd annual eCrime researchers summit* (pp. 37-44). ACM. doi:10.1145/1299015.1299019

Downs, J. S., Holbrook, M. B., & Cranor, L. F. (2006, July). Decision strategies and susceptibility to phishing. In *Proceedings of the second symposium on Usable privacy and security* (pp. 79-90). ACM. doi:10.1145/1143120.1143131

Dunham, K. (2008). *Mobile malware attacks and defense*. Syngress.

El-Din, R. S., Cairns, P., & Clark, J. (2014). Mobile Users' Strategies for Managing Phishing Attacks. *Journal of Management and Strategy*, 5(2), 70. doi:10.5430/jms.v5n2p70

Felt, A. P., Finifter, M., Chin, E., Hanna, S., & Wagner, D. (2011, October). A survey of mobile malware in the wild. In *Proceedings of the 1st ACM workshop on Security and privacy in smartphones and mobile devices* (pp. 3-14). ACM. doi:10.1145/2046614.2046618

Görling, S. (2006, October). The myth of user education. In *Virus Bulletin Conference* (Vol. 11, p. 13).

Halevi, T., Lewis, J., & Memon, N. (2013). Phishing, Personality Traits and Facebook. *arXiv preprint arXiv:1301.*7643.

Herzberg, A., & Gbara, A. (2004). *Trustbar: Protecting (even naive) web users from spoofing and phishing attacks.*

How To Spot Spoof (fake) eBay+PayPal Phishing Emails. (n.d.). Retrieved December 2014, from http://www.ebay.co.uk/gds/how-to-spot-spoof-fake-ebay-paypal-phishing-emails/10000000001711994/g.htmls

Informa Telecoms and Media. (2009). Informa Telecoms & Media report. Technical Report, London.

Jagatic, T. N., Johnson, N. A., Jakobsson, M., & Menczer, F. (2007). Social phishing. *Communications of the ACM*, 50(10), 94-100.-100, October 2007.

Jakobsson, M. (2007). The human factor in phishing. *Privacy & Security of Consumer Information*, 7, 1–19.

Jakobsson, M. (2011). *Why Mobile Security is not Like Traditional Security.*

Jakobsson, M., & Myers, S. (Eds.). (2006). *Phishing and countermeasures: understanding the increasing problem of electronic identity theft*. John Wiley & Sons. doi:10.1002/0470086106

Kirlappos, I., & Sasse, M. A. (2012). Security Education against Phishing: A Modest Proposal for a Major Rethink. *IEEE Security and Privacy Magazine*, 10(2), 24–32. doi:10.1109/MSP.2011.179

Kumaraguru, P., Sheng, S., Acquisti, A., Cranor, L. F., & Hong, J. (2010). Teaching Johnny not to fall for phish. *ACM Transactions on Internet Technology*, 10(2), 7. doi:10.1145/1754393.1754396

Love, S. (2005). *Understanding mobile human-computer interaction*. Oxford, UK: Butterworth-Heinemann.

Micro, T. (2013). *Mobile security*. Retrieved December 2014, from apac.trendmicro.com

Mohebzada, J. G., El Zarka, A., Bhojani, A. H., & Darwish, A. (2012, March). Phishing in a university community: Two large scale phishing experiments. In *Innovations in Information Technology (IIT), 2012 International Conference: Abu Dhabi* (pp. 249-254). IEEE.

Moody, G., Galletta, D., Walker, J., & Dunn, B. (2011). Which Phish Get Caught? An Exploratory Study of Individual Susceptibility to Phishing. *Proceedings of the International Conference on Information Systems, ICIS 2011*, Shanghai, China.

Muir, J. (2003). Decoding mobile device security. *Computerworld*, 14.

Oxford Dictionaries on-line. (n.d.). Retrieved December 2014, from http://oxforddictionaries.com/

Parrish, J. L. Jr, Bailey, J. L., & Courtney, J. F. (2009). *A Personality Based Model for Determining Susceptibility to Phishing Attacks*. Little Rock: University of Arkansas.

Pattinson, M., Jerram, C., Parsons, K., McCormac, A., & Butavicius, M. (2012). Why do some people manage phishing e-mails better than others? *Information Management & Computer Security, 20*(1), 18–28. doi:10.1108/09685221211219173

Phishing Scams. (n.d.). Retrieved March 2014, from http://www.onguardonline.gov

Protecting You against Phishing. (n.d.). Retrieved March 2013, from http://www.vodafone.co.uk/about-this-site/our-privacy-policy/protecting-our-customers/phishing

Schiller, J. H. (Ed.). (2003). *Mobile communications*. Pearson Education.

Secure Mail Anti-Phishing. (n.d.). Retrieved December 2014, from http://www.hsbc.com/1/2/online-security/phishing

Security Cartoon. (2013). Retrieved February 2103, from http://Securitycartoon.com

Security For The Post-PC Era. Mobile Security. (2013). Retrieved March 2103, from http://www.Look-out.com

Sheng, S., Magnien, B., Kumaraguru, P., Acquisti, A., Cranor, L. F., Hong, J., & Nunge, E. (2007, July). Anti-phishing phil: the design and evaluation of a game that teaches people not to fall for phish. In *Proceedings of the 3rd symposium on Usable privacy and security* (pp. 88-99). ACM. doi:10.1145/1280680.1280692

Srikwan, S., & Jakobsson, M. (2008). Using cartoons to teach internet security. *Cryptologia, 32*(2), 137–154. doi:10.1080/01611190701743724

University of Exeter, School of Psychology. (2012). The psychology of scams: Provoking and Committing Errors Of Judgment. Devon, UK

Vishwanath, A., Herath, T., Chen, R., Wang, J., & Rao, H. R. (2011). Why do people get phished? Testing individual differences in phishing vulnerability within an integrated, information processing model. *Decision Support Systems, 51*(3), 576–586. doi:10.1016/j.dss.2011.03.002

Weirich, D., & Sasse, M. A. (2001, September). Pretty good persuasion: a first step towards effective password security in the real world. In *Proceedings of the 2001 workshop on New security paradigms* (pp. 137-143). ACM. doi:10.1145/508171.508195

Workman, M. (2008). Wisecrackers: A Theory- Grounded Investigation of Phishing and Pretext Social Engineering Threats to Information Security. *Journal of the American Society for Information Science and Technology, 59*(4), 662–674. doi:10.1002/asi.20779

Wright, R., Chakraborty, S., Basoglu, A., & Marett, K. (2010). Where did they go right? Understanding the deception in phishing communications. *Group Decision and Negotiation*, *19*(4), 391–416. doi:10.1007/s10726-009-9167-9

Wu, M., Miller, R. C., & Garfinkel, S. L. (2006, April). Do security toolbars actually prevent phishing attacks? *In Proceedings of the SIGCHI conference on Human Factors in computing systems* (pp. 601-610). ACM. doi:10.1145/1124772.1124863

Ye, Z. E., Smith, S., & Anthony, D. (2005). Trusted paths for browsers. [TISSEC]. *ACM Transactions on Information and System Security*, *8*(2), 153–186. doi:10.1145/1065545.1065546

Ying, L., Dinglong, H., Haiyi, Z., & Rau, P. (2007). *Users' Perception of Mobile Information Security*. Hacker Journals White Papers.

Zhang, Y., Hong, J. I., & Cranor, L. F. (2007, May). Cantina: a content-based approach to detecting phishing web sites. In *Proceedings of the 16th international conference on World Wide Web* (pp. 639-648). ACM. doi:10.1145/1242572.1242659

KEY TERMS AND DEFINITIONS

Cell Phone: Is a phone that can make and receive telephone calls over a radio link while moving around a wide geographic area.

Education: Is a form of learning in which the knowledge, skills, values, beliefs and habits of a group of people are transferred from one generation to the next through storytelling, discussion, teaching, training, or research.

HCISEC: Is the study of interaction between humans and computers, or human–computer interaction, specifically as it pertains to information security.

Literature Review: Is an evaluative report of information found in the literature related to a selected area of study. The review should describe, summarize, evaluate and clarify this literature. It should give a theoretical base for the research and help the authors determine the nature of their research.

Personality Traits: Are the habitual patterns of behavior, thought, and emotion.

SMishing: SMS Phishing (SMishing) is a form of criminal activity using social engineering techniques. Phishing is the act of attempting to acquire personal information such as passwords and credit card details by masquerading as a trustworthy entity in an electronic communication.

SMS: Short Message Service (SMS) is a text messaging service component of phone, Web, or mobile communication systems.

Chapter 5
Security Issues in Mobile Wireless Ad Hoc Networks:
A Comparative Survey of Methods and Techniques to Provide Security in Wireless Ad Hoc Networks

Arif Sari
European University of Lefke, Cyprus

ABSTRACT

The purpose of this chapter is to investigate and expose methods and techniques developed to provide security in wireless ad hoc networks. Researchers have proposed variety of solutions for security problems of Wireless Mobile Ad-Hoc Networks (MANET) against Distributed Denial of Service (DDoS) attacks. Due to the wireless nature of the channels and specific characteristics of MANETs, the attacks cannot be defeated through conventional security mechanisms. An adversary can easily override its medium access control protocol (MAC) and continually transfer packages on the network channel and the access point node(s) cannot assign authorization access to shared medium. These attacks cause a significant decrease on overall network throughput, packet transmission rates and delay in the MAC layer since other nodes back-off from the communication. In this chapter the proposed methods are applied for preventing and mitigating different wireless ad hoc network attacks are investigated and effectiveness and efficiency of these mechanisms are exposed.

INTRODUCTION

Security is one of the major problems of network systems. Secure communication becomes significant challenge for Mobile Wireless Ad Hoc Networks (MANET) due to their dynamic network topology and lack of centralized infrastructure. The varieties of attacks cause potential threats from different aspects, however, Denial of Service attacks (DoS) or Distributed Denial of Service attacks (DDoS) are two of the most harmful attacks against functionality and stability of network systems and MANETs are more

DOI: 10.4018/978-1-4666-8345-7.ch005

vulnerable to these attacks due to limited resources that forces them to be greedy in resource utilization. These attacks aims to paralyze the member of the network (a node) or the entire network, by flooding excessive volume of traffic to consume the key resources of the member of the network or the entire network.

Solving security issues in these networks become more critical since financial aspects of the DoS and DDoS attacks becomes noticeable and since the application areas covers military, disaster relief operations, mine site operations and robot data acquisitions. Such networks can be used to enable next generation of battlefield applications envisioned by the military including situation awareness systems for maneuvering war fighters, and remotely deployed unmanned micro-sensor networks. MANETs can provide communication for civilian applications, such as disaster recovery and message exchanges among medical and security personnel involved in rescue missions.

Majority of the research efforts in the literature have been taken to solve an effective and applicable security mechanism problems of MANETs, which would detect the flooding attack, mitigate the affects and provide traceback mechanism. Research efforts on MANETs provided security through different mechanisms.

Based on the wide range of survey and analysis of current MANETs DDoS attacks and security system strategies, the major purposed solutions composed of two-tier architecture which has a little complexity that obeys the nature of MANETs. On many surveys, the proposed solutions require some modifications on routing protocols (such as AODV, DSR, DSDV), or require some cooperation or support from non-system node(s), or in some studies controlling the access and authorization through assigning through certification authorities (CA). These proposed solutions and strategies against DoS attacks can be classified under different categories and especially Jamming attacks are investigated by the researchers in the literature since these attacks consume the nodes power and processing abilities to keeping them busy by injecting huge amount of traffic on the network (Nguyan, et.al, 2000).

DoS defence methods have been proposed since long time, but most of them remain theoretical with no actual implementation or could not produce satisfied results and performance when applied on MANETs. Many of these methods need to be implemented simultaneously and collaboratively on several nodes, making them difficult to implement especially on nodes which are distributed and need to maintain round-the-clock Internet connectivity. In addition to this, this implementation becomes more difficult once we consider distributed framework and the stability of Internet connection problems arises on MANETs. Moreover, adopted solutions introduce relative complexity, overhead and delay to the network, by adding features such as digital signatures and encryption. The security methods rely on random or probabilistic means to detect legitimate traffic and discard it, which necessities that a certain percentage of legitimate packets would be dropped in the process. While this might not be a serious downside, it reduces the overall Quality of service on providing security.

Recent wireless research indicates that the wireless MANET presents a larger security problem than conventional wired and wireless networks. A Jamming attacks exhausts the victim's network resources such as bandwidth, computing power, battery etc. The victim is unable to provide services to its legitimate clients and network performance is greatly deteriorated. This chapter provides a wide range of literature survey of existing methods and approaches to providing security in MANETs.

5.1 SECURITY THREAT ASPECTS AND DESIGN CHALLENGES OF MOBILE AD HOC NETWORKS

In recent years, home or small office networking and collaborative computing with laptop computers in a small area have also emerged as other major potential areas of where the use of MANET could be useful. In this introductory chapter on ad-hoc networks we discuss some of the issues related with security aspects and along with some general and foundation topics that provide context for the rest of the chapters that follow in this thesis. This chapter begins by first looking into the security aspects and design challenges of MANETs. The continuation of this section covers discussion of different types of vulnerabilities in MANET environment. Section 2.2 provides a detailed comparative survey of existing methods and techniques of implementing security on MANETs. In section 2.3, previous studies on securing MANETs and examples of specific security strategies against DDoS and DoS attacks are highlighted and classified.

There is variety of research conducted on securing mobile ad hoc networks in the literature. The Mobile ad hoc network is an active mobile device is called node which is free to move independently in any location the users wants to take it, and will of course repeatedly change its links to the other devices (Katz, 2002). Because of several characteristics which makes MANETs vulnerable against attacks from variety of perspectives, researchers face difficulties of implementing proper security scheme on MANETs.

The security threats that prevail in a traditional wired and wireless network environment also hold true for wireless ad-hoc networks but are further aggravated due to unpredictable and dynamic nature of such networks. There are also some security issues that are peculiar only to MANET such as a nasty neighbour relaying packets or a malicious node disrupting the routing infrastructure. Further, wireless link characteristics also introduce reliability problems due to limited wireless transmission range, the broadcast nature of the wireless medium, mobility induced packet losses, and data transmission errors (Zhou and Haas, 1999).

MANETs require the four standard attributes in order to provide wide range of security on the network (Gasser et al., 1989). These are the; Availability; which requires that the system stays up and in a working state, and provides the right access and functionality to each user. This security aspect is the target of DoS or DDoS attacks. Confidentiality; which requires that the information will not be read or copied by unauthorized parties. Authentication and other access control techniques are also used to achieve this goal. Authenticity, which requires that the communication peer is really the legitimate node and is exactly whom we expect to talk to (not an unauthorized node), and that the content of a message is valid. Integrity, which requires that communication data between nodes must not be modified by any unauthorized, unanticipated or unintentional parties.

There are varieties of threats available on the field of Mobile ad-hoc Networks. In this section, several security threats will be discussed that are prevalent in an ad-hoc network environment [Rafique, 2002).

Denial of Service is the first and the most famous threat for MANETs. This threat prevents the normal use of management or communication facilities of the network. This is a threat against the availability of the system. Availability means that all necessary components are operable and all the necessary services are available when a user requires them. In ad-hoc environment, Availability concept has 2 different aspects, i.e., is the medium available when it is needed and is the services offered by a node available to its users when expected, in spite of attacks (Kong et al., 2001). In the DoS attack, the attacker can deny service to the nodes in a given area by jamming the radio frequencies they use. On the other hand, the attack can be internal or external from the node's perspective. In an internal attack a legitimate node behaves maliciously to subvert the communication between two or more nodes. In an external attack, an unauthorised node attempts to break or prevent the message flow between two nodes. Such nodes may generate incorrect routing information, replay old routing information or even deform old routing information (Luo et al., 2000). In the former case, appropriate mechanisms and services must exist to detect and eliminate the compromised malicious node. In the latter case, appropriate authentication and authorisation services must exist to prevent an unauthorised node from participating in the network.

In Unauthorised Disclosure of Information attacks, an attacker tries to learn the contents of the transmitted message. A confidentiality service is necessary to protect the transmitted data from such attacks and protect the contents of the data. Several levels of protection can be identified. The broadest service protects all the data transmitted in the network for a period of time. However complexity and applicability must be taken into consideration in such cases. Narrower forms of this service can also be defined, including protection of a single message or even specific fields within a message. This type of solution will protect only the transmitted message and not the entire communication line. In an ad-hoc network, the links are wireless and are error prone. Use of such wireless links renders an ad-hoc network susceptible to link attacks ranging from passive eavesdropping to active impersonation. The other aspect of confidentiality is the protection of traffic flow from analysis. The protection mechanisms that maintain confidentiality requires attacker not be able to observe the characteristics of the network traffic such as transmission of source and destination address, frequency, length or other characteristics. The leakage of such information could have fatal consequences. For instance, in battlefield ad-hoc networks, traffic analysis can have devastating effects. In such situations, the routing information must also remain confidential because this information might be valuable to enemies to identify and locate their targets in a battlefield (Luo et al., 2000).

As mentioned before, the security of transmitted message is one of the important aspects of confidentiality. Appropriate encryption (symmetric or public key) must be in place to protect the secrecy of transmitted information. Through the help of efficient key management infrastructure, these encryption mechanisms provide secrecy of the message. There are several issues in providing such an infrastructure for ad-hoc networks. We discuss these issues later sections of this study.

The Unauthorised Modification of Information means that some portion of the legitimate message is altered somehow, or that message are delayed or reordered, to produce an unauthorised effect. An integrity service is necessary to ensure that a message being transferred (with or without encryption) is never corrupted. In an ad-hoc network environment, a message could be corrupted because of benign failures, such as radio propagation impairment, or because of malicious attacks on the network (Luo et al., 2000). The applicability of Integrity can be possible for a single message, selected fields within a message or to a stream of messages. When integrity is applied to a stream of messages then this process is called connection-oriented integrity (Luo et al., 2000). This approach ensures that messages are received as sent, with no duplication, insertion, modification, reordering, or replays. The links in ad-hoc networks are vulnerable to errors and prone to active attacks, and hence the use of connection-oriented integrity can be justified. An integrity service is often implemented using so called Checksums and hashing functions. Checksum or hashing-hash sum is a count of number of bits in a transmission unit that is included with the unit so the receiver can check to see whether the same number of bits was received. TCP and UDP layers provide checksum and hash-sum functions to ensure integrity.

Unauthorised Access to Information includes unauthorised access to resources on the network as well as within a system. This may occur in conjunction with a masquerading attack. The attacker has successfully masqueraded himself with another entity, and gain access to resources of the network which are otherwise denied to it. An access control service provides the ability to limit and control access to host systems applications, resources and networks, and to limit what entity might do with the information contained. In ad-hoc networks access control can involve mechanisms with which the formation of groups is controlled (Zhang and Lee, 2000). For example, in cluster driven ad-hoc networks, an access control service must exist that determines when nodes may form, destroy, join, or leave clusters. This makes a strict control for joining into network or make modification on the network resources.

Access Control Service is represented by an access control policy that is essentially a set of rules that define the conditions under which initiators may access targets (Zhang and Lee, 2000). The access control rules are used to determine the requests decisions whether to accept or deny. The variety of access control approaches mentioned in the literature by the researchers. For example Discretionary access control (DAC) allows the restriction of access to objects based on the identity of subjects or groups of subjects. The Mandatory access control (MAC) contains formal authorisation policy that controls the access to the objects. While MAC is more general than DAC and controls the operations of DAC, and DAC used by the user to control access to other subjects, both DAC and MAC are often applied together for efficient and effective security. In addition to that Role Based Access Control (RBAC) applies the concept of roles within subjects (Zhang and Lee, 2000).

A masquerading attack takes place when one entity pretends to be another entity. An authentication scheme must be in place to the recipient that a message is from the source that it claims to be. In an ad-hoc network a node performs routing functions apart from being an end recipient for a transmission flow. The malicious node that attacks to network can misdirect or modify the routing information thus causes interruption on the communication among nodes in the network. For better security inter node authentication is required which means, each node must authenticate each other prior to exchange routing information and after this step, end to end authentication step should be followed. It must also be ensured that the communication between these two nodes is not interfered with in such a way that a third node can masquerade as one of the two legitimate parties for the purpose of unauthorized transmission and reception .

Repudiation of Actions is a kind of a threat against accountability and occurs when the sender (or the receiver) denies having sent (or received) the information. A no repudiation service must be in place that prevents either the sender or receiver from denying a transmitted message. For that reason, when a message is sent, the receiver can prove that the message was in fact sent by the alleged sender. Similarly, when a message is received, the sender can prove that the alleged or presumed receiver in fact received the message. When one node receives a false message from another node, this service allows it to blame the other node of sending the false message and enables all the other nodes to know that the offending node is compromised (Kong et al., 2001).

A key management is another issue once the above mentioned problems are highlighted. A problem in providing the above mentioned security services are to facilitate the provision of a key management infrastructure. Key management addresses the problem of creation, generation and distribution of keys that are necessary for the implementation of a security service. Wired and traditional wireless networks assign the responsibility of key management to a static and trusted authority, which normally is a part of fixed infrastructure. Such an entity does not exist in an ad-hoc environment where the nodes dynamically form a network without the support and power of any fixed authority or infrastructure. The dynamic nature of ad-hoc networks insinuate that nodes move in an out of the networks frequently making it necessary to change the keys in securing communications more often than in other networks. This also indicates that the regular key management framework used in traditional networks will not be applicable to this situation. There are several approaches to providing a key management service mentioned in the literature by the researchers. Often a public key infrastructure is deployed because of its superiority in distributing keys and in achieving integrity and non-repudiation (Luo et al., 2000). However, a public key infrastructure based scheme requires the presence of a certification authority (CA) for key management (Schwingenschlögl, and Horn, 2002). The CA has a public/private key pair, with its public key known to every node in the network, and signs certificates binding public keys to nodes. The public key system requires that the Certification Authority (CA) be available on line, to confirm and revoke public key certificates. The presence of a single CA leads to bottleneck problems leading to a single point of failure in the network. It also becomes the most obvious point of attack since a compromise of the CA compromises the entire network. Finally, such an infrastructure requires that a single reliable, trusted entity is available on-line, an assumption that appears unrealistic in an ad-hoc environment. The problem of key management is further provoked in multicast based communications i.e., situations involving multi-party communications. Any key management scheme deployed for such networks must have the following properties:

1. **Scalability:** To accommodate dynamic groups of arbitrary size.
2. **Low Computational Complexity:** To accommodate nodes having limited resources.
3. **Not Relying on Dedicated Trusted Nodes:** To accommodate rapidly changing topological conditions.

In the above section, we have identified the types of threats that can rise in a mobile ad-hoc environment. For a particular environment, one needs to determine which threats are more applicable. For instance, in group-based communication, uttermost care must be taken to prevent the key management infrastructure from being compromised by attackers. In military based communication, care should be taken to protect the information flow from traffic analysis. For commercial scenarios like a wireless payment system over mobile ad-hoc, strong authentication and authorization schemes must coexist with the confidentiality service. In most of the cases, physical attacks against the nodes must also be considered. This can be a very serious security fact that as the attacker can get access to hardware and software known to the network and can possibly perform successful authentication, eavesdrop messages or inject arbitrary or malicious data into the network which may lead to collapse in entire network (Rabin, 1998). It may be necessary for such networks to deploy Intrusion Detection Systems (IDS) to detect and respond to computer misuse and attacks conducted by the adversary.

Counteracting the relevant security threats involves provision and enforcement of appropriate security services and mechanisms as discussed above. The overall set of security measures required to neutralize the identified threats forms the security policy. The security architecture supported by this policy must be able to support a wide range of systems and applications, and therefore it is intended that it should support a wide range of security services that can be used and combined in different ways to meet different security policies in the entire network.

In conclusion of this section, design and deployment of the effective security framework for wireless ad-hoc networks requires investigation of various criteria. For that reason, this thesis contains the investigation of different attacks and security mechanisms in MANETs, proposed security architectures by researchers in the literature, e.g., network architectures and routing protocols that are specifically targeted to assist in security, determination and classification of compromised nodes and establishing the trusted node

5.2 DETAILED COMPARATIVE ANALYSIS OF EXISTING METHODS AND TECHNIQUES OF IMPLEMENTING SECURITY IN MANETs

In this section, an overview of the existing methods and techniques are criticized and compared in the field of MANET security issues.

The paper by the researcher presented a short literature study over papers on ad-hoc networking to show that many of the new generation ad-hoc networking proposals are not yet able to address the actual security problems they face (Shoup, 2000). The author indicates that ad hoc networking proposals of modern era up till now are not able to completely describe the security problems of ad hoc networks. According to the author, environment-specific implementations of the required approaches in implementing security have not yet been fully realised.

Researchers have examined the major security issues related to the wireless ad-hoc networks (Desmedt and Frankel (1990). According to them that from the time ad-hoc environment of network are controlled by tight bounds on power budget and the CPU cycles, and by the communication of intermittent nature, this combination builds an authentication, naming and denial of service irrelevant. The combination identifies some of the recently originated attacks i.e. sleep deprivation torture, & shortfalls of the acceptable primitives for the cryptographic protocols. According to the researchers, providing confidentiality is not a more difficult task compared to providing authentication. They mentioned that if the problems regarding to authentication are solved, protecting confidentiality becomes very simply by just encrypting the session, no matter what material related to keying is available. They present the secure transient association approach which indicates the association between the controller and the peripheral device. This relationship indicates the capacity of a controller to control a peripheral device during its ownership duration of the peripheral device. When device controlled by the new controller, it does as new master orders to act and stop obeying the previous one consequently makes this relationship transient.

As it is mentioned above, researcher claims that one way of securing the ad hoc network is a "duckling model" (Stajano and Anderson, 1999). In this model, duckling is the slave device and duck is the mother which is the master controller. Firstly, duckling recognizes it's as first entity which sends it a secret key on a secure channel fro example by physical contact. This entire process is called imprinting. The duckling slave device always obeys its mother, which tells it whom to talk to by reference to an access control list. The bond between mother and duckling is broken by death after which the duckling accepts another imprinting. Death may be caused by the mother itself, a timeout or any specific event. The whole security chain corresponds to a tree topology formed of hierarchical master-slave relationships. The root of the tree is a human being controlling all devices in its subtree. As it is well known that, in hierarchical networks there are nodes that have different roles than others (Desmedt and Frankel 1990).

However this specific approach proposed by researchers for providing security has some issues. For example if there is a breakage in one relationship then the relationship of the whole subtree is broken. So, it requires the constant involvement of a human for the maintenance of security, which is not be feasible in a lot of cases. So network maintenance should be considered while designing a proposed solution for mobile ad hoc network environments.

According to research by authors has proposed a scalable intrusion tolerant security solution for infrastructureless wireless mobile ad hoc networks (Venkatraman and Agrawal 2001). The proposed system has designed to be fully decentralized in order to operate in a large-scale network. The main idea behind this scheme is to maximise the service availability in each network locality which is crucial for supporting ubiquitous services for mobile users. If this proposed method investigated from the cryptographic perspective, the design is based on the concepts of threshold secret sharing and secret share updates. From the system aspect, the architecture is fully distributed and localised.

However, there are several drawbacks associated with this scheme. In this scheme researchers used k-bounded coalition offsetting technique to enable scalable distributed certificate generation. But when a node V_j receives a certificate request from V_i, its records may not provide enough information on Vi. This may be because the interaction between V_i and V_j does not last long enough. Moreover, V_i may not exist in V_j records at all if they just met. At this point, there are 2 possibilities. First, V_j may serve to the V_i's request since it has not bad records about Vi. Other option is to drop the request since there is no reliable information available about the request owner. In addition to that, the simulation experiment conducted by the researchers shows that for both centralised and hierarchical solutions incur in high delay which entails difficulties in predicting future expiration time in certificate renewal.

Researchers have followed the design guidelines provided in other researchers (Venkatraman and Agrawal 2001), and proposed a new scheme with a number of new contributions (Binkley and Trost, 2001). The proposed scheme makes a local trust model by expanding the adversary model which a system can handle. In his trust model, an entity (for example entity K) is trusted in the condition that trusted entities claim within a specified duration "Tcert". These K entities are in general are among the entity's one-hop neighbours. The authors claim that the proposed scheme is self-securing design approach in which multiple nodes collaboratively provide authentication services for any node in the network. The proposed scheme is designed to handle DoS attacks and node break-ins (Binkley and Trost, 2001).

There are quite a few deficiencies in this approach. The model assumes that each node has minimum K number of legitimate neighbours. The theory is critical for certification services to be strong against the adversaries. Availability of the services is also determined by the parameter K. The three mentioned factors of the model are joined and characterized by a single parameter K. This sort of coupling effect to reduces the flexibility of the model's scheme. In a specific scenario, these factors aspects may have contradictory goals. For example, security may require K to be minimum 10, but the service availability may require the K to be maximum 7, where as network can only certify 5 legitimate neighbours. This situation creates new challenges that need to be addressed. The model also makes an unrealistic assumption that each node is equipped with a few local detection mechanisms to recognize the misbehaving nodes among its one hop neighbourhood (Binkley and Trost, 2001).

The research shows a survey for intrusion detection and trace back response techniques against attacks (Marti et al., 2000). This research inspected the weaknesses of ad-hoc networks and gives a conclusion that an ad-hoc network is mainly exposed to DoS attack, because of its features including open medium, cooperative algorithms, dynamic changing topology, lacking the centralised monitoring and management point, and lacking a clear line of defence. According to researchers, building a highly secure wireless ad hoc network, a suitable intrusion detection and response technique must be applied. They claim that there is need of further research to adapt the intrusion detection and response technique to any ad-hoc network environment. The recent intrusion detection techniques discussed which is distributed and co-operative and also uses an approach of statistical anomaly detection. According to them the processes of trace analysis & anomaly detection must be done locally of each node and by the cooperation with each node in the network if possible. Further, the process of intrusion detection must take place in all the networking layers in the integrated cross layer manner. This technique is specified to intrusion detection and cannot be used as a generic security model (Marti et al., 2000).

The paper by researchers suggests some algorithms to use as build blocks against the DoS attacks on ad-hoc networks (Johnson and Maltz, 1996). Given the self-controls faced by such networks, the paper also inspects the feasibility of such algorithms on the environments of mobile ad-hoc network. It mentions that different algorithms can be used which can deal with the secret and function sharing and RSA threshold schemes like Capkun et al. (2003) and Hubaux et al. (2001). The paper also describes that how these algorithms can meet the given demands of ad-hoc networks.

Researchers proposed a new security mechanism by identifying the new challenges and opportunities faced by the ad-hoc networking environment and proposed so called threshold cryptography scheme to provide secure communication within network (Luo et al., 2000). The proposed secure communication method is inspired from the study of another proposed security method (Asokan and Ginzboorg, 2000). The paper mainly discusses on secure routing and secure key management establishment concepts. In particular techniques to prevent denial of service attacks from occurring in the routing process are discussed. These techniques take advantage of the redundancies in ad-hoc network topology and use diversity coding on multiple routes to tolerate both benign and Byzantine failures.

According to the researchers, this work represents the first step of their research to analyse the security threats, to understand the security mechanisms for ad-hoc networks, and to identify existing techniques, as well as to propose new mechanisms to secure ad-hoc networks (Luo et al., 2000). The idea suggested by this approach is to distribute trust to a set of nodes by letting them share the key management service, in particular the ability to sign certificates. This is done using threshold cryptography which proposed by the researchers in the literature (Asokan and Ginzboorg, 2000). An (n, t+1) threshold cryptography scheme allows parties to share the ability to perform a cryptographic operation so that any t+1 parties can perform this operation jointly whereas it is infeasible for at most t parties to do so. Using this scheme, the private key k of the CA (certification authority) is divided into n shares (s1, s2, ...,sn), each share being assigned to a special node. Using this share, a set of t+1 special node is able to generate a valid certificate. As long as t or less special nodes are compromised and do not participate in generating certificates the service can operate. Even if the compromised nodes deliver incorrect data the service is able to sign certificates (Luo et al., 2000).

In the proposed method (Luo et al., 2000) the user identity is authenticated by CA. In a case of single centralised CA, this scheme works well. But this proposed scheme may face problems in a distributed CA environment. This scheme shows a scenario in which, collaborative CAs are arranged and deployed as access point for the security services. So, the users have to prove their identity to all the special nodes to prevent compromised node passing on the faulty information but if it signs that the certificates without proving the identity the model cannot be used for highly-value transactions. There are a number of characteristics of this model which make it ineffective. High mobility makes frequent route changes thus in this way contacting the local CA in a timely manner is insignificant. Moreover, in an ad-hoc network, a local CA can be multihops away and also can move. This situation not only complicates the dynamic repartitioning of a network, but also complicates the problem of tracing and tracking the local CA server. Multihop communication over an error-prone wireless channel depicts the data transmission to a high loss rate. The whole act reduces the success ratio sand which increases the average service latency.

According to the work mentioned by Bellovin and Merrit (1992), an effective operation of the ad-hoc networks is mainly dependant on maintaining the appropriate routing information in a distributed way to avoid a malicious node from becoming misrepresented, suppressing or misrouting the data packets. To work against this attack, researcher has introduced a technique for inter-router authentication and meanwhile problems like handle replay that can prevail using existing the schemes. This technique has been integrated into a routing protocol to minimize the security threats to routing protocols. According to author the technique uses Ad Hoc On-Demand Distance Vector Routing (AODV) routing protocol and is evenly applicable to other demand driven routing protocols.

The scheme in Bellovin and Merrit (1992) works whenever the route from a source A to a destination B needs to be found, the route discovery process is initiated. The process has several steps that contain route discovery messaging between the source and destination or intermediate nodes. The scheme provides a means for authenticating route discovery messages to ensure that route table does not contain any false routing information. Researchers have simulated this scheme and shown the results. This technique has a drawback that it does not perform a good authentication during the time propagation of route requests but optionally it provides reliability by using message authentication codes. Unfortunately, a message authentication code can only approves for the integrity but can not stop the replay attack.

Researchers has acknowledged some security goals of modern ad-hoc routing protocols, and anticipated some causes of threats to the mentioned routing protocols (Kong et al., 2001). For that reason, it has suggested some possible approaches to prevent the routing attacks in mobile ad-hoc networks with a key management framework. Specifically, researcher suggested some solutions for protecting the internal and external attacks to these ad-hoc networks. He suggests "that encrypting routing messages with a private key algorithm and authenticate them by using the digitally signed message digests with windowed sequence numbers can prevent the external attack. For internal attacks he suggests that redundant paths, "aging out of false routing information, and dismiss the routing information at each node are all employed to combat against internal attacks.

For the ad-hoc networks (Diffie and Hellman 1976), has designed an authenticated routing protocol at the link layer which specifically addresses the link security issues. He presents two key ideas in his research report. First of all, he suggests providing a fix to decrease the spoofing problems linked with the Address Resolution Protocol. Providing a fix and exchanging the Address Resolution Protocol with a protocol where beacons are used to verify approach. This type of protocol is always naturally integrated with the Mobile IP as the agent already uses a beacon system for communicating. In the second solution he provides, "the beacons binding IP and MAC addresses are authenticated". This stops the unauthorised entities to access the network resources and also reduce the danger of attacks like link-layer spoofing. These authentication beacons improve the Mobile IP security. These approaches by researcher also do not deal with the threats of replay attacks. The attackers can record a link layer authenticated beacon at one foreign agent and later he can retransmit it. In the result, the victim may not be presented and remains unaware of the attack. The protocol described in this approach just protects the routing connectivity but unable to protect the user data. An attacking host may just simply listen to the passing traffic. This work is very easy to do and extremely difficult to detect, and it works despite the consequences that how a hosts learn will each other's MAC addresses (Diffie and Hellman 1976).

The paper has suggested the Pathrater technique for the prevention of DoS attacks on ad hoc networks (Weimerskirch and Thonet, 2001). This study has inspired from the paper presented by Torgerson and Leeuwen (2001),which related with Dynamic Source Routing in Ad-hoc networks. In this technique run by each node on an ad hoc network combines the knowledge of misbehaving nodes with the link of reliability of data to pick the most reliable route expectedly. The author suggests a method to prevent misbehaving or malicious nodes to participate in the network. Through categorising nodes based on their dynamically measured behaviour. The watchdog method is proposed by the researchers to detect misbehaving nodes and a Pathrater that helps routing protocols to avoid these nodes. As mentioned before, these two features are added as extensions to Dynamic Routing Algorithm (DSR) by Torgerson and Leeuwen (2001). A drawback with this technique is that as the Pathrater cannot detect a misbehaving node in the existence of different types of collisions such as ambiguous collisions, receiver collisions, limited transmission power, false misbehaviour and partial dropping. The limitation with this method is since it depends on knowing the exact path a data packet has passed through, so implementation of this is only possible on top of a source routing protocol.

To prevent Mobile Ad Hoc Networks from the DoS attacks researchers has proposed several repository construction algorithms (Papadimitratos and Haas, 2002). These algorithms take into consideration the features of certificate graphs in the sense that the choices of certificates which are stored by each service user depends on the connectivity of that user and also depends on his certificate graph neighbours. The success or failure of this technique extremely dependent on construction of some local certificate repositories and depends on the features of certificate graphs. A certificate graph is a type of graph whose vertices are represented by the public keys of the users and the edges are represented by the public key certificates issues by the service users. Like in the any of the approach which uses certificate chains, this approach also assumes that trust is transitive that is not practiced quite regularly in the real life situation. The author suggests fixing to this problem by assuming the paths of multiple certificates and by using the authentication metrics.

The study by Levijoki (2000), describes some problems related to the securing ad hoc networks form DoS attack. The work presented here is similar to the presented in Papadimitratos and Haas (2002) with more detailed description of algorithms. The proposed method suggest to develop the idea of a self-organized public key infrastructure and certificates are stored and distributed by the users instead of using certificate directory.

This proposed system offered by researchers has several drawbacks. First of all, to ensure the safety of system, each entity's identity should be checked in real times before the certificates are issued to users. Additionally the approach assumes that each node in the recommendation chain is completely checked by the certificate requester trusts. In the end a considerable amount of computing power and considerable time is consumed to get a certificate which is passing through the chain of certificates. In the process of checking the received certificate for authentication and signing it before forwarding it each node in the chain must perform the operations of public key. This process cannot be prepared parallel but can only be done one after the other (Levijoki, 2000).

In a paper by Patrikakis, Masikos and Zouraraki (2004), a new key agreement scenario is described and various solutions to the key agreement problem in this scenario are examined. The encrypted key exchange method presented in a research paper is extends to multi-party case (Royer and Toh, 1999). This method is based on the assumption that the composition of the group does not change during the session. On the other hand, this work has similarity which has presented a fault-tolerant version of multiparty Diffie-Hellman Key agreement protocol (Wood and Stankovic, 2002). The particular scheme addressed the scenario of group of people who want to set up a secure session in a meeting room without any support infrastructure.

The major disadvantage of this proposed scheme, authentication is done outside the IT system e.g., the group members authenticate themselves by showing their passports or through common knowledge like friendship or knowing each other. So this method may not be applicable for those situations when there are more than one group exist or the group of people don't know each other.

The work proposed by researchers provided an authentication service in an ad-hoc network environment and claims that authentication is a core element for secure communication (Nichols and Lekkas, 2002). This scheme is proposed for low value transactions and cooperation and feedback system introduces quality and responsibility while hardware requirements for the devices are quite low. However, there are some problems with this approach. In this approach, for preventing channel establishment, a path in the network of trusted entities is replaced by the shared knowledge or is trusted with third party. There is as high probability of any malicious entity in the network of trusted entities as much as longer the particular path stays. Thus there is a lot of effort required to find out the efficient algorithms and making a well-sized repository lists. Another challenge in this approach is the essential feedback system. The proposed feedback system has to work to detect fraud quickly and take appropriate action to prevent repeated attacks.

The report prepared by Sandia laboratories, is focused on security issues arise from wrapping authentication mechanisms around ad hoc routing data (Schuller, 2003). The researchers indicate that, appending signatures to the routing messages of currently existing protocols is not sufficient to prevent adversaries to insert false routing information into network. In this report, the authors have illustrated a repeater attack and prove that even if the network has sophisticated authentication mechanisms placed on the routing messages, the adversary can bring down the entire multi-hop network. This happens through the distributed repeaters that placed by the adversary throughout the network and hears the network traffic and transmits the traffic to all other repeaters that in the network. The routing protocol may behave as though nothing had happened since the adversary's repeaters have only increased the broadcast range and not violated any security features. These adversary's repeaters broadcast the messages to all other repeaters and this action gives the nodes the false belief that the diameter of the network is much smaller than that it actually is.

The authors argue that the provision of comprehensive secure communication requires that both discovery and data forwarding be safeguarded (Wenyuan et al, 2005). The scheme proposes a secure routing protocol (SRP) that counters malicious behaviour that targets the discovery of topological information. The authors proposed a protocol called Secure Message Transmission protocol (SMT) to provide flexible, end to end secure data forwarding scheme that naturally compliments SRP. In essence, this work is proposed to secure against non-colluding adversaries and does not aim to authenticate intermediate nodes that forward "Route requests" and thus do not handle authorization.

In a research proposed by Blum and Eskandarian (2004), is identified some of the challenges in providing authentication, authorisation and accounting in wireless ad hoc networks through classifying them. This is a review paper that cites the work of another research paper, to propose some remedial solutions (Luo et al., 2000).

5.3 PREVIOUS STUDIES ON SECURING MANETs AGAINST DoS AND DDoS ATTACKS

A DoS attacker can cause the congestion in a network by either producing an unnecessary amount of traffic by itself, or generating the excessive amount of traffic by the other nodes. In the wireless networks, DoS attacks are very difficult to prevent or protect. These attacks can cause a harsh degradation on performance of network. In this section, the types of DoS and DDoS attacks and the possible preventions against these attacks are discussed.

According to the research study, master minds of DoS attacks usually target the sites or services hosted on the high-profile web servers like banks, gateways of credit card payment, and also the root name servers (Stubblefield, Ioannidis and Rubin, 2002). A common way of attack is saturating the target machine with external communications requests, like it can't respond to the legitimate traffic, or it may respond so slowly as to be made effectively unavailable. According to these authors attacks like these generally lead to an overload of server. According to these authors generally, DoS and DDoS attacks are implemented either by forcing the targeted network to reset, or consuming that particular network's resources with the intention that it no longer is able to provide its intended service or block the communication media between its intended users or the victim to obstruct adequate communicate (Stubblefield, Ioannidis and Rubin, 2002).

As variety of prevention and detection methods discussed and analysed in the section 2.2, the variety of attacks can be clearly understood in the light of comparative critical analysis. Because of the variety of attacks in MANETs, the attacks are classified based on different aspects. This section mainly covers DoS and DDoS attacks in order to provide an insight about the importance of problem in this field of science and importance of proposed solution. The attacks are classified and categorized in this section as well. On the other hand, the security strategies against these attacks proposed by researchers are also categorised according to their characteristics.

The attack types are classified and categorised as follows; Legitimate Based Classification, Interaction Based Classification, Network Protocol Stack Based Attack Classification, Cryptography Attacks, and AODV protocol Attacks. Each and every attack category will be discussed in the further subsections. As it is mentioned in the section 2.1, MANETs required four standard security attributes and these attributes were availability, confidentiality, authenticity and integrity. In order to provide a secure MANET environment, the existence of such attributes is compulsory. Each of these concepts has explained in the section 2.1. In addition to this, likewise the attack classification, the security strategies against DDoS and DoS attacks proposed by researchers are also classified.

These strategies are classified as attacker side strategies, victim side strategies, and intermediate strategies.

In legitimate based classification, according to the legitimate status of a node, an attack could be external or internal. The external attacks are committed by nodes that are not legal members of the network or group, while the internal attacks are from a compromised member inside the network called as "selfish node". These attackers are aware of the security strategies and are even protected by them. The internal attacks pose a higher threat to the network.

Interaction based classification is another category. In terms of interaction, an attack could be passive or active. The Figure 1 illustrates the categorisation of active and passive attacks. Passive attacks do not disrupt the communication. Instead, they intercept and capture the packets to read the information where this information might be personal or related with security issues. On the other hand, active attackers inject packets into the network to interfere or interrupt the network communication among nodes, overload the network traffic; fake the legitimate node or package, consume the participating nodes processing power and battery, obstruct the operation or cut off certain nodes from their neighbours so they can not use the network services effectively anymore. Denial of Service or Distributed Denial of Service attacks are active attacks as shown in the Figure 1.

The attacks could also be classified according to the target layer in the protocol stack. The Table 1 illustrates the protocol based attack classification. As it is shown on the Table 1, the protocol stack layer is separated according to attack types. Each and every attack belongs to one of the layer in the stack layer. The stack layer contains layers which are Application Layer Attacks, Transport Layer Attacks, Network Layer Attacks, Link Layer Attacks, Physical Layer Attacks and Multi-Layer Attacks (Katz, 2002).

Figure 1. Taxonomy of MANET attacks

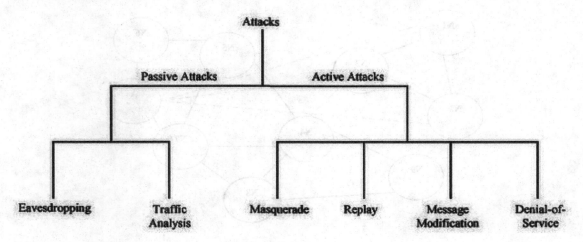

The physical layer attacks are targeting the physical layer of a wireless node, an attacker can easily intercept and read the message contents from open radio signals (Ramaswamy et al., 2003 ; Barbir, Murphy and Yang, 2004). An attacker can interfere the communication by generating powerful transmission to overwhelm the target signals. The jamming signals do not follow the protocol definition, and they can be meaningless random noise and pulse (Yi et al., 2005).

The network layer is responsible of taking traffic from the transport layer and prepare it for the data link layer which leads to realization of end-to-end delivery of packets between nodes. The attackers are targeting the link layer and generate meaningless random packets to grab the channel and cause collisions (Vigna, 2004). In such situation, if the impacted node keeps trying to resend the packet, it will exhaust its power supply; The attacker can passively eavesdrop on the link layer packets; The link security protocol Wireless Encryption Protocol (WEP) is vulnerable too, the initialization vector (IV) flaw in the WEP protocol makes it easier for an attacker to launch a cryptanalytic type attack (CERT, 1998).

Variety of new protocols introduced in MANETs, different types of attacks are targeted these vulnerabilities of these protocols. "Black hole" attacks targeted Distance Vector type routing protocols (Ramaswamy, et al., 2003; Just, Kranakis and Wan 2003). The black hole attacker responds to all Route

Table 1. MANET protocols and attacks classification

MANET Protocols and Attacks	
Application Layer Attacks	Repudiation, Backdoor, Virus, Data corruption or deletion
Transport Layer Attacks	Session hijacking, SYN flooding, Desynchronization
Network Layer Attacks	Blackhole, Byzantine, Misdirection, Resource consumption, flooding, Location disclosure, packet dropping, Rushing, Spoofing, Wormhole, Selfish
Link Layer Attacks	Collision, Disruption MAC(802.11), Unfairness, Exhausting, Monitoring
Physical Layer Attacks	Eavesdropping, Interceptions, Jamming, Tampering
Multi-layer attacks	DoS, impersonation, replay, man-in-the-middle

Figure 2. Man-in-the-middle attack - black hole attack

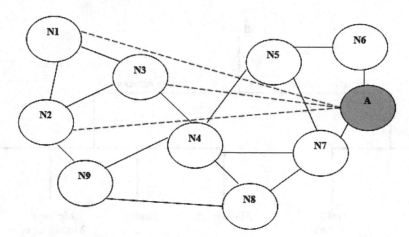

Requests (RREQ) with a shortest Route Reply (RREP). Once the black hole attacker grabs the route, it may drop all the packets, or selectively forward some of the packets to hide the malicious nature. It is also the first step in the man-in-the-middle attacks which is illustrated in the Figure 2 (Hu, Perrig, and Johnson, 2003).

In Figure 2 Black hole attack, Attacker A claims to have shortest route to N1, N2, and N3 Cooperative black hole attacks over AODV and defence system is investigated and discussed in the study by researchers (Al-Shurman, Yoo and Park, 2004 ; Conti,Gregori and Maselli, 2003).

"Byzantine" attackers respond to the RREQ with wrong route information to disrupt or degrade the routing services, such as creating routing loops, forwarding packets through non-optimal paths, or selectively dropping packets (Molva and Michiardi, 2002).

Flooding methods used by DoS and DDoS attackers in wired network have the same effect on the MANET environment (Stoica et al., 2002).

"Location disclosure" attackers disclose the security-sensitive location information of nodes or the topology of the network (Lazos, 2005).

"Misdirection" attackers lead the packets to a wrong way and toward the victim. This is similar to the "Smurf attack" mentioned in (Charles, 2005).

"Packet dropping" attackers disrupt the network communication, and they are very difficult to detect. This attack is often working alone with other attack methods to amplify and increase the damage (Lawson, 2005).

"Resource consumption" or so-called "Sleep deprivation" attackers try to waste the power of the legitimate nodes by requesting excessive route discovery, forwarding useless packets to the victim node, or endlessly "dangling" useless packets between two distant attackers.

"Rushing" attackers have more power and quicker links than legitimate nodes in the network. They may forward RREQ and RREP faster and this allows them to be involved in the routes always as attacker A follows this method which is faster and more powerful than other nodes. The Figure 3 illustrates the Rushing Attack (Hu, Perrig, Johnson, 2003 ; Graf, 2005).

The "Selfish" nodes, as mentioned before, join into network but do not cooperate. These nodes save the battery life, CPU cycles and other resources for their own packets and processes. This behaviour cause inefficient networking while not damaging other participating nodes of the network. There are varieties of researches conducted to differentiate selfish or misbehaving nodes in the network (Black Box Corp, 2003).

Figure 3. Rushing attack

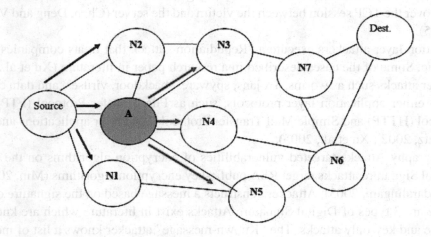

The "Spoofing" attackers impersonate a legitimate node to misrepresent the network topology to cause network loops or partitions (Ferguson and Senie, 2000 ; Humphries and Carlisle, 2002). As it is shown in the Figure 4, the "Wormhole" attackers forward packets between each other by a tunnel instead of hop based routing method defined by the protocol in the research paper (Lazos et al., 2005 ; Min, 2004). This tunnel control messages may cause interruption on routing. The Wormhole attacks are harsh threats for MANETs on-demand routing protocols. This attack may cause prevention of discovery actual routes other than through the wormhole. The Figure 4 illustrates the Wormhole attack. In the literature, research papers mention about defence strategies against Wormhole attack. However these strategies are often based on space or time relativity, such as geographical leashes, temporal leashes or a graph theoretic approach (Min, 2004 ; Wang, 2004).

All these attacks that are mentioned above related with Physical layer attacks. The second layer is Transport Layer. The "desynchronization" attackers sends fabricated packets exceeding the sequence number to either node of the connection and break an existing connection between two nodes. This may lead one of the nodes to send retransmission request for the missed frames which may cause an unnecessary traffic (Kaufman, Perlman and Speciner, 2002).

Figure 4. The Wormhole attack

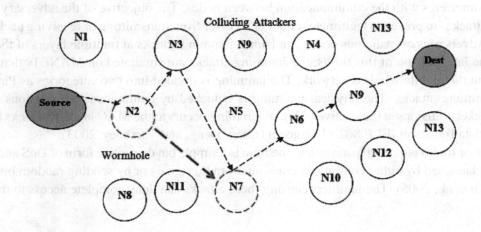

Another transport layer attack is a "Session Hijacking" attack. The attacker impersonates the victim node and takes over the TCP session between the victim and the server (Chen, Deng and Varshney, 2003 ; (Lawson, 2005).

The application layer attackers execute a "Repudiation" attack that treats companies that relies on electronic traffic. Some of the cases described in a research paper in literature (Xu et al., 2005). Other application layer attacks such as worms, Trojans, spywares, backdoor, viruses, and data corruption and deletion, target either application layer protocols, such as File Transfer Protocol (FTP), Hyper Text Transfer Protocol (HTTP) and Simple Mail Transfer Protocol (SMTP) or applications and data files on the victims (Katz, 2002 ; Xu et al., 2005).

The Cryptography Attacks targeted vulnerabilities of encryption algorithms on the related protocols. The Digital Signature attacks target RSA public-key encryption algorithms (Min, 2004 ; Convery, Miller and Sundaralingam, 2003). Attacker constructs a message based on the signature of a legitimate message. There are 3 types of Digital Signature Attacks exist in literature which are known-message, chosen-message and key-only attacks. The "Known-message" attacker knows a list of messages previously signed by the victim. The "Chosen-message" attacker can choose a specific message that it wants the victim to sign. The "Key-only" attacker knows the public verification algorithm only (Min, 2004).

The "Hash collision" attacks target hash algorithms, such as SHA-1, MD4, MD5, HAVAL-128, and RIPEMD, to construct a valid certificate corresponding to the hash collision (Wang, et al., 2003).

Pseudorandom number attacks reverse engineer the pseudorandom number generator used by the public key mechanisms in order to break the cryptography (Humphries, Jeffrey and Carlisle, 2002).

The AODV protocol is specifically designed as a routing protocol for MANETs and other ad-hoc networks. This protocol has many advantages while it is intrinsically vulnerable to many attacks. The classification is illustrated in the Figure 5 (Lazos et al., 2005).

The vulnerability on DoS attacks in link layer IEEE 802.11 has been investigated widely by the researchers in the literature (Karygiannis and Owens, 2002). The malicious or misbehaving node keeps the most of binary exponential back off scheme. In order to happen as expected malicious node damage frame easily by putting few extra bits on the frame and transmits the package to the network through other participating nodes. Malicious node keep the wireless medium busy and start loaded frames transmitting which tend to capture the wireless channel by sending data non-stop as result neighbours nodes back-off endlessly. Therefore other nodes find the wireless medium busy and keep back-off so the performance of the network degrades this way.

The most popular attack model of IEEE 802.11 is Jamming Attacks. Jamming is defined as a DoS attack that interferes with the communication between nodes. The objective of the adversary causing a jamming attack is to prevent a legitimate sender or receiver from transmitting or receiving packets on the network. Adversaries or malicious nodes can launch jamming attacks at multiple layers of the protocol suite. In the later section of this thesis, the Jamming attacks are simulated on MANETs that results in collisions in the mobile wireless network. The jamming is divided into two categories as Physical and Virtual Jamming attacks. The physical jamming is launched by continuous transmissions and/or by causing packet collisions at the receiver. Virtual jamming occurs at the MAC layer by attacks on control frames or data frames in IEEE 802.11 protocol (Chen, Deng, and Varshney, 2003).

Physical or Radio jamming in a wireless medium is a simple but disruptive form of DoS attack. These attacks are launched by either continuous emission of radio signals or by sending random bits onto the channel (Xu et al., 2005). The jammers causing these attacks can deny complete access to the channel

Figure 5. Attacks on AODV protocol in MANETs

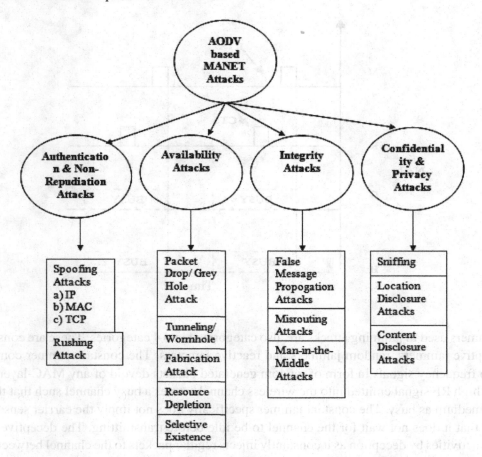

by monopolizing the wireless medium. The nodes trying to communicate have an unusually large carrier sensing time waiting for the channel to become idle. This has an adverse propagating effect as the nodes enter into large exponential back-off periods.

Virtual Jamming Attacks can be launched at the MAC layer through attacks on the RTS/CTS (Request to Send/Clear to Send) frames or DATA frames (Chen, Deng and Varshney, 2003; Thuente and Acharya, 2006). A significant advantage of MAC layer jamming is that the attacker node consumes less power in targeting these attacks as compared to the physical radio jamming. Here, we focus on DoS attacks at the MAC layer resulting in collision of RTS/CTS control frames or the DATA frames. In virtual jamming attack malicious node sent RTS packets continuously on the transmission with unlimited period of time. During this entire process malicious node effectively jam the transmission with a large segment of transmission on the wireless channel with small expenditure of power. This attack is much effective than physical layer jamming as this attack consume less battery power compare to the other physical layer jamming attack. For example node M is a malicious node and it starting sending a false RTS packet to node R with a large frame. When nodes G and H receive packet on wireless channel they both become blocked for a certain amount of time as apply for node M as shown in the Figure 6 (Rahman and Gburzynski, 2006).

Figure 6. Virutal jamming attack

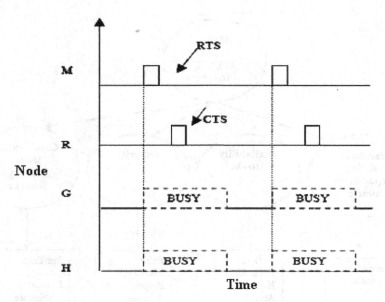

The jammers used in jamming attacks are also categorized into 4 categories. These are constant jammers, deceptive jammers, random jammers and reactive jammers. The constant jammer continuously emits radio frequency signals in form of random generated packets devoid of any MAC-layer protocol or rules. A high RF signal emitted into the wireless channel creates a busy channel such that the sender senses the medium as busy. The constant jammer specifically does not imply the carrier sense scheme; this means that it does not wait for the channel to be idle before transmitting. The deceptive jammers perform its activities by deception as it constantly injects regular packets to the channel between sequential transmissions without any interval of time instead of sending out random bit. It transmits semi-valid packets that contains valid message header but useless pay load. This behaviour leads to a deceptive environment that all other participating nodes notice that the channel contains a valid traffic. Random jammers send radio signals within specific periods. These periods are specified as "awake" and "sleep". Once the jammer is awake, it transmits the signals and once it's in "sleep" condition, it does not transmit any signals. The major aim of such mechanism is to create an energy efficient attack while saving its energy during sleeping mode by turning its radio off. Reactive Jammers targeting receiver channel by sending radio signal when it detects that the channel is busy which means that the reactive jammers do not conserve energy unless they detect the channel.

5.4 SECURITY STRATEGIES AGAINST DoS AND DDoS ATTACKS ON MOBILE AD HOC NETWORKS

As mentioned in the section 2.1, the provision of effective and efficient security can be provided through considering availability, confidentiality, authenticity and integrity concepts. A practically operating MANET must consider the trade-off between the deployment feasibility of a security patch and the system efficiency. And often, the feasibility is considered over the efficiency (Ferguson and Senie, 2000 ; Sans,

Table 2. Classification of strategies against DoS attacks

Attacker-Side Strategies	Victim-Side Strategies	Intermediate Strategies
Mostly Protocol based protection. The protection is provided through modifying the communication protocols and analyze/ differentiate the authorized traffic transmitted over network and controlling e.g. AODV, DSR.	Mainly Certification and Key management authority based protection. The protection is provided through authorization by assigning certificates to participating nodes.	Security is provided through participated nodes in the network. These nodes called intermediate nodes.

2000). The feasibility of a deployment (accessibility and cost) mostly depends on the deployment location. Based on this concept, the security strategies are classified as attacker-side strategies, victim-side strategies, and intermediate strategies (Lakshminarayanan, 2003). This taxonomy makes more practical sense to evaluate a security strategy than other taxonomies, e.g. activity level or cooperation degree (Mirkovic, Prier and Reiher, 2002). The Table 2 represents the classification of the strategies with sample proposed examples offered by other researchers.

The Attacker-side strategies is the first classification for classifying attacks (Zhou, Schneider and Renesse, 2002; Benccsath and Vajda 2004; Leiwo, Aura and Nikander, 2000 ; Yau, Wang and Karim, 2002). It puts the incoming control to the edge routers. So that the packets going out into the network are only the legitimate ones. The disadvantage is that it requires not only a large-scale deployment of ingress control, but also the cooperation among the network clusters which requires a complex architecture that is against the nature for MANETs.

The Victim-side strategies are those strategies that an authentication system is built up by the victim, then it may let only the legitimate traffic have the access, or allocate resources to the requests only after they are authenticated (Li et al., 2004 ; Ioannidis and Bellovin, 2002 ; Savage et al. 2000). The disadvantages are that it requires the client to take extra legitimate application for the access, and DoS congestion may occur before the traffic reaches the victim so the strategy fails. The implementation of such strategy must be taken into consideration carefully against DDoS attacks.

Intermediate strategies require multiple intermediate nodes to support the secure system for the target. These intermediate nodes can work as a proxy to forward and filter the packets, or as the traffic monitors to detect the attack patterns. Another usage of the intermediate nodes is to form a multi-tier architecture, which can provide a unified security service (or other MANET services) interface towards client nodes (Schnackenberg, Djahandari, and Sterne, 2000). In our architecture, we will be also using participating nodes in the network in order to provide security against DoS attacks.

The effective strategy can be a combination of the characteristics of the above mentioned strategies which requires large amount of testing and verifying to solve the dilemma of performance and complexity.

Figure 7. Classification of detection mechanisms

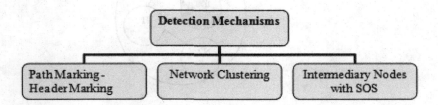

The strategies and methods proposed by researchers to provide security, detection and backtracing against DoS and DDoS attacks are classified in this study. The DoS and DDoS strategy examples are given in the light of the strategy classification shown in the Table 2.

In addition to this Figure 7 illustrates the classification of known detection methods and each of the method that researchers have proposed in the literature.

Researchers have proposed variety of methods to provide security in MANETs against DoS and DDoS attacks. In addition to security, the methods proposed by researchers focus on providing backtracing facilities in order to detect the source of the attack and block the incoming attack from the point of inception. Statistical-based Detection and Backtracing methods are proposed by Yaar,, Perrig,, and Song, (2004) and used packet header marking in order to reduce overhead problem in the network for detection and backtracing facilities. This strategy works through packet sampling and picks particular percentage of the packets on the network in order to analyze and provide security. When DoS attack happens, the flood of attack packets can rapidly provide sufficient information about incoming packages through packet header marking and it gives sufficient information for backtracing purposes. In addition to this, other researchers also proposed similar security strategies through header marking or path marking methods mentioned in the literature (Anderson, Roscoe and Wetherall, 2004 ; Keromytis and Rubenstein, 2002).

The Network Clustering is another proposed method by the researchers in the literature which works through clustering the nodes into small groups called community and puts the boundary controllers at the edge of each community. This controllers help nodes to communicate with each other among different clusters and provide information to trace back the DoS attacks. In order to provide such mechanism, researchers have proposed Intruder Detection and Isolation Protocol (IDIP) (Schnackenberg, Djahandari, and Sterne, 2000). The Figure 8 represents the groups-communities and Intruder detection system and Isolation Protocol working mechanism.

Figure 8. IDIP intrusion detection system

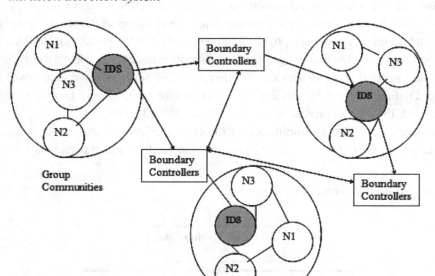

Figure 9. Proposed i3 communication

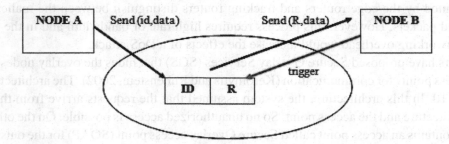

On the other hand, researchers have proposed another strategy method so called "mobile-agent-based architecture" which is fully distributed and randomly selecting the migration path (Stoica et al. 2002; Bencsáth, and Vajda, 2004; Leiwo, Aura and Nikander, 2000). As it is represented on Table 2 security in MANETs can be provided through managing authorization and differentiation of authorized traffic. The researchers have proposed a method to differentiate unauthorized traffic through specifying an authorization key to the important service requesters (Yaar,, Perrig,, and Song, 2004; Anderson, Roscoe and Wetherall, 2004). However it does nothing to the triggers are used for the secure and efficient routing (Min, 2004). The secure authorized traffic and secure communication is provided through this mechanism. The proposed method by the researchers is illustrated in the Figure 9.

This proposed method by researchers have caused high rate of overhead during handshake process of specification of authorization key problem. On the other hand, the public triggers must be known by the clients or the specified servers have to announce them which lead to the DoS attacks. On the other hand, this method has not implemented in the Application Layer, which requires modification on the Network Layer for all other actors of the network such as client nodes and server nodes. It is compulsory to consider the Wormhole attacks which belongs to Network Layer and as it has mentioned that strategy is not modified for the Application layer which contains Backdoors and Trojans and Viruses, the all other actors will be vulnerable to these attacks.

Figure 10. SOS architecture

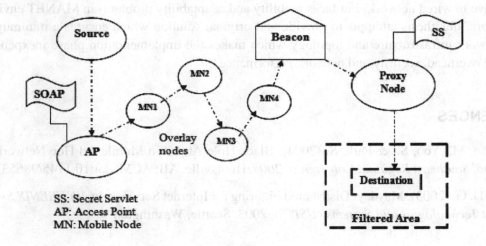

SS: Secret Servlet
AP: Access Point
MN: Mobile Node

The traceback mechanism is provided through edge routers and tracking routers. The suspicious traffic is rerouted by the edge routers and tracking routers distinguish between the malicious packets and authorized packets. However, this process requires high rate of bandwidth and in the case of DoS attack, the networking overhead would increase the effects of a DoS attack.

Researchers have proposed Secure Overlay Services (SOS) that hides the overlay nodes and opens a couple of access points for communication (Keromytis and Rubenstein, 2002). The architecture is shown in the Figure 10. In this architecture, the system assumed that the requests arrive from the nodes that know the architecture and the access point. So no unauthorized access is possible. On the other hand, the architecture contains an access point called Secure Overlay access point (SOAP) for the outside requests. These outside requests are forwarded by the access point to the forwarding proxy nodes called "Secret Servlets" in the architecture. These secret servlets nodes deliver the requests to the service provider. When a DoS attack is generated on the network, only the legitimate and authorized traffic can get into the system by this way. The proposed SOS method is more generalized by the researchers and proposed as a security mechanism called "Mayday" (Andersen, 2003).

As it is known that, overlay architectures provide communication and connectivity even though under the attack which is one of the advantages of the SOS architecture. However the SOS strategy protects only the specific entity of the system and cannot provide communication out of the overlay. In addition to this, packets transmitted through secure overlay access point can be spoofed and attack to secret servlets. In addition to that, there is not load balancing system available among nodes to provide equal workload share. So system may even crash with more complex flow of traffic. The SOS method is also proposed for the Internet and it will have performance, mobility and deployment problems for implementing in Mobile Ad Hoc Networks.

The most of the proposed methods by researchers discussed in this chapter required modification on communication protocols or architecture or even both. The modification and upgrade of the communication protocols seems like an absolute solution for prevention against DoS and DDoS attacks. However, the process of implementing such project may fail because of non-participating nodes refuse the upgrade or modification. On the other hand, network protocol modifications may fail the applications running on the network. For instance, modification on network layer affects the link layer and layers above it and interfaces between them. Controlling the attack traffic through edge routers and using tunnels to forward this traffic is useful. However it requires protocol modification and it may require high rate of bandwidth which may lead an amplification effect of DoS attack on the network. The proposed SOS method is useful and effective in wired networks but faces mobility and adaptability problems in MANET environment.

Therefore, this thesis attempts to provide and original solution which ensures a minimum impact on the network infrastructure and topology which makes the implementation phase inexpensive with reasonable overhead, security and network performance.

REFERENCES

Al-Shurman, M., Yoo, S., & Park, S. (2004). Black Hole Attack in Mobile Ad Hoc Networks. In *the 42nd Annual Southeast Regional Conference. 2004*. Huntsville, AB: ACM. doi:10.1145/986537.986560

Andersen, D. G. (2003). Mayday: Distributed Filtering for Internet Services. In *4th USENIX Symposium on Internet Technologies and Systems (USITS)*. 2003. Seattle, Washington.

Anderson, T., Roscoe, T., & Wetherall, D. (2004). Preventing Internet Denial-of-Service with Capabilities. *Computer Communication Review, 34*(1), 39–44. doi:10.1145/972374.972382

Asokan, N., & Ginzboorg, P. (2000). Key Agreement in Ad-hoc networks. *Computer Communications, 23*(17), 1627–1637. doi:10.1016/S0140-3664(00)00249-8

Barbir, A., Murphy, S., & Yang, Y. (2004). *Generic Threats to Routing Protocols 2004, IETF Internet draft.* Available at: http://www.ietf.org/internet-drafts/draft-ietfrpsec-routing-threats-07.txt. Last accessed: 29/09/14.

Bellovin, S. M., & Merrit, M. (1992). Encrypted Key Exchange: *Password-Based Protocols Secure Against Dictionary Attacks. IEEE Symposium on Research in Security and Privacy.*

Bencsáth, B., & Vajda, I. (2004). Protection Against DDoS Attacks Based On Traffic Level Measurements. In *International Symposium on Collaborative Technologies and Systems.* 2004. San Diego, CA.

Binkley, J., & Trost, W. (2001). Authenticated Ad-hoc Routing at the Link Layer for Mobile Systems. *Wireless Networks, 7*(2), 139–145. doi:10.1023/A:1016633521987

Black Box Corp. (2003). *Network Security, A White Paper. 2003.* Available at: http://www.blackbox.com/Tech_Support/White-Papers/Network-Security2.pdf

Blum, J., & Eskandarian, A. (2004). The Threat of Intelligent Collisions. *IT Professional, 6*(1), 24–29. doi:10.1109/MITP.2004.1265539

Capkun, S., Buttyan, L., & Hubaux, J. P. (2003). Self Organized Public-Key Management for Mobile Ad Hoc Networks. *IEEE Transactions on Mobile Computing, 2*(1), 52–64. doi:10.1109/TMC.2003.1195151

CERT. (1998). *Smurf Attack CERT Annual Report.* Available at CERT: http://www.cert.org/advisories/CA-1998-01.html. Last accessed: 29/09/14.

Charles, C. T. (2005). *Security Review of the Light-Weight Access Point Protocol. 2005.* IETF CAPWAP Working Group.

Chen, D., Deng, J., & Varshney, P. K. (2003). Protecting wireless networks against a denial of service attack based on virtual jamming, in MOBICOM -Proceedings of the Ninth Annual International Conference on Mobile Computing and Networking, ACM, 2003.

Conti, M., Gregori, E., & Maselli, G. (2003). Towards Reliable Forwarding for Ad Hoc Networks. In Personal Wireless Communications, IFIP-TC6 8th International Conference, PWC 2003. Venice, Italy: Springer. p. 790--804. doi:10.1007/978-3-540-39867-7_71

Convery, S., Miller, D., & Sundaralingam, S. (2003). *Cisco SAFE: Wireless LAN Security in Depth 2003.* CISCO Whitepaper.

Desmedt, Y., & Frankel, Y. (1990). Threshold Cryptosystem. Advances in Cryptology Crypto 89 G. Brassard Ed., Springer Verlag, pp 307-15, August. doi:10.1007/0-387-34805-0_28

Diffie, W., & Hellman, M. (1976). New Directions in Cryptography. *IEEE Transactions on Information Theory, IT-22*(6), 644–654. doi:10.1109/TIT.1976.1055638

Ferguson, P., & Senie, D. (2000). *Network Ingress Filtering: Defeating Denial of Service Attacks Which Employ IP Source Address Spoofing*. IETF. Available on http://www.rfc-archive.org/getrfc.php?rfc=2827

Fletcher, T., Richardson, H. W. K., Carlisle, M. C., & Hamilton, J. A. (2005). Jr. Simulation Experimentation with Secure Overlay Services. In *Summer Computer Simulation Conference*. 2005. Philadelphia, PA.

Gasser, M., Goldstein, A., Kaufman, C., & Lampson, B. (1989). The Digital distributed system security architecture. In *Proceedings of the National Computer Security Conference*, pp. 305-319, 1989.

Graf, K. (2005). *Addressing Challenges in Application Security*. Watchfire White Paper. Retrieved from http://www.watchfire.com

Hu, Y.-C., Perrig, A., & Johnson, D. B. (2003). Rushing Attacks and Defense in Wireless Ad Hoc Network Routing Protocols. In 2nd ACM Wireless Security (WiSe'03). 2003. pp. 30-40. doi:10.1145/941311.941317

Hubaux, J. P., Gross, T., Boudec, J. Y., & Vetterli, M. (2001, January). Toward self-organized mobile ad hoc networks: The terminodes project. *IEEE Communications Magazine*, *39*(1), 118–124. doi:10.1109/35.894385

Humphries, J. W. & Carlisle, M.C. (2002). Introduction to Cryptography. *ACM Journal of Educational Resources in Computing, 2*(3), 2.

Ioannidis, J., & Bellovin, S. M. (2002). Implementing Pushback: Router-Based Defense Against DDoS Attacks. In *Network and Distributed System Security Symposium*. 2002. San Diego, CA. pp.79-86.

Johnson, D. B., & Maltz, D. A. (1996). In T. Imielinski & H. Korth (Eds.), *Dynamic source routing in ad hoc wireless networks, in mobile Computing* (pp. 153–181). Kluwer Academic Publishers.

Just, M., Kranakis, E., & Wan, T. (2003). Resisting Malicious Packet Dropping in Wireless Ad Hoc Networks. In ADHOCNOW'03. 2003. Montreal, Canada. doi:10.1007/978-3-540-39611-6_14

Karygiannis, T., & Owens, L. (2002). Wireless Network Security 802.11 Bluetooth and Handheld Devices, National Institute of Standards and Technology Special Publication, 800-48, Nov 2002, Available at: http://csrc.nist.gov/publications/nistpubs/800-48/NIST_SP_800-48.pdf

Katz, J. (2002). Efficient Cryptographic Protocols Preventing "Man-in-the-Middle" Attacks. 2002, PhD Dissertation, Columbia University.

Kaufman, C., Perlman, R., & Speciner, M. (2002). Network Security Private Communication in a Public World. 2002: Prentice Hall PTR. p. 752.

Keromytis, A. D., & Rubenstein, D. (2002). SOS: Secure Overlay Services. In ACM SIGCOMM'02. 2002. Pittsburgh, PA.

Kong, J., Zerfos, P., Luo, H., Lu, S., & Zhang, L. (2001). Providing Robust and Ubiquitous Security Support for Mobile Adhoc Networks, in Ninth International Conference on Network Protocols (ICNP), 2001, pp. 251–260, also available at http://citeseer.nj.nec.com/kong01providing.html

Lakshminarayanan, K., Adkins, D., Perrig, A., & Stoica, I. (2003). Taming IP Packet Flooding Attacks. In *2nd ACM Workshop on Hot Topics in Networks*. 2003. Cambridge, MA: ACM Press pp. 45-50.

Lawson, L. (2005). Session Hijacking Packet Analysis. 2005, SecurityDocs.com Report.

Lazos, L., Poovendran, R., Meadows, C., Syverson, P., & Chang, L. W. (2005) Preventing Wormhole Attacks on Wireless Ad Hoc Networks: A Graph Theoretic Approach. In *IEEE Wireless Communications and Networking Conference*. 2005. pp. 1193-1199. doi:10.1109/WCNC.2005.1424678

Leiwo, J., Aura, T., & Nikander, P. (2000). Towards Network Denial Of Service Resistant Protocols. In 15th International Information Security Conference 2000. Beijing, China. pp. 301-310. doi:10.1007/978-0-387-35515-3_31

Levijoki, S. (2000). Authentication, Authorization and Accounting in Ad-hoc networks Department of Computer Science Helsinki University of Technology 26th of May 2000 http://www.hut.fi/~slevijok/aaa.htm

Li, J., Sung, M., Xu, J., & Li, L. E. (2004). Large-Scale IP Traceback in High-Speed Internet: Practical Techniques and Theoretical Foundation. In IEEE Symposium on Security and Privacy 2004. Oakland, California, USA. 115.

Luo, H., Kong, J., Zerfos, P., Lu, S., & Zhang, L. (2000). *Self Securing Ad-hoc Wireless Networks. IEEE Symposium on Computers and Communications (ISCC'02)*.

Marti, S., Giuli, T., Lai, K., & Baker, M. (2000). Mitigating Routing Misbehaviour in Mobile Ad-hoc Networks. In *Proceedings of the ACM International Conference on Mobile Computing and Networking MobiCom*.

Min, S. (2004). A Study on the Security of NTRUSign Digital Signature Scheme. 2004, Master Thesis in Information and Communications University, Korea.

Mirkovic, J., Prier, G., & Reiher, P. (2002). Attacking DDoS at the Source In the 10th IEEE International Conference on Network Protocols. 2002: IEEE Computer Society. pp. 312-321.

Molva, R., & Michiardi, P. (2002). Security in Ad Hoc Networks. In Personal Wireless Communications, IFIP-TC6 8th International Conference. 2002. Venice, Italy: Springer. pp. 756-775. doi:10.1007/978-3-540-39867-7_69

Nguyan, D., Zhao, L., Uisawang, P., & Platt, J. (2000). Security Routing Analysis For Mobile Ad-hoc Networks. Interdisciplinary Telecommunications Program of Colorado University, Spring 2000.

Nichols, R. K., & Lekkas, P. C. (2002). Wireless Security: Models, Threats, and Solutions 1ed. 2002: McGraw-Hill Professional. pp. 657.

Papadimitratos, P., & Haas, Z. J. (2002). Secure Routing for Mobile Ad-hoc Networks. In *Proceedings of the SCS Communication Networks and Distributed Systems Modelling and Simulations Conference (CNDS 2002)*, San Antonio, TX, January 27-31, 2002.

Patrikakis, C., Masikos, M., & Zouraraki, O. (2004). Distributed Denial of Service Attacks. *The Internet Protocol J.*, *7*(4), 13–35.

Rabin, T. (1998). A Simplified Approach to Threshold and Proactive RSA. In. Lecture Notes in Computer Science: Vol. 1462. *Advances in Cryptology – Crypto 98 Proceedings* (pp. 89–104). Springer-Verlag. doi:10.1007/BFb0055722

Rafique, K. (2002). *A Survey of Mobile Ad Hoc Networks. ELEN 695, Presented to Dr. Campbell.* Available at: http://www.columbia.edu/itc/ee/e6951/2002spring/Projects/CVN/report13.pdf

Rahman, A., & Gburzynski, P. (2006). *Hidden Problems with the Hidden Node Problem.* Available at: http://citeseerx.ist.psu.edu/viewdoc/download?doi=10.1.1.61.365&rep=rep1&type=pdf

Ramaswamy, S., Fu, H., Sreekantaradhya, M., Dixon, J., & Nygard, K. (2003). Prevention of Cooperative Black Hole Attack in Wireless Ad Hoc Networks. In International Conference on Wireless Networks 2003. 2003. pp.570-575.

Royer, E., & Toh, C. (1999). A Review of Current Routing Protocols for Ad Hoc Mobile Wireless Networks. *IEEE Personal Communications, 6*(2), 46–55. doi:10.1109/98.760423

Sans. (2000). *Egress Filtering v 0.2. 2000, SANS.* Available at: http://www.sans.org/y2k/egress.htm

Savage, S., Wetherall, D., Karlin, A., & Anderson, T. (2000). Practical Network Support for IP Traceback. In the 2000 ACM SIGCOMM Conference. 2000. Stockholm, Sweden. pp. 295-306.

Schnackenberg, D., Djahandari, K., & Sterne, D. (2000). Infrastructure for Intrusion Detection and Response. In DARPA Information Survivability Conference and Exposition. 2000. pp. 1003-1011.

Schuller, J. (2003). *Understanding Wireless LAN Technology and Its Security Risks.* Available at GIAC: http://www.giac.org/practical/GSEC/Julie_Schuller_GSEC.pdf

Schwingenschlögl, C., & Horn, M.-P. (2002). Building Blocks for Secure Communication in Ad-hoc Networks. In *Proceedings of the 4th European Wireless (EW'02) Florence*, Italy.

Shoup, V. (2000). Practical Threshold Signatures. In. Lecture Notes in Computer Science: Vol. 1807. *Advances in Cryptology-Eurocrypt 2000 proceedings* (pp. 207–221). Springer Verlag. doi:10.1007/3-540-45539-6_15

Stajano, F., & Anderson, R. (1999). The Resurrecting Duckling: Security Issues for Ad-Hoc Wireless networks. In *Proceedings of the 7th International Workshop on Security Protocols*.

Stoica, I., Adkins, D., Zhuang, S., Shenker, S., & Surana, S. (2002). Internet Indirection Infrastructure. In ACM SIGCOMM Conference 2002. Pittsburgh, PA, USA. pp.73-88.

Stubblefield, A., Ioannidis, J., & Rubin, A. D. (2002). Using the Fluhrer, Mantin, and Shamir attack to break WEP. In Symposium on Network and Distributed System Security. 2002. Also available at http://www.isoc.org/isoc/conferences/ndss/02/proceedings/papers/stubbl.pdf. Last accessed: 29/09/14

Thuente, D., & Acharya, M. (2006). Intelligent jamming in wireless networks with applications to 802.11b and other networks, in *Proceedings of the 25th IEEE Communications Society Military Communications Conference (MILCOM)*, October 2006.

Torgerson, M. and Leeuwen, B.V., (2001). Routing Data in Wireless Ad-hoc Networks. Sandia laboratories report SAND2001-3119 October 2001.

Venkatraman, L., & Agrawal, D. P. (2001). An Optimized Inter-Router Authentication Scheme for Ad-hoc networks. In *Proceedings of the 13th International Conference on Wireless Communications*, pp. 129-1, Calgary, Canada.

Vigna, G., Gwalani, S., Srinivasan, K., Elizabeth, M., Royer, B., & Kemmerer, R. (2004). An Intrusion Detection Tool for AODV-based Ad hoc Wireless Networks. in *20th Annual Computer Security Applications Conference (ACSAC'04)*. 2004: IEEE Computer Society pp. 16-27. doi:10.1109/CSAC.2004.6

Wang, X., Feng, D., Lai, X. and H. Yu (2004). Collisions for Hash Functions MD4, MD5, HAVAL-128 and RIPEMD. 2004, Cryptology ePrint Archive.

Weimerskirch, A., & Thonet, G. (2001). A Distributed Lightweight Authentication Model for Ad-hoc Networks. In the Proceedings of the 4th International Conference on Information Security and Cryptology (ICICS 2001) December 6-7 2001 Korea.

Wood, A. D., & Stankovic, J. A. (2002). Denial of Service in Sensor Networks. *Computer*, *35*(10), 54–62. doi:10.1109/MC.2002.1039518

Xu, W., Wade, T., Yanyong, Z., & Timothy, W. (2005). The Feasibility of Launching and Detecting Jamming Attacks in Wireless Networks. In 6th ACM International Symposium on Mobile Ad Hoc Networking and Computing 2005. Urbana-Champaign, IL, USA: ACM Press pp. 46-57.

Xu, W., Trappe, W., Zhang, Y., & Wood, T. (2005). The feasibility of launching and detecting jamming attacks in wireless networks, in MobiHoc '05: Proceedings of the 6th ACM international symposium on Mobile ad hoc networking and computing, pp. 46–57, 2005.

Yaar, A., Perrig, A., & Song, D. (2004). SIFF: A Stateless Internet Flow Filter to Mitigate DDoS Flooding Attacks. In the IEEE Security and Privacy Symposium. 2004. Philadelphia, Pennsylvania, USA ACM Press New York, NY, USA pp. 241-252. doi:10.1109/SECPRI.2004.1301320

Yau, S. S., Wang, Y., & Karim, F. (2002). Development of Situation-Aware Application Software for Ubiquitous Computing Environment. In 26th International Computer Software and Applications Conference on Prolonging Software Life: Development and Redevelopment 2002: IEEE Computer Society. pp. 233-238. doi:10.1109/CMPSAC.2002.1044557

Yi, P., Dai, Z., Zhong, Y., & Zhang, S. (2005). Resisting Flooding Attacks in Ad Hoc Networks. In Proceedings of the International Conference on Information Technology: Coding and Computing (ITCC'05) 0-7695-2315-3/05, IEEE, 2005.

Zhang, Y., & Lee, W. (2000). Intrusion detection in wireless ad-hoc networks, The 6th Annual International Conference on Mobile Computing and Networking, pp. 275–283, 2000.

Zhou, L., & Haas, Z. J. (1999). *Securing Ad-hoc Networks. IEEE Networks, Special Issues on Network Security* (pp. 24–30). November/December.

Zhou, L., Schneider, F. B., & Renesse, R. V. (2002). COCA: A Secure Distributed On-line Certification Authority. *ACM Transactions on Computer Systems*, *20*(4), 329–368. doi:10.1145/571637.571638

KEY TERMS AND DEFINITIONS

Denial of Service (Dos): A type of an attack that aims to make computer system unavailable that provides services to other nodes on the network through flooding useless traffic.

MANET: Connection of number of self-configured mobile devices or nodes throrugh wireless media with an dynamic infrastructurelss environment.

Network Defence Mechanisms: Physical or software mechanism provided by network administrator in order to detect, mitigate and prevent system against network security attacks.

Network Security Attacks: Any method, action or process conducted to compromise the network security to illegally use, modify or alter remote data for variety of reasons and can be classified generally as active or passive attacks.

Network Security: Combination of rules and policies implemented by network administration to prevent unatuhorized access, modification,misue, or alteration of data, or denial of a computer network resources.

RTS/CTS: It is an mechanism used by the 802.11 Wirleess Networks and protocols to reduce frame collisions created through hidden nodes on the network that has malicious activities.

Wireless Networks: A typical network that sender and reciever connected to each other through radio waves to manintain communicaton and has no physical wired communication infrastructure.

Chapter 6
Legal Issues:
Security and Privacy with Mobile Devices

Brian Leonard
Alabama A&M University, USA

Maurice Dawson
University of Missouri – St. Louis, USA

ABSTRACT

Privacy and security are two items being woven into the fabric of American law concerning mobile devices. This chapter will review and analyze the associated laws and policies that are currently in place or have been proposed to ensure proper execution of security measures for mobile and other devices while still protecting individual privacy. This chapter will address the fact that as the American society significantly uses mobile devices, it is imperative to understand the legal actions surrounding these technologies to include their associated uses. This chapter will also address the fact that with 9/11 in the not so distant past, cyber security has become a forefront subject in the battle against global terrorism. Furthermore, this chapter will examine how mobile devices are not like the devices of the past as the computing power is on par with that of some desktops and the fact that these devices have the ability to execute malicious applications. In addition, this chapter will discuss the reality, significance, legal and practical affects of the fact that suspicious programs are being executed offensively and security based attacks can be performed as well with the use of programs such as Kali Linux running on Android.

LEGAL BACKGROUND

Privacy and security are two ideals that are woven into the very fabric of the United States (U.S.) law. This is evidenced by the fact that they are principles that are embodied in the U.S. Constitution (*U.S. Const.*, 1787). However, supporting and protecting these ideals is not without challenge, especially as technology and innovation make it increasingly more difficult to navigate these ideals and to continue to protect them. In a post-9/11 era, privacy and security have become increasingly challenging and in some cases have become difficult to reconcile with one another. One such area, is that of the safety and security of the Internet, including the mobile devices that are used more and more to access and

DOI: 10.4018/978-1-4666-8345-7.ch006

transact business and personal matters via the Internet. The dilemma faced by the U.S. is attempting to provide for the protection of the U.S. and its citizens from cyber attacks on the one hand, and trying to ensure that in so doing, the U.S. government does not become too intrusive into the lives of individuals and businesses on the other hand. This difficulty is most likely the reason why the U.S. still has yet to develop consistently broad national policy regarding cyber-security and the protection of U.S. citizens from cyber attacks. Moreover, the swiftness with which technology changes, and new threats emerge, have made it even more difficult for U.S. law and policy to develop comprehensive safeguards to protect the nation's and it's citizens' secure information.

INDUSTRY-SPECIFIC LAWS

Although comprehensive policy remains a challenge, there have been strides made in the passage of laws in specific industries and areas where the U.S. government and by representation, most U.S. citizens have acknowledged and likely accepted the need for national regulation regarding the security and safety of information. An early attempt at protecting electronic information from unauthorized access, is the Electronic Communications Privacy Act ("ECPA"). This Act criminalizes the unauthorized access of the electronic communications of another without the owner's or recipient's permission (Electronic Communications Privacy Act, 1988). Although probably not contemplated by the Act in its inception, mobile devices which transmit electronic communications in the form of e-mail and other forms of communication are likely covered by the ECPA (Electronic Communications Privacy Act,1988). However, this Act does not go far enough in that it does not deal more specifically with the more sophisticated nature of cyber attacks today.

Next, health information is probably for many the most important area of information that needs protection from attacks. Through the Health Insurance Portability and Accountability Act ("HIPAA"), the U.S. Government has provided for the creation of national standards for both the practical and technical security of health information (Health Insurance Portability and Accountability Act, 2000); Security Rule and Privacy Rule, 2003). Through subsequent standards adopted by the U.S government, these technical standards include such safeguards as the use of encryption, passwords, and other means of protecting health information from cyber attacks (Health Insurance Portability and Accountability Act, 2000; Security Rule and Privacy Rule, 2003).

Furthermore, post 9/11, the U.S Government formed the Department of Homeland Security through the Homeland Security Act ("HSCA"). Among other things, this act requires steps to be taken to protect it from terrorist attacks to include cyber attacks (Homeland Security Act, 2006). The Act provides for standards to protect the nation's defense network as well as to share information with private industries and organizations to protect against cyber threats in the private sector (Homeland Security Act, 2006). Along with the HSCA, the Federal Information Security Management Act ("FISMA"), requires all federal agencies to take measures to protect their networks, electronic information, and devices from cyber attacks (Federal Information Security Management Act, 2006). Lastly, the Gramm–Leach–Bliley Act ("GLB") requires banks and financial institutions to maintain the security of financial information and transactions (Gramm–Leach–Bliley Act, 2000).

As is clear from their industry-specific application, outside of national security and defense (HSCA), health services (HIPAA), federal agencies (FISMA), and financial services (GLB), all of these measures fall short in providing for comprehensive reform and policy regarding the protection of individual users of mobile devices and other devices from cyber attacks.

CURRENT CYBER-SECURITY EFFORTS ANDTHREATS

The U.S. government has identified multiple risks associated with cyber terrorism and its impacts. Cyber warfare is not limited to computer grid systems but all systems that are vulnerable such as mobile devices. Lewis (2002) states that the literature on cyber security assumes that the associated vulnerabilities of critical infrastructures and computer networks are the same.

FEDERAL EFFORTS

To that end, there have been some efforts by the U.S. government to deal with the area of cyber-attacks and cyber-security measures. Under his executive authority, for example, the President has issued an Executive Order - Improving Critical Infrastructure Cybersecurity (Executive Order No.13636, 2013) (the "Order"). This Order provides for among other things, information sharing among federal agencies and with the private sector, to include dissemination of reports regarding critical infrastructure assets, consultation, civil liberty protection, critical infrastructure risk reduction, cyber-security framework development, voluntary cyber-security program creation, and critical infrastructure cyber-security risk identification (Executive Order No.13636, 2013).

As required by the Order, the document, *Framework for Improving Critical Infrastructure Cybersecurity*, version 1.0,(the "Framework") was developed and issued within one year of the Order, on February 12, 2014. In 41 pages the Framework addressed the issues outlined by the Order (National Institute of Standards and Technology, 2014). The Framework makes clear that it is a living document and due to the constant changing nature of cyber threats that may occur, the Framework would also need to evolve and remain a fluid document (National Institute of Standards and Technology, 2014). The Framework's Core elements are Functions, Categories, Subcategories and Informative References (National Institute of Standards and Technology, 2014). The Functions of the Framework's Core are to Identify, Protect, Detect, Respond, and Recover (National Institute of Standards and Technology, 2014).

After research, it was determined that three agencies, the Environmental Protection Agency ("EPA"), the Department of Health and Human Services ("HHS"), and the Department of Homeland Security ("DHS") were required to submit reports regarding their specific areas of critical infrastructure ("the Reports") (*Assessing Cybersecurity Regulations*, 2014). The White House). The DHS report was comprised of three (3) areas: maritime critical infrastructure cyber-security standards, chemical facility anti-terrorism standards, and transportation critical infrastructure cyber-security standards (U.S. Department of Homeland Security, 2014). The EPA report focused on water and wastewater critical infrastructure cyber-security standards, and the HHS report focused on food and drug critical infrastructure cyber-security standards, and cyber-security standards and exercises designed to handle attacks on medical devices and health organizations. (U.S. Department of Health and Human Services, 2014,) While the federal government acknowledges that there is still more work to do, it is proud of the progress it has made in the area of cyber-security measures for critical infrastructure (The White House, 2014).

While the Order, the Framework, and the Reports are an important step toward national policy on cyber-security, they are limited to those areas considered critical infrastructure, or those areas and/or industries, both physical and virtual, that are "...so vital to the United States that the incapacity or destruction of such systems and assets would have a debilitating impact on security, national economic security, national public health or safety, or any combination of those matters..." (Executive Order No.13636,

2013). There is a pretty good chance that use of smartphones, tablets, or other mobile devices might not fall into that category. In addition, even in the case of critical infrastructure, the Order specifically excludes any regulation of critical infrastructure security beyond what is already existing under current law, meaning, that it only requires certain actions to be taken but does not provide for greater policy or legal protection than what is already provided by other laws. Moreover, since it is only an Executive Order, it is applicable only to the federal agencies under the executive branch of government's control anyway (Executive Order No.13636, 2013).

STATE EFFORTS

In order to have significant, comprehensive and national policy regarding cyber-security for mobile devices, it is without question, a matter that the U.S. government is likely better equipped to handle and address. However, state efforts are still important and can be useful in this area. Not surprising, for example, the state of California has taken measures to include the passing of a law requiring businesses and organizations that experience a security breach to provide notice of the breach to those affected (Notice of Breach of Security Act, 2003). In addition, the state of California has also passed a provision requiring that businesses that maintain users' secure information, to enact "reasonable" levels of security to prevent the unauthorized access or disclosure of that information, which includes protection from cyber and other attacks on such information (California Assembly Bill No. 1950, 2004). As with the federal initiatives, it is likely that even these steps alone are not sufficient to protect users of mobile devices from cyber attacks.

However the state of California's Attorney General's Office has issued certain public awareness campaigns aimed at helping its citizens protect against cyber attacks using mobile devices. For example, its "Getting Smart about Smartphones" Campaign provides information sheets with Tips for Parents and Tips for Consumers. These information sheets warn parents and consumers of the risks of Apps, and encourages the screening, controlling, and reporting of Apps, as California law requires Apps to have a privacy policy (State of California Department of Justice Office of the Attorney General, 2013,). Furthermore, the Tips for Consumers remind consumers to not only check their Apps, but to check their Network, and that just like the desktop computer, smartphones remain vulnerable to attack from spyware, malware, and hackers. (State of California Department of Justice Office of the Attorney General, 2013, State of California Department of Justice Office of the Attorney General) Similar campaigns could go a long way to inform and educate users of mobile devices about the risks of cyber attacks.

PROPOSED REGULATIONS

Unfortunately, the lack of a national uniform policy regarding cyber security of mobile and other devices largely exists due to the lack of consensus in the U.S. government on the best way to provide such security and protection and at the same time avoid over-involvement of government in citizen's private affairs. This can be see in the failure of legislative efforts on both sides of the isle in Congress and by the President. For example, the Cyber-Intelligence Sharing and Protection Act (CISPA) was passed by the House of Representatives, but not favored by the Senate or the President, over concerns that in requiring the sharing of information, it also failed to protect critical infrastructure, as well as waived several civil liberties and threatened individual privacy. (Cyber-Intelligence Sharing and Protection Act, 2012; Lardinois, 2012,). Similarly, the Cyber-security Act of 2012 was passed by the Senate and had Presidential support, in an attempt to provide for greater protection from cyber-security attacks. However, just like the CISPA, this bill faced opposition, largely due to concerns over the bill's alleged increased regulation of businesses. (Cybersecurity Act, 2012; *Cybersecurity Bill Wins Key Senate Vote*, 2012).

MODEL NATIONAL POLICY

Despite the failed legislative efforts to adopt national legislation and policy regarding cyber-security for mobile and other devices, there appears to at least be a consensus among the federal legislative and executive branches, of the necessity to enact some federal provision dealing with cyber-security in general. Given the importance and frequency of use of smartphones, tablets and other devices, any federal provision dealing with cyber-security would also most assuredly need to address mobile device security. This is because, as indicated by California's Attorney General, for the purposes of cyber-security, mobile devices are just as vulnerable as desktop computers and similar devices to attack. The main impediment then is what shape such regulation should take, taking into account the individual civil liberties and privacy concerns, business regulation concerns, and the protection of critical infrastructure concerns.

At the outset, a theoretical model policy on cyber-security for mobile and similar devices, would most likely need to emanate from the federal government. While each state has an interest in developing its own policy, a national policy would likely be more consistent and easier to navigate for most consumers and businesses, rather than a state by state approach. Furthermore, a national model policy on cyber-security likely has legal support and is authorized by the U.S. Constitution, under the Commerce clause's authority to regulate matters that travel in or affect interstate commerce, which would include not only e-commerce but the use of mobile devices almost by definition (*U.S. Const.* 1787). Furthermore, there are likely numerous federal statutes and federal agencies that provide a basis for and could enforce a national model policy on cyber-security for mobile devices. However one possible agency that could be utilized in this national model policy is the the Federal Trade Commission ("FTC"), which was created by and enforces the Federal Trade Commission Act ("FTA"), and other rules promulgated by the FTC.

The FTC seems to be a wise choice not only for enforcing such a model national policy on cyber-security on mobile devices, but it also can assist in evaluation and implementation of such a model national policy. This is because as a bipartisan independent agency, the FTC is uniquely suited to handle the various disputes that have plagued Congress and the President in attempting to come to a consensus about the larger issue of cyber-security and the smaller issue of cyber-security for users of mobile devices. (Federal Trade Commission Act, 1914) Moreover, one of the FTC's primary roles is consumer protection. Consequently the most likely victims of cyber-security attacks and breaches upon mobile devices are consumers, and thus the agency charged with protection of consumers seems to be the likely choice to promulgate and enforce standards of a national model policy to address this issue. Furthermore, the FTC has already taken steps to protect consumers from cyber-attacks through cases it has presented against Twitter and Wyndam, for example. (U.S. Federal Trade Commission, 2011; Egan, 2014).

In addition, the FTC could engage in public education and awareness campaigns designed to assist consumers in becoming more knowledgeable about the existence of and how to prevent cyber attacks similar to those used by California's Attorney General's office mentioned above. While the FTC can develop specific standards, through the public comment and hearing process, there still needs to be a national model policy which lays the framework for the FTC to utilize. The good news is that there is already a starting point for such a framework in place. However, the Framework developed as a result of the Order issued by the President would need to be expanded to include consumer protection and more specifically the threat of cyber-security attacks on mobile devices used by consumers in order to be developed into a national model policy. This can likely be done with the aid of the FTC, as well as private entities or public interest organizations committed to protecting and ensuring the integrity of mobile devices for their continued use. Once the consumer protection and mobile device provisions are added to the Framework, the final pieces to be added would be provisions to protect individual privacy and business autonomy, which could follow the previous examples of HIPAA and GLB, since these laws are industry-specific, to address such concerns. Critical infrastructure protection is already provided for in the Framework and thus this concern has already been addressed by the document. Once completed, the revised Framework would still need bipartisan support from both houses of Congress and the President, before being adopted. If that can be done, then the U.S. could finally have a national model policy on cyber-security for mobile devices. The national policy could allow states to model their own policy after the national policy, where necessary, but could retain certain minimum standards necessary to ensure continuity and comprehensiveness nation-wide.

Finally, as always the courts as the third and final branch of the federal government would serve their ever-important role of interpreting such provisions of the national policy to ensure that the privacy and other legal concerns are adequately protected as they have done in the past, while still preserving the ideal of cyber-security for consumers using mobile devices (*U.S. Const.*, 1787; Marbury v. Madison, 1803).

GOVERNMENT TECHNICAL GUIDANCE

The National Institute of Standards and Technology (NIST) is charged with promoting innovation and industrial competitiveness by advancing measurement science, standards, and technology to enhance America's economic security. Additionally, it is charged with improving the quality of life. NIST's Computer Security Division publishes the Special Publications (SP) 800 Series that are general interest to the computer security community. These publications represent collaborative efforts between industry, government, and academia. NIST Special Publication (SP) 800-124, Guidelines on Cell Phone and PDA Security provides general insights into securing these devices (Jansen & Scarfone, 2008). Jansen and Scarfone (2008) provide guidance about the threats and technology risks associated with mobile devices to includes potential methods for mitigation. Ayers, Brothers, and Jansen (2013) drafted guidelines for mobile forensics which is important as the U.S. has the right to use forensics techniques at any port of U.S. entry at that particular entry point. An older guidelines NIST SP 800-19 Mobile Agent Security, published Oct 1999, was one of the first guidelines to address security for mobile agent security. Jansen and Karygiannis (1999) identified generic security objectives and various measures for countering the identified threats. It is important to note that the SP 800-19 address specifically mobile code execution.

Other key NIST guidance such as SP 800-164 Guidelines on Hardware-Rooted Security in Mobile Devices provide guidance on how mobile devices can provide strong security assurance to end users and organizations (Draft) (Chen et al, 2012). The aim of the guidance document is to further industry efforts to implement these primitives and capabilities (Chen et al, 2012). As much of the other NIST SPs this SP provides a baseline of security technologies that can be implemented that will aid in securing mobile devices that are used in enterprise environments. The key capabilities in this SP is broken into three sections which are the following: 1) device integrity, 2) isolation, and 3) protected storage. Device integrity is the absence of corruption in the firmware, hardware, and software in a mobile device. Integrity is one of the three pillars in the Availability, Integrity, and Confidentiality (AIC) triad that Information Assurance (IA) is built upon. Isolation prevents unintended interaction between Information Owners on the same device (Chen et al, 2012). The Information Owner is not to be confused with the Device Owner. Protected storage deals with preserving the confidentiality and integrity of the data while in use, and at rest. However encrypting data has ramifications such as being jailed in certain countries for refusal to give up encryption keys.

Bring Your Own Device (BYOD)

Understanding the legal issues and ramifications are ever more important as organizations are pushing for Bring Your Own Device (BYOD) and security and privacy are a significant factor (Miller et al, 2012). When we think of mobile devices it is essential that the hyperconnectivity trend is taken as a factor (Dawson et al, 2014). As mobile devices connect with corporate networks while still enabling services such as Bluetooth pose a real threat. To be secure and compliant organizations must re-evaluate their wireless security models (Welch & Lathrop, 2003). BYOD will need to address licensing as virtualization must occur for partitioning and security. BYOD has yet to address issues surrounding a data link or confidential data bleed over. An approved architecture must be created to satisfy the policies and laws of that state. Furthermore this architecture must be scalable.

CONCLUSION

In conclusion, legal issues in the area of cyber-security and privacy with respect to mobile devices will have to be continually reviewed and updated where necessary to address and adapt to the changing technological environment. However, a model national policy that provides legal protection, provides for legal standards, promotes education, and information sharing, would be an important and critical first step to protecting consumers and users of mobile devices from the ever-present threat of cyber attacks. Changing trends such as BYOD will force organizations to determine how data is secured and segregated.

REFERENCES

Ayers, R., Brothers, S., & Jansen, W. (2013). Guidelines on Mobile Device Forensics (Draft). *NIST Special Publication*, *800*, 101.

California Assembly Bill No. 1950, (2004). Cal. Civ. Code § 1798.82

Chen, L., Franklin, J., & Regenscheid, A. (2012). Guidelines on Hardware-Rooted Security in Mobile Devices (Draft). *NIST Special Publication*, *800*, 164.

ConstU.S.. art. IV (1787).

ConstU.S.. Pmbl(1787).

U.S. Const. amend. IV (1791).

Cyber-Intelligence Sharing and Protection Act, (2013). H.R. 3523, 112th Congress (2011-2012), (2012), H.R. 624,113th Congress (2013-2014)

Cybersecurity. (2014). Retrieved June 14, 2014 from http://www.phe.gov/Preparedness/planning/cip/Pages/eo13636.aspx

Cybersecurity Act of 2012, (2012). S. 2105, 112th Congress (2011-2012).

Cybersecurity bill wins key Senate vote, upi.com. (2012). Retrieved June 14, 2014 from http://www.upi.com/Top_News/US/2012/07/26/Cybersecurity-bill-wins-key-Senate-vote/UPI-57801343345113/

Cybersecurity Framework. (2014). Retrieved June 14, 2014 from http://www.dhs.gov/publication/eo-13636-improving-ci-cybersecurity

Dawson, M., Omar, M., Abramson, J., & Bessette, D. (2014). The Future of National and International Security on the Internet. In A. Kayem & C. Meinel (Eds.), *Information Security in Diverse Computing Environments* (pp. 149–178). Hershey, PA: Information Science Reference; doi:10.4018/978-1-4666-6158-5.ch009

Department of Health and Human Services. (2014). *HHS Activities to Enhance.* Author.

Department of Homeland Security. (2014). *Section 10(a) and 10(b) Report on the United States Coast Guard (USCG) and Maritime Critical Infrastructure Cybersecurity Standards,Section 10(b) Report on the Department of Homeland Security's Chemical Facility Anti-Terrorism Standards (CFATS)Section 10(b) Report on the Transportation Security Administration's (TSA's) Approach to Voluntary Industry Adoption of the NIST.* Author.

Egan, M. (2014). *Judge Rules FTC Can Sue Wyndham Over Cyber Security Lapses.* Retrieved June 16, 2014 from http://www.foxbusiness.com/industries/2014/04/08/us-ftc-can-sue-hotel-group-over-poor-data-security-court-rules/

Electronic Communications Privacy Act of 1986, (1988). 18 U.S.C. §§ 2510-2511

Exec. Order No. 13636, (2013). 78 FR 11737, 11737 -11744

Federal Trade Commission Act, (1914). 15 USC §§ 41-58

FTC Accepts Final Settlement with Twitter for Failure to Safeguard Personal Information. (2014). Retrieved June 16, 2014 from http://www.ftc.gov/news-events/press-releases/2011/03/ftc-accepts-final-settlement-twitter-failure-safeguard-personal

Gramm–Leach–Bliley Act of 1999, (2000). 15 U.S.C. §§ 6801-6809; 6821-6827

Harris, S., & Meyers, M. (2002). *CISSP.* McGraw-Hill/Osborne.

Health Insurance Portability and Accountability Act of 1996, (2000). 42 U.S.C. §§1320d-1320d-9

Health Insurance Portability and Accountability Act of 1996, Privacy and Security Rule, (2003). 45 C.F.R. §§ 164.102-164.534

Homeland Security Act of 2002, (2006). 6 U.S.C. §§ 101-613 Federal Information Security Management Act of 2002, (2006). 44 U.S.C. §§ 3541-3549

Janczewski, L., & Colarik, A. (2008). *Cyber Warfare and Cyber Terrorism*. Hershey, PA: IGI Global; doi:10.4018/978-1-59140-991-5

Jansen, W., & Karygiannis, A. T. (1999). *SP 800-19. Mobile Agent Security*. Gaithersburg, MD: National Institute of Standards & Technology.

Jansen, W., & Scarfone, K. (2008). Guidelines on cell phone and PDA security. *NIST Special Publication*, *800*, 124.

Lardinois, F. (2012), *U.S. House passes controversial CISPA cybersecurity bill 248 To 168*. Retrieved June 14, 2014 from http://techcrunch.com/2012/04/26/u-s-house-passes-cispa-248-to-168/

Lewis, J. A. (2002). *Assessing the risks of cyber terrorism, cyber war and other cyber threats*. Center for Strategic & International Studies.

Marbury v. Madison, (1803). 5 U.S. 137

Miller, K. W., Voas, J., & Hurlburt, G. F. (2012). BYOD: security and privacy considerations. *It Professional, 14*(5), 53-55.

National Institute of Standards and Technology (NIST). (2014). *Framework for Improving Critical Infrastructure Cybersecurity*. United States of America.

Notice of Breach of Security Act, (2003). Cal. Civ. Code § 1798.29

Sarker, S., & Wells, J. D. (2003). Understanding mobile handheld device use and adoption. *Communications of the ACM, 46*(12), 35–40. doi:10.1145/953460.953484

State of California Department of Justice Office of the Attorney General. (2013). *Getting smart about smartphones, tips for parents*. Retrieved June 14, 2014 from http://oag.ca.gov/privacy/facts/online-privacy/smartphones-parents

The White House. (2014). *Assessing Cybersecurity Regulations*. Retrieved June 14, 2014 from http://m.whitehouse.gov/blog/2014/05/22/assessing-cybersecurity-regulations

U.S. Const. art. I, § 8, cl. 1 (1787).

U.S. Const. art. I, § 8, cl. 3 (1787).

U.S. Const. art. III, §§ 1-2 (1787).

U.S. Environmental Protection Agency. (2014). *Section 10(b) report on the environmental protection agency's water and wastewater critical infrastructure cyber-security preparedness*. Retrieved June 14, 2014 from http://water.epa.gov/infrastructure/watersecurity/upload/EO_13696_10-b-_EPA_response.pdf

Welch, D., & Lathrop, S. (2003, June). Wireless security threat taxonomy. In *Information Assurance Workshop* (pp. 76-83). IEEE.

KEY TERMS AND DEFINITIONS

Authentication: Security measure designed to establish the validity of a transmission, message, or originator, or a means of verifying an individual's authorization to receive specific categories of information (Harris, 2002).

Availability: Timely, reliable access to data and information services for authorized users (Harris, 2002).

Confidentiality: Assurance that information is not disclosed to unauthorized individuals, processes, or devices (Harris, 2002).

Cyber Terrorism: Attacks with the use of the Internet for terrorist activities, including acts of deliberate, large-scale disruption of computer networks, especially of personal computers attached to the Internet, by the means of tools such as computer viruses, worms, Trojans, and zombies (Janczewski & Colarik, 2008).

Device Owner: Entity that has purchased and maintains ownership of device (Chen et al, 2012).

Information Owner: An application-specific provider, a digital product provider, or an enterprise that allows access to resources from mobile devices, (Chen et al, 2012).

Integrity: Quality of an IS reflecting the logical correctness and reliability of the OS; the logical completeness of the hardware and software implementing the protection mechanisms; and the consistency of the data structures and occurrence of the stored data. Note that, in a formal security mode, integrity is interpreted more narrowly to mean protection against unauthorized modification or destruction of information (Harris, 2002).

Mobile Device: This device type is usually referred to as a handheld, handheld device or handheld computer (Sarker & Wells, 2003).

Non-Repudiation: Assurance the sender of data is provided with proof of delivery and the recipient is provided with proof of the sender's identity, so neither can later deny having processed the data (Harris, 2002).

Chapter 7
Survey in Smartphone Malware Analysis Techniques

Moutaz Alazab
Isra University, Jordan

Lynn Batten
Deakin University, Australia

ABSTRACT

Smartphone Malware continues to be a serious threat in today's world. Recent research studies investigate the impacts of new malware variant. Historically traditional anti-malware analyses rely on the signatures of predefined malware samples. However, this technique is not resistant against the obfuscation techniques (e.g. polymorphic and metamorphic). While the permission system proposed by Google, requires smartphone users to pay attention to the permission description during the installation time. Nevertheless, normal users cannot comprehend the semantics of Android permissions. This chapter surveys various approaches used in Smartphone malware detection and Investigates weaknesses of existing countermeasures such as signature-based and anomaly-based detection.

INTRODUCTION

The production and use of smartphone devices are increasing rapidly, with technological advancements resulting in lighter and more powerful devices. In 2015, the growth in smartphone popularity convinced society, on both a macro and micro level, to turn away from traditional computers in exchange for what the smartphone market was offering (Halleck, 2014).

Nowadays, consumers are not restricted to only making phone calls and sending text messages via their mobile phones. The smartphone market offers a number of features that were previously unheard of, with the consumer being able to browse the internet, upload and share their photos, access and send emails, view social networking sites such as Facebook and Twitter, and have the convenience of countless applications offering everything from online banking to online market.

Smartphones are the most in-demand phone amongst consumers across the entire phone market (Gartner, 2015). The growth in popularity has prompted manufacturers to develop the phone's functionality

DOI: 10.4018/978-1-4666-8345-7.ch007

even further, which explains the existence of company giants such as HTC, Apple and Samsung who are competing to release more improved and advanced smartphones.

With this dramatic growth in the smartphone market (Bureau, 2012; Svajcer, 2014), there has been a detection of high amounts of prohibited malicious applications designed to specifically target smartphones. For example, the most common type of malware is known as a Trojan. This specific malware appears to be clean, but in fact can harm the smartphones without the user even noticing. The authors of such malicious applications are able to produce malevolent files by gaining access to operating system documents of the smartphones targeted. Such documents are used to find gaps that they can penetrate, and then used to create smartphone malware. In addition, the developments of smartphone applications are considerably more complicated than the development of traditional windows software. In comparison, this makes smartphone malware more complicated to understand.

Smartphone misconduct through cybercriminals is not a new area, with the latest reports CNCCS (2013); (Fossi et al., 2011; Victor Chebyshev & Roman Unuchek, 2014) showing that various kinds of malicious codes are being developed for the mobile handsets. The well-known antivirus engine Kaspersky produced a report Kaspersky (2012) on the IT threat evolution, which indicated that smartphone attacks are becoming more frequent, and attention has been given to target open source operating systems, such as the Android. In their report, findings confirm that almost 150,000 "zero day" malicious applications harm the Android operating system annually, with 49% of those smartphone malware being a centralised Trojan, which has the capability of stealing users' data by connecting smartphones to a remote server.

The damage caused by malicious applications usually has two results:

- Malware that causes physical damage to the smartphone handset by taking up memory space and switching on extra features such as the Bluetooth. This, in turn, damages smartphone speed and performance. This kind of malware primarily affects the handset's resources i.e. battery life, CPU speed and memory capacity.
- The software effect, where some other malicious binary may cause innumerable problems to confidential data, includes the threat of hackers accessing and stealing the mobile user's private emails, passwords, contacts, photos, videos and various other personal files. It can also affect the mobile user's service bill, with hardware glitches that yield calls and messages that result in the user exceeding their usual fixed bill.

Smartphone antivirus applications are becoming widely deployed amongst smartphone users, and have proven to be very efficient in offering protection against different types of smartphone malware threats. Commercial smartphones are all protected by antivirus engines and firewalls. Indeed there are various real-time anti-malware and anti-theft protection for smartphones, accessible in the smartphone markets, which are free to the consumer. These antivirus applications usually protect users from harmful Viruses, Trojans, Spyware and help to preserve the safety of the mobile users' private data. There are incomplete forms of protection available for these devices that can offer cellular network firewalls and antivirus protection (Zhao, Zhang, Ge, & Yuan, 2012; Zhou & Jiang, 2012). Malicious writers produce malevolent files to exploit new weaknesses, security retailers have to find it first and then react with a new antivirus signature(s) that require smartphones users to complete the installation through the Internet (Wi-Fi or cellular network). Therefore, fresh malicious attacks do not have the time they need to spread throughout smartphones.

The smartphone market is not only fighting against malicious authors, but is also facing threats by innumerable groups such as LulzSec and AnonSec. At present, there are various tools and malicious applications that can explore smartphone weaknesses such as Super Bluetooth Hack, SpoofTooph and Zitmo. Those tools are used as efficient malware to harm smartphone users' data.

Zitmo, an alternative name of "Smartphone Zeus", is an example of a malicious tool. It appeared in late 2011 and aims to steal online banking data by spying on the incoming mobile transaction authorization number (mTAN), and will then forward it to a remote web server. Figure 1 shows a snapshot of the Zitmo source code. In general, banks try to secure online user transactions by using several methods. Typically, banks request the customer to login to their account by entering dissimilar username and password for security measures. An additional security step is for customers to provide an mTAN before completing a transaction. This is a code which is sent from the bank to a user via SMS to approve the online transaction. The method of sending them a TAN code through SMS has weaknesses that can be abused by Zitmo. Zitmo has the capacity to monitor the incoming messages and then extract the mTAN code. After the content of mTAN is extracted from the message, Zitmo will directly send the mTAN number to a predetermined server or via SMS. Against Zitmo threats, the federal financial institutions examinations council (FFIEC) recommended banks to reconsider the mTAN authentication (Schwartz, 2011). The new system uses a security tokens, username and involves entering the password instead of using the SMS. This is more secure, as the SMS can be easy triggered while security tokens is extremely difficult for malicious authors to crack.

Figure 1. Snapshot from the Zitmo source code

```
if ( localBundle != null)
{
    object[] arrayOfObject = (object[]) localBundle.get("pdus");
    if (arrayOfObject != null)
      new SmsBlockerThrea(arrayOfObject).start();       trigger the incomming
}                                                        messages
.
.
.

SmsMessage localSmsMessage = SmsMessage.createFromPdi((byte[]this.pdus[i]);
string str1 = localSmsMessage.getOrginatingAdress();
string str2 = localSmsMessage.getMessageBdy();          extract the content of
.                                                       the messages
.

ServerSession.postRequst (new UrlEncodedFormEntity(localArrayList));
.
.                                                       start the server sesssions

Public static String initUrl()
{
    return http://softthrifty.com/security.jsp           send the message
}
```

The structure of this paper is as follows: Section 2 we discuss Approaches for identifying smartphone malware and recent smartphone malware intrusion detections in two sections: Misused-based detection and Anomaly-based detection. Section 3 presents the literature and summarises smartphone analysis in terms of the features: extraction static analysis and dynamic analysis. Section 4 summarises the paper and states the conclusions.

TAXONOMY OF SMARTPHONE MALWARE DETECTION

The purpose of malware detection is to detect and to reduce the number of smartphone attacks. Modern malware detection methods can be separated into two groups labelled 'Misuse-based detection' and 'Anomaly-based detection'.

Smartphone malware detection includes:

- Analysing smartphone operating system.
- Checking applications in both official market and non-official markets.
- Recognizing repackaged applications.
- Investigating abnormal behaviour.
- Analysing and monitoring smartphone SD card.
- Detecting and classifying malware.

The two methods of misuse-based detection and anomaly-based detection generally require either static analysis or dynamic analysis to extract particular features from the executable malware. Misuse-based detection, used by antivirus companies, has the benefits of identifying known smartphone malware accurately with a false low alarm rate. Nevertheless, the method is unable to protect smartphone users against new attacks (Alazab et al., 2012). In comparison, anomaly-based detection identifies both known and unknown attacks without any difficulty. However, the anomaly-based detection technique requires a complex set of steps to be implemented, such as defining a subset of structured rules.

Misuse-Based Detection

Misuse-based detection (also known as signature-based detection) works in a similar manner to antivirus engines. Misuse-based detection has the strength of identifying the malware during real-time in very high detection rates. The signature is usually generated by extracting the package names and file names of malware that has been formerly predetermined using the hash value of an algorithm.

Current AV methods were developed in response to malware attacking desktop computers and laptops (Ravi & Manoharan, 2012). While there are many indications that different kinds of malware are being developed for portable platforms, such as smartphones (A. Alazab, Alazab, Abawajy, & Hobbs, 2011; M. Alazab, Venkataraman, & Watters, 2010; Lu et al., 2012). Recent smartphone malware countermeasure tools, such as antivirus software and intrusion detection, have high processing and energy consumption, require a lot of time to analyse, and the signature database needs to be constantly updated in order to protect users against malware.

In traditional computer malware analysis, antivirus software monitors all kinds of operations such as writing, reading and copying in the file system. Monitoring the file system operations allows the antivirus to block specific event or file during the running time, and also allows the antivirus to predict a malicious threat before it can actually damage users' data. As soon as a malicious file is downloaded in the hard drive, an antivirus responds using different techniques. For instance, a report of the well-known antivirus company Kaspersky indicated that computer malware analysis uses three scanning techniques as followed: signature analysis, heuristic analysis and check against KSN lists (Kaspersky, 2013).

Antiviruses for the Android operating system follow a completely different strategy for detecting the malevolent files, because the file system operations cannot be monitored in the Android operating system (Fedler, Schutte, & Kulicke, 2013). The strategy used in the Android antivirus software is primarily to scan the package name or filename of the installed applications against a predefined obscure black list (Adolphi & Langweg, 2012; Fedler et al., 2013).

When comparing the strategy used by computer anti-malware products with the strategy used by Android antivirus applications, we observe that the computer anti-malware uses techniques not found in the Android antivirus applications such as the heuristic analysis. Android anti-malware has resorted to scanning the package names and package filenames against a predefined black list database (Adolphi & Langweg, 2012; Fedler et al., 2013). While matching the filename or package names against a blacklist database does not exist in the computer anti-malware products.

The problem in the Android antivirus products is that antiviruses rely on the package and applications names of the installed applications for detecting the malicious applications. While comparing only the package names and file names against the black list can be easily evaded; the malicious authors' needs only to change the package name to avoid the installed protection mechanism and the application's code will remain the same (Adolphi & Langweg, 2012).

At this time, the main technique used by smartphone antivirus engines is signature matching and patterns (Fedler et al., 2013; Hidalgo., 2011; Ketari & Khanum, 2012). An antivirus application either has either to be installed on a smartphone device or has to be located in the cloud, which requires users to upload data and applications, over the server to keep them protected against malware attacks.

Misuse-based detection has the benefits of discovering malicious contents before the system is actually infected with the malware, and can accurately identify a malicious binary during the running time. However, the main challenge of misuse-based detection is that every single signature needs an entry in the database. This means a comprehensive database may contain thousands of entries.

An Android application is available to users as a zipped file, identified as the Android application package file (APK). If a user wishes to install an application from either an official or non-official market in their handset, the application will be installed in the following directory /Data/App/. The installed applications can be readable by other files, which allows antivirus engines to read and scan other applications and to look for malicious signatures. Usually smartphone antivirus software scans the systems and common parts of code within the packaged file to match the signature against predefined databases. Figure 2 demonstrates how the misuse-based detection works in the Android operating system. Smartphone users can download applications from official markets such as the Apple store and Google play (Google, 2014). Users can also download applications from non-official markets such as 1Mobile market, AndroidDrawer market, TorrApk market and SlideME market.

Google provides a centralised market in their operating system that allows the user to download and install applications by themselves. During installation an Android application, the PackageManager that is responsible for querying and manipulating installed packages and related permissions, will organise the process via extracting the demanded permissions from visible applications and installing them into the system. Note, if an application desires to access private data such as contacts, email, messages, and photos.

Figure 2. Architecture of the misuse-based detection

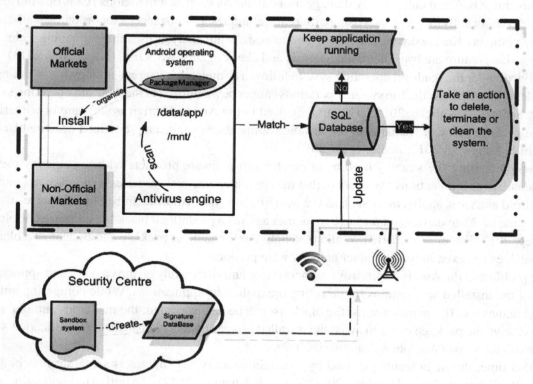

The application has to declare the access during the installation process through showing the user a list of permissions about what the application will access. Once an application is installed from either official markets or non-official markets, the installed application will be positioned in the following path /Data/App/. Refer to Figure 3; which verifies where the installed applications are located in the Android operating system. The applications are stored in /Data/App/ can be removed from the system, but it needs acceptable permission from the user to interact within the operating system. In contrast,

Figure 3. The installed application's path in the Android operating system

```
C:\Users\Moutaz>adb shell
# cd data/app
cd data/app
# pwd
pwd
/data/app
# ls *.apk
ls *.apk
ApiDemos.apk
CubeLiveWallpapers.apk
GestureBuilder.apk
SoftKeyboard.apk
#
```

system applications, which reside within every Android device (see Figure 4) are stored on /System/App. The system applications are different to (/Data/App/) which are independent of label task and cannot be deleted from the operating system. The system applications should be able to perform operations such as interfacing directly with the telephony API (Enck, Ongtang, & McDaniel, 2009).

Figure 4. The system applications that come up with Android operating system

```
C:\Users\Moutaz>adb shell ls /system/app
Phone.apk
Development.apk
Email.apk
Calculator.apk
SdkSetup.apk
Camera.apk
Protips.apk
MediaProvider.apk
Contacts.apk
SystemUI.apk
NetSpeed.apk
CertInstaller.apk
PackageInstaller.apk
Browser.apk
UserDictionaryProvider.apk
DeskClock.apk
Term.apk
Settings.apk
SpeechRecorder.apk
SpareParts.apk
Mms.apk
ContactsProvider.apk
CustomLocale.apk
DrmProvider.apk
TelephonyProvider.apk
Launcher2.apk
AccountAndSyncSettings.apk
Gallery.apk
DownloadProviderUi.apk
PinyinIME.apk
SoundRecorder.apk
TtsService.apk
LatinIME.apk
PicoTts.apk
Fallback.apk
LiveWallpapersPicker.apk
ApplicationsProvider.apk
Music.apk
OpenWnn.apk
SettingsProvider.apk
VpnServices.apk
DefaultContainerService.apk
QuickSearchBox.apk
HTMLViewer.apk
DownloadProvider.apk
```

In the work conducted by Adolphi and Langweg (2012), the authors provide an overview of current smartphone operating security software in terms of firewalls and antivirus engines. The authors evaluate their work by taking three different operating systems as follows: Android, iOS and Windows phone. Intended for the Android operating system, the authors investigate five antivirus engines downloaded from the Google Play store to determine the functionality of the antivirus engines. Adolphi and Langweg checked the time when scans are performed, where the antivirus scanned for malware, and what the antivirus engines scan for. The five antivirus engines investigated were predicted as: AVG Antivirus Free 2.11.1, Antivirus Free 1.3.4, Avast Mobile Security 1.0.2129, Lookout Security & Antivirus 7.11.1-a7cf123 and Norton Antivirus & Security 2.5.0.398. The authors confirm in their experiments that each one of the selected antivirus engines scanned the following in the Android operating system: the installed package names against an obscure list, filenames within a black list, certain writable locations of the system & external media and the content of executable files with malware definition files.

There are two ways in which antivirus products execute scanning:

- Antivirus programs that run a scan of the device itself. In this scheme, the antivirus scanner is centred in the handset and requires users to regularly update with the latest malicious code signature, in order to keep the user protected. If there is an antivirus application installed on the handset, the antivirus will initially scan the package names for each installed application, and then compare the package name against a predefined obscure black list. Some of the anti-scanners check the permission structure within each application layer, Java classes, method names, package name.
- The second type of program executes scanning on the cloud server but does not require the signatures to be updated, nor complex analysis engines to be run on every handset. In the cloud program, each user sends their applications and files to the network server for analysis, and then the antivirus program will quarantine or delete the malicious application based on a warning report returned by the cloud server. The difficulty of such programs from a consumers' perspective is that cloud scanning gives the provider access to the users' data. It might be hard for the consumer to find a cloud provider whom they can trust as these providers have access to their devices and private data. Cloud-based antimalware techniques can, at best, only detect 70% of malware threats to a smartphone (Fatskunk, 2013).

Smartphone malware detection and analysis are a critical area. Antivirus applications are being used as a primary solution for keeping smartphone devices safe. The problem is that smartphone devices have few resources and might not support the power to run and execute scans. An example would be the Android antivirus products; they look for a signature such as the package names and file names of malicious applications. Nevertheless the signature can be easily evaded by the malicious authors. On the other hand, cloud based scanning would be efficient to protect user data against malicious attacks. Although the cloud based technique requires users to upload their data to perform scanning, most of the users are not comfortable uploading their data over the cloud, because they would be prevented from controlling their own personal data. This lack of control causes mistrust in cloud storage.

Furthermore, there is the problem of availability and integrity within the cloud. User data runs the risk of becoming compromised as data is in the servers of the service providers; these servers are in locations that are unknown to a data owner. The service providers provide the users with the assurance of the safe protection of the data in the servers that are controlled and monitored by the service providers; however, users are not assured that data will be as protected as the data is in the on-premises. When data is in the on-premises, users can oversee the activities done on the data, and the people involved in the data process. However, when users outsource or upload data in the cloud to perform scanning, there is visibility of the entities handling the data but lack of visibility of the data processing. This creates a lack of confidence in regard to data, protection and shared access to data.

Even though the misuse-based detection is commonly used by the anti-virus applications, there is a requirement to employ the anomaly-based detection as misuse-based detection suffers from the following:

1. **Detection Rates:** Current antivirus engines suffer from a low detection rate and therefore have limited capacity to protect users' data against malicious attacks. At best, the engines can detect 79.6% of the malicious samples as shown in Zhou and Jiang (2012). Jiang's 2012 report, from the NC State University, determined the functionality of the Android antivirus products and the Google verification service. Jiang randomly picked up malicious samples from 49 different families to estimate the capacity of third-party antivirus engines. The following ten antivirus engines were evaluated: Avast, AVG, Trend Micro, Symantec, BitDefender, ClamAV, F-Secure, Fortinet, Kaspersky and Kingsoft. The author shows that the overall detection rates of these representative anti-virus engines range from 51.02% to 100% Jiang (2012).

2. **High False Positive:** This occurs when the antivirus engine incorrectly identifies clean files as malicious type. For example, as discussed earlier antivirus industries update their signature regularly; most often, the antivirus manufacturer checks a new signature several times before deploying it, since, if there is anything wrong with an established signature, it will cause several problems to the operating system. It might be that the AV wrongly flagged packed files as actual malware. In September 2012, the well-known Sophos industry detected their own updates (Advisory: Shh/Updater-B) as false-positive malware (Whittaker, 2012). After one month of releasing the false alarm, Sophos demands users to run the AutoUpdate to fix the mistaken updates (Sophos, 2012). This issue has denied other installed applications such as Adobe and Java from updating and running.

    Another problem in smartphone devices is that antivirus software look for specific contents within the application, such as 'name, size, SHA1 value, version, and the URL associated with it' (Jiang, 2012). However, the application name and hashes value can be easily altered, which might create false positives. For example, false positives might occur when a clean application request a common call functions of malicious application, such as interacting with the telephony manager, keyboard, Bluetooth, battery or messages.

3. **High False Negative:** The main weakness of the misuse-based detection is that a system has to be familiar with malicious pattern and signatures of malicious contents in advance of scanning. A false negative happens when the system has a vulnerability and the scanner fails to identify the system vulnerabilities. A false alarm occurs when the smartphone is infected with malware and the scanner cannot identify the malicious pattern.

4. **Crashes:** Malicious applications can be designed to check if there is any antivirus application installed and then terminate it by acquiring privileged access. If a malicious application obtains privileged access to the operating system, the application can exploit the operating system's vulnerability, and even terminate or wipe any installed application. Commwarrior is an example of such a malicious application and is the first detected smartphone malware that can terminate the installed antivirus application (Mills, 2011).

5.   **Performance Consumption:** Antivirus scanners require complex steps and might consume system resources such as battery, memory and CPU for their operation (Zonouz et al., 2013). The impact of the antivirus applications on mobile devices has been studied by Dawson (2012); (Radvilavicius et al., 2012). The authors conducted several investigations on how to optimise the antivirus performance.

The authors of Egele et al. (2008) conducted a study which provides an overview of dynamic analysis used to analyse potentially malicious samples. The authors confirm that attackers can transform clean executable applications into syntactically different malicious binaries, which allows attackers to create thousands of malicious applications daily.

Large amounts of research has been conducted for the testing and optimization of misuse-based detection. The authors of Venugopal and Hu (2008) presented a signature-based smartphone malware detection. In their work, the authors show the presented approach uses less than 50% of the memory used by the Clam antivirus. In other work carried out by Xianyong and Yangmin (2012), the authors present a signature-based detection scheme for mobile ad hoc networks. It is clear there is a lack of existing countermeasures for identifying malicious binaries leading to a requirement to discuss the anomaly-based detection, which is elaborated in the next section.

Anomaly-Based Detection

Intrusion detection approaches play progressively vital roles in smartphone security. This section discusses current intrusion detection approaches used in smartphones and demonstrates the various challenges related to smartphone intrusion detection.

Anomaly-based detection is a security mechanism, aiming to classify system activity or applications as either normal or anomalous, by monitoring applications' behaviours or other features. The anomaly-based detection method comprises three stages: collecting level, training level and detecting level. In the first level of anomaly-based detection, the analyser collects predetermined data that is pre-classified to either normal or anomalous. In the next level, he/she will train the collected data and test them to find if there is any specific clean activity. In the final level of anomaly-based detection, by comparing any unknown behaviour against the clean behaviour, it is possible to discriminate normal activities from abnormal activities.

Anomaly-based detection is considerably more efficient, compared with misuse-based detection, as it can anticipate new malware attacks. On the other hand, the misuse-based detection only identifies known patterns within the malicious files. The benefit of customising anomaly-based detection to every operating system version makes the system harder to exploit. Conversely, the weakness of anomaly-based detection is that it consumes abundant system resources that may affect the smartphones' performance. The high percentage of false alarm rates makes anomaly-based detection a challenge to implement (A. Alazab et al., 2011).

Smartphone intrusion detection systems have been used in research literature and can be divided into three groups: Host intrusion detection system (HIDS), Network intrusion detection system (NIDS) and Security monitoring server. Figure 5 illustrates the smartphone malware protection mechanisms used by literature. In HIDS, the aim is to customise software or a framework to apply a specific approach. HIDS relies on analysing the source code of applications or monitoring the behaviour of applications. On the other hand, NIDS works behind a firewall as a second defence by linking the mobile device to cellular and wireless networks during the analysis, and the network traffic is monitored.

Figure 5. Architecture of the misuse-based detection

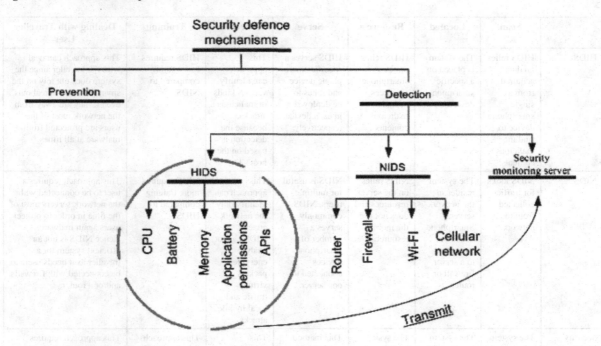

- **Host Intrusion Detection System (HIDS):** Is a security reactive mechanism built on installing on software, application, and framework in each smartphone device to keep the smartphone protected from malware. The installed mechanism aims to analyse and track particular events such as API sequences, system calls, CPU performance, logical ordering, low-level communication, file system, and battery power consumption. Commonly, most of the research applies the sandbox environment to monitor such events and then to apply detection.

HIDS technique can protect a local area connection from common types of attacks such as Denial of Service (DOS), backdoor, worm, network abuse, remote procedure call and FTP attacks. However, the main disadvantage of HIDS is that it consumes the smartphone resources: memory space, processing and battery resources.

- **Network Intrusion Detection System (NIDS):** Is a security proactive technique, which can be installed in particular points such as, on the server, router or firewall as an interface between the smartphone device and network. This technique can be used as a second defence by tracking wireless including wireless and Bluetooth or mobile networks (CDMA, 3G) to protect the user from malicious activity during smartphone requests. NIDS serves a large number of smartphone devices and can be used as a prevention to block malware before it reaches the smartphone.
- **Security Monitoring Server:** In the work conducted by Alazab and Batten (2012), the authors apply HIDS to transmit the API calls, object state, call flows, code graph and code injection at a runtime to an external security monitoring server to perform the online detection.

Table 1. Comparison between intrusion detection systems in the smartphone handset

	Scan	Located	Resources	Serve	Detection Methods	Training	Dealing with Traveller User
HIDS	HIDS relies on data acquired from a single smartphone device to find the malicious contents.	The system is placed on a specific smartphone device.	HIDS relies on the smartphone resources to find malicious contents.	HIDS serves a specific smart phone device and it has to be deployed in each device respectively.	This approach can identify various kinds of malicious attacks, because the detection is based on the host's log.	HIDS requires less training compared to NIDS	This approach can deal with the traveller since the system does not rely on the smart phones whereabouts, even if they are away from the network most of the users are protected from malware at all times.
NIDS	NIDS looks for traffic collected from the network.	The system resides in the network server. Smartphone has to be connected to a server, firewall or router.	NIDS relies on the server resources and does not use the mobile resources.	NIDS is useful for multiple users. NIDS commonly serves a number of smartphone devices connected to one server.	This approach can identify only the network attacks. NIDS cannot analyze encrypted packets, virtual traffic and local mobile attacks.	NIDS requires more training compared to HIDS	This approach requires a user to be connected with the network servers most of the time in order to protect users again malware. Hence NIDS is not an efficient system for a traveller as it needs users to be connected with firewalls and/or a router.
Security Monitoring Server	The system relies on data acquired from a smartphone device, which is then transmitted to the server.	The system reside on both handset and server. The system looks for a system log, which is then transmitted to the server which then performs the online detection.	The system relies more on the server resources along, but with some support from smartphone resources to extract features.	This method can be deployed to serve multiple users or can be customised to work for a specific handset.	This approach recognizes most of the smart phone malware attacks. Since detection relies on the smartphone's logs and the network server to build a detection based on the extracted features.	This approach does not require much training in comparison to NIDS because the training is based on the feature that extracted from the HIDS.	This approach requires users to stay connected to the monitoring server. Therefore, this approach is not ideal for travellers.

Both misuse-based detection and anomaly-based detection have their share of pros and cons. anomaly-based detection can create patterns of malicious applications, which might be useful to provide the signature-based detection with those patterns. Despite this fact, an anomaly-based detection system is proficient in identifying smartphone malware, however, anomaly-based detection suffers from the following (refer to Table 1):

1. **Scan:** The strategy used to find malicious contents is different in each type of the intrusion detection. For instance, HIDS has to be deployed in each device separately; the intrusion system in this case traces and analyses activities associated with a particular smartphone device, such as behaviours, system calls, and unusual operations of the mobile device. Usually, HIDS works in parallel with NIDS, as the HIDS aims to find undetected threats by NIDS. While, NIDS resides on the network

server; the system monitors activities associated with incoming and outgoing traffic packets within the network layer. The NIDS relies on the information gained from tcpdump, which gives information about the packet.

2. **Location and Resources:** The central part of any intrusion detection system is where to locate the intrusion detection system and what features the detection system will look for. In fact current intrusion detection systems will take one of the two approaches HIDS or NIDS. HIDS is placed on a smartphone device to look for malicious content through a log collected from the individual smartphone device. The problem with the HIDS is that mobile devices do not have a fixed infrastructure to handle intrusion detection cases. In contrast, NIDS resides in the network server; the system relies on a real-time incoming and outgoing traffic analysis. The problem with the NIDS approach is it cannot be functional in a new environment, as it needs the mobile user to stay connected with firewalls and/or a router.

3. **Training:** Anomaly-based detection consists of three phases: collecting phase, training phase and detecting phase. In the first phase of anomaly-based detection, the analyser collects predetermined data that is pre-classified to either normal or anomalous. Both HIDS and NIDS require training in order to identify new attacks.

4. **Detection Methods:** The purpose of an intrusion detection system is to differentiate malicious applications from non-malicious applications based on features collected from predetermined applications. The most crucial aspect of the intrusion detection system is to determine which feature can provide the most accurate results and eliminate disruptions (Tsanas, Little, McSharry, Spielman, & Ramig, 2012; Yerima, Sezer, McWilliams, & Muttik, 2013). API sequence calls have been successfully used to build a detection engine for malware (Alazab & Venkatraman, 2013; Alazab et al., 2011; Alazab. M, 2014; Han, Kim, & Im, 2012; Iwamoto & Wasaki, 2012), as the sequence call can be used to identify the malicious applications and classify smartphone malware to their families.

5. **Dealing with Traveller:** NIDS requires users to stay connected to the monitoring server. Hence, NIDS is not an efficient system for a traveller. HIDS is considerably preferable to deal with a traveller, since the system does not rely on the smartphone location, as detection is based on the logs collected from the local host.

TAXONOMY OF FEATURES EXTRACTION

There are two main categories of analysis and feature extraction that are often used by security vendors; there are static feature extraction and dynamic feature extraction. Figure 6 gives an overview of static and dynamic analyses. Static analysis relies on the study of the application binary without executing it. While, dynamic analysis relies on tracking the application behaviour during its execution. Most malware analysis relies on feature extraction and building of feature sets of the malware.

Static Feature Extraction

Static Analysis: is the procedure of analysing source code without executing the application itself. Static analysis can provide different information about the source code such as function calls, control flow graph and structuring of the code. This technique has the strength of understanding how malicious applications react with the system during a fully automated analysis of functions calls, permissions or by looking at the entire source code.

Figure 6. Smartphone malware analysis

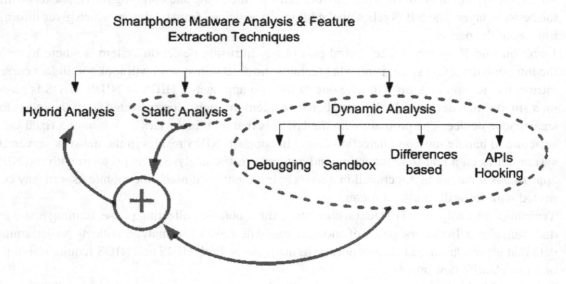

The responsibilities of static analysis can be separated into three categories:

1. **Identifying Bugs in Applications:** Android's developers have to meet the basic quality expectations of their applications. In fact, there are various tools which the static analysis can use to look for bugs in the code, such as FindBugs, which is a program that looks for bugs in a Java code.
2. **Plagiarism Detection Applications:** Static analysis can use similar measures to detect plagiarism applications. In research work conducted by Desnos (2012), the author provides an algorithm based on static analysis to find similarities and differences of methods amongst two applications. In the proposed work, the author used normalised compression distance (NCD) to find the similarity distance between two Android applications based on their code.
3. **Detecting Where Malicious Code Is Located in an Application:** By precisely identifying where the malicious functions are located in the code, it can give an analyser a potential clue about further malware variants within the same family.

All Android applications have common features, which are often used for automated static analysis:

- Control Flow Analysis.
- Package Name.
- Application Program Interface.
- Permissions.
- Inter-Process Communication.
- Xml Files.
- Java Classes.
- Function Calls.

Modern anti-malware scanners rely on static features extracted from application source code (Schmidt et al., 2008; Tian, 2011). One of the main challenges that can be seen on the Android operating system smartphone platform is that some Trojan exploit has the ability of accessing the Command and Control (C&C) server. If that happens, the handset might accept and execute commands from a remote C&C server to the smartphone handset, and that will allow malware to download and upload files when it is controlled by the server (Trendmicro, 2012). This means that malicious applications can transform the original application to become completely malicious during the runtime. Therefore, static analysis will be impractical in this case, as it simply shows that an application demands a server or web page, without showing what happens after the connection.

Obfuscation techniques make source code hard to read and challenging to recognize. Android software development kit (SDK) contains a tool named Proguard (Google, 2012), which can be used to obfuscate android applications at the compiling-stage on the lowest level by removing unused code and renaming classes without changing the behaviour of the application. Proguard can be implemented at the Java classes before creating applications, this phase (obfuscation technique) is used before the application is transformed to the final stage (Dalvik Bytecode). Figure 7 describes the steps of applying an obfuscator to Android applications during the developing phase. Attackers might use these tools to make their applications harder to analyse via renaming the classes, packages, methods or by removing debug information such as altering local variable names.

Analysing Android applications statically is the way to collect information and identify the malware by returning an application to its original state. The approach of reversing the Android application is to recreate the Java class from the Dalvik byte code. Currently, there are several tools that can be implemented to execute static analysis in the Android platform: IDA Pro, Smali/BackSmali, Androguard, Apktool and Dex2jar.

Figure 7. Applying obfuscation technique in the Android applications

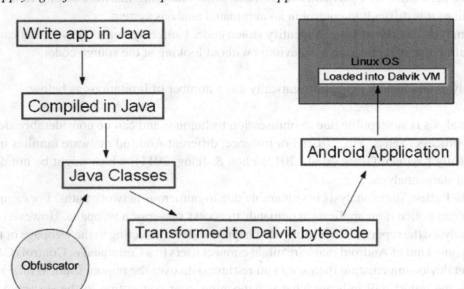

Pros and Cons of Static Analysis

In this section, we discuss further both static analysis and feature extraction that can be useful for smartphone malware detection. Static analysis offers various information about the source code; including instructions, function calls, control flow graphs, permissions, and class graphs.

Static analysis and feature extraction statically has various benefits as outlined below:

1. In the last decade, malicious applications have been created to disarm an antivirus engine (Mills, 2011). In reality, both of the static and dynamic analyses can find if an application attempts to turn off an anti-malware scanner. Static analysis in this case works as a proactive mechanism, and can warn if a malicious application tries turning off an anti-malware scanner without disabling the antivirus itself. Thus, static analysis would be proficient in dealing with this kind of malevolent application. In contrast, dynamic analysis works as a reactive mechanism, and will notice those kinds of malicious applications after the system is actually infected.
2. Static analysis offers the ability to examining the source code structure, and pathways to inspecting methods call graph such as Gephi (Gephi, 2013). This can help to ensure the code adheres to usual standards, and can identify bugs that are not easy to detect.
3. **Hardware Resources:** Static analysis consumes fewer of resources compared to dynamic analysis. The analysis is usually implemented in off-mobile device that has huge computing resources. In contrast, dynamic analysis usually consumes mobile resources as the analysis is conducted in a real device or in emulator environment.
4. **Dealing with Large Data:** Static analysis has the strength of processing a large dataset, as it can be implemented in a fully automated process.
5. **What the Analysis Looks For:** Static analysis, it is expected to look into the entire source code or find specific content within the code. However, dynamic analysis can only run on the commands that were performed in a particular set of runs. Note analysing malware during running is time-consuming; it is difficult to control in an automated analysis system.
6. Static analysis can be valuable to identify stolen code. Unlike dynamic analysis that can be useful to identify only an application's behaviours without looking at the source code.

Static analysis and feature extraction statically has a number of limitations as below:

1. Static analysis is susceptible due to obfuscation techniques and can be considerably slow in challenging process (Yan & Yin, 2012). For instance, different Android malware families implements dynamically payload (Grace etl al., 2012; Zhou & Jiang, 2011), which might be not detected on common static analysis.
2. **Multiple Paths:** Static analysis is vulnerable due to numerous network paths. For example, static analysis can notice if an application demands to access server or a webpage. However, during the static analysis, the report will not show what happens after connecting to the webpage or that server. In fact, some kind of Android malware might connect users to a Command & Control (C&C) server to collect device information then send and retrieve data over the remote shell. While, in dynamic analysis, the report will indicate what is happening after connecting to the server. An example of this kind of malware is "Android.LuckyCat" shown in Figure 8, which provides a snapshot of Android.LuckyCat's source code for sending user's information over the server.

Figure 8. Analysis of Android Lucky Cat

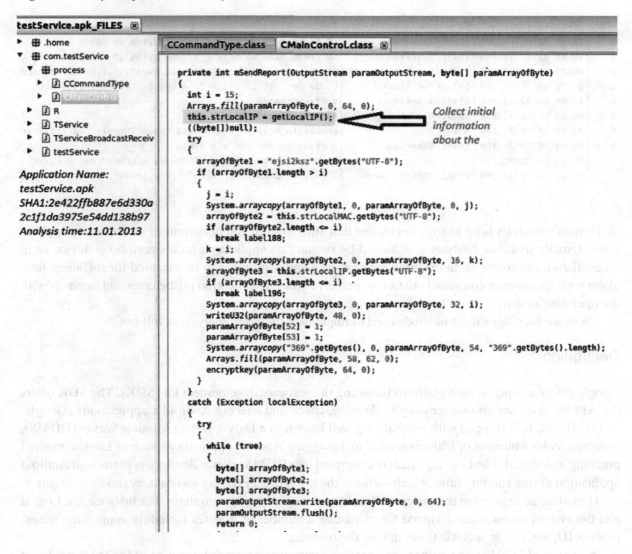

Both analysis on static and dynamic can deliver different information about malicious executable. For example, static analysis provides more understanding about the source code of malicious samples, and can provide different statistics. While dynamic analysis provides more understanding to the behaviour of the application under investigation.

Dynamic Feature Extraction

In this section, we further discuss dynamic analysis and feature extraction that can be useful for smartphone malware detection. Dynamic analysis provides various information such as system calls, permissions, API calls and application's behaviours, which might be valuable to any detection system. In this section, we introduce four significant techniques commonly used for dynamic analysis. Furthermore, we demonstrate various challenges proposed by literature concerning dynamic analysis.

Figure 9. Logcat tools for debugging Android applications

Level	Time	PID	Tag	Text
D	06-05 16:32:19.325	115	dalvikvm	GC freed 7354 objects / 500856 bytes in 981ms
D	06-05 16:32:19.795	19481	dalvikvm	GC freed 3194 objects / 379856 bytes in 497ms
D	06-05 16:32:19.816	19481	LocationManager	Constructor: service = android.location.ILocationManage
I	06-05 16:32:20.169	19481	MobclickAgent	Could not get location from GPS or Cell-id, lack ACCESS
D	06-05 16:32:21.096	19481	GamePlayer	surfaceCreated
D	06-05 16:32:21.096	19481	GamePlayer	surfaceChanged:800 w:h 480
D	06-05 16:32:21.128	19481		unable to unlink '/data/data/com.AFTDMedia.copter1/shar
D	06-05 16:32:21.156	19481	GamePlayer	surfaceChanged:800 w:h 480
I	06-05 16:32:21.167	115	ActivityManager	Displayed activity com.AFTDMedia.copter1/.MainActivity:
I	06-05 16:32:21.266	19481	MobclickAgent	{"body":{"launch":[{"date":"2012-06-05","time":"16:32:1

Dynamic analysis is an analysis technique that aims to study the behaviour of smartphones applications. Usually dynamic analysis is achieved by running an application on a smartphone device or in an emulation environment. In dynamic analysis each application has to be executed for sufficient time along with appropriate command control, to perceive how an application misbehaves and interacts with the operating system.

There are four significant methods used to implement dynamic analysis as follows:

Debugging

Google offers an open source platform including the software development kit (SDK). The SDK offers the API libraries and tools necessary to develop, check and execute Android's applications (Google, 2013). The SDK is shipped with a debugging tool known as a Dalvik Debug Monitor Server (DDMS), which provides a number of features related to debugging Android applications such as Logcat, method profiling and thread. The Logcat, which is integrated into DDMS, allows developers to trace an Android application during running time, which includes the level, time, PID, tag and data, as shown in Figure 9.

The extracted features or the system calls rely on the operating system status. For instance, the Logcat and the system monitor are designed for extracting a number of features including application status, process ID, tag, etc. at specific times during the runtime.

In Dini et al., (2012), the authors presented a security framework known as "MADAM" to detect malicious applications on the Android during the runtime. In their research work, the authors employ a hijack system call from the operating system and the Logcat, to investigate the number of sent SMS messages and trace the system calls. The authors then applied machine-learning algorithms on those extracted features. The authors achieved 93% detection rate with 5% positive rate on 10 malicious applications collected from the wild and 50 clean applications.

API Hooking

Hooking is the process of invoking API calls that an application requested during the analysis. Hooks usually are injected during runtime into the kernel space. This technique is commonly used by antivirus vendors to trace the operating system behaviour and to detect zero day malware (Father, 2004).

Box 1. Implementing API hooking on the Android SDK

```
SomeAPIMethod () {
...
// injected code to extract methods.
HTTP.SendData (getCurrentMethodName());
...
}
```

API hooking is one of the most appropriate procedures to gaining valuable information such as blocking on the call, investigation of object state and call flows, code graphs and code during runtime. Commonly, API hooking is composed by using two techniques as follows: hook method and hook server. The hook method injects a function in the SDK driver and target processes during the runtime in the SDK. Hook server aims to ship invoked methods to a predetermined place such as Http. Please refer to Box 1 for more explanation of the steps on applying API hooking.

Difference-Based

In this kind of dynamic analysis, a snapshot has to be taken from the operating system and the registry in advance of and after the analysis. Both snapshots have to be compared to detect the modification on the operating system. Note that the difference-based technique can be used efficiently for exploring the rootkit.

Sandbox

Sandbox is an isolated environment that aims to trace a specific event such as behaviour, system call, API call, CPU, battery and memory usages. Tracing an application in sandbox surroundings, may lead to identification of the malicious samples and keep the environment uncontaminated. It is expected from the analysis that a report will provide an application's behaviour during the execution.

In research work conducted by Lantz (2011), the author provides an open source sandbox to monitor android's applications by collecting logs from the Logcat. The presented tool delivers various information such as: data leakage detection, sent SMS, phone calls, usage of cryptography API, logging file and socket operations.

In the work conducted by Alazab et al. (2012), the authors investigated the behaviour of malicious and clean applications. The authors showed a simple and effective way to determine if family names have been correctly assigned by current anti-virus vendors using sandbox environment. Their results indicate that traditional anti-virus mechanisms are not always able to correctly identify malicious Android applications. They also found that three popular Games applications, which were pre-classified as clean applications by five robust AV engines (i.e. Sophos, Symantec, F-Secure, TrendMicro and MacAfee), leaked sensitive information about the smartphone device.

Pros and Cons of Dynamic Analysis

Dynamic analysis has various advantages, which are described below:

1. Dynamic analysis is very convenient to implement in the Android devices because of the following:
   a. Android is an open source operating system.
   b. There are several operating system versions available as follows: KitKat, Jelly Bean, Ice Cream Sandwich, Honeycomb, Gingerbread, Froyo, Eclair, Donut and Cupcake. By using dynamic analysis for testing, it is possible to choose any of the aforementioned versions to check the vulnerability of the operating system.
   c. Analysis can be done within the Android emulator that preserves the analysis environment away from malicious contamination.
2. Android malware perform obfuscation techniques to evade the AV-vendors. Dynamic analysis is proficient to detect obfuscation code compared to static analysis.
3. Dynamic analysis can be used to collect different types of information such as an initial overview of the malicious application behaviour (Lantz, 2011).
4. Dynamic analysis can be useful for analysing in case an application leaks of user data such as the IMEI and IMSI.

Dynamic analysis has a number of limitations as below:

1. Evasion techniques: Some of the malicious applications are able to identify the emulation environment to evade the analysis, as a result the malware refuses to run.
2. Application Control: Each application has to be run for a sufficient time along with the appropriate command control. As a result, there is no way of knowing if an application analysed correctly, and an analyser cannot estimate how long an application needs to be run.
3. Cut-off time to end the execution process: In dynamic analysis there should be enough time to execute each application to collect sufficient behaviours in order to conduct further analysis. However an analyser cannot estimate for how long an application needs to be run, some research work Shih-Yao and Sy-Yen (2007) disclosed that five minutes enough to execute each application and be able to collect sufficient behaviours to conduct further analysis. Other research works indicated that even one minute (Alazab et al., 2012); Bayer et al., (2010) would be enough to extract behaviours. The length of time that an application has to be run is unknown. In contrast, static analysis looks at the execution time and is based on the source code of an application. Hence, static will end by looking at the entire source code.

CONCLUSION

In summary, this literature review surveyed smartphone malware analysis approaches. According to the literature, it is clear there is a lack of existing countermeasures for identifying malicious applications. Before providing such a detection system, it is critical to understand how malicious applications work and what kinds of evasion techniques they are able to implement. This chapter presented a summary of the most recent analysis approaches used to counter malicious applications targeting smartphone devices.

Modern mechanisms of where to apply malware detection can be separated into two categories as follows. The first: applying detection in the network side and in the smartphone to identify the new malware samples. Applying detection in the network side has the benefits of serving large numbers of smartphone devices, blocks malware before it spreads on the network and does not consume the smartphone resources.

However, applying detection on the network side is impractical because of the following: the proposed solution cannot detect all kinds of smartphone malware attacks, needs more training compared to other approaches, and requires users to have network access to apply detection.

The second category is applying detection in the smartphone itself, which is valuable for detecting various kinds of malicious applications; this has a high detection rate, requires little training compared to detection in the network side, can work without network access and can block malicious applications of making phone calls or sending premium messages. However, applying detection in the smartphone device often consumes resources such as battery, CPU and battery.

Smartphone antivirus applications can be divided into two groups as follows: Misuse-based detection and anomaly-based detection. Misuse-based detection works by scanning particular patterns, raw byte sequences, port numbers, unique functions and classes, port type. Misuse-based detection has the benefits of identifying known patterns within the code. However, it cannot detect unknown malware variants, encrypted communications, botnets, and allocates a large amount of memory for process.

The second group is the anomaly-based detection where the system is able to detect irregular behaviour, which allows identifying new malware variants. However, this has various weaknesses as follows: hard to train dataset with respect to dynamic environment and usually results in higher false positive rates compared to the misuse-based detection (Hoang, Hu, & Bertok, 2009).

As discussed earlier, smartphone malware applications have become complex and hard to analyse due to the growth in the smartphone markets. The authors of such malicious applications are able to produce malicious files by gaining access to operating system documents of the smartphones being targeted. Such documents are used to find gaps that they can penetrate, and then use to create smartphone malware. Hence, the main security concerns in the 2015 is to find security techniques that can distinguish smartphone malware from non-malware (CNCCS, 2013; ESET, 2013; Rathi, 2013; Singh, 2012). The well-known antivirus engine Panda, produced a report (ESET, 2013), which indicated that smartphones malicious applications which target online banking to increase. We are expected to see advance malware performing system call hooking for intercepting API calls from banking applications and capturing users' information in the upcoming years.

REFERENCES

Adolphi, B., & Langweg, H. (2012). Security Add-Ons for Mobile Platforms. In A. Jøsang & B. Carlsson (Eds.), *Secure IT Systems* (Vol. 7617, pp. 17–30). Springer Berlin Heidelberg. doi:10.1007/978-3-642-34210-3_2

Alazab, A., Alazab, M., Abawajy, J., & Hobbs, M. (2011). *Web application protection against SQL injection attack.* Paper presented at the 7th International Conference on Information Technology and Applications.

Alazab, M. (2014). *Analysis on Smartphone Devices for Detection and Prevention of Malware. (Doctor of Philosophy).* Deakin University, Deakin University.

Alazab, M., & Batten, L. (2012). Synchronized-blocking mode, Technical report.

Alazab, M., Monsamy, V., Batten, L., Lantz, P., & Tian, R. (2012). *Analysis of Malicious and Benign Android Applications.* Paper presented at the International Conference on Distributed Computing Systems Workshops (ICDCSW), 2012 32nd. doi:10.1109/ICDCSW.2012.13

Alazab, M., Venkataraman, S., & Watters, P. (2010, 19-20 July 2010). *Towards Understanding Malware Behaviour by the Extraction of API Calls.* Paper presented at the Cybercrime and Trustworthy Computing Workshop (CTC), 2010 Second.

Alazab, M., & Venkatraman, S. (2013). Detecting malicious behaviour using supervised learning algorithms of the function calls. *International Journal of Electronic Security and Digital Forensics*, 5(2), 90–109. doi:10.1504/IJESDF.2013.055047

Alazab, M., Venkatraman, S., Watters, P., & Alazab, M. (2011). *Zero-day malware detection based on supervised learning algorithms of API call signatures.* Paper presented at the Ninth Australasian Data Mining Conference: AusDM 2011, Ballarat, Australia.

Alazab, M., Venkatraman, S., Watters, P., Alazab, M., & Alazab, A. (2012). Cybercrime: The Case of Obfuscated Malware. In C. Georgiadis, H. Jahankhani, E. Pimenidis, R. Bashroush, & A. Al-Nemrat (Eds.), *Global Security, Safety and Sustainability & e-Democracy* (Vol. 99, pp. 204–211). Springer Berlin Heidelberg. doi:10.1007/978-3-642-33448-1_28

Bayer, U., Kirda, E., & Kruegel, C. (2010). *Improving the efficiency of dynamic malware analysis.* Paper presented at the In proceedings of the 2010 ACM Symposium on Applied Computing, Sierre, Switzerland. doi:10.1145/1774088.1774484

Bureau, D. n. (2012). Android malware threatens 2013. *Android malware threatens 2013*. Retrieved Dec.28, 2012, from http://www.dqweek.com/dq-week/report/154801/android-malware-threats-2013

Chebyshev, V., & Unuchek, R. (2014). Mobile Malware Evolution. *securelist*. Retrieved Apr. 10, 2015, from http://securelist.com/analysis/kaspersky-security-bulletin/58335/mobile-malware-evolution-2013/

CNCCS. N. C. S. A. (2013). *Smartphone Malware: report pandasecurity*. Retrieved http://press.pandasecurity.com/usa/wp-content/uploads/2011/06/CNCCS-Smartphone-Malware-Full-Report-Translated-06-7-11-FINAL.pdf

Dawson, M. (2012). Cyber Security and Mobile Threats: The Need for Antivirus Applications for Smart Phones more. *JISTP, 5*(14), 40-60.

Desnos, A. (2012). *Android: Static Analysis Using Similarity Distance.* Paper presented at the International Conference on System Science (HICSS), 2012 45th Hawaii.

Dini, G., Martinelli, F., Saracino, A., & Sgandurra, D. (2012). *MADAM: a Multi-Level Anomaly Detector for Android Malware.* Paper presented at the International Conference on Mathematical Methods, Models and Architectures for Computer Network Security. doi:10.1007/978-3-642-33704-8_21

Egele, M., Scholte, T., Kirda, E., & Kruegel, C. (2008). A survey on automated dynamic malware-analysis techniques and tools. *ACM Computing Surveys*, 44(2), 1–42. doi:10.1145/2089125.2089126

Enck, W., Ongtang, M., & McDaniel, P. (2009). Understanding android security. *Security & Privacy, IEEE*, 7(1), 50–57. doi:10.1109/MSP.2009.26

ESET. (2013). *Trends for 2013 Astounding growth of mobile malware*. Retrieved Jan.15, 2013, from http://go.eset.com/us/resources/white-papers/Trends_for_2013_preview.pdf

Father, H. (2004). Hooking Windows API-Technics of hooking API functions on Windows. *CodeBreakers J, 1*(2).

Fatskunk. (2013). *The Challenge of Smarthone Malware*. Retrieved Jan.05, 2013, from http://www.fatskunk.com/what-is-mobile-malware

Fedler, R., Schutte, J., & Kulicke, M. (2013). *On the effectiveness of malware protection on android an evaluation of android antivirus app*. Technical Report by Fraunhofer AISEC. Retrieved Apr.30, 2013, from http://www.aisec.fraunhofer.de/en/about-us.html

Fossi, M., Egan, G., Haley, K., Johnson, E., Mack, T., Adams, T., . . . McKinney, D. (2011). Symantec internet security. *threat report trends for 2010, 16*, 20.

Gartner. (2015). Gartner Says Smartphone Sales Surpassed One Billion Units in 2014. *Newsroom*. Retrieved Apr. 10, 2015, from http://www.gartner.com/newsroom/id/2996817

Gephi. (2013). *The Open Graph Viz Platform*. Retrieved Jan.09, 2013, from http://gephi.org/

Google. (2012). *ProGuard*. Retrieved Jul.17, 2012, from http://developer.android.com/tools/help/proguard.html

Google. (2013). *Get the Android SDK*. Retrieved Jan.10, 2013, from http://developer.android.com/sdk/index.html

Google. (2014). *Google Play*. Retrieved Jan. 29, 2014, from https://play.google.com/

Grace, M., Zhou, Y., Zhang, Q., Zou, S., & Jiang, X. (2012). *RiskRanker: scalable and accurate zero-day android malware detection*. Paper presented at the 10th international conference on Mobile systems, applications, and services, Low Wood Bay, Lake District, UK. doi:10.1145/2307636.2307663

Halleck, T. (2014). We Spend More Time On Smartphones Than Traditional PCs. *International Business Times*. Retrieved Apr. 10, 2015, from http://www.ibtimes.com/we-spend-more-time-smartphones-traditional-pcs-nielsen-1557807

Han, K.-S., Kim, I.-K., & Im, E. (2012). Malware Classification Methods Using API Sequence Characteristics. In KimK. J.AhnS. J. (Eds.), *Proceedings of the International Conference on IT Convergence and Security 2011* (Vol. 120, pp. 613-626). Springer Netherlands. doi:10.1007/978-94-007-2911-7_60

Hidalgo, B. (2011). *Behavior-based malware detection system for the Android platform*. (Master's project). Linkoping University, Linkoping, Sweden.

Hoang, X. D., Hu, J., & Bertok, P. (2009). A program-based anomaly intrusion detection scheme using multiple detection engines and fuzzy inference. *Journal of Network and Computer Applications, 32*(6), 1219–1228. doi:10.1016/j.jnca.2009.05.004

Iwamoto, K., & Wasaki, K. (2012). *Malware classification based on extracted API sequences using static analysis*. Paper presented at the Asian Internet Engineeering Conference, Bangkok, Thailand. doi:10.1145/2402599.2402604

Jiang, X. (2012). *An Evaluation of the Application ("App") Verification Service in Android 4.2* Technical Report. Retrieved from http://www.cs.ncsu.edu/faculty/jiang/appverify/

Kaspersky. (2012). Android Under Attack: Malware Levels for Google's OS Rise Threefold in Q2 2012. *Kaspersky.* Retrieved Jan.04, 2013, from http://www.kaspersky.com/about/news/press/2012/Android_Under_Attack__Malware_Levels_for_Googles_OS_Rise_Threefold_in_Q2_2012

Kaspersky. (2013). *File Anti-Virus.* Retrieved Apr. 30, 2013, from http://support.kaspersky.com/learning/courses/kl_102.98/chapter2.2/section1

Ketari, L., & Khanum, M. A. (2012). A Review of Malicious Code Detection Techniques for Mobile Devices. *International Journal of Computer Theory and Engineering, 4*(2).

Lantz, P. (2011). *An Android Application Sandbox for Dynamic Analysis.* (Master's Thesis at Department of Electrical and Information Technology), Lund University, Sweden.

Lu, T., Zheng, K., Fu, R., Liu, Y., Wu, B., & Guo, S. (2012). A Danger Theory Based Mobile Virus Detection Model and Its Application in Inhibiting Virus. *Journal of Networks, 7*(8), 1227–1232. doi:10.4304/jnw.7.8.1227-1232

Mills, E. (2011). *Android hole could be used to disable antivirus apps.* Retrieved Jan.09, 2013, from http://news.cnet.com/8301-27080_3-20115108-245/android-hole-could-be-used-to-disable-antivirus-apps/

Radvilavicius, L., Marozas, L., & Cenys, A. (2012). Overview of Real-Time Antivirus Scanning Engines. *Journal of Engineering Science and Technology Review, 5*(1), 63–71.

Rathi, A. (2013). *Android Malware will Increase in 2013.* Retrieved Jan.15, 2013, from http://newamazingtech.blogspot.com.au/p/about-us.html

Ravi, C., & Manoharan, R. (2012). Malware Detection using Windows API Sequence and Machine Learning. *International Journal of Computers and Applications, 43*(17), 12–16. doi:10.5120/6194-8715

Schmidt, A. D., Schmidt, H. G., Clausen, J., Yuksel, K. A., Kiraz, O., Camtepe, A., & Albayrak, S. (2008). *Enhancing security of linux-based android devices.* Paper presented at the 15th International Linux Kongress. Lehmann.

Schwartz, M. J. (2011). Zeus Banking Trojan Hits Android Phones. *informationweek.* Retrieved Apr. 29, 2013, from http://www.informationweek.com/security/mobile/zeus-banking-trojan-hits-android-phones/231001685

Shih-Yao, D., & Sy-Yen, K. (2007). *MAPMon: A Host-Based Malware Detection Tool.* Paper presented at the International Symposium on Dependable Computing, 2007. PRDC 2007. 13th Pacific Rim

Singh, S. (2012). *Malware target on Android OS set to increase in 2013.* Retrieved Jan.15, 2013, from http://articles.economictimes.indiatimes.com/2012-12-25/news/35999218_1_malware-android-os-flash-drives

Sophos. (2012). *Fixing Sophos AutoUpdate after required files were deleted or moved by Sophos Anti-Virus due to a false positive.* Retrieved Jan. 05, 2013, from http://www.sophos.com/en-us/support/knowledgebase/118323.aspx

Svajcer, V. (2014). Sophos Mobile Security Threat Report. *Sophos Mobile Security Threat Report.* Retrieved Apr. 10, 2015

Tian, R. (2011). *An Integrated Malware Detection and Classification System.* PhD Thesis at Deakin University. Melbourne, Australia.

Trendmicro. (2012). *Adding Android and Mac OS X Malware to the APT Toolbox.* Trend Micro Incorporated Research Paper. Retrieved from http://www.trendmicro.com/cloud-content/us/pdfs/security-intelligence/white-papers/wp_adding-android-and-mac-osx-malware-to-the-apt-toolbox.pdf

Tsanas, A., Little, M. A., McSharry, P. E., Spielman, J., & Ramig, L. O. (2012). Novel Speech Signal Processing Algorithms for High-Accuracy Classification of Parkinson's Disease. *Biomedical Engineering. IEEE Transactions on, 59*(5), 1264–1271. doi:10.1109/TBME.2012.2183367

Venugopal, D., & Hu, G. (2008). Efficient signature based malware detection on mobile devices. *Mobile Information Systems, 4*(1), 33–49. doi:10.1155/2008/712353

Whittaker, Z. (2012). *Sophos antivirus detects own update as false positive malware.* Retrieved Jan.05, 2013, from http://www.zdnet.com/sophos-antivirus-detects-own-update-as-false-positive-malware-7000004565/

Xianyong, M., & Yangmin, L. (2012, 6-8 June 2012). *A novel verifiable threshold signature scheme based on bilinear pairing in mobile Ad Hoc Network.* Paper presented at the International Conference on Information and Automation (ICIA), Shenyang.

Yan, L. K., & Yin, H. (2012). *DroidScope: Seamlessly Reconstructing the OS and Dalvik Semantic Views for Dynamic Android Malware Analysis.* Paper presented at the 21st USENIX Conference on Security Symposium.

Yerima, S. Y., Sezer, S., McWilliams, G., & Muttik, I. (2013). *A New Android Malware Detection Approach Using Bayesian Classification.* Paper presented at the IEEE 27th International Conference on Advanced Information Networking and Applications (AINA), Barcelona. doi:10.1109/AINA.2013.88

Zhao, M., Zhang, T., Ge, F., & Yuan, Z. (2012). RobotDroid: A Lightweight Malware Detection Framework On Smartphones. *Journal of Networks, 7*(4), 715–722. doi:10.4304/jnw.7.4.715-722

Zhou, Y., & Jiang, X. (2011). *An Analysis of the AnserverBot Trojan.* Retrieved Jan.10, 2013, from http://www.csc.ncsu.edu/faculty/jiang/pubs/AnserverBot_Analysis.pdf

Zhou, Y., & Jiang, X. (2012). *Dissecting Android Malware: Characterization and Evolution.* Paper presented at the Security and Privacy (SP), 2012 IEEE Symposium on. doi:10.1109/SP.2012.16

Zonouz, S., Houmansadr, A., Berthier, R., Borisov, N., & Sanders, W. (2013). Secloud: A cloud-based comprehensive and lightweight security solution for smartphones. *Computers & Security, 37*(0), 215–227. doi:10.1016/j.cose.2013.02.002

KEY TERMS AND DEFINITIONS

Anomaly-Based Detection: Is a mechanism, aiming to classify unseen application as either normal or anomalous by defining a subset of structured rules of what is considered as normal and anomalous.

Data Mining: Is an intelligence approach that analyses a given database from different aspects and views in an automated fashion, allowing the construction of a model that provides useful information and correlation about the analysed database. These results help in providing a deep understanding of the current data behaviour, characteristics, dependencies, relations and rules. In addition, the results provide the ability to predict future expected values depending on the database analysis results.

Dynamic Analysis: Is an analysis technique that aims to study a smartphone applications' behaviour during run-time. During the analysis, each application has to be executed for sufficient time, along with appropriate command control, to perceive how an application misbehaves and reacts with the operating system.

Malicious Software (Malware): Is any software that aims to harm a digital system. This might disturb the system functionality, recruiting the system to conduct malicious activities or steal personal information from system's users.

Malware Signature: Is a pattern (byte sequence, package names, hash value and filenames) of malicious applications generated by an antivirus company to identify harmful applications.

Misuse-Based Detection: (Also known as signature-based detection) is a mechanism to search and match application against a predefined black list database of signatures, it is also a traditional method and first line defense to detect known malware of the most antivirus engines.

Smartphone Malware: Is malicious software that is specifically designed to exploit smartphone platforms to affect the functionality, availability and the integrity of the system. The types of this malicious software exist in different forms as Viruses, Trojan, Rootkits, Worms, Spyware and others. These malwares can designate attacks to different smartphone OSs, allowing it to exploit and compromise large numbers of smartphone devices.

Static Analysis: Is the procedure of analysing source code of application without executing it. Static analysis can provide various information about the source code such as basic blocks, function calls, control flow graph and structuring of the code. This technique has the strength of understanding all possible execution paths by approximating application behaviour.

Chapter 8
Trust Management in Mobile Ad Hoc Networks for QoS Enhancing

Ryma Abassi
City of Communication Technologies, Tunisia

ABSTRACT

In a collaborative environment such as MANET, nodes reliability evaluation is vital. Trust Management can be used to ensure such healthy collaboration it offers a formal and unified framework for trust specification and interpretation. Establishing trustworthy relationships is generally done by maintaining a reputation for each node computed based on direct observations or neighbors' observations exchanged using recommendations. Unfortunately, for malicious reason, such method may be faked by cheaters: several nodes collude in order to rate each other with the maximum value and decrease other nodes' reputations by giving negative recommendations. The main contribution of this chapter is then, the proposition of a trust based environment for MANET and securing it against collusion attack in order to enhance the network QoS. This is achieved using three steps: (1) the definition of a formal trust based environment (2) the addition of a process handling collusion attack and (3) the extension of the whole proposition by a delegation process allowing nodes functionalities sharing.

INTRODUCTION

MANETs (Mobile Ad hoc NETworks) are wireless mobile nodes dynamically self organizing in arbitrary and temporary network topologies. Their nodes can be internetworked without a pre-existing communication infrastructure. Therefore, such networks are designed to operate in widely varying environments, from military networks to low-power sensor networks and other embedded systems. Dynamic topologies, bandwidth constraints, energy-constrained operations, wireless vulnerabilities, and limited security are among the main MANET characteristics.

DOI: 10.4018/978-1-4666-8345-7.ch008

Initial MANET routing protocols, such as AODV proposed by Perking and Royer (1999), OLSR Jacquet *et al.* (1998), etc. were not designed to withstand malicious nodes within the network or outside attackers nearby with malicious intent Cordasco and Wetzel (2008) Hence, due to these specific characteristics and to the unreliable medium in MANETs, some security mechanisms must be defined. In the literature, some works have been proposed for securing MANET Arijita *et al.* (2012); Quershi *et al.* (2011); Babu *et al.* (2008); Marmol & Perez (2009); Grafii *et al.* (2007); Cordasco & Wtezel (2008); Sachan & Mohen Khilar (2011); Mathews *et al.* (2011). They can be classified into two categories: those based on cryptography and those based on trust. The cryptography-based systems apply cryptographic methods to the existing protocols to distinguish between legitimate nodes and malicious ones. The main advantage of cryptography based systems is that they allow securing routing information from tampering. However, they suffer from a high computational cost and they can't identify nodes with malicious intention. Trust-based systems take advantage from the intrinsic properties of routing protocols to detect malicious nodes i.e. they behave as an intrusion detection system. This is achieved by using node's reputation to mitigate misbehaving. Reputation is maintained through direct observations as well as reputation messages exchanged with other nodes.

Trust enables collaborating nodes to counter their uncertainty and suspicion by establishing trustworthy relationships. Due to the criticality of used concepts, trust is associated to a unified approach allowing its specification and formalization called Trust Management (TM) Blaze *et al.* (2002). Hence, we define trust relations between a *Trustor* (trust provider) and a *trustee* (trust beneficiary) as a binary decision relationship allowing their collaboration in a given situation with a given security level. This level is proportional to *trustee's* reputation i.e. a perception a party creates through past actions about its intentions and norms. Reputation is obtained through direct observations made by the node itself and/or by indirect observations. These latter correspond to the received appreciations from neighbors who have had interactions in the past and have evaluated and rated each others.

Paradoxically, success of trust based schemes depends on cooperation among the nodes. In fact, the TM process may constitute a security weakness due to its vulnerability to the collusion attack where several malicious nodes may collaborate in order to decrease a benevolent node's reputation.

Moreover, resources availability in MANET is a fundamental and a vital constraint. Availability concerns essentially the network nodes as well as routing and other forwarding actions accessibility. Generally, nodes lifetime is consumed by legitimate traffic. In practice, and in a hostile environment, it also can be shortened or even depleted by deny of service attacks penalizing the routing process.

In this work, we propose a trust environment using reputations in order to detect colluders and consequently enhance the network QoS. The first contribution of this chapter, concerns then the proposition of a model built over three activities constituting the basic steps of any system lifecycle: establishment, update and revocation. In order to establish a trust relation, we propose two schemas. In the first one, a trust request is evaluated and a trust level is affected to the established relation based on reputation computing and maintaining. In the second scheme, recommendations are used in order to ensure trust transitivity and a recommendation level is assigned to the established relation. Update activity concerns the modification of the considered relation i.e. trust level, recommendation level and reputation. Finally, revocation activity concerns the removal of an established trust relation.

The second contribution deals with collusion attack and more precisely with the proposition of a process detecting colluders as well as a process punishing such behavior. Hence, an appropriate attack modeling is proposed. Detection is made by assessing recommendations variance compared with the recommendations average. Punishment discards detected colluders and prevents them from participating in future communications.

The third contribution of this work is the extension of the previously proposed trust environment with a delegation process. This process was designed in order to allow the perpetuity of routes without neither stopping packets transfer nor novel route calculation. The purpose of this delegation is to allow a node with a short lifetime, a '*grantor*' delegating its functionalities to another one, a '*grantee*' avoiding a novel route definition. Due to the criticality of the delegation task, it must be made within a secure environment i.e. between trustworthy nodes. Hence, we managed delegation during its initialization, negotiation and revocation based on trust relations. More precisely, delegation is initialized through a *grantee* election procedure based on a reputation calculation process. Negotiation is achieved by exchanging credentials requests as well as credentials responses. A notification of route modification is then sent to involved nodes to incite them updating their routing tables. Finally, revocation of delegations and consequently all its associated actions is achieved as needed.

The rest of this chapter is organized as follows. First, we recall, in Section II, some existing works dealing with trust management for MANET environment as well as MANET QoS enhancing. A new trust Management model is detailed in Section III. In Section IV, a process securing against collusion attack is presented. This is achieved by detecting colluding nodes and discarding them from further communication using a formal modeling of collusion attack and its environment. Delegation concept introduced in Section V, offers all needed basics for QoS enhancing in a MANET. Some simulations and results showing the feasibility and the effectiveness of our proposal are given in Section VI. Finally, Section VII concludes this chapter.

Related Work

Several works dealt with TM in MANET. Blaze *et al.* (2002) introduced a management scheme for IPsec based on TM and on the use of KeyNote. Let's recall that keynote is a unified approach for specifying and interpreting security policies and credentials that allows direct authorization of security-critical actions. Rabahi *et al.* (2005) proposed to monitor the behavior of nodes' neighbors and then to compute the nodes reputation based on the information collected by the monitoring. However, their mechanism allows only malicious packet dropping detection without any proposition to discard involved malicious nodes. Sun *et al* (2006). proposed a framework to quantitatively measure trust, model trust propagation and defend trust evaluation systems against malicious attacks. According to these three works, three TM models emerged: policy based, social based and reputation based models. Policy based models such as KeyNote Blaze *et al.* (2002) are used for systems access control where peers use credential verification to establish a trust relationship. Let's note that according to this model, trust is unilateral i.e. only the resource-owner request to establish trust. Social based systems such as Regret (Sabater & Sierra 2002), are based on social relationships between peers when computing trust and reputation values. They form conclusions about peers through analyzing a social network. Reputation based systems such as EigenRep introduced in Kamvar *et al.* (2003), are based on measuring reputation: they evaluate the trust in the peer and the trust in the reliability of the resource. "CORE", a collaborative reputation mechanism (Michiardi & Molva, 2002), was designed in order to use the "Watchdog" mechanism as a monitoring mechanism. This latter, allows maintaining a reputation table at each node to keep track of reputation values of other nodes. Only positive rating factors can be distributed among nodes since a selfish node may send false negative rating factors to other nodes and may cause disruption of the reputation system. This mechanism devises a penalty action towards a selfish node by denying all services given to it. CONFIDANT Cooperation Of Nodes: Fairness In Dynamic Ad-hoc NeTworks was proposed by Buchegger and Boudec (2002) based on four main components namely a monitor, a reputation system, a path manager, and a trust manager.

Paradoxically, trust schemas may be vulnerable to some attacks. This kind of attack targets the trust process securing routing protocols. Because the high interest perceived by the researchers, several works dealing with collusion attack in MANET were made. Most of them were interested by OLSR based environment where nodes collude during communications.

Kannhavong *et al.* (2006) introduced a collusion attack model against OLSR as well as a technique to detect the attack by utilizing information of 2-hops neighbors. In fact, according to this model, a node must be able to learn topology up to 3-hops in order to check whether link info advertised by its 1-hop neighbors is reliable or not. However, in this proposition, a node is not able to differentiate between mobility induced topology change and the collusion attack. CAP-OLSR a Collusion Attack Prevention protocol for OLSR was introduced by Babu *et al.* (2008). This protocol prevents the collusion attack based on trust information. The proposed trust modeling uses information theoretic framework. Nodes establish trust relations among them using direct observations and uncertainty calculation as well as using recommendations gathered from other nodes. Entropy functions have been used to represent the uncertainty involved in a node's behavior. Recommendations are exchanged through two new introduced messages, Trust Request (TREQ) and Trust Reply (TREP).

The main contribution of this chapter is then, three-folds. First, we present a formal TM model. Second, a collusion detection and prevention process is introduced. Third, a delegation scheme is associated to the whole model.

TRUST MANAGEMENT MODEL

In this section, we introduce a trust management model based on trust characteristics'. This model is built over the concepts of trust level, reputation and recommendation as well as three phases: trust establishment, trust update and trust revocation.

Trust Basics

Defining the trust concept is a challenging task since it may have different applications which may cause divergence in terminology. According to the Cambridge Advanced Learner's Dictionary, trust is "the belief or confidence in the honesty, goodness or skill of a person, organization or thing". Kyung *et al.* (2008) precise that trust concerns the extent to which one party is willing to participate in a given action with a given partner, considering the risks and incentives involved. Hence, according to the IUT, an entity can be said to 'trust' a second entity "when the first entity makes the assumption that the second entity will behave exactly as the first entity expects". Moreover, Dimitrakos *et al.* (2001) specify that trust must be related to a given service and define trust of a party A in a party B for a service X as "the measurable belief of A in B will behave dependently for a specified period within a specific context". For our concern, we define trust as a binary decision relationship between two entities allowing their collaboration in a given situation with a given security level Abassi and El Fatmi (2012-a). The main advantage of such definition is that it can be adapted to several communication aspects since it includes the main trust basic characteristics. In fact, this definition handles the trust and distrust concepts through the term binary decision. The term situation can refer to several communication needs where subjectivity is implicitly included in security level meaning that this trust is not absolute but provides a certain degree of security according to collaborating entities. Let's note that in the rest of this chapter, the service provider is called *Trustor* while the subject requiring access to the Trustor's services is called trustee.

Six trust properties were introduced in the literature by Gardison (2003). Our modeling is constructed based on these properties:

- **Asymmetry:** A trust relation is asymmetric. In fact, if A trust B that doesn't implies that B trusts A, too.
- **Reflexivity:** Trust is reflexive meaning that each entity trusts itself.
- **Context Dependence:** A trust relation concerns a precise action on a precise object and cannot be generalized to other actions or objects.
- **Permanence:** A trust relation is dynamic i.e. it is valid while its constraints are valid.
- **Scalability:** Trust is scalable since it may evolve during communication. This evolution implies trust level modification which also implies a modification of entities reputation. Trust level gives the trust degree while reputation designates the general appreciation of a given entity.
- **Transitivity:** Tries to respond to the following question: if A trusts B and B trusts C then does A trust C? Intuitively, one is tempted to say that a trust relation is not transitive since it is a subjective relation. However, under some constraints this property can hold such as modeled in following sections.

The defined concepts will be used, in the following, in order to model the whole trust lifecycle and mainly the trust establishment, update and revocation.

Trust Establishment

In order to establish a trust relation, two schemas can be used (1) directly through a request (2) in a transitive way through a recommendation.

In the first scheme, the *trustee* submits a trust request to the concerned *Trustor* using the following syntax:

$$Trust(T, t, a, o, [c]) \rightarrow level$$

where '*T*' stands for the *Trustor*, '*t*' for the *trustee*, '*a*' the action concerned by the trust, '*c*' the constraints of the trust relation and '*level*' for the trust level. Let's note that '[ ]' are used in order to indicate optional fields.

A *Trustor* receiving this request asks for the agreement of the trust policy. This latter verifies the validity of the constraints; checks the trustee's accreditations and recommendations and finally returns an adequate trust level.

The second trust establishment scheme is based on the use of trust transitivity. As introduced above, a trust relation can be transitive based on the exchange of recommendations as well as the calculation of recommendation levels. Hence, if A trusts B and B trusts C then A can trust C *iff* B recommends C. This is depicted by Figure 1 where given A, B, and C such that B trusts C and A trusts B:

1. C requests the establishment of a trust relation with A and presents B as a recommender.
2. A sends a recommendation request *recd-req* to B.
3. B can either recommend C or not and sends its response using *recd-resp* to A.
4. According to received recommendations, a trust relation can be established between A and C.

Figure 1. Recommendation modeling

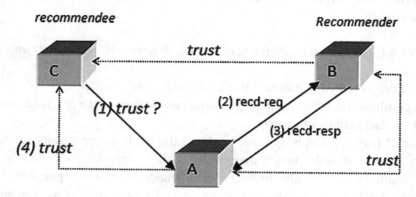

Hence, the trust relation is enriched with a recommendation field as follows:

$$Trust(T, t, a, o, [c], [recd]) \rightarrow level$$

Formally, the recommendation request is expressed as follows:

$$recd - req(R, r, a, o, [c])$$

where 'R' is the recommender, 'r' the *recommendee*, 'a' is the action, 'o' the object of the recommendation, 'c' are associated constraints. The response can be formalized as follows:

$$recd - resp(R, r, a, o, [c], recd - level)$$

where '*recd-level*' is the recommendation level computed by *R*. Let's note that this response is also used when a node broadcasts a trust level modification for a given node in order to inform others of a good or bad behave and to incite them to change their own reputations, too.

Moreover, recommendation is associated with two conditions that must be both fulfilled:

1. The *recommender* and the *recommendee* have a trust relation with a positive level: *Trust (T,t, a, o)→ level* such that *level > 0*
2. The recommendation and the trust relation have the same context.

Trust (T,t, a, o)→ level, Recommend (R, r, a', o', [c])→ resp Such that *a=a'* and *o=o'*

Trust Level Modeling

A trust relation isn't permanent which may induce an increase or a decrease of the trust on a given node. This characteristic can be expressed through trust levels.

Let's have a set L of trust levels whose elements represent degrees of trust and which can range from -3 to 3. We chose the use of quantitative values in order to have more expressiveness concerning trust relation evaluation. In addition, we divided this interval into three parts: [-3, 0[, {0} and] 0, 3] depending on the knowledge that *Trustor* has about the *trustee*. Hence, given $l \in L$,

- ***l ∈ [-3, 0[***: Characterizes a distrust relation where the *Trustor* doesn't accept the establishment of a trust relation with the requesting *trustee*. This can be the case when the *trustee* has a bad reputation and is judged untrustworthy.
- ***l = {0}***: Characterizes a trust relation where the *Trustor* doesn't have any information about the *trustee* reputation and even the presented accreditations come from unknown entities (for the *Trustor*). In this case, *Trustor* establishes the requested relation and assigns to it a neutral level. The choice to associate zero to an unknown *trustee* was made in order to ovoid isolating him (starvation problem).
- ***l ∈]0, 3]***: Characterizes a trust relation where the presented accreditations or recommendations are accepted by the *Trustor* and where the *trustee* is judged trustworthy. These three values are assigned as follows: '1' characterizes a low trust relation, '2' characterizes a medium trust relation and '3' characterizes a high trust relation.

Reputation Calculation

Trust levels are used in order to evaluate nodes reputations rep_i in a given context. After calculating reputation of node i, it is balanced by a corresponding weight w_i as follows:

$$if \; rep_i \in [-3, 0] \; Then \; w_i := 0$$

$$if \; rep_i == 1 \; Then \; w_i := 1$$

$$if \; rep_i == 2 \; Then \; w_i := 2$$

$$if \; rep_i == 3 \; Then \; w_i := 3$$

Each node having communicated with the involved *trustee* sends its appreciation to the *Trustor* that computes then, its own reputation value for this *trustee*. Two cases are conceivable:

1. The *Trustor* has already its own reputation of the *trustee* and hence will only update it.
2. The *Trustor* doesn't have a reputation value for the *trustee* and hence, will compute it from gathered values.

In the first case, when the *Trustor* has already its own evaluation of the trustee's reputation and is updating it, the new reputation is computed as follows:

$$rep_{a,b} = \left| \frac{3 \times repl_{a,b} + \sum_{i}^{n \backslash \{a,b\}} w_i \times rep_{i,b}}{|n|+1} \right|$$

where w_i is the weight associated to the node i, n is the set of entities, $|n|$ is the number of evaluating entities, $rep_{i,b}$ is the reputation given by i to b. The value $repl_{a,b}$ is the existing reputation i.e.. to be updated. It is, by default, weighted by 3 because it corresponds to the reputation that the *Trustor* already has and since by definition trust is a reflexive relation, then it trusts itself completely. Given that m is the number of communications between a and b, $fw_{a,b}^k$ a satisfaction value when node b forwards packets from node a for the kth times, $repl_{a,b}$ is calculated as follows:

$$repl_{a,b} = \left| \frac{\sum_{k=1}^{m} repl_{a,b} + fw_{a,b}^k}{\sum_{k=1}^{m} repl_{a,b}} \right|$$

Finally, we extended the neighbor table in order to store the reputation and the weight of each neighbor such as depicted by Table 1.

For instance, let's consider nodes A, B, C, D and E maintaining respectively Table A, Table B, Table C and Table D as shown in Table 2.

Table 1. Neighbor table extension

NodeID	Reputation	Weight
2	3	3
12	-1	0

Table 2. Neighbor tables example

Table A			Table B			Table C			Table D		
Node	$Rep_{A,node}$	W_{node}	Node	$Rep_{B,node}$	W_{node}	Node	$Rep_{C,node}$	W_{node}	Node	$Rep_{D,node}$	W_{node}
B	-3	0	A	2	2	A	-3	0	A	0	0
C	1	1	C	-3	0	B	2	2	B	3	3
D	0	0	D	1	1	D	0	0	C	1	1
			E	2	2	E	1	1	E	3	3

Let's consider that A is computing the C's reputation: A receives the feedback of B $rep_{B,C} = -3$ as well as the feedback of D $rep_{D,C} = 1$ in addition to its own appreciation. The updated reputation is then:

$$rep_{A,C} = \left| \frac{(3 \times 1) + (0 \times -3) + (0 \times 1)}{3} \right| = 1$$

For the second case, when the *Trustor* doesn't have an initial appreciation value and will compute it from gathered values only, we propose the following formula:

$$rep_{P_{a,b}} = \left| \frac{\sum_i^{n \setminus \{a,b\}} w_i \times rep_{i,b}}{|n|} \right|$$

Thus, for the previous example, A computes the reputation of node E according to the feedbacks received from B, C and D as follows:

$$rep_{A,E} = \left| \frac{(0 \times 2) + (1 \times 1) + (0 \times 3)}{3} \right| = 0$$

Once established, trust relation may evolve during communication. This is handled by the trust update process.

Trust Update

The second step in the trust lifecycle is trust update. Update concerns the potential modifications that may arise when nodes collaborate. In fact, according to the collaboration history, we may need to favor trustworthy nodes or penalize untrustworthy ones. Hence, trust update process can modify the several trust concepts described above mainly, trust level, recommendation level and reputation.

Trust Level Update

Once initialized, trust level value can be updated according to the *Trustor* feedback or other *Trustors* recommendations. In the first case, the *Trustor* modifies its trust level following its collaboration with the concerned *trustee*. The modification can be '+α' in order to increase the trust value or '-α' in order to decrease it knowing that these modifications cannot be combined for the same event and that it corresponds to the event severity degree. In a MANET environment, two negative events can be observed: dropping a packet and not forwarding a packet. An appropriate α value will then be attributed to each event.

In the second case, the trust level is modified following received recommendations from other *Trustors*. However, in order to avoid any overloading traffic, we assume that recommendations are sent only when a change in the sign of the trust level occurs e.g. the level becomes positive whereas it was negative and reciprocally.

Recommendation Update

Recommendation level may be updated if the associated trust level changes. In fact, a modification of the trust level of the relation involving the *Recommendor* and the *recommendee* leads to the modification of the *recommendee's* weighting and to the recommendation level, too.

Reputation Update

Reputation value can be updated on demand or in reaction.

It is said on demand when the *Trustor* broadcasts a reputation request asking for *trustee's* reputation. As a response each concerned node sends back its reputation evaluation. This is modeled as follows:

$$Rep - req(T, t) \rightarrow level$$

The reputation update is said in reaction when it is triggered by a node feedback during its communication with the concerned node. In fact, if the sign of the trust level is inverted then the involved *Trustor* broadcasts this information to other nodes to incite them updating their reputation values. This is modeled by the following:

$$Update(T, t, level)$$

where *level* corresponds to the reputation of t such as perceived by T ($rep_{T,t}$). In such case, the node changes its reputation without any other feedbacks from other nodes and the new reputation value will be simply the new trust level perceived by the node

$$rep_{T,t} = level$$

In MANET, when a node detects that its neighbor is dropping packets, it changes the corresponding trust level and broadcasts this information to other nodes to incite them changing their reputation appreciation for this node in order to isolate it. Let's recall that this detection is made using a Watchdog mechanism which is able to differentiate between link failure and a misbehaving node.

Trust Revocation

The last activity in trust lifecycle concerns trust revocation. It can be considered as a special case of trust update whereas the trust relation is simply dropped. More precisely, trust revocation can be triggered by a *Trustor* request or by a constraint violation. In the first case, a *Trustor* requests to revoke an established trust relation in which it is involved. In the second case, a violation of the constraints associated to a trust relation leads to an automatic revocation of this relation.

DEALING WITH COLLUSION ATTACK

According to Arijita (2012), success of trust based schemes depends on cooperation among the nodes. In fact, the TM process may constitute a security weakness due to its vulnerability to the collusion attack where several malicious nodes collaborate in order to decrease a benevolent node's reputation such as presented in Kannhavong *et al.* (2006); Babu *et al.* (2008); Marmol & Perez (2009); Grafii *et al.* (2007).

Collusion Attack Modeling

There are certain attack models we are not addressing in this work. Therefore, we made some assumptions here:

1. Reputation and local trust values are securely protected.
2. At least, two nodes have to cooperate to achieve such attack.
3. Colluders can always collaborate with each other and attack the network.
4. A colluder may not be neighbor with the *Trustor*. This is because the recommendation request is broadcasted and any node in the network may respond.
5. Each colluder must be neighbor with at least another colluder.
6. A colluder may not be neighbor with the *trustee*. In fact, a colluder is cheating so it can do it even when it is not neighbor with the *trustee* and didn't communicate with it before.
7. Two colluding behaviors are considered: the continuous and the camouflaged.

More precisely, we focus on collusion attack in which two or more attackers collaborate to disturb the TM process. Attackers rated each other with the maximum value and on the other hand, decrease the reputation of benevolent nodes by giving negative recommendations about them. Hence, in the rest of this work, a collusion attack is seen as a group of nodes selectively giving wrong recommendations for a given node (victim) in order to decrease its reputation and consequently to discard it from communication. This is depicted by Figure 2 where the network is composed by six nodes from which three are colluders (4, 5 and 6). Solid lines are used for node visibility.

Figure 2. Collusion attack in a trust based environment

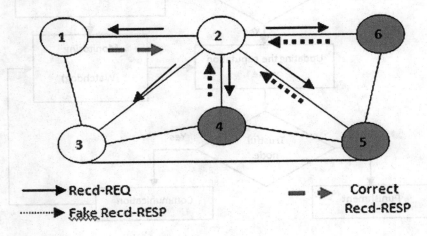

In this figure, node 2 broadcasts a recommendation request *Recd-REQ* asking for node 3's reputation. Nodes 4, 5 and 6 collude in order to under evaluate the reputation of node 3 by sending fake responses. A similar scenario may be applied in order to overvalue the reputation of a node. In this case, node 2 broadcasts a recommendation request *Recd-REQ* asking for node 4's reputation. Nodes 6 and 5 collude by sending fake responses in order to be sure that 4 will be chosen as a *trustee*.

Collusion Attack Prevention

The process depicted by Figure 3 is proposed in order to avoid collusion attack. In fact, when a node needs to evaluate the trustworthiness of an unknown node, it uses its neighbors table in order to select trustworthy nodes to which it will send the recommendation requests *recd-req*. Two cases are conceivable: (1) no trustful node responds because none has already communicated with this node (2) there are some trustful responding nodes.

In the first case, this node i.e. *trustee* is affected by a neutral reputation that will be updated after communications through direct observations. In the second case, recommendations are used in order to calculate a first estimation of this reputation. If the node is considered trustful, then communications will be triggered in parallel with the monitoring process else the punishment process is triggered.

Figure 3. Prevention process

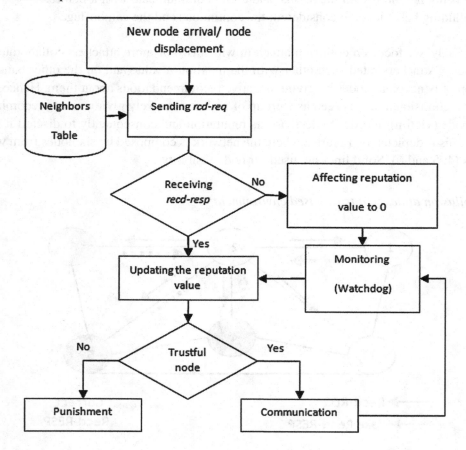

Collusion Attack Detection

Obviously, colluders' recommendations are divergent from legitimate ones. Hence, in order to detect colluders, a reputation variance is calculated. This latter serves as a quality measure of the reputation value computed based on recommendations. Assessing this deviation may contribute to colluders' detection.

Let's have x_i is the obtained reputation by node x on node y's using its behavior and received recommendations at the instant i. The associated weight is w_i,

Let's have $X : \Omega \to R$, we measure how far a set of reputations is spread out using the following variance where

$$E(X) = \sum_{x_i \in X(\Omega)} x P(X = x_i)$$

$$V(X) = E((X - E(X)^2)$$

Variance measures the deviation between a reputation and the average of received reputations. Moreover, in order to assess the reliability of the estimate, this variance is used in order to create a confidence interval I as follows:

$$I = \pm E(X) - \frac{\sigma(X)}{\sqrt{n}}$$

where n corresponds to the number of recommending nodes and $\sigma(n)$ is the variance square root. This latter is triggered by every node having to calculate the deviation of another node R when receiving recommendation responses for a given *recommendee r*.

To detect colluders, a threshold value δ_v is used indicating the maximum allowed variance. Using the presented metrics, the whole detection process is described by the inference system shown in Box 1.

Box 1.

init	$\dfrac{}{\varnothing, D, n[R], \varnothing}$	
recurcall	$\dfrac{recd - resp(R, r, level), D, n[R]}{\varnothing, D_1, n_1[R], V}$ *where* $V = \mathrm{var}\,iance - measure(level, D)$	$if\ V > \delta_v\ n_1[R] = n[R] + 1\ else\ D = D \cup level$
stop	$\dfrac{recd - resp(R, r, level), D, n[R]}{R, \varnothing, n[R], V}$	$if\ n[R] > 3$

Figure 4. Proposed delegation life cycle

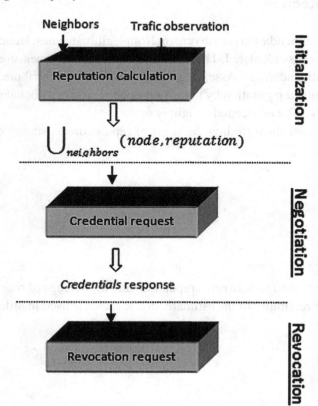

Let's consider a finite domain P containing all received recommendation responses. The rules presented in this system apply to a triplet (*recd-resp*; D and n[R]) whose first component *recd-resp* is a received recommendation response from R concerning r with the level *level*, the second component D is a subset of P and the third component n[R] is the number of detected variances for the concerned node R.

The main recursive rule deals with variance calculation. In fact, given a received *recd-resp*, D and number of variance already detected (lesser than three), a variance V is calculated. Each time this latter is greater than the predefined threshold, the number n[R] is incremented and the concerned level is added to D. The system stops when n[R] reaches the value 3.

We denote by |-* the reflexive application of inference rules of Figure 4 and by x $>^{*3}$ y the fact that three instances of x are greater than y. In the following, we prove that the inference system of Figure 4 terminates and is correct.

Theorem 1 (Termination): For a given MANET, while there are colluders, they are detected. Proof:

Initially,

$$\forall R \setminus n[R] < 3 \Rightarrow R = \varnothing \Rightarrow no\ colluder\ is\ detected\ .$$

During each iteration,

$$\begin{cases} if\ v > \delta_v \Rightarrow n[R] + + \\ if\ n[R] > 3 \Rightarrow colluder\ detected \Rightarrow system\ stops \end{cases}$$

Hence, the system always terminates.

Theorem 2 (Correctness): Having that the system terminates, whatever a node is detected as colluder, it is really a colluder.

$$if \forall R \setminus V(level, D) >^{*3} \delta_v \vdash^* R$$

Proof. The termination proof was made previously. In addition, *if $V(level, D) > \delta_v$* three times then the node that gave this recommendation is deviating. Therefore, R is a colluder.

As we noted previously, we tolerate that a node gives divergent recommendations three times and thus in order to minimize the false positive detections. However, once the third divergence is reached, the node is declared as colluder and a punishment process is triggered. This latter is detailed in the next sub-section.

Collusion Attack Punishment

Initially, each node has a reputation; the blacklist contains nodes having a reputation lesser that 0 and the gray list those for which we observed one or two variances.

Having that each node makes its own observations, when the number of variances reaches the value three for a given suspect node T, the node verifies whether its own observation (gathered using the watchdog) is different from the received response summed with the variance. Two cases are then conceivable: (1) the node is a colluder or (2) the node is divergent because other nodes collude. This is automated by the inference system below.

In the first case, the suspect node is detected as a colluder and is punished by decreasing its reputation and blacklisting it. Let's note that the use of watchdog is motivated by the fact that each node trusts its own observation. In parallel, the collusion attack victim t is rehabilitated by changing its reputation to zero i.e. neutral. This choice was made in order to minimize the risk of rehabilitating an attacker pretending to behave properly given that the neutral reputation annuls the node's weight in the trust-based environment temporarily.

In the second case, as we said above, a divergent but innocent node is detected because other nodes collude. In such case, the node is simply removed from the *greylist* and its variance number n is decremented (See Box 2).

In order to be able to detect colluders, a recommendation table is used for the storage of received recommendation responses as depicted by Table 2.

Box 2.

$$
\begin{array}{lll}
init & \dfrac{\rule{3cm}{0.4pt}}{rep_{ID}, B, rep_{t}, G, n[ID]} & \\[3ex]
recurcall & \dfrac{watchdog(T,t), level, V}{rep'_{ID}, B \cup ID_{rep}, G \setminus ID, n'[ID]} & if\ watchdog(T,t) > level + V \quad where \begin{cases} rep'_{ID} = -3 \\ rep'_{t} = 0 \\ n'[ID] = n[ID] -- \end{cases} \\[3ex]
stop & \dfrac{\varnothing}{stop} & if\ no\ other\ rules\ apply
\end{array}
$$

This table is temporary in that sense that only last responses are stored. It contains a *recd-level*, the corresponding trustee and the recommendation sender. For instance, as seen in Table 3, the current node received a *recd-level* concerning *trustee* 3 with the value 2 from node 4 and a *recd-level* concerning *trustee* 3 with the value 1 from node 0.

Benefiting from Delegation in a Trust Based Model

In a collaborating environment, entities may need to give some of their authority to other entities in order to allow service perpetuity and avoid any unavailability. Delegation process can be used for such purpose since it allows sharing permissions and beliefs between entities. The node initiating the delegation is called '*grantor*' while the delegation beneficiary is called '*grantee*'. In a trust based system, delegation can be achieved through the use of credentials. Credentials are defined by Ben Ghorbel-Talbi *et al.* (2007) as properties of entities that are described in a semantic language and signed by other entities. Hence, the previously introduced assertion can be updated as follows:

$$Trust(T, t, a, o, [c], [recd], [cred]) \rightarrow level$$

where '*cred*' corresponds to the presented credential.

Though trust is very important for the sharing of permissions, managing delegations is rather difficult. In the rest of this chapter, we propose a modeling of delegation concepts in a trust based environment.

Table 3. Recommendation table example

Recd-Level	Trustee	Recd Sender
2	3	4
1	3	0

Delegation Characteristics

In order to propose a complete framework dealing with delegation, we began by identifying the delegation characteristics and thus, through a review of some existing works such as Ben Ghorbel-Talbi *et al.* (2007) ; Ding and Peterson (1995); Crampton and Khambham-mettu (2008); Abassi and El Fatmi (2012-b) dealing with such topic. The identified characteristics comprise mainly permanence, monotonicity, multiplicity, depth and revocation.

- *Permanence*: refers to delegation types in terms of their time duration. This is modeled in our approach using constraints. Indeed, while constraints are valid, delegation is valid whereas when a constraint is no longer valid, the associated delegation is revoked, too.
- *Monotonicity*: refers to the state of the authorization that the *grantor* possesses after the delegation. A monotonic delegation, called grant, means that upon delegation the *grantor* maintains the delegated power. With a non-monotonic delegation, a transfer, upon delegation the *grantor* loses the delegated power throughout the delegation. This is modeled in our approach using two different requests that are differently handled by the model. Let's note that the term delegation will be used in the rest of this chapter to refer to grant/transfer common characteristics.
- *Multiplicity*: refers to the number of people to whom a *grantor* can delegate. This is modeled in our approach using a number fixed by the *grantor* and managed by the SP.
- *Depth*: defines whether or not each delegation can be further delegated and how many times. This is modeled in our approach using a depth level specifying when it is different from zero, the number of authorized delegations. Moreover, each time the permission is re-delegated, this number is automatically decreased until it reaches 0.
- *Revocation*: refers to the process by which a *grantor* can take away the privileges that he delegated to another user.

Credential Modeling

The basic idea behind trust based delegation is that a *"Trustor* trusts a *trustee* to make decisions on its behalf, with respect to a resource or service that the *Trustor* owns or controls" such as introduced by Crampton and Khambham-mettu (2008). In this work, we propose to extend the trust based delegation concept to cover the actions that *Trustor* can perform on objects, too. Hence, three delegation types can be differentiated. In the first type, the *Trustor* delegates the permission to achieve some actions on its behalf such as establishing new trust relations or forwarding packets. In the second type, the *Trustor* delegates to its *trustee* the permission to delegate a received permission. In the third type, the *Trustor* delegates to its *trustee* the permission to achieve some actions on its behalf and to delegate them, too. Since delegation is made through credentials exchange, three credential types corresponding to three delegations types introduced above are proposed. In fact, a *grantor* can delegate:

1. The right to execute actions only. This corresponds to an *execution credential*.
2. The right to delegate only. This corresponds to a *delegation credential*.
3. The right to execute actions and delegate too. This corresponds to a *general credential*.

These three credentials can be requested using a CREDENTIAL-REQUEST message formalized as follows:

$$CREDENTIAL - REQ(ID, G, g, cxt, t, m, [dp])$$

where '*ID*' is the credential identifier, '*G*' stands for the *grantor* giving the credential to the *grantee* '*g*' for the context '*cxt*' referring to a triplet *(a, o, [c])* designing respectively the delegated action 'a' on a given object 'o' following some constraints 'c'. This credential has type 't', is destined to '*m*' subjects, and can eventually be re-delegated '*dp*' times.

Credential type 't' can be one of the following such as introduced above:

$$t := \text{'execution'} \mid \text{'delegation'} \mid \text{'general'}$$

Once this request is received, the *grantee* sends back a CREDENTIAL-RESPONSE if it accepts the delegation otherwise nothing is returned:

$$CREDENTIAL - REP(ID, G, gt)$$

When the number of authorized re-delegations *dp* is different from zero, a credential chain can be created. In such case, the credential chain length has to be checked: each time a credential is delegated, the trust policy must verify if its *dp* value is different from zero then *dp* is decreased else the delegation is prohibited.

Revocation is used in order to delete an already shared credential. The *grantor* sends then the following message to the trust policy removing by the fact the associated credential:

$$CREDENTIAL - RVK(ID, G, g)$$

In the rest of this chapter, a trust based delegation modeling based on the introduced characteristics as well as on the delegation life cycle is introduced. The proposed scheme ensures routes' perpetuity while maintaining a minimum generated overhead. It is built upon three main steps: initialization, negotiation and revocation.

Trust Based Delegation Lifecycle Modeling

Trust based delegation lifecycle has three steps as depicted by Figure 4: the initialization of the delegation, its negotiation and finally the revocation of an established delegation. Initialization collects all needed information about nodes in order to select the *grantee* of the delegation while negotiation checks whether a delegation can be granted in which case, it is established. A successful completion of these steps leads to some specific impacts on the existing communication system such as security rule addition, action execution, etc. Once unneeded, delegation may be revoked.

Table 4. Exchanged messages

Message	Meaning
Rcd-REQ	A node is requesting recommendation levels from its neighbors for a given node.
Rcd-RESP	A node is replying by sending its recommendation level for a given node.
Change-route	A node is requesting to change its ID by the trustee ID in the routing tables of its neighbors.

Trust Based Delegation Initialization

The initialization component is in charge of collecting local and global information about the past behavior of each node in order to establish trust relationship among them. An information collector and a reputation calculation engine are then used. The collector performs a local and a global observation of neighbors' nodes. Local observation is carried out by the node itself by observing generated packets, let's say g, as well as forwarded packets, let's say f, for a given neighbor. Then, periodically, this node computes f/g and stores the obtained result in the ratio column of its Reputation Table. This ratio represents at this level the neighbor's reputation.

Global observations are collected from neighbors' nodes through the reception of recommendations. A recommendation is given by a node to another one in order to reinforce its reputation provided that the two nodes have already a trust relation. It is requested by a node broadcasting a recommendation request message formalized as follows:

$$Recd - REQ(ID, trustee)$$

A node receiving this request, returns a recommendation response Recd-RESP to the *Trustor* containing a recommendation level *recd-level* depicting its level and corresponding to the trustee's *t* reputation such as perceived by the node identified by its ID for a given context cxt described through an action on an object.

$$Recd - RESP(ID, Trustor, trustee, cxt, recd - level)$$

Once collected, this information is sent to the reputation calculation engine which is in charge of calculating the corresponding reputation.

These two messages as well as all proposed ones are summarized in Table 4.

Trust Based Delegation Negotiation

When the energy of a node participating to packets forwarding reaches a critical threshold, it initiates a negotiation process. This is done as depicted by the inference system shown in Box 3.

Given a Trustor's reputation table R, the node having the highest reputation is chosen to be *trustee*. When this latter accepts this delegation, the *Trustor* shares with it its reputation table and broadcasts a CHANGE-ROUTE message to its neighbors. This message, presented in Table 2 is formalized as follows:

$$CHANGE - ROUTE(Trustor, trustee)$$

Box 3.

$$init \quad \overline{\varnothing, R}$$

$$recurcall \quad \frac{R, d\lg- req(t_{prev})}{t, R_{parsed}} \quad where \begin{cases} R_{parsed} = R \setminus t \\ \forall t' \in R,\ rep_t > rep, \end{cases} \quad if\ d\lg- req(t_{prev}) = no$$

$$sucess \quad \frac{R, d\lg- req(t)}{t_{new},\ R_{parsed}} \quad where\ R_{parsed} \subseteq R \quad if\ d\lg- req(t_{prev}) = no$$

$$fail \quad \frac{R, \varnothing}{\varnothing, R_{arsed}} \quad where\ R_{parsed} = R$$

Each node receiving the CHANGE-ROUTE message replaces the Trustor's ID by the trustee's ID in its routing table.

Let's note that this negotiation has a nice side effect if a node does not accept a delegation request. In fact, in such case, its reputation is decreased since it can be considered as a selfish node.

Once defined, the inference system presented in Figure 7 has to be verified. Two properties are used: safety and vivacity.

Theorem 3 (Safety): For a given *Trustor*, at most only one *trustee* has to be elected.

Proof. Initially, no *trustee* is elected. Using the *recurcall* rule, the node with the highest reputation is chosen (the first one in the reputation table R) and a delegation request is sent to this node. Once a positive response received, the success rule is triggered and consequently the inference system stops. Hence, only one *trustee* can be elected.

Theorem 4 (Vivacity): A response has to be given in a finite time.

Proof. (Trivial) The *recurcall* rule is applied at most |R| times: $R_{parsed}=R$. Hence, even if a *trustee* isn't found, the system stops. Trust based delegation revocation

Given that the delegation is triggered due to battery problem, it is obvious that it may be revoked. For MANETs, this revocation can be reduced to the resurgence of the *Trustor* in the network. This latter will be detected by its neighbors thanks to Hello messages.

SIMULATION AND DISCUSSION

Simulation Environment

Simulations were made using the Network Simulator NS2 version 2.35 and the following environment's characteristics.

- **Topology:** We consider a MANET composed of 50 mobile nodes randomly placed on an open field of 1000 m × 1000 m. Nodes use IEEE 802.11 MAC protocol and the bandwidth is 2 Mbps.
- **Routing Algorithm:** We used the reactive algorithm AODV.
- **Mobility:** Nodes move according to random waypoint model with a velocity uniformly distributed between 0 and 20 m/s. Each of the node moves from a random location to a randomly chosen destination initially. On arriving, the node will stop for a pause time then move to next random destination. By varying pause time we achieve different network mobility.
- **Traffic Model:** During each simulation, a number of nodes want to exchange data packets CBR (Constant Bit Rate). The packet size is 512 bytes exchanged. These packets are broadcast at regular intervals (every the 0.25 s) between the beginning and the end of the transmission. Transmission scenarios are generated automatically using the script provided with cbrgen.tcl NS-2.
- **Misbehaving Model:** Periodically, nodes are turned off. This is made after a given time where the node launches the negotiation process.

Furthermore, the following performance metrics were used for experimental results evaluation.

- **Packet Loss Ratio:** Ratio of total transmitted packets and lost packets in the network.
- **Reputation Value Variation:** Concerns the reputation of a node such as seen by other nodes.
- **Detection Rate:** Ratio of total numbers of malicious nodes detected and total malicious nodes present in the network.
- **False Positive Rate:** Ratio of benevolent nodes detected as being colluders and real malicious nodes.
- **Overhead:** Number of control and routing packets.
- **Energy Consumption:** Battery drainage over the time.

Discussion

In the following, we present the results of our simulations compared with initial AODV implementation and thus according to different scenarios. These latter are grouped into network configuration scenarios and network mobility scenarios. Changing network configuration implies varying the nodes number whereas changing network mobility implies varying pause times.

Trust Model/Collusion Prevention and Detection

The experiment depicted in Figure 5 was made according to five scenarios, the first one without any colluder and the last four scenarios with an increasing percentage of colluders (this percentage is obtained according to recommending nodes). Let's note that in this simulation, the victim is a well behaving node.

Figure 5. Reputation values' variation over time for different colluders rate

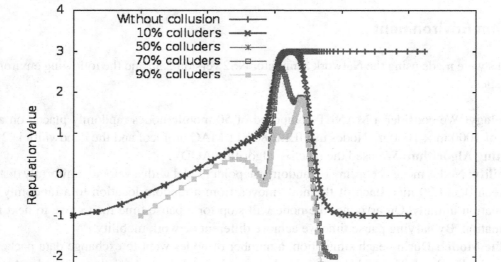

Figure 6. Reputation values' variation without the presence of colluders

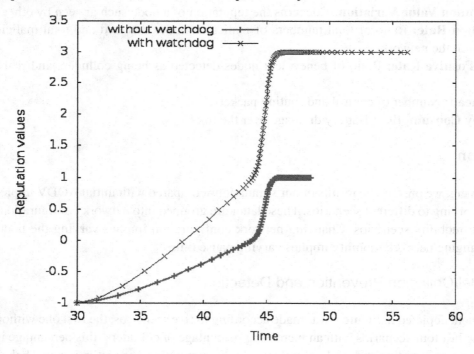

Figure 7. Variation in reputation value in presence of colluders

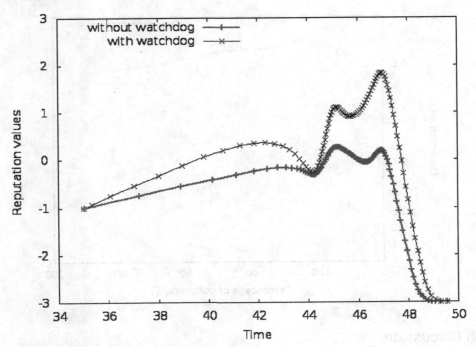

Figure 5 shows that without colluders, reputation is stationary. In fact, it starts with value "-1" and is increased until reaching a stable value which is in this case "3". This is due to the fact, that reputation is modified progressively based on watchdog and received recommendations. Moreover, when there is a collusion attack, the reputation value decreases dramatically. More precisely, as the ratio of colluders with respect to total number of nodes increases reputation values decrease. This decrease is not abrupt neither sudden because the watchdog value is more important when calculating a node's reputation.

Figure 6 shows that reputation values are sensibly lesser when watchdog isn't used even without any colluder. This is due to the fact that each node performs its own observations concerning its neighbors and that this appreciation is pondered by its weight when it is recommending another node. The weight itself is obtained thanks to the appreciation of node receiving the recommendation and can be zero if the node didn't observed this node yet.

The same simulation is achieved in presence of colluders such as depicted by Figure 7. We note that the reputation values calculated based on recommendations only are lesser to the one calculated based on watchdog and recommendations. In fact, when the node has its own observations even in presence of colluders, the calculated reputation will be more realistic. However, when only recommendations are used, the reputation will be more faked.

A second experiment was carried out to determine the colluders' detection rate of our proposal. As shown in Figure 8, the detection rate of colluders is around 100%. For example, when the percentage of colluders is 10% we detect 100% of them where when their percentage is 90%, we detect 70% of them.

In order to verify the effectiveness of our detection, we evaluated the number of false positive detected varying with the number of colluders. As depicted in Figure 9, the false positive rate increases with the number of colluders but remains very negligible compared with colluders' number.

Figure 8. Colluder detection rate varying with the number of colluders

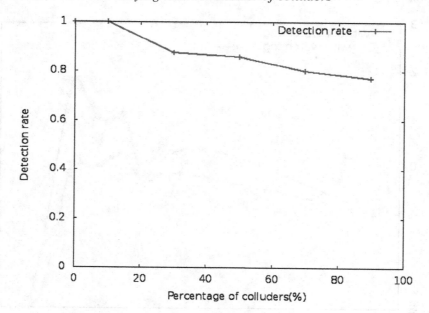

Delegation Discussion

Figure 10 shows the lost packets ratio for the initial configuration i.e. 50 nodes with a pause time equals to 2.00s. One can observe that the performance of AODV and our implementation is the same for the first 1000 packets. However, for the next 1500 packets, our simulation presents a lesser ratio of lost packets. This is due to the fact that routes are not simply broken and re-created but are maintained through delegation. Hence, when a node failed, its neighbors switch automatically on the second established route (through the elected trustee).

Figure 11 depicts the performances with 25 nodes. One can remark that our implementation is more efficient than the first scenario. In fact, the number of lost packets decreases with the number of nodes having that exchanged packets is lesser.

The second simulation results concerns the impact of mobility. This latter corresponds to a pause time modification. Figure 12 shows the packet loss ratio for the same configuration as previously with a modified pause time equals to 4.00s. One can observe that AODV and our implementation have substantially the same performances and that modified AODV is even better after 700 sent packets. This is due to the switching on trustee's route after a node failure whereas in AODV a new route is calculated before obtaining packet loss stability at around 900 packets.

Figure 13 depicts the last scenario where nodes are not very mobile i.e. the pause time is equal to 10.00s. Similarly to the precedent scenario, the effectiveness of AODV and our implementation are very close with a slight distinction to our proposal.

Obtained results demonstrate that our trust-based delegation scheme can improve significantly routes reliability. For all cases, the packet loss ratio is lower for AODV with delegation which proves the effectiveness of this delegation. Parameters as nodes number and pause time influence the packet delivery ratio, where their higher values decrease the delivery

Figure 9. False positive rate varying with real number of colluders

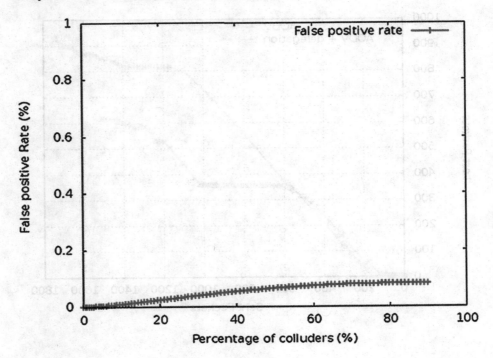

Figure 10. Packet Loss Ratio with 50 nodes, pause time=2.0s

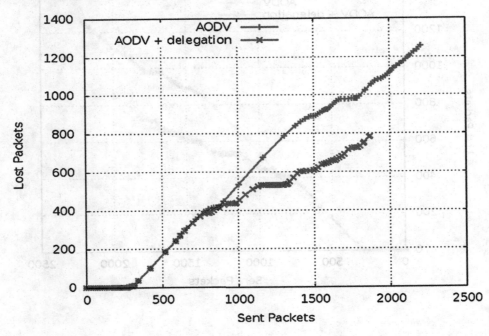

Figure 11. Packet Loss Ratio with 25 nodes, pause time=2.0s

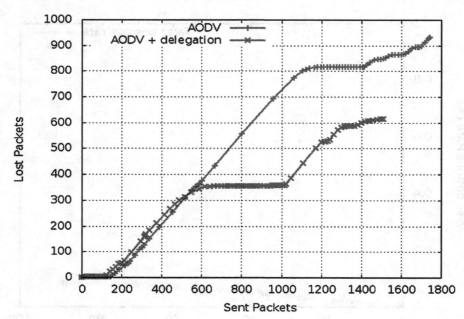

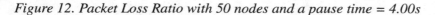

Figure 12. Packet Loss Ratio with 50 nodes and a pause time = 4.00s

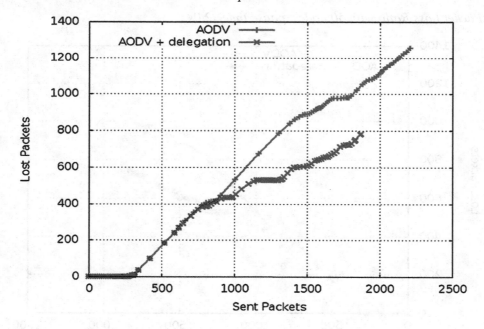

Figure 13. Packet Loss Ratio with 50 nodes and a pause time =10.00 s

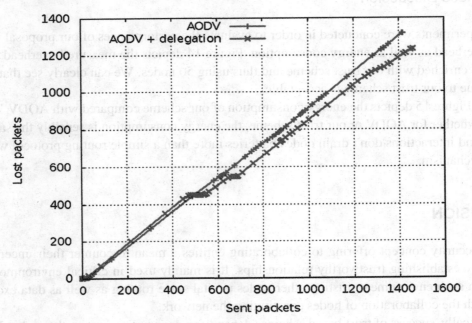

Figure 14. Packet overhead compared with total transmitted packets

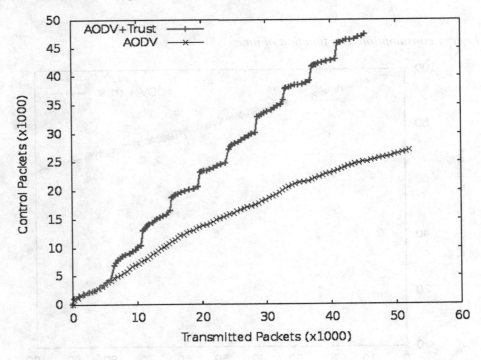

Effectiveness Discussion

The last experiments were conducted in order to evaluate the performances of our proposal in terms of induced overhead as well as energy consumption. Figure 14 depicts the measured overhead for AODV and AODV enriched with our trust scheme and thus using 50 nodes. We can clearly see that the added overhead due to our trust scheme is acceptable.

Finally, Figure 15 depicts the energy consumption of our scheme compared with AODV. The results show that whether for AODV or our trust scheme, the energy consumption is sensibly the same: added messages and interactions don't drain nodes batteries more than a simple routing protocol without any security mechanism.

CONCLUSION

Trust is a security concept offering to collaborating entities a mean to counter their uncertainty and suspicion by establishing trustworthy relationships. It is mainly used in critical environment such as MANET. In such environment trusting other nodes is vital since routing as well as data exchange are handled with the collaboration of nodes constituting the network.

Paradoxically, success of trust based schemes depends on cooperation among the nodes. In fact, the trust management process may constitute a security weakness due to its vulnerability to the following attack: several malicious nodes may collaborate in order to decrease a benevolent node's reputation or to increase a malicious node's reputation. That's what is usually called a collusion attack.

Figure 15. Energy consumption as a function of time

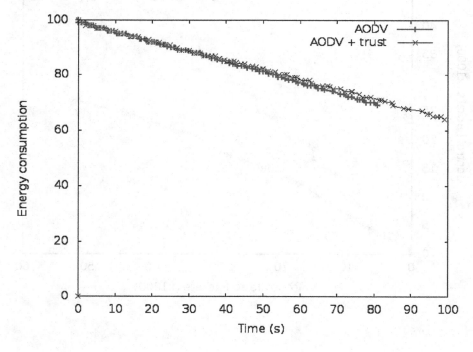

In this chapter, we proposed a TM scheme for MANET QoS enhancing. More precisely, we presented a formal trust model based on the concepts of reputation, recommendation, trust establishment, update and revocation. This model was extended with collusion attack prevention, detection and punishment process where each step was formally defined using adequate inference systems. The last part of this chapter dealt with a delegation process used in order to minimize the packet loss due mainly to node displacement/loss. This process was built over three steps: initialization, negotiation and revocation. Several simulations experiments were achieved and demonstrate the feasibility and the effectiveness of our proposal. First, the packet loss ratio varying with the number of nodes as well as the pause time compared with AODV was evaluated and revealed that packet loss decreases with our proposition. Second, the colluder detection rate varying with the number of colluders was evaluated and obtained results shows that this rate is included between 100% when the number of colluders is lesser than 20% of the total number of nodes in the network and 80% when the number of colluder is approximately around 90% of the network nodes. Third, false positive rate, overhead and energy consumption were evaluated. Obtained results are encouraging since the false positive rate is lesser than 10%, the overhead and energy consumption are close to the ones generated by AODV without any addition.

In future works, the proposed environment can be enriched in order to handle more complex attacks such as Sybil camouflage where a number of colluders perform camouflage attack together, whitewashing attacks where a misbehaving node is able to *whitewash* its low trustworthiness by starting a new session with the initial reputation value, etc. The challenge is then how to adapt and/or enrich the proposal in order to handle various strategic attacks.

REFERENCES

Abassi, R., & Guemara El Fatmi, S. (2012a). Towards a Generic Trust Management Model. In *Proceedings of the 19th International Conference on Telecommunication, ICT 2012*, Jounieh, Lebanon.

Abassi, R., & Guemara El Fatmi, S. (2012b). A Trust based Delegation Scheme for Ad Hoc Networks. In *Proceedings of the 7th International Conference on Risks and Security of Internet and Systems CRISIS 2012*, Cork, Ireland.

Arijita, B., Sarmistha, N., & Chandreyee, C. (2012). Reputation based trust management system for MANET. *3rd International Conference on Emerging Applications of Information Technology*, pp.376-381.

Babu, K., Franklin, A., & Murthy, S. (2008). On the Prevention of Collusion Attack in OLSR-based mobile ad hoc networks. In *Proceedings of the International Conference of Networks*, pp 1-6.

Ben Ghrobel-Talbi, M., Cuppens, F., Cuppens-Boulahia, N., & Bouhoula, A. (2007). Managing Delegation in Access Control Models. 15th International Conference on Advanced Computing & Communication (AD'COM 2007), Guwahati, India, pp. 744-751. doi:10.1109/ADCOM.2007.105

Blaze, Ioannis & Keromytis. (2002). Trust Management for IPsec. *ACM Transactions on Information and System Security*, 5(2).

Buchegger & Boudec. (2002). Performance analysis of the confidant protocol (cooperation of nodes: Fairness in dynamic ad-hoc networks). In *Proceedings of MOBIHOC'02*.

Cambridge Advanced Learner's Dictionary. (n.d.). Retrieved June, 2014 http://dictionary.cambridge.org/

Cordasco, J., & Wetzel, S. (2008). Cryptographic versus trust-based methods for MANET routing security. *Electronic Notes in Theoretical Computer Science, 197*(2), 131–140. doi:10.1016/j.entcs.2007.12.022

Crampton, J., & Khambham-mettu, H. (2008). Delegation in Role-Based Access Control. *International Journal of Information Security, 7*(2), 123–136. doi:10.1007/s10207-007-0044-8

Dimitrakos, Matthews, & Bicarregui. (2001). *Towards security and trust management policies on the web*. In ERCIM Workshop 'The Role of Trust in e-Business' in conjunction with IFIP I3E Conference, CLRC Rutherford Appleton Laboratory, Oxfordshire.

Ding, Y., & Petersen, H. (1995). *A new approach for delegation using hierarchical delegation tokens*. University of Technology Chemnitz-Zwickau Department of Computer Science.

Grafii, K., Mogre, P. S., Hollick, M., & Steimetz, R. (2007). Detection of Colluding Misbehaving Nodes in Mobile Ad hoc and Wireless Mesh Networks. In *Proceedings of IEEE Globecom*, pp. 5097-5101. doi:10.1109/GLOCOM.2007.966

Grandison, T. (2003). *Trust Management for Internet Applications*. (PhD thesis). Imperial College London, London, UK.

International Telecommunication Union. ITU-T Recommendation X.509. (2000). Retrieved June 2014, http://www.itu.int/ITU-T/recommendations/rec.aspx?rec=11735&lang=en

Jacquet, P., Muhlethaler, P., & Qayyum, A. (1998). *Optimized Link State Routing Protocol*. Internet Draft. Retrieved from June 7, 2014 https://tools.ietf.org/html/draft-ietf-manet-olsrv2-19

Kamvar, S. & Garcia-Molina. (2003). EigenRep: Reputation Management in P2P Networks. Proceedings of the Twelfth International World Wide Web Conference, Budapest.

Kannhavong, B., Nakayama, H., & Jamalipour, A. (2006). A Collusion Attack against OLSR-based Mobile Ad Hoc Networks. In Proceedings of IEEE GLOBECOM Conference. doi:10.1109/GLOCOM.2006.262

Kyung Kim, T., & Suk Seo, H. (2008). *A Trust Model using Fuzzy Logic in Wireless Sensor Network*. World Academy of Science, Engineering and Technology.

Marmol, F. G., & Perez, G. M. (2009). Security threats scenarios in trust and reputation models for distributed systems. *Computers & Security, 28*(7), 545–556. doi:10.1016/j.cose.2009.05.005

Mathews, Sudarsan, Kannan, & Karthik. (2012). A Secure and Energy Enhanced Protocol for Routing in Mobile Ad-Hoc Networks. *International Journal of Scientific & Engineering Research, 3*(11).

Michiardi & Molva. (2002). CORE: a collaborative reputation mechanism to enforce node cooperation in mobile ad hoc networks. In *Proceedings of the Communication and Multimedia Security Conference*.

Perkins & Royer. (1999). Ad-hoc On-Demand Distance Vector Routing. In *Proceedings of the Second IEEE Workshop on Mobile Computer Systems and Applications*. doi:10.1109/INFOCOM.2006.154

Qureshi, Min & Kouvatsos. (2011). Countering the collusion attack with a multidimentionnal decentralized trust and reputation model in disconnected MANETs. Journal of Multimedia Tools and Applications, Springer.

Rabahi, Y., Mujica-V, V. E., & Sisalem, D. (2005), A Reputation-Based Trust Mechanism for Ad hoc Networks. In *ISCC '05: Proceedings of the 10th IEEE Symposium on Computers and Communications (ISCC'05)*, pages 37–42, Washington, DC, USA doi:10.1109/ISCC.2005.17

Sabater, & Sierra. (2002). Reputation and social network analysis in multi-agent systems. First International Joint Conference on Autonomous Agents and Multi-Agent Systems, Bologna, Italy

Sachan & Mohan Khilar. (2011). Securing AODV Routing Protocol in MANET Based on Cryptographic Authentication Mechanism. *International Journal of Network Security & Its Applications*, 3(5).

Sun, Y. L., Han, Z., Yu, W., & Liu, K. J. R. (2006). A Trust Evaluation Framework in Distributed Networks: Vulnerability Analysis and Defense against Attacks. [Spain.]. *IEEE INFOCOM, 2006*, 1–13.

KEY TERMS AND DEFINITIONS

Collusion Attack: A security attack where a node lies in order to decrease the reputation of a malicious node and/or increase the reputation of a malicious node.

Credential: A qualification proving that a node is suitable for a given situation.

Delegation: A node gives its own privileges to another node.

Grantee: The beneficiary of a delegation.

Grantor: The initiator of a delegation.

MANET: A mobile network where there is no preexisting infrastructure and where all the network components can move.

Recommendation: The opinion of a given node regarding another node.

Reputation: The appreciation of a node calculated by another one based on its past behavior and interactions.

Trust: A relation where nodes can rely on each other.

Chapter 9
Insider Threats:
Detecting and Controlling Malicious Insiders

Marwan Omar
Nawroz University, Iraq

ABSTRACT

Malicious insiders are posing unique security challenges to organizations due to their knowledge, capabilities, and authorized access to information systems. Data theft and IT sabotage are two of the most recurring themes among crimes committed by malicious insiders. This paper aims to investigate the scale and scope of malicious insider risks and explore the impact of such threats on business operations. Organizations need to implement a multi layered defensive approaches to combat insider risks; safeguarding sensitive business information from malicious insiders require firstly, an effective security policy that communicates consequences of stealing or leaking confidential information in an unauthorized manner. Secondly, logging and monitoring employee activity is essential in detecting and controlling system vulnerabilities to malicious insiders. Thirdly, conducting periodic and consistent insider vulnerability assessments is critical to identifying any gaps in security controls and preventing insiders from exploiting them. And lastly, but certainly not least, taking extra caution with privileged users is important to proactively protecting information infrastructure from insider risks.

INTRODUCTION AND BACKGROUND

Recent security research studies have clearly shown that insider threats are posing a major security risk to organizational information assets. In fact; about 70% of threats to an organization's network and network-based infrastructure originate from inside (Sugata, 2010). While many business organizations invest their most dear computational as well as monetary resources to fortify their network against outside malicious attacks; they forget or rather fail to pay close attention to the great threats posed by insiders who can advertently abuse or exceed their authorized access to organizational information systems and ultimately steal or modify sensitive business data for financial gains and other malicious goals. Fur-

DOI: 10.4018/978-1-4666-8345-7.ch009

thermore; Insider threats have become a common and popular trend targeting private sector companies as well as government agencies for reasons that range from financial gains and IT sabotage to business advantage and industrial espionage (Barrios, 2013).

The insider threat challenge continues to receive increasing attention by both industry experts and scholars alike due to its devastating consequences which usually result in theft of sensitive business data and cause privacy, credibility, and reputation issues. A root cause of the insider threat issue stems from the fact that business organizations, and government agencies alike, do not seem to have adequate security defenses in place to detect and prevent insider attacks. This coupled with the fact that insiders have access to the "crown jewels" and valuable information assets that are inaccessible by outsiders; this certainly entices insiders to abuse their privileged access to those data and commit attacks. Organizations typically rely on security policies, auditing and log monitoring tools, and traditional access control mechanisms to combat insider threats; unfortunately those techniques cannot withstand emerging insider threats which are becoming highly sophisticated and usually remove their foot prints after committing insider attacks.

What Is Insider Threat and Who Are Malicious Insiders?

According to CERT, a malicious insider is a current or former employee, contractor, or business partner who has or had legitimate and authorized access to organization's information systems and advertently misused or abused that privilege to compromise the confidentiality, integrity, and availability of organizational information assets (CERT, 2009).Employees with malicious intentions represent the insider threat to business organizations and government agencies and they usually commit deliberate acts for a variety of reasons such as job dissatisfaction, employment termination, workplace conflicts with co-workers and managers, or it could be due to influences by outsiders who have their own malicious objectives and want to exploit insiders' authorized access to confidential business information which in turn could be for industrial espionage or IT sabotage or business advantage.

It's important to note that insider threats may fall under two main categories: intentional insider threat and unintentional insider threat; as it's equally important to acknowledge that both are a problem and both can have devastating consequences on organizational information resources. Nonetheless; both threats are exploited by the same entity which is organization's personnel (current or former employees, contractors, business partners, etc.) whom are considered the source of greatest threat because they are usually entrusted with valuable and confidential business data which can entice them to exploit and exceed this privilege for their own personal advantage(Carroll, 2006). Unintentional insider threat is usually manifested in non -adherence or lack of security policy and non- conformance to security awareness and training programs. Intentional insider threat, on the other side, usually originates from malicious intentions and seeks to harm organization's information assets. This kind of threat is certainly more dangerous and more consequential since it deliberately accesses information in an unauthorized manner; malicious insiders are usually technically capable and may use a combination of social engineering techniques along with sophisticated technical expertise to gain unauthorized access to organization's valuable information resources.

Scope and Scale of Insider Threats

The significance of insider threats poses a great risk to an organization's security posture that it cannot be overlooked. Malicious insiders, unlike hackers, are hard to be identified and monitored therefore it's easy for those insiders to conceal their deliberate malicious actions within organization's information infrastructure. Trusted insiders (employees, clients, contractors, vendors, etc.) whom are normally provided with credentials (e.g. user name and password) have access to organization's information system and the entire network; this privilege, in turn, enables as well as entices willful malicious insiders to compromise the confidentiality, integrity, and availability of those information resources (Yang & Wang, 2011). Furthermore; malicious insiders do not have to worry about breaking defenses because they are already inside the network/system which really gives them an advantage over outside hackers. Therefore; the insider threat has repeatedly been called the greatest threat to network information resources, and yet this is often overlooked in a rush to protect the perimeter with ever-increasingly sophisticated defense controls and security measures (Warkentin&Willison, 2009).

Malicious insiders usually use their intimate knowledge of company's information resources along with their authorized access to the system to commit malicious, deliberate unauthorized acts; Webster Report, showed that most of Robert Hanssen's exploits involved the use of authorized access to commit deliberate unauthorized action. One of Mr.Hanssen's attacks involved hacking into his supervisor's workstation in an unauthorized manner; his intimate knowledge of the organization and its information resources (such as knowing where each work station is located, how its configured, and what security measures it has) enabled him to commit this malicious act. More recent reports confirm that ready and immediate access to knowledge about the system and acquaintance with other authorized users is the third advantage an inside adversary has and may exploit (Haigh, Harp, O'Brien, Payne, Gohde, & Maraist, 2009).It's important to note that insiders' threats are increasing in scale, scope, and sophistication as they seem to be happening and targeting business organizations more frequently given the fact that we are facing a fragile global economy where waves of layoffs are happening regularly which provokes employees to harm their current or former employer's information infrastructure as a revenge. To make matters worse, business competitors and adversaries may use dishonest insiders as an attack vector to steal trade secrets and strategic plans. Insider threats have evolved, over time, from simple malicious acts of abusing privileges to highly organized and highly sophisticated threats where they target private sector as well as government agencies for broader malicious intentions such as IT sabotage, industrial espionage, and financial gains. Cert researchers at Carnegie Melon University collected, studied and analyzed about 118 cases of insider incidents and presented a breakdown of classes of insider threats which is illustrated in Figure 1 (Cert, 2009). They stated that the main trends and patterns of insider threat goals that have surfaced during the last few years were centered on IT sabotage, theft or modification for financial gains, and business advantage.

Related Work

There have been research studies conducted by researchers to closely examine insider threats and evaluate their impact on organizations and government agencies. The main objective of those studies was to enhance our understanding of this type of threat and consequently offer preventive measures to combat insider threats. In a study conducted by Anderson, eight general approaches to control and mitigate insider threat were proposed (Anderson, 1999). Jabbour & Menasce (2009) presented a security scenario

Figure 1.

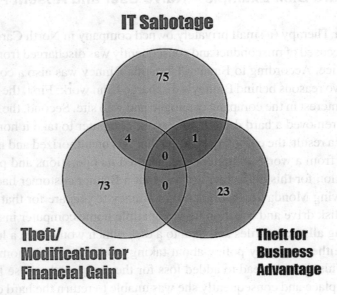

to enable privileged users to compromise the system they protect along with an assessment theory for Insider Threat Security Architecture (ITSA); the researchers, then, discussed ways in which the same scenario can be mitigated using the ITSA model. Preventing malicious insiders from compromising confidential data at the database application level was another insider threats study which was conducted by Chagarlamudi, Panda & Hu (2009).

Researchers at the Carnegie Mellon University have always been known for focusing their efforts on the insider threat phenomena; specifically conducted within the IT and telecommunications sector (Kowalski, Cappelli & Moore, 2008). The study focused on the characteristics, motives and behaviors of the insiders and the consequences for both the insiders and the organizations. Some recommendations for the prevention of insider attacks for the IT industry were provided. This study was also retrospective in nature and was based on 52 documented attacks that occurred within the IT and telecommunications sector between 1996 and 2002 (Kowalski et al., 2008). The size of targeted organizations varied greatly. The majority of organizations had fewer than 500 employees (62%); however 30% were large organizations with over 10,000 employees. All of the organizations were private sector businesses. In half of the instances where intellectual property was stolen, the insider was employed by a company that had confidentiality policies in place (Kowalski et al., 2008).

EXAMPLES OF MALICIOUS INSIDER THREAT INCIDENTS AND THEIR IMPACT

Examining and evaluating some of the common insider threat cases will help in identifying some of the characteristics and properties of insiders which, in turn, can be very valuable in predicting trends and understanding any common themes or practices used by malicious insiders. This will assist and benefit both researchers and industry experts alike. Looking at some of the recent insider incidents will also help studying insider's motives and intentions for committing such crimes as it may be a good tool to identify trends and techniques used by malicious insiders.

Example 1: The Hard Disk Example – Naïve User and Absent Policy

On April, 2003, Banner Therapy (a small privately owned company in North Carolina, USA) employee Christina Binney was accused of misconduct and consequently was discharged from her employment and told not to return to office. According to Banner, Christina Binney was also a co-founder of it. Banner stated that there were two reasons behind Binney's discharge from work: First, the company disputed her assertion of copyright interest in the company catalogue and web site. Second, the company claimed that she had impermissibly removed a hard drive from a work computer to take it home and use its content for a client meeting. As a result, the company claimed that this unauthorized and intentional act (removing the hard disk drive from a work computer) had crippled its operations and put its valuable data at risk. Binney's justification for this deliberate act was that a Banner customer had requested a meeting on Friday for the following Monday morning, and for Binney to prepare for that meeting, she decided to take the entire hard disk drive and use it on her compatible home computer instead of going through the hassle of transferring all needed files and data to a disk which would take a long time. At the time, Banner Therapy had neither company policy about taking work equipment home nor established any computing protocols. This, in turn, lead to added loss for the company because Binney was prevented from entering the work place and consequently she was unable to return the hard disk drive to company as she claimed she was planning to do so. (Probst, Hunker, Gollmann, & Bishop, pp. 1-20, 2010)

Example 2: The Email Example, Ordinary User Generates an Extraordinary Amount of E-Mails

October, 2007 was the time for Alex Green to change jobs; to prepare for the change; he decided to change his designated e-mail address to a department of homeland security intelligence bulletin subscription which would then allow him to update his subscription to that bulletin. While doing so, he mistakenly and inadvertently hit "reply all" and touched off a listserv free-for-all when his request arrived in the electronic mail boxes of several thousand governments and private sector security specialists. As results, there were more than 2.2 million e-mails pinging among approximately 7,500 recipients which forced the e-mail server to shut down. This inadvertent incident was described as a mini distributed denial of service attack; although, the bulletin content was unclassified, this inadvertent act of responding to all did not prevent the compromise of department contacts and information. Individual subscribers with security clearance and classification remained anonymous until they hit the "reply" button responding from work accounts which naturally contained their auto signatures. This incident truly introduced the risk of impersonating government employees whom hold sensitive and confidential positions. (Probst, Hunker, Gollmann, & Bishop, pp. 1-20, 2010)

Example 3: Former Employee Stealing Confidential Information

This deliberate act of information theft occurred when an employee decided to stay at the office after hours just two days prior to his resignation; the former employee, who was a member of product team, had already planned to work for a competitor and as a result he advertently decided to download hundreds of confidential files for projects to which he was not assigned from the company's server onto his desktop computer. To hide any evidence of this malicious act, he decided to copy the files to CDs and delete the files from his desktop. After his former employer noticed and realized (through log files) that there has been a large number of file deletions from his desktop computer; company decided to initiate an investigation to further examine the former employee's activity. This former employee was smart enough to find out about this investigation before it even took place. Consequently he deleted all those files from his new employer's desktop computer. Therefore, authorities were unable to find those files on his new desktop computer. Fortunately; this malicious act did not cause any financial losses but it highlighted the imminent risk posed by insiders especially those who no longer work for their employers. (Cert, 2009)

Example 4: Privileged System Administrator Incurs Severe Financial Loss to His Former Company

A system administrator, disgruntled and unhappy with his diminished role in a thriving defense manufacturing firm whose computer network he alone had developed and managed, centralized the software that supported the company's manufacturing processes on a single server, he then managed to coerce a coworker to give him the only backup tapes for that software. This inappropriate attitude and negative behavior in dealing with co-workers resulted in system administrator's termination. Unfortunately, this termination had disastrous consequences on his organization because he had already planted a logic bomb which then was detonated by former system administrator and caused the deletion of the only remaining copy of the critical software from the organization's server. The scale and scope of this somewhat unique malicious insider incident exceeded 10 million dollars according to the victim organization and lead to about 80 employee layoffs. (Insider threat study, 2005)

MOTIVES AND TECHNIQUES USED FOR CARRYING OUT INSIDER ATTACKS: HUMAN AND BEHAVIORAL ISSUES

Understanding the intentions and motives of insiders for attacking information systems is paramount to designing robust defense techniques to combat such insider threats. Job dissatisfaction, layoffs, and terminations have often being cited by researchers as primary reasons to engage in unethical actions and break into their systems; on the other side, employees with malicious intentions and other employees who are influenced by competitors or other adversaries also have their share in committing deliberate acts of compromising confidential organizational information to achieve personal gains. Games & Michael (2008) indicated that the most common psychological theme for insider attacks was "greed, revenge for perceived grievances, ego gratification, resolution of personal or professional problems, to protect or advance their careers, to challenge their skill, express anger, impress others, or some combination". It's worth noting that different categories of insiders (e.g. full time employees, part time workers, consultants, business partners, and vendors) may have different motives for attacking company's information systems; some of the most commonly observed causes of attacks are: financial gains, secure future employment, and personal grievances from job termination and job dissatisfaction.

Theft or Modification of Information for Financial Gains

Financial gains remain the most prominent motive for insiders to commit attacks on their organizations especially given the fact that we live in a digital age where sensitive corporate data (such as strategic plans, marketing strategies, and customer financial information) are considered the crown jewels and can be sold for a high price in black markets. What further motivates malicious insiders to commit this deliberate act is the fact that those valuable data is easily accessible anytime, anywhere given the fact that most business organizations provide remote access for their employees to access information resources. Any employee with malicious intentions can simply use a removable device such as USB to take out confidential information without anyone noticing it. In March 2002, a "logic bomb" deleted 10 billion files in the computer systems of an international financial services company. The incident affected over 1300 of the company's servers throughout the United States. The company sustained losses of approximately $3 million, the amount required to repair damage and reconstruct deleted files. Investigations by law enforcement professionals and computer forensic professionals revealed the logic bomb had been planted by a disgruntled employee who had recently quit the company because of a dispute over the amount of his annual bonus (Randazzo, Keeney, Kowalski, Cappelli & Moore, 2005)

Theft of Information for Business Advantage

This class of insider threat involves stealing confidential business data by current or former employees, business partners, consultants, or contractors. Their goal is to advertently use their privileged access to the system to steal sensitive or proprietary business data from their organization and use it for business advantage. The ultimate goal of malicious insiders in this category would be to use the confidential information to obtain a better job with a competitor or to start their own competing business or even to sell to competitors for a price (CERT, 2009). It's important to note that insiders who commit this kind of malicious activity hold sensitive positions such as financial, technical, and managerial roles where they have immediate access to confidential information and they misuse or exceed their privileged access to the system to commit this deliberate act. Also, once they steal the confidential information, they usually resign to start their own competing business or join another competing company. The extent of this category of malicious activity can be far reaching to include leaking information to foreign companies or governments which usually inflicts severe financial losses for the victimized organization. This goes to show that the ultimate intention of this class of attack is also financial where perpetrators sold confidential corporate information and achieved monetary gains.

What Are the Best Practices Used by Organizations to Stop Insider Threats and Are They Effective?

Since insiders have legitimate and authorized access to system resources; it makes it even more difficult to identify malicious insiders because they are exposed to confidential organizational information as part of their daily tasks. Malicious insiders often abuse this privilege and use their knowledge of security controls to subvert defense measures and leak or steal mission critical data. Therefore; to combat this unique security threat, organizations need to implement their best security measures for detecting and responding to deliberate insider risks.

First and foremost, organizations need to enforce clear security policies and guidelines to minimize the risk posed by both intentional and unintentional security incidents. One of the most common and effective security controls employed by organizations to address insider threats is a robust access control mechanism; business organizations tend to implement the rule of least privilege which indicates that employees should only have access to information resources necessary to perform their daily tasks. Furthermore; access control mechanisms enable companies to specify and implement monitoring and auditing requirements (Iyer, Dabrowski, Nakka, & Kalbarczyck, 2008)

One of the limitations posed by access control techniques is their inability to prevent privileged system users (such as system administrators) from committing deliberate malicious actions such as leaking mission critical information and selling them to competitors or adversaries. Also, limiting access for legitimate users to system informational resources could impede their productivity and efficiency. Principle of least privilege and separation of duties are two of the most commonly enforced controls to manage and minimize the risk of insider threats. Organizations need to ensure that employees only have access to the resources necessary for their job function as they also should continuously verify and check for any user activities outside of the normal scope of daily activities so that internal malicious users do not cross boundaries of their daily job duties (Green, 2014).

Auditing security logs is another strategy used by companies to detect and deter insider threats; Logs contain detailed information which can be correlated with particular events happening within organization's information systems and networks. Security technologies such as firewalls, routers, intrusion detection systems, and antivirus software applications generate numerous logs; business organizations rely on those logs and analyze them for identifying any potential malicious insider activity, violations to security policies, and security incidents. Organizations also heavily rely on audit logs to identify user authentication attempts and extract information generated about other security devices about potential cyber- attacks; this mechanism for mitigating malicious insider risks is effective in capturing suspicious activity because it provides a way to collect data, analyze it, and present it which could help in the prosecution process when insiders have committed cyber –crime (Kuman & Morarjee, 2014).

The shortcoming of this security approach is that there is a huge amount of logs generated everyday by all security devices which makes it challenging to manage and analyze in a timely manner; this in turn makes it difficult to identify and respond to potential malicious insider activity in a proactive manner. Some companies deploy log management software to effectively store and analyze computer security log files and best use them for detecting and addressing suspicious user activity. (Roy, Tomar, & Singh, 2010)

Recommendations to Business Organizations Based on the Investigation

One of the most essential techniques for detecting and mitigating insider threats is through effective real time event monitoring systems; a monitoring system could be in the form of an event log analyzer where it can monitor internal user activity and report any suspicious activities that may lead to internal attacks. The monitoring application would also help IT security professionals to track specific and critical events in real time thus provide capabilities to establish baseline parameters and pin point potential internal malicious activity. Furthermore; to maximize the benefit of such monitoring mechanism, business organization need to establish meaningful security policies to determine what needs to be monitored and at what levels of system architecture. Also, data collected from various security devices may need to be further analyzed to aid in detecting any insider misuse given the fact that some sensitive information system encrypt their critical data and therefore its necessary to conduct through log analysis before attempting to identify and detect malicious insiders.

Another defensive approach would be to be cautious with privileged users such as system administrators and IT managers; privileged employees are not only aware of loosely enforced company's policies and procedures but they are also aware of system's security flaws and know how to exploit those flaws to commit malicious actions. Therefore; business organizations need to pay additional attention to those advantageous individuals, this could be by establishing technical controls to log, monitor, and audit their online actions in addition to enforcing proactive and strict security measures following their termination such as account termination and ensuring that their access to any information resources is disabled.

Conducting insider threats vulnerability assessment is also a good security strategy to protect organizations against malicious insiders; companies need to implement vulnerability assessment measures to understand how vulnerable they are to insider risks and develop mitigation techniques based on the assessment. It's also important for organizations to incorporate vulnerability assessment plans into a wide enterprise risk assessment strategy and identify the most critical information resources against both insiders and outsiders.

Another non- technical defensive measure would be by enforcing and clearly communicating security policies and procedures to employees at all levels of organization; malicious insiders are usually on the look out to exploit any gaps in security policies and guidelines, therefore companies should address this risk by consistently and strictly enforcing technical and organizational policies. This proactive security technique is likely to prevent any data modification or leakage by disgruntled employees or employees who are not happy with their compensation and benefits. Business organizations with effective security controls will be better able to mitigate suspicious employee behaviors and ultimately minimize the risk and impact of information theft and insider IT sabotage.

CONCLUSION

The forgone discussion has explored insider threats and shed light on some of the consequences of compromising corporate data by insiders. The risk of insider malicious threats is increasingly becoming a major enterprise security issue and receiving much attention and care from business leaders because insiders have knowledge, capabilities, and, above all, legitimate access to confidential organizational information resources. This paper addressed risks associated with malicious insiders from a technical perspective and proposed some technical solutions to combat malicious insiders and minimize the impact of compromising sensitive business information. Data theft for financial gains and IT sabotage by disgruntled employees are among the most common motives for insiders to abuse their privileged access to systems and compromise sensitive digital resources. Monitoring and logging employee online activity is one of the effective techniques to control insider threats, also taking extra caution with privileged system users such as system administrators is intended to mitigate some insider risks. Establishing sound security policies and effectively communicating them with employees at all levels is also essential to protecting organizations from insiders with malicious intentions.

REFERENCES

Barrios, R. (2013). A Multi-Level Approach to Intrusion Detection and Insider Threat. *Journal of Information Security.*, *4*(1), 54–65. doi:10.4236/jis.2013.41007

Carroll, M. (2006). "Information Security: Examining and managing the Insider Threat", *Proceedings of the 3rd annual conference on Information security curriculum development*, pp. 156-158. 2006. doi:10.1145/1231047.1231082

Cert. (2009). *"Common Sense Guide to Prevention and Detection of Insider Threat"*. Retrieved from http://www.ncix.gov/issues/ithreat/csg-v3.pdf on Dec 3rd, 2011

Chagarlamudi, M., Panda, B., & Hu, Y. (2009). *"Insider Threat in Database Systems: Preventing Malicious Users. Activities in Databases.* In *Proceedings of the 2009 Sixth International Conference on Information Technology: New Generation*, Las Vegas, pp. 1616-1620, 2009. doi:10.1109/ITNG.2009.67

Green, D. (2014). Insider threats and employee deviance: Developing an updated typology of deviant workplace behaviors. *Issues in Information Systems, 15*(II), 185–189.

Greitzer, F.L., Moore, A.P., Cappelli, D.M., Andrews, D.H., Carroll, L.A., & Hull, T.D. (2011). Combating Insider Threats. *IEEE Security & Privacy, 6*(1), 45-60.

Haigh, J. T., Harp, S. A., O'Brien, R. C., Payne, C. N., Gohde, J., & Maraist, J. (2009) Adventium Labs., Minneapolis, MN. *"Trapping Malicious Insiders in the SPDR Web"*. *Proceedings of the 42nd Hawaii International Conference on System Sciences* – 2009.

Iglesias, J., Angelov, P., Ledezma, A., & Sanchis, A. (2012). Creating evolving user behavior profiles automatically. *IEEE Transactions on Knowledge and Data Engineering, 24*(5), 854–867. doi:10.1109/TKDE.2011.17

Insider Threat Study. (2005). Retrieved on Dec 2nd, 2011 from www.secretservice.gov/ntac/its_report_050516.pdf

Iyer, R., Dabrowski, P., Nakka, N., & Kalbarczyck, Z. (2008). *Pre-configurable Tamper-resistant Hardware Support Against Insider Threats: The Tested ILLIAC Approach. Insider Attack and Cyber Security* (pp. 133–152). Springer.

Jabbour, G., & Menasce, D. A. (2009). *The Insider Threat Security Architecture: A Framework for an Integrated, Inseparable, and Uninterrupted Self-Protection Mechanism. International Conference on Computational Science and Engineering.*

James, S., & Michael, R. (2008). Insider Threats to Information Systems. *SAIS (2008) Proceedings.* Retrieved from http://aisel.aisnet.org/sais2008/26

Kowalski, E.F., Cappelli, D.M., & Moore, A.P. (2008). *Insider Threat Study: Illicit Cyber Activity in the Information Technology and Telecommunications Sector.* Joint SEI and U.S. Secret Service Report, January 2008.

Kuman, D., & Morarjee, K. (2014). Insider data theft detection using decoy and user behavior profile. International Journal of Research in Computer Applications and Robotics. 2(2), 51-55.

Probst, C., Hunker, J., Gollmann, D., & Bishop, M. (2010). "Insider Threats in Cyber Security" (Advances in Information Security) (pp 20-30). New York: Springer. doi:10.1007/978-1-4419-7133-3

Probst, C., Hunker, J., Gollmann, D., & Bishop, M. (2010). Aspects of Insider Threats. *Advances in Information Security, 49*(10), 1–15.

Randazzo, M. R., Keeney, M., Kowalski, E., Cappelli, D., & Moore, A. (2005). *Insider Threat Study: Illicit Cyber Activity in the Banking and Finance Sector.* U.S. Secret Service and CERT Coordination Center: Software Engineering Institute.

Roy, R., Tomar, D., & Singh, N. (2010). An Approach to Understand the End User Behaviour through Log Analysis. *International Journal of Computers and Applications, 5*(Issue.11), 27–34. doi:10.5120/953-1330

Salya, A., & Ravi, M. (2013). Survey on defense against insider misuse attacks in the cloud. *International Journal of Advanced Computing, 5*(1), 20-25.

Sanyal, S., & Gupta, S. (2010). "New Frontiers of Network Security: The Threat Within," *Second Vaagdevi International Conference on Information Technology for Real World Problems*, 2010. pp.63-66 doi:10.1109/VCON.2010.19

Warkentin & Willison. (2009). *"Motivations for Employee Computer Crime: Understanding and Addressing Workplace Disgruntlement through the Application of Organizational Justice"*. Retrieved on Dec 3rd, 2011, from http://scholar.googleusercontent.comscholar?q=cache:B4zLaLcU80QJ:scholar.google.com/+Warkentin+Willison,+2009+insider+threats&hl=en&as_sdt=0,44

Yang, S., & Wang, Y. (2011). System Dynamics Based Insider Threats Modeling. *International Journal of Network Security & Its Applications, 3*(3), 1–13. doi:10.5121/ijnsa.2011.3301

KEY TERMS AND DEFINITIONS

Data Theft: The act of stealing confidential or sensitive business data for the purpose of selling it or using it in other ways to harm the organization's reputation and financial standing.

Insider Threat: Is a malicious threat to an organization that comes from people within the organization, such as employees, former employees, contractors or business associates, who have inside information concerning the organization's security practices, data and computer systems.

IT Sabotage: The deliberate act of preventing Information Technology processes from achieving its intended results.

Malicious Insider: Is current or former employee, contractor who intends to abuse his permissions to harm and affect the confidentiality, integrity, or availability of the organization's information or information systems.

Privileged Employees: An employee who has the privilege to access certain computational resources due to his/her position or title within the organization.

Security Controls: Measures or tools used to protect information resources from adversaries.

Security Policy: Is a clearly defined document that outlines specific procedures that need to be enforced by upper management to contribute to the protection of digital assets.

Vulnerability Assessment: The process of identifying security holes or weaknesses in an information systems before hackers exploit such weaknesses.

Chapter 10
Authorship Analysis:
Techniques and Challenges

Athira U.
LBS Center for Science and Technology, India

Sabu M. Thampi
IIITMK, India

ABSTRACT

Authorship Analysis is the process of examining documents to determine the stylistic details underlying the document and hence inferring about the characteristics of the author of document in order to attribute the authorship to a particular author or to confirm the authenticity of a claimed authorship. The popularity of online communications has paved way to the promotion of numerous fraudulent acts. These illegal activities can be curbed to an extent by identifying the source of the postings, which is made possible by finding the real authors of online documents.Applicability of authorship analysis in the field of forensic linguistics also gathers great importance today. The automation of, process aimed at analyzing the authorship of forensic documents, eases the linguists of the high manual effort spent in analyzing documents and is also advantageous in terms of its accuracy. Here we discuss about the existing methods that have been used so far to deal with automation of authorship analysis and the challenges faced by them.

INTRODUCTION

Authorship Analysis is the process of finding the author of a given document by analyzing the writing style followed in the document. It has been used to attribute authorships of many literary works in early days. The ancient example of authorship analysis was demonstrated by King Vikramadithya to find the greatest poet of his assembly, Kalidasa who was found absconding. The excellent comprehension of king in the poet's style enabled him to identify the source of certain lines written by delitescent Kalidasa.

Authorship analysis is mainly based on the assumption that each author is featured by a unique idiolect, which means a distinct and unique way of usage of language. The author's text reflects this characteristic and hence can be used to identify the authorship of a document (Rygl, 2013). The major

DOI: 10.4018/978-1-4666-8345-7.ch010

task behind the authorship analysis is to find out feature set representative of the idiolect of the author. Just like the unique finger print of a person, this feature set should be a unique write print capable of identifying an individual. This includes usage of function words, vocabulary richness, common terms used, frequency of n- lettered words and so on. As an example it is to be noted that the famous writer J.KRowling, the author of a series of seven fantasy novel Harry Potter, has a distinctive trait of usage of terms and spellings and also vocabulary set consists of terms characterizing her own unique style. Terms like "mudblood" is indeed the writer's own creativity. Similar is the case of Shakespeare who formulated terms suiting situations and characters. The same quality turned out to be a crucial evidence of identifying the so called "Unabomber", Ted Kaczynski the serial murderer. The convict wrote a letter to New York Times stating that he will detest from bombing if they were to publish his manifesto named Industrial Society and its future. The writing style followed in the manifesto was identified by his brother and sister- in- law which made the inquiry pretty easy. The phrase "cool-headed logician" was peculiar to Ted Kaczynski and was identified by his brother. Careful analysis of all literary works can reveal such hidden specialties of an author, which are to be captured correctly to represent the author characteristic. Authorship analysis aims at this type of analysis.

To begin with scientific studies, it has been used, to verify the authorship of certain plays of Shakespeare (Malone, 1787) . This analysis was a part of finding answer to the questioned closeness of works by Christopher Marlowe and William Shakespeare. Later several works were done on the same problem to prove the authorship of the disputed works. Similarly a statistical analysis was conducted by Scholar Kenneth Greyston and the statistician Gustav Herdan, in 1959–1960, to study the vocabulary usage of the contributors of Bible:The New Testament. A radical change in traditional approach of authorship analysis was observed in the methodologies followed by Mosteller and Wallace in 1964 to attribute authorship of the disputed federalist paper. Federalist papers were written as a part of swaying the population in NewYork to endorse the U.S Constitution in 1787-1788. Alexander Hamilton, John Jay and James Madison were the contributors of the paper comprising of 77 short essays. Later this together with 8 other essays pertaining the same area were compiled to form a book and was published in 1788. Out of 85 articles, 51 were written by Hamilton, 5 by John Jay, Madison wrote 14 papers and 3 papers were contributed by Madison and Hamilton. But there was an uncertainty regarding the authorship of 12 papers and it was doubted to be that of either Madison or Hamilton (Fung, 2003).Various analyses were conducted using Federalist paper as the data set. From then onwards methods for authorship attribution were rather computational than computer aided. The discussion so far dealt with the literary works. But the analysis of authorship finds its widespread applicability in several realms of real world scenario and hence procured a great scope of research.

As a part of curbing the spread of illegal postings including terrorism through cyber space, a research initiative named Dark Web Project has been undertaken by University of Arizona. They aim at establishing an immune intelligent system tolerant to the illicit content in the web as well as identifying such contents from web (Yang et al., 2012). The same strategy can be followed in identifying online fraudulence like impersonations and phishing sites.

The areas where finding the author of a document is very crucial, as in the case where language is used as evidence, make room for the need of automating the whole process of authorship analysis which is usually done manually by a linguist. It has been proved that suicide note classification using machine learning methods outperformed the decision of mental health professionals in predicting the forgery associated with suicide notes (Pestian et al, 2010). American Academy of Matrimonial Lawyers

Figure 1. Problem areas of authorship analysis

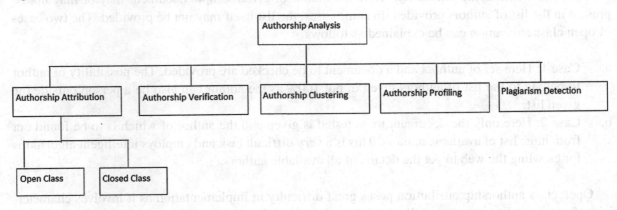

now accept electronic communication as evidence as per law. These all point to the urgency of a fully automated intelligent authorship analysis system that eases the tasks of linguists in identifying the real author of a document and also improve the accuracy of identification.

Background

Authorship Analysis can be divided into five major areas namely

- Authorship Attribution
  - Closed Class
  - Open Class
- Authorship Verification
- Authorship Clustering or Authorship Collaboration
- Authorship Profiling
- Plagiarism Detection (Zhao, 2007)

Authorship Attribution

This involves finding the author of given sample of text. The author may be one among set of authors given or it can be any possible author. Based on this, the problem can be sub divided into two areas namely closed class and open class (Zhao, 2007).

Closed class authorship attribution: Here the authors need to be found out from a set of given authors. The given sample document is authored by one of the authors in the given list of authors. Closed class attribution can be

a. Binary Authorship Attribution: Out of the two available candidates we need to identify the correct author of the unknown document

b. Multi-class authorship attribution: Here more candidate authors will be provided and we are supposed to find out the possible author for a given unknown document. (Halliday et al., 1965)

Open class authorship attribution: Here the author of given sample document may or may not be present in the list of authors provided. In some cases, the list itself may not be provided. The two cases of open class attribution can be explained as follows

a. Case 1: Here set of authors and a document to be checked are provided. The possibility of author to belong to the list of authors given in not 100% as the author can also be a person outside the given list.
b. Case 2: Here only the document to be tested is given and the author of which is to be found out from huge list of available authors. This is a very difficult task and employs intelligent algorithms for crawling the web to get the details of all available authors.

Open class authorship attribution poses great difficulty in implementation as it involves characterizing features of an author as well as another class featuring "not-the -author". This second class is very difficult to represent as it involves many characteristics not depictive of an author, which means a combination of various characteristics of all other authors. Formation of such a class is a difficult task.

Based on the area of application, authorship attribution can again be classified into traditional authorship attribution and non-traditional authorship attribution (Zhao, 2007).

Traditional authorship attribution: It deals mainly with solving controversies relating to literary works. The same works as has been done on the works of Shakespeare and Marlowe. Here more manual work is required for the analysis and purely statistical methods have been employed so far.

Non Traditional authorship attribution: It deals mainly with computational methods for detecting the author of a document and employs machine learning algorithms and alternations of existing classification algorithms. These are particularly suitable for finding the authorship of forensic documents and other short texts. Less works have been performed in finding the authorship of short documents.

Authorship Verification

This is a process of verifying or confirming whether a particular document is authored by a claimed author. Here also we can define two major cases of verification as follows

Case 1: This is the case where the authorship of a document by a single author in question is either accepted or rejected (Van, 2004). Thus the sample consists of several previous works by the author and comparison of questioned document is made with these samples and is confirmed to be that by the author if it satisfies certain threshold criteria.

Case 2: This case points to a scenario where, we are provided with the sample documents of suspected author as well as several document sample of a set of other authors. Thus the authorship is confirmed based on the similarity exhibited by the sample document with style of all authors given in the set of authors. If the document similarity with the style as that of the suspected author outperforms all other author's style, then authorship can be confirmed (Iqbal et al., 2010).

Authorship verification is the most challenging problem area in the field of authorship analysis and the work from the part of the research community is less in this case (Koppel & Schler, 2004).

Authorship Clustering or Authorship Collaboration

Authorship Clustering refers to the process of finding out whether a given document is singly authored or a contribution of multiple authors (Graham et al., 2005). This can be identified by comparing different segments of the documents to analyze its style. If the document is stylistically similar throughout, then it is singly authored otherwise multi-authored. Both unsupervised (Akiva & Koppel, 2012) and supervised (Koppel & Schler, 2004) methods have been employed for clustering a multi- authored document.

Authorship Profiling

Authorship profiling analyzes the socio-linguistic feature of a document and then infers details like gender, native language, age, location, personality pertaining to the author. This finds relevance in the field of forensic linguistics, security issues in cyber world and commercial settings (Argamon et al., 2009). The process resides to the assumption that people belonging to the different genre type and socio-linguistic conditions resorts to different ways of language usage. The identification of these features can be helpful in cases of crime identification.

Plagiarism Detection

This is included optionally as a part of authorship analysis. It exhibits its applicability in the area of academics (Zhao, 2007) . Plagiarism detection checks for the authenticity of the authorship claimed in the case of academic related articles. Apart from the analysis of literary works and other documents, plagiarism detection deals mainly with documents of formal nature and hence may not reflect the original style of author but can be influenced by the review of an article by scholars. Thus can be used only find the copy and paste strategy followed by the authors.

Here we will be discussing about the existing methods of authorship analysis and all the drawbacks and challenges involved in this area. The chapter focuses on highlighting the importance of authorship analysis in providing measures that can curb online fraudulence and spread of illegal propaganda via online media. The chapter is divided into different sections that describe procedure followed in authorship analysis, challenges faced by existing methods in this area, future research directions and conclusion.

PROCEDURES OF AUTHORSHIP ANALYSIS

The major steps involved in the process of authorship analysis can be listed down as follows (Zheng et al., 2006).

1. Message Collection
2. Feature Extraction
3. Model Generation
4. Author Identification

Figure 2. Procedures of authorship analysis

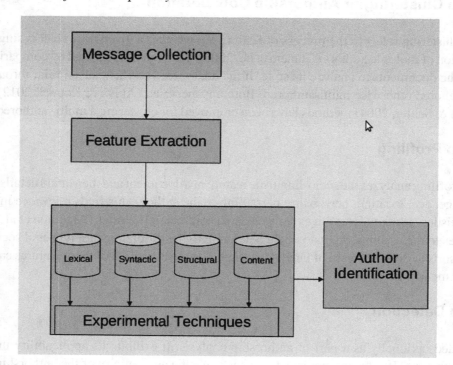

Message Collection

The process of message collection is characterized by collecting all relevant articles capable of providing an accurate author profile. This includes literary works in the case of traditional authorship attributes and other relevant documents like personal notes in the case of forensic investigations. Availability of the documents varies with authors. The message collection part is easy in case of authorship analysis of literary works. This is due to the availability of long texts and more texts. But at the same time this part becomes a challenge when it comes to crime document investigations like analyzing threat notes, analysis of suicidal notes etc.

Obtaining a standard test bed for authorship analysis is a real challenge. But there are several test corpuses, that have been used effectively by many for authorship analysis. Below mentioned is some of the commonly used data set.

Reuters Corpus Volume 1 (RCV1): It is a corpus for English language comprising of 800,000 newswire stories. It has been used for research purpose including text categorization as well as Authorship identification. The texts in the corpus are small thus facilitating the testing of analysis methods applicable for short texts as in the case of forensic linguistics, E-mail messages. In (Houvardas & Stamatatos, 2006) (Khmelev & Teahan, 2003) (Madigan et al., 2005) this corpus has been used as data set.

TREC- Data: It is a collection of newswire articles in which many of the articles contain the author information provided in its meta data. In (Zhao & Zobel, 2005) this has been mentioned as a challenging corpus as here the authors might use varying style as each author may write both features and reviews.

Algorithm for collecting data from Internet: (Rygl & Horák, 2011) describes an algorithm for collecting data from internet and saving it in database. The algorithm is aimed at accelerating the ease of obtaining online documents for authorship analysis and thus improving the accuracy of machine learning algorithms. This algorithm has been developed as a part of ART (Authorship Recognition Tool).

The Writing Sample Database: It includes samples collected from about 98 persons including males and females of age group 18 to 49 (Chaski, 1997).

PAN Corpus: This corpus primarily provided for authorship identification consists of 189 documents in 3 different languages Greek,English and Spanish. The method followed in (Halvani et al., 2013) considers this as the corpus for identification task.

Literary Works: Many analyses use the historical plays and works by famous authors as collection. Shakespeare plays, BIBLE, Federalist papers, and plays by other authors include the literary works commonly used.

Feature Extraction

Feature extraction is the underpinning of the whole process of authorship analysis. The accuracy of identification depends mainly on the features selected. This renders feature selection a good scope of research. Authorship analysis experiments focus on the different types of features selected for defining the author characteristics. Based on the previous works conducted in this area, we are providing a general classification of feature sets.

Feature sets are mainly divided into following categories

1. Lexical features
2. Syntactic features
3. Character features
4. Semantic features
5. Application-specific features

Lexical Features

The lexical features are token based features and they are of two types: word based and character based. It takes into account the number of times a particular word is used by an author or number of characters per word, number of character per sentence and so on. Word-length and sentence length are also considered as a feature (Abbasi & Chen, 2005). Vocabulary richness of an author is another important trait. Lexical features are also characterized by features formed by word-n grams and word elongations. This feature also focuses on the identification of, an author, based on the common mistakes (spelling) made by him. But this feature can be used only in the case where text length is greater than 1000 words, thus not suitable for short texts in forensic linguistics. But its use accompanied by other rich features provides good result (Stamatatos et al., 1999).

Syntactic Features

Syntactic features mainly include function words, word roots, punctuations (Abbasi & Chen, 2005), parts-of-speech, chunks, sentences and phrase structure, rewrite rule frequencies followed by an author (Stamatatos, 2009).Unlike in ordinary text classification, where function words are discarded, in authorship analysis it is of much importance. This is because function words usage is a unique feature associated with an author as it is done unconsciously by each author (Stamatatos et al., 1999). Most of the researchers have relied on this method as an excellent feature set. The success of function words as feature set has been well illustrated in (Argamon & Chen, 2005) (Zhao & Zobel, 2005). The usage of function word finds its wide applicability in the case of forensic linguistics. Challenge lies in selecting the function words to be used for analysis.

Character Features

Features defined at the character level also find a widespread applicability as feature set. This includes character n-grams, usage of special characters, alphabetical characters, digit characters, upper case and lower case character usage frequency. The usage of character based feature set offers various advantages as this feature set is also capable of capturing lexical information as well as some sort of contextual information. It is highly resistant to noises as misspelled versions of a word produce common character n-grams. N-Gram is a component comprising of 'n' successive characters. The n-grams used for analysis can be of fixed length as well as variable length. This feature also enables to identify common mistake made by an author (Stamatatos, 2009). The successful implementation of authorship analysis with character feature has been illustrated in (Kjell et al., 1994) .

Semantic Features

Semantic features mainly deal with structural aspect of sentence. It can be word structure at paragraph level or message level or it can be technical structure like font size, font color, embedded images and hyper-links (Abbasi & Chen, 2005) . These features consider synonyms of a particular term and also terms used in association with certain phrases. This feature varies with each author. An author may have a characteristic semantics of his own. The identification of such features can enable easy tracking of author of a particular document. The experiments conducted in (Gamon, 2004) points to the fact that the semantic features together with lexical and syntactic feature can effectively improve the accuracy of analysis.

Application-Specific Features

These are features that rely on context based usage of style. This is of much relevance in the case of email mining. But this cannot be a best feature as documents written by two different authors on same domain can be more similar than two documents belonging to different domains written by same author. But still if the candidate documents available for a particular author is based on same thematic area this method can be efficient in identifying context specific keywords associated with an author (Stamatatos, 2009).

Once the features have been formulated, our major task is concentrated on finding the best feature from a given set of features. Feature extraction need to be performed. The general observation is that accuracy kept increasing as more number of features was used. But the performance degraded as number of features increased beyond a certain limit (De Vel et al., 2001). This is due to the effect of overfitting. Thus we must resort to dimensionality reduction for better results by getting rid of the defects.

Dimensionality reduction aims at selecting the best features out of the several numbers of features available. For this, either we can follow an exhaustive search or heuristic search. But exhaustive search becomes less applicable in the case of large feature set. Dimensionality reduction can be implemented by means of machine learning approaches namely Principle component analysis (Abbasi & Chen, 2006), Genetic algorithm (De Vel et al., 2001), ID3, Naive- Bayes, Selecting the most significant n-grams (Houvardas & Stamatatos, 2006). PCA outperformed all methods in dimensionality reduction in majority of experiments. Thus it is often chosen for reducing the feature set.

Model Generation

This step aims at creating a framework using the feature set formed after dimensionality reduction. The methods followed include statistical, computational and machine learning approaches.

Statistical Methods

Simple statistics: Here simple statistics of writing pattern were observed. These measures involve word-length frequencies, sentence length frequencies, vocabulary statistics, number of words used once, twice etc. The word-length frequency determines stylistic similarity by adopting the method described by T. C. Mendenhall (Mendenhall, 1887).

$$1 - \frac{\sum_{i=1}^{\infty}(W_i^{d_1} - W_i^{d_2})}{2} \tag{1}$$

Here d1 and d2 refers to two documents and wi refers to the frequency of occurrence of words with length i in the document. The summation of difference in the frequency count of words with different lengths is calculated and is taken as a similarity measure. The above formula can be modified by changing word length to sentence length and find similarity in terms of length of sentence in each document. Vocabulary richness is another statistical measure that is usually found out by calculating Simpson index (Simpson, 1949) .

$$\sum(W_i)\left(\frac{i}{tot}\right)\left(\frac{i-1}{tot-1}\right) \tag{2}$$

Here Wi refers to the number of words with frequency i and tot denotes the total number of words in the document.

Cusum(Cumulative Sum Technique): This method finds its applicability in case of small texts for authorship clustering. The method considers the frequencies of various writing habits followed by an author. (Farringdon, 2004) describes the application of cusum technique by choosing a text content of the author and then finding the difference between the sentence length [in terms of number of words] of each sentence with the average sentence length of the text sample. The cumulative sum of the calculation is plotted as a graph. The graph displays how the writing differs from average. Then words of common habit are made use of. Here 'common habit' may refer to words starting with vowel or it can be n-lettered words or any distinguishing characteristics. The same strategy followed for plotting the sentence length graph is followed here also. That is, average word count of 'similar habit words' is found out and then the difference between the average and count of 'same habit words' in each sentence is found out. Then cumulative sum is calculated and plotted in graph. These measures are also plotted cumulatively. Finally these two graphs are scaled together to find whether they overlap or not. If the entire sample is written by same author the graphs should be overlapping, otherwise it will not. But the method faces several criticisms as the method requires editing sentences that are too long and too short. This might affect the writing style of an author (Haan, 1998).

Chi Square: This method is supposed to give more accurate results in comparison with word length distribution and sentence length distribution (Yang & Pedersen, 1997). It is a statistical method where we find the difference between frequencies observed value and expected value. The value x2 is given by

$$x^2 = \sum \frac{(O-E)^2}{E} \tag{3}$$

Here O refers to observed frequency and E refers to expected frequency (Butler, 1985). The method proceeds by finding out statistical significance which gives us the extent to which null hypothesis is false or the extent to which our hypothesis is true. But there can always be a risk of proving the null hypothesis false but our own hypothesis may not be true. To ensure the correctness we can always set a threshold value above which will satisfy for a particular hypothesis to be true (Witte, 2012). This method is used in most of the modern applications including text categorization and is considered to be simple and less time consuming compared to other methods.

Computational Methods

Principal Component Analysis: It is a computational method which has found its application in the field of authorship analysis. PCA has been successfully implemented to find out the authorship of documents in (Jamak et al., 2012). The method is used to select the most suitable feature patterns capable of representing the author write print. The result proved that the method was successful in finding out unique author characteristics based on counting the number of short words per paragraph. Though the method finds application in many areas, it cannot be claimed to be flawless as pointed in (Hoover, 2001) where, D.L Hoover infers that PCA is not suitable for Authorship Attribution in the case of more than two authors, The accuracy of the method is determined by the selection of optimum number of common words or function words and that varies according to the author. This is most problematic in the case of anonymous authors. But the method can be modified adequately to suit the application and thus we can also enhance the accuracy.

Markov chain: Markov model relies on the probability of nth word/character which is determined from previous n-1 words/characters. First order Markov chains have been used successfully in case of authorship analysis. This is applied at character level. The method involves plotting the transition matrix that contains the transition for one character to the next and the characters being the features. Thus when a new document for which the authorship is to be determined arrives, it is checked for the transition characteristic of its characters and based on that the best author is chosen)(Zhao, 2007). But Markov model has a problem of occurrence of zero probability which is observed in a case where a sentence does not contain a particular bi-gram. The problem is even worsened in the case of tri-gram, quadri-grams and so on. Thus we need to apply some smoothing techniques to deal with the zero probability issue, by assigning some non-zero value for an observed zero probability bi-gram or tri-gram. The common methods include add-one smoothing, Witten-Bell discounting, Good Turing discounting and backoff (Care, 2003).

Machine Learning Approaches

The later advances in the field of authorship analysis throws light to the usage of machine learning approaches like C4.5(Zheng et al., 2006),Neural Networks(Zheng et al., 2006), SVM (Zheng et al., 2006), Kullback-Leibler Divergence(Zhao, 2007). The approach obtains its result by applying various classification techniques on given sample based on some set of predefined metrics. C4.5 algorithm is a modified version of decision tree induction algorithm. The method is rule based and they follow greedy approach. Decision trees are self explanatory and the algorithms aim at generating trees from the leaf of which we can identify different classes. But in (Quinlan, 1993) the oversensitivity to training set, attributes and noise has been specified as its disadvantage. Neural networks on the other hand are classification methodology that is based on the strategy of back propagation. Back propagation aims at learning from training samples by processing them iteratively and comparing the actual result with observed result and thereby reducing the mean squared error between the expected value and obtained value. Kullback-Leibler divergence technique measures the divergence between different author styles and the style of the questioned document. Authorship is attributed to that author whose style has minimum divergence with that of the document. Though the computational cost associated with this method is much less compared to that of SVM and other Bayesian methods, the method is less effective in the case of large document sets. SVM is a classification model proposed by Vapnik (Vapnik, 2000) and is based on Structural Risk Minimization. The method has been successfully implemented in various classification problems. Of all these methods SVM (support vector machine) is supposed to give more accurate results. Thus SVM is most popularly used for model generation in authorship analysis.

Author Identification

Once the model has been generated, the final task is to attribute authorship to correct author. This phase is the final part of whole process of authorship analysis, which gives as result the author of document. Attribution can be by three means: Profile based methods, instance based approaches and hybrid approaches (Stamatatos, 2009).

Profile Based Method

Here author features are collected from different documents and are combined to form a single corpus representative of feature of an author. This corpus is then used as input into a model which selects the corresponding author of an unknown document. They can be either

Probabilistic Models

The model attempts to find the probability of a document to be written by all candidate authors and authorship is attributed to that author for which the probability is maximum. A successful implementation of this sort of model was accomplished in (Peng et al.,2004) where an extension of Naive Bayes algorithm has been used.

Compression Models

Here the documents known to be authored by a particular author i is collected together to form a single file xi. This is made to undergo a compression algorithm to obtain an output C(xi). In order to determine the authorship of an unknown document x, it is added to xi of all authors. Then again compression algorithm is applied to the new file to get C(xi +x) for each author. Then the difference value d(x,xi) is calculated for each author as C(xi +x)-C(xi). Authorship can be attributed to that author for which similarity is maximum, which means difference is minimum. The factor d(x,xi) gives the difference in the bitwise size of the compressed files C(xi) and C(xi +x)(Zhao,2007). The compression method produces results whose accuracy is determined by the length of the file. Thus more the length more is the accuracy. In (Goodman, 2002) reasonable criticisms regarding the method, regarding its slowness in producing the results and lesser accuracy compared to Naive Bayes Technique, has been pointed out.

CNG and Variants

Common N-Gram based methods are very popular among the various profile based methods. In (Hassan & Chaurasia, 2012) a method has been defined where we consider the most frequently occurring n-grams. The similarity measure can be defined as the difference in the frequency of ith n-gram of the training data and corresponding n-gram of unknown text. This is calculated for all i's . Thus overall similarity can be obtained from this measure. Another measure has been defined in (Kešelj et al., 2003) . But all these methods face a general problem of class imbalance. That is the methods prove to be inefficient in the case where the number of candidate documents for each author in the training sample is not equal.

Instance Based Method:

Here each separate document contributes individually to the classification model, rather than forming a single corpus. The model considers each document separately and a vector associated with each document is formulated. These vectors together formulate a model, with which a novel document can be analyzed. The method triggers for the need to break a single document (if it is the only one available) into many units for training the classifier. They can be of following types

Vector Space Models

Here the available documents and the questioned documents will be represented as vectors. The similarity measure refers to the angle between the two vectors (vector representing training document and vector representing the questioned document). The lesser the angle the more will be the similarity. The authorship decision is made based on the similarity of the vector spaces formulated. It includes the models like SVM and other machine learning approaches where texts and styles can be represented as vector models. The details of the methods can be found in (Sebastiani, 2002). But these models also suffer from class imbalance problem, which affects the analysis in the case of forensic documents.

Similarity-Based Models

The method finds similarity between two documents by comparing the pairwise similarity features of a questioned text and available training documents. Then the best similar document is found out by implementing nearest neighbor algorithm. A method named 'Delta' has been implemented successfully in (Burrows,2002). The method proceeds by finding the z-distribution associated with suitable function words chosen and then finds the z-score of these function words by calculating the difference of the frequencies of these words from norm. Finally the authorship is attributed to that author whose document style bears minimum delta measure with the questioned document. The method suits long literary works than short texts.

Meta-Learning Models

One of the best known Meta learning method is the one proposed by (Koppel et al.,2007) called 'Unmasking'. The method aims at eliminating the features that are most relevant in distinguishing an author's style and then subjecting the entire set of documents for cross-validation. It checks for the speed of degradation of accuracy of prediction. The rate of degradation is observed to be fast in the case where all documents are written by same author while slow in the case of documents written by different authors. The method finds success in long literary texts while showing reduced effectiveness in the case of short texts.

Hybrid Approach

Combines the features of both instance based and profile based methods. Feature vector of each documents of an author is formulated. Then average is taken to form a single vector associated with an author. This is used for comparison against the vector associated with unknown text.

The above mentioned are the methods for implementing authorship analysis. But these methods suffer from problems which include lack of successful implementations suitable for short documents of forensic nature. These limitations can be summarized as follows

CHALLENGES IN AUTHORSHIP ANALYSIS

There are several challenges associated with authorship analysis. The analysis of authorship is based on stylometric techniques, which in turn is marked by several methodological issues, problems related to linguistic documents (Juola, 2006), and problems pertaining evaluation of analysis.

Methodological Issues

The stylometric analysis faces a problem of less acceptability by many researchers like Rudman, who point out that the demerits associated with the technique is more compared to its advantages. The rating made in terms of accuracy does not satisfy the required range of credibility. This interpretation results from following considerations.

The writing style of an individual is influenced by so many features and dependent on factors like age, gender, educational qualification, social background and it may change over time. This poses a challenge in authorship identification (Brennan & Greenstadt, 2009) . This actually paves way for methods in identifying the characteristics of author, as one can infer the social status or educational background or nativity of a person from his writing style. But this turns out to be a disadvantage in the cases of formulation of an author profile. Author profile can be formed by combining all available articles of an author. If this combination involves articles written in different style, then it will affect the accuracy.

Special care need to be taken while collecting documents for authorship analysis. The documents should correctly portray the real writing habits of an author. This can be guaranteed only if the documents pertaining to an author is selected in such a way that it belongs to different domains in which he has laid his hands on and does not concentrate on one particular subject. If the documents collected deals with discussion regarding one particular subject, then an article by the same author belonging to different subject may be wrongly attributed. Similarly article written by different author, but discussing the same subject may be wrongly attributed to this author.

Sample that represents the features for identifying an author has another challenge of containing quoting or usages by other authors. For example an author may site wordings by different author or he may even use sentences of a different user. This can affect the credibility of system developed using such sample collection. Many authorship analysis studies conducted so far, refines the sample by removing such quotings from article. This demands for an extra task of editing the text but can improve the accuracy.

Another technical difficulty associated with sample collection can be outlined as follows. As mentioned previously in section 1, problem caused by open-class authorship attribution still remains unsolved. This is because it is impossible to search through all possible documents by an author. The case 1 scenario of open class authorship attribution requires classes for set of possible authors given in the list and another class that represents "not any one of the authors mentioned in the list". This class is very difficult to formulate as it should include all possible author characteristics available. If this class is not correctly formulated, then there can be a chance of wrong attribution of authorship to an author in the list. Similar is the case 2 scenario of open class attribution where we are given a single piece of document with no author list. Here we need to search through all author characteristics. This sort of general class formulation poses great difficulty in authorship attribution.

Availability of style modifiers and other word applications also pose challenge to authorship analysis as the style of an author may be modified by the application thus giving a style or idiolect which is no longer similar to that of the author.

Issues in Forensic Linguistics

Disadvantages associated with forensic documents are many. The basic difference between criminal authorship and literary authorships is that the type of texts in case of criminal authorships is short, incidental, spontaneous, addressed to a limited audience, production limited by space and time and emotional. While literary texts tend to be long, non-spontaneous, addressed to a big audience and planned. This poses a complexity in finding out authors associated with criminal texts.

The field of stylometry faces challenges including lack of credibility and lack of admissibility, especially in the area of forensic linguistics. The credibility is based on the accuracy of prediction. The method used for prediction should be applicable in the case of forensic documents. The accuracy in terms of long literary works would not suffice for this (Juola, 2006). The credibility of attribution is also backed by the understanding of the method used for analysis. For example if the analysis is based on some vector based methodology like SVM, its explanation in terms of word vectors and its planes would not be satisfactory for non technical audience for whom the explanation should be in terms of words and the similarity criteria used for analysis. Such an explanation would provide with ample reasons for supporting the attribution of authorship when used as evidence in courts.

Similar is the problem of admissibility. The jurisdictions in court of laws should meet up the standards laid down by the legal system prevailing in that court. Thus the authorship attribution techniques used should also abide by those standards. Only then can the attribution foster the legal admissibility.

Apart from all the above there can be cases of attacks against authorship analysis. The attacks mainly come in two forms namely obfuscation attacks and imitation attacks. Obfuscation attacks hide the real identity of an author. Thus tracking the source becomes difficult (Brennan & Greenstadt, 2009). Imitation attacks aim at tarnishing the image of an author by purposefully imitating the style followed by that author. Thus the author's identity is misused to propagate the concept of attacker.

Lack of Standard Test Bed for Evaluation

Every technique implemented need to be evaluated for its accuracy and scalability. In case of authorship analysis, there is a challenge in the evaluation of the technique as there is a lack of standard test bed. The test corpus formulated so far has been based on particular application, thus making it application-specific. For example, the work done to evaluate the closeness of stylistic features of Marlowe and Shakespeare, demands collection of those documents. These documents are to be compiled manually to suit the application. The limitation is most evident especially in the field of forensic linguistics. The techniques employed in multiple dataset poses problem in comparison of different methodologies. This situation causes difficulty in making a decision regarding the best attribution method. Availability of a standard bench mark is essential for contributing to the evaluation of the scalability of technique developed beyond trivial cases (Zhao, 2007).

FUTURE RESEARCH DIRECTIONS

There is a broad spectrum of area where authorship analysis holds significant relevance. These areas call for a full-fledged research in Authorship Analysis. The automation of Authorship Analysis can result in fruitful applications in numerous areas. The following discussion outlines the common areas of applicability of authorship analysis.

Forensic Linguistics

Authorship analysis finds wide spread application in the fields where language serves as evidences (Teresa & Coulthard, 2011). Language serves as evidence in the cases where we are seeking for authorship of literary works as well as criminal authorship. The importance of language in these fields has been explained in section 1.The previous section points to the fact that its applicability in forensic analysis faces major challenges. But current scenario with increased online fraudulence demands the need of automation of authorship analysis. Further, analyzing documents have proved to be very crucial in finding the real criminals behind different forgeries and fraudulence. (Chaski, 1997) describes about several cases where finding out the author of the document turned out to be the crucial evidence. The examples mentioned include Unabomber case, death of Michael Hunter, prosecutions involving forged checks, forged suicidal notes, threatening letters.

Web Security

Authorship analysis proves to be a successful measure for identifying the authors of illegal postings in web. This can in some way contribute to control the drastic spread of online terrorism and cyber-crimes. Propagating pornography, offensive postings, misleading sites etc cause security breach and hinder the inherent privacy of users. Biometric features like footprint, thumb impression, and other physical features prove to be evidences in the case of real world crime scenario. But in the case of crimes over internet, an effective mechanism to track real criminal is yet to be developed (Ma et al., 2014). "Dark web Project" is one such effort to prevent cyber terrorism. Works to curb the attacks on web by groups have been done to prevent phishing sites (Layton et al., 2012) . There is a recent trend of increased spam messages and increased traffic due to unsolicited emails. The e-mail facility has also been used to spread illegal propagandas. This can be put to control by computer forensics techniques. One such effective work has been illustrated in (Teng et al., 2004). Computer based attacks like spread of worms, viruses, and plagiarism of code etc poses threat to online- security. This can be dealt in with software forensic analysis. Authorship of such mails can be determined and hence the severity of damage can be controlled by tracking such sources. Authorship analysis techniques can be applied in such areas (Gray et al., 1997). Possible applications of authorship analysis in the area of cyber crime detection includes detection of fraudulent acts like online impersonation, to find out the author of text messages in mobile phone, possible solutions to curb Cyber security flaws etc (Teresa & Coulthard, 2011). Another application is to apply it to verify the authorship of emails and electronic messages (De Vel et al., 2001).

Identification of Socio Linguistic Characteristics

The applicability of authorship analysis can be extended from mere identification of author characteristics to identification of group characteristics. This includes identifying socio linguistic features from a document to get details about the author. These details consist of information like age, gender, nativity, educational qualifications and social background pertaining an author. Identification of social identity group is another important application of authorship analysis. This can be very much useful in the case of scientific collaborative networks where authors of same academic, or research interest can cooperate together to publish their ideas. Identification of group characteristics is very useful in this case (Booker, 2008). These characteristic identifications also support forensic investigations. Tracing the ethnicity of author, determining mother tongue of an author from a document, communication pattern recognition etc are applications where socio linguistic feature identification takes a major role. Determining the mental health of a person based on the language usage has also been a promising application of authorship analysis.

Determining Age of Document

This area is much controversial area and is based on assumption that a person's writing style changes over time. There will be change in the usage of vocabulary. A clear cut variation has been observed in the writing style followed by Shakespeare in his early writing as well as latest ones)(Zhao, 2007).The same has been observed for many authors. Thus authorship analysis can be used for identification of period of creation of an article. Similar is the change that takes place in the case of language. New terms and new usages can emerge over time and there will be new additions to the dictionary. Thus there will be variations in documents written in early days and recent documents. This area thus demands a great research scope.

CONCLUSION

The chapter deals with a brief description about what authorship analysis is. It can be summarized as an analysis carried out to find the real author of a document by analyzing the writing style of a person. The writing style followed by a person is reflected throughout his articles. This fact is exploited to formulate the style of a person from his existing documents. This style model is then checked against the style followed ion a new document. This is the strategy followed in the case of authorship attribution and verification. Authorship clustering aims at finding the multiple authors of a single document.

The analysis conducted here focuses mainly on the different authorship attribution methods. The chapter also discusses about the general challenges of authorship. Out of these issues, imitation attacks are the most challenging problem that is in search of a 'silver bullet'.

Most of the methods discussed here deal with text documents which are long and thus it is easy for analysis. But the methods that deal with documents that are short are less and not yet popular. Detailed study regarding these methods is to be conducted for the effective application in the field of forensic linguistics and crime investigations. The technique is based on stylometric analysis and the success depends on the selection of effective style markers which means an optimal feature set selection.

Though stylometric analysis faces several criticisms, the area of authorship analysis is of great relevance in today's scenario. This is because the field is marked by great research scope as can be understood from its immense applications. The automation of authorship analysis methods can ease the work of linguists. Handwriting recognition holds no more relevance when it comes to digital era. Further in some cases, style recognition can prove to be more efficient than finding out finger dexterity.

The relevance of the research in area is heightened by the recent research initiatives that focus on this area. These include ALIAS (Automated Linguistic Identification and Assessment System). The system developed software named ALIAS for forensic linguistic analysis. Considerable research is also being conducted by team lead by Dr. Hsinchun Chen of University of Arizona. EVL Lab, Centre for Forensic Linguistics (Aston University), and CLEF Conference and Labs of the Evaluation Forum also provide significant research contributions in this area. Thus authorship analysis and stylometry exhibits a wide scope of research.

REFERENCES

Abbasi, A., & Chen, H. (2006). Visualizing authorship for identification. In *Intelligence and Security Informatics* (pp. 60–71). Springer Berlin Heidelberg.

Abbasi, A., & Chen, H. (2005). Applying authorship analysis to extremist-group web forum messages. IEEE Intelligent Systems, 20(5), 67–75.

Akiva, N., & Koppel, M. (2012, August). *Identifying Distinct Components of a Multi-author Document* (pp. 205–209). EISIC.

Argamon, S., Koppel, M., Pennebaker, J. W., & Schler, J. (2009). Automatically profiling the author of an anonymous text. *Communications of the ACM, 52*(2), 119–123.

Argamon, S., & Levitan, S. (2005, June). Measuring the usefulness of function words for authorship attribution. In *Proceedings of the Joint Conference of the Association for Computers and the Humanities and the Association for Literary and Linguistic Computing*.

Booker, L. B. (2008). Finding identity group "fingerprints" in documents. In *Computational Forensics* (pp. 113–121). Springer Berlin Heidelberg.

Brennan, M. R., & Greenstadt, R. (2009, April). *Practical Attacks Against Authorship Recognition Techniques*. IAAI.

Burrows, J. (2002). 'Delta': A measure of stylistic difference and a guide to likely authorship. *Literary and Linguistic Computing, 17*(3), 267–287.

Butler, C. (1985). Article. *Statistics in Linguistics, 9*, 112–113.

Care, M. (2003). *Authorship Attribution: a Comparison of Three Methods*. (Doctoral dissertation). Universidade de Sheffield.

Chaski, C. E. (1997). Who wrote it? Steps toward a Science of Authorship Identification. *National Institute of Justice Journal, 233*, 15–22.

De Vel, O., Anderson, A., Corney, M., & Mohay, G. (2001). Mining e-mail content for author identification forensics. *SIGMOD Record, 30*(4), 55–64.

Farringdon, J. M. (2004). *How to be a Literary Detective: Authorship Attribution: A brief introduction to cusum analysis*. Available online at http://members. aol. com/qsums/QsumIntroduction. html

Fung, G. (2003, October). The disputed Federalist Papers: SVM feature selection via concave minimization. In *Proceedings of the 2003 Conference on Diversity in Computing* (pp. 42-46). ACM.

Gamon, M. (2004, August). Linguistic correlates of style: authorship classification with deep linguistic analysis features. In *Proceedings of the 20th international conference on Computational Linguistics* (p. 611). Association for Computational Linguistics.

Goodman, J. (2002). *Extended comment on language trees and zipping*. arXiv preprint cond-mat/0202383.

Graham, N., Hirst, G., & Marthi, B. (2005). Segmenting documents by stylistic character. *Natural Language Engineering*, *11*(4), 397–415.

Gray, A., Sallis, P., & MacDonell, S. (1997). *Software forensics: Extending authorship analysis techniques to computer programs*.

Grayston, K., & Herdan, G. (1959). The authorship of the Pastorals in the light of statistical linguistics. *New Testament Studies*, *6*(1), 1–15.

Haan, P. D. (1998). A review of 'analysing for authorship'. *Forensic Linguistics*, *5*, 69–76.

Halliday, M. A. K., McIntosh, A., & Strevens, P. (1965). *The linguistic sciences and language teaching* (pp. 5–6). Longmans.

Halvani, O., Steinebach, M., & Zimmermann, R. (2013). *Authorship Verification via k-Nearest Neighbor Estimation*.

Hassan, F. I. H., & Chaurasia, M. A. (2012). N-Gram Based Text Author Verification. *International Proceedings of Computer Science & Information Technology*, *36*.

Hoover, D. L. (2001). Statistical stylistics and authorship attribution: An empirical investigation. *Literary and Linguistic Computing*, *16*(4), 421–444.

Houvardas, J., & Stamatatos, E. (2006). N-gram feature selection for authorship identification. In Artificial Intelligence: Methodology, Systems, and Applications (pp. 77-86). Springer Berlin Heidelberg.

Iqbal, F., Khan, L. A., Fung, B., & Debbabi, M. (2010, March). E-mail authorship verification for forensic investigation. In *Proceedings of the 2010 ACM Symposium on Applied Computing* (pp. 1591-1598). ACM.

Jamak, A., Savatić, A., & Can, M. (2012). Principal component analysis for authorship attribution. *Business Systems Research*, *3*(2), 49–56.

Juola, P. (2006). Authorship attribution. Foundations and Trends in information *Retrieval, 1*(3), 233-334.

Kešelj, V., Peng, F., Cercone, N., & Thomas, C. (2003, August). N-gram-based author profiles for authorship attribution. In *Proceedings of the conference pacific association for computational linguistics, PACLING* (Vol. 3, pp. 255-264).

Khmelev, D. V., & Teahan, W. J. (2003, July). A repetition based measure for verification of text collections and for text categorization. In *Proceedings of the 26th annual international ACM SIGIR conference on Research and development in informaion retrieval* (pp. 104-110). ACM.

Kjell, B., Woods, W., & Frieder, O. (1994). Discrimination of authorship using visualization. *Information Processing & Management*, *30*(1), 141–150.

Koppel, M., & Schler, J. (2004, July). Authorship verification as a one-class classification problem. In *Proceedings of the twenty-first international conference on Machine learning* (p. 62). ACM.

Koppel, M., Schler, J., & Bonchek-Dokow, E. (2007). Measuring Differentiability: Unmasking Pseudonymous Authors. *Journal of Machine Learning Research*, *8*(6).

Layton, R., Watters, P., & Dazeley, R. (2012, October). Unsupervised authorship analysis of phishing webpages. In Communications and Information Technologies (ISCIT), 2012 International Symposium on (pp. 1104-1109). IEEE.

Ma, J., Li, Y., & Teng, G. (2014). CWAAP: An Authorship Attribution Forensic Platform for Chinese Web Information. *Journal of Software*, *9*(1), 11–19.

Madigan, D., Genkin, A., Lewis, D. D., Argamon, S., Fradkin, D., & Ye, L. (2005, June). Author identification on the large scale. In *Proc. of the Meeting of the Classification Society of North America*.

Malone, E. (1787). *A Dissertation on the three parts of King Henry VI., tending to shew that those plays were not written originally by Shakspeare*. Gale Ecco, Print Editions.

Mendenhall, T. C. (1887). The characteristic curves of composition. *Polar Science*, *11*, 237–246.

Mosteller, F., & Wallace, D. (1964). *Inference and disputed authorship: The Federalist*.

Peng, F., Schuurmans, D., & Wang, S. (2004). Augmenting naive Bayes classifiers with statistical language models. *Information Retrieval*, *7*(3-4), 317–345.

Pestian, J., Nasrallah, H., Matykiewicz, P., Bennett, A., & Leenaars, A. (2010). Suicide Note Classification Using Natural Language Processing: A Content Analysis. Biomedical informatics insights, 2010(3), 19-28.

Quinlan, J. R. (1993). *C4. 5: programs for machine learning* (Vol. 1). Morgan Kaufmann.

Rygl, J. (2013, January). *Determining Authorship of Anonymous Texts*. PhD thesis proposal, Masaryk University, (pp.2-3).

Rygl, J., & Horák, A. (2011). *A Framework for Authorship Identification in the Internet Environment*.

Sebastiani, F. (2002). Machine learning in automated text categorization. [CSUR]. *ACM Computing Surveys*, *34*(1), 1–47.

Simpson, E. H. (1949). Measurement of diversity. *Nature*.

Stamatatos, E. (2009). A survey of modern authorship attribution methods. *Journal of the American Society for Information Science and Technology*, *60*(3), 538–556.

Stamatatos, E., Fakotakis, N., & Kokkinakis, G. (1999, June). Automatic authorship attribution. In *Proceedings of the ninth conference on European chapter of the Association for Computational Linguistics* (pp. 158-164). Association for Computational Linguistics.

Teng, G. F., Lai, M. S., Ma, J. B., & Li, Y. (2004, August). E-mail authorship mining based on SVM for computer forensic. In *Proceedings of 2004 International Conference on Machine Learning and Cybernetics, 2004*. (Vol. 2, pp. 1204-1207). IEEE.

Teresa, M.T., & Coulthard, M. (2011, September). Forensic Plagiarism Detection and Authorship Attribution: on the linguists' achievements and the challenges for computerized analysis. *CLEF 2011 - PAN'5 2011 Lab Forensic Linguistics Panel*, 19-22.

Van Halteren, H. (2004, July). Linguistic profiling for author recognition and verification. In *Proceedings of the 42nd Annual Meeting on Association for Computational Linguistics* (p. 199). Association for Computational Linguistics.

Vapnik, V. (2000). *The nature of statistical learning theory*. Springer.

Witte, J. (2012) Author identification techniques, *Charter college, 4*:13-14.

Yang, M., Kiang, M., Chen, H., & Li, Y. (2012). Artificial immune system for illicit content identification in social media. *Journal of the American Society for Information Science and Technology, 63*(2), 256–269.

Yang, Y., & Pedersen, J. O. (1997, July). A comparative study on feature selection in text categorization. In ICML (Vol. 97, pp. 412-420).

Zhao, Y. (2007). *Effective authorship attribution in large document collections*. PhD thesis, School of Computer Science and Information Technology, RMIT University, Melbourne, Aus content analysis. Biomedical informatics insights 2010.3 (2010): 19.

Zhao, Y., & Zobel, J. (2005). Effective and scalable authorship attribution using function words. In *Information Retrieval Technology* (pp. 174–189). Springer Berlin Heidelberg.

Zhao, Y., & Zobel, J. (2005). Effective and scalable authorship attribution using function words. In *Information Retrieval Technology* (pp. 174–189). Springer Berlin Heidelberg.

Zheng, R., Li, J., Chen, H., & Huang, Z. (2006). A framework for authorship identification of online messages: Writing-style features and classification techniques. *Journal of the American Society for Information Science and Technology, 57*(3), 378–393.

ADDITIONAL READING

Baayen, H., Van Halteren, H., & Tweedie, F. (1996). Outside the cave of shadows: Using syntactic annotation to enhance authorship attribution. *Literary and Linguistic Computing, 11*(3), 121–132.

Bratley, P., & Lusignan, S. (1978). Computers and the Humanities. *Computer, 11*(8), 6–7.

Love, H. (2002). *Attributing authorship: an introduction*. Cambridge University Press.

KEY TERMS AND DEFINITIONS

Authorship Analysis: It is the process of examining documents to determine the stylistic details underlying the document and hence inferring about the characteristics of the author of document in order to attribute the authorship to a particular author or to confirm the authenticity of a claimed authorship.

Authorship Attribution: This involves finding the author of given sample of text. The author may be one among set of authors given or it can be any possible author.

Authorship Clustering: It refers to the process of finding out whether a given document is singly authored or a contribution of multiple authors.

Authorship Profiling: It is the analysis of a document to infer the socio-linguistic features of the author and to arrive at a conclusion regarding the details like gender, native language, age, location, personality pertaining to the author.

Authorship Verification: This is a process of verifying or confirming whether a particular document is authored by a claimed author.

Class Imbalance Problem: The disadvantage associated with attribution methods, which results in need for equal number of sample documents in the test set as well as training set.

Forensic Linguistics: Area of crime investigation where language is evidence, thus involves analysis documents like threat notes, suicidal notes, ransom notes etc.

Idiolect: Distinct and unique way of usage of language by a person. It varies with each person.

Socio linguistic features: These details consist of information like age, gender, nativity, educational qualifications and social background pertaining an author.

Stylometry: Branch of study that aims at studying the features or characteristics associated with an author by analyzing the documents written by him.

Chapter 11
The Need for a Dualist Application of Public and Private Law in Great Britain Following the Use of "Flame Trolling" During the 2011 UK Riots:
A Review and Model

Ivan Mugabi
Centre for Research into Online Communities and E-Learning Systems, UK

Jonathan Bishop
Centre for Research into Online Communities and E-Learning Systems, UK

ABSTRACT

Since time immemorial, the legal systems of Great Britain have often been spoken of highly as pinnacles of democracy. However, the split between criminal law and tort law have often caused problems where the police has often focused on the prosecution of people in poverty and where only the wealthy can afford to use the system. This chapter discusses the extent and limitations of existing measures to tackle computer-related crime, particularly with regards to the abusive kind of Internet Trolling, namely "flame trolling." The chapter recommends further research to establish whether it should be the case that in a society based on dualism that criminal and civil cases should be held at the same time, and that in both instances those being accused of an offence or tort should be allowed to bring a counter-claim. It is discussed that in such a system the cases that would be brought are where there is a clear victim who had no part in the offence against them, such as murder, rape, theft and burglary, which are usually carefully planned and orchestrated acts.

DOI: 10.4018/978-1-4666-8345-7.ch011

INTRODUCTION

It is often said that Great Britain has one of the best legal systems in the world. At present it is made up of three legal jurisdictions, namely the law of England & Wales, Welsh law and Scottish law. Following the 2014 Scottish independence referendum there were calls for a separate jurisdiction of English law as it became clear there would be more powers devolved to Scotland. This might lead to the jurisdiction of England & Wales being broken up, with devolved parliaments in each nation, meaning Acts of the UK Parliament will only be used for issues that affect all nations. All of these existing legal systems have a wide range of similarities, since they are based on a statute and case law model which is a typical feature of common law patronage and therefore sharing the same Supreme Court.

Unfortunately for legislative democracies of this kind, taking account of the role of technology and the effect it has can take a long time. Although it could be argued that existing law is capable of dealing with offences arising out of social media (Bishop, 2010; Bishop, 2013a), the lack of the right for the judiciary to fill the gaps where public law (i.e. statute) does not provide for an act to be an offence causes problems. That is because it takes a long time for the law to update to take account of changes relating to e-democracies. But even the judiciary are not immune to problems, as judges may make decisions in absence of complete information leading to miscarriages of justice. If the courts had the power to fill in the gaps in the law, then there would need to me an easy means for elected politicians to tell these judges what decision they would be expected to make if a law already existed. This would avoid the creation of a democratic deficit where unelected judges, who lack the legitimacy that elected politicians have, could make decisions without being accountable for them.

In many cases legal action is commenced by the authorities for it to then be lost on grounds of technicalities in absence of existing law. An example is issues arising about whether precise set of acts constitutes an 'offence' rather than the pivotal argument resolving on whether it was a 'crime' from the point of view of both the complainant and the court, regardless of whether a law exists or does not exist. The former is possible under the European Convention of Human Rights, even with the provision of Article 6 giving the right to a fair trial without being charged with a crime that didn't exist when it was committed. This was vividly exemplified in the case of Pinochet v Bow Street Metropolitan Stipendiary Magistrate and Others (ex parte Pinochet Ugarte) (No. 3) [2000] 1 A.C. 147; [1999] 2 W.L.R. 827; [1999] 2 All E.R. In this case the applicant's acts were offences in the literal sense but have not been incriminated until the 9 September 1988, when section 134 of the Criminal Justice Act 1988 came into force.

Essentially, an efficient legal system ought to be perceived based on the notion of injury suffered by the complainant as the criterion for a crime to exist (i.e. malum reus), which is called a 'bleasure' (Bishop, 2011a; Bishop, 2014a; Bishop, 2014b; Bishop, 2014f). Such an interpretation of the European Convention on Human Rights should only be allowed providing that it does not impinge on the Convention and other rights of the accused and thus cause injury to them through being denied their rights. The dualistic approach in the UK ought to be flexible in allowing merits of monism approach as with private law rather than a strictly dualistic designed interpretation of statutory provisions which largely concentrates on the contextual and literal interpretation of 'offences'. The proposed approach would be more efficient and would secure greater justice for those who feel trespassed against such as through being harmed by online postings of defamatory statements, acts of assaults and other forms of trespass to person.

BACKGROUND

The UK Riots of August 2011 started in London and were subsequently coordinated though online social networks that consequentially resulted in the organisation of a number of flash mobs via Twitter (Baker, 2012; Vis, 2013). As the coverage commenced, its cumulative frequencies skyrocketed over social media platforms, and it was not long before the escalating contagion effect took force and others simultaneously got involved. The devastation and destructive effects of the incident should not be overlooked as it not only culminated into burning of numerous ancient buildings but also squandered remnants of coveted treasures that had been guarded jealously over the test of time across the tragic times in London history. Along with it were the many tragic stories, like a musician whose prize possessions of musical instruments engulfed the media equally. Many reasons have been developed to account for occurrence of the riots. The most convincing include changes made by the Coalition Government to welfare support, which have meant no one under 35 could get enough state help to rent more than a bedsit (Jensen, 2013). The heyday of New Labour's anti-poverty measures were well and truly over. Many young people were stuck in short-hold housing contracts they could hardly get rid of. Many took to the streets in search of goods to sell, others to release pent up frustration, not seen in the UK ever since the epoch of peasantry revolt (Prescott, 1998). The violence that was witnessed on streets during the 2011 London riots was unheard of by the UK executive; more used to such problems being prevalent in other countries where the executives have dispensed military forces in bid to end lawlessness. And indeed at the zenith of the chaotic scenes, threats of shutting down the Internet were made by the UK Prime Minister David Cameron, no different to governments overthrown in the Arab Spring Uprisings (Solo & Bishop, 2011; Solo & Bishop, 2014). Equally, the judiciary made sure they "made examples" of the youths who were brought before their courts (Bishop, 2013a; Bishop, 2013b). Many lay judges in magistrates courts were faced with their first real test of judgement, beyond being presented each week with the same young benefit claimants, targeted by the police who lack the resources and will to take on white collar crime.

The UK Riots were seized upon by UK politicians as a way to fuel their political agendas (Hancock & Mooney, 2013). For most Conservatives it was proof of New Labour's 'broken society'. For most Labour opposition members, riots emerged as a notable proof that for absolute failure of Coalition policies. One Labour MP, Alex Cunningham even went so far as to incite disorder by telling the youths to "get stuck in." Cunningham surprisingly was left scot-free without prosecution, but a youth who did something similar on Facebook, Anthony Gristock from Cardiff, was brought before the courts at the earliest opportunity (Bishop, 2013a; Bishop, 2013b). This suggests that the legal system as it stands has distinct flaws and a move towards reforms is long overdue in order to provide for equality before the law and the courts.

Prior to the election of the Coalition Government, the New Labour Governments between 1997 and 2010 created over 3,000 new statutory offences (Bishop, 2010). These included within the Protection from Harassment Act 1997, and the Communications Act 2003 (Bishop, 2013a). It is worth mentioning that the each of these Acts codified certain acts to constitute offences. It is imperative to note that even though devolved Great Britain nations have holistically adopted these enactments, the discrepancies in levels of enforcement are still evident (Ross, 2008). In Wales for instance one of the first acts towards the imposition of fixed penalty orders was to increase the fine, while this was not the case with others.

The Corporate Homicide and Corporate Manslaughter Act 2007 has been used to capture the liability of companies in the cases of criminal recklessness or loss of Life (Field & Jones, 2011). Yet it has become clear that the public law system has become ineffective at resolving the rapid advancement of trespasses against citizens for which there are 'gaps in the law,' which more public law won't resolve and for which private law is not a cost effective option for most people (Bishop, 2010; Couldry, Markham, & Livingstone, 2005). Public law would normally make the police and other public authorities act more reasonable when handling matters that might affect the civil liberties or could result into breach of duty of care. It could be noted that on several occasions this has not seemed to be the case. It must be appreciated that administrative law conceptualises the police and other authorities to be accountable to the public since there are entrusted with duties and roles for and on the behalf of the public.

Open Public Services and the Law

One might expect the question to be asked, 'what impact might the opening up of public services have on the UK legal system?' If public law was more likely to be applied this would water down the public right to challenge decisions in the distinctive parameters of private law. For instance, under public law it is, unlikely that tortuous acts, that have been excluded from codes of criminal offences for acts of such commissions or omissions to be considered unlawful, as was confirmed in Fagan v Metropolitan Police Commissioner (Reed & Smith, 2004), where an intentional act was necessary. Similarly the requirements for intent were considered in the case of Ashley v Chief Constable of Sussex [2008] AC Vol.1 962, [2008] Vol. 3 All Eng 573 the aspect of intention acts in these cases has been regarded be necessary in tort is concerned. In a tort claim by the family of James Asherly, a majority of the UK supreme-court (HL) held that this claim was sustained suitable for trial (Kristy Horsey and Erika Rackely, 382-383). In the case of R (on the application of Laporte) v Chief Constable of Gloucestershire 2006 WL 3485404, the police were able to get away with stopping miners who presumably intended to engage in the strike. The case was followed by the appeal where the court believed that the behaviour of the police was justifiable in order to ensure that pre-emptive action was taken against the miners. This could be seen to show a situation of trespass to person in tort that could comprise false arrest. Although the case illuminates how law might as well be used to by the public constraint acts of civil liberties, the danger of the police's trespass to person might be apparent in some of the cases.

The Bullingdon Principle and 'Dualism'

In this chapter it is asserted that legal frameworks should be based on dualism. Dualism is the principle that where a law applies to a person from one group or class, the same rule should be applied in an equivalent manner to a related but different group or class. For instance, following the 2011 UK riots, the Coalition Government brought in the Welfare Reform Act 2012, which led to the creation of the 'under-occupancy penalty,' also known as the 'bedroom tax' (Leighton, Keenan, & McAnulty, 2013). This penalty means that should those living in council or social housing have more rooms than the Coalition Government felt they deserved, they would have to forfeit their housing subsidies by an arbitrary amount. Following on from this the same government proposed 'Prepaid Benefit Cards,' which aimed to restrict purchases of welfare claimants to exclude cigarettes and alcohol. Under dualism, equivalent rules would be introduced for Members of Parliament (MP) who claim expenses and the wealthy who claim tax breaks. In the case of the former, the second homes they would be entitled to would be subject to the same rules as Housing Benefit, and in the case of the latter, they may face a 'mansion tax' for those properties they are either not using or not using at an optimal level. Equally MPs would be restricted from spending their salaries at the House of Commons Bar, and the rich would be required to report their spending on alcohol and cigarettes for the year and declare it as a payment-in-kind so they are taxed on it. There is however a non-government-imposed phenomena in society, which is that those with the most wealth as well as those with least wealth, both have less concern for the consequences of their actions. The authors call this the 'Bullingdon Principle.'

The Bullingdon Club is an exclusive student club based at a major university in the United Kingdom which has as its membership those who are part of wealthy family and is open by invitation only and the 'uniforms' for it cost £3000 alone (Davison, 2011). The club is known for its exploits in damaging public property, notably a fight in the cellar of a public house which was left laden in blood (Atkinson, 2006). While it is known that an increase in income equality can play a vital role in reducing crime, never the less prospects of law enforcement are also instrumentally important (dos Santos, 2009). This Bullingdon Principle can be seen to represent a situation where the closer one's disposable income is to the extremities of the distribution of wealth, the less likely one is to worry about the consequences of one's actions. This analogical dichotomy typically illustrates members with relatively high levels of income are usually less concerned about the effect of their actions on other members of the society, something found to be the case with Internet trolling for those living in the South East of England (Bishop, In Press). The respected newspaper, *The Guardian*, reported on 13 August 2011 edition, how a wealthy businessman's daughter had been caught-up in the London riots and detailed account of how others had faced minute costs as low as £85, only £10 above the standard fixed penalty notice extended in use for such unlawful acts under the Antisocial Behaviour Act 2003. Even so, one mother was quoted in the same article lamenting in despair about her son who was caught up in the riots, *"I'll take his Xbox off him. That hurts more than anything in the world,"* she said. These narratives demonstrate how the simultaneous criminalisation of a massive influx of people in society not only costs courts in terms of time, but it may also constrain the efficacy of its resources at that time. It is therefore commendable to advocate for more efficient system of promoting lawfulness through creation of incentives and disincentives to reduce offences as opposed to the instilling a fear of punishment. A similar view has been explained by (Millie, 2011).

LIMITATIONS IN THE BRITISH LEGAL SYSTEM FOR DEALING WITH COMPUTER-RELATED CRIME

One area where it is always said that statute lags behind advancing criminal acts is computer related crime, such as case where the data subjects have fallen prey to direct and indirect acts of data misuse especially inflicted by the data controllers. However, this is not substantiated by the research. More so, the New Labour Government introduced over 3,000 new offences between 1997 and 2010, with these computer related offences notably including numerous enactments in this narrow area of computer related crime (Bishop, 2010). Despite the appreciatively swift development in codification of these statutory offences, many are neither efficiently prosecuted nor adequately enforced. This includes the Regulation of Investigatory Powers Act 2000, which gives law enforcement authorities a duty to request for the relevant and identification data with respect personal details of parties alleged to engage in commission of computer related offences. It was reported in the Guardian on 10 October 2014 that mobile phone operators, EE, Vodafone and Three, provide direct access for the authorities to access personal data from their customer's mobile phones, whereas with O2 they had to justify their requests on a case-by-case basis.

In the case of Brookes v Facebook (2012), a member of the public, namely Nicola Brookes, attempted to get such a right in civil law to request the details of those who post abuse about someone online, which in relation to Facebook she was granted. When it was discovered that one of her alleged abusers was a police officer from Manchester, called Lee Rimell, the evidence requirements for using his IP address as proof of wrongdoing were raised above what is normally expected. Following this case the Defamation Act 2013 was created for which Section 5 allows for members of the public to obtain the details of their abusers where they allege the person defamed them. As defamation cases are expensive to bring, this information could then be used to bring a civil case for harassment or stalking under Section 3 of the Protection from Harassment Act 1997.

Problems with Tort Law in the Digital Age

A defect in of the law of tort is that it focuses on proximity of the parties before the grant of damages to them, and the fact that the grant of the claims by another party in tort is dependent on if the party involved had the closer degree of relationship, causes problems in its use in the present age. A test on this basis was applied in *Frost and other v. Police Constable of South Yorkshire* [1998] QB 254. The group of state police officials that had brought action on following the injuries that were sustained in the process, of the match the CA also stated allowing, by a majority, appeals by four police officials of their claims for psychiatric injury sustained as a result of tending victims of their employer's negligence arising out of the disaster at Hillsborough Stadium, Sheffield on April 15, 1989. The involvement of each police official had been caused by the efforts to save the loss of life, the criteria that was adopted in each was to consider the police men who were in close locality of the rescue point. This case was being reviewed by an inquiry at the time of writing.

Although the rules of proximity are relevant in meeting the limiting multiplicity of claimants, another challenge also arises. In the determination of the degrees of closeness, it could well be complicated by certain parties, who could be friends, but affected by eventual acts of a tortuous accident. In this respect, the law in relation to proximity may need further reconsideration. For instance, Marc Reeves (Twitter: @marcreeves) while remote from the burning of the 144 year old House of Reeves store in Croydon during the 2011 UK Riots, tweeted on 8 August his distress at seeing the store his ancestor founded being burnt to the ground. So this makes it quite clear there needs to be some alternative measure of proximity, beyond the geographical measure, which is not appropriate in the media age, where television imagery can capture as much of the reality as being in the location being captured. Proximity may need to be measured on the basis of say how many degrees of separation the claimant is from the tort victim that determines it. For instance, if an actor's mother is involved in a tragic event, and even if that actor is the other side of the world from their mother it will affect them. The level of shock and metal disturbance is very likely to be just as much as if they received the news via telephone, email, or any other social communication online networked assuming the news receiver were in their own locality (Bishop, 2014e). Equally in cases where an actor is six degrees removed from a victim, such as the person's only linkage of the shock being attainable through a series of friends, then the proximity of them in the physical world will have little effect on how much they grieve for that person. It therefore seems more appropriate that proximity, in terms of psychiatric injury, be based on the strength of social ties between the injury of the primary victim and the secondary victim. Indeed, it has been found that much R.I.P trolling of memorial websites is done because the so-called trolls do not like the insincerity of grief being expressed by people who never knew the person who has died (Phillips, 2011; Walter, Hourizi, Moncur, & Pitsillides, 2011).

THE NEED FOR A DUALIST REFORM OF THE BRITISH LEGAL SYSTEMS

Following on from the last section, it is worth looking into the critical examination of the criminological study with respect to the growth of Internet trolling by Dadak (2011). Dadak (2011) discusses how the relevant pieces of trolling legislation, such as the Communications Act 2003, can be used to prosecute those who troll to intentionally or purposely harm others - called flame trollers (Bishop, 2012a; Bishop, 2014d). Dadak (2011) further argues that although this legislative approach seems to be firmly based on the national laws, the complexities are aggravated by the fact that these laws do not have applicability across frontiers. Indeed, there are many issues in dealing with Internet trolling in an international context, such as because police forces are not always aware of the avenues open to them (Bishop, 2013d).

In a dualist legal system there would be no consideration about whether to prosecute someone who committed a trolling offence on grounds such as media pressure, that person's wealth or status, or any other non-judicial basis. For example, Matthew Woods, who was a teenager when he was convicted, was sentenced to prison for 14 weeks for re-posting an offensive joke about missing child April Jones, which he got from a website called Sickipedia. Under dualism, the law enforcement agencies would have had to go back to the original source and bring a case against them also. An example of dualism not being in existence can be seen in the case of a student union officer at the University of Central Lancaster called Joey Guy, who also posted an offensive joke about April Jones – all he had to do was apologise. All these messages were no more than Magnitude 1 or 2 on the Trolling Magnitude Scale (Bishop, 2013a; Bishop, 2013b). It could be argued that unless the law enforcement agencies were going to prosecute all who posted Magnitude 1-2 messages about April Jones then they should bring none. The postings by Matthew Woods would not have met the thresholds in the subsequent guidance issued by the Crown Prosecutor in the UK (Starmer, 2013). Woods is the victim of the unfortunate timing of his re-posting, which he did not intend to have a wide audience, and which is no longer prosecutable (Starmer, 2013).

Legal Issues Surrounding Computer-Related Crime in an International Context

The situation with regards to computer-related crime cases in the United Kingdom is not that much different if compared and contrasted with cases decided in the United States jurisdictions. Take for example the controversial case of United States v Drew (No. 08-CR-00582-UA, 2009 WL 2872855). This case related to a child, Megan Meier, who committed suicide, where character evidence revealed that she had a history of depression. But what was also particularly remarkable about the tragic act was that it was claimed to be a consequence of an express rejection online and break up with her boyfriend, Josh Evans. It was alleged that Josh Evans had sent a vivid and supposedly shocking message using the Myspace social network, where he said that he wanted nothing more to do with her (Accardi, 2009; Henderson, 2009; Quinche, 2011). Certainly on the face of it, the most obvious conclusion was that nobody was really to blame for her suicide. It transpired that there was no such person as Josh Evans. And that surely the seemingly factual and yet fictitious online relationship had been deliberately set up by one Lori Evans, the mother of a girl with whom Megan Meier had quarrelled with while at school, with the aim of the social network site for securing information on Meier and using it to humiliate her, a plan that unfortunately was all too successful. With hope that Evans might be prosecuted for the death was quickly dashed by the authorities, who concluded that she had committed no offence contrary to the criminal code of Missouri. In the United Kingdom, the case of Hannah Smith was near identical.

Hannah Smith was alleged to have committed suicide following cyberbullying on the website, Ask.fm. It later transpired that she was trolling herself. In another instance, Michelle Chapman was sent to jail for trying to frame her parents for trolling, when it was her posting the messages.

It has been argued that the British courts would not differ at all to the US in handling such cases on computer related crimes, hacking and online trolling, and indeed it has been said that cases decided in British jurisdictions have strong similarities with the decision of USA v Dew (Stannard, 2010). This however causes one to wonder why enactments on computer-related crimes like trolling and hacking have still encountered hindrances to effective enforcement.

(Carrabis & Haimovitch, 2011) make a sufficient exposition of more legal reforms that were caused by the incident of Meier case, of which America laws, save for Florida apparently adopted threefold objective test approach in deciding the computer related offences. This is as follows; (1) the required mens rea of the cyberbully; (2) the mandatory use of electronic means of communication; and (3) that the communications were severe, hostile, and repeated. It might be argued that there need to be greater reforms in computer laws of Great Britain that are similar to those in America. Having said that, it is worth noting this may be affected by non-enforcement as a result of failed institutional mechanisms, and not the absence of appropriate statutes (Bishop, 2013a).

With respect to the consultative initiatives in UK, the Open Public Services White Paper issued in 2011 by the 2010 UK Coalition Government, has been criticised for being long overdue, but an essential stage in market involvement in the provision of public services further than ever before (Griffiths, 2011). In 2000, the UK appeals court (CA), in the case of *Kent v. Griffiths*, held that an unreasonably delayed response by an ambulance service to an emergency call could be actionable in negligence (Williams, 2007). Unlike Williams claims, this should not be seen as the significant precedent they attribute to it. In Donoghue v Stevenson (HL, 1932 AC) Lord Atkinson established the "neighbour principle" which was defined to include the following; *"taking reasonable care to avoid acts or omissions which you (the probable defendant) can reasonably foresee are most likely to injure damage or cause loss to your neighbour."* Rationally it is quite clear in this case that a person entrusted with a public service obligation meets the definition of neighbour, as someone who should exercise skills and duty of care, since others (i.e. constituting the public) are likely to be affected by his acts or omissions. In this respect such a person will be expected to be mindful of the other parties that are envisaged to be inflicted by his or her actions. The case is indeed significant as it will imply, The Donoghue case was fundamental in the realisation of negligence as a tort, which has been simply defined as an act that violates a norm in a common law jurisdiction, such as the UK which specifies how one must act with reasonable due care in relation to others of which the actor may not necessary have had a prior contractual basis of understanding for the bleasure (i.e. loss, injury or damage) to occur (Goldberg, 2011). This category of law is called private law, and in fact much of the modern aspects of health care law and most of its writing concern the vital attributes such as medical or professional negligence, "best interests" and consent (Wolfe & Logan, 2009). The doctor's failure to execute medical work in the "best interest" of the patient has been held to be actionable in tort under professional negligence. The duty law of tort has been extended to refine matters of professional liability. Most important that standard of care to trained personnel like the medical worker will usually exceed that of reasonable person test. This was tested and examined the case of Grant v Australian Knitting Mills Limited and others [1936] A.C. 562. In Whiten (A party suing by his mother and litigation friend) v St. George Health Care (NHS) Trust [2011] EWHC 2066 (QB), it was held that where the claimant had suffered from the physical damage following the negligence of the doctor that worked on the mother in the delivery process. Such psychiatric damage has been shown to be closely linked associated with reduced functioning in working memory, conscience, and other factors which may contribute towards attributes society imposed criminality if not addressed through corrective therapy (Bishop, 2011c; Bishop, 2012c).

THE ROLE OF LAW OF TORTS IN SUPPLEMENTING PUBLIC LAW FOR A DECRIMINALISED SOCIETY

It is fallacious to think there is any coherent social order beyond the social constructions someone makes of the legal, economic and scientific civilisation systems, the jurisdiction of which such individuals find themselves subjected by virtue of the concept of their domiciliary residence. The modern UK society is unfortunately positioned on the pedestal of assuming that practices of small groups can be generalised to overlook the interests of wider populations dominant in political and academic thinking. This may be the reason underlying the policy of criminalising of those carrying out misdemeanours, a bye-product of ineffective use of civilisation systems. It must be mentioned this approach must therefore be itself ineffective in acknowledging the distinction of misdemeanours from felonies that are more grave offences (Myers, 1982). This deserves to be respected in all the aspects of criminal objectives from deterrence to rehabilitating the offenders. Concepts like "Gamification" therefore, which bring elements of gaming into systems like these where they otherwise may not be part, can improve user experience and user engagement with them (Deterding, Sicart, Nacke, O'Hara, & Dixon, 2011). Where such concepts were applied to public services, such as with the 'competition' envisaged by New Labour (Shaw, 2009) as a way to increase productivity under the notion of customer-led policies, or the 'self-governance' envisaged by the Coalition, the optimum strategy that would otherwise inevitably result from the Nash equilibrium (Nash, 1950). This will be clear to all, yet from a more realistic and logical perspective, the maximum benefit derived from the system will be variably different from each person. The reason is predominately associated with effects of the asymmetrical concept and its relationship on nature of information available to the actors within the system. This certainly affects their ability to benefit from it (Akerlof, 1970), although academics and the diversity of academic literature has been attributed this to several factors such as to the digital divide (Hersberger, 2003), limited education (Howcroft, 1999), and cognitive and working memory limitations, which results to inadequate access to all relevant and sufficient information more so when positioned in a bargaining situation (Bishop, 2011b).

Actus Reus without Mens Rea

In the law of torts it is often not important whether someone intended to commit a guilty act (i.e. the mental element is immaterial). In principle the commission of an act which causes a loss or damage or personnel injury to someone will suffice and amount to a 'bleasure' (Bishop, 2014a; Bishop, 2014b; Bishop, 2014f). This is a typically vital element that constitutes action and claims under tort law, yet of which, there are only a limited amount justifiable grounds to encompass internet crimes as compared to criminal law that would be the most appropriate forum of dealing with Internet trolling as opposed to the 'action' and 'state of mind' approach traditionally used in criminal law. Needing to prove mens rea should be an obstacle in the prosecution of flame trollers, as people often easily get unknowingly and electronically trapped up in the moment in a high state of online information flow and communication interchange processes (Csikszentmihalyi, 1990) ultimately some online actors may be often unaware of the technical and electronic controller of their online actions.

Law of tort has largely tapered on the duty of care front, while it could have equally justifiable links with elements of criminal law. Such links are fundamentally instrumental to enforcement of criminal law. The offenders in this respect could have committed an offence (i.e. had actus reus) as well as the guilty state of mind of committing that offence (i.e. mens rea). In the case of the 2011 UK riots, the actions of demonstrators might cause injuries that constitute action of trespass to person. In criminal law, this has been coined in the flowery phrases of actual bodily harm, although the law of tort hardily considers the concept of intention, this will not undermine the role this branch of law might play to enforce criminal law. The case of *King v Bristow Helicopters Ltd [2002]* 2002 Scot (D) 3/3 found that injuries against the person, whether physical or mental (i.e. bleasures) were prosecutable under tort law. Difficulties with the way police prioritise cases, based more on punishing people than restorative justice for victims, mean that there is often little come back for those who have suffered some loss. It might therefore be that a deminimis rule could be introduced where the police or other law enforcement authorities only bring cases where there has been a bleasure of some sort (i.e. proving malum reus) for which remedies can be brought for victims beyond punishment.

Tracey Ormsby v The Chief Constable of Strathclyde Police [2008] WL 4264270 is a suitable example. In this action the pursuer, a former constable with Strathclyde Police Force, claimed damages for bleasures said to have been sustained as a result of the alleged mishandling of a police operation at Govanhill Baths, Glasgow in August 2001. There was a further hearing relating to supplementary submissions for the defendant. The issues before court included deciding if the senior officer in charge was accountably for allegations of negligent handling during the operation, and if so, did it cause the pursuer loss, injury and damage, and if so, to what extent. In this respect, to decide matters that related to negligence and breach of this duty of care, the court made reference to Police (Health and Safety) Act 1997 c. 42, In the course of analysis this case, the court rightly observed that, when considering issues of duty and standard of care, account should be paid to the likely inherent danger of encouraging overly defensive policing, something which would be contrary to the wider public interest.

Another important reform might be avoiding the unnecessary and excessive criminalisation, especially of youths, which has been a problem since the hype around 'Internet trolling' began (Bishop, 2014d; Bishop, In Press). It is recommendable that the police authorities should only exercise such powers of arrest only in presence of strongly irrefutable evidence and more so after following the criminal procedure rules, to bring a charge. This could mean that some police constables could be dispensed with and replaced with local authority civil enforcement officers, accountable to Sergeants, who make the decision about whether to arrest. A Sergeant therefore being the first contact with the power to arrest may exercise this more effectively. Such a reform will ensure that cases are brought only when there is a chance of securing evidence to get restorative justice for victims, assuming they are indeed a victim by their allegations being proven to have merit.

The Concept of 'Malum Reus' in the Law of Tort

Malum reus refers to an emerging principle in common law that one is only liable for a supposed guilty act if one causes injury to another (Bishop, 2013a). In most soft-law jurisdictions relating to Internet trolling, such as those covered by the Advertising Standards Authority or the Press Complaints Commission, there needs to have been some 'offense' experienced or some other loss by the complainant in order for action to be brought. It is clear that the existence of some groups on the Internet, like a group on Facebook set up to tell sick 'baby jokes' were never intended to be seen by those who would be offended by them.

Applying the case of DPP v Connolly, where it was found that had surgeons who performed abortions received the propaganda showing images of foetuses and not pharmacists who issued the contraceptive pill then no crime would be committed. Therefore this case established that malum reus was necessary in order for articles to be 'grossly offensive,' as did the case of DPP v Chambers, also known as the Twitter joke trial, which said in order for something to be grossly offensive it had to cause apprehension. This may be reflected in tort law as being where an act would cause harm to someone of normal fortitude.

The Concept of 'Pertinax Reus' in the Criminal Law System

Pertinax reus refers to a commonality in criminal law relating to harassment and other legal areas that evidence the performance of a guilty act over a sustained period. Indeed this makes a stronger case for an offense being committed than a single guilty act. In the case of the Protection from Harassment Act 1997, there needs to be a number of "related" cases of flame trolling in order for someone to be prosecuted under this Act. A similar offence of "persistent misuse" of a communications network, such as for flame trolling is in the Communications Act 2003. In addition it has been a typical traditional in the common law for past offences to be suitable for proving the likelihood of an offence being committed in similar circumstances (i.e. actus reus).

Reforming the Use of Mens Rea in the British Legal Systems

It may be appropriate that the concept of 'mens rea' be used as a way to rule out cases that do not meet a threshold beyond a 'deminimis' value. The use of mens rea could therefore look at whether the person acted with good faith or bad faith and whether they were caught up in the moment, or actually went out of their way to flame troll.

To prosecute for flame trolling in most cases it would only be necessary to prove actus reus (that the person actually did the guilty act). If it could be proven that the victim sustained an injury such as a 'bleasure' (i.e. proved malum reus) then they would be entitled to compensation to an appropriate level usually associated with a fine. This concept is presented in Table 1 below. This table is based on an adaptation of the framework in (Bishop, 2012b).

THE ROLE OF GAMIFICATION TO UNDERSTAND PRE-LEGAL INTERVENTIONS

It has been precisely postulated that are only two things certain in life; 'death and taxes' (Kallbekken & Sælen, 2011). However, two other things are also certain; one being that citizens whether rich or poor will seek to maximize the amount of time they can spend enjoying their life with as many resources as they can acquire; and the second aspect seeking to minimise their tax liability while maximising their return from the state. This is done, according to (Picciotto, 2007), by players seeking to act opportunistically in interpret the rules to their advantage, but in a 'formalist and technicist' manner, that is to say, by referring only to the apparent internal logic of the rule system, whose vocal attention is based on justifying the ethical nature of the choices made. Elements of 'gaming' and 'equilibrium' are therefore typical and profoundly built in the structure of any economic system, whether built on the system of 'self-interest' claimed by game-theorists using cognitivist psychology (Griffith, 2002; O'Neill, 1995), or the most gratifying and least discomforting use of artefacts (e.g. knowledge, conversation, goods) proposed by equatricists using post-cognitivist psychology (Bishop, 2011b).

Table 1. Types of Internet troller, the types of posts and gamification remedies

Troller Type	Common Types of Trolling	Gamification Remedy
Big Man	Messages to prove others wrong, or rebuking people for breaking one of their rules, such as posting off-topic. The Big Man's way to 'pwn' others is for the website or individual to ban or block them respectively.	'levels[1]', 'learning[2]', 'points[2]'
Snert	Messages to attack others and make them feel inadequate. Spiteful messages for the sole purpose of attacking someone they are jealous of.	'group identity[1]', 'fun[2]', 'love[2]'
E-Venger	Messages to get back at someone for a wrong they have done against the user, including returning to a community to avenge those who wronged them.	'punishments[2]', 'rewards[2]'
Iconoclast	Messages of 'fact' to dash others' certainties or worldviews, and in some cases to directly or indirectly get content removed. Their aim is to give a 'more accurate' picture.	'leader-boards[1]', 'badges[2]'
Chatroom Bob	Messages that appear friendly and kind, but which are designed to gain someone's trust so exploit them, such as to get them to send nude photos or otherwise groom them for another purpose.	'power[1]', 'mastery[2]'
Elder	Messages that prove the persons cynicism about the community or the world. They will provoke new users into flaming in such a way to confirm their biases.	'meaning[2]', 'autonomy[1]'

Interface Cues: [1] authority cues [2] bandwagon cues

Framework for Using Gamification and Tort Law to Reduce Flame Trolling

Any factors that limit the full access to human cognition has been known to affect human ability to carry out tasks, expert evidence has been used in proving questions of limited cognitive capacity to act in such cases. This includes, Cullen v General Medical Council [2004] CO/5467/2004. Table 1 below presents the various types of Internet troller that make up online communities (Bishop, 2008; Bishop, 2013c), the type of trolling they do, and the most appropriate methods for helping them reduce the amount of flame trolling they carry out (A. J. Kim, 2011; H. S. Kim & Sundar, 2011).

The analogy of the neighbour that might cause themselves a bleasure while in the rush to protect another's baby, might be the best way to explain the effect of necessity in the context of the other extraneous circumstances. It is worth mentioning that trespassing in the common law context has been broadly categorised into three major class namely Trespass done to the person, Trespass done on someone's property and tress to land, as in the case of Burt v Chelsea hospital.

IMPLICATIONS AND FUTURE RESEARCH DIRECTIONS

This chapter focused mainly on reforming the law on the basis of extending the use of torts, but it also has implications for criminal law cases. Under dualism, where complainant and respondent are treated the same, then as can happen with a civil tort claim it might be that the person defending allegations against them should be permitted to file a counter-claim against their accuser, which might result in fewer cases being brought by the authorities that were not of merit. This would mean that law enforcement time could be spent on ensuring that those who actually victims of crimes – where there is no possibility of them being equally as guilty as the person they are accusing – such as theft, burglary, murder, and most cases of rape, where there is on the whole a planned element where the accused knew ahead of committing the offence that they were going to do so. Further research is needed to establish how there may be greater fusion of criminal and civil law, and how the legal system could be further based on dualism.

DISCUSSION

Even though the legal systems of Great Britain have been seen as some of the best in the world, there is however a number of key failings in the manner in which crimes against others are dealt with. And this awakens public outcry to the state of unhelpfulness and inefficacy as apparently manifested by the system in dealing with Internet trolling. Great Britain's system of criminal law crimes (i.e. a wrong against a person that is unlawful), and so often the criteria for determining as to whether a person gets justice is predominantly dependent on whether the police considers it a priority or whether they have the funds to bring a civil case for a tortuous obligation.

This chapter uses the established 'Trolling Magnitude Scale' to help law enforcement authorities prioritise which flame trolling offences to institute criminal action and which ones should be considered least important for purposes of lodging criminal prosecutions. The authors show how the current legal system can be best optimised to deal with flame trolling, and how if reasonable yet marginal changes were made to it, could transform the entire system be more effective by assurance of adequate compensation to victims of computer-related crime through tort law and in other instances creating a leeway for prosecution the perpetrators of computer abusive tendencies using criminal law.

It is clear that as instances of flame trolling are only likely to go up, as world government's 'austerity measures' being to bite those in poverty, that the Bullingdon Principle is only going to become more apparent. This principle states that the closer someone is to the extremities of wealth the more likely they are to be unconcerned by the consequences of their actions. This should be a warning to governments that unless they tackle things like youth poverty and the growing gap between the richest and the poorest that flame trolling will be an escalating reality for years and generations to come.

ACKNOWLEDGMENT

The authors would like to thank all those who provided comment and feedback on earlier drafts of this chapter. The research that led to this chapter was highly influential in the development of another paper on dualism following the 2011 UK riots, which was sole authored by the second author (Bishop, 2014c).

REFERENCES

Accardi, K. (2009). Is violating an internet service provider's terms of service an example of computer fraud and abuse: An analytical look at the computer fraud and abuse act, lori drew's conviction and cyberbullying. *W.St.UL Rev., 37*, 67.

Akerlof, G. A. (1970). The market for" lemons": Quality uncertainty and the market mechanism. *The Quarterly Journal of Economics, 84*(3), 488–500. doi:10.2307/1879431

Atkinson, R. (2006). Spaces of discipline and control: The compounded citizenship of social renting. *Housing, Urban Governance and Anti-Social Behaviour: Perspectives. Policy & Practice*, 99–116.

Baker, S. A. (2012). From the criminal crowd to the "mediated crowd": The impact of social media on the 2011 english riots. *Safer Communities, 11*(1), 40–49. doi:10.1108/17578041211200100

Bishop, J. (2008). Increasing capital revenue in social networking communities: Building social and economic relationships through avatars and characters. In C. Romm-Livermore & K. Setzekorn (Eds.), *Social networking communities and eDating services: Concepts and implications* (pp. 60–77). Hershey, PA: IGI Global.

Bishop, J. (2010). Tough on data misuse, tough on the causes of data misuse: A review of new labour's approach to information security and regulating the misuse of digital information (1997–2010). *International Review of Law Computers & Technology, 24*(3), 299–303. doi:10.1080/13600869.2010.522336

Bishop, J. (In Press). Digital teens and the 'antisocial Network': Prevalence of troublesome online youth groups and internet trolling in great Britain. *International Journal of E-Politics,* Carrabis, A. B., & Haimovitch, S. D. (2011). Cyberbullying: Adaptation from the old school sandlot to the 21st century world wide web-the court system and technology law's race to keep pace. *J.Tech.L.& Pol'Y, 16,* 143.

Bishop, J. (2011a). All's WELL that ends WELL: A comparative analysis of the constitutional and administrative frameworks of cyberspace and the united kingdom. In A. Dudley-Sponaugle & J. Braman (Eds.), *Investigating cyber law and cyber ethics: Issues, impacts and practices ( ).* Hershey, PA: IGI Global.

Bishop, J. (2011b). *The equatrics of intergenerational knowledge transformation in techno-cultures: Towards a model for enhancing information management in virtual worlds. (Unpublished MScEcon).* Aberystwyth, UK: Aberystwyth University.

Bishop, J. (2011c). The role of the prefrontal cortex in social orientation construction: A pilot study. *The British Psychological Society's Sustainable Well-being Conference,* Wrexham, GB.

Bishop, J. (2012a). Scope and limitations in the government of wales act 2006 for tackling internet abuses in the form of 'Flame trolling'. *Statute Law Review, 33*(2), 207–216. doi:10.1093/slr/hms016

Bishop, J. (2012b). Tackling internet abuse in great britain: Towards a framework for classifying severities of 'flame trolling'. *The 11th International Conference on Security and Management (SAM'12),* Las Vegas, NV.

Bishop, J. (2012c). Taming the chatroom bob: The role of brain-computer interfaces that manipulate prefrontal cortex optimization for increasing participation of victims of traumatic sex and other abuse online. *Proceedings of the 13th International Conference on Bioinformatics and Computational Biology (BIOCOMP'12),* Las Vegas, NV.

Bishop, J. (2013a). The art of trolling law enforcement: A review and model for implementing 'flame trolling' legislation enacted in great britain (1981–2012). *International Review of Law Computers & Technology, 27*(3), 301–318. doi:10.1080/13600869.2013.796706

Bishop, J. (2013b). The effect of deindividuation of the internet troller on criminal procedure implementation: An interview with a hater. *International Journal of Cyber Criminology, 7*(1), 28–48.

Bishop, J. (2013c). Increasing capital revenue in social networking communities: Building social and economic relationships through avatars and characters. In J. Bishop (Ed.), *Examining the concepts, issues, and implications of internet trolling* (pp. 44–61). Hershey, PA: IGI Global. doi:10.4018/978-1-4666-2803-8.ch005

Bishop, J. (2013d). Internet trolling and other cyberlaw issues in the UK and the international arena. In D. H. Goldhush, K. Ossian, T. F. Claypoole, J. K. Sherwood, D. Schnapp, C. Bal & J. Bishop (Eds.), Understanding developments in cyberspace law (2013th ed., pp. 109-120). Eagan, MI: West Publishing Co.

Bishop, J. (2014a). 'U r bias love:' Using 'bleasure' and 'motif' as forensic linguistic means to annotate twitter and newsblog comments for the purpose of multimedia forensics. *The 11th International Conference on Web Based Communities and Social Media,* Lisbon, PT.

Bishop, J. (2014b). 'YouTube if you want to, the lady's not for blogging': Using 'bleasures' and 'motifs' to support multimedia forensic analyses of harassment by social media. *Oxford Cyber Harassment Research Symposium*, Oxford, GB.

Bishop, J. (2014c). Internet trolling and the 2011 UK riots: The need for a dualist reform of the constitutional, administrative and security frameworks in great britain. *European Journal of Law Reform,* *16*(1), 154–167.

Bishop, J. (2014d). Representations of 'trolls' in mass media communication: A review of media-texts and moral panics relating to 'internet trolling'. *International Journal of Web Based Communities*, *10*(1), 7–24. doi:10.1504/IJWBC.2014.058384

Bishop, J. (2014e). Trolling is not just a art. it is an science: The role of automated affective content screening in regulating digital media and reducing risk of trauma. In M. M. Cruz-Cunha & I. M. Portela (Eds.), *Handbook of research on digital crime, cyberspace security, and information assurance* (pp. 424–435). Hershey, PA: IGI Global.

Bishop, J. (2014f). Using the legal concepts of 'forensic linguistics,' 'bleasure' and 'motif' to enhance multimedia forensics. *The 13th International Conference on Security and Management (SAM'14)*, Las Vegas, NV.

Couldry, N., Markham, T., & Livingstone, S. (2005). *Media consumption and the future of public connection*. London, UK: London School of Economics and Political Science.

Csikszentmihalyi, M. (1990). *Flow: The psychology of optimal experience*. New York: Harper & Row.

Dadak, R. (2011). Quashing the beast. *Solicitor's Journal, 155*(36), 9.

Davison, J. (2011). Literacy and social class. *Debates in English Teaching,*, 169.

Deterding, S., Sicart, M., Nacke, L., O'Hara, K., & Dixon, D. (2011). Gamification: Using game-design elements in non-gaming contexts. Paper presented at the *Proceedings of the 2011 Annual Conference on Human Factors in Computing Systems*, New York, NY. 2425-2428. doi:10.1145/1979742.1979575

dos Santos, M. R. (2009). Labor supply, criminal behavior and income redistribution. *Brazilian Review of Econometrics*, *29*(2), 5–6.

Field, S., & Jones, L. (2011). Death in the workplace: Who pays the price? *Colorado Lawyer, 32*(6), 166–173.

Goldberg, J. C. P. (2011). Does the world still need united states tort law? or did it ever?: Tort in three dimensions. *Pepp.L.Rev., 38*, 321–597.

Griffith, S. J. (2002). Deal protection provisions in the last period of play. *Fordham Law Review, 71*, 1899.

Griffiths, S. (2011). The retreat of the state: Conservative 'modernisation' and the public services. *Public Policy Research, 18*(1), 23–29. doi:10.1111/j.1744-540X.2011.00637.x

Hancock, L., & Mooney, G. (2013). "Welfare ghettos" and the "Broken society": Territorial stigmatization in the contemporary UK. *Housing. Theory and Society, 30*(1), 46–64.

Henderson, A. M. (2009). High-tech words do hurt: A modern makeover expands missouri's harassment law to include electronic communications. *Missouri Law Review, 74*, 379.

Hersberger, J. (2003). Are the economically poor information poor? does the digital divide affect the homeless and access to information? *Canadian Journal of Information and Library Science, 27*(3), 45–64.

Howcroft, D. (1999). The hyperbolic age of information: An empirical study of internet usage. *Information Communication and Society, 2*(3), 277–299. doi:10.1080/136911899359592

Jensen, T. (2013). Riots, restraint and the new cultural politics of wanting. *Sociological Research Online, 18*(4), 7. doi:10.5153/sro.3158

Kallbekken, S., & Sælen, H. (2011). Public acceptance for environmental taxes: Self-interest, environmental and distributional concerns. Energy Policy, Kim, A. J. (2011). Do you know the score on gamification? The Gamification Summit 2010, San Francisco, CA.

Kim, H. S., & Sundar, S. S. (2011). Using interface cues in online health community boards to change impressions and encourage user contribution. Paper presented at the *Proceedings of the 2011 Annual Conference on Human Factors in Computing Systems*, 599-608. doi:10.1145/1978942.1979028

Leighton, A., Keenan, M., & McAnulty, U. (2013). 'In all fairness...?' Housing policy and welfare reform.

Millie, A. (2011). Big society, small government: The british coalition government and tackling anti-social behaviour. *Crime Prevention and Community Safety, 13*(4), 284–287. doi:10.1057/cpcs.2011.17

Myers, M. A. (1982). Common law in action: The prosecution of felonies and misdemeanors*. *Sociological Inquiry, 52*(1), 1–15. doi:10.1111/j.1475-682X.1982.tb01235.x PMID:11618150

Nash, J. F. (1950). Equilibrium points in n-person games. *Proceedings of the National Academy of Sciences of the United States of America, 38*(1), 48–49. doi:10.1073/pnas.36.1.48 PMID:16588946

O'Neill, B. (1995). Weak models, nil hypotheses, and decorative statistics. *The Journal of Conflict Resolution, 39*(4), 731–748. doi:10.1177/0022002795039004007

Phillips, W. (2011). LOLing at tragedy: Facebook trolls, memorial pages and resistance to grief online. *First Monday, 16*(12). doi:10.5210/fm.v16i12.3168

Picciotto, S. (2007). Constructing compliance: Game playing, tax law, and the regulatory state. *Law & Policy, 29*(1), 11–30. doi:10.1111/j.1467-9930.2007.00243.x

Prescott, A. (1998). Writing about rebellion: Using the records of the peasants' revolt of 1381. Paper presented at the *History Workshop Journal, 1998*(45) 1-28. doi:10.1093/hwj/1998.45.1

Quinche, F. (2011). Cyber-harcèlement. jeunes et violences" virtuelles. *Jeunes Et Médias-Les Cahiers Francophones De L'Éducation Aux Médias-N° 1, 1,* 143.

Reed, A., & Smith, G. (2004). Omission to act can amount to an assault or battery. *Journal of Criminal Law, 68*(6), 459–465. doi:10.1350/jcla.68.6.459.54142

Ross, A. (2008). Why legislate for sustainable development? an examination of sustainable development provisions in UK and scottish statutes. *Journal of Environmental Law, 20*(1), 35–68. doi:10.1093/jel/eqm019

Shaw, E. (2009). The consumer and new labour: The consumer as king? *The Consumer in Public Services: Choice, Values and Difference,*, 19.

Solo, A. M. G., & Bishop, J. (2011). The new field of network politics. Paper presented at the *The 2011 International Conference on E-Learning, E-Business, Enterprise Information Systems & E-Government (EEE'11),* Las Vegas, NV. 442-444.

Solo, A. M. G., & Bishop, J. (2014). Conceptualizing network politics following the arab spring. In A. M. G. Solo (Ed.), *Handbook of research on political activism in the information age* (pp. 231–238). Hershey, PA: IGI Global. doi:10.4018/978-1-4666-6066-3.ch014

Stannard, J. E. (2010). Sticks, stones and words: Emotional harm and the english criminal law. *Journal of Criminal Law, 74*(6), 533–556. doi:10.1350/jcla.2010.74.6.668

Starmer, K. (2013). *Guidelines on prosecuting cases involving communications sent via social media.* London, GB: Crown Prosecution Service.

Vis, F. (2013). Twitter as a reporting tool for breaking news: Journalists tweeting the 2011 UK riots. *Digital Journalism, 1*(1), 27–47. doi:10.1080/21670811.2012.741316

Walter, T., Hourizi, R., Moncur, W., & Pitsillides, S. (2011). Does the internet change how we die and mourn? an overview. *Omega, 64*(4), 12. PMID:22530294

Williams, K. (2007). Litigation against english NHS ambulance services and the rule in kent v. griffiths. *Medical Law Review, 15*(2), 153–175. doi:10.1093/medlaw/fwm001 PMID:17517759

Wolfe, D., & Logan, R. (2009). Public law and the provision of healthcare. *Judicial Review, 14*(2), 210-223. Retrieved from http://libezproxy.open.ac.uk/login?url=http://search.ebscohost.com/login.aspx?direct=true&db=a9h&AN=44834301&site=eds-live&scope=site

KEY TERMS AND DEFINITIONS

Actus Reus: The principle that in order for someone to be convicted of an offence the action they are accused of committing needs to be proven to have occurred.

Bleasure: An imposed physical or mental injury that has a substantial impact on a person's wellbeing on a long-term basis.

Bullingdon Principle: The concept that the close one is to the extremities of wealth (i.e. being rich or poor) then the less likely one is to be concerned about the consequences of one's actions.

Flame Trolling: The posting of provocative or offensive messages to the Internet with the intention of causing harm to another person.

Malum Reus: The principle that a person must have caused injury to someone else in order to have committed an offence.

Open Public Services: Services provided to the public that need not be run by the government, but which can be taken over by the public should they wish to run them.

Pertinax Reus: The principle that in order for someone to be convicted for a minor offence it needs to be shows that they have committed the specific behaviour on more than one occasion.

UK Riots: The UK Riots occurred in August 2011 following the mass publication of an image of the aftermath of the police killing of Mark Duggan.

Chapter 12
Native Language Identification (NLID) for Forensic Authorship Analysis of Weblogs

Ria Perkins
Aston University, UK

ABSTRACT

This chapter introduces Native Language Identification (NLID) and considers the casework applications with regard to authorship analysis of online material. It presents findings from research identifying which linguistic features were the best indicators of native (L1) Persian speakers blogging in English, and analyses how these features cope at distinguishing between native influences from languages that are linguistically and culturally related. The first chapter section outlines the area of Native Language Identification, and demonstrates its potential for application through a discussion of relevant case history. The next section discusses a development of methodology for identifying influence from L1 Persian in an anonymous blog author, and presents findings. The third part discusses the application of these features to casework situations as well as how the features identified can form an easily applicable model and demonstrates the application of this to casework. The research presented in this chapter can be considered a case study for the wider potential application of NLID.

1. BACKGROUND

1.1 Introduction

Forensic Linguistics, Authorship Analysis and Native Language Identification

Native language identification is an aspect of forensic linguistic authorship analysis. Forensic linguistics is a branch of applied linguistics that relates to legal situations and processes. Loosely defined it relates to any overlap between language or linguistics, and legal or criminal situations. Coulthard, Grant and Kredens (2010) suggest that forensic linguistics, is application of linguistics in three main areas; "writ-

DOI: 10.4018/978-1-4666-8345-7.ch012

Figure 1. Authorship profiling

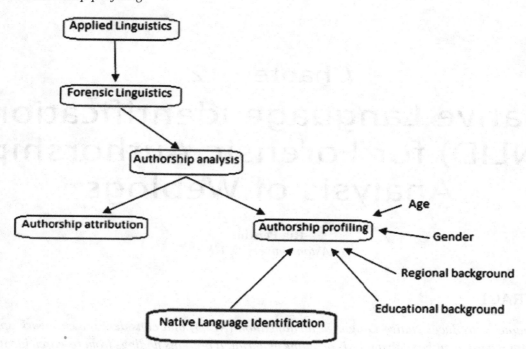

ten legal texts, spoken legal practices and the provision of evidence for criminal and civil investigations and courtroom disputes" (Coulthard et al., 2010, p. 529). For this research forensic linguistics is often considered a section of applied linguistics rather than a completely separate discipline. Forensic linguistic consultants are predominantly linguists, who apply their knowledge to forensic situations or contexts.

Native language identification (NLID) is a very specific question within the wider field of forensic linguistics, falling under the area of authorship analysis which relates specifically to the last of the three main areas of forensic linguistic interest that were identified by Coulthard, Grant and Kredens (2010); that being the provision of evidence. Authorship analysis has two main sub-areas; profiling and authorship attribution, of which native language identification belongs to the second (Figure 1 below shows the location of NLID to forensic linguistics and its sub-fields).

Authorship attribution seeks to answer which person out of a fixed group of suspects is the most likely author of an anonymous document. This usually requires a closed group of suspects and a comparison between the questioned or disputed texts and texts that are known to have been written by each suspect. A typical case might involve threatening emails being sent to a company, the content of which might indicate the author is most likely an employee of the company. The forensic linguist could then compare linguistic features within the threatening emails (questioned texts) and compare them to emails known to be authored by each of the employees (known texts), to determine which employee is the most likely author. Authorship profiling is the other area of authorship analysis, it is similar in many ways, but does not require a closed pool of suspects. A famous case of authorship profiling is the devil strip case (Leonard, 2005). Linguist Dr Roger Shuy was consulted on a case regarding a kidnapped girl whose parents had received a ransom note reading:

Do you ever want to see your precious little girl
again? Put $10,000 cash in a diaper bag. Put it
in the green trash kan on
the devil strip at corner 18th and Carlson.
Don't bring anybody along.
No kops!! Come alone! I'll be watching you
all the time. Anyone with you,
deal is off and dautter is dead!!!

He was asked by law enforcement if he could determine any information from the text which might be able to guide the investigation. He noticed many interesting features which indicated the note was likely authored by a well-educated man from Akron Ohio. It is rare to be able to determine such an accurate location, this case was fortunate in that the use of the term 'devil strip' is localised to a very specific dialect, that of Akron, Ohio. Seemingly deliberate misspellings and other features within the text helped with the wider profile, which was discovered to exactly fit one of the suspects, who it later transpired had indeed written the note (Shuy, 2001). Authorship profiling draws predominantly from sociolinguistics, which is grounded in the theory that our language and linguistic choices are influenced by a great range of social factors; as our social experiences and backgrounds are relatively unique, so too is our language. Authorship profiling can seek to answer a range of questions depending on the case or specific context. Areas often considered include; age, education level, gender, regional background and native language (or L1). Forensic linguistics works from a functional rather than prescriptive approach to grammar, in that it is concerned with how language is used by individuals and within certain social groups, as opposed to how it *should* be used. The forensic linguist does not make psychological observations about the author or their intentions; however they can seek to determine information relating to social aspects and origins. Native Language Identification can be considered an area of authorship profiling, there might be cases when it also forms part of authorship attribution cases, but it is primarily a profiling question. Despite this is has only garnered limited academic interest from this perspective so far.

Grant (2008) draws the parallel between sociolinguistic profiling and psychological profiling in their application within the legal process, highlighting that sociolinguistic profiling, like psychological profiling is unlikely to be admissible as evidence in the UK judicial and court system (Grant, 2008; R. Perkins & Grant, 2013), however they can provide much benefit at an investigative level. Authorship profiling has been of much use to law enforcement agencies across a wide variety of cases. NLID also has a great potential to benefit law enforcement agencies or organisations (LEOs) with certain cases, especially when used as a tool for authorship analysis. However, the areas of law enforcement that would likely benefit most significantly from research into NLID are those that deal especially with non-native speakers, particularly intelligence agencies. Due to the nature of intelligence work, casework in this field is rarely published; however it is still possible to allow intelligence applications to shape research into NLID through collaboration with relevant and interested agencies and departments, this can be seen with reports such as Grant, Kredens, & Perkins (2010).

Threat and Case History

Research in the area of forensic authorship profiling, like many other areas of forensic linguistics, is motivated by its application in casework situations. Forensic linguists who specialize in forensic authorship analysis are regularly approached to consult in casework for a wide range of clients, including private firms, individuals or law enforcement agencies (LEOs). The cases on which forensic linguists consult on are needs-driven and reflect the socio-political climate, it is interesting to note that increasingly cases revolve around language data produced as part of computer mediated communication, as well as cases involving speakers of multiple languages. Multilingualism is becoming increasingly prevalent, with there now being more multilingual than monolingual speakers in the world (Thomason, 2001). While it is difficult to define exactly what level of expertise constitutes being a speaker of a second language, it is estimated that the number of second language (L2) English speakers could outnumber the number of native English (L1) speakers (Bhatia & Ritchie, 2004), this trend continues into the virtual sphere, with approximately 80% of the 40 million internet users communicating in English (Bhatia & Ritchie, 2013). It is therefore logical to conclude that a considerable number of English language forensic texts are likely to be produced (or at least possibly produced) by non-native English speakers. Bhatia and Ritchie (2013) highlighted this growing link between computer mediated communication, multilingualism and forensic linguistics, stating "In a world connected by social media and globalization, the role of the study of multilingualism in forensic linguistics is increasing rapidly."(Bhatia & Ritchie, 2013, p. 672).

Any text produced has the potential to become a forensic text depending on the context (Coulthard et al., 2010; Olsson, 2004), for example a mundane to-do list could become a *forensic* text, if it became relevant to an investigative situation. This study focuses on data from blogs, one key reason for this is to best reflect genuine forensic linguistic data. There are already numerous documented cases in which forensic authorship analysis has aided law enforcement agencies in cases involving computer mediated communication. In 2001 Prof. Malcolm Coulthard was consulted to give an expert opinion on whether messages sent from Danielle Jones's mobile after her disappearance, were authored by her or her uncle, Stuart Campbell, who was suspected of murdering her then sending the messages to try and cover his tracks. Coulthard ascertained that there were features in the text that indicated the suspect messages were inconsistent with Danielle's style of writing and therefore unlikely to have been written by her (Grant, 2010). Since then, there have been more cases involving computer mediated communication in which forensic linguistics authorship analysis has aided law enforcement officers at either the investigative or evidentiary level. More recently there have been cases involving online data and emerging social software. Forensic linguists have consulted on cases involving email, blogs, twitter, WhatsApp, and MSN messenger. Forensic linguistics has a lot to offer in the realms of research driven support for aiding law enforcement agencies (LEOs) working to counter and prosecute digital crime and cyber terrorism, this has led to increasing co-operation between forensic linguists and LEOs.

The concept of determining a person's native language (L1) from how they use a second language (L2) is not new, neither is the link to potential forensic applications. Conan Doyle (1892) incorporated it into his short story Scandal in Bohemia, when Sherlock Holmes deduced the origins the author of an anonymous note from a combination of physical evidence, and the linguistic structures used in the note. "And the man who wrote the note is a German. Do you note the peculiar construction of the sentence--'This account of you we have from all quarters received.' A Frenchman or Russian could not have written that. It is the German who is so uncourteous to his verbs." (Doyle, 1892, p. 8). Holmes is performing a very basic native language identification here, based on a comparison of German and

English grammatical structures and an understanding that a person's L1 might exhibit an influence over their L2 production. Similar situations have been documented in genuine cases, the earliest being the 1930's trial of Bruno Hauptmann. Hauptmann, a German immigrant living in America, was accused of kidnapping and killing the 20 month old son of the famous aviator, Charles Lindbergh. After the boy disappeared, ransom notes were sent to the Lindbergh's demanding money in exchange for the return of their son. The police and FBI were led to suspect Bruno Hauptman, who later stood trial and was executed for the crime. During the trial handwriting experts drew on a combination of orthographic and linguistic information contained within the ransom notes to conclude that they were most likely written by a native German speaker. It is also interesting to note that the International Herald Tribune wrote of Hauptmann's court appearance in 1935, that he "spoke slowly, with a strong German accent and frequent Germanic grammatical constructions — such, incidentally, as appeared in the ransom notes he is alleged to have written." (The International Herald Tribune, 2010). While the testimonies given by the handwriting experts would unlikely fulfil today's criteria for expert evidence, this case clearly shows that NLID has a place within the wider legal system.

More recently, German linguist Hannes Kniffka discussed a case in which he used formulations in an anonymous author's writing to indicate information about their L1 (Kniffka, 1996). Kniffka had been consulted concerning a case of threatening letters being sent within a German company. The content indicated that the author was likely an employee of the company. During his analysis, Kniffka noticed that the notes contained some unique linguistic constructions within the German language use, including; unusual spelling errors with umlauts, awkward lexical collocations and non-idiomatic use of German proverbs. His conclusion was that despite the author having a high level of German fluency, it was likely their second language rather than their native language. Till then the chief suspect had been one of the L1 German employees. The company also contained two non-native German speakers; one French and one American. The police put these two new suspects under observation and later caught the American employee in the process of writing another threatening letter. Hubbard (1996) also details a case of forensic authorship analysis incorporating NLID. In 1988 the Johannesburg headquarters of a South African chain store received ten extortion letters. The letters demanded payment of $500,000 or the author threatened to poison food on the store's shelves and to alert the media. A fake payment was organised following the demands in the letter, however police lost track of the payment. The man who lived directly next to the stated drop site became the main suspect. He was a medical doctor (and also claimed to hold an engineering doctorate) with German-English parentage, who had spent most of his life in Romania, but claimed Polish as his L1, requesting a Polish court interpreter. During the trial the defence advocate hired a professor of English, who performed various analyses; most notably a basic form of error analysis, to determine that it was unlikely that the doctor had written the extortion notes. The prosecution then approached Hubbard, whose analysis and evidence entailed three main parts: "(a) a critique of the evidence led by the defence witness; (b) a stylometic analysis; and (c) an error analysis" (Hubbard, 1996, p. 125). The accused was found guilty of the extortion charges, leading Hubbard to observe that "error analysis can have forensic value" (Hubbard, 1996, p. 137). Although NLID is distinct from error analysis, in that it accounts for all the features in the language, not just errors, there are still parallels that can be drawn.

It is likely that there are even more cases involving elements of NLID which have not been documented in publically accessible literature. This is even more probable when the link to extremism and terrorism is considered; as such cases often cannot be discussed in public fora. NLID does not specifically answer all the questions that are raised by these cases, but we can see the potential of NLID as a useful tool for forensic authorship analysis. There are documented cases that would benefit from greater research into NLID, indicating that research into Native Language Identification would be of great benefit to future cases.

1.2 Literature Review

Native Language Identification has received very limited attention from academic research, despite its considerable potential for practical application (Koppel, Schler, & Zigdon, 2005). The research that has examined NLID takes a mainly computational approach. Koppel, Schler and Zigdon (2005) are often considered as having pioneered the research in this field (Wong, Dras, & Johnson, 2011). They used a combination of text mining and error analysis to determine authors' likely L1's or native languages. Basing their research on the International Corpus of Learner English, they focused on Czech, French, Bulgarian, Russian and Spanish speakers writing in English. They used function words, letter n-grams, and errors and idiosyncrasies as the base for the development of an automated system. Tsur & Rappoport, (2007) developed upon the work by Koppel, Schler and Zigdon (2005), extending it to consider links between word choice and L1 phonological structures. Estival et al. (2007) looked at a wide range of sociolinguistic factors in authorship analysis including native language identification. All these studies rely heavily on student data, which holds difficulties for application in forensic contexts. Forensic data rarely involves student data, and is normally a considerably different genre making the data not particularly comparable. There are also fewer variables (for example the lack of disguise or threatening topics). There are also dangers with fully automated approaches, as they risk ignoring the capacity for complexity of linguistic variables. A fully automated classification system removes the important layer of a linguist analysing the data and hence understanding what the features are and why they have occurred. If you have a fully automated system, there is the possibility that when it is applied to real-life forensic data it may not be able to account for new factors (such as disguise or more threatening topics) and that this may confuse the results. If a linguist is actively involved in the process (rather than relying on a 'black-box' system) this should be reduced. Past cases involving NLID that have been published, most notably Hubbard (1996) and Kniffka (1996) are very much based on an individual linguist's analysis. They both set out the methodology they utilized in the cases, but there is a very limited focus on research and building tools to aid with wider NLID cases. This research seeks to combine the two approaches and develop a methodology that is easily applicable and relevant for potential future research.

One area of linguistics that is of considerable interest to NLID is the concept of interlanguage which is predominantly discussed within the realm of pedagogy and second language acquisition or contact linguistics (specifically with relation to multilingualism). Interlanguage has long been of interest to linguists, predominantly those taking a pedagogical perspective and aiming to improve English language teaching. Despite the difference in aims, it is the nearest sizeable body of existing research which can inform the current approach to NLID. The term *interlanguage* was initially coined in 1972 by Selinker, however, the concept it referred to had existed and been discussed in differing terms prior to that. Most notably Weinreich (1953) discussed "Interlingual identifications", as well as *interference*, a term he defined as implying "the introduction of foreign elements" (Weinreich, 1953, p. 1) into a second language. One of the main focus points of existing interlanguage research was to better understand where learner errors came from in order to eliminate or reduce them. While this area provides an important theoretical underpinning to NLID research it is relevant to note that there is a lack of consensus in exactly what factors can and do cause interlingual features in learner language. Researchers have cited potential influences from factors such as learning techniques, other languages learnt and the potential (and controversial) existence of a universal grammar. De Angelis when discussing this stated that "our understanding of what can and cannot be transferred from one non-native language to another in the process of acquisition remains quite limited to date" (Angelis, 2005, p. 380). Although she was specifically discussing transfer between second languages, it serves to highlight the lack of ability to account for all the influences on second language production. Here the different aims of NLID for forensic authorship purposes and existing interlanguage really come to bear. NLID, like forensic authorship analysis on general, is more concerned with documenting the features that are present within the language of L1 Persian speakers, rather than why they are there. For this reason (as demonstrated in Figure 2 below) the potential existence of a universal grammar, cultural influences, or impact from teaching styles means this research will allow for numerous potential influences on interlanguage and second language production, so as not to exclude any potential interlanguage features. This also supports the motivation for a data-driven approach that enables the documentation of any features of the language of this social group.

Another key difference between existing interlanguage research and NLID is the application and how that is reflected in data selection. Existing research focuses understandably on student data, mirroring the intended application of the findings. Interestingly the existing computational NLID research is also based on student data. This presents a key problem for NLID research as the intended application is focused on forensic data. As stated previously, any text can become a forensic text if the context is right, however the majority of documented cases of forensic authorship analysis rarely relate to texts produced in an educational environment. Genre has a key role in influence the linguistic choices an individual makes when authoring a document, it could reasonably be expected that an individual's student essay would contain significantly different features from a threatening email by the same person. There are numerous ethical and practical difficulties with attaining genuine forensic data, but it is of benefit to choose a genre of texts to study that is nearer to the genre expected.

Early research on interlanguage was not explicitly based on research; rather it was seemingly grounded in linguists' experience and intuition. This creates many potential difficulties for forensic linguistic situations as forensic linguistics is mainly interested in how language is actually used, rather than on preconceptions of how it is, or should be used. This research, like the existing NLID research,

Figure 2. Interlanguage influence

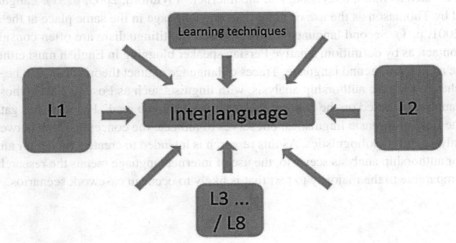

uses corpora (collections of texts) as data. The use of corpora and corpus linguistics has undoubtedly "revolutionised the study of language, and of the applications of language over the last few decades." (Hunston, 2002, p. 1). Corpus linguistics has many advantages (Stubbs, 1996). One major benefit is that rather than creating hypotheses then looking for evidence in the data to support them, a corpus approach encourages more unbiased analysis, showing how language is actually used, rather than focusing on misperceptions of how it is used or how it should be used. For this reason a corpus based approach is of much use to forensic linguistic research. Coulthard highlighted the importance of corpora to forensic linguistic research stating that "any improved methodology must depend, to a large extent, on the setting up and analysing of corpora." (Coulthard, 1994, p. 40). The growth of the internet and computer mediated communication in daily life makes the need to focus on online texts more important, as can be witnessed through the establishment of continually growing fields such as computer forensics and internet forensics (Berghel, 2003), as well as through the need for books such as this one. It is therefore appropriate that the data source for this research is internet language. The main difference between student data and blog data is that student data is elicited whereas blog data is collected. Elicited data has certain advantages as there is greater control over topic choice, a better possibility to collect background data, and reduced chance of a participant giving a false profile. Conversely collected data has not been written for that specific purpose, meaning that the researcher has less control over the data and surrounding information. The internet also facilitates the collection of larger amounts of valuable relevant data. Computer mediated communication can be considered a distinct genre (or genres). Text from the internet has the benefit that the medium of the internet has fewer regulations and elicits a more relaxed style, congruent with the 'real-life' data necessary for this research. Crystal has widely discussed the much publicised informality of internet language, he illustrated the situation by writing "The electronic medium [...] presents us with a channel which facilitates and constrains our ability to communicate in ways that are fundamentally different from those found in other semiotic situations." (Crystal, 2001, p. 5) This relates to Labov's work on field methods for sociolinguistic research, in which he determined that style is related to the amount of attention a speaker pays to their speech and in turn that the less attention is paid to speech, the more systematic data it provides for linguistic analysis (Labov, 1984). The internet and online communication has a key role in globalization and language contact, it has been termed the "defining technology of globalization" (Blommaert, 2010, p. loc. 1537). Winford writes that "[a]nother type of "distant" contact leading to lexical borrowing can be found in the spread of global avenues of communications such as radio, television, and the internet." (Winford, 2003, p. 31). Language contact was explained by Thomason as the use of more than one language in the same place at the same time" (Thomason, 2001, p. 1). Second language acquisition and multilingualism are often considered forms of language contact, as by definition, a native Persian speaker blogging in English must either be multilingual or have acquired a second language. Traces of language contact theories can also be seen within some approaches to forensic authorship analysis, with linguists such as Foster (2001) whose approach to authorship analysis is based on the concept that 'you are what you read'. His work has gathered criticism within the field of forensic linguistics, but serves to indicate the conceptual link between forensic authorship analysis and sociolinguistics. As this research is intended to create a model for analysis in an investigative or authorship analysis scenario, the use of internet language means the research is built on data that is comparable to the majority to text that is likely to occur in casework scenarios.

2. NLID STUDY

2.1 Study Design

The research in this chapter was carried out by the primary author at Aston University (Perkins, 2012), it formed part of a larger NLID study which comprises multiple studies around the theme. The main aim of this research is to determine if linguistic features in L2 writing can be used to indicate an author's native tongue. The focus was on L1 Persian speakers blogging in English. The main questions asked were:

- Which specific features best indicate authorship by an L1 Persian speaker,
- Can the features identified distinguish influence from Persian as opposed to closely related languages,
- Can we develop a method of NLID for casework situations, and
- With what degree of accuracy can we draw conclusions about an author's L1.

The best approach to answer these questions was to develop a study with different sections. The first comprising two corpora; one of L1 Persian texts and one of L1 English texts, in order to determine which features were indicative of L1 Persian authorship. The next study looked at closely related languages. There was also a third study which considered the concept of an author disguising their language, due to practical constraints this sub-study will not be discussed fully in this chapter[1].

The concepts of first and second languages which are pivotal to the data collection of this research might initially seem relatively straight forward, but this is not always the case. Due to the increase in multilingualism and factors such as globalisation, there are many people with very complex linguistic backgrounds; a high proportion of people are now bi- or multilingual, and it is common for an individual to come into contact with languages that they do not necessarily speak (through the media or travel). This has been discussed extensively by linguists such as Leung, Harris, & Rampton, (1997) and Rampton (1990). While they discuss many pertinent issues their observations focus primarily on language learning environments; offering few solutions for data collection. It was considered most practical that in this research an author's L1 or native language was considered to be the language they themselves identified as being their native language. The terminology used varied considerably, with *native language* or *mother tongue* being the most frequent. If an author claimed multiple native languages then they were not considered to be an L1 speaker of the relevant language, however if they stated speaking other languages to a lesser ability the language they were still accepted as L1 speakers of the language they identified as their native language. With relation to this work L2 or *second language* is used to refer to any language that is not the first, or L1. The complexity of identifying L1 speakers of specific languages, coupled with the possibility of an author giving a false linguistic background gives rise to the possibility of irregularities in the data. These are diminished through manual data collection and the application of consistent criteria throughout the data gathering, as well as collecting a sizeable amount of data for each corpus so that any irregularities would be statistically insignificant.

In order to understand what features are unique to L1 Persian speakers it is important to have a control corpus of L1 English speakers also blogging in English. This enables us to compare the data sets and see how the features differ between the native Persian and native English speakers. All data were collected using Google searches and comprised publicly accessible weblogs written in English. The blogs were by individual authors (rather than multiple co-authors) and not ostensibly edited by anyone else. This enabled a more accurate understanding of the linguistic history of the person who had produced the text and reduced external variables. Data was collected manually to ensure a high reliability of correct L1 identification. The data for Study One comprise two groups; English language weblogs by L1 Persian speakers and English language weblogs by L1 English speakers. A total of 25 authors were chosen for each corpus (L1 Persian and L1 English) and approximately 2,000 words were collected for each author. The data for Study Two comprised the L1 Persian corpus collected for Study One, and an extra corpus of L1 speakers of Azeri and Pashto (the motivations behind focusing on these languages is discussed later). Study Two was a sub-study and practical limitations meant that a reduced number of authors and reduced volume of text could be considered. A total of 1,000 words for 10 separate authors (five L1 Azeri and five L1 Pashto) were collected.

Due to the lack of existing research in this specific field, there was very limited methodological precedent. Part of the research therefore, involved developing a reliable methodology for NLID. The majority of related existing research took a 'top-down' perspective, in that features were chosen then those specific features were analysed in the text. This research combines a 'top-down' and a 'bottom-up' approach in which the features identified were data-driven. The first stage of analysis comprised identifying potential features within the corpora, this was done by a close analysis of a sample of texts where possible marked, unusual or unnatural language use was noted and then features were created to describe it (a total of over 300 features were identified, many of which related to very precise descriptive markers). It should be noted that this was not just error analysis, but any marked use of language could be a feature (even hyper-correctness). These features were then converted into a linguistic feature tree which could be used to identify and code any potential feature features within the texts. It was discovered that the initial features identified could be arranged into groups the following main groups; Position and Ordering, Adjective, Adverb, Article, Capitalisation, Conjunction, Lexical, Preposition, Pronoun, Punctuation, and Verbal. Within each of these groups the features could be accounted for by being either; *marked* presence, *marked absence, marked construction, marked choice* or *marked ordering and positioning* (not all of these features were present in the data, resulting in a total of 29 mid-level features present). The final framework of the feature tree meant that could be expanded to accommodate any potential new features as well as those already identified. Under each of these overarching groupings the features were coded even more descriptively to give more detail about the features present and highlight more subtle trends and patterns. This lower level of coding and the more specific analysis is not being discussed in this chapter due to practical constraints; it is also the subject of further ongoing research. The feature tree also included a feature for possible influence, for example if the word *word* was spelt as *wrod* it if easily understood as likely to be a typing error, rather than a genuine error. There is a danger however that in making an assumption such as this, certain trends or features could be missed (or misattributed). Therefore it would be marked as an error in lexical construction, as well as being marked as possibly influenced by a typing error. In this way the two aims of coding any section of the texts is; to describe a feature, and where relevant to explain it. In many cases it was impossible to describe how the language was marked without making assumptions about the author's intentions, for this reason there was a feature set of *unsure/problematic to classify*. This accounted for a high number of features as would be expected. The strong advantage of the structure of this feature tree is that its scope to account for more features within its structure means that it could be applied to similar analysis of other languages or data. As the methodology for each study was kept as consistent as possible, all corpora were coded with the same coding system.

As discussed previously, the first stage of analysis comprised feature identification based on a sample of the data and the development of a coding system. The next stage involved coding all the data according to the system developed; this was done manually but aided by use of the qualitative software program NVivo. The third stage was a statistical analysis using logistic regression, to determine which of the features identified were the most discriminating between the groups. Study Two built on Study One, using the same feature tree and coding system and mirroring the analysis as much as possible.

2.2 Findings

Study One Findings

The initial observations of the feature counts demonstrated which features were the most prevalent (Figure 3 below). The fact the some of the features are higher in the L1 English data serves to highlight that the features being focused on were not just errors, but usage patterns.

The frequency counts enable certain interesting insights to the data, but the real importance is their discriminatory ability rather than frequency. In order to determine how good the features were at discriminating between the groups, a logistic regression analysis was undertaken. Logistic regression analysis is a classification model based on probabilities, it uses the distribution of features to predict the linear probability that a given author would belong to a certain group, the two groups constituting two discreet possible outcomes. The computer programme SPSS enables quick logistic regression analysis, and also evaluates the model for predictive ability. The analysis showed that using all 29 features identified at the

Figure 3. Feature frequencies

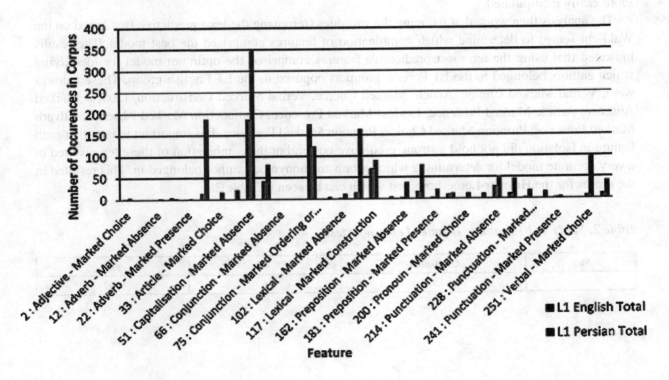

Table 1. Study 1 - Lower level features Hosmer-Lemeshow test

Step	Chi-Square	df	Sig.
1	.000	8	1.000

mid-level, resulted in a model that has a theoretical accuracy of 100%, correctly assigning all authors to the correct groups. This in combination with the Hosmer-Lemeshow test (Table 1), indicates that the model is overly fitted to the specific data. Over-fitting indicates that while the feature and model are good for this data, the model may not be applicable to other data and cases. As this research is intended for application in forensic authorship situations it is important that the model is accurate, but not over-fitted to the specific data.

The Hosmer-Lemeshow test and the Model Summary evaluate the fit of the model. A significance score lower than 0.05 indicates that the model does not fit the data well. A score of 1.000 as can be seen here, shows that the model is over fitted to the data, so would not be generalisable to other data. The ideal significance score is over 0.05 but less than 1.000. The analysis indicates that the model would be more reliable with a reduced number of variables (which equates to linguistic features). The Wald-Chi statistic gives the significance of each feature, indicating how predictive each individual feature is. Each feature had a very low Wald-Chi square score, as well as a significance value very close to one. This shows that although the features are exceedingly predictive when all 29 features are used in the model together, when taken in isolation even the most predictive feature is not highly predictive of group membership. This is good from an application point of view as it means the strength of the models comes from the combination of features, rather than single features which are more easily manipulated.

The analysis then worked at reducing the variables (removing the least predictive first based on the Wald-chi score) to determine which combination of features comprised the best model. The results indicated that using the ten most predicative features comprised the optimum model for identifying which authors belonged to the L1 Persian group as opposed to the L1 English group. These features were; Verbal Marked Choice, Article Marked Choice, Verbal Marked Construction, Lexical Marked Absence, Article Marked Presence, Lexical Marked Presence, Conjunction Marked Absence, Adverb Marked Presence, Pronoun Marked Choice, Pronoun Marked Presence. It is important to note that each feature in isolation did not hold a strong predictive power, but the combination of these ten resulted in a very accurate model for determining which group an anonymous author belonged in. This resulted in the scores for the Hosmer-Lemeshow Test which can be seen in Table 2.

Table 2. Study 1. 10 Features Hosmer Lemeshow test

Step	Chi-Square	df	Sig.
1	3.128	6	.793

Table 3. Study 1 - Optimum model classification table

Classification Table[a]							
	Observed			Predicted			
				L1 Group (1=English, 2=Persian)			Percentage Correct
				1	2		
Step 1	L1 Group (1=English, 2=Persian)		1	23	2		92.0
			2	2	23		92.0
	Overall Percentage						92.0
a. The cut value is .500							

The Chi-square value is 3.128 with a significance value of 0.793. This is considerably higher than 0.05 yet less the 1.000 indicating that the model comprising the ten selected is very reliable, but not over fitted to the data. This is also supported by the Model Summary which includes the Cox and Snell R Square and Nagelkerke R Square values which are pseudo R square statistics. They signify approximately how much of the variability in the data is explained by the chosen features, which in this case is between 59.5 percent and 79.3 percent. As these percentages are quite high it means the model is fairly accurate.

The Classification Table (Table 3) states how many authors were assigned to each group according to the features they exhibit (predicted) and which group they actually originally belonged to (observed). This table demonstrates that out of the total of 50 authors, only 4 were incorrectly attributed as belonging to the wrong group. Each author (or case) is assigned a predicted group purely from the features contained within the data for that author; no reference is paid to the distribution of other authors. In order to better understand which cases were misattributed we can examine the Casewise List. Table 4 is a modified version showing only the values only for the misattributed cases.

A predicted probability over 0.5 (where the score is between 0 and 1) results in the author being predicted as belonging to Group 2, the group of L1 Persian speakers. A score of less than 0.5 results in the author being assigned to Group 1, the group of L1 English speakers. Of the two L1 English speakers that were attributed as belonging to the L1 Persian, their probabilities are both close to the 0.5 threshold. Case 11 had a probability of 0.532, which is only 0.032 over the cut-off point and Case 15 has a probability of 0.726 which is 0.226 over the 0.5 boundary. Both two cases are within the bottom 4 cases that

Table 4. Study 1 - Optimum model casewise list

Casewise List						
Case	Selected Status[a]	Observed	Predicted	Predicted Group	Temporary Variable	
		L1 Group (1=English, 2=Persian)			Resid	ZResid
11	S	1**	.532	2	-.532	-1.066
15	S	1**	.726	2	-.726	-1.628
33	S	2**	.073	1	.927	3.576
40	S	2**	.073	1	.927	3.576
a. S = Selected, U = Unselected cases, and ** = Misclassified cases.						

were attributed to Group 2 (the L1 Persian speakers). Conversely the two L1 Persian speakers that were predicted as belonging to the L1 English group (Group 1) had probabilities that placed them more firmly within that group, and were not as close to the 0.5 boundary line.

Study 2 Findings

Study One clearly demonstrated that NLID is possible and that these features have a high reliability, but it does not explain whether it is possible to distinguish closely related languages. In order to test this, an additional corpus of blogs written by L1 speakers of related languages was collected and analysed. The two languages chosen were Pashto and Azeri as they are completely distinct languages from Persian and have a significant number of speakers in the Iranian Plateau. Unlike some of the lesser spoken languages they were also able to produce enough data for this study. Pashto (also known as Afghani) is the official language of Afghanistan. It is a central Iranian language belonging to the Indo-Iranian language family (Persian is a Southwestern-Iranian language also of the Indo-Iranian language family). Azeri (also known as Azerbaijani) is a Turkic language, it is spoke predominantly in Azerbaijan and northern Iran, but it also an official language in Russia. Pashto represents a language that is from the same language family as Persian, whereas Azeri represents a language that is slightly further away on the linguistic family tree, yet is culturally similar. Both languages have a significant proportion of their speakers in the same geographical area as Persian, meaning that they can be considered geographically and culturally close, this is important given the forensic context. They also have relatively large number of native speakers, meaning they are able to yield enough data for this research. As discussed previously practical constraints and the fact the languages are less widely spoken meant that a reduced volume of data was collected for this data as opposed to Study One. Despite this the data collection and methodology were designed to be as consistent as possible to that of Study One. As with Study One there were two corpora, one of L1 Persian speakers writing in English, and one labelled *otherlanguages* which contained the L1 Azeri and L1 Pashto authors. Data was collected for a total of ten authors; five L1 Azeri and five L1 Persian. Where possible up to 2,000 words of data were collected for each author, but as this was not always possible a minimum of 200 words was set. Feature counts were later normalised to calculate the average total per 2,000 words, this accounted for the difference in volume and enabled direct comparisons.

Initial findings showed that as expected there were differences in the feature frequencies compared to the Study One corpora. As in Study One though the key focus was on which features were the best discriminators rather than the most frequent, to determine this binary logistic regression was used. Using all 29 features in Study One resulted in a model that was over-fitted to the data, it was unsurprising that the same was the case for Study Two. The Hosmer-Lemeshow test resulted in a chi-square score of less than 0.000 and a significance approaching 1.000, demonstrating that the model was over fitted and contained too many features. Despite the over-fitting of the model, as was seen before, the individual features had a very low determining power when taken in isolation. The features were ranked according to their Wald-chi square statistic, and then reduced to determine which combination produced the optimum model. It was found that the optimum model comprised the 12 features with the highest Wald-chi scores. These features are: Pronoun Marked Presence, Verbal Marked Choice, Lexical Marked Choice, Conjunction Marked Absence, Conjunction Marked Presence, Lexical Marked Presence, Preposition Marked Absence, Lexical Marked Absence, Pronoun Marked Absence, Adverb Marked Absence, Lexical Marked Construction, and Verbal Marked Construction. Using these features in the model resulted in a significance of 0.922 and a Chi-square score of 2.571 in the Hosmer-Lemeshow Test. A significance

Table 5. Study 2. 12 features classification table

	Observed		Predicted		
			Classification Table[a]		
			Study2otherlanguages		Percentage Correct
			Persian	Azeri and Pashto	
Step 1	Study2otherlanguages	Persian	23	2	92.0
		Azeri and Pashto	4	6	60.0
	Overall Percentage				82.9
a. The cut value is .500					

score that is close to 1, without reaching it, means that the model is accurate without being over-fitted. The Nagelkerke R square and the Cox and Snell R square scores indicate that the model using the twelve features accounts for between 44.5 and 63.8 percent of the variability.

The following classification table (Table 5) demonstrates that using the optimum model of 12 features resulted in six of the authors being attributed to the wrong group. Two L1 Persian authors out of 25 were falsely identified as belonging to the *otherlanguages* group, and four out of ten authors in the *otherlanguages* group were identified as L1 Persian speakers.

Of the Azeri and Persian authors that were misidentified as being L1 Persian; two were Azeri speakers and two were Pashto. Table 6 demonstrates that the wrongly assigned texts all had predicted probabilities that were relatively close to the 0.5 boundary, so were only just in the probability range of the other group. Texts that had a predicted probability of less than 0.5 were assigned to the L1 Persian speaker group (Group 2) and a predicted probability of over 0.5 meant the author was indicated as belonging to Group 3, the group of other language speakers.

The predicted probability values for the two Pashto authors are lower than the values for the two Azeri authors, meaning that they have a great predicted probability of belonging to the L1 Persian text. This could be linked to the fact that Pashto and Persian are more linguistically similar than Azeri and Persian, but it should be noted that this is a preliminary study focusing on distinguishing between Persian and

Table 6. Study 2. 12 features misattributed authors casewise list

Case	Author (L1)	Observed	Predicted	Predicted Group	Temporary Variable	
		Casewise List				
		Study2 otherlanguages			Resid	ZResid
34	AH: (Persian)	2**	.662	3	-.662	-1.400
36	AJ: (Persian)	2**	.510	3	-.510	-1.019
53	BA: (Azeri)	3**	.485	2	.515	1.030
54	BB: (Azeri)	3**	.347	2	.653	1.371
56	BD: (Pashto)	3**	.110	2	.890	2.846
57	BE: (Pashto)	3**	.276	2	.724	1.618
** = Misclassified cases.						

closely related languages, not a full study into these other languages. In order to investigate this more fully further research with more data from L1 Azeri and L1 Pashto authors would be needed. Two L1 Persian authors were misattributed to the *otherlanguages* group. Again they were both close to the 0.5 threshold. It is possible that these two authors had some degree of influence from either Azeri or Pashto, especially due to the geographical locations of the languages; however, this level of information is not available for the collected data. The prevalence of Persian in the areas that Azeri and Pashto are commonly spoken would imply that many L1 Azeri and L1 Pashto speakers will have an influence from L1 Persian. It is therefore not surprising that more authors from the otherlanguages Group were attributed as L1 Persian speakers, than the other way around.

3. NLID FOR CASEWORK / APPLICATION AND FUTURE

3.1 Summary and Implications of Findings

This research demonstrated that interlingual features in non-native (L2) writing can be used to indicate an author's native tongue. Taking a new approach it helped develop a new methodology for NLID research, which can be (and is being) developed on through further research. A template of features was developed and all features were data-driven. Study One ascertained which features were the most predictive for indicating authorship by an L1 Persian speaker blogging in English demonstrating that the optimum model to distinguish L1 Persian authorship from L1 English comprised the following features; Verbal Marked Choice, Article Marked Choice, Verbal Marked Construction, Lexical Marked Absence, Article Marked Presence, Lexical Marked Presence, Conjunction Marked Absence, Adverb Marked Presence, Pronoun Marked Choice, Pronoun Marked Presence. Study Two was a scoping study which examined whether the features identified would be able to distinguish between related languages. The analysis mirrored that of Study One, but utilised a smaller amount of data. It determined that the features were able to distinguish between L1 Persian authors and authors of related languages. It was determined that the optimum model comprised the following twelve features: Verbal Marked Choice, Article Marked Choice, Verbal Marked Construction, Lexical Marked Absence, Article Marked Presence, Lexical Marked Presence, Conjunction Marked Absence, Adverb Marked Presence, Pronoun Marked Choice, Pronoun Marked Presence.

This research also considered the degree of accuracy with which we can draw conclusions based on the analysis involved. It was the case in both studies that the features identified tended towards overfitting rather than a lack of reliability. The optimum model for Study One has a Chi-square value of 3.128 with a significance value of 0.793. This is considerably higher than 0.05 yet less than 1.000 indicating that using the ten selected features generates a model that is very reliable, but not over fitted to the data. The Cox and Snell R Square and Nagelkerke R Square values signify approximately how much of the variability within the data is explained by the chosen features, which for this model is between 59.5 percent and 79.3 percent. The higher the percentage (or the closer the score is to one) the more accurate the model is. This is supported by the fact that in using the 10 features that comprised the optimum model for this study, it was possible to correctly predict which group 92% of the authors belonged to. For Study Two the optimum model resulted in a significance of 0.922 and a Chi-square score of 2.571 in the Hosmer-Lemeshow Test, with the Nagelkerke R square and the Cox and Snell R square scores indicating that this model (using the twelve features most predictive features) accounts for between 44.5 and 63.8 percent of the variability, as well as correctly assigning 82.9% of authors to the correct group.

The findings of this research support the concept discussed in section one that it is possible to identify a person's L1 or native language, from the linguistic choices they make in a second language. They also indicate that it is possible to do this to a relatively high level of accuracy. There is a demonstrated potential for native language identification as a part of forensic authorship analysis to be of great assistance at an investigatory level.

3.2 Application to Casework Situation

During the process of this research project the lead author was contacted with a question about related casework. The case highlighted that in order to truly provide support in forensic authorship analysis casework situations, the results had to be extracted in an easily implementable form. The statistical output also gives us the *B* value for each feature (see Table 7), which relates to how much the presence of that particular feature alters the probability of membership to each group. The polarity indicates which group the feature relates to. A positive B value in Study One increased the probability that the author belonged to the second group, that of L1 Persian speakers. In Study Two a negative B value increases the probability of L1 Persian authorship. In both studies the following 3 features indicated an increased probability that the author belonged to the L1 Persian speakers group: Conjunction Marked Absence, Pronoun Marked Presence, and Lexical Marked Presence.

This information enables much greater understanding of the features and avoids a 'black-box' approach to analysis. It is also possible to use these optimum models and the information contained in the table about to perform analysis in case-work situations. The option to focus on these features in isolation, as opposed to finding comparison data and fully coding multiple corpora at the full range of features (over 300), means that the model is implementable in casework scenarios which from experience tend to necessitate relatively quick analysis. This is best demonstrated through a practical example. The following is a short extract from a blog that did not form part of the data for this research. Ideally a forensic linguist will

Table 7. Study 1 and 2 - optimum model features

Rank	Study One	Wald	B	Study Two	Wald	B
1	Verbal Marked Choice	4.101	1.727	Conjunction Marked Absence	3.535	4.364
2	Article Marked Choice	3.355	2.628	Pronoun Marked Presence	2.463	6.313
3	Verbal Marked Construction	1.629	-1.058	Preposition Marked Absence	2.134	-1.632
4	Lexical Marked Absence	0.853	1.355	Lexical Marked Choice	2.109	0.242
5	Article Marked Presence	0.84	1.161	Lexical Marked Absence	0.852	-2.52
6	Lexical Marked Presence	0	26.623	Lexical Marked Construction	0.83	0.103
7	Conjunction Marked Absence	0	-53.241	Lexical Marked Presence	0.657	-1.691
8	Adverb Marked Presence	0	-74.842	Verbal Marked Construction	0.385	-0.383
9	Pronoun Marked Choice	0	80.921	Pronoun Marked Absence	0.352	0.385
10	Pronoun Marked Presence	0	-16.168	Verbal Marked Choice	0.053	0.073
11				Conjunction Marked Presence	0	-40.801
12				Adverb Marked Absence	0	-26.574

gather as much data as possible for authorship analysis, however this is not always possible. Coulthard (1994) estimated that forensic texts tend to be between 400 and 700 words in length. The increase of forensic data linked to computer mediated communication, such as text messages or tweets, means that even briefer texts are becoming more relevant to forensic contexts (Silva & Laboreiro, 2011). It is unlikely that such a short text would constitute good forensic data, but it serves as a good example here.

My name is Jaleh but my friends call me Jamigen, I am a student at the University of Tehran [Pardis] where I *265* studying in the Faculty of Law and Political Sciences. My professor is Davoud Agahie. I *251* start this blog site as a school project. I *251* provide information on world affairs but mostly I know my own country Iran the best. My native language is Persian but I know some English and Arabic. This blog site will *251* write in English since I *265* trying to speak and write English better. I will update this blog *122* site often. (Jaleh, 2011)

The features are marked in the text with *numbers* that correspond to the relevant features (see list below). The text contains the following features:

- *251* = Verbal Marked Choice x3 occurrence
- *265* = Verbal Marked Construction x2 occurrence
- *122* = Lexical Marked Presence x1 occurrence

Each study much be considered in turn. Firstly, the features relating to Study 1 can be input to the following equation to determine the probability that the text was authored by an L1 Persian speaker

Likelihood of membership to second group = (B value of feature for specific study x number of occurrences) + (B value of next feature x number of occurrences) [...]

Study 1 Likelihood of L1 Persian author = (1.727 x 3) + (-1.058 x 2) + (26.623 x 1) = 5.181 + -2.116 + 26.623 = 29.688 times more likely to be L1 Persian

This demonstrates, that despite the reduced volume of text, the features indicate that the author is an L1 Persian speaker which matches what the author identified with. The likelihood ratio constitutes moderate evidence by the standards of Champod & Evett, (1999)'s scale.

Study 2 likelihood of L1 otherlanguages author = (0.073 x 3) + (-0.383 x 2) + (-1.691 x 1) = -2.238 times more likely to be an L1 other languages speaker = 2.238 times more likely to be an L1 Persian speaker

This again is in keeping with the blogger's self-identification as an L1 Persian speaker. The reduced likelihood ratio only constitutes limited evidence on Champod and Evett's 1999 scale for evaluating likelihood scales as evidence. However, the facts that even with a very small section of text, the results are as expected, supports the reliability of the features and their use in forensic situations. It is likely that a greater volume of text would yield more features, and hence the weight of evidence might increase. NLID is intended to be a tool for linguists only, however to fully code the data with the full range of features as discussed previously would require a very specific level of expertise with this specific analysis, making NLID less of a widely implementable tool for forensic authorship analysis. Focusing on these reduced variables is more implementable both time wise and practically.

3.3 Conclusion

Native language identification (NLID) has much potential as a tool to aid forensic authorship analysis, which in turn holds much promise for law enforcement agencies seeking to prevent, investigate and ultimately prosecute online crime or terrorism. Despite this NLID has not been the subject of much research. This is starting to change and it is starting to attract growing interest from law enforcement agencies, at both application and research level. Forensic authorship has already proved to be of much interest and benefit to parties working to prevent and prosecute computer mediated crime and there are indicators that the same can be said for native language identification. When discussing the progression of the wider field of forensic linguistics Coulthard (1994) wrote that "the future [for forensic linguists] must lie in the creation of a better standardized and more widely used methodology." (Coulthard, 1994, p. 40), this can also be applied to the more specific focal area of NLID. The research seeks to promote this and encourage further, competing ideas and methodologies surrounding NLID. The practical application is a vital aspect of NLID and future research should be guided by this. Language and language use is constantly evolving, this is mirrored in the evolution of forensic casework. For this reason native language identification is posited as a methodology that must evolve and grow. Forensic linguistics is still a relatively new discipline; this means that the interface between forensic linguists and law enforcement agencies is still evolving as many people are not yet aware of forensic linguistics. Similarly there might be situations in which forensic linguistics and NLID might be of benefit, but have not become recognised within forensic linguistics yet. A broad evolutionary approach must be taken. NLID has drawn on other areas of linguistics, and it is likely that the analysis and findings might be of use to wider areas of linguistics. For example the B values indicate which features increase the likelihood that an author is more likely to a certain group, this could be compared to existing interlanguage research and comparative linguistics. Although the research presented here is intended to mainly have implications for forensic authorship analysis, findings such as these might be of benefits to other areas of sociolinguistic research, bridging the gaps.

The coding system devised, contained considerably more information that could be thoroughly discussed here. On-going research is already taking place to analyse this as well as to expand and develop the project as discussed so far. The research presented in this chapter has a relatively narrow focus; that of L1 Persian speakers writing in English. There are of course many other languages that would be of interest to law enforcement agencies. That is before we even consider influences evident in other languages (for example an L1 English speaker writing in Persian). The list of potential future research areas relating to NLID is considerable. The research presented here, forms a part of a wider project investigating a wide range of NLID related questions and considering a variety of languages. The key direction of ongoing research at the moment is distinguishing influence from languages that are closely related linguistically and culturally, considering a much broader range of languages than previously, and working towards a more automated model which is easily implementable.

It is clear that there are many potential directions in which this research can be expanded, and suggestions for the future that are contained in here should not be considered as limiting, as it is impossible to discuss all areas of potential benefit. Perhaps the key element of this research is that it intends to spark a debate, and the potential future for NLID as discussed here, is just one perspective. In order to truly grow and develop to its full potential, input from and collaboration with a range of academics and practitioners is needed.

REFERENCES

Berghel, H. (2003). The discipline of Internet forensics. *Communications of the ACM, 46*(8), 15. doi:10.1145/859670.859687

Bhatia, T. K., & Ritchie, W. C. (2004). Bilingualism in the Global Media and Advertising. In T. K. Bhatia & W. C. Ritchie (Eds.), *The Handbook of Bilingualism* (pp. 513–546). Oxford: Blackwell Publishing Ltd.

Bhatia, T. K., & Ritchie, W. C. (2013). Multilingualism and Forensic Linguistics. In *The Handbook of Bilingualism and Multilingualism* (pp. 671–701). Malden, Oxford: Blackwell Publishing Ltd.

Blommaert, J. (2010). *The Sociolinguistics of Globalization*. Cambridge: Cambridge University Press. doi:10.1017/CBO9780511845307

Champod, C., & Evett, I. W. (1999). A. P. A. Broeders (1999) "Some observations on the use of probability scales in forensic identification. *International Journal of Speech Language and the Law, 6*(June), 228–241.

Coulthard, M. (1994). On the use of corpora in the analysis of forensic texts. *Forensic Linguistics, 1*(1), 27–43.

Coulthard, M., Grant, T., & Kredens, K. (2010). Forensic Linguistics. In B. Johnstone, R. Wodak, & P. Kerswill (Eds.), *The SAGE Handbook of Sociolinguistics* (pp. 529–544).

Crystal, D. (2001). *Language and the Internet. New York*. Cambridge: Cambridge University Press. doi:10.1017/CBO9781139164771

De Angelis, G. (2005). Interlanguage Transfer of Function Words. *Language Learning, 55*(3), 379–414. doi:10.1111/j.0023-8333.2005.00310.x

Doyle, A. C. (1892). *The Adventures of Sherlock Holmes*. New York: Harper and Brothers.

Estival, D., Hutchinson, B., Gaustad, T., Pham, S. B., Radford, W., & Nsw, S. (2007). Author Profiling for English Emails, 263–272.

Foster, D. (2001). *On the Trail of Anonymous*. New York: Henry Holt & Company.

Grant, T. (2008). Approaching questions in forensic authorship analysis. In J. Gibbons & M. T. Turell (Eds.), *Dimensions of Forensic Linguistics* (pp. 215–229). Philadelphia, PA: John Benjamins Publishing Company. doi:10.1075/aals.5.15gra

Grant, T. (2010). Text Messaging Forensics: Txt 4n6: Idiolect free authorship analysis? In M. Coulthard & A. Johnson (Eds.), *The Routledge Handbook of World Englishes* (pp. 508–522). London, New York: Routledge. doi:10.4324/9780203855607.ch33

Grant, T., Kredens, K., & Perkins, R. (2010). Identifying an Author ' s Native Language Phase 2 + Finding and training the bilingual language expert. Birmingham.

Hubbard, E. H. H. (1996). Errors in Court: A Forensic Application of Error Analysis. In H. Kniffka, S. Blackwell, & M. Coulthard (Eds.), *Recent Developments in Forensic Linguistics* (pp. 123–140). Frankfurt Am Main: Peter Lang GmbH.

Hunston, S. (2002). *Corpora in Applied Linguistics*. Cambridge: Cambridge University Press. doi:10.1017/CBO9781139524773

Jaleh. (2011). *Jamigen's Iranian Affairs Blog Site*. Retrieved July 19, 2011, from http://jamigen.com/index.htm

Kniffka, H. (1996). On Forensic Linguistic "Differential Diagnosis.". In H. Kniffka, S. Blackwell, & M. Coulthard (Eds.), *Recent Developments in Forensic Linguistics* (pp. 75–122). Frankfurt Am Main: Peter Lang GmbH.

Koppel, M., Schler, J., & Zigdon, K. (2005). Determining an author's native language by mining a text for errors. In *Proceedings of the eleventh ACM SIGKDD international conference on Knowledge discovery in data mining - KDD '05* (pp. 624–628). New York: ACM Press. doi:10.1145/1081870.1081947

Labov, W. (1984). Field Methods of the Project on Linguistic Change and Variation. In J. Baugh & J. Sherzer (Eds.), *Language in Use: Reading in Sociolinguistics* (pp. 29–53).

Leonard, R. A. (2005). Forensic Linguistics. *The International Journal of the Humanities*, *3*, 65–70.

Leung, C., Harris, R., & Rampton, B. (1997). The Idealised Native Speaker, Reified Ethnicities, and Classroom Realities. *TESOL Quarterly*, *31*(3), 543–560. http://www.ncbi.nlm.nih.gov/pubmed/21344620 doi:10.2307/3587837

Olsson, J. (2004). *Forensic Linguistics. An Introduction to Language, Crime and the Law*. London, New York: Continuum.

Perkins, R., & Grant, T. (2013). Forensic linguistics. In Encyclopedia of Forensic Sciences. doi:10.1016/B978-0-12-382165-2.00030-1

Perkins, R. C. (2012). *Linguistic Identifiers of L1 Persian speakers writing in English. NLID for Authorship Analysis* Unpublished doctoral dissertation. Aston University, Birmingham, U.K.

Rampton, M. B. H. (1990). Displacing the "native speaker": Expertise, affiliation, and inheritance. *ELT Journal*, *44*(2), 97–101. http://eltj.oupjournals.org/cgi/doi/10.1093/elt/44.2.97 doi:10.1093/elt/44.2.97

Selinker, L. (1972). Interlanguage. *IRAL*, *10*(1-4), 209–231. doi:10.1515/iral.1972.10.1-4.209

Shuy, R. (2001). Forensic Lingusitics. In M. Aronoff & J. Rees-Miller (Eds.), The Handbook of Linguistics (Kindle., pp. 683–691). Oxford & Malden: Blackwell Publishing Ltd.

Silva, R. S., & Laboreiro, G. (2011). Automatic Authorship Analysis of Micro-Blogging Messages. *ReCALL*, 161–168.

Stubbs, M. (1996). *Text and Corpus Analysis*. Oxford: Blackwell Publishing Ltd.

The International Herald Tribune. (2010). From the International Herald Tribune - 100, 75, 50 Years Ago - NYTimes.com. *International Herald Tribune*. Retrieved December 04, 2012, from http://www.nytimes.com/2010/01/25/opinion/25iht-oldjan25.html?_r=1

Thomason, S. (2001). *Language Contact: An Introduction*. Baltimore: Georgetown University Press. doi:10.1016/B0-08-043076-7/03032-1

Tsur, O., & Rappoport, A. (2007). Using Classifier Features for Studying the Effect of Native Language on the Choice of Written Second Language Words. In P. Buttery, A. Villavicencio, & A. Korhonen (Eds.), *Cognitive Aspects of Computational Language Acquisition* (pp. 9–17). Madison: Omnipress. doi:10.3115/1629795.1629797

Weinreich, U. (1953). *Languages in contact*. The Hague: Mouton & Co.

Winford, D. (2003). *An Introduction to Contact Linguistics*. Oxford: Wiley-Blackwell.

Wong, S. J., Dras, M., & Johnson, M. (2011). Exploring Adaptor Grammars for Native Language Identification, (July), 699–709.

KEY TERMS AND DEFINITIONS

Authorship Analysis: Authorship analysis comprises authorship attribution and authorship profiling, it is the analysis of linguistic features within an anonymous or disputed text(s), to help indicate authorship.

Authorship Profiling: Authorship profiling can be considered a branch of authorship analysis. It relates to the analysis of linguistic features to extrapolate information about an anonymous author and is based on concepts from sociolinguistics.

Computer Mediated Communication: Computer mediated communication is discipline of applied linguistics focusing on communication through electronic media.

Forensic Linguistics: Forensic linguistics is the application of linguistics to legal or forensic contexts.

Interlanguage: For the purpose of this research *interlanguage* is considered the influence of one language on an individual's production of another language.

L1: L1 refers to the language a person identifies as being their native language or mother tongue.

Multilingualism: Multilingualism relates to individuals (or social groups) that have a high proficiency at more than one language.

Sociolinguistics: Sociolinguistics is a branch of linguistics concerned with the social context of language. The main underlying premise is that language and social aspects are inextricably interlinked.

ENDNOTE

[1] The question was asked whether a person trying to disguise their language to falsely give the impression that they were an L1 Persian speaker, would be classified as such with this system. Existing literature indicates that it is very difficult to disguise language as their "effort usually involves the more conscious aspect of language use rather than the major features analysed in the linguistic profile." (Shuy, 2001, Loc. 10105). The findings of this sub-study supported this indicating that "there is a considerable difference between the language and features produced by a genuine L1 Persian speaker and those of someone pretending to be an L1 Persian speaker." (Perkins, 2012, p120). While this was only an exploratory study, it indicates that the features are reliable in this respect.

Chapter 13
The Critical Need for Empowering Leadership Approaches in Managing Health Care Information Security Millennial Employees in Health Care Business and Community Organizations

Darrell Norman Burrell
Florida Institute of Technology, USA

Taara Bhat
George Mason University, USA

Darryl Williams
Walden University, USA

Clishia Taylor
National Graduate School of Quality Management, USA

ABSTRACT

According to the Ponemon (2012) Third Annual Benchmark Study on Patient Privacy & Data Security, 94 percent of healthcare organizations surveyed suffered at least one data breach; 45 percent experienced more than five in the past two years. Data breaches cost the U.S. healthcare industry an average of $7 billion annually (Ponemon, 2012). Electronic health records are becoming more pervasive at hospitals and clinics in the United States. Meanwhile, healthcare organizations are taking small steps toward meaningful exchange and secure data security of patient information. This has created a need for new expertise in health data security from a newly degreed and young in information security professionals from the "Millennial Generation". This chapter explores the attraction, recruitment, and retention of younger-generation professionals with critical and emerging health information security skills.

DOI: 10.4018/978-1-4666-8345-7.ch013

INTRODUCTION

The challenges facing health care organizations and health care professionals today are more complex than at any other time in our history, particularly within the context of new technologies, globalization, social, political, and economic changes (Burns, Bradley, & Weiner, 2011). The traditional challenges of managing costs, access and quality are still on the forefront of today's health care leaders (Burns, Bradley, & Weiner, 2011). According to Burns, Bradley, and Weiner, (2011) health care organizations, professionals and practitioners face current challenges including:

1. Federal and state legislation
2. Increased emphasis on efficient use of resources
3. Increased emphasis of quality
4. Increased emphasis on cost effectiveness
5. Increased emphasis on patient health outcomes
6. Advanced technology
7. Information systems, digital health care records, and digital records security
8. Changing patient demographics and diversity
9. Skilled labor shortages

Today's health care manager not only has to be competent in the traditional practices of management and leadership but also competent, knowledgeable and strategic in his/her approach to adapting their organization to the changing and often confusing challenges confronting today's health care environment. Effective health care management requires both the traditional components of effective management and leadership along with the specific and unique components of a changing and evolving health care system (Burns, Bradley, & Weiner, 2011). According to the Ponemon report (2012), 94 percent of healthcare organizations surveyed suffered at least one data breach; 45 percent experienced more than five in the past two years. Data breaches cost the U.S. healthcare industry an average of $7 billion annually (Ponemon, 2012). Health care organizations are also challenged with addressing:

1. Strategic proactive protection plans for data and information breaches.
2. The development of new data and Encryption approaches.
3. Implement monthly or quarterly vulnerability assessments to reduce the threat of hackers.
4. The most prominent security protection priorities and organizational resources investments
5. The development of mobile security policies and protections for employees that access organizational records with mobile devices.
6. Strategic approaches for the effective use of cloud computing applications.
7. Ensure the Incident Response Plan (IRP) covers business associates, partners, cyber liability insurance.
8. Conduct security awareness with staff and build an organizational culture of information security (Rhodes-Ousley, 2013).

Many health organizations are facing the challenges of reduced budgets, increased retirements, and lost critical organizational expertise. On one end of the employment pipeline, a younger workforce is developing a new set of values and expectations, creating new recruiting and employee retention issues.

The progression from an older, traditional, highly experienced workforce to a younger, more portable, employee generation has created critical challenges (Delong, 2004). Addressing these challenges are critical for organizations that are faced with patient safety, information security, delivery of clinical services, and the improvement of patient health outcomes. Electronic health records are becoming more pervasive at hospitals and clinics in the United States. Meanwhile, healthcare organizations are taking small steps toward meaningful exchange of patient information. The digital transformation of healthcare holds great promise for dramatically improving the quality of care while holding down costs by providing timely access to potentially live-saving information. HIPAA Omnibus Rule, with tougher privacy and security requirements and tougher penalties, called attention yet again to the need for healthcare organizations to ramp up their efforts to safeguard patient information (US Government Printing Office, 2013). This has created a need for new expertise of health information professionals from the "Millennial Generation". These professionals have different interests from previous generations in terms of work environments and cultures (Lancaster & Stillman, 2010)

These younger professionals have undergraduate and graduate degrees in Cyber-Security, Information Assurance, and Information Security that have just been created in the last 10 years. They also have certifications in Security + and Information Systems Audit and Control Association (ISACA) certifications. But in order to attract, recruit, and retain this younger generation of professionals with these critical and emerging skills, managers must consider alternative approaches that look to empower employees over micromanaging and controlling them.

Command and control approaches can present challenges with employees that are from younger generation. Members of the millennial generation occupy an increasingly prominent segment of today's workforce (Lancaster & Stillman, 2010). It is vital that new management approaches are explored and adopted to figure out the best ways to inspire and motivate Millennials while helping them accomplish their personal goals and aspirations (Lancaster & Stillman, 2010). Millennials don not share the same values or career motivators as their predecessors (Lancaster & Stillman, 2010). As hospitals, clinics and other healthcare organizations implement electronic health records and participate in health information exchange, they are working to develop robust information security measures to assure patients that their information will be protected and win their trust and in order to be effective, they need these younger employees and their emergency expertise.

Generally recognized as the cohort born after 1980, Millennials differ from baby boomers and Gen X in the workplace in three primary ways (McMahon, Miles, & Bennett, 2011). Probably the most striking difference is the role work occupies in their lives. Work isn't as important to Millennials as it was to previous generations. Today's younger workers are more covetous of leisure time and describe work as less central to their lives (McMahon, Miles, & Bennett, 2011). They are generally more outgoing and assertive than previous generations, and thrive on immediate feedback and affirmation from top-level management. (McMahon, Miles, & Bennett, 2011). Organizations with managers that do not respect their views or value ideas are those that will have challenges with retaining Millennials.

According to Lancaster and Stillman (2010), each generation's views are socialized and shaped by significant events experienced while growing up. Some of the significant things that have influenced the Millennials are:

1. **Parents have focused on them-** For this generation the family focus moved back on children after the previous generation latchkey kids, children of divorce, and kids with two working parents found themselves growing up on their own.

2. **Attacks in America and 9/11-**During their most formative years, Millennials witnessed the bombing and devastation of the bombing in Oklahoma City, 9/11, and the shootings at Columbine High School. They never experienced the times when you could meet a friend or family member who was flying right at the gate when they got off the plane.

3. **Engaged parents-**The Millennials were raised by active, involved parents who were often labeled "helicopter parents" for the way they hovered and intervened in their children's affairs to ensure that their children would grow up safely, receive fair treatment, and have many opportunities.

4. **Scheduled, structured lives-**Parents and teachers micromanaged their schedules to ensure that they would be stimulated by a variety of experiential learning experiences and developmental activities, which often left little free time.

5. **Diversity-**Because of increased immigration and globalization, children grew up in the 1990s and 2000s interacting with other ethnicities and cultures than ever before. This has changed their comfort level with different groups and races compared to previous generations but also creates a lack of understanding for the challenges and history of strife as it relates to race and ethnic relations in this country.

6. **Heroism-** Emerging out of those acts of violence, Millennials watched the re-emergence of the American hero. Policemen, firemen, firefighters, and mayors were pictured on the front page of the newspaper, featured on TV specials, and portrayed in art and memorabilia.

According to Lancaster and Stillman (2010) these events have created a generation of employees with a different work ethic than any other, certainly different from their Gen X colleagues. Here are the main components of their work ethic:

1. **Self-assured-**Raised by parents believing in the importance of self-esteem, they characteristically consider themselves intellectually ready to overcome challenges even if they lack experience. Managers who believe in "paying your dues," or that the only opinions are worth listening to should come from someone with extensive work experience could find conflict with a Millennials "let me try to solve this problem attitude."

2. **Optimistic-**They expect a workplace that is challenging, collaborative, creative, fun, and financially rewarding. They see situations from a framework of great things that can happen and not bad things that can go wrong.

3. **Accomplishment focused-**Many Millennials arrive at their first day of work with a vision of where they want to be with dates and times listed with each milestone. If they don't see progress, they will look for opportunities elsewhere.

4. **Community service oriented-** They are constantly focused on big picture societal issues. They are focused on work and activities that allow them to make a difference and have an impact.

5. **Collaborative-** Millennials are used to working in teams and sharing knowledge, so workplace with closed department silos or that do not support collective knowledge sharing are not cultures that they prefer.

6. **Justice oriented-** Millennials want to work in environments and for supervisors that are fair, ethical, honest, and transparent.

According to Espinoza (2010) "No matter how good companies are at attracting Millennials, however, keeping them still comes down to the relationship between manager and millennial. Numerous studies reveal that people leave managers, not companies."

Douglas McGregor

Consider many of the traditional approaches to as it relates to management and how these approaches can present challenges to managing Millennials. Among the world's most sought after human motivation and organizational theorist, Douglas McGregor (1906-1964) was one of the most prominent philosophers during his time. McGregor was a Management professor at Antioch College in MIT Sloan School of Management from 1948-1954. During his tenure there, he also served as the president of the School of Management. Additionally, Douglas has other teaching experiences, such as the Indian Institute of Management in Calcutta. Not only was McGregor an educator, but a publisher as well. Particularly, one of his most profound writings in 1960 was his book *The Human Side of Enterprise.*

In light of this phenomenal perspective from McGregor, he believed that in organizations, the management theory most managers utilized was either theory X or theory Y. Theory Y closely followed the Dr. Abraham Maslow's Humanistic Theory, most commonly known as The Hierarchy of Needs and applied it to scientific management principles. Likewise, Theory X focused on a different motivational principle, that being, motivation via the authoritative management style. Each viewpoint is dedicated to understanding the two types of employees typical manager are exposed to, therefore, providing a framework from which aspiring managers can investigate, invest in others or test out assumptions.

Management and Scientific Knowledge

According to McGregor (1960) "Every professional is concerned with the use of knowledge in the achievement of objectives". For this reason, he asserts that the engineer designs equipment, doctors' diagnoses and prescribe medications for their ill patients, and lawyers serve their clients. More specifically, the aforementioned professionals rely heavily on an existing body of knowledge and colleagues for guidance as means to meet the needs and objectives society. Personal experience is also ancillary in the leadership or council of individuals or companies. McGregor (1960) postulates that, "The degree to which the professional relies upon the first two of these rather than the third is one of the ways in which the professional may be distinguished from the layman.

Furthermore, McGregor (1960) believed that "One of the major tasks of management is to organize human effort in the service of the economic objectives of the enterprise". For this reason, "Every management decision has behavioral consequences." (McGregor, 1960). Additionally, McGregor postulated that the success of management depends significantly upon the manager's ability to predict and control human behavior in order to accomplish interdependent goals. Alternatively, McGregor purported that "In literally thousands of ways, we predict with a high degree of accuracy what other will do, and we control their behavior in the sense that our actions lead to the desired consequences" (McGregor, 1960).

Essentially, if a company is successful, it can be safely surmised that a manager was able to influence individuals within their organization and direct their efforts into producing, selling, or servicing at a profit for the company. Nevertheless, McGregor discovered that there were very few managers who were "satisfied with their ability to predict and control the behavior of the members on their organizations" (McGregor, 1960). In light of this perspective, McGregor firmly believed that "The social sciences could contribute more effectively than they have to managerial process with respect to the human side of enterprise" (McGregor, 1960). The social sciences provide an abundant amount of resources, however, McGregor did not agree with primitive methods of organizational management nor did he agree with its applicability. McGregor asserted, "I am not particularly impressed with the arguments that social scientists do not publish their findings in language intelligible to the layman" (McGregor, 1960). In other words, the professional should not have to be scientist to understand the literature, rather, "he must be sophisticated enough to make competent use of scientific knowledge" (McGregor, 1960).

The Reliance on Theory

One of the most significant reasons why management in corporations has been relatively slow to the reliance of social science knowledge is self-direction. More specifically, McGregor further elucidates this statement by asserting "Every manager quite naturally considers himself his own social scientist. His personal experience with people from childhood on has been so rich that he feels little real need to turn elsewhere for knowledge of human behavior" (McGregor, 1960). Following this further, it would appear that theoretical knowledge would seem unrelated to the management, with a formed bias that it would not solve the complex realities in which one would deal. In this situation, McGregor observed that management was more comfortable with personal experience based knowledge in which it was considered "more practical and useful" (McGregor, 1960).

Nevertheless, almost every managerial decision is based on some sort of "assumption, generalizations, and hypotheses – that is to say on theory" (McGregor, 1960). This natural response is the foundation upon which many assessments have been made by management. For this reason, decision without careful thought could result in conflicting outcomes. Bill 'Obrien (1990), Hanover CEO made a profound statement regarding human resource management. They are as follows:

In the traditional authoritarian organization, the dogma was managing, organizing and controlling. In the learning organization, the new "dogma" will be vision, values and mental models. The healthy corporations will be the ones which can systematize ways to bring people together to develop the best possible mental models for the situation at hand.

Ironically, this methodology closes follows and agrees with McGregor's vision in management with respect to human enterprise, which predates the statement by 30 years. Furthermore, McGregor delves deeper into the implied psychology in management style when they utilize their "personal and practical" solutions to enterprise management. McGregor likened this sort of thinking to "Let's accept my theoretical assumptions without argument or test." (McGregor, 1960). Unfortunately, McGregor has observed this management approach and furthers explained that "The common practice of proceeding without explicit examination of theoretical assumptions leads, at times, to remarkable inconsistencies in managerial behavior" (McGregor, 1960).

In addition to reliance on "personal and practical" procedures in management styles, McGregor also found another method of denying the significance of theory in management behavior. This caveat is well known as "insisting that management is an art rather than a science" (McGregor, 1960). However, the argument was not if management were a science or not. More importantly, McGregor's focus was whether management could "utilize scientific knowledge in the achievement of those objectives" (McGregor, 1960). For the most part, science is motivated by the expansion of knowledge. Likewise, managements' primary concern is the accomplishment of practical goals. Nevertheless, according to McGregor "to continually insist that management is an art is frequently no more than a denial of the systematic, tested knowledge to practice. As long as the manager fails to question the validity of his personal assumptions, he is unlikely to avail himself of what is available in science" (McGregor, 1960) There is a plethora of data available in the social sciences, but the problem is how the information is contradictory to how one would like to "personally and practical" manage. Therefore, it is at times rejected, especially, since one could "always find imperfections and inadequacies in scientific knowledge" (McGregor, 1960).

Control Is Selective Adaption

McGregor observed another reason that most management strategies fail to make adequate use of the social science knowledge at the time. This is in respect to the common misconception concerning "nature of control in the field of human behavior" (McGregor, 1960). For example, in the profession of engineering, the control entails in adjustments to the natural law. In other words, "It does not mean making nature do our bidding" (McGregor, 1960). In light of this phenomenon, there is an interesting perspective in how management views human behavior and mechanical engineering. Being that, "We do not dig channels in the expectation that water will flow uphill" and "We do not use kerosene to put out a fire" (McGregor, 1960). Equally important, when designing a particular engine, engineers realize and accept the fact that gases expand once they are heated; the engineers do not attempt to make elements behave differently. In respect to the physical viewpoint, McGregor (1960) understood that "control involves the selection of means which are *appropriate* to the nature of the phenomena with which we are concerned"

McGregor believed that the aforementioned approach should be the same in the human field. However, his observation found that most managers attempt to make water flow uphill. In management, there are numerous efforts to control human behavior. Nevertheless, their poor use of *selective adaptations*, as asserted by McGregor (1960) "is in direct violation of human nature". Profusely, businesses strain to make people behave in certain ways without a sincere concern for the natural law of human nature. McGregor's vantage point on this matter discerned that managers are as likely to be successful as an engineer would be ignoring the natural laws of physics.

In addition to flawed systematic approach, McGregor noticed that typically, business organizations use the practical logic of incentives. That is to say, "People want money, and they will work harder to get it" (McGregor, 1960). When in fact, these incentive plans "do not take into account of several well-demonstrated characteristics of behavior in the organizational setting" (McGregor, 1960) which are as follows:

1. *Most people also want the approval of their fellow workers and, if necessary, they will forgo increased pay to obtain this approval.*
2. *No managerial assurances can persuade workers that incentive rates will remain inviolate regardless of how much they produce*
3. *The ingenuity of the average worker is sufficient to outwit any system of controls devised by management.*

McGregor did acknowledge that good incentive plans were plausible enough to bring about a "moderate" level of productivity, however, he felt it would only be about 15%. Similarly, this type of program could produce other behavior as well, such as, "deliberate restrictions of output, hidden jigs and fixtures, hidden production, fudged records, grievances over rates and standards" (McGregor, 1960). Consequently, antagonism towards the managers who administers the plan could introduce new issues into the organization. These include, but are not limited to integrity, fairness, indifference to company collaborations.

Moreover, another possible issue that arises within an organization that employ coerced human control methodologies is accountability. More specifically, when the company fails to reach the results desired, the blame is often placed everywhere else, instead of where it should be. McGregor believed that the failure is significantly related to the poor choice in methods of control. Considering our previous analogy of the engineer and laws of nature, we must remember, "the engineer does blame the water for not flowing uphill or gases for expanding rather than contracting when heating" (McGregor, 1960). Irrespective of this fact, McGregor noticed in organizations, "When people respond to managerial decisions in undesired way, the normal response is to blame them" (McGregor, 1960) and not the company's failure to choose adequate means for control.

In management, being able to accurately predict and control are equally important to the task management of engineers or medicine. According to McGregor (1960) "human behavior is predictable" however, he believed that depends on the "correctness of underlying theoretical assumptions." McGregor believed emphatically that "There is, in fact, no prediction without theory; all management decisions and actions rest on assumptions about behavior. However, the issue is how management reaching the conclusion of how human reactions.

In either event, McGregor was extremely optimistic about improved human behavior control in businesses and other organizations when appropriate selective adaptation to human nature were applied and not trying to "make human nature bend to our will." (McGregor, 1960) The improved competence of managerial decisions in respect to human behavior could be realized once accountability is accepted blame isn't placed on the employees or people for "failing to behave according to our predictions" (McGregor, 1960). This is especially true when the very nature of human behavior is completely ignored within organizations. By becoming more sensitive to human values and creating ethical codes that support "social responsibility." healthier control in respect to human behavior with in organizations appears more plausible.

Theory X

The traditional view of direction and control, as affirmed by McGregor, is Theory X. Again, McGregor (1960) postulates, "Behind every managerial decision or action are assumptions about human nature and human behavior". The following will outline the traditional outline of McGregor theory of direction and control (See Figure 1).

1. The average human being has an inherent dislike of work and will avoid it if he can.
2. Because of this human characteristic of dislike of work, most people must be coerced, controlled, directed, threatened with punishment to get them to put forth adequate effort toward the achievement of organizational objectives
3. The average human being prefers to be directed, avoid responsibility, possesses little ambition, and wants security above all. (McGregor, 1960)

In light of the aforementioned paternalism of organizations that utilize Theory X, McGregor (1960) asserted that "The philosophy of management by direction and control – regardless of whether it is hard or soft – is inadequate to motivate because the human needs on which this approach relies are relatively unimportant motivators of behavior in our society today". More

Figure 1.

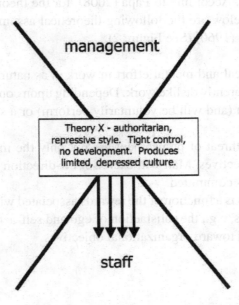

'Theory X'

management

Theory X - authoritarian, repressive style. Tight control, no development. Produces limited, depressed culture.

staff

specifically, direction and control are inimical and are not satisfactory methods of encouraging people for those whose important needs are social and egoistic. With this in mind, it is not out of the question to consider some of the causes and effects of organizations utilizing insufficient motivators.

For example, individuals who are deprived of occasions to satisfy at the work place, especially if these are their important motivating factors, could result in unfavorable behaviors. These conducts could include, but are not limited to "indolence, passivity, unwillingness to accept responsibility, resistance to change, willingness to follow the demagogue, unreasonable demands for economic benefits" (McGregor, 1960). According to McGregor, it is possible that companies who employ these organizational directions and control methodologies may be "in a web of their own weaving" (McGregor, 1960)

Essentially, Theory X is a limiting managerial strategy that fails to recognize human nature, although, it asserts to. These flawed assumptions fail to see the true potential within humans. Even in child rearing, it is unanimously recognized that parents must control must be "progressively modified to adapt to the changed capabilities and characteristics of the human individual as he develops from infancy to adulthood" (McGregor, 1960). This approach acknowledges that human adults do possess that ability of continued learning and growth. In light of this revelation, McGregor (1960) concludes, "so long as the assumptions of Theory X continue to influence managerial strategy; we will fail to discover, let alone utilize, the potentialities of the average human being" (McGregor, 1960).

Theory Y

The assumptions in McGregor's Theory Y affirm the integration of individual and organizations goals. McGregor believed that under this particular strategy, human potential within organizations may be revealed without direct control. According to Papa (2008), for the theory Y employee "to them, work is as natural as play". Listed below are the following theoretical assumptions regarding Theory Y, as asserted by Douglas McGregor (1960) (See Figure 2).

1. The expenditure of physical and mental effort in work is as natural as play or rest. The average human being does not inherently dislike work. Depending upon controllable conditions, work may be a source of satisfaction (and will be voluntarily perform) or a source of punishment (and will be avoided if possible).
2. External control and the threat of punishment are not only the means for bringing about effort toward organizational objectives. Man will exercise self-direction and self-control in the service of objective to which he is committed.
3. Commitment to objectives is a function of the rewards associated with their achievement. The most significant of such rewards, e.g., the satisfaction of ego and self-actualization needs, can be direct products of effort directed toward organizational objectives

Figure 2.

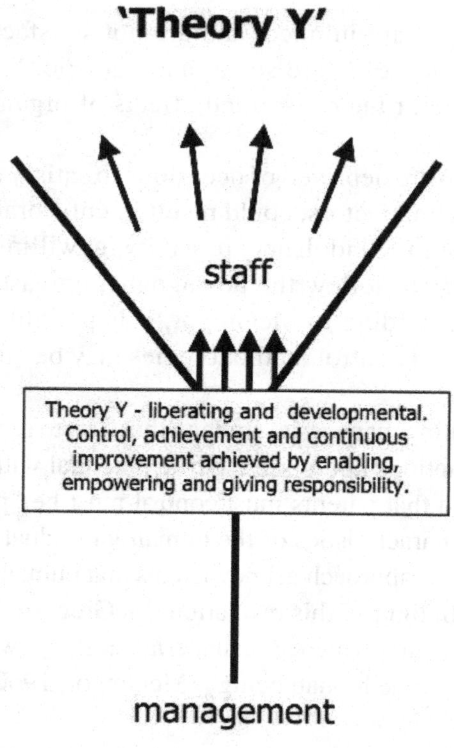

4.   The average human being learns, under proper conditions, not only to accept but also to seek responsibility. Avoidance of responsibility, lack of ambition, and emphasis on security are generally consequences of experience, not inherent human characteristics.

5.   The capacity to exercise a relatively high degree of imagination, ingenuity, and creativity in the solution of organizational problems is widely, not narrowly, distributed in the population.

6.   Under the conditions of modern industrial life, the intellectual potentialities of the average human being are only partially utilized.

Theory Y is more of an optimistic perception of the average human being. Contrary to Theory X, this particular managerial strategy is "More dynamic rather than static" according to McGregor (1960). This process is open to selective adaptation and does not attempt to assume total control over the employee. That is to say, the employees are presumed to be valuable assets, rather than expendable slaves. McGregor, however, did agree that implementation would not be easier. Nevertheless, he did note that it would provoke managerial "deeply ingrained habits of though and action" (Senge, 1990).

Essentially, the principle of integration is Theory Y. Mary Parker Follett, renowned social worker, management consultant, and pioneer in the field of organizational theory and organizational behavior asserted during a phenomenal speech in 1933 at the London School of Economics, which adds value to Theory Y comprehension. Follett postulated "there are three ways of settling differences".....

1.   By *domination*: A victory of one side over the other. You stay where you are. This is usually not good for the long run, for the side that is defeated will simply wait for its change to dominate. Only one side gets what they want.

2.   By *compromise*: This is how most controversies are settled, however, each side gives up a little to have peace. In the end, you deal with no new values. Neither side gets what they want.

3.   By *integration*: Provides progress within organizations. Something new has emerged, the third way, some beyond the either-or. All parties work together to achieve a common goal (Graham, 1995)

Many organizations still manage from those early approaches outlined by McGregor and others. Despite the global recession, the war for employee talent is fierce. All organizations must have an integrated approach to effectively recruit, manage, and retain Millennials. This requires different approaches to management and employee development (McGrath, 2009).

Millennials have no interest in time-honored ideas of being managed or supervised. Therefore, one must adopt a coaching approach to management instead of micro-management and authoritative approaches to management (McGrath, 2009) Millennials want freedom to work when and where they choose, and they don't believe face time in the office is important as long as work is being performed. Much of this is the result of being raised during the technology boom, with social networks and other online communication tools playing a large role in this mindset (McGrath, 2009) Millennials are, however, much more comfortable and open to communicating their interest in knowing "What are you doing for me beyond just paying my salary and providing benefits?" Surprisingly, money is not a primary motivator; most Millennials put time at the top of the list (McGrath, 2009) Millennials demand work-life balance. Millennials are socially and environmentally conscious, requiring free time for volunteerism and charitable work (McGrath, 2009)

According to a 2011 Pew study, 49 percent of Millennial took a job they didn't want just to pay bills. To organizations, this only means that most of their employees are not engaged in their job, which makes the task of managing even more challenging (Taylot et. al, 2012). According to Lynch, it is important for an organization to develop strategies to attract, develop, and retain this new generation. Given that most Millennials are roughly $20,000 in debt, offering compensation packages at or above industry norms will prove to be fruitful in efforts geared towards recruitment (Lynch, 2008). Furthermore, according to Baker, it is important to foster collaborative efforts in the workplace that will diminish the gap between the Millennials and Baby Boomers (Brack, 2008). Not only will this collaboration increase appreciation for diversity, it will also diminish misconceptions and potentially prepare Millennia's to assume positions leading the Baby Boomers (Brack, 2008). Baker also goes on to state that Millennials are usually in search of a fun and flexible community atmosphere at the workplace (Brack, 2008). Millennials are also in a constant search of more knowledge (Brack, 2008). If organizations could provide more coaching and continuing education programs, Millennials will most likely be more interested in applying what they learn in the classrooms to the job, thereby, increasing productivity and employee engagement.

Millennials want participate in how they are managed which is a dramatic departure from the Theory X command and control management or micromanagement approaches that have been traditionally used in organizations. Employee engagement has delivered a powerful focus to many organizations' employee cultural and management assessment programs. Beyond mere job satisfaction, employee engagement contributes to positive outcomes such as longer retention, higher individual performance, achievement of organizational results and customer loyalty. (Penrose, 2007).

According to Penrose (2007) Employee engagement includes:

- *Shared Values: Do the company and its employees conduct day-to-day business based on a common set of values?*
- *Effective Leadership: How well do managers communicate and walk the talk?*
- *Motivational Recognition: Are employees recognized for a job well done in ways that have special meaning to them?*
- *Contribution to Success: Do employees understand how their work contributes to the organization's overall success?*
- *Involvement: Are employees involved in decision-making that affects their work?*
- *Personal Development: Are there opportunities for employees to grow and advance?*
- *Economic Self-Interest: Do employees think their pay and benefits are fair and competitive in the marketplace? (Penrose, 2007).*

Kaner and Lind's (1996) idea of participative (or participatory) management, otherwise known as employee engagement or participative decision making, encourages the involvement of stakeholders at all levels of an organization in the analysis of problems, execution of change approaches, development of strategies, and implementation of solutions. This approach is vastly different than the command and control approaches that have been traditionally used in organizations. Employees are invited to share in the decision-making process of the firm by participating in activities such as setting goals, determining work schedules, and making suggestions. Other forms of participative management include forming self-managed teams, quality circles, and soliciting survey feedback. Participative management, however, involves more than allowing employees to take part in making decisions. It also involves management treating the ideas and suggestions of employees with consideration and respect (Kaner and Lind, 1996).

According to Kaner and Lind (1996) creativity and innovation are two important benefits of participative management. By allowing a diverse group of employees to have input into decisions and methods of doing things, the organization benefits from the synergy that comes from a wider choice of options. When all employees, instead of just managers or executives, are given the opportunity to participate, the chances are increased that a valid and unique idea will be suggested (Kaner and Lind, 1996).

According to Kaner and Lind (1996) successful participation requires organizational change in the behaviors of managers to approach employee involvement with an open mind. They must be open to new ideas and alternatives in order for participative management to work. It is important to remember that although the manager may not agree with every idea or suggestion an employee makes, how those ideas are received is critical to the success of participative management. Managers must also be willing to give up some power and some level of their control. Employees must also embrace change by engaging actively in the participation process (Kaner and Lind, 1996). An example of this is appreciative Inquiry, which is a process that allows employees to participate in the organizational change and development process.

According to Kaner and Lind (1996) four processes influence participation and employee engagement. The further down these processes move, the higher the level of involvement by employees. The four processes include:

1. Information sharing, which is concerned with keeping employees informed about organizational the financial health, successes, initiatives, and approaches.
2. Seeking employee feedback on decision-making and organizational strategy.
3. Seeking employee feedback in determining work schedules to deciding on budgets or processes.
4. Show a willingness to give up some level of control and power to empower employees (Kaner and Lind, 1996).

The kinds of approaches that are most effective with the youngest generation of employees are aligned with leadership approaches like Servant Leadership, which was coined by Robert Greenleaf (2012). It calls for leaders to be more pragmatic in their roles by leading others by being a servant first. The servant leader must empower employees to be part of the process that outlines how they are managed and must be responsive to the needs of those who benefit from their service (Greenleaf, 2012). The servant leader is "one who is a servant first" (Greenleaf, 2012, p. 21). This approach requires managers to treat employees like their own customers that have needs to be served. This includes removing the barriers that limit their ability to accomplish work. Getting employees the resources they need to be effective and using their influence and contacts as a manager to make the team effective more effectively. This process also includes engaging in climate surveys, assessments, and creating feedback loops that allow employees to share their perspectives in ways that management actually acts up.

Below is a simple assessment (Burrell Valued Employee Engagement Assessment Survey) tool that employees can complete to share insights on how management engages and values employees.

Burrell Valued Employee Engagement Assessment Survey

Using the 5-point scale below, rate each question based on your organization's level of engagement on a:
_5 = Frequent level _4 = Reasonable level _3 = Fair level _2 = Infrequent level _1 = Never

1. To what extent do you feel that you have a say and flexibility in how your do your job and how you function in your job role?

   _5 _4 _3 _2 _1

2. To what extent do you feel that you are supported by your organization and supervisors with realistic expectations and appropriate resources that are needed to be the most effective with completing your job duties?

   _5 _4 _3 _2 _1

3. To what extent do you feel that your expertise, experience, and work contributions are valued by your supervisors and organization?

   _5 _4 _3 _2 _1

4. To what extent do you feel that the supervisors and organization provides regular and consistent acknowledgement and appreciation for quality of your work when you have done an outstanding job?

   _5 _4 _3 _2 _1

5. To what extent do you feel that your viewpoints, opinions, and ideas related to improving work processes, work efficiency, work conditions, and work culture are solicited and heard by your supervisors and the organization?

   _5 _4 _3 _2 _1

6. To what extent do you feel that your supervisors show concern and interest about you and your career beyond your current job duties and job role?

   _5 _4 _3 _2 _1

7. To what extent does your supervisors acknowledge your work related strengths and offer you opportunities to grow those strengths through professional development training opportunities or through new job related projects?

   _5 _4 _3 _2 _1

8. To what extent do you feel that the behaviors and actions of your supervisors match with the written values and mission of the organization?

   _5 _4 _3 _2 _1

9.   To what degree do you feel that there are other significant upward job opportunities in the organization that would allow you to use your education, expertise, and experience in the future?

_5 _4 _3 _2 _1

10.   To what degree do you feel that supervisors show you honest and genuine respect in the workplace?

_5 _4 _3 _2 _1

5 Levels of Leadership

Engaging and valuing this newest generation of employees requires that supervisors gain new knowledge and apply new approaches. John Maxwell's (2011) manifesto, "The 5 Levels of Leadership," reinstates the skills and abilities necessary for an organization to progress through four levels in order to attain the fifth level of leadership, otherwise known as the pinnacle. Maxwell (2011) provides a practical model that moves beyond authoritative and command and control approaches and moves towards employee engagement that could be effective with managing younger generation employees by providing a roadmap of how a leader that engages employees should function and behave as he or she moves from a level one manager that is about command and control styles of management to a level five manager that is effective at engaging employees (See Figure 3).

Level 1 of Maxwell's manifesto focuses on position. Maxwell states that a position is only the first step towards leadership. It is an opportunity granted to an individual by someone who believes in an individual's potential (Maxwell, 2011, p. 41). Moreover, the leadership position is an opportunity to shape and mold oneself based on "inner character and integrity of ambition (Maxwell, 2011, p. 45)." However, once a leader relies on position to push people, he/she has invited failure. A level 1 leader should shift from position to potential and rules to relationships in order to continue growing and eventually reach level 2 (Maxwell 2011, p. 79)." Therefore, even though level 1 is the most essential step for any leader, it can easily be lost if the leader assumes the position without transforming the position.

Table 1. Scoring scale Burrell valued employee engagement assessment survey

41–50 points	It seems extremely likely that personnel in the organization feel very valued and engaged by their management and feel very committed to their organization and supervisor. Employees feel invigorated about the work that they do and their role in the organization.
31–40 points	It seems likely that personnel feel valued and engaged to a certain degree by their management and feel very committed to their organization and supervisor.
21–30 points	It seems likely that personnel feel marginally valued and engaged to a certain degree by their management and feel very committed to their organization and supervisor.
11–20 points	It seems very likely that the prevailing feeling on the part of personnel that their expertise and work contributions are not valued and employees are not actively engaged by their supervisors. Employees have a limited amount of commitment to the organization and their supervisor.
0–10 points	It extremely likely that employees are have adverse perspectives and feelings about the work culture, the management, and the potential of their future in the organization. Employees have low commitment to the job and the organization. Employees do not feel energized or excited about the job or work climate.

Developed in 2010 by Darrell Norman Burrell as result of research done in conjunction of a doctoral dissertation at A.T. Still University.

Figure 3.
(Source: Maxwell, 2011, p.6)

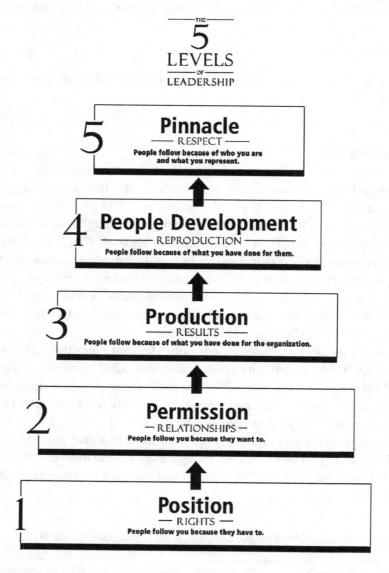

It is assumed that in order to be leader, he or she must lead his/her people. The people who make up the team being led are a very essential part of one's leadership experience. Hence, level 2 explains why it is necessary to build relationships between a leader and those being led as a solid foundation for overall success. A leader who shares positive relations with his/her workers will lead more effectively because the team will listen and be inspired by someone whom they can relate to. Contrary to popular belief, "people-not position-are a leader's most valuable asset (Maxwell, 2011, p. 74)." Some leaders who are naturally good with people, will breeze level 2, while others may need to learn people skills in order to get through level 2. Since a more personable attitude may be misconstrued in goal oriented situations, it is important to strike a healthy balance between caring, or valuing an individual(s) being led and candor, valuing an individual(s) potential. Even though strong relationships form a foundation for any successful leader, it is necessary to use this foundation as a springboard to capture results.

Luck may have brought an individual to level 1, good wit may have brought a leader to level 2, but only hard work will bring a leader to level 3. Level 3 stresses the importance of production for a leader. The ability to produce results and capture goals not only serves as motivation for others, but it also verifies a leader's credibility. Although a leader's success is motivational to others, it doesn't necessarily ensure that the team will also be successful. "Leadership is defined by what a person does with and for others (Maxwell, 2011, p. 146)." Therefore, in order to be a successful level 3 leader, he or she must use personal productivity to motivate and encourage the team to produce their goals and vision. To reach the upper levels of leadership that create elite organizations, leaders must transition from producers to developers. After reaching success on level 3, a leader is keen to look for ways to further grow their organization. Most leaders focus their attention and stop at the on the wrong place, level 3. Instead, level 4 stresses the development of people on the team.

A leader seeking to further enhance the success of his/her organization must seek the best in each individual on the tem, thereby enhancing the success of the team overall. A level 4 leader will not only seek to enhance themselves, but will also seek to create other successful leaders on the team. "With the addition of more good leaders, the organization's current efforts improve (Maxwell, 2011, p. 189)." Creating other successful leaders entails placing the right people in the right position. "A leader must understand how those players best fit on the team and put them there. To do that, he must have a clear picture of each individual's strengths and weaknesses, and understand how they fit the needs of the team (Maxwell, 2011, p. 208)."

Level 5, or the Pinnacle, creates legacy within an organization. "The Pinnacle level is not a resting point for leaders to stop and view their success. It is a reproducing place from which they make the greatest impact of their lives (Maxwell, 2011, p. 231)." It is easy for any leader to believe he/she has reached success, and must now retire. However, it is essential that he/she realize that there is still much to be accomplished. Leaving a legacy is no easy task, in fact, far from it. There are few leaders who have left a lasting legacy. As Maxwell states, "the ultimate leader is one who is willing to develop people to the point that they eventually surpass him or her in knowledge and ability (Maxwell, 2011, p. 244)." A level 5 manager is truly a manager that focuses effectively on employee engagement. It is the level 5 manager that will have the propensity for success with Millennial employees.

The development of supervisors that develop approaches that are effective in engaging and empowering employees. It does not matter how good organizations are at attracting Millennials with the needed critical health information security expertise if their supervisors are not capable of creating a culture that would make young employees want to stay. Can supervisors make the leadership style adaptations necessary to deliver on organizational promises and workforce psychological contracts? According to Espinoza (2010) Managers, because they have the most responsibility, have to adjust first. That does not mean Millennials do not need to change but the reality is that these information security professionals with this expertise are in high demand and will have a plethora of job options. Having young professionals that understand the complexities and nuances of information security is critical to all health care organizations. The challenge is not just about finding them and hiring them. What is critical is creating a supervisory climate that will make them want to stay, contribute, grow, and stay committed to the organization, its mission, its leadership, and its values.

REFERENCES

Brack, J. (2012). *Maximizing millenials in the workplace.* (Master's thesis). University of North Carolina.

Burns, L., Bradley, E., & Weiner, B. (2011). *Shortell and Kaluzny's Healthcare Management: Organization Design and Behavior.* New York: Cengage Learning.

Delong, D. (2004). *Lost Knowledge: Confronting the Threat of an Aging Workforce.* London: Oxford University Press. doi:10.1093/acprof:oso/9780195170979.001.0001

Drucker, P. F. (1992). *Managing for the future: The 1990s and beyond.* New York, NY: Truman Talley Books/Plume.

Espinoza, C. (2010, March). *Managers Key to Retaining Millennials.* Talent Management.

Graham, P. (1995). *Mary Parker Follett: prophet of management - a Celebration of Writings from the 1920s.* Boston, Mass: Harvard Business School Press.

Greenleaf, R. (2012). *The Servant as Leader.* Seattle, WA: Amazon Digital Services.

Kaner, S., & Lind, L. (1996). *Facilitator's Guide to Participatory Decision-making.* Gabriola Island, BC, Canada: New Society Publishers.

Kreitner, R., & Kinicki, A. (2007). *Organizational Behavior* (7th ed.). New York, New York: McGraw-Hill.

Lyncaster, L., & Stillman, D. (2010). *The M-Factor: How the Millennial Generation Is Rocking the Workplace.* Los Angeles, CA: Harper Collins.

Lynch, A. (2008). *ROI on generation Y employees.* Bottom Line Conversations, LLC. Retrieved from http://www.knoxvillechamber.com/pdf/workforce/ROIonGenYWhitePaper.pdf

Maxwell, J. (2011). *The 5 levels of leadership.* New York, NY: Hachette Book Group.

McGrath, M. (2009, October). How to Motivate Millennials. *Talent Management Magazine.*

McGregor, D. (1960). *The Human side of Enterprise.* New York: McGraw Hill.

McMahon, B, Miles, S. & Bennett, N. (2011, June). *Managing the Millennials.* Talent Management.

Penrose, J. (2007, July). Tracking Employee Engagement. *Talent Management Magazine.*

Ponemon Institute. (2012). *Third Annual Benchmark Study on Patient Privacy & Data Security.* Portland, Oregon: Ponemon Institute.

Rhodes-Ousley, M. (2013). *Information Security.* Washington, DC: McGraw Hill.

Senge, P. (1990). *The Fifth Discipline: The Art and Practice of the Learning Organization.* New York: Doubleday.

Taylor, F. W. (1911). The Principles of Scientific Management. *Fundaments of Scientific Management.* New York: Harper and Brothers. US government Printing Office. (2013, January 25). [US Government Printing Office.]. *Federal Register, 78*(17).

Yukl, G. (1994). *Leadership in organizations.* Upper Saddle River, NJ: Prentice Hall.

Chapter 14
Learning Management Systems:
Understand and Secure Your Educational Technology

Sharon L. Burton
American Meridian University,
USA

Darrell N. Burrell
Florida Institute of Technology,
USA

Dustin Bessette
National Graduate School of
Quality Management, USA

Rondalynne McClintock
Claremont Graduate University,
USA

Kim L. Brown-Jackson
National Graduate School of
Quality Management, USA

Shanel Lu
National Graduate School of
Quality Management, USA

ABSTRACT

Learning management systems (LMSs) are significant in offering highly collaborative, widely accessible, and manageable learning solutions. It is feasible that learning solutions stakeholders pursue an in-depth understanding of the LMS and the vulnerabilities surrounding technology-enabled learning and teaching. The over 300 types of active LMSs, proprietary or open source, are not off limits to hackers. Past research shows that hackers compromise technology systems to ascertain personal identifiable information and interfere with the integrities of post-secondary institutions. Stakeholders must understand how to safeguard the LMS. To address LMS cybercrime concerns, this text reviews vulnerability information on over 12 LMS features. After reading this text, stakeholders will gain increased insight into their works to thwart security related LMS incidents. This text can support stakeholders' knowledge in actions to take prior to the LMS reaching unacceptable vulnerability levels. Researchers and practitioners will benefit from this text's perspective on the LMS and mitigating risk.

INTRODUCTION

Education and learning are not about immediate learner results. Education and learning are components that shape a lifetime, and form a pathway for possibilities into the future. The upsurge of computers, information and communication technologies, and swift development of the Internet drive colleges and universities to alter their educational programs. Technology persists to have a key impact on institutions

DOI: 10.4018/978-1-4666-8345-7.ch014

of higher learning (Glenn, 2008). The embracing of technology mediated learning, in particularly LMSs, and web-based applications resulted in a major transformation in the way researchers work together on a universal scale (Glenn, 2008).

A conduit for channeling education is the LMS, an integrated computer system that can be web-based. Learning management systems are essential tools in the higher education arena and in many businesses. According to Vogten and Koper (2014), LMSs have sufficient authenticity in an information-based society that is continually embracing cloud technology. Through the swift development of information technologies, learning management systems are one of the most significant modernisms for delivering education. The primary purpose of this ubiquitous learning management system is to provide strategic virtual educational environments and opportune communication channels between instructors and students. This virtual dimension in education supports educational institutions and learners in conquering barriers such as time and space.

Despite the affects, LMSs are popular to study because the systems continuously evolve. If this unremitting change remains inappropriately managed, the change can lead to data compromise. This text explains the LMS, the value of the LMS to a technology strategy, and browser neutrality. Further, the text provides information on the general components of the LMS, and LMS quality such as the software as a service phenomenon, as well as operational sustainability. As posited by Al-Busaidi, 2009; Cheng, 2011; Wang & Chiu, 2011, LMS quality is related to the attributes of the system (i.e., functionality, interactivity). For the purpose of this text, functionality is the specific use or set of usages in that the LMS was designed and developed.

This LMS examination supports thought leaders - Chief Learning Officers, Chief Information Officers, and other Learning and IT professionals in efforts to understand better the LMS, and comprehend vulnerabilities of such systems, combat information leakage, and guard against data contamination. This text provides these thought leaders, as well as stakeholders, with information to guide policymaking, and comprehend how to analyze data for adopting new systems and mitigating risks. After reading this text, practitioners and academicians will be able to enhance their understanding of LMS vulnerabilities from an operational standpoint, not as IT professionals.

WHAT IS THE LEARNING MANAGEMENT SYSTEM ABOUT?

The LMS, a system that has gained a solid position in colleges and universities internationally (Glenn, 2008), and is known by multiple names (Goyal & Purohit, 2010). Names include but are not limited to course management system - CMS (Lane, 2009; Unal & Unal, 2011), learning management system - LMS (Caminero, Hernandez, Ros, Tobarra, Robles-Gomez, Pastor, 2013; Hustad & Arntzen, 2013), and content management system - CMS (Black, 2011). Additional names given by Monarch Media Inc. (2010) are virtual learning environments (VLE), and collaborative learning environments.

The LMS can be a web-based distance education system (Deperlioglu, Sarpkaya, & Ergun, 2011), as well. Organizations are continuously looking towards technology as a way to better manage infrastructure and improve delivery of IT services and applications. Whether as a proprietary or an open source system, LMSs can affect the core business of teaching, learning, and managing learning delivery.

In 2008, Glenn reported the results of a survey providing that "60%" (p. 5) of the survey respondents said "technological change occurring in our midst will alter the perception of the college campus from a one-dimensional (physical) concept to a multi-dimensional (physical and online) one" (p. 5). Not only have college campuses altered due to learning technology, businesses have altered, too. The materialization of Information and Communication Technologies (ICTs) make the availability of new tools for users to direct data, knowledge, and facts (Conde, Rodriguez-Conde, Alier, & Garcia-Halgodo, 2014). Distinct differences exist between the names that LMSs are referred, even though the functionality is blurred.

The course management system is an element of online learning (Tella, 2011). The CMS offers a space for education and teaching activities to occur. The system makes possible for instructors, and learners to post learning content, contribute in forums and educational discussions, retain a grade book, maintain a roster, track learners, and engage in and manage educational activities in an online distance education environment. According to Martins and Kellermanns (2004), the CMS is a compilation of information and communication technologies. This team provided that the CMS includes, bulletin boards, chat rooms, content repositories, e-mail, instant messaging, and document-sharing systems (Martins and Kellermanns, 2004). An example of a course management system is Blackboard (Yin, Lien, & Werner, 2009).

The content management system is a tool for creating, editing, publishing, and tracking learning objects (Nasinar & Rasheed, 2014). Content includes audio files, lessons, complete courses, text documents, and video files. Pickett (2000) referred to content as data made available on websites. With the content management system, users can develop content, upload it to the database, publish the content for users, and then track content usage. Per (Connell, 2013), content management systems can be used to manage library websites. An example of content management systems is WordPress.

Figure 1. Information Flow for the Content Management System provides a graphic for the usage of the system

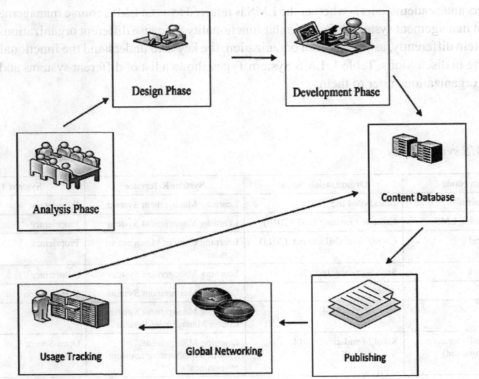

The LMS, a tool that is essential for online distance education, is an instrument for providing forums, email, evaluation tools such as questionnaires, and a grading system (Caminero, Hernandez, Tobarra, Robles-Gomez, & Pastor, 2012). According to (Pastor, Hernandez, Robles-Gomez, Caminero, & Hernandez, 2011), the LMS is a tool for video conferencing. The LMS progressed from a system to handle administrative tasks associated with online distance education to being the foundation of multiple functions" … talent development, including on [-] boarding, on-the-job performance support, and social learning" (Lindenberg, 2014, p. 28). In the selection of an LMS, it is important to investigate organizations' current and future needs, involve key stakeholders as early in the process as possible, as well as design, develop, and implement a LMS selection and an implementation plan. The LMS provides flexibility and the capability for learners to study at their pace within any-place and anytime models (Hustad & Arntzen, 2013).

Security of LMSs are managed through digital rights management (DRM). DRM rules rights of entry for control technologies that can be utilized with the goal to limit digital content usage (Nasinar & Rasheed, 2014). Per Pal (2014), the DRM was established as a system for the safety of digital works. Further, DRM's creation was to safeguard the unsanctioned duplication and illegal circulation of copyrighted digital products (Pal, 2014). The world-wide-web is used ubiquitously. DRM prevents users from pirating (Sinha, Machado, & Sellman, 2010), and acting on unauthorized and illegal actions such as copying and selling marketed digital information and products.

LMSs are used in different ways and their capabilities are variable (Conde, Rodriguez-Conde, Alier, & Garcia-Halgodo, 2014). The understanding that each technological tool has a set of exclusive purposes means that a goal was implicit in the analysis, design, development, and implementation. Thus, an objective ensued from the goal that bound or specified the tools' usages. Each LMS has impacts to teaching. The system determines the teaching impact. Through this text, what should be understood by practitioners and academicians is whether the LMS is referred to as an LMS, course management system, or a content management system there is similar functionality. Because different organizations may refer to their system differently, as well as each organization, the key is to understand the functionalities when participating in discussions. Table 1. LMS System Types shows a list of different systems and how their associated organizations refer to them.

Table 1. LMS system types

System Name	Organization Name	System Reference	System Type
Blackboard Learn™	Blackboard Inc. (2014)	Learning Management System	Proprietary
Latitude Learning LMS	Latitude Learning LLC. (2014)	Learning Management System	Proprietary
Learning Cloud	Cornerstone OnDemand. (2014)	Learning Content Management System	Proprietary
Learning@work	Saba Software, Inc. (2014)	Learning Management System	Proprietary
.LRN	.LRN ™	Learning Management System	Open Source
Moodle LMS/CMS	Moodle ™. (2014)	Learning Management System/ Course Management System	Open Source
Sakai LMS (collaborative learning environment)	Sakai Foundation. (2014)	Learning Management System (collaborative learning environment)	Open Source

Figure 2. Learning Management System provides a graphic for the usage of the system

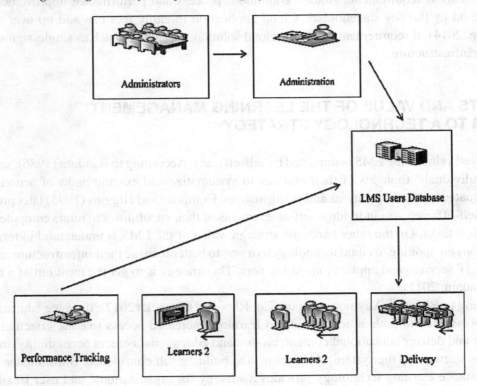

Systems can be proprietary or open source (Boehle, 2007; Monarch Media Inc., 2010). Examples of proprietary systems are Latitude Learning, Blackboard, Cornerstone OnDemand, and Saba.

Open source systems are those wherein the systems' codes are available to the general public and is free to be changed at no cost. Also, no license or hardware costs are connected with open source technology. Examples of open-source systems are Moodle - Modular Object-Oriented Dynamic learning Environment, Sakai, and .LRN. Open-source systems primarily were connected to institutions of higher education; however, these systems are now a part of government, corporate training departments, and non-profit agencies (Monarch Media Inc., 2010).

The proprietary and the open-source systems boast security features. One measure organizations use when deciding on whether to implement a proprietary or open-source system is cost. Per Boehle (2007), the difference between the LMS and the CMS is that LMSs are business applications and CMSs key focus is content. Today, organizations are using both the LMS and the CMS.

Prior to the cloud, LMSs ran through software functionality. Deciphering which LMS model to implement requires planning. According to Lowe (2014), implementing LMS software has its higher costs during a start-up due to the number of licenses required and the implementation. Generally, there needs to be a license for each user. The cost of the license can be $500.00 per person. A point to understand is that software implementation becomes less costly as the system ages.

On the other hand, software functionality is shifting to cloud technology (Jouini, Aissa, Rabai, and Mili (2012). In understanding this shift, non-IT leaders need an understanding of this technology move from software functions to SaaS and cloud applications. LMS cloud applications can be expensive;

therefore, business requirements guiding continuous process and performance improvements have to be understood by the key stakeholders. Cloud application monthly fees can add up over a period of time (Lowe, 2014). If requirements dictate a cloud solution, technology such as single-sign-on can help protect the infrastructure.

BENEFITS AND VALUE OF THE LEARNING MANAGEMENT SYSTEM TO A TECHNOLOGY STRATEGY

The perceived value of the LMS is impacted by self-efficacy. According to Bandura (1986), self-efficacy refers to individuals' thoughts of their abilities to systematize and execute paths of action needed to reach designated types of operations and performances. Compeau and Higgins (1995) later provided that computer self-efficacy was individual self-assessments of their capabilities to relate computer aptitudes to accomplish tasks. On the other hand, the strategic value of the LMS is understood in terms of ICT. Organizations are looking to cloud technology as a way to better manage their infrastructure and improve delivery of IT services and applications to learners. The strategy is to get the most out of a technology venture (Kadam, 2011).

According to Bhuasiri, Xaymoungkhoun, Zo, Rho, and Ciganek (2012), distance education affords a variety of benefits to include individualized learning, increased access to data, effectual avenue to standardize and deliver educational content, on-demand educational content accessibility, interactivity between the learner and the system, self-pacing, and building self confidence. Bhrommalee (2012) offers that distance learning technology provides a strategy for organizational and user flexibility (i.e., anytime and any-place learning), and convenient and diverse learning environments (i.e., learners in multiple locations can train at the same time). In comparison to conventional learning styles, distance education learning can offer time-effective methods and possibly decrease costs for facilities, education, travel (i.e., airfare, hotel, per diem) printed materials, and labor (Bhuasiri et al., 2012). Cost and time savings equal value.

As a non-IT practitioners, users and leaders will need to have not only an understanding of the benefits and value of the LMS. These users and leaders will need an understanding of browser neutrality, components of the LMS and their vulnerabilities, and cloud technology. Understanding is needed to ensure appropriate requirements gathering, development, testing, and implementation of solutions.

BROWSER NEUTRALITY, THE LMS, AND SECURITY

Browser neutrality means that a website or web application looks and acts the same when viewed in all web browsers. In other words, with browser neutrality, the Web is more visually attractive; it is accessible through different interfaces without difficulty (Gardner, 1998). The choice of a web browser include, but are not limited to Internet Explorer, Mozilla, Safari, Chrome, Opera, and Bing. In regards to the LMS, inconsistent web-browser development can lead to distance learning applications appearing and performing differently. The difference can be a negative. Negativity includes allowing cyber attacks of LMS systems, causing issues such as pixels to look different, LMS screens not to advance, LMS tests not to open, and test scores not to calculate correctly.

Geier (2013) recommends maintaining an up-to-date browser as these browsers will maintain security patches. Security patches help to safeguard computers. Also, users should ensure not to use outdated operating systems. Why? Once operating systems are outdated, the software owners no longer service the system. An example of an outdated operating system is Microsoft's Window XP. Per Reisinger (2014), Microsoft stopped its support of Windows XP; therefore, users still operating the platform should not expect Microsoft to provide a security patch. The lack of a security path will eventually lead to cyber concerns.

COMPONENTS OF THE LMS AND THEIR VULNERABILITIES

LMS functional areas can include numerous features. The importance of each feature depends upon the institution or business requiring the LMS service. Software vulnerability is no more than the propensity to be intercepted by malicious manipulations, in other words disruption. The disruptive increase in cloud computing, mobility, and connective technologies indicates that enterprise applications no longer look or perform the way they previously performed. This section provides general LMS features so users can understand the functionality that could become vulnerable within the LMS. Ensuring most favorable LMS performance is challenging because organizations may lack the suitable visibility into their users' experiences.

Enhancements in practitioners' understandings of LMS vulnerabilities allow stakeholders to have increased insights into their works to thwart security related accidents. This information can support stakeholders' knowledge in actions to take prior to the LMS reaching unacceptable vulnerability levels.

SOFTWARE AS A SERVICE A PHENOMENON

Software vendors of a plethora of sizes and specialties continue to promote Software as a service (SaaS). Institutions of higher learning and businesses are more content with retrieving and managing their data and information over the Internet. Information technology services are being outsourced so much that institutions and businesses are viewing IT as an expense as opposed to an asset. Companies employing on demand offerings are not only cutting costs, these companies are attaining competitiveness, (Demirkan, Cheng, & Bandyopadhyay, SaaS as a phenomenon, 2010). With the attractiveness of cost savings and space savings, a multitenant public cloud is deemed a novel and troublesome milieu (Lango, 2014).

Host Server as a Security Measure

Institutions of higher learning and organizations can purchase a LMS through two avenues. These organizations can license the LMS software and then host the software on their pre-determined servers internally. The other avenue was reviewed in the topic, A Cloud Application as a Security Measure. The advantages e-learning offers to the end user include availability, confidentiality, as well as information

Table 2. General LMS Functional Features for general LMS categories and their descriptions

Functional Features	Description
Assessments	Pre-test, Post-test, Quizzes, Self-assessments
Course and Resource Management	Supports the capability to add external training, CEUS, certifications, informal training, codes to training, and more
Catalog Usage	Supports the capability to enable categories and sub-categories to be assigned to a course catalog structure, as well as the capability to search at a subcategory level
Curriculum, Learning Plans, & Certification Management	Supports the capability to enable grouping of learning activities in a curriculum, certification or learning plan, as well as set due dates for entire plan completions Supports the capability to allow one role to take courses from another role
Skills & Competency Management	Supports the capability to support skills and competency inventories at multiple levels, as well as enable skill gap analysis and reporting
e-Learning Content Creation/ Management	Supports the capability for learners to self-register and unregister for e-learning offerings
Surveys and Assessment	Supports the capability to enable importing of test questions either from a local or shared drive, or from a third party vendor, directly into a question bank Supports the capability for built-in test and survey creation tools
Enrollment and Registration Administration	Supports the capability to notify learners of their enrollments by email through mobile technology and non-mobile technology
E- Commerce	Supports the capability to send pre-scripted and free style notices to companies about billing instances
Reporting and Analytics	Supports the capability to run reports in real time, as well as enable reporting on all learning activities
User Interface	Supports the capability to support user configuration of interface design by organizational hierarchy, organizational units, and job titles
Hosting & Support	Supports the capability to host delivery services such as SaaS, as well as interoperability with other modules/applications
Administration	Supports the capability for data exchanges of inbound and outbound feeds
User Management	Supports the capability for flexibility in creating audiences or groups
Communication and Workflow	Supports the capability to manage notifications and reminders by organization, as well as the ability to send notices throughout the hierarchy
Security	Supports the capability for token ring functionality and the authentication with third party tools Supports the capability to turn on/off data fields
LMS Features	Explanation of the Features
Synchronous Communication	chat, whiteboard, teleconferencing

integrity. Some of the limitations of operating, or hosting, a LMS through the organization's servers is the vulnerability to security threats that impact these advantages (Iacob, 2013). There are several types of security attacks that can present themselves to a host server. A common threat, a Denial of Service (DoS) attack, can fill memory capacity, cancel or redirect information, or disable supporting services (Voznak and Safarik, 2012). In e-learning environments maintained on organizationally hosted servers, security management practices combined with environmental security standards mitigate many of the threats to host servers.

Cloud Application as a Security Measure

Another avenue for purchasing a LMS is through a hosted service. With a hosted service, the software is maintained on the vendors' servers accessible through the Internet. Cloud computing services are divided into three main categories: Software as a service (SaaS), Platform as a service (PaaS), and Infrastructure as a service (IaaS) (Ertaul et al., 2010). The commonality among these externally hosted formats is that they provide availability and convenient access to a shared pool of resources.

The term *Cloud* refers to accessing information through Internet. Cloud computing is a model that allows users to pay only for the resources that they use, and transfer the burden of maintaining the infrastructure of servers to the external host. SaaS, (Katzan & Dowling, 2010) is a hosted service that allows users to access a provider's software that is operated and maintained externally, in the cloud. PaaS is a delivery model that allows a user/provider to deploy a software application into the cloud without the need to manage the underlying infrastructure. Many cloud based LMSs run on this platform. IaaS is a service that allows a user access to different types of content – software, programs, firewalls – without purchasing or maintaining data center resources. The user generally pays on a per-use basis.

To bring the understanding of the cloud to light, many users are familiar with the Internet in regards to sending email. The sending of email, in most cases, is a cloud computing service. With cloud computing services, the home of applications initiates on external servers, in the cloud. User access is through the Internet. SaaS providers service applications through a range of architectural levels. These levels are supported by the capability to sustain multiple clients and software configurability. Four architectural levels were identified. The amount of levels in any definite operational environment is founded upon the cloud configuration and its uniqueness. As posited by Mangiuc (2010), a cloud platform makes available the facility for a software application developer to construct applications that operate in the cloud. With this said, the services employed by the application developer are available in the cloud.

Levels of Service for SaaS

SaaS is one of the three key categories for cloud computing service. The additional two are Infrastructure-as-a-service (IaaS), and Platform-as-a-service (PaaS). Because this text concerns LMS vulnerability, Saas was further reviewed. Generally, four levels are involved with SaaS. With the first level, users within a client domain address a single instance of an application running on a server. Each client/instance, running on the same server, is completely independent of other client/instances. Every software instance is separately customized for each client. The level one method is the traditional hosted service operating in the cloud. Next is the second level. The server hosts an individual instance of the software for every client. On the other hand, the instance is a configurable version of the same code base. This process reduces maintenance costs and contributes to enhanced economy-of-scale. Another level is the third level. Here vendors can run a sole instance of an application that is shared by numerous clients. The feature set for every client is determined by configurable metadata, and authorization/security policies to insure/declare the separation of user data. The last level is the fourth one. With this level, vendors can run a sole instance of an application shared by numerous clients on a server farm with fabric for load balancing. The determinations of the cloud's architectural levels are determined by the providers'/clients' businesses, architectural, and operational models.

Single Sign-On as a Security Measure

Single sign-on is the ability to use one point of entry for various Internet accessed accounts. This capability, designed to reduce the burden of managing several accounts and passwords, can inadvertently lead users to develop password strategies, which can reduce the security of their protected information (Sun et al., 2010). Single sign-on systems separate the role of the identity provider from the role of the relaying party allowing users to leverage using one identity across multiple platforms. The identifying provider issues credentials to the user, while the relaying party essentially verifies the credentials. When configured, single sign-on can provide a sense of security for users; however, these configurations can be problematic for organizations, which must maintain duplicate sets of user data (Lewis and Lewis, 2010).

OPERATIONAL SUSTAINABILITY AND THE LEARNING MANAGEMENT SYSTEM

Institutions of higher learning are within a regulatory and compliant environment that must adhere to guidelines and bylaws set to protect sensitive information that could result in cybercrimes. An example of these guidelines and bylaws are the National Institute of Standard Technology (NIST), Computer Security Resource Center (CSRC) and Federal Information Security Management Act (FISMA) (Updegrove, 2009). In many instances, personal identifiable information (PII) can be compromised leaving LMS systems vulnerable for internal and external system hackers to retrieve sensitive data. According to Baker (2009), the U.S government and private institutions must set standards and securities to protect the information transmitted through cyberspace, the Internet. This revelation was determined through the President Obama administration that declared the nation, including public sectors and academic institutions, address the urgency to safeguard the privacy and civilian rights of our citizens (Baker, 2009). It is the obligation of institutions of higher learning to adopt operational sustainability practices (Baker, 2009). Adopting operational sustainability practices will ensure requirements are within technology security standards.

The path to develop high-level securities that will protect LMSs is the driving force (Burley, Eisenburg, & Goodman, 2014) to creating an operational sustainability plan. To safeguard LMSs from technological vulnerabilities, it is viable for institutions of higher learning to adopt defense practices that form a holistic operational sustainability approach. To create an operational sustainability approach, methods, tools, and techniques utilizing cryptography and access control within various components are imperative to secure and protect information and data (Shoffner et al., 2013). The components of strategic security planning, workforce planning, operational planning, and business process management will allow institutions of higher learning to establish best practices in assisting with increasing cyber-protections of LMSs.

Strategic Security Planning

Strategic security planning provides clarity about the organizational goals and purpose to protect its data and information by following certain guidelines and bylaws –NIST, CSRC, and or FISMA (Abdalkrim, 2013; Updegrove, 2009). Developing a strategic security plan to mitigate risk is a difficult quest for stakeholders (Ferraro, 2014). Determining the right internal protection system that contains protection properties to maintain and collaborate with current systems may pose setbacks to making quantifiable decisions. The preliminary tasks that stakeholders face are defining the amount of information technology (IT) security that is required to safeguard sensitive information. Another task is determining the amount of security measures that will have the most longevity and control systems. The last task is establishing improvement on levels of security (Carin, Cybenko, & Hughes, 2008). To ensure that theories and hypothesis are being measured adequately, adopting Quantitative Evaluation of Risk for Investment Efficient Strategies, Queries methodology can strengthen decision evaluations (Carin, et al., 2008). Using the Queries methodology will allow a thorough risk assessment that will provide clarity to stakeholders upon executing a strategic security plan.

Workforce Planning

When creating a workforce of stakeholders, the demand for well-trained and adequate professionals is necessary. Stakeholders must be fluent in regulatory and compliant conditions that speak to critical cybersecurity matters. In many cases, specialized IT professionals who desire to transition into management positions can enhance the opportunity of being well-diverse teams of stakeholders (McDaniel, 2013). To address cybersecurity matters, stakeholders must hold years of cyber security experience, IT certifications, licensure, and skill-based competency exams that will enforce operational and tactical needs surrounded by cybersecurity (Burley, Eisenbery, & Goodman, 2014). As posited by Ginter (2013), it is crucial that stakeholders are able to identify any threats and vulnerabilities that can infiltrate firewall security. Designing the workforce with diverse skills and talent that encompasses professional aptitude in operations and cybersecurity will reduce risk to network systems (Anderson & Evans, 2013).

To assist with optimizing stakeholder's roles as decision makers, developing on-going educational training is highly recommended (Pusey & Sadera, 2011). It is vital that organizations incorporate ongoing training to gain preparedness for cyber-attacks (Levy, Ramim, & Hackney, 2013). Security threats are constantly evolving as hackers and predators are becoming more system knowledgeable. In order for stakeholders and system analyst to remain informative, strategies for Education, Training, and Awareness, ETA will assist organizations and stakeholders with addressing the latest security threats and risk. By allowing stakeholders and decision-makers ETA, opportunities to safeguard LMSs will have viable protection (McDaniel, 2013).

Operational Planning

Once all stakeholders are informed of the strategic plan, establishing a Disaster Recovery Plan, DRP, and Business Continuity Planning, BCP, is essential (Omar, Alijani, & Mason, 2011). Within operational planning, making a current analysis of the educational technology environment will be beneficial to understanding future desired processes (Adam et al., 2013). According to Carcary (2013), the operational goal of creating technological security standards is reducing any disruption or consequences that may leave data information available for hackers. To integrate models and tools to negate a vulnerable infrastructure (Neumann, 1997), a well designed network infrastructure and security controls must be in place. Some examples of these security controls are following approved standard configuration guides, implementing security templates, and enforcing strict security systems policies on the systems network. Adhering to a DRP and BCP will assist institutions of higher learning with the capabilities to restore and recover sensitive information that could be potentially affected by natural disasters, power outages, or cybercrimes (Omar, Alijani, & Mason, 2011).

Business Process Management

Many business operations implement Six Sigma, Total Quality Management, or Kaizen tools and techniques to improve business processes. However, IT Infrastructure Library, ITIL sets the path for best practices within IT operations (Marrone, Gacenga, Cater-Steel, &Kolbe, 2014). As strategic security plans are implemented into operations, the next process is to initiate the plans into business processes. ITIL ensures that operations integrate new process initiatives according to security guidelines set-forth by regulations that will enforce a more structured LMS migration and monitoring. According to Marrone et al., to encourage this development, institutions of higher learning must understand the following

1.   How is the Business-IT alignment perceived at different levels of maturity of the ITIL implementation?
2.   How does the total number of realized benefits develop as the maturity of the ITIL implementation increases (2014, p. 364)?

Using these guidelines when executing implementation of new processes, will provide measureable outcomes that will determine system upgrade efficiencies (Ahmad, Amer, Qutaifan, & Alhilali, 2013). The purpose of ITIL is to design a roadmap that will provide critical details upon process implementation. If the new process proves to have limitations and challenges, decision-makers will have the opportunity to adjust or modify current strategies.

Figure 3 provides an overview of the process of strategic security planning that will determine the decisions to implement processes to sustain regulatory and compliant conditions. Through strategic planning, goals to strengthen LMSs will be the focal point of new policies. Institutions of higher learning are constantly evolving to accommodate the need of adult-learner students. With educational technology, it is an opportune time to ensure that academic institutions develop proactive approaches to provide security measures that will implement safety measures (Eoyang, 2004). For institutions of higher learning to be compliant with regulatory conditions, stakeholders must adhere to operational efficiencies that will promote sustainability (Ullah, Lai, & Majoribanks, 2013). As institutions of higher learning embrace sustainable concepts, increasing positive reputations and public recognition is the by-product (Lim, Stratopoulos, & Wirjanto, 2013). Once stakeholders implement strategies that enforce the need to develop high security levels, achieving security continuity will be validated in public view (Lim, et al., 2013). To achieve a holistic approach to gaining quality efficiencies, applying best practices within strategic security planning, workforce planning, operational planning and business process management will provide sustained concepts toward a prosperous future.

DISCUSSION AND CONCLUSION

Maintaining a modern website that runs efficiently requires a well thought through cyber security plan tied to operational sustainability. Nonetheless, maintaining a smoothly run LMS is vital to keeping users in an environment involving extremely strong competition, and a technology-driven world. This text provided practitioners and academicians insights to the LMS, cyber-security, and operational sustainability. Examiners of this information should be better equipped to guide others in LMS security and operational sustainability understanding.

Figure 3. Strategic security planning

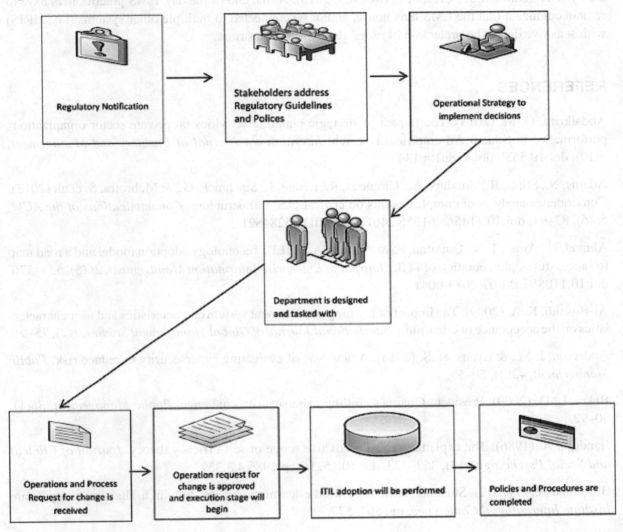

Vulnerability related concerns are critical to consider at the very beginning of any LMS adoption. According to Hommel (2010), this security concern is due to features related to security and privacy policies, which already exist at runtime, being hard to add to LMSs. IT professionals may review vulnerability models to access risk. On the other hand, non-IT practitioners need a method to consistently review and partner with IT to ensure the LMS continues to run efficiently. Partnering can and does include tracking spikes, and system malfunctions.

Criminals are consistently seeking avenues to force themselves into systems and gain access to users' data. Breaches to access information such as legal names, mailing addresses, email addresses, telephone numbers, and other key identifying features are avenues to overtake identities. Understanding security involving LMSs, and invoking well thought through plans. As given by (Whalen & Bell, 2014) the task to identify exact procedures for managing cyber crime is very difficult. The difficulty lies in the attacks having different characteristics, and consistently maintaining the plan through evolved iterations of cyber attacks. Organizations could notably decrease and alleviate risk using proven standards for administrating systems (Dawson, Jr., Crespo, & Brewster, 2013). At the end of the day, LMS practitioners have to remain cognizant that the LMS may house, and/or be connected to multiple other systems (i.e., HRIS) with sensitive data. The protection of users' data is very important.

REFERENCES

Abdalkrim, G. M. (2013). The impact of strategic planning activities on private sector organizations performance in Sudan: An empirical research. *International Journal of Business and Management*, *8*(10). doi:10.5539/ijbm.v8n10p134

Adams, N., Stiles, R., Zimdars, A., Timmons, R., Leung, J., Stachnick, G., & Mehrotra, S. et al. (2013). Consequence analysis of complex events on critical U.S. infrastructure. *Communications of the ACM*, *56*(6), 83–91. doi:10.1145/2461256.2461276 PMID:25284821

Ahmad, N., Amer, T. N., Qutaifan, F., & Alhilali, A. (2013). Technology adoption model and a road map to successful implementation of ITIL. *Journal of Enterprise Information Management*, *26*(5), 553–576. doi:10.1108/JEIM-07-2013-0041

Al-Busaidi, K. A. (2009). The impact of learning management system characteristics and user characteristics on the acceptance of e-learning. *International Journal of Global Management Studies*, *1*(2), 75–91.

Anderson, J. M., & Evans, K. S. (2013). A new way of evaluating cybersecurity to reduce risk. *Public Management*, *42*(3), 50–53.

Baker, L. D. (2009). President Obama's chilling cybersecurity challenge. *Public Management*, *38*(1), 90–92.

Bandura, A. (1986). The explanatory and predictive scope of self-efficacy theory. *Journal of Clinical and Social Psychology*, *4*(3), 359–373. doi:10.1521/jscp.1986.4.3.359

Bhrommalee, P. (2012). Students' attitudes toward e-learning: A case study in a Thai university. *Clute Institute International Conference*, pp. 567–577.

Bhuasiri, W., Xaymoungkhoun, O., Zo, H., Rho, J. J., & Ciganek, A. P. (2012). Critical success factors for e-learning in developing countries: A comparative analysis between ICT experts and faculty. *Computers & Education*, *58*(2), 843–855. doi:10.1016/j.compedu.2011.10.010

Black, E. L. (2011). Selecting a web content management system for an academic library website. *Information Technology & Libraries*, *30*(4), 185–189.

Blackboard Inc. (2014). A learning management system that brings your vision to life. *Blackboard*. Retrieved from http://www.blackboard.com/platforms/learn/overview.aspx

Boehle, S. (2007). Is open source right for you? *Training (New York, N.Y.)*, *44*(7), 36.

Burley, L. D., Eisenberg, J., & Goodman, E. S. (2014). Would cybersecurity professionalization help address the cybersecurity crisis? *Communications of the ACM*, *57*(2), 24–27. doi:10.1145/2556936

Caminero, A. C., Hernández, R. R., Ros, S. S., & Tobarra, L. l. (2013). Robles.-Gómez, A. A., & Pastor, R. R. (2013). Comparison of LMSs: Which is the most suitable LMS for my needs? *International Journal of Emerging Technologies In Learning*, *8*, 829–836. doi:10.3991/ijet.v8iS2.2758

Carcary, M. (2013). IT risk management: A capability maturity model perspective. *Electronic Journal of Information Systems Evaluation, 16*(1).

Carin, L., Cybenko, G., & Hughes, J. (2008). Cybersecurity strategies: The QuERIES methology. *IEEE Computer Society, 41*(8), 20–26. doi:10.1109/MC.2008.295

Cheng, Y.-M. (2011). Antecedents and consequences of e-learning acceptance. *Information Systems Journal, 21*(3), 269–299. doi:10.1111/j.1365-2575.2010.00356.x

Compeau, D. R., & Higgins, C. A. (1995). Computer self-efficacy: Development of a measure and initial test. *Management Information Systems Quarterly, 19*(2), 189–211. doi:10.2307/249688

Conde, M. A., Garcia, F., Rodriguez-Conde, M. J., Alier, M., & Garcia-Halgodo, A. (2014). Perceived openness of Learning Management Systems by students and teachers in education and technology courses. *Computers in Human Behavior, 31*, 517–526. doi:10.1016/j.chb.2013.05.023

Connell, R. (2013). Content Management Systems: Trends in Academic Libraries. *Information Technology & Libraries, 32*(2), 42–55. doi:10.6017/ital.v32i2.4632

Cornerstone On Demand. (2014). Learning management. *Learning Cloud.* Retrieved from http://www.cornerstoneondemand.com/global-business/talent-management/learning-management-cloud

Dawson, M. E., Crespo, M., & Brewster, S. (2013). DoD cyber technology policies to secure automated information systems. *International Journal of Business Continuity and Risk Management, 4*(1), 1–22. doi:10.1504/IJBCRM.2013.053089

Demirkan, H., Cheng, H., & Bandyopadhyay, S. (2010). Coordination strategies in an SaaS supply chain. *Journal of Management Information Systems, 26*(4), 119–143. doi:10.2753/MIS0742-1222260405

Deperlioglu, O., Sarpkaya, Y., & Ergun, E. (2011). Development of a relational database for Learning Management Systems. *Turkish Online Journal of Educational Technology - TOJET, 10*(4), 107-120.

Ertaul, L., Singhal, S., & Saldamli, G. (2010). Security challenges in cloud computing. In Security and Management (pp. 36-42).

Ferraro, M. F. (2014). "Groundbreaking" or broken? An analysis of sec cybersecurity disclosure guidance, its effectiveness, and implications. *Albany Law Review, 77*(2), 297–347.

Gardner, D. (1998). Newest HTML spec folds in benefits of DHTML. *InfoWorld, 20*(1), 47.

Geier, E. (2013). Four ways to make Internet Explorer more secure. *PC World, 31*(9), 189–191.

Ginter, A. (2013). Securing industrial control systems. *Chemical Engineering (Albany, N.Y.), 120*(7), 30–35.

Glenn, M. (2008). The future of higher education: How technology will shape learning. In D. D'Agostino (Ed.), Economist Intelligence Unit Report. New York, NY: The New Media Consortium; Retrieved from http://graphics.eiu.com/upload/The%20Future%20of%20Universities.pdf

Goyal, E., & Purohit, S. (2009). Study of using learning management system in a management course. *SIES Journal of Management, 6*(2), 11–20.

Hommel, W. (2010). Security and privacy management for learning management systems. In Y. Kats (Ed.), *Learning management system technologies and software solutions for online teaching: Tools and applications* (pp. 37–56). Hershey, PA: IGI Global; doi:10.4018/978-1-61520-853-1.ch003

Hustad, E., & Arntzen, A. (2013). Facilitating Teaching and Learning Capabilities in Social Learning Management Systems: Challenges, Issues, and Implications for Design. *Journal of Integrated Design & Process Science, 17*(1), 17–35. doi:10.3233/jid-2013-0003

Iacob, J. L. N. M. (2013). Information security management in e-learning. *Knowledge Horizons, 5*(2).

Jouini, M., Aissa, A. B., Rabai, L. B. A., & Mili, A. (2012). Towards quantitative measures of information security: A cloud computing case study. *International Journal of Cyber-Security and Digital Forensics, 1*(3), 248–262.

Kadam, Y. (2011). Security Issues in Cloud Computing A Transparent View. *International Journal of Computer Science Emerging Technology, 2*(5), 316–322.

Katzan, H. Jr, & Dowling, W. A. (2010). Software-as-A-service economics. *The Review of Business Information Systems, 14*(1), 27–37.

Kumar, G., & Chelikani, A. (2011). Analysis of security issues in cloud based e-learning.

Lane, L. M. (2009). Insidious pedagogy. How course management systems impact technology. *First Monday Peer-Reviewed Online Journal.* Retrieved from http://firstmonday.org/ojs/index.php/fm/article/view/2530/2303

Lango, J. (2014). Toward software - defined SLAs. *Communications of the ACM, 57*(1), 54–60. doi:10.1145/2541883.2541894

Latitude Learning, L. L. C. (2014). Our clients love our LMS. *Latitude Learning.* Retrieved from http://www.latitudelearning.com

Levy, Y., Ramim, M. M., & Hackney, R. A. (2013). Assessing ethical severity of e-Learning systems security attacks. *Journal of Computer Information Systems, 53*(3), 75–84.

Lewis, K. D., & Lewis, J. E. (2010). Web single sign-on authentication using SAML. [IJCSI]. *International Journal of Computer Science Issues, 7*(4).

Lim, J., Stratopoulos, C. T., & Wirjanto, S. T. (2013). Sustainability of a firm's reputation for information technology capability: The role of senior IT executives. *Journal of Management Information Systems, 30*(1), 57–96. doi:10.2753/MIS0742-1222300102

Lindenberg, S. (2014). Finding the right LMS fit. *T+D, 68*(4), 28.

Lowe, K. M. (2014). How to make the SaaS decision. *Chief Learning Officer, 13*(2), 38–47.

LRN. (n.d.). *About LRN.* Retrieved from http://dotlrn.org/about/

Mangiuc, D. M. (2010). Modelul "software as a service" si posibilele sale aplicatii în domeniul auditului financial. *Audit Financiar, 8*(8), 29-39. Retrieved from http://search.proquest.com/docview/729259251?accountid=62746

Marrone, M., Gacenga, F., Cater-Steel, A., & Kolbe, L. (2014). IT service management: A cross-national study of ITIL adoption. *Communications of the Association for Information Systems, 34*, 865–892.

Martins, L. L., & Kellermanns, F. (2004). A model of business school students' acceptance of a web-based course management system. *Academy of Management Learning & Education, 3*(1), 7–26. doi:10.5465/AMLE.2004.12436815

McDaniel, A. E. (2013). Securing the information and communications technology global supply chain from exploitation: Developing a strategy for education, training, and awareness. *Issues in Informing Science & Information Technology, 10*, 313–324.

Monarch Media Inc. (2010). The open-source LMS. *Open-Source Learning Management Systems: Sakai and Moodle.*

Moodle. (2014). Decision FAQ. *Documentation*. Retrieved from http://docs.moodle.org/27/en/index.php?search=cms&title=Special%3ASearch

Nasinar, M. A., & Rasheed, A. A. (2014). Dynamic security technique for content management repository system. *International Journal of Research in Advent Technology, 2*(1), 10–15.

Neumann, P. G. (1997). Identity-related misuse. *Communications of the ACM, 40*(7), 112–112. doi:10.1145/256175.256196

Omar, A., Alijani, D., & Mason, R. (2011). Information technology disaster recovery plan: Case Study. *Academy of Strategic Management Journal, 10*(2), 127–141.

Pal, A. K. (2014). Application of digital rights management in library. *DESIDOC Journal of Library & Information Technology, 34*(1), 11–15. doi:10.14429/djlit.34.5490

Pastor, R., Hernandez, R., Ros, S., Robles-Gomez, A., Caminero, A. C., & Castro, M. (2011). A video-message evaluation tool integrated in the unedited e-learning platform. *Proceedings of the 41st ASEE/IEEE Frontiers in Education Conference (FIE)*, Rapid City, SD, F3C-1 – F3C-6.

Pickett, J. P. (2000). *The American Heritage dictionary of the English language* (4th ed.). Boston: Houghton Mifflin Company.

Pusey, P., & Sadera, W. A. (2012). Cyberethics, cybersafety, and cybersecurity: Preservice teacher knowledge, preparedness, and the need for teacher education to make a difference. *Journal of Digital Learning in Teacher Education, 28*(2).

Reisinger, D. (2014). 10 Ways to protect yourself from the zero-day IE exploit. *Eweek, 1*.

Saba Software, Inc. (2014). LMS. *Learn@work*. Retrieved from http://www.saba.com/us/lms/

Shoffner, M., Owen, P., Mostafa, J., Lamm, B., Wang, X., Schmitt, C., & Ahalt, S. C. (2013). The secure medical research workspace: An IT Infrastructure to enable secure research on clinical data. *CTS Clinical & Translational Science, 6*(3), 222–225. doi:10.1111/cts.12060 PMID:23751029

Sinha, R., Machado, F., & Sellman, C. (2010). Don't think twice, it's all right: Music piracy and pricing in a DRM-free environment. *Journal of Marketing, 74*(2), 40–54. doi:10.1509/jmkg.74.2.40

Sun, S. T., Boshmaf, Y., Hawkey, K., & Beznosov, K. (2010, September). A billion keys, but few locks: the crisis of web single sign-on. *Proceedings of the 2010 Workshop on New Security Paradigms*, Concord, MA, 61-72. doi:10.1145/1900546.1900556

Tella, A. (2011). Reliability and factor analysis of a blackboard course management system success: A scale development and validation in an educational context. *Journal of Information Technology Education*, *10*, 1055–1080.

Ullah, A., Lai, R., & Majoribanks, T. (2013). A proposed model for business sustainability based on business and information technology. *Journal of Software*, *8*(11), 2796–2806. doi:10.4304/jsw.8.11.2796-2806

Unal, Z., & Unal, A. (2011). Evaluating and comparing the usability of web-based course management systems. *Journal of Information Technology Education*, *10*, 1019–1038.

Updegrove, A. (2009). How we'll get the job done: An interview with NIST's Dr. George W. Arnold. Standards Today, 8(3), 32-39.

Vogten, H., & Koper, R. (2014). Towards a new generation of Learning Management Systems. Paper presented at the Proceedings of the 6th International Conference on Computer Supported Education, Barcelona, Spain, 514-519.

Voznak, M., & Safarik, J. (2012). DoS attacks targeting SIP server and improvements of robustness. *International Journal of Mathematics and Computers in Simulation*, *6*(1), 177–184.

Wang, H. C., & Chiu, Y. F. (2011). Assessing E-Learning 2.0 System Success. *Computers & Education*, *57*(2), 1790–1800. doi:10.1016/j.compedu.2011.03.009

Whalen, D. T., & Bell, G. (2014). The cybersecurity challenge. *NACD Directorship*, *40*(3), 75.

Yin, L., Lien, N., & Werner, J. M. (2009). Learning in virtual groups: Identifying key aspects of a course management system affecting teamwork in an it training course. *Information Technology, Learning and Performance Journal*, *25*(2), 30–41.

KEY TERMS AND DEFINITIONS

Academician: An intellectual, scholarly person. A teacher at a college or university.

Cybersecurity: Cyber security is the information that is securely stored in computing servers such as public and private networks, computers and smartphones.

Infrastructure-as-a-Service (IaaS): Infrastructure as a Service is a provision model in which an business outsources the tools utilized to support operations, to include data storage, hardware, networking components, and servers.

Learner: Refers to adult students who have or are currently taking a year of distance learning courses.

Platform-as-a-Service (PaaS): Platform-as-a-service (PaaS) mechanizes the relationship, configuration, deployment, and continual management of applications in the cloud.

Software-as-a-Service (SaaS): Software set out as a hosted service and accessed over the world-wide-web.

Technology Mediated-Learning: Term used to define different ways of employing computers in learning and instruction.

Chapter 15

The Innovation and Promise of STEM–Oriented Cybersecurity Charter Schools in Urban Minority Communities in the United States as a Tool to Create a Critical Business Workforce

Darrell Norman Burrell
Florida Institute of Technology, USA

Janet Simmons
The National Graduate School of Quality Management, USA

Aikyna Finch
Strayer University, USA

Sharon L. Burton
Florida Institute of Technology, USA

ABSTRACT

This text is an on-going study to provide current information regarding developing underrepresented student populations through STEM specific Charter schools to fulfill pipeline shortages. Current findings show that African Americans are underrepresented in high paying Science, Technology, Engineering, and Mathematics (STEM) fields, especially in cybersecurity. The U.S. pipeline of minority students studying STEM falls short in producing the next generation of cybersecurity professionals; thus, a salient need exists to design, pilot, and test a program to grow the minority student pipeline in the cybersecurity field. The charter school movement is one of the fastest growing education reforms with the ability to make a dramatic impact in the U.S. and internationally. Because charter schools often organize around a mission, theme, or curricular and enjoy freedoms, in organizational structure, mission, and academic program, with all held to high standards, this text proposes cybersecurity charter schools to fill technology voids. This organizational structure, mission, and academic programming, will enable students to become immersed in hands-on, real world applications allowing for experiential learning, which can develop students with cybersecurity expertise, technical knowledge, and skills, and competencies needed to take and pass cybersecurity and information security related certification assessments.

DOI: 10.4018/978-1-4666-8345-7.ch015

INTRODUCTION

African Americans unemployment rate is consistently twice that of Caucasians (Desilver 2013). One of the challenges is the need to develop specialized job expertise in career areas that are in demand and high paying in urban African-American communities. Knowledge, critical thinking skills, and leadership in science, technology, engineering and mathematics (STEM) fields are in high demand, especially in the cybersecurity profession (See Figure 1).

African Americans remain one of the most underrepresented minority groups in computer science and computer engineering-related fields (Washington, 2011). The percentage of African-Americans earning STEM degrees has fallen during the last decade. African-Americans are 12 percent of the U.S. population and 11 percent of all students beyond high school. In 2009, they received just 7 percent of all STEM bachelor's degrees, 4 percent of master's degrees, and 2 percent of PhDs, according to the National Center for Education Statistics (Washington, 2011). From community college through PhD level, the percentage of STEM degrees received by African-Americans in 2009 was 7.5 percent, down from 8.1 percent in 2001(Washington, 2011). The numbers are striking in certain fields. In 2009, African-Americans received 1 percent of degrees in science technologies (Washington, 2011). The underrepresentation of African Americans in STEM college degree programs and STEM jobs begins at the K-12 educational level, as successful graduates with the expertise in the areas of computer science, information security, and computer engineering are the necessary building blocks for successful careers.

Demand for trained cybersecurity and computer science professionals who work to protect organizations from cybercrime is high nationwide, but the shortage is particularly severe in the federal government, which does not offer salaries as high as the private sector (Halzack, 2014). The nationwide shortage of cybersecurity professionals particularly for positions within the federal government creates risks for national and homeland security, according to a new study from the RAND Corporation (Halzack, 2014). The Washington metropolitan area had more than 23,000 total job postings for cybersecurity positions in 2013, a figure that far surpassed the number of cyber postings in any other region. New York, which

Figure 1. Unemployment rates by race: Seasonally adjusted

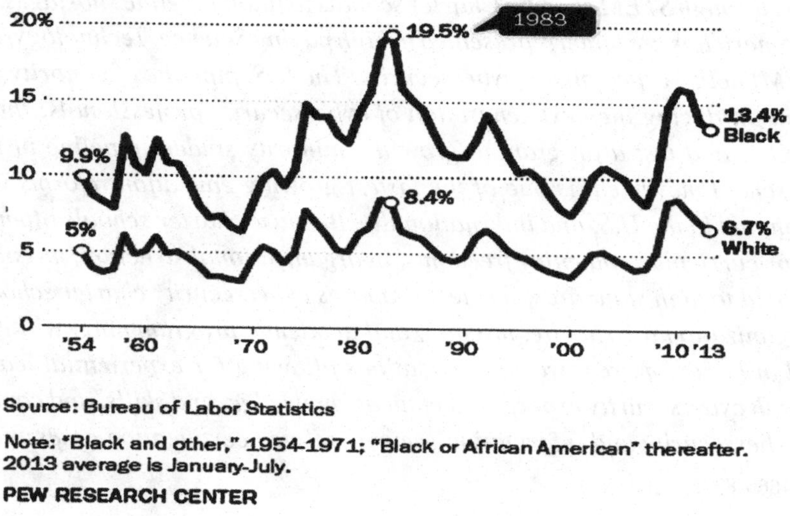

Source: Bureau of Labor Statistics

Note: "Black and other," 1954-1971; "Black or African American" thereafter. 2013 average is January-July.

PEW RESEARCH CENTER

Figure 2. Top cities ranked by total postings (Courtesy of Burning Glass Technologies)

	City (MSA)	Total Postings	% Growth (2007-2013)		City (MSA)	Total Postings	% Growth (2007-2013)
1	Washington D.C.	23,457	90%	14	Denver	3,482	200%
2	New York	15,632	68%	15	Detroit	3,093	84%
3	San Francisco/San Jose	12,697	96%	16	Minneapolis	2,929	42%
4	Chicago	9,723	131%	17	Phoenix	2,885	114%
5	Dallas	7,669	140%	18	St. Louis	2,506	82%
6	Los Angeles	7,123	58%	19	Miami	2,496	29%
7	Boston	6,336	99%	20	Charlotte	2,410	127%
8	Atlanta	5,883	213%	21	Virginia Beach/Norfolk	2,335	74%
9	Baltimore	4,514	135%	22	Portland (OR)	1,981	119%
10	Seattle	4,470	85%	23	Austin	1,979	172%
11	Philadelphia	4,032	-4%	24	Tampa/St. Petersburg	1,932	58%
12	San Diego	3,665	112%	25	San Antonio	1,841	68%
13	Houston	3,648	67%				

had the second-highest number of postings, had just over 15,000. The San Francisco-San Jose metro area, which includes Silicon Valley, had over 12,000 (Halzack, 2014). Many of these jobs are in or near major cities with large African-American and minority populations and high unemployment rates. Figure 2 shows large metropolitan areas ranked by the number of cybersecurity job posted in 2013.

Employers across the nation are facing extreme shortages of cybersecurity experts with strong hands-on technical skills. This means going back to the high school/middle school level and developing effective teaching and learning programs to both educate and expose students in an attempt to help they develop interests and skills in the field (University of Delaware, 2014)

One solution could be the development of public charter high schools in these minority communities that have an academic focus on computer science and cybersecurity that not only allow African American and minority students to gain expertise in the field but could also be tied to students gaining cybersecurity certifications of significant value to employers while still in high school.

The charter school movement is one of the fastest growing education reforms in the country and it has the ability to make a dramatic impact on educational reform in the US and internationally. The growth of these schools requires the development of new leadership skills for educational administrators. The charter school movement also has bipartisan political support nationally and in the states that have enacted charter school laws. The federal government encourages the development and implementation of charter schools through the Public Charter Schools Program (PCSP), a major grant program administered by the U.S. Department of Education.

Charter schools are publicly funded elementary or secondary schools that have been freed from some of the rules, regulations, and statutes that apply to other public schools, in exchange for some type of accountability for producing certain results, which are set forth in each charter school's charter.

Beginning with two charter schools in Minnesota in 1991, there were almost 3,000 charter schools by 2004, operating in 37 states plus the District of Columbia and Puerto Rico, and enrolling approximately 750,000 students. By the 2002-03 school years, 39 states and the District of Columbia had charter school laws in place, and more than 2,700 charter schools were operating nationally, serving hundreds of thousands of students from every socioeconomic and demographic segment of the U.S. population. However, more than one-third of those schools had been in operation for three years or less, while more than 400 other charter schools had gone out of business between 1991 and 2003 (Palmer and Gau, 2003).

GROWTH OF CHARTER SCHOOLS IN THE US

The growth of new charter schools requires the development of new administrators with new skills. The charter school movement also has bipartisan political support nationally and in the states that have enacted charter school laws. The federal government encourages the development and implementation of charter schools through the Public Charter Schools Program (PCSP), a major grant program administered by the U.S. Department of Education.

Charter schools are publicly funded elementary or secondary schools that have been freed from some of the rules, regulations, and statutes that apply to other public schools, in exchange for some type of accountability for producing certain results, which are set forth in each charter school's charter.

Beginning with two charter schools in Minnesota in 1991, there were almost 3,000 charter schools by 2004, operating in 37 states plus the District of Columbia and Puerto Rico, and enrolling approximately 750,000 students. By the 2002-03 school years, 39 states and the District of Columbia had charter school laws in place, and more than 2,700 charter schools were operating nationally, serving hundreds of thousands of students from every socioeconomic and demographic segment of the U.S. population. However, more than one-third of those schools had been in operation for three years or less, while more than 400 other charter schools had gone out of business between 1991 and 2003 (Palmer and Gau, 2003).

Federal support for charter schools began in 1995 with the authorization of the Public Charter Schools Program (PCSP), administered by the U.S. Department of Education (ED). The PCSP funds the state grant program discussed in this report, supports charter school research and demonstration programs and underwrites national charter school conferences (Nelson, Berman, Ericson, Kamprath, Perry, Silverman, and Solomon, 2000).

In the educational setting the conversations on change centers on objects of different levels of leadership- individuals, groups, organizations, systems, and the like - because these objects are arranged in a nested hierarchy of administrative levels: the individuals are in groups, which are components of organizations (classes, departments, schools, districts), which are in turn components of larger organized (regional, national) systems, and so on. To fully understand the magnitude of institutional and organizational change there needs to be an exploration and understanding of the nuances of change. Leonard J Waks, in his 2007 article, "The Concept of Fundamental Educational Change," outlined that change that must be navigated by leadership is described as,

Stage 1: Misalignment. Changes, whether internal to the institution or taking place elsewhere in the social system, bring the institution out of alignment with other social institutions.

Stage 2: Protest. Some individuals and groups experience frustrations and express dissatisfaction, but entrenched and more powerful agents deny their demands. The older institution no longer functions as taken-for-granted background; however, but now emerges as a figure subject to reflection and criticism, implying that the institution has already changed significantly, in that the norms, and the organizations they ordain, are being rejected.

Stage 3: Ad Hoc Alternatives. New ideas proliferate and resources are mobilized for new forms of outside-the-box actions, even prior to the emergence of concrete mechanisms for broader implementation. Agents at least think and speak about withdrawing from organizations ordained by the older institution and begin seeking to handle their needs in various innovative ad hoc ways.

Stage 4: Entrepreneurship. "Institutional entrepreneurs" then specify new ideas and action patterns in forms more suitable for public commitment and institutionalization. They take some of the ideas developed in stage 3, and add or subtract elements to broaden their appeal. Public discussion of these ideas further undermines older institutional forms, as debate further weakens their taken-for-granted character.

Stage 5: Responsible Innovation. Some of these specified innovations are brought into existence by responsible agents who can be held accountable.

Stage 6: Social Construction. A process of social construction and negotiation is initiated, in which some of these innovations are rewarded and others rejected, depending upon their acceptability to various stakeholders in terms of evolving beliefs and values. In this process, innovative operational moves and innovative vocabularies become inter-defined.

Stage 7: Institutionalization. Rewarded innovations gain further commitments of resources and participants. Their ideas become more influential and their practices become models for further innovations. Innovations selected in this way continue through cycles of constructive adjustment and feedback until they are gradually institutionalized, becoming part of the accepted, more differentiated institutional pattern and gradually losing their character as innovative or different.

Stage 8: Reorganization. Some older organizations adapt structurally to lay claim to a role in the new institutional pattern, others remain unchanged but serve niche clientele, and others disappear. (Waks, 2007).

Public education in the US is a multifaceted, multilayered system of institutions organizations, decision-makers, educators, parents and students. Every school, school district and state exists in—and is affected by—a complex web of laws, policies and conflicting demands from different stakeholders. Charter schools are a relatively new arrival on this scene and have matured within the same milieu of highly diverse school missions, accountability expectations, state laws, and federal policies that affect the rest of public schooling. These schools represent the clearest example of nuances of change outlined by Waks (2007).

Charter schools open for a variety of reasons. Some of these reasons, according to Nelson et al. (2000), included realizing an alternative vision of schooling (75 percent) and serving a special population of students (28 percent). Furthermore, charter school founders focus on more than test scores, including "how kids should be raised, the cultural content of the curriculum, the democratic or authoritative ways in which teachers relate to parents" (Finn et al., 2000, p.7). Charter schools provide choice and educational options for parents who are on the jurisdiction of poor performing schools but may lack the financial ability to send their children to private schools.

The phrase "charter school movement" is often used but is somewhat misleading because this reform comprises a variety of actors and institutions across the country. Since state charter school laws do not require a particular program or instructional approach, the missions and educational philosophies of charter schools vary, as do the types of students and communities they serve, the accountability requirements they face and the degree of flexibility they enjoy. For example, some charter schools deliver instruction through independent study, distance learning, and home schooling programs. Many of the differences are due to differences in state laws and regulations. One should keep in mind this high degree of variation when comparing charter schools with traditional public schools (Finch, Burrell, and Luna, 2009).

A central tenet of the charter school movement is to provide "opportunities for educators and parents [emphasis added] to create the kinds of schools they believe make the most sense" (Nathan, 1996, p.1). Moreover, respondents in the charter schools visited for this evaluation typically referred to high levels of parent involvement and multiple avenues for parents to become involved.

Charter schools have widespread political support because this educational reform has come to symbolize different things to diverse groups with contradictory agendas (Wells et al., 1999). Because charter school policies are a vehicle for change, rather than a particular approach or design, they can be considered "an opportunity, not a blueprint" (Nathan, 1996). Although state charter laws vary, all share a common set of assumptions: (1) that accountability for outcomes will improve school performance and (2) that high levels of autonomy will allow schools to better meet student needs and as a result, improve performance. Beyond these common assumptions, charter schools vary, by design, in a number of ways. For example, they may be either new schools or public or private conversions; they may be authorized by local districts or other agencies (e.g., universities); and they may target special populations of students or highlight particular curricular or instructional philosophies.

Charter schools have five key features, according to Finn, Manno and Vanourek (2000, p.15):

- They can be created by almost anyone.
- They are exempt from most state and local regulations, essentially autonomous in their operations.
- They are attended by youngsters whose parents choose them.
- They are staffed by educators who are also there by choice.
- They are liable to be closed for not producing satisfactory results.

In general, those who wish to operate a charter school submit a proposal outlining the components of the school's plan, including the instructional approach, the governance and financial arrangements, the specific educational outcomes, and the way in which the charter school will measure these outcomes (Geske, Davis, and Hingle, 1997). A legally designated authorizing body then determines if it will "charter" the school and as part of the bargain, hold it accountable to the terms of its charter. While charter schools may be similar to some specialty or magnet schools, they differ in the existence of performance agreements developed with their individual authorizers (Hill, Lake and Celio, 2002). In contrast to the typical configuration of elementary, middle, and high schools, charter schools are more likely to contain either grades K-8 or grades K-12. More than one-third (35 percent) of charter schools are K-8 or K-12 schools, compared with 8 percent of other public schools. Interviews with charter school staff and parents indicated that the K-8 and K-12 configurations might be in response to the desire for students to avoid the difficult transitions between school-levels (Renchler, 2002). Charter schools are public schools that operate independently of local school districts. They are open to all students, free of charge; if there are more students than slots available, enrollment is determined by blind lottery.

Charter school founders are generally parents or community leaders, who come together to start a different kind of public school in their community. Often charter public schools are organized around a specific mission, theme or curricular focus. In exchange for specific freedoms (in organizational structure, mission, and academic program), charter public schools are held to high standards.

CURRICULUM FRAMEWORKS

Student could be immersed in hands on applications that allow for experiential learning as tools to develop students with expertise in Cybersecurity in ways that teach them key concepts and also prepare them to take and pass cyber and information security tests like Security + and Information Systems Audit and Control Association (ISACA) certifications.

The key frameworks of the core curriculum in cybersecurity would focus on the following topic areas:
Windows Basics:

- Identify basic computer components
- Describe information security
- Go through the Windows "boot" sequence
- List the different Windows versions
- Explain the basic architecture of Windows
- Describe why "default installations" left alone are bad
- Describe Windows installation limitations
- Use Windows utilities to determine settings
- Use third-party tools to determine settings

Windows Networking:

- List the differences between various types of networks
- Identify common network devices
- Describe the fundamentals of DNS
- Understand basic routes and routing

Services/DR/shadow copies:

- Explain basic service components
- Explain ports and service mappings
- Describe the services attack vector
- Identify Windows default services
- Understand the enabling/disabling of services
- Identify tools to check services
- Understand the importance of backups
- Understand the importance of restores

Authentication/Access Controls/basic crypto:

- Understand strong password management and creation
- Understand password cracking techniques
- Understand system permissions and rights
- Understand strong cryptography and its uses
- Understand the importance of file integrity

Servers -File Server:

- Understand your server's role
- Understand why multiple roles present vulnerabilities
- Understand each services unique vulnerability
- Understand strong configuration options for services
- Understand the importance of server placement within your network
- Understand the placement of IDS/IPS devices within your network

Locking down Servers with utilities -add on utilities:

- Understand your server's role
- Understand why multiple roles present vulnerabilities
- Understand each services unique vulnerability
- Understand strong configuration options for services
- Understand the importance of server placement within your network
- Understand the placement of IDS/IPS devices within your network
- Explain the purpose and basic operation of (TCP/IP)
- Identify Windows networking configuration tools
- Explain basic components of wireless networking

Accounts Basics:

- Identify basic properties of Windows user accountsUnderstand the basics of user account permissions and privilegesUnderstand the different built-in Windows user accounts
- Know the difference between a local account and networked (domain) account
- Know what tools are used to create local user accounts
- Explain a few Windows 7 groups
- Explain security issues with the administrator account

Threats and Vulnerabilities:

- Describe the concept of threats, vulnerabilities, and exploits, and their relation to each other
- Explain the concept of risk.
- Describe the concept of dealing with risk issues
- Explain motivations for hackers/attackers
- Explain forms of hacking techniques
- Review the Microsoft System and Security Center
- Describe the Windows firewall

Threats and Vulnerabilities/Patching:

- Describe how threats, vulnerabilities and exploits are related to patching
- Understand why attacks are targeted toward un-patched systems
- Explain "why do we patch?"
- Understand different patching methods
- Describe the Microsoft patch process
- Understand the anti-virus update installation process

DNS, Routes, Workgroups/Domain:

- Explain workgroups and domains
- Understand a domain controller
- Understand organizational units
- Explain active directory and trusts

In application, students would learn how to apply the expertise outlined by Rhodes-Ousley (2013) that include:

1. How to develop strategic proactive protection plans for data and information breaches.
2. How to develop of new data and Encryption approaches.
3. How to implement monthly or quarterly vulnerability assessments to reduce the threat of hackers.
4. The most prominent security protection priorities and organizational resources investments.
5. The development of mobile security policies and protections for employees that access organizational records with mobile devices.

6. Strategic approaches for the effective use of cloud computing applications.
7. How to create effective Incident Response Plans (IRP).
8. How to conduct security awareness training with staff and build an organizational culture of information security (Rhodes-Ousley, 2013).

Experiential learning involves a series of activities that allow a student to experience learning growth through trial and error, collaboration, and reflective learning experience which helps them to fully learn new skills and knowledge (Roberts, 2011).

According to Roberts (2011) effective applied and experiential learning allows students to engage in the following steps:

1. "Doing"- Students experience and explore by engaging in a process of role playing and problem solving in the core subject area.
2. "What Happened?"- Students Share and Reflect the results, reactions and observations with their peers related to their hands on exploration. The sharing equates to reflecting on what they discovered and relating it to past experiences, which can be used for future use.
3. "What's Critical and what's significant?"- Student process and Analyze. Describing and analyzing their experiences allow students to relate them to future learning experiences.
4. "What's the context?"- Students Generalize to relate the experience with previous experiences, real world examples to find trends or common truths in the experience, and identify learning principles that emerged.
5. "Now what?' – Students Apply what they learned in the experience (and what they learned from past experiences and practice) to a similar or different situation. Also, students will discuss how the newly learned process can be applied to other situations. Students will discuss how issues raised can be useful in future situations and how more effective behaviors can develop from what they learned. This is the stage where students develop dexterity as a result of the he combination of all the earlier stages (Roberts, 2011).

EDUCATIONAL AND LEADERSHIP DEVELOPMENT RAMIFICATIONS

K-12 education has been through many changes in the past 10 years. The No Child Left Behind Act has opened many doors to innovative education structures, techniques and ideas. One of the structures that have benefited from the Act is the Charter School. Many parents today are losing faith in the public schools and are looking for schools with specialized curriculums designed for the specific needs of the students (Nathan, 1996). Because of this, many educators have seen the need and there many charter schools of specialties emerging on the scene.

Charter schools are more likely to serve minority and low-income students than traditional public schools but less likely to serve students in special education. Charter schools, by design, have greater autonomy over their curriculums, budgets, educational philosophies, and teaching staff than do traditional public schools (Finch, Burrell, Luna, 2009).

The emergence of new schools has also created a need for new school structures and new leadership skills. Because charter schools are supported by the use of public funds, they have certain rules that must be followed like a public school. The difference is that they have more freedom and/or flexibility to tailor the curriculum to the individual student. The structure on which the charter school is based often has a propensity to determine whether or not the school will run efficiently not to mention if the plan for the school will receive a charter from the school board.

Leadership and structure can be extremely influential factors to the success of a charter school, in addition to curriculum, student growth and academic achievement. The structure of the charter school has been influenced by the choice of instruction, the orientation of the founder and the issue of autonomy from the bureaucracy.

There are 37 states that offer charter schools and these schools can be grouped into main categories: Conversion and Startup schools. Now the main categories can be broken down into two sub-categories based on instruction: Classroom- and non-classroom-based schools. Charter schools can incorporate both types of instruction but to be considered a non-classroom–based charter school the student is not required to be on site and with a certified teacher 80% of the time allotted for instruction (Buddin and Zimmer, 2005).

There is also the advantage of smaller classes and uses of innovative learning techniques such as technology and independent study. Because the average enrollment of a charter school is 250 students, it makes for a more conducive learning environment. It lets the teacher focus on the individual learning needs of each student and promotes academic excellence. This is especially beneficial for students who at risk and/or have learning disabilities (Harris, 2002).

The use of technology and independent study are different ways that are used to enhance the learning of that was underserved in the conventional public schools. Both of these options can be used to support the student who learns on a different level than that of the rest of the class but still can benefit from having peer interaction. The use of home study involves the parents in the learning experience of the child. The study is overseen by a certified teacher but it is up to the parent and the child to get the work done. This works well with students who are anti-social and overly disruptive in the classroom setting (Nathan, 1996).

THE ORIENTATION OF THE FOUNDERS AND LEADERS

There are usually two different types of leadership origins for Charter schools which are mission-oriented and marketing-oriented (Henig, Holyoke, Brown, and Lacireno-Paquet, 2005). Schools that have a leadership philosophy that is focused on the mission are usually people who were dissatisfied with the conventional schools. They are also founded as nonprofit entities looking for other outlets to serve the community. The leadership focus on these skills are value based or principal based with an academic curriculums that is often infused with teachings focused on character development. Mission-oriented charter school founders usually have leadership focuses that are geared towards social change in underserved or needy populations. In this case the school founders perpetuate a leadership focus on the needs of the students in the school and this focus is reflected in the staff and the structure of the school (Henig, Holyoke, Brown, and Lacireno-Paquet, 2005).

Charter school founders can also have a leadership focus on strategic marketing where the school provides a quality education while simultaneously operating as an institution that capitalizes on niche not being served in the regional marketplace (Henig, Holyoke, Brown, and Lacireno-Paquet, 2005). Often schools with marketing orientated leadership philosophies are usually people who run as a for-profit charter school. These charter schools are usually founded by large corporations.

THE PUBLIC SCHOOL STRATEGY

Public schools in the United States are beginning to develop curricula that support STEM programs, but many do not focus on cybersecurity specifically and/or specifically ensuring underrepresented students have access. Few K–12 educators are teaching topics that would prepare students to be cyber-capable employees or cybersecurity-aware college students. The US must invest early in a student's academic journey to motivate them to pursue STEM careers. Fields like cybersecurity require years for technical skills to manifest, so investments should be deliberate, tracked and maintained so students can reach their full potential (Charleston County School District, 2014).

Many public high schools do not have the budgets to infuse additional cybersecurity curricula, teachers, equipment, software and/or training to increase the pipeline of students. Public school districts like the Charleston County School District (CCDS) in South Carolina quickly caught on to the need to develop programs to specifically support local, regional and national workforce personnel shortages. The CCSD is the second largest school system in South Carolina representing a unique blend of urban, suburban, and rural schools that span 1,000 square miles of coastal lands. CCSD serves more than 46,000 students in 84 schools and several specialized programs. CCSD offers a diverse, expanding portfolio of options—including neighborhood, charter, and magnet schools—and is divided into elementary, middle, secondary, "Innovation Zone" and Promise Neighborhood Learning Communities, each led by an associate or assistant associate superintendent (Charleston County School District, 2014).

CCSD launched the Lowcountry Tech Academy program in the spring of 2013, to give public school students career and technology options in several STEM areas to include cybersecurity. CCSD's African American student population during the 2013-2014 school year equaled approximately 43% of the 46,000 enrolled, providing a larger pool of African American students. The program provides career technology learning with the right amount of technology and education learning experiences. The success of the program comes from the program's design, which brings in the right instructors who have current, real world experiences and industry partners to also provide instructions and offer internships and work based learning opportunities to the students. After completing four courses in cybersecurity, students are called completers and are encouraged and ready to take industry certifications (Charleston County School District, 2014).

New Jersey's Red Bank Regional High School in Little Silver, New Jersey has delivered many success stories in its move to a focus on STEM. Recently, its cybersecurity team won a national cybersecurity competition, awarding $12,000 to the school. Red Bank Regional High School's student body draws from 17 different school districts and offers three separate academies in Visual and Performing Arts, Finance and Technology. The school accepts tuition and in-district students who demonstrate their abilities through audition and academic record. In 2007, the district was awarded a $1.25 million Federal Grant for the development of small learning communities, which resulted in students having an opportunity to select from among newly developed academies as well: Math and Science, Sports Medicine and Management, Humanities and Social Sciences, and International and Cultural Studies (Red Bank Regional High School, 2013).

Similar to Lowcountry Tech Academy in Charleston, Red Bank Regional High School also has integrated cybersecurity curricula and students are able to commit to a cybersecurity pathway, with a program that includes an introduction to computer systems and networking courses and then the program advances to a dual credit cybersecurity course and culminates with digital forensics. The school's computer science and engineering programs allow students to focus on areas the computer science, computer applications, applied technology, computer networking and pre-engineering areas, which provides the skills needed for students to take and pass many of the cybersecurity-related certifications required by today's employers (Red Bank Regional High School, 2013).

Efforts must be made to ensure underrepresented students have adequate resources and access to quality STEM programs. Public schools in many regions have developed programs and capabilities to bridge that gap; however, results have not shown that these programs can deliver an increase in skilled and knowledgeable students, prepared to pursue careers in high demand fields like cybersecurity. Charter schools offer options to communities that are improperly zoned, with ethnically unbalanced student populations; do not have a focus on providing curricula focused on in-demand, high paying professions; and school districts that lack funding and resources to provide students the tools they need to survive and thrive in a technology rich world. Charter schools, by design, have greater autonomy over their curriculums, budgets, educational philosophies, and teaching staff than do traditional public schools (Finch, Burrell, and Luna 2009). This autonomy allows the focus to be put on the student, the educational need, and skills requirements for student success. Charter schools may provide the solution to the US' ability to quickly and effectively increase the underrepresented student population in high paying and in high demand professions.

REFERENCES

Braunlich, C., & Looney, M. Center for Education Reform (2002). Charter schools 2002: Results from CER's Annual Survey of America's Charter Schools. Washington, DC.

Chabrow, E, (2011, October 11) Women, Minorities Scarce in IT Security Field: Profession Does Not Mirror Rest of American Workforce. Government Information Security.

Charleston County School District. (2014). *About Us*. Retrieved from http://www.ccsdschools.com/About_Us/

Desilver, D. (2013, August 21). Black unemployment rate is consistently twice that of whites. Washington DC: The Pew Research Center.

Finch, A., Burrell, D., & Luna, B. (2009). *An Analysis of the Growth, Emergence, and Development of Leaders and Leadership Philosophies of Charter Schools in the United States*. The John Shepherd Journal of Practical Leadership.

Finn, C., Manno, B., & Vanourek, G. (2000). *Charter schools in action*. Princeton, N.J.: Princeton University Press.

Franklin, B., & Glascock, C. (1996, October). *The relationship between grade configuration and student performance in rural schools*. (ERIC document ED 403083). Paper presented at the Annual Conference of the National Rural Education Association, San Antonio, Texas.

Garcia, G. F., & Garcia, M. (1996, November). Charter schools—Another top-down innovation. *Educational Researcher*, *25*, 34–36.

Geske, T. G., Davis, D., & Hingle, P. (1997). Charter schools: A viable public school choice option? *Economics of Education Review*, *16*(1), 15–23. doi:10.1016/S0272-7757(96)00039-8

Greene, J., Forster, G., & Winters, M. (2003). *Apples to apples: An evaluation of charter schools serving general student populations*. (Education Working Paper 1). New York, N.Y.: Manhattan Institute for Policy Research.

Halzack, S. (2014, March 5). Evidence that the D.C. area really is a hotbed for cybersecurity jobs. Capital Business

Hassel, B., and Herdman, P. (2000, April). *Charter school accountability: A guide to issues and options for charter authorizers*. Charlotte, N.C.: Public Impact.

Hill, P., Lake, R., & Celio, M. B. (2002). *Charter schools and accountability in public education*. Washington, D.C.: The Brookings Institution.

Hill, P., Lake, R., Celio, M. B., Campbell, C., Herdman, P., & Bulkley, K. (2001). *A study of charter school accountability*. Washington, D.C.: U.S. Department of Education, Office of Educational Research and Improvement.

RPP International and University of Minnesota. (1997). *A study of charter schools: First-year report*. Washington, D.C.: U.S. Department of Education, Office of Educational Research and Improvement.

Jane, H. (2003). The role of shared values and vision in creating professional learning communities. *National Association of Secondary School Principals. NASSP Bulletin*, *87*(637), 21–34. doi:10.1177/019263650308763703

Jeannine, L. F. (2002). Organizational structures and perceived cultures of community-charter schools in Ohio. *Phi Delta Kappan*, *83*(7), 525–531. doi:10.1177/003172170208300712

Jeffrey, R. H., Thomas, T. H., Heath, B., & Natalie, L.-P. (2005). The influence of founder type on charter school structures and operations. *American Journal of Education*, *111*(4), 487–588. doi:10.1086/431181

Nathan, J. (1996). *Charter schools: Creating hope and opportunity for American education*. San Francisco: Jossey-Bass Publishers.

Nelson, B., Berman, P., Ericson, J., Kamprath, N., Perry, R., Silverman, D., & Solomon, D. (2000). *The state of charter schools 2000: Fourth-year report*. Washington, D.C.: U.S. Department of Education, Office of Educational Research and Improvement.

Palmer, L. B., and Gau, R. (2003, June). *Charter school authorizing: Are states making the grade?* Washington, D.C.: Thomas B. Fordham Institute.

Red Bank Regional High School. (2013). *Red Bank Regional High School Profile 2013,* Retrieved from http://www.rbrhs.org/Services/Guidance/Profile.pdf

Renchler, R. (2002). *School organization: Grade span Trends and issues (ERIC document ED 472994)*. Washington, D.C.: Office of Educational Research and Improvement.

Richard, B., & Ron, Z. (2005). Student achievement in charter schools: A complex picture. *Journal of Policy Analysis and Management, 24*(2), 351–371. doi:10.1002/pam.20093

Roberts, J. (2011). *Beyond Learning by Doing: Theoretical Currents in Experiential Education*. London: Routledge.

Sandra, H. (2002). Children with special needs and school choice: Five stories. *Preventing School Failure, 46*(2), 75–78. doi:10.1080/10459880209603350

University of Delaware. (2014, July 17). University to host US Cyber Challenge summer camp, competition. UD Daily. Retrieved from http://www.udel.edu/udaily/2015/jul/cyber-camp-071714.html

U.S. Department of Education. (2000). *Evaluation of the public charter schools program: Year one evaluation report*. Washington, D.C.: Office of the Under Secretary, Planning and Evaluation Service, Elementary and Secondary Program Division.

Waks, L. (2007). The concept of fundamental educational change. *Educational Theory, 57*(3), 277–295. doi:10.1111/j.1741-5446.2007.00257.x

Washington, Jesse (2011, October 23). STEM Education And Jobs: Declining Numbers Of Blacks Seen In Math, Science. *The Huffington Post*.

Wayne, K. H. (2003). An analysis of enabling and mindful school structures: Some theoretical, research and practical considerations. *Journal of Educational Administration, 41*(1), 87–109. doi:10.1108/09578230310457457

KEY TERMS AND DEFINITIONS

Charter Schools: An independently operated public school granted more plasticity in its approach to operations, in return for enhanced accountability for performance.

Curriculum: Lessons and academic matter taught in a specific course/program, or school.

Cybersecurity: The body of technologies, processes, and practices intentioned to guard computers, networks, programs, and information from attack, impairment or unauthorized access.

Ethnically Unbalanced: Statistically, the number of students may not be equal, whether higher or lower.

STEM: Science: Technology, Engineering, Math.

Strategic Marketing: Marketing that provides a quality education while simultaneously operating as an institution that capitalizes on a niche not being served in the regional marketplace (Henig: Holyoke, Brown, & Lacireno-Paquet, 2005).

Urban High Schools: Ground-breaking independent high schools with a duty to fuel a passion for learning in students and to inspire them.

Chapter 16
Communication, Technology, and Cyber Crime in Sub–Saharan Africa

Dustin Bessette
National Graduate School of Quality Management, USA

Randall E. Sylvertooth
National Cybersecurity Institute at Excelsior College, USA

Jane A. LeClair
National Cybersecurity Institute at Excelsior College, USA

Sharon L. Burton
Florida Institute of Technology, USA

ABSTRACT

As a region that is rapidly developing its technology base, Sub-Saharan Africa is experiencing many of the issues associated with the benefits of cyber technology as well as its many negative sides. This paper discusses mobile and internet technologies currently being utilized in Sub-Saharan Africa as well as some of the major cybersecurity concerns threatening networks in the region that are associated with the new economic growth on the African continent. Such topics will include a viable increased awareness of news, historical events, and recent gatherings of information on this main topic.

INTRODUCTION

The field of cybercrime has hit the mainstream of the economic world by storm. Cybercrime has overwhelmingly been a high risk for communication devices in developing countries, such as those in Sub-Saharan African. Cybercrime has even surpassed illegal drug trafficking as a major criminal offense in many developed countries. So what does this mean for the under-developed countries? Development and keen protection must be at its highest level based on circumstances and internal process changes. In other words, developing countries need to invest in order to protect themselves based on underlying illegal activities such as cyber-attacks from internet sources. This chapter will identify the history of cybercrime in Sub-Saharan African countries, specify cyber themes, show national security awareness

DOI: 10.4018/978-1-4666-8345-7.ch016

and reasons for government regulation, and provide solutions and recommendations for successful developing countries. This chapter will also assist with correlating the national security awareness towards a global enterprise of cybercrimes in other Sub-Saharan African countries.

BACKGROUND

One of the fastest growing economies in the world today can be found on the continent of Africa, particularly in Sub-Saharan Africa. In the last five years, Africa has seen its mobile, internet, and technology industry explode with the introduction of undersea fiber optic cables and international companies providing internet and mobile service to the various countries and their civilian populations. Macharia (2014) notes that, "Africa's growth in mobile and internet access has been rising faster over the last decade than any other region of the world" (p. 18). While there has been rapid economic growth on the continent, it still remains plagued with decades of civil war, government corruption, poverty, disease, and terrorism. The recent activities of Boko Haram and the Ebola epidemic are clear indicators that negative forces continue to be alive and well in Africa. Despite these issues, the economic improvement in Sub-Saharan Africa has been met with cautious excitement from the civilian population who have great hopes of gaining economic success and prosperity (Nwabueze, 2014).

There has been a growing demand for internet service and mobile technology in Sub-Sahara Africa. In the past decade across the region, Macharia (2014) writes, "…mobile phone penetration has grown from 1% in 2000 to 54% in 2012" (p.18). This rapid expansion, however, is providing cyber criminals an increased opportunity to make money from unsuspecting individuals utilizing the Internet in both the business and private sectors. On the cybercrime issue in Nigeria, Ndubueze, Mazindu, Emmanuel, & Okoye write: "Cyber crime has become a serious problem in Nigeria, culminating in the listing of Nigeria as third on the roll of the top ten cyber crime hot spots in the world by a 2009 Internet Crime Report" (2013, p. 225). Kshetri (2010) observes that a similar problem exists in the growing Internet areas of Kenya and notes that "Kenya experienced about 800 bot attacks per day in July 2009, which is projected to increase to 50,000 per day after the fiber connectivity goes live" (p. 1063).

Goodman, (2010) writes that the problem of cyber crime may actually be continent wide and notes:

As the use and utility of mobile phones in Africa continues to rise, so too will security vulnerabilities. Unless properly addressed, security vulnerabilities endemic to the use of the information and communications technologies (ICTs) will be magnified by a number of factors unique to Africa, possibly leading to a tsunami of information insecurity across the continent. (p. 24)

The increase in Sub-Saharan African cybercrime is a result of poor resources from local law enforcement and government security services to combat the threat. The void created by inadequate government infrastructure presents a lucrative operating environment for global cyber criminals looking for less risky endeavors than in their home nations. In addition to a permissive environment, much of the cybercrime occurring in the region can also be attributed to a lack of understanding from the business and civilian populations on how to best protect their private and business information from cyber theft.

Individuals and businesses are unwittingly purchasing or downloading pirated software infected with malware to their mobile devices and computers resulting in the theft of funds from banks or businesses. Businesses have not introduced needed technology such as sound firewalls and encryption nor have they been using intrusion detection tools to catch would be thieves. In a study conducted by the National University of Singapore (NUS), the two greatest cyber threats to Sub-Saharan Africa are software infected with malware and software piracy. The study also revealed that 60% of consumers stated that malware, loss of data, files and personal information were the greatest concerns (Biz Community, 2014).

The Kenyan government is currently working with Microsoft to deter theft of proprietary information and copyright infringement. The theft and consolidation of identity in Kenyan banks is an everlasting problem. "According [to] Kaspersky Lab experts, 20% of computers being used in Kenya are vulnerable to malware and the number is rapidly rising. The large exposure to cyber threats is mainly related to the absence of patch management of the systems and to the presence of older OS versions" (Paganini, 2012). The South African government states that cybercrime is now a "National Crisis in South Africa." The government is facing threats from hackers on government computers as well as police websites, and the banking industry is losing millions. ("Cybercrime Is a 'National Crisis' in South Africa" 2014) The greatest threats to Sub-Saharan Africa are threats to countries' infrastructures from cyber criminals hacking into banks, government agencies, businesses, software piracy and malware attacks.

The nations within Sub-Saharan Africa, from Angola to Zimbabwe, are still struggling to meet the basic needs of the civilian population and are often ill-equipped to address the cybercrime wave that is threatening the newly emerging businesses that are springing up all over Africa. "According to the Norton Cybercrime Report 2012 cybercrime is growing at an alarming rate with over 556 million worldwide victims per year, which equates to over 1.5 million victims per day, or about 18 victims per second. South Africa has been ranked as having the third highest number of cybercrime victims after China and Russia" (The Reality of Cybercrime in Africa, 2014).

Much of the technology being utilized relies on the aid of mobile devices, internet service hot-spots, and portable routing devices. To date, most African countries have not identified any major organized crime rings, rather they have found various groups or individuals sophisticated enough to launch cyber attacks either inside or outside of the continent. The 2012 Norton Cybercrime Report also states that cybercrime will increase as unemployment increases and as the internet becomes more available to the general population. A recent study by Wolfpack Information Risk found South Africa's annual loss resulting from cybercrime in three sectors to be R2.65 billion. South Africa's banks suffered tens of millions of rand worth in losses due to a major breach of customer card data by criminal syndicates that infected electronic point-of-sale (POS) terminals using a variant of the Trojan horse malicious software called Dexter (Bit Cyber, 2013). Dexter' works by collecting credit card information at the point of sale—during the transaction—which is in turn used to create fraudulent credit cards. Discussing 'Dexter' and its variants, Mimoso writes that "Point-of-sale systems present hackers with a target-rich environment. The systems are often reachable online and are usually guarded with default or weak passwords that are child's play for a brute force or dictionary attack" (Mimoso, 2013).

Africa in many ways is in the same position as most western countries with regard to cybercrime. In America, many large, well known banks and corporations have been hit in recent years with front-page-news cyber attacks. Recently, Target department stores were hit costing the store millions of dollars as well as loss in consumer confidence (Zolkos, 2014). Cybercrime does not necessarily occur with internet transactions alone, but can occur physically at the point of sale. However, access to the internet and exploding business opportunities have put the bourgeoning African economy at risk of failure. This is due to lack of both money and cybersecurity professionals available to create a more robust and secure enterprise for businesses and government alike.

The governing bodies in Sub-Saharan African countries need to concentrate on ethical issues related to the Internet, business, and cybersecurity. The moral and ethical dilemmas confronted by governments when addressing cyber-related issues are increasingly complex. Cyber crime can bring wealth to some while at the same time cause financial ruin to others. The economic impact, both positive and negative, on a community can cloud thinking when rational choices are to be made. In other words, it is often too late when a cyber attack or breach occurs before a country thinks about expending high amounts of energies to combat it. This is often the case for "reactive" thinking instead of "preventative" planning. The ethical concern here is based on the high value and concern countries need to place on security in order to exploit a general awareness of cybercrime. When countries do not factor security costs into their security equation, they are creating many unprepared and vulnerable environments for attacks.

The governments of Sub-Saharan African countries must understand the dire necessity of combating cyber attacks. Without a sustained future plan for cybersecurity, a nation will be totally defenseless in the face of the rapid advancement of technology in the world. The cost factor for sustainable global cybersecurity can be expensive if procurements do not allow for adjusted cost-effective software to be allowed into a country. Governments in Sub-Saharan African nations need to develop a sustained system within their security limits, which assists cyber security as a high cost factor.

Evidence has shown that the need for cybersecurity in this information age is necessary in most third world countries. It is important to evaluate the research and information in today's society based that all items discussed have valid points and are consistent with the theme of cybersecurity. Cyber crime has gained significant international mobility (Al Bawaba, 2013) and may even be related to the growing issue of cyber terrorism in the new uprising economies such as Sub-Saharan African counties. Current research gives reason as to why terrorism takes place in this geographic location. Mainly, the terrorist attacks target large infrastructures such as government headquarters, defense systems, and large financial banks. The main objective of cyber-terrorist is to seek out power and control for undetermined reasons based on motives that drive terrorizing activities.

Some of the Sub-Saharan African countries do not have large amounts of wealth or power based the economic drive they are in. Some of them do not even have conceptual control on some of the larger worldly decisions being made by other countries. So why should cybersecurity become a driving interest to many of these low economic countries? Mainly, cybersecurity ensures the future of one country is safe in terms of technology and infrastructure. Negative outsides forces have the ability to hack into and mutate information on internal software's defense systems such that they have the ability to shut down an entire defense system from the inside out. This is a major concern to a majority of smaller defense systems in Sub-Saharan African countries based on the fact that many of them do not have the technology infrastructure to support such a change. Sub-Saharan African countries need to successfully adapt an anti-cyber system that engages and stops all vital information from being illicitly spread. The vital information that hackers most likely want to obtain are passwords for finances, names, dates of birth and birth records, and also business plan information. This information could later be leveraged to gain higher access and commit further crimes. This system needs to function in such a way that it is able to then track where the information is leaking from and being transferred to.

SOLUTIONS AND RECOMMENDATIONS

It is important to note that each Sub-Saharan African country has a different method of cyber communication based on the allowance of technology for that country. For instance, not all Sub-Saharan African countries have quality mobile communication via cell phones and high-speed internet. This factor alone hinders the capability of hackers to get into and corrupt any data stored within the country or a database. Without internet access, hackers cannot gain access to information on the personal, business, or governmental level, which means that in some instances underdeveloped nations are not high targeted priorities for hackers. As technology is embraced by nations, the need for security also increases and hackers have begun to notice loopholes in these systems being closed. Outdated software and technology are just easy methods for entry in the cyber world. Hackers realize that the ability to access vital information is and will become even more difficult in the future due to new security measures. Not only will the level of difficulty restrain their activities, but the cost factor and availability to obtain hacking software will also become a serious challenge.

Many countries are seeking to develop an approach to the issue of cybersecurity that is at least informed and seeks to diminish cyber theft. They are making technology available that can help individuals, businesses, and communities protect themselves from hackers. Knowledgeable forces recognize and understand the importance of cybersecurity and how new preventive measures that are being taken into consideration can detour hacking from even taking place. Being able to take measurable steps before any cyber attack takes place is the only way that these countries will get ahead of the curve. If they wait until an attack occurs, it will already be too late. When an attack occurs, there is a good possibility that most of the information the hackers need has already been taken and stored elsewhere. Any one of these small occurrences has the ability to stunt economic growth for a Sub-Saharan African country.

With education on the rise, it is important to implement a plan of action for successful future endeavors. Part of the foreseen economic growth for Sub-Saharan African countries is growth in educational fields such as online learning, distance learning, and M-learning. M-learning has been derived as a leading platform for institutions to formulate and coordinate cyber learning. As M-learning continues to escalate so does the emergence of new threats, such as viruses, rootkits, and Trojans (Marwan & Dawson, 2013). The need to improve existing software in the educational arena is a continuous and non-stop battle that has been placed on the forefront of this industry. Overall, the education systems inside many of the Sub-Saharan African countries are vulnerable in terms of how hackers can obtain and steal information. A model of survival for many of the new and empowering institutions and universities that support the M-learning field is needed.

CONCLUSION

In the end, technology in Sub-Saharan African countries will increase at a phenomenal rate based on the improving economies of those nations as they become increasingly engaged in the global economy. However, with increased dependence on technology come the concomitant problems with which developed nations already struggle. Within the last decade, cybersecurity has increasingly become a global national security crisis. There are increased cyber-attacks from cyber criminals seeking financial gain, state sponsored actors seeking security information and state secrets, and 'hacktivists' (individuals seeking to change environmental or political policies within their own countries). Developed nations have for some time been dealing with issues of cybersecurity. As developing nations increase their dependence on technology and the Internet, they will have to devote more attention to the issue. Sub-Saharan Africa must make cybersecurity one of its highest priorities if the region hopes to move its economy safely and confidently in a positive direction.

REFERENCES

Africa, A. (2014). The reality of cybercrime in Africa. Informational. *Alert Africa*. Accessed April 28. http://alertafrica.com/

Avaya Data Network Solutions. (2014). Technology products. *Avaya Data Network Solutions*. Accessed April 28. http://www.avaya.com/usa/products/networking

Al Bawaba. (2009, Jul 13). Rise in cyber crime, cyber terrorism and cyber espionage tied heavily to data-stealing malware. Retrieved from thefreelibrary.com/Rise+in+Cyber+Crime,+Cyber+Terrorism +and+Cyber+Espionage+Tied...-a0203518026

Brck. (2014). Technology. *Brck*. Accessed April 23. http://www.brck.com/specifications/

Cisco. (2014). Technology products. *Cisco*. Accessed April 23. http://palop.comstor.com/content/vendors/cisco

Community, B. (2014, March, 24). *Ties Between Malware Software and privacy,* Retrieved from http://www.bizcommunity.com/Article/196/542/111169.htm

Cyber, B. (2013, November, 11). *"Dexter Malware" A New Threat in Kenya Banking,* Retrieved from http://bitcyber.wordpress.com/2013/11/11/dexternalware/

Dawson, M. E. Jr, Crespo, M., & Brewster, S. (2013). DoD cyber technology policies to secure automated information systems. *International Journal of Business Continuity and Risk Management, 4*(1), 1–22. doi:10.1504/IJBCRM.2013.053089

Elu, J. U. (2012). Terrorism in Africa and South Asia: Economic or existential good? *Journal of Developing Areas, 46*(1), 345–358. doi:10.1353/jda.2012.0008

Goodman, S., & Harris, A. (2010). The coming African tsunami of information insecurity. *Communications of the ACM, 53*(12), 24–27. doi:10.1145/1859204.1859215

GSMA. (2013). Sub-Saharan Africa mobile economy 2013. Retrieved from *GSMA*. http://www.gsma-mobileeconomyafrica.com/Sub-Saharan%20Africa_ME_ExecSummary_English_2013.pdf

Hamilton Research. (2011, Jan. 17). *Submarine cables reach 4.4% of Africa's population, terrestrial fibre networks reach 31%.* Author. Retrieved from http://www.africabandwidthmaps.com/?p=1735

Harper College. (2014). *Sub Saharan African countries.* Accessed September 30. http://www.harpercollege.edu/mhealy/mapquiz/ssa/ssacoufr.htm

Hersman, E. (2014). *Erik Hersman CEO at BRCK.* Social Media. *Linkedin.* Accessed April 23. http://ke.linkedin.com/in/erikhersman

Huawei. (2014). Technology products. *Huawei*. Accessed April 23. http://enterprise.huawei.com/en/products/index.htm

i-Com. (2014). Interactive Communication. Mobile Cellular Router. *I-com Interactive Communication Managed Service.* Accessed April 23. http://www.icom.co.bw/icom_cat_desc.php?cid=17

IT News Africa. (2012, August 21). *Top ten largest telecoms companies in Africa*. Retrieved from http://www.itnewsafrica.com/2012/08/top-ten-largest-telecoms-companies-in-africa/

Kshetri, N. (2010). Diffusion and effects of cyber-crime in developing economies. *Third World Quarterly*, *31*(7), 1057–1079. doi:10.1080/01436597.2010.518752

Library of Congress. (2014). *List of Sub-Saharan African countries. Africana Collections*. Accessed April 23. http://www.loc.gov/rr/amed/guide/afr-countrylist.html

Macharia, J. (2014). Internet access is no longer a luxury. *Africa Renewal*. Retrieved from http://www.un.org/africarenewal/magazine/april-2014/internet access-no-longer-luxury.

Marwan, O., & Dawson, M. E., Jr. (2013). *Research in progress- defending android smartphones from malware attacks*. Paper presented at the 2012 Third International Conference on Advanced Computing & Communication Technologies, Gymkhana Club, HUDA Sector 4, Rohtak. Retrieved from http://jpinfotech.org/wp-content/plugins/infotech/file/upload/pdf/559Research-in-Progress--Defending-Android-Smartphones-from-Malware-Attacks-pdf.pdf

Mimoso, M. (2013). *New Dexter point-of-sale malware campaigns discovered*. Retrieved from the Internet at.

Ndubueze, P., Mazindu, I., Emmanuel, U., & Okoye, U. (2013). Cyber crime victimization among internet active Nigerians: An analysis of socio-demographic correlates. *International Journal of Criminal Justice Sciences.*, *8*(2), 225–234.

2012.   Norton, C. C. R. (2012, January 1). Retreived May 3, 2014, from http://now-static.norton.com/now/en/pu/images/Promotions/2012/cybercrimeReport/2012_Norton_Cybercrime_Report_Master_FINAL_050912.pdf

Nwabueze, C., & Ekwughe, V. (2014). Nigerian newspapers' coverage of the effect of Boko Haram activities on the environment. *Journal of African Media Studies.*, *6*(1), 71–89. doi:10.1386/jams.6.1.71_1

Paganini, P. (2012). Cyber security landscape in Africa. *Security Affairs*. Retrieved from http://security-affairs.co/wordpress/9746/security/cyber-security-landscape-in-africa.html

Pickering, S., McCulloch, J., & Wright-Neville, D. (2008). Counter-terrorism policing: Towards social cohesion. *Crime, Law, and Social Change*, *50*(1-2), 91–109. doi:10.1007/s10611-008-9119-3

Reisinger, D. (2014). Target's massive data breach: 10 things you need to know. eWeek. 1/13/2014, p. 8.

Staffeld, M. (2013). Terrorism, instability, and democracy in Asia and Africa. *Air & Space Power Journal*, *27*(2), 178–180.

Tamarkin, E. (2014). South Africa must pay more attention to cybercrime. Retrieved from http://www.issafrica.org/iss-today/south-africa-must-pay-more-attention-to-cybercrime

Tentena, P. (2014). Cyber crime on the increase in Africa. Retrieved from http://www.busiweek.com/index1.php?Ctp=2&pI=868&pLv=3&srI=69&spI=221&cI=11

Thawte. (2014). Cybercrime is a 'national crisis' in South Africa 2014.Business News. *Thawte*. Accessed April 23. https://www.thawte.com/about/news/?story=450371

Ward, M. (2014). Africa's digital revolution: Full speed ahead. *World Policy Blog*. Retrieved from http://www.worldpolicy.org/blog/2014/03/04/africas-digital-revolution-full-speed-ahead

Zolkos, R., & Kenealy, B. (2014). Target tested by huge holiday data breach. *Business Insurance*, *48*(1).

KEY TERMS AND DEFINITIONS

Cost-Effective Software: Low cost software, with very little maintenance, that can be easily installed and adapted by businesses, users, and the government.

Cybersecurity: The use of processes and practices that develop through a network of computers, communications, programs, and platforms to prevent data from being attacked, hacked, and/or damaged by unauthorized person(s).

Cyber-Terrorism: The motivated and widespread use of computers to attain and acquire information via technology and cause mass disruption and fear in society.

Developing Countries: A country with low-economic status that seeks to become technologically savvy and economically viable.

M-Learning: Learning and communication through multiple devices such as cell phones, lap tops, tablets, etc.

Mobile Phone: Cell phone or mobile device that is able to transmit communication from one user to another/multiple users.

Terrorism: The wide use and acts of violence in the pursuit of power and political leadership.

APPENDIX 1

Table 1. List of Sub-Saharan African Countries

Angola	Côte d'Ivoire	Madagascar	Seychelles
Benin	Djibouti	Malawi	Sierra Leone
Botswana	Equatorial Guinea	Mali	Somalia
Burkina Faso	Eritrea	Mauritania	South Africa
Burundi	Ethiopia	Mauritius	Sudan
Cameroon	Gabon	Mozambique	South Sudan
Cape Verde	The Gambia	Namibia	Swaziland
Central African Republic	Ghana	Niger	Tanzania
Chad	Guinea	Nigeria	Togo
Comoros	Guinea-Bissau	Réunion	Uganda
Congo (Brazzaville)	Kenya	Rwanda	Western Sahara
Congo (Democratic Republic)	Lesotho	Sao Tome and	Zambia
	Liberia	Principe	Zimbabwe
		Senegal	

(Library of Congress, 2014)

Figure 1. Map of Africa

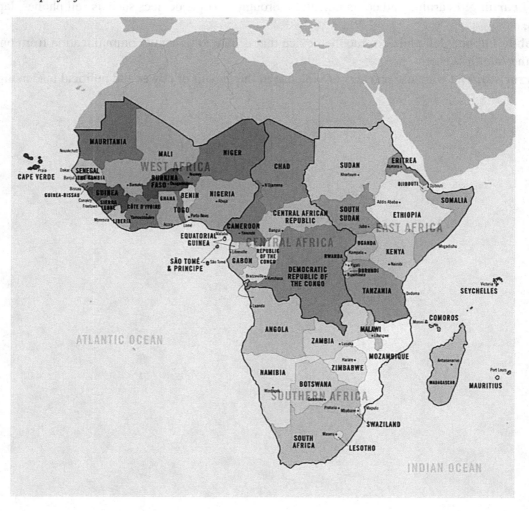

APPENDIX 2

Mobile GSM Providers in Subs-Saharan Africa by Rank

("IT News Africa," 2012)

- MTN South Africa- 176 million subscribers across 16 countries in Africa.
- Vodacom Group (South Africa) 23 million subscribers.
- Telkom (South Africa) South Africa's largest fixed- line and wireless service provider operating in 38 countries throughout the African continent. The South African government has a 39% stake in the company.
- Orascom Telecom (Egypt) One of the largest operating GSM networks in the Middle East, Africa, Canada and Asia. 51% of the company is owned by Russia's Vimpelcom and is the 6th largest mobile telecom provider in the world.
- Maroc Telecom (Morocco) The main telecommunications company in Morocco and is partly owned by Vivendi. Maroc has 17.1 million subscribers.
- MTN Nigeria (Nigeria) 43 million subscribers.
- Orascom Telecom Algerie (Algeria) 16.5 million subscribers.
- Mobinil (Egypt) France Telecom (Orange) owns 94% of the company. As of 2010 Mobinil had 30 million subscribers.
- Safaricom (Kenya) At the end of 2010 the company had 12 million subscribers, most of who reside in Narobi.
- Telecom (Egypt) 12 million subscribers.

Subscribers: 253 million as of 2012.(GSMA, 2013)
Connections: 502 million as of June 2013.(GSMA, 2013)
Two thirds of the population are still without mobile service.(GSMA, 2013)
Technology in Sub-Saharan Africa; Mobile devices, GSM, fiber cabling, routers and Wi-Fi

According to Africa Renewal.com, "there are more than 754 million connections in sub-Saharan Africa and over 35 mobile network operators in Africa. Several countries, such as Seychelles, Tunisia, Morocco and Ghana, have mobile subscription rates in excess of 100%. Tunisia, at 120%, has 10.8 million more cell-phone connections than it has citizens" (Macharia, 2014).

An open internet hub for businesses and individuals is called the iHub, which is a prominent and powerful tool that is used throughout Africa, particularly in Nairobi, Kenya where individuals can access business markets, emerging technologies and companies interested in creating and investing in Africa. iHub was founded by Erik Hersman in 2010 (Hersman, 2014).

APPENDIX 3

Submarine and Fiber Optic Cable Connections

Submarine cables landing in sub-Saharan Africa currently reach 37.4 million people within a 25-km range of landing stations, equivalent to 4.4% of the total population. This will increase to 46.6 million (5.5%) once additional landing points for the WACS, ACE, and SEAS submarine cables have been completed in 2011 and 2012.

The thirteen submarine cable systems with landings in sub-Saharan Africa have a total design capacity of 14.0 Tbps, which will now almost double to 25.8 Tbps by the end of 2012, but the key is delivering this capacity to customers.

Africa's terrestrial fibre optic networks reach some 259.3 million people within a 25-km range of operational fibere nodes, some 30.8% of the population. Once fibre network which is currently under construction is completed, this will grow to 313.3 million (37.2%), and if network which is currently planned or proposed is completed, this will increase again to 388.2 million (46.1%). (Hamilton Research, 2011)

APPENDIX 4

Routers and Wi-Fi Technology

BRCK: Erik Hersman the founder of the previously mentioned iHub also owns a company named Ushahidi. Ushahidi, created a small, lightweight portable router called the BRCK router. The BRCK router is known to work well in tough environments such as extreme heat, dust and limited connectivity. According to the BRCK website, the router "makes accessing the internet simple and reliable wherever you are. It's a rugged, cloud managed, full-featured modem/router with built in fail-overs and programmable GPIO expansion" ("Brck" 2014).

BRCK Specifications ("Brck" 2014)

- 802.11 b/g/n Wireless
- 10/100Mbps WAN/LAN Port
- Wi-Fi Bridge and Client modes
- WPA/WPA2 PSK, WPA Enterprise, and WEP Encryption
- DHCP, NAT, DMZ, Port Forwarding, and Access Control
- OpenVPN Client/Server
- NFS/FTP Network Attached Storage
- Auto Network Failover

i-Com: i-Com was founded in 2001 and boasts on it's website that it "offers a cost saving solution cellular calls initiated from fixed lines. It installs cellular routers connected to the organizations PABX . Calls will be routed directly to the mobile network."(i-Com, 2014).

Huawei: A Chinese global communication conglomerate that provides three types of routers. Huawei also provides switches, access routes, transport networks, WLAN, Security Gateways, Fiber Infrastructure, and a host of other products and services in Sub-Saharan Africa, North America, China, Europe, Asia Pacific, Latin American and the Commonwealth of Independent States. ("Huawei," 2014)

- AR150, AR160, AR200 Enterprise Routers
- AR530 Industrial Switching Router
- NE20E-S Series Multi-Service Router

Avaya: An American company that provides a host of communication services including Ethernet Routing Switch 8800 series and 4000series ("Avaya Data Network Solutions," 2014).

CISCO: An American company that provides a host of communications and secure services as well as the 3800,2800,1800 and 800 Series Integrated Service Routers ("Cisco," 2014).

Related References

To continue our tradition of advancing information science and technology research, we have compiled a list of recommended IGI Global readings. These references will provide additional information and guidance to further enrich your knowledge and assist you with your own research and future publications.

Acharjya, D. P., & Mary, A. G. (2014). Privacy preservation in information system. In B. Tripathy & D. Acharjya (Eds.), *Advances in secure computing, internet services, and applications* (pp. 49–72). Hershey, PA: Information Science Reference; doi:10.4018/978-1-4666-4940-8. ch003

Agamba, J., & Keengwe, J. (2012). Pre-service teachers' perceptions of information assurance and cyber security. [IJICTE]. *International Journal of Information and Communication Technology Education*, *8*(2), 94–101. doi:10.4018/jicte.2012040108

Aggarwal, R. (2013). Dispute settlement for cyber crimes in India: An analysis. In R. Khurana & R. Aggarwal (Eds.), *Interdisciplinary perspectives on business convergence, computing, and legality* (pp. 160–171). Hershey, PA: Business Science Reference; doi:10.4018/978-1-4666-4209-6.ch015

Agwu, E. (2013). Cyber criminals on the internet super highways: A technical investigation of different shades and colours within the Nigerian cyber space. [IJOM]. *International Journal of Online Marketing*, *3*(2), 56–74. doi:10.4018/ijom.2013040104

Ahmad, A. (2012). Security assessment of networks. In *Wireless technologies: Concepts, methodologies, tools and applications* (pp. 208–224). Hershey, PA: Information Science Reference; doi:10.4018/978-1-61350-101-6.ch111

Ahmed, N., & Jensen, C. D. (2012). Security of dependable systems. In L. Petre, K. Sere, & E. Troubitsyna (Eds.), *Dependability and computer engineering: Concepts for software-intensive systems* (pp. 230–264). Hershey, PA: Engineering Science Reference; doi:10.4018/978-1-60960-747-0.ch011

Al, M., & Yoshigoe, K. (2012). Security and attacks in wireless sensor networks. In *Wireless technologies: Concepts, methodologies, tools and applications* (pp. 1811–1846). Hershey, PA: Information Science Reference; doi:10.4018/978-1-61350-101-6.ch706

Al-Ahmad, W. (2011). Building secure software using XP. [IJSSE]. *International Journal of Secure Software Engineering*, *2*(3), 63–76. doi:10.4018/jsse.2011070104

Al-Bayatti, A. H., & Al-Bayatti, H. M. (2012). Security management and simulation of mobile ad hoc networks (MANET). In H. Al-Bahadili (Ed.), *Simulation in computer network design and modeling: Use and analysis* (pp. 297–314). Hershey, PA: Information Science Reference; doi:10.4018/978-1-4666-0191-8.ch014

Al-Bayatti, A. H., Zedan, H., Cau, A., & Siewe, F. (2012). Security management for mobile ad hoc network of networks (MANoN). In I. Khalil & E. Weippl (Eds.), *Advancing the next-generation of mobile computing: Emerging technologies* (pp. 1–18). Hershey, PA: Information Science Reference; doi:10.4018/978-1-4666-0119-2.ch001

Al-Hamdani, W. A. (2011). Three models to measure information security compliance. In H. Nemati (Ed.), *Security and privacy assurance in advancing technologies: New developments* (pp. 351–373). Hershey, PA: Information Science Reference; doi:10.4018/978-1-60960-200-0.ch022

Al-Hamdani, W. A. (2014). Secure e-learning and cryptography. In K. Sullivan, P. Czigler, & J. Sullivan Hellgren (Eds.), *Cases on professional distance education degree programs and practices: Successes, challenges, and issues* (pp. 331–369). Hershey, PA: Information Science Reference; doi:10.4018/978-1-4666-4486-1.ch012

Al-Jaljouli, R., & Abawajy, J. H. (2012). Security framework for mobile agents-based applications. In A. Kumar & H. Rahman (Eds.), *Mobile computing techniques in emerging markets: Systems, applications and services* (pp. 242–269). Hershey, PA: Information Science Reference; doi:10.4018/978-1-4666-0080-5.ch009

Al-Jaljouli, R., & Abawajy, J. H. (2014). Mobile agents security protocols. In *Crisis management: Concepts, methodologies, tools and applications* (pp. 166–202). Hershey, PA: Information Science Reference; doi:10.4018/978-1-4666-4707-7.ch007

Al-Suqri, M. N., & Akomolafe-Fatuyi, E. (2012). Security and privacy in digital libraries: Challenges, opportunities and prospects. [IJDLS]. *International Journal of Digital Library Systems*, *3*(4), 54–61. doi:10.4018/ijdls.2012100103

Alavi, R., Islam, S., Jahankhani, H., & Al-Nemrat, A. (2013). Analyzing human factors for an effective information security management system. [IJSSE]. *International Journal of Secure Software Engineering*, *4*(1), 50–74. doi:10.4018/jsse.2013010104

Alazab, A., Abawajy, J. H., & Hobbs, M. (2013). Web malware that targets web applications. In L. Caviglione, M. Coccoli, & A. Merlo (Eds.), *Social network engineering for secure web data and services* (pp. 248–264). Hershey, PA: Information Science Reference; doi:10.4018/978-1-4666-3926-3.ch012

Alazab, A., Hobbs, M., Abawajy, J., & Khraisat, A. (2013). Malware detection and prevention system based on multi-stage rules. [IJISP]. *International Journal of Information Security and Privacy*, *7*(2), 29–43. doi:10.4018/jisp.2013040102

Alazab, M., Venkatraman, S., Watters, P., & Alazab, M. (2013). Information security governance: The art of detecting hidden malware. In D. Mellado, L. Enrique Sánchez, E. Fernández-Medina, & M. Piattini (Eds.), *IT security governance innovations: Theory and research* (pp. 293–315). Hershey, PA: Information Science Reference; doi:10.4018/978-1-4666-2083-4.ch011

Alhaj, A., Aljawarneh, S., Masadeh, S., & Abu-Taieh, E. (2013). A secure data transmission mechanism for cloud outsourced data. [IJCAC]. *International Journal of Cloud Applications and Computing*, *3*(1), 34–43. doi:10.4018/ijcac.2013010104

Ali, M., & Jawandhiya, P. (2012). Security aware routing protocols for mobile ad hoc networks. In K. Lakhtaria (Ed.), *Technological advancements and applications in mobile ad-hoc networks: Research trends* (pp. 264–289). Hershey, PA: Information Science Reference; doi:10.4018/978-1-4666-0321-9.ch016

Ali, S. (2012). Practical web application security audit following industry standards and compliance. In J. Zubairi & A. Mahboob (Eds.), *Cyber security standards, practices and industrial applications: Systems and methodologies* (pp. 259–279). Hershey, PA: Information Science Reference; doi:10.4018/978-1-60960-851-4.ch013

Aljawarneh, S. (2013). Cloud security engineering: Avoiding security threats the right way. In S. Aljawarneh (Ed.), *Cloud computing advancements in design, implementation, and technologies* (pp. 147–153). Hershey, PA: Information Science Reference; doi:10.4018/978-1-4666-1879-4.ch010

Alshaer, H., Muhaidat, S., Shubair, R., & Shayegannia, M. (2014). Security and connectivity analysis in vehicular communication networks. In D. Rawat, B. Bista, & G. Yan (Eds.), *Security, privacy, trust, and resource management in mobile and wireless communications* (pp. 83–107). Hershey, PA: Information Science Reference; doi:10.4018/978-1-4666-4691-9.ch005

Alzamil, Z. A. (2012). Information security awareness at Saudi Arabians' organizations: An information technology employee's perspective. [IJISP]. *International Journal of Information Security and Privacy*, 6(3), 38–55. doi:10.4018/jisp.2012070102

Anyiwo, D., & Sharma, S. (2011). Web services and e-business technologies: Security issues. In O. Bak & N. Stair (Eds.), *Impact of e-business technologies on public and private organizations: Industry comparisons and perspectives* (pp. 249–261). Hershey, PA: Business Science Reference; doi:10.4018/978-1-60960-501-8.ch015

Apostolakis, I., Chryssanthou, A., & Varlamis, I. (2011). A holistic perspective of security in health related virtual communities. In *Virtual communities: Concepts, methodologies, tools and applications* (pp. 1190–1204). Hershey, PA: Information Science Reference; doi:10.4018/978-1-60960-100-3.ch406

Arnett, K. P., Templeton, G. F., & Vance, D. A. (2011). Information security by words alone: The case for strong security policies. In H. Nemati (Ed.), *Security and privacy assurance in advancing technologies: New developments* (pp. 154–159). Hershey, PA: Information Science Reference; doi:10.4018/978-1-60960-200-0.ch011

Arogundade, O. T., Akinwale, A. T., Jin, Z., & Yang, X. G. (2011). A unified use-misuse case model for capturing and analysing safety and security requirements. [IJISP]. *International Journal of Information Security and Privacy*, 5(4), 8–30. doi:10.4018/jisp.2011100102

Arshad, J., Townend, P., Xu, J., & Jie, W. (2012). Cloud computing security: Opportunities and pitfalls. [IJGHPC]. *International Journal of Grid and High Performance Computing*, 4(1), 52–66. doi:10.4018/jghpc.2012010104

Asim, M., & Petkovic, M. (2012). Fundamental building blocks for security interoperability in e-business. In E. Kajan, F. Dorloff, & I. Bedini (Eds.), *Handbook of research on e-business standards and protocols: Documents, data and advanced web technologies* (pp. 269–292). Hershey, PA: Business Science Reference; doi:10.4018/978-1-4666-0146-8.ch013

Askary, S., Goodwin, D., & Lanis, R. (2012). Improvements in audit risks related to information technology frauds. [IJEIS]. *International Journal of Enterprise Information Systems*, 8(2), 52–63. doi:10.4018/jeis.2012040104

Aurigemma, S. (2013). A composite framework for behavioral compliance with information security policies. [JOEUC]. *Journal of Organizational and End User Computing*, 25(3), 32–51. doi:10.4018/joeuc.2013070103

Avalle, M., Pironti, A., Pozza, D., & Sisto, R. (2011). JavaSPI: A framework for security protocol implementation. [IJSSE]. *International Journal of Secure Software Engineering*, 2(4), 34–48. doi:10.4018/jsse.2011100103

Axelrod, C. W. (2012). A dynamic cyber security economic model: incorporating value functions for all involved parties. In M. Gupta, J. Walp, & R. Sharman (Eds.), *Threats, countermeasures, and advances in applied information security* (pp. 462–477). Hershey, PA: Information Science Reference; doi:10.4018/978-1-4666-0978-5.ch024

Ayanso, A., & Herath, T. (2012). Law and technology at crossroads in cyberspace: Where do we go from here? In A. Dudley, J. Braman, & G. Vincenti (Eds.), *Investigating cyber law and cyber ethics: Issues, impacts and practices* (pp. 57–77). Hershey, PA: Information Science Reference; doi:10.4018/978-1-61350-132-0.ch004

Baars, T., & Spruit, M. (2012). Designing a secure cloud architecture: The SeCA model. [IJISP]. *International Journal of Information Security and Privacy*, 6(1), 14–32. doi:10.4018/jisp.2012010102

Bachmann, M. (2011). Deciphering the hacker underground: First quantitative insights. In T. Holt & B. Schell (Eds.), *Corporate hacking and technology-driven crime: Social dynamics and implications* (pp. 105–126). Hershey, PA: Information Science Reference; doi:10.4018/978-1-61692-805-6.ch006

Bachmann, M., & Smith, B. (2012). Internet fraud. In Z. Yan (Ed.), *Encyclopedia of cyber behavior* (pp. 931–943). Hershey, PA: Information Science Reference; doi:10.4018/978-1-4666-0315-8.ch077

Bai, Y., & Khan, K. M. (2011). Ell secure information system using modal logic technique. [IJSSE]. *International Journal of Secure Software Engineering*, 2(2), 65–76. doi:10.4018/jsse.2011040104

Bandeira, G. S. (2014). Criminal liability of organizations, corporations, legal persons, and similar entities on law of portuguese cybercrime: A brief discussion on the issue of crimes of "false information," the "damage on other programs or computer data," the "computer-software sabotage," the "illegitimate access," the "unlawful interception," and "illegitimate reproduction of the protected program". In I. Portela & F. Almeida (Eds.), *Organizational, legal, and technological dimensions of information system administration* (pp. 96–107). Hershey, PA: Information Science Reference; doi:10.4018/978-1-4666-4526-4.ch006

Barjis, J. (2012). Software engineering security based on business process modeling. In K. Khan (Ed.), *Security-aware systems applications and software development methods* (pp. 52–68). Hershey, PA: Information Science Reference; doi:10.4018/978-1-4666-1580-9.ch004

Bedi, P., Gandotra, V., & Singhal, A. (2013). Innovative strategies for secure software development. In H. Singh & K. Kaur (Eds.), *Designing, engineering, and analyzing reliable and efficient software* (pp. 217–237). Hershey, PA: Information Science Reference; doi:10.4018/978-1-4666-2958-5.ch013

Belsis, P., Skourlas, C., & Gritzalis, S. (2011). Secure electronic healthcare records management in wireless environments. [JITR]. *Journal of Information Technology Research*, 4(4), 1–17. doi:10.4018/jitr.2011100101

Bernik, I. (2012). Internet study: Cyber threats and cybercrime awareness and fear. [IJCWT]. *International Journal of Cyber Warfare & Terrorism*, 2(3), 1–11. doi:10.4018/ijcwt.2012070101

Bhatia, M. S. (2011). World war III: The cyber war. [IJCWT]. *International Journal of Cyber Warfare & Terrorism*, 1(3), 59–69. doi:10.4018/ijcwt.2011070104

Blanco, C., Rosado, D., Gutiérrez, C., Rodríguez, A., Mellado, D., Fernández-Medina, E., & Piattini, M. et al. (2011). Security over the information systems development cycle. In H. Mouratidis (Ed.), *Software engineering for secure systems: Industrial and research perspectives* (pp. 113–154). Hershey, PA: Information Science Reference; doi:10.4018/978-1-61520-837-1.ch005

Bobbert, Y., & Mulder, H. (2012). A research journey into maturing the business information security of mid market organizations. In W. Van Grembergen & S. De Haes (Eds.), *Business strategy and applications in enterprise IT governance* (pp. 236–259). Hershey, PA: Business Science Reference; doi:10.4018/978-1-4666-1779-7.ch014

Boddington, R. (2011). Digital evidence. In D. Kerr, J. Gammack, & K. Bryant (Eds.), *Digital business security development: Management technologies* (pp. 37–72). Hershey, PA: Business Science Reference; doi:10.4018/978-1-60566-806-2.ch002

Bossler, A. M., & Burruss, G. W. (2011). The general theory of crime and computer hacking: Low self-control hackers? In T. Holt & B. Schell (Eds.), *Corporate hacking and technology-driven crime: Social dynamics and implications* (pp. 38–67). Hershey, PA: Information Science Reference; doi:10.4018/978-1-61692-805-6.ch003

Bouras, C., & Stamos, K. (2011). Security issues for multi-domain resource reservation. In D. Kar & M. Syed (Eds.), *Network security, administration and management: Advancing technology and practice* (pp. 38–50). Hershey, PA: Information Science Reference; doi:10.4018/978-1-60960-777-7.ch003

Bracci, F., Corradi, A., & Foschini, L. (2014). Cloud standards: Security and interoperability issues. In H. Mouftah & B. Kantarci (Eds.), *Communication infrastructures for cloud computing* (pp. 465–495). Hershey, PA: Information Science Reference; doi:10.4018/978-1-4666-4522-6.ch020

Brodsky, J., & Radvanovsky, R. (2011). Control systems security. In T. Holt & B. Schell (Eds.), *Corporate hacking and technology-driven crime: Social dynamics and implications* (pp. 187–204). Hershey, PA: Information Science Reference; doi:10.4018/978-1-61692-805-6.ch010

Brooks, D. (2013). Security threats and risks of intelligent building systems: Protecting facilities from current and emerging vulnerabilities. In C. Laing, A. Badii, & P. Vickers (Eds.), *Securing critical infrastructures and critical control systems: Approaches for threat protection* (pp. 1–16). Hershey, PA: Information Science Reference; doi:10.4018/978-1-4666-2659-1.ch001

Bülow, W., & Wester, M. (2012). The right to privacy and the protection of personal data in a digital era and the age of information. In C. Akrivopoulou & N. Garipidis (Eds.), *Human rights and risks in the digital era: Globalization and the effects of information technologies* (pp. 34–45). Hershey, PA: Information Science Reference; doi:10.4018/978-1-4666-0891-7.ch004

Canongia, C., & Mandarino, R. (2014). Cybersecurity: The new challenge of the information society. In Crisis management: Concepts, methodologies, tools and applications (pp. 60-80). Hershey, PA: Information Science Reference. doi:10.4018/978-1-4666-4707-7.ch003

Cao, X., & Lu, Y. (2011). The social network structure of a computer hacker community. In H. Nemati (Ed.), *Security and privacy assurance in advancing technologies: New developments* (pp. 160–173). Hershey, PA: Information Science Reference; doi:10.4018/978-1-60960-200-0.ch012

Cardholm, L. (2014). Identifying the business value of information security. In T. Tsiakis, T. Kargidis, & P. Katsaros (Eds.), *Approaches and processes for managing the economics of information systems* (pp. 157–180). Hershey, PA: Business Science Reference; doi:10.4018/978-1-4666-4983-5.ch010

Cardoso, R. C., & Gomes, A. (2012). Security issues in massively multiplayer online games. In M. Cruz-Cunha (Ed.), *Handbook of research on serious games as educational, business and research tools* (pp. 290–314). Hershey, PA: Information Science Reference; doi:10.4018/978-1-4666-0149-9.ch016

Carpen-Amarie, A., Costan, A., Leordeanu, C., Basescu, C., & Antoniu, G. (2012). Towards a generic security framework for cloud data management environments. [IJDST]. *International Journal of Distributed Systems and Technologies*, 3(1), 17–34. doi:10.4018/jdst.2012010102

Caushaj, E., Fu, H., Sethi, I., Badih, H., Watson, D., Zhu, Y., & Leng, S. (2013). Theoretical analysis and experimental study: Monitoring data privacy in smartphone communications. [IJITN]. *International Journal of Interdisciplinary Telecommunications and Networking*, 5(2), 66–82. doi:10.4018/jitn.2013040106

Cepheli, Ö., & Kurt, G. K. (2014). Physical layer security in wireless communication networks. In D. Rawat, B. Bista, & G. Yan (Eds.), *Security, privacy, trust, and resource management in mobile and wireless communications* (pp. 61–81). Hershey, PA: Information Science Reference; doi:10.4018/978-1-4666-4691-9.ch004

Chakraborty, P., & Raghuraman, K. (2013). Trends in information security. In K. Buragga & N. Zaman (Eds.), *Software development techniques for constructive information systems design* (pp. 354–376). Hershey, PA: Information Science Reference; doi:10.4018/978-1-4666-3679-8.ch020

Chandrakumar, T., & Parthasarathy, S. (2012). Enhancing data security in ERP projects using XML. [IJEIS]. *International Journal of Enterprise Information Systems*, 8(1), 51–65. doi:10.4018/jeis.2012010104

Chapple, M. J., Striegel, A., & Crowell, C. R. (2011). Firewall rulebase management: Tools and techniques. In M. Quigley (Ed.), *ICT ethics and security in the 21st century: New developments and applications* (pp. 254–276). Hershey, PA: Information Science Reference; doi:10.4018/978-1-60960-573-5.ch013

Chen, L., Hu, W., Yang, M., & Zhang, L. (2011). Security and privacy issues in secure e-mail standards and services. In H. Nemati (Ed.), *Security and privacy assurance in advancing technologies: new developments* (pp. 174–185). Hershey, PA: Information Science Reference; doi:10.4018/978-1-60960-200-0.ch013

Chen, L., Varol, C., Liu, Q., & Zhou, B. (2014). Security in wireless metropolitan area networks: WiMAX and LTE. In D. Rawat, B. Bista, & G. Yan (Eds.), *Security, privacy, trust, and resource management in mobile and wireless communications* (pp. 11–27). Hershey, PA: Information Science Reference; doi:10.4018/978-1-4666-4691-9.ch002

Cherdantseva, Y., & Hilton, J. (2014). Information security and information assurance: Discussion about the meaning, scope, and goals. In I. Portela & F. Almeida (Eds.), *Organizational, legal, and technological dimensions of information system administration* (pp. 167–198). Hershey, PA: Information Science Reference; doi:10.4018/978-1-4666-4526-4.ch010

Cherdantseva, Y., & Hilton, J. (2014). The 2011 survey of information security and information assurance professionals: Findings. In I. Portela & F. Almeida (Eds.), *Organizational, legal, and technological dimensions of information system administration* (pp. 243–256). Hershey, PA: Information Science Reference; doi:10.4018/978-1-4666-4526-4.ch013

Chowdhury, M. U., & Ray, B. R. (2013). Security risks/vulnerability in a RFID system and possible defenses. In N. Karmakar (Ed.), *Advanced RFID systems, security, and applications* (pp. 1–15). Hershey, PA: Information Science Reference; doi:10.4018/978-1-4666-2080-3.ch001

Cofta, P., Lacohée, H., & Hodgson, P. (2011). Incorporating social trust into design practices for secure systems. In H. Mouratidis (Ed.), *Software engineering for secure systems: Industrial and research perspectives* (pp. 260–284). Hershey, PA: Information Science Reference; doi:10.4018/978-1-61520-837-1.ch010

Conway, M. (2012). What is cyberterrorism and how real is the threat? A review of the academic literature, 1996–2009. In P. Reich & E. Gelbstein (Eds.), *Law, policy, and technology: Cyberterrorism, information warfare, and internet immobilization* (pp. 279–307). Hershey, PA: Information Science Reference; doi:10.4018/978-1-61520-831-9.ch011

Corser, G. P., Arslanturk, S., Oluoch, J., Fu, H., & Corser, G. E. (2013). Knowing the enemy at the gates: Measuring attacker motivation. [IJITN]. *International Journal of Interdisciplinary Telecommunications and Networking*, 5(2), 83–95. doi:10.4018/jitn.2013040107

Crosbie, M. (2013). Hack the cloud: Ethical hacking and cloud forensics. In K. Ruan (Ed.), *Cybercrime and cloud forensics: Applications for investigation processes* (pp. 42–58). Hershey, PA: Information Science Reference; doi:10.4018/978-1-4666-2662-1.ch002

Curran, K., Carlin, S., & Adams, M. (2012). Security issues in cloud computing. In L. Chao (Ed.), *Cloud computing for teaching and learning: Strategies for design and implementation* (pp. 200–208). Hershey, PA: Information Science Reference; doi:10.4018/978-1-4666-0957-0.ch014

Czosseck, C., Ottis, R., & Talihärm, A. (2011). Estonia after the 2007 cyber attacks: Legal, strategic and organisational changes in cyber security. [IJCWT]. *International Journal of Cyber Warfare & Terrorism*, 1(1), 24–34. doi:10.4018/ijcwt.2011010103

Czosseck, C., & Podins, K. (2012). A vulnerability-based model of cyber weapons and its implications for cyber conflict. [IJCWT]. *International Journal of Cyber Warfare & Terrorism*, 2(1), 14–26. doi:10.4018/ijcwt.2012010102

da Silva, F. A., Moura, D. F., & Galdino, J. F. (2012). Classes of attacks for tactical software defined radios. [IJERTCS]. *International Journal of Embedded and Real-Time Communication Systems*, 3(4), 57–82. doi:10.4018/jertcs.2012100104

Dabcevic, K., Marcenaro, L., & Regazzoni, C. S. (2013). Security in cognitive radio networks. In T. Lagkas, P. Sarigiannidis, M. Louta, & P. Chatzimisios (Eds.), *Evolution of cognitive networks and self-adaptive communication systems* (pp. 301–335). Hershey, PA: Information Science Reference; doi:10.4018/978-1-4666-4189-1.ch013

Dahbur, K., Mohammad, B., & Tarakji, A. B. (2013). Security issues in cloud computing: A survey of risks, threats and vulnerabilities. In S. Aljawarneh (Ed.), *Cloud computing advancements in design, implementation, and technologies* (pp. 154–165). Hershey, PA: Information Science Reference; doi:10.4018/978-1-4666-1879-4.ch011

Dark, M. (2011). Data breach disclosure: A policy analysis. In M. Dark (Ed.), *Information assurance and security ethics in complex systems: Interdisciplinary perspectives* (pp. 226–252). Hershey, PA: Information Science Reference; doi:10.4018/978-1-61692-245-0.ch011

Das, S., Mukhopadhyay, A., & Bhasker, B. (2013). Today's action is better than tomorrow's cure - Evaluating information security at a premier indian business school. [JCIT]. *Journal of Cases on Information Technology*, 15(3), 1–23. doi:10.4018/jcit.2013070101

Dasgupta, D., & Naseem, D. (2014). A framework for compliance and security coverage estimation for cloud services: A cloud insurance model. In S. Srinivasan (Ed.), *Security, trust, and regulatory aspects of cloud computing in business environments* (pp. 91–114). Hershey, PA: Information Science Reference; doi:10.4018/978-1-4666-5788-5.ch005

De Fuentes, J. M., González-Tablas, A. I., & Ribagorda, A. (2011). Overview of security issues in vehicular ad-hoc networks. In M. Cruz-Cunha & F. Moreira (Eds.), *Handbook of research on mobility and computing: Evolving technologies and ubiquitous impacts* (pp. 894–911). Hershey, PA: Information Science Reference; doi:10.4018/978-1-60960-042-6.ch056

De Groef, W., Devriese, D., Reynaert, T., & Piessens, F. (2013). Security and privacy of online social network applications. In L. Caviglione, M. Coccoli, & A. Merlo (Eds.), *Social network engineering for secure web data and services* (pp. 206–221). Hershey, PA: Information Science Reference; doi:10.4018/978-1-4666-3926-3.ch010

Denning, D. E. (2011). Cyber conflict as an emergent social phenomenon. In T. Holt & B. Schell (Eds.), *Corporate hacking and technology-driven crime: Social dynamics and implications* (pp. 170–186). Hershey, PA: Information Science Reference; doi:10.4018/978-1-61692-805-6.ch009

Desai, A. M., & Mock, K. (2013). Security in cloud computing. In A. Bento & A. Aggarwal (Eds.), *Cloud computing service and deployment models: Layers and management* (pp. 208–221). Hershey, PA: Business Science Reference; doi:10.4018/978-1-4666-2187-9.ch011

Dionysiou, I., & Ktoridou, D. (2012). Enhancing dynamic-content courses with student-oriented learning strategies: The case of computer security course. [IJCEE]. *International Journal of Cyber Ethics in Education*, 2(2), 24–33. doi:10.4018/ijcee.2012040103

Disterer, G. (2012). Attacks on IT systems: Categories of motives. In T. Chou (Ed.), *Information assurance and security technologies for risk assessment and threat management: Advances* (pp. 1–16). Hershey, PA: Information Science Reference; doi:10.4018/978-1-61350-507-6.ch001

Dougan, T., & Curran, K. (2012). Man in the browser attacks. [IJACI]. *International Journal of Ambient Computing and Intelligence*, 4(1), 29–39. doi:10.4018/jaci.2012010103

Dubey, R., Sharma, S., & Chouhan, L. (2013). Security for cognitive radio networks. In M. Ku & J. Lin (Eds.), *Cognitive radio and interference management: Technology and strategy* (pp. 238–256). Hershey, PA: Information Science Reference; doi:10.4018/978-1-4666-2005-6.ch013

Dunkels, E., Frånberg, G., & Hällgren, C. (2011). Young people and online risk. In E. Dunkels, G. Franberg, & C. Hallgren (Eds.), *Youth culture and net culture: Online social practices* (pp. 1–16). Hershey, PA: Information Science Reference; doi:10.4018/978-1-60960-209-3.ch001

Dunkerley, K., & Tejay, G. (2012). The development of a model for information systems security success. In Z. Belkhamza & S. Azizi Wafa (Eds.), *Measuring organizational information systems success: New technologies and practices* (pp. 341–366). Hershey, PA: Business Science Reference; doi:10.4018/978-1-4666-0170-3.ch017

Dunkerley, K., & Tejay, G. (2012). Theorizing information security success: Towards secure e-government. In V. Weerakkody (Ed.), *Technology enabled transformation of the public sector: Advances in e-government* (pp. 224–235). Hershey, PA: Information Science Reference; doi:10.4018/978-1-4666-1776-6.ch014

Eisenga, A., Jones, T. L., & Rodriguez, W. (2012). Investing in IT security: How to determine the maximum threshold. [IJISP]. *International Journal of Information Security and Privacy*, 6(3), 75–87. doi:10.4018/jisp.2012070104

Eyitemi, M. (2012). Regulation of cybercafés in Nigeria. In *Cyber crime: Concepts, methodologies, tools and applications* (pp. 1305–1313). Hershey, PA: Information Science Reference; doi:10.4018/978-1-61350-323-2.ch606

Ezumah, B., & Adekunle, S. O. (2012). A review of privacy, internet security threat, and legislation in Africa: A case study of Nigeria, South Africa, Egypt, and Kenya. In J. Abawajy, M. Pathan, M. Rahman, A. Pathan, & M. Deris (Eds.), *Internet and distributed computing advancements: Theoretical frameworks and practical applications* (pp. 115–136). Hershey, PA: Information Science Reference; doi:10.4018/978-1-4666-0161-1.ch005

Farooq-i-Azam, M., & Ayyaz, M. N. (2014). Embedded systems security. In *Software design and development: Concepts, methodologies, tools, and applications* (pp. 980–998). Hershey, PA: Information Science Reference; doi:10.4018/978-1-4666-4301-7.ch047

Fauzi, A. H., & Taylor, H. (2013). Secure community trust stores for peer-to-peer e-commerce applications using cloud services. [IJEEI]. *International Journal of E-Entrepreneurship and Innovation*, 4(1), 1–15. doi:10.4018/jeei.2013010101

Fenz, S. (2011). E-business and information security risk management: Challenges and potential solutions. In E. Kajan (Ed.), *Electronic business interoperability: Concepts, opportunities and challenges* (pp. 596–614). Hershey, PA: Business Science Reference; doi:10.4018/978-1-60960-485-1.ch024

Fernandez, E. B., Yoshioka, N., Washizaki, H., Jurjens, J., VanHilst, M., & Pernu, G. (2011). Using security patterns to develop secure systems. In H. Mouratidis (Ed.), *Software engineering for secure systems: Industrial and research perspectives* (pp. 16–31). Hershey, PA: Information Science Reference; doi:10.4018/978-1-61520-837-1.ch002

Flores, A. E., Win, K. T., & Susilo, W. (2011). Secure exchange of electronic health records. In A. Chryssanthou, I. Apostolakis, & I. Varlamis (Eds.), *Certification and security in health-related web applications: Concepts and solutions* (pp. 1–22). Hershey, PA: Medical Information Science Reference; doi:10.4018/978-1-61692-895-7.ch001

Fonseca, J., & Vieira, M. (2014). A survey on secure software development lifecycles. In *Software design and development: Concepts, methodologies, tools, and applications* (pp. 17–33). Hershey, PA: Information Science Reference; doi:10.4018/978-1-4666-4301-7.ch002

Fournaris, A. P., Kitsos, P., & Sklavos, N. (2013). Security and cryptographic engineering in embedded systems. In M. Khalgui, O. Mosbahi, & A. Valentini (Eds.), *Embedded computing systems: Applications, optimization, and advanced design* (pp. 420–438). Hershey, PA: Information Science Reference; doi:10.4018/978-1-4666-3922-5.ch021

Franqueira, V. N., van Cleeff, A., van Eck, P., & Wieringa, R. J. (2013). Engineering security agreements against external insider threat. [IRMJ]. *Information Resources Management Journal*, 26(4), 66–91. doi:10.4018/irmj.2013100104

French, T., Bessis, N., Maple, C., & Asimakopoulou, E. (2012). Trust issues on crowd-sourcing methods for urban environmental monitoring. [IJDST]. *International Journal of Distributed Systems and Technologies*, 3(1), 35–47. doi:10.4018/jdst.2012010103

Fu, Y., Kulick, J., Yan, L. K., & Drager, S. (2013). Formal modeling and verification of security property in Handel C program. [IJSSE]. *International Journal of Secure Software Engineering*, 3(3), 50–65. doi:10.4018/jsse.2012070103

Furnell, S., von Solms, R., & Phippen, A. (2011). Preventative actions for enhancing online protection and privacy. [IJITSA]. *International Journal of Information Technologies and Systems Approach*, 4(2), 1–11. doi:10.4018/jitsa.2011070101

Gaivéo, J. (2011). SMEs e-business security issues. In M. Cruz-Cunha & J. Varajão (Eds.), *Innovations in SMEs and conducting e-business: Technologies, trends and solutions* (pp. 317–337). Hershey, PA: Business Science Reference; doi:10.4018/978-1-60960-765-4.ch018

Gaivéo, J. M. (2013). Security of ICTs supporting healthcare activities. In M. Cruz-Cunha, I. Miranda, & P. Gonçalves (Eds.), *Handbook of research on ICTs for human-centered healthcare and social care services* (pp. 208–228). Hershey, PA: Medical Information Science Reference; doi:10.4018/978-1-4666-3986-7.ch011

Gelbstein, E. E. (2013). Designing a security audit plan for a critical information infrastructure (CII). In C. Laing, A. Badii, & P. Vickers (Eds.), *Securing critical infrastructures and critical control systems: Approaches for threat protection* (pp. 262–285). Hershey, PA: Information Science Reference; doi:10.4018/978-1-4666-2659-1.ch011

Gódor, G., & Imre, S. (2012). Security aspects in radio frequency identification systems. In D. Saha & V. Sridhar (Eds.), *Next generation data communication technologies: Emerging trends* (pp. 187–225). Hershey, PA: Information Science Reference; doi:10.4018/978-1-61350-477-2.ch009

Gogolin, G. (2011). Security and privacy concerns of virtual worlds. In B. Ciaramitaro (Ed.), *Virtual worlds and e-commerce: Technologies and applications for building customer relationships* (pp. 244–256). Hershey, PA: Business Science Reference; doi:10.4018/978-1-61692-808-7.ch014

Gogoulos, F. I., Antonakopoulou, A., Lioudakis, G. V., Kaklamani, D. I., & Venieris, I. S. (2014). Trust in an enterprise world: A survey. In M. Cruz-Cunha, F. Moreira, & J. Varajão (Eds.), *Handbook of research on enterprise 2.0: Technological, social, and organizational dimensions* (pp. 199–219). Hershey, PA: Business Science Reference; doi:10.4018/978-1-4666-4373-4.ch011

Goldman, J. E., & Ahuja, S. (2011). Integration of COBIT, balanced scorecard and SSE-CMM as an organizational & strategic information security management (ISM) framework. In M. Quigley (Ed.), *ICT ethics and security in the 21st century: New developments and applications* (pp. 277–309). Hershey, PA: Information Science Reference; doi:10.4018/978-1-60960-573-5.ch014

Goldschmidt, C., Dark, M., & Chaudhry, H. (2011). Responsibility for the harm and risk of software security flaws. In M. Dark (Ed.), *Information assurance and security ethics in complex systems: Interdisciplinary perspectives* (pp. 104–131). Hershey, PA: Information Science Reference; doi:10.4018/978-1-61692-245-0.ch006

Grahn, K., Karlsson, J., & Pulkkis, G. (2011). Secure routing and mobility in future IP networks. In M. Cruz-Cunha & F. Moreira (Eds.), *Handbook of research on mobility and computing: Evolving technologies and ubiquitous impacts* (pp. 952–972). Hershey, PA: Information Science Reference; doi:10.4018/978-1-60960-042-6.ch059

Greitzer, F. L., Frincke, D., & Zabriskie, M. (2011). Social/ethical issues in predictive insider threat monitoring. In M. Dark (Ed.), *Information assurance and security ethics in complex systems: Interdisciplinary perspectives* (pp. 132–161). Hershey, PA: Information Science Reference; doi:10.4018/978-1-61692-245-0.ch007

Grobler, M. (2012). The need for digital evidence standardisation. [IJDCF]. *International Journal of Digital Crime and Forensics*, 4(2), 1–12. doi:10.4018/jdcf.2012040101

Guo, J., Marshall, A., & Zhou, B. (2014). A multi-parameter trust framework for mobile ad hoc networks. In D. Rawat, B. Bista, & G. Yan (Eds.), *Security, privacy, trust, and resource management in mobile and wireless communications* (pp. 245–277). Hershey, PA: Information Science Reference; doi:10.4018/978-1-4666-4691-9.ch011

Gururajan, R., & Hafeez-Baig, A. (2011). Wireless handheld device and LAN security issues: A case study. In D. Kerr, J. Gammack, & K. Bryant (Eds.), *Digital business security development: Management technologies* (pp. 129–151). Hershey, PA: Business Science Reference; doi:10.4018/978-1-60566-806-2.ch006

Ha, H. (2012). Online security and consumer protection in ecommerce an Australian case. In K. Mohammed Rezaul (Ed.), *Strategic and pragmatic e-business: Implications for future business practices* (pp. 217–243). Hershey, PA: Business Science Reference; doi:10.4018/978-1-4666-1619-6.ch010

Hagen, J. M. (2012). The contributions of information security culture and human relations to the improvement of situational awareness. In C. Onwubiko & T. Owens (Eds.), *Situational awareness in computer network defense: Principles, methods and applications* (pp. 10–28). Hershey, PA: Information Science Reference; doi:10.4018/978-1-4666-0104-8.ch002

Hai-Jew, S. (2011). The social design of 3D interactive spaces for security in higher education: A preliminary view. In A. Rea (Ed.), *Security in virtual worlds, 3D webs, and immersive environments: Models for development, interaction, and management* (pp. 72–96). Hershey, PA: Information Science Reference; doi:10.4018/978-1-61520-891-3.ch005

Halder, D., & Jaishankar, K. (2012). Cyber crime against women and regulations in Australia. In *Cyber crime: Concepts, methodologies, tools and applications* (pp. 757–764). Hershey, PA: Information Science Reference; doi:10.4018/978-1-61350-323-2.ch404

Halder, D., & Jaishankar, K. (2012). Cyber victimization of women and cyber laws in India. In *Cyber crime: Concepts, methodologies, tools and applications* (pp. 742–756). Hershey, PA: Information Science Reference; doi:10.4018/978-1-61350-323-2.ch403

Halder, D., & Jaishankar, K. (2012). Definition, typology and patterns of victimization. In *Cyber crime: Concepts, methodologies, tools and applications* (pp. 1016–1042). Hershey, PA: Information Science Reference; doi:10.4018/978-1-61350-323-2.ch502

Hamlen, K., Kantarcioglu, M., Khan, L., & Thuraisingham, B. (2012). Security issues for cloud computing. In H. Nemati (Ed.), *Optimizing information security and advancing privacy assurance: New technologies* (pp. 150–162). Hershey, PA: Information Science Reference; doi:10.4018/978-1-4666-0026-3.ch008

Harnesk, D. (2011). Convergence of information security in B2B networks. In E. Kajan (Ed.), *Electronic business interoperability: Concepts, opportunities and challenges* (pp. 571–595). Hershey, PA: Business Science Reference; doi:10.4018/978-1-60960-485-1.ch023

Harnesk, D., & Hartikainen, H. (2011). Multi-layers of information security in emergency response. [IJISCRAM]. *International Journal of Information Systems for Crisis Response and Management*, *3*(2), 1–17. doi:10.4018/jiscrm.2011040101

Hawrylak, P. J., Hale, J., & Papa, M. (2013). Security issues for ISO 18000-6 type C RFID: Identification and solutions. In *Supply chain management: Concepts, methodologies, tools, and applications* (pp. 1565–1581). Hershey, PA: Business Science Reference; doi:10.4018/978-1-4666-2625-6.ch093

He, B., Tran, T. T., & Xie, B. (2014). Authentication and identity management for secure cloud businesses and services. In S. Srinivasan (Ed.), *Security, trust, and regulatory aspects of cloud computing in business environments* (pp. 180–201). Hershey, PA: Information Science Reference; doi:10.4018/978-1-4666-5788-5.ch011

Henrie, M. (2012). Cyber security in liquid petroleum pipelines. In J. Zubairi & A. Mahboob (Eds.), *Cyber security standards, practices and industrial applications: Systems and methodologies* (pp. 200–222). Hershey, PA: Information Science Reference; doi:10.4018/978-1-60960-851-4.ch011

Herath, T., Rao, H. R., & Upadhyaya, S. (2012). Internet crime: How vulnerable are you? Do gender, social influence and education play a role in vulnerability? In *Cyber crime: Concepts, methodologies, tools and applications* (pp. 1–13). Hershey, PA: Information Science Reference; doi:10.4018/978-1-61350-323-2.ch101

Hilmi, M. F., Pawanchik, S., Mustapha, Y., & Ali, H. M. (2013). Information security perspective of a learning management system: An exploratory study. [IJKSR]. *International Journal of Knowledge Society Research*, *4*(2), 9–18. doi:10.4018/jksr.2013040102

Hommel, W. (2012). Security and privacy management for learning management systems. In *Virtual learning environments: Concepts, methodologies, tools and applications* (pp. 1151–1170). Hershey, PA: Information Science Reference; doi:10.4018/978-1-4666-0011-9.ch602

Hoops, D. S. (2012). Lost in cyberspace: Navigating the legal issues of e-commerce. [JECO]. *Journal of Electronic Commerce in Organizations*, *10*(1), 33–51. doi:10.4018/jeco.2012010103

Houmb, S., Georg, G., Petriu, D., Bordbar, B., Ray, I., Anastasakis, K., & France, R. (2011). Balancing security and performance properties during system architectural design. In H. Mouratidis (Ed.), *Software engineering for secure systems: Industrial and research perspectives* (pp. 155–191). Hershey, PA: Information Science Reference; doi:10.4018/978-1-61520-837-1.ch006

Huang, E., & Cheng, F. (2012). Online security cues and e-payment continuance intention. [IJEEI]. *International Journal of E-Entrepreneurship and Innovation*, *3*(1), 42–58. doi:10.4018/jeei.2012010104

Ifinedo, P. (2011). Relationships between information security concerns and national cultural dimensions: Findings in the global financial services industry. In H. Nemati (Ed.), *Security and privacy assurance in advancing technologies: New developments* (pp. 134–153). Hershey, PA: Information Science Reference; doi:10.4018/978-1-60960-200-0.ch010

Inden, U., Lioudakis, G., & Rückemann, C. (2013). Awareness-based security management for complex and internet-based operations management systems. In C. Rückemann (Ed.), *Integrated information and computing systems for natural, spatial, and social sciences* (pp. 43–73). Hershey, PA: Information Science Reference; doi:10.4018/978-1-4666-2190-9.ch003

Islam, S., Mouratidis, H., Kalloniatis, C., Hudic, A., & Zechner, L. (2013). Model based process to support security and privacy requirements engineering. [IJSSE]. *International Journal of Secure Software Engineering*, *3*(3), 1–22. doi:10.4018/jsse.2012070101

Itani, W., Kayssi, A., & Chehab, A. (2012). Security and privacy in body sensor networks: Challenges, solutions, and research directions. In M. Watfa (Ed.), *E-healthcare systems and wireless communications: Current and future challenges* (pp. 100–127). Hershey, PA: Medical Information Science Reference; doi:10.4018/978-1-61350-123-8.ch005

Jansen van Vuuren, J., Grobler, M., & Zaaiman, J. (2012). Cyber security awareness as critical driver to national security. [IJCWT]. *International Journal of Cyber Warfare & Terrorism*, *2*(1), 27–38. doi:10.4018/ijcwt.2012010103

Jansen van Vuuren, J., Leenen, L., Phahlamohlaka, J., & Zaaiman, J. (2012). An approach to governance of CyberSecurity in South Africa. [IJCWT]. *International Journal of Cyber Warfare & Terrorism*, *2*(4), 13–27. doi:10.4018/ijcwt.2012100102

Jensen, J., & Groep, D. L. (2012). Security and trust in a global research infrastructure. In J. Leng & W. Sharrock (Eds.), *Handbook of research on computational science and engineering: Theory and practice* (pp. 539–566). Hershey, PA: Engineering Science Reference; doi:10.4018/978-1-61350-116-0.ch022

Johnsen, S. O. (2014). Safety and security in SCADA systems must be improved through resilience based risk management. In *Crisis management: Concepts, methodologies, tools and applications* (pp. 1422–1436). Hershey, PA: Information Science Reference; doi:10.4018/978-1-4666-4707-7.ch071

Johnston, A. C., Wech, B., & Jack, E. (2012). Engaging remote employees: The moderating role of "remote" status in determining employee information security policy awareness. [JOEUC]. *Journal of Organizational and End User Computing, 25*(1), 1–23. doi:10.4018/joeuc.2013010101

Jung, C., Rudolph, M., & Schwarz, R. (2013). Security evaluation of service-oriented systems using the SiSOA method. In K. Khan (Ed.), *Developing and evaluating security-aware software systems* (pp. 20–35). Hershey, PA: Information Science Reference; doi:10.4018/978-1-4666-2482-5.ch002

Kaiya, H., Sakai, J., Ogata, S., & Kaijiri, K. (2013). Eliciting security requirements for an information system using asset flows and processor deployment. [IJSSE]. *International Journal of Secure Software Engineering, 4*(3), 42–63. doi:10.4018/jsse.2013070103

Kalloniatis, C., Kavakli, E., & Gritzalis, S. (2011). Designing privacy aware information systems. In H. Mouratidis (Ed.), *Software engineering for secure systems: Industrial and research perspectives* (pp. 212–231). Hershey, PA: Information Science Reference; doi:10.4018/978-1-61520-837-1.ch008

Kamoun, F., & Halaweh, M. (2012). User interface design and e-commerce security perception: An empirical study. [IJEBR]. *International Journal of E-Business Research, 8*(2), 15–32. doi:10.4018/jebr.2012040102

Kamruzzaman, J., Azad, A. K., Karmakar, N. C., Karmakar, G., & Srinivasan, B. (2013). Security and privacy in RFID systems. In N. Karmakar (Ed.), *Advanced RFID systems, security, and applications* (pp. 16–40). Hershey, PA: Information Science Reference; doi:10.4018/978-1-4666-2080-3.ch002

Kaosar, M. G., & Yi, X. (2011). Privacy preserving data gathering in wireless sensor network. In D. Kar & M. Syed (Eds.), *Network security, administration and management: Advancing technology and practice* (pp. 237–251). Hershey, PA: Information Science Reference; doi:10.4018/978-1-60960-777-7.ch012

Kar, D. C., Ngo, H. L., Mulkey, C. J., & Sanapala, G. (2011). Advances in security and privacy in wireless sensor networks. In H. Nemati (Ed.), *Security and privacy assurance in advancing technologies: New developments* (pp. 186–213). Hershey, PA: Information Science Reference; doi:10.4018/978-1-60960-200-0.ch014

Karadsheh, L., & Alhawari, S. (2011). Applying security policies in small business utilizing cloud computing technologies. [IJCAC]. *International Journal of Cloud Applications and Computing, 1*(2), 29–40. doi:10.4018/ijcac.2011040103

Karokola, G., Yngström, L., & Kowalski, S. (2012). Secure e-government services: A comparative analysis of e-government maturity models for the developing regions–The need for security services. [IJEGR]. *International Journal of Electronic Government Research, 8*(1), 1–25. doi:10.4018/jegr.2012010101

Kassim, N. M., & Ramayah, T. (2013). Security policy issues in internet banking in Malaysia. In *IT policy and ethics: Concepts, methodologies, tools, and applications* (pp. 1274–1293). Hershey, PA: Information Science Reference; doi:10.4018/978-1-4666-2919-6.ch057

Kayem, A. V. (2013). Security in service oriented architectures: Standards and challenges. In *Digital rights management: Concepts, methodologies, tools, and applications* (pp. 50–73). Hershey, PA: Information Science Reference; doi:10.4018/978-1-4666-2136-7.ch004

K.C, A., Forsgren, H., Grahn, K., Karvi, T., & Pulkkis, G. (2013). Security and trust of public key cryptography for HIP and HIP multicast. [IJDTIS]. *International Journal of Dependable and Trustworthy Information Systems, 2*(3), 17–35. doi:10.4018/jdtis.2011070102

Kelarev, A. V., Brown, S., Watters, P., Wu, X., & Dazeley, R. (2011). Establishing reasoning communities of security experts for internet commerce security. In J. Yearwood & A. Stranieri (Eds.), *Technologies for supporting reasoning communities and collaborative decision making: Cooperative approaches* (pp. 380–396). Hershey, PA: Information Science Reference; doi:10.4018/978-1-60960-091-4.ch020

Kerr, D., Gammack, J. G., & Boddington, R. (2011). Overview of digital business security issues. In D. Kerr, J. Gammack, & K. Bryant (Eds.), *Digital business security development: Management technologies* (pp. 1–36). Hershey, PA: Business Science Reference; doi:10.4018/978-1-60566-806-2.ch001

Khan, K. M. (2011). A decision support system for selecting secure web services. In *Enterprise information systems: Concepts, methodologies, tools and applications* (pp. 1113–1120). Hershey, PA: Business Science Reference; doi:10.4018/978-1-61692-852-0.ch415

Khan, K. M. (2012). Software security engineering: Design and applications. [IJSSE]. *International Journal of Secure Software Engineering, 3*(1), 62–63. doi:10.4018/jsse.2012010104

Kilger, M. (2011). Social dynamics and the future of technology-driven crime. In T. Holt & B. Schell (Eds.), *Corporate hacking and technology-driven crime: Social dynamics and implications* (pp. 205–227). Hershey, PA: Information Science Reference; doi:10.4018/978-1-61692-805-6.ch011

Kirwan, G., & Power, A. (2012). Hacking: Legal and ethical aspects of an ambiguous activity. In A. Dudley, J. Braman, & G. Vincenti (Eds.), *Investigating cyber law and cyber ethics: Issues, impacts and practices* (pp. 21–36). Hershey, PA: Information Science Reference; doi:10.4018/978-1-61350-132-0.ch002

Kline, D. M., He, L., & Yaylacicegi, U. (2011). User perceptions of security technologies. [IJISP]. *International Journal of Information Security and Privacy, 5*(2), 1–12. doi:10.4018/jisp.2011040101

Kolkowska, E., Hedström, K., & Karlsson, F. (2012). Analyzing information security goals. In M. Gupta, J. Walp, & R. Sharman (Eds.), *Threats, countermeasures, and advances in applied information security* (pp. 91–110). Hershey, PA: Information Science Reference; doi:10.4018/978-1-4666-0978-5.ch005

Korhonen, J. J., Hiekkanen, K., & Mykkänen, J. (2012). Information security governance. In M. Gupta, J. Walp, & R. Sharman (Eds.), *Strategic and practical approaches for information security governance: Technologies and applied solutions* (pp. 53–66). Hershey, PA: Information Science Reference; doi:10.4018/978-1-4666-0197-0.ch004

Korovessis, P. (2011). Information security awareness in academia. [IJKSR]. *International Journal of Knowledge Society Research, 2*(4), 1–17. doi:10.4018/jksr.2011100101

Koskosas, I., & Sariannidis, N. (2011). Project commitment in the context of information security. [IJITPM]. *International Journal of Information Technology Project Management, 2*(3), 17–29. doi:10.4018/jitpm.2011070102

Kotsonis, E., & Eliakis, S. (2013). Information security standards for health information systems: The implementer's approach. In *User-driven healthcare: Concepts, methodologies, tools, and applications* (pp. 225–257). Hershey, PA: Medical Information Science Reference; doi:10.4018/978-1-4666-2770-3.ch013

Krishna, A. V. (2014). A randomized cloud library security environment. In S. Dhamdhere (Ed.), *Cloud computing and virtualization technologies in libraries* (pp. 278–296). Hershey, PA: Information Science Reference; doi:10.4018/978-1-4666-4631-5.ch016

Kruck, S. E., & Teer, F. P. (2011). Computer security practices and perceptions of the next generation of corporate computer users. In H. Nemati (Ed.), *Pervasive information security and privacy developments: Trends and advancements* (pp. 255–265). Hershey, PA: Information Science Reference; doi:10.4018/978-1-61692-000-5.ch017

Kumar, M., Sareen, M., & Chhabra, S. (2011). Technology related trust issues in SME B2B E-Commerce. [IJICTHD]. *International Journal of Information Communication Technologies and Human Development*, 3(4), 31–46. doi:10.4018/jicthd.2011100103

Kumar, P., & Mittal, S. (2012). The perpetration and prevention of cyber crime: An analysis of cyber terrorism in India. [IJT]. *International Journal of Technoethics*, 3(1), 43–52. doi:10.4018/jte.2012010104

Kumar, P. S., Ashok, M. S., & Subramanian, R. (2012). A publicly verifiable dynamic secret sharing protocol for secure and dependable data storage in cloud computing. [IJCAC]. *International Journal of Cloud Applications and Computing*, 2(3), 1–25. doi:10.4018/ijcac.2012070101

Kumar, S., & Dutta, K. (2014). Security issues in mobile ad hoc networks: A survey. In D. Rawat, B. Bista, & G. Yan (Eds.), *Security, privacy, trust, and resource management in mobile and wireless communications* (pp. 176–221). Hershey, PA: Information Science Reference; doi:10.4018/978-1-4666-4691-9.ch009

Lawson, S. (2013). Motivating cybersecurity: Assessing the status of critical infrastructure as an object of cyber threats. In C. Laing, A. Badii, & P. Vickers (Eds.), *Securing critical infrastructures and critical control systems: Approaches for threat protection* (pp. 168–189). Hershey, PA: Information Science Reference; doi:10.4018/978-1-4666-2659-1.ch007

Leitch, S., & Warren, M. (2011). The ethics of security of personal information upon Facebook. In M. Quigley (Ed.), *ICT ethics and security in the 21st century: New developments and applications* (pp. 46–65). Hershey, PA: Information Science Reference; doi:10.4018/978-1-60960-573-5.ch003

Li, M. (2013). Security terminology. In A. Miri (Ed.), *Advanced security and privacy for RFID technologies* (pp. 1–13). Hershey, PA: Information Science Reference; doi:10.4018/978-1-4666-3685-9.ch001

Ligaarden, O. S., Refsdal, A., & Stølen, K. (2013). Using indicators to monitor security risk in systems of systems: How to capture and measure the impact of service dependencies on the security of provided services. In D. Mellado, L. Enrique Sánchez, E. Fernández-Medina, & M. Piattini (Eds.), *IT security governance innovations: Theory and research* (pp. 256–292). Hershey, PA: Information Science Reference; doi:10.4018/978-1-4666-2083-4.ch010

Lim, J. S., Chang, S., Ahmad, A., & Maynard, S. (2012). Towards an organizational culture framework for information security practices. In M. Gupta, J. Walp, & R. Sharman (Eds.), *Strategic and practical approaches for information security governance: Technologies and applied solutions* (pp. 296–315). Hershey, PA: Information Science Reference; doi:10.4018/978-1-4666-0197-0.ch017

Lin, X., & Luppicini, R. (2011). Socio-technical influences of cyber espionage: A case study of the GhostNet system. [IJT]. *International Journal of Technoethics*, 2(2), 65–77. doi:10.4018/jte.2011040105

Lindström, J., & Hanken, C. (2012). Security challenges and selected legal aspects for wearable computing. [JITR]. *Journal of Information Technology Research*, 5(1), 68–87. doi:10.4018/jitr.2012010104

Maheshwari, H., Hyman, H., & Agrawal, M. (2012). A comparison of cyber-crime definitions in India and the United States. In *Cyber crime: Concepts, methodologies, tools and applications* (pp. 714–726). Hershey, PA: Information Science Reference; doi:10.4018/978-1-61350-323-2.ch401

Malcolmson, J. (2014). The role of security culture. In I. Portela & F. Almeida (Eds.), *Organizational, legal, and technological dimensions of information system administration* (pp. 225–242). Hershey, PA: Information Science Reference; doi:10.4018/978-1-4666-4526-4.ch012

Mantas, G., Lymberopoulos, D., & Komninos, N. (2011). Security in smart home environment. In A. Lazakidou, K. Siassiakos, & K. Ioannou (Eds.), *Wireless technologies for ambient assisted living and healthcare: Systems and applications* (pp. 170–191). Hershey, PA: Medical Information Science Reference; doi:10.4018/978-1-61520-805-0.ch010

Maple, C., Short, E., Brown, A., Bryden, C., & Salter, M. (2012). Cyberstalking in the UK: Analysis and recommendations. [IJDST]. *International Journal of Distributed Systems and Technologies*, 3(4), 34–51. doi:10.4018/jdst.2012100104

Maqousi, A., & Balikhina, T. (2011). Building security awareness culture to serve e-government initiative. In A. Al Ajeeli & Y. Al-Bastaki (Eds.), *Handbook of research on e-services in the public sector: E-government strategies and advancements* (pp. 304–311). Hershey, PA: Information Science Reference; doi:10.4018/978-1-61520-789-3.ch024

Martin, N., & Rice, J. (2013). Spearing high net wealth individuals: The case of online fraud and mature age internet users. [IJISP]. *International Journal of Information Security and Privacy*, 7(1), 1–15. doi:10.4018/jisp.2013010101

Martino, L., & Bertino, E. (2012). Security for web services: Standards and research issues. In L. Jie-Zhang (Ed.), *Innovations, standards and practices of web services: Emerging research topics* (pp. 336–362). Hershey, PA: Information Science Reference; doi:10.4018/978-1-61350-104-7.ch015

Massonet, P., Michot, A., Naqvi, S., Villari, M., & Latanicki, J. (2013). Securing the external interfaces of a federated infrastructure cloud. In *IT policy and ethics: Concepts, methodologies, tools, and applications* (pp. 1876–1903). Hershey, PA: Information Science Reference; doi:10.4018/978-1-4666-2919-6.ch082

Maumbe, B., & Owei, V. T. (2013). Understanding the information security landscape in South Africa: Implications for strategic collaboration and policy development. In B. Maumbe & C. Patrikakis (Eds.), *E-agriculture and rural development: Global innovations and future prospects* (pp. 90–102). Hershey, PA: Information Science Reference; doi:10.4018/978-1-4666-2655-3.ch009

Mazumdar, C. (2011). Enterprise information system security: A life-cycle approach. In *Enterprise information systems: Concepts, methodologies, tools and applications* (pp. 154–168). Hershey, PA: Business Science Reference; doi:10.4018/978-1-61692-852-0.ch111

McCune, J., & Haworth, D. A. (2012). Securing America against cyber war. [IJCWT]. *International Journal of Cyber Warfare & Terrorism*, 2(1), 39–49. doi:10.4018/ijcwt.2012010104

Melvin, A. O., & Ayotunde, T. (2011). Spirituality in cybercrime (Yahoo Yahoo) activities among youths in south west Nigeria. In E. Dunkels, G. Franberg, & C. Hallgren (Eds.), *Youth culture and net culture: Online social practices* (pp. 357–380). Hershey, PA: Information Science Reference; doi:10.4018/978-1-60960-209-3.ch020

Miller, J. M., Higgins, G. E., & Lopez, K. M. (2013). Considering the role of e-government in cybercrime awareness and prevention: Toward a theoretical research program for the 21st century. In *Digital rights management: Concepts, methodologies, tools, and applications* (pp. 789–800). Hershey, PA: Information Science Reference; doi:10.4018/978-1-4666-2136-7.ch036

Millman, C., Whitty, M., Winder, B., & Griffiths, M. D. (2012). Perceived criminality of cyber-harassing behaviors among undergraduate students in the United Kingdom. [IJCBPL]. *International Journal of Cyber Behavior, Psychology and Learning*, 2(4), 49–59. doi:10.4018/ijcbpl.2012100104

Minami, N. A. (2012). Employing dynamic models to enhance corporate IT security policy. [IJATS]. *International Journal of Agent Technologies and Systems*, 4(2), 42–59. doi:10.4018/jats.2012040103

Mirante, D. P., & Ammari, H. M. (2014). Wireless sensor network security attacks: A survey. In *Crisis management: Concepts, methodologies, tools and applications* (pp. 25–59). Hershey, PA: Information Science Reference; doi:10.4018/978-1-4666-4707-7.ch002

Mishra, A., & Mishra, D. (2013). Cyber stalking: A challenge for web security. In J. Bishop (Ed.), *Examining the concepts, issues, and implications of internet trolling* (pp. 32–42). Hershey, PA: Information Science Reference; doi:10.4018/978-1-4666-2803-8.ch004

Mishra, S. (2011). Wireless sensor networks: Emerging applications and security solutions. In D. Kar & M. Syed (Eds.), *Network security, administration and management: Advancing technology and practice* (pp. 217–236). Hershey, PA: Information Science Reference; doi:10.4018/978-1-60960-777-7.ch011

Mitra, S., & Padman, R. (2012). Privacy and security concerns in adopting social media for personal health management: A health plan case study. [JCIT]. *Journal of Cases on Information Technology*, 14(4), 12–26. doi:10.4018/jcit.2012100102

Modares, H., Lloret, J., Moravejosharieh, A., & Salleh, R. (2014). Security in mobile cloud computing. In J. Rodrigues, K. Lin, & J. Lloret (Eds.), *Mobile networks and cloud computing convergence for progressive services and applications* (pp. 79–91). Hershey, PA: Information Science Reference; doi:10.4018/978-1-4666-4781-7.ch005

Mohammadi, S., Golara, S., & Mousavi, N. (2012). Selecting adequate security mechanisms in e-business processes using fuzzy TOPSIS. [IJFSA]. *International Journal of Fuzzy System Applications*, 2(1), 35–53. doi:10.4018/ijfsa.2012010103

Mohammed, L. A. (2012). ICT security policy: Challenges and potential remedies. In *Cyber crime: Concepts, methodologies, tools and applications* (pp. 999–1015). Hershey, PA: Information Science Reference; doi:10.4018/978-1-61350-323-2.ch501

Molok, N. N., Ahmad, A., & Chang, S. (2012). Online social networking: A source of intelligence for advanced persistent threats. [IJCWT]. *International Journal of Cyber Warfare & Terrorism*, 2(1), 1–13. doi:10.4018/ijcwt.2012010101

Monteleone, S. (2011). Ambient intelligence: Legal challenges and possible directions for privacy protection. In C. Akrivopoulou & A. Psygkas (Eds.), *Personal data privacy and protection in a surveillance era: Technologies and practices* (pp. 201–221). Hershey, PA: Information Science Reference; doi:10.4018/978-1-60960-083-9.ch012

Moralis, A., Pouli, V., Grammatikou, M., Kalogeras, D., & Maglaris, V. (2012). Security standards and issues for grid computing. In N. Preve (Ed.), *Computational and data grids: Principles, applications and design* (pp. 248–264). Hershey, PA: Information Science Reference; doi:10.4018/978-1-61350-113-9.ch010

Mouratidis, H., & Kang, M. (2011). Secure by design: Developing secure software systems from the ground up. [IJSSE]. *International Journal of Secure Software Engineering*, 2(3), 23–41. doi:10.4018/jsse.2011070102

Murthy, A. S., Nagadevara, V., & De', R. (2012). Predictive models in cybercrime investigation: An application of data mining techniques. In J. Wang (Ed.), *Advancing the service sector with evolving technologies: Techniques and principles* (pp. 166–177). Hershey, PA: Business Science Reference; doi:10.4018/978-1-4666-0044-7.ch011

Nabi, S. I., Al-Ghmlas, G. S., & Alghathbar, K. (2012). Enterprise information security policies, standards, and procedures: A survey of available standards and guidelines. In M. Gupta, J. Walp, & R. Sharman (Eds.), *Strategic and practical approaches for information security governance: Technologies and applied solutions* (pp. 67–89). Hershey, PA: Information Science Reference; doi:10.4018/978-1-4666-0197-0.ch005

Nachtigal, S. (2011). E-business and security. In O. Bak & N. Stair (Eds.), *Impact of e-business technologies on public and private organizations: Industry comparisons and perspectives* (pp. 262–277). Hershey, PA: Business Science Reference; doi:10.4018/978-1-60960-501-8.ch016

Namal, S., & Gurtov, A. (2012). Security and mobility aspects of femtocell networks. In R. Saeed, B. Chaudhari, & R. Mokhtar (Eds.), *Femtocell communications and technologies: Business opportunities and deployment challenges* (pp. 124–156). Hershey, PA: Information Science Reference; doi:10.4018/978-1-4666-0092-8.ch008

Naqvi, D. E. (2011). Designing efficient security services infrastructure for virtualization oriented architectures. In H. Nemati (Ed.), *Pervasive information security and privacy developments: Trends and advancements* (pp. 149–171). Hershey, PA: Information Science Reference; doi:10.4018/978-1-61692-000-5.ch011

Neto, A. A., & Vieira, M. (2011). Security gaps in databases: A comparison of alternative software products for web applications support. [IJSSE]. *International Journal of Secure Software Engineering*, 2(3), 42–62. doi:10.4018/jsse.2011070103

Ngugi, B., Mana, J., & Segal, L. (2011). Evaluating the quality and usefulness of data breach information systems. [IJISP]. *International Journal of Information Security and Privacy*, 5(4), 31–46. doi:10.4018/jisp.2011100103

Nhlabatsi, A., Bandara, A., Hayashi, S., Haley, C., Jurjens, J., & Kaiya, H. ... Yu, Y. (2011). Security patterns: Comparing modeling approaches. In H. Mouratidis (Ed.), *Software engineering for secure systems: Industrial and research perspectives* (pp. 75-111). Hershey, PA: Information Science Reference. doi:10.4018/978-1-61520-837-1.ch004

Nicho, M. (2013). An information governance model for information security management. In D. Mellado, L. Enrique Sánchez, E. Fernández-Medina, & M. Piattini (Eds.), *IT security governance innovations: Theory and research* (pp. 155–189). Hershey, PA: Information Science Reference; doi:10.4018/978-1-4666-2083-4.ch007

Nicho, M., Fakhry, H., & Haiber, C. (2011). An integrated security governance framework for effective PCI DSS implementation. [IJISP]. *International Journal of Information Security and Privacy*, 5(3), 50–67. doi:10.4018/jisp.2011070104

Nobelis, N., Boudaoud, K., Delettre, C., & Riveill, M. (2012). Designing security properties-centric communication protocols using a component-based approach. [IJDST]. *International Journal of Distributed Systems and Technologies*, 3(1), 1–16. doi:10.4018/jdst.2012010101

Ohashi, M., & Hori, M. (2011). Security management services based on authentication roaming between different certificate authorities. In M. Cruz-Cunha & J. Varajao (Eds.), *Enterprise information systems design, implementation and management: Organizational applications* (pp. 72–84). Hershey, PA: Information Science Reference; doi:10.4018/978-1-61692-020-3.ch005

Okubo, T., Kaiya, H., & Yoshioka, N. (2012). Analyzing impacts on software enhancement caused by security design alternatives with patterns. [IJSSE]. *International Journal of Secure Software Engineering*, 3(1), 37–61. doi:10.4018/jsse.2012010103

Oost, D., & Chew, E. K. (2012). Investigating the concept of information security culture. In M. Gupta, J. Walp, & R. Sharman (Eds.), *Strategic and practical approaches for information security governance: Technologies and applied solutions* (pp. 1–12). Hershey, PA: Information Science Reference; doi:10.4018/978-1-4666-0197-0.ch001

Otero, A. R., Ejnioui, A., Otero, C. E., & Tejay, G. (2013). Evaluation of information security controls in organizations by grey relational analysis. [IJDTIS]. *International Journal of Dependable and Trustworthy Information Systems*, 2(3), 36–54. doi:10.4018/jdtis.2011070103

Ouedraogo, M., Mouratidis, H., Dubois, E., & Khadraoui, D. (2011). Security assurance evaluation and IT systems' context of use security criticality. [IJHCR]. *International Journal of Handheld Computing Research*, 2(4), 59–81. doi:10.4018/jhcr.2011100104

Pal, S. (2013). Cloud computing: Security concerns and issues. In A. Bento & A. Aggarwal (Eds.), *Cloud computing service and deployment models: Layers and management* (pp. 191–207). Hershey, PA: Business Science Reference; doi:10.4018/978-1-4666-2187-9.ch010

Palanisamy, R., & Mukerji, B. (2012). Security and privacy issues in e-government. In M. Shareef, N. Archer, & S. Dutta (Eds.), *E-government service maturity and development: Cultural, organizational and technological perspectives* (pp. 236–248). Hershey, PA: Information Science Reference; doi:10.4018/978-1-60960-848-4.ch013

Pan, Y., Yuan, B., & Mishra, S. (2011). Network security auditing. In D. Kar & M. Syed (Eds.), *Network security, administration and management: Advancing technology and practice* (pp. 131–157). Hershey, PA: Information Science Reference; doi:10.4018/978-1-60960-777-7.ch008

Patel, A., Taghavi, M., Júnior, J. C., Latih, R., & Zin, A. M. (2012). Safety measures for social computing in wiki learning environment. [IJISP]. *International Journal of Information Security and Privacy, 6*(2), 1–15. doi:10.4018/jisp.2012040101

Pathan, A. K. (2012). Security management in heterogeneous distributed sensor networks. In S. Bagchi (Ed.), *Ubiquitous multimedia and mobile agents: Models and implementations* (pp. 274–294). Hershey, PA: Information Science Reference; doi:10.4018/978-1-61350-107-8.ch012

Paul, C., & Porche, I. R. (2011). Toward a U.S. army cyber security culture. [IJCWT]. *International Journal of Cyber Warfare & Terrorism, 1*(3), 70–80. doi:10.4018/ijcwt.2011070105

Pavlidis, M., Mouratidis, H., & Islam, S. (2012). Modelling security using trust based concepts. [IJSSE]. *International Journal of Secure Software Engineering, 3*(2), 36–53. doi:10.4018/jsse.2012040102

Pendegraft, N., Rounds, M., & Stone, R. W. (2012). Factors influencing college students' use of computer security. In H. Nemati (Ed.), *Optimizing information security and advancing privacy assurance: New technologies* (pp. 225–234). Hershey, PA: Information Science Reference; doi:10.4018/978-1-4666-0026-3.ch013

Petkovic, M., & Ibraimi, L. (2011). Privacy and security in e-health applications. In C. Röcker & M. Ziefle (Eds.), *E-health, assistive technologies and applications for assisted living: Challenges and solutions* (pp. 23–48). Hershey, PA: Medical Information Science Reference; doi:10.4018/978-1-60960-469-1.ch002

Picazo-Sanchez, P., Ortiz-Martin, L., Peris-Lopez, P., & Hernandez-Castro, J. C. (2013). Security of EPC class-1. In P. Lopez, J. Hernandez-Castro, & T. Li (Eds.), *Security and trends in wireless identification and sensing platform tags: Advancements in RFID* (pp. 34–63). Hershey, PA: Information Science Reference; doi:10.4018/978-1-4666-1990-6.ch002

Pieters, W., Probst, C. W., Lukszo, Z., & Montoya, L. (2014). Cost-effectiveness of security measures: A model-based framework. In T. Tsiakis, T. Kargidis, & P. Katsaros (Eds.), *Approaches and processes for managing the economics of information systems* (pp. 139–156). Hershey, PA: Business Science Reference; doi:10.4018/978-1-4666-4983-5.ch009

Pirim, T., James, T., Boswell, K., Reithel, B., & Barkhi, R. (2011). Examining an individual's perceived need for privacy and security: Construct and scale development. In H. Nemati (Ed.), *Pervasive information security and privacy developments: Trends and advancements* (pp. 1–13). Hershey, PA: Information Science Reference; doi:10.4018/978-1-61692-000-5.ch001

Podhradsky, A., Casey, C., & Ceretti, P. (2012). The bluetooth honeypot project: Measuring and managing bluetooth risks in the workplace. [IJITN]. *International Journal of Interdisciplinary Telecommunications and Networking, 4*(3), 1–22. doi:10.4018/jitn.2012070101

Pomponiu, V. (2011). Security in e-health applications. In C. Röcker & M. Ziefle (Eds.), *E-health, assistive technologies and applications for assisted living: Challenges and solutions* (pp. 94–118). Hershey, PA: Medical Information Science Reference; doi:10.4018/978-1-60960-469-1.ch005

Pomponiu, V. (2014). Securing wireless ad hoc networks: State of the art and challenges. In *Crisis management: Concepts, methodologies, tools and applications* (pp. 81–101). Hershey, PA: Information Science Reference; doi:10.4018/978-1-4666-4707-7.ch004

Pope, M. B., Warkentin, M., & Luo, X. R. (2012). Evolutionary malware: Mobile malware, botnets, and malware toolkits. [IJWNBT]. *International Journal of Wireless Networks and Broadband Technologies, 2*(3), 52–60. doi:10.4018/ijwnbt.2012070105

Prakash, S., Vaish, A., Coul, N. G. S., Srinidhi, T., & Botsa, J. (2013). Child security in cyberspace through moral cognition. [IJISP]. *International Journal of Information Security and Privacy, 7*(1), 16–29. doi:10.4018/jisp.2013010102

Pye, G. (2011). Critical infrastructure systems: Security analysis and modelling approach. [IJCWT]. *International Journal of Cyber Warfare & Terrorism, 1*(3), 37–58. doi:10.4018/ijcwt.2011070103

Rahman, M. M., & Rezaul, K. M. (2012). Information security management: Awareness of threats in e-commerce. In M. Gupta, J. Walp, & R. Sharman (Eds.), *Threats, countermeasures, and advances in applied information security* (pp. 66–90). Hershey, PA: Information Science Reference; doi:10.4018/978-1-4666-0978-5.ch004

Rak, M., Ficco, M., Luna, J., Ghani, H., Suri, N., Panica, S., & Petcu, D. (2012). Security issues in cloud federations. In M. Villari, I. Brandic, & F. Tusa (Eds.), *Achieving federated and self-manageable cloud infrastructures: Theory and practice* (pp. 176–194). Hershey, PA: Business Science Reference; doi:10.4018/978-1-4666-1631-8.ch010

Ramachandran, M., & Mahmood, Z. (2011). A framework for internet security assessment and improvement process. In M. Ramachandran (Ed.), *Knowledge engineering for software development life cycles: Support technologies and applications* (pp. 244–255). Hershey, PA: Information Science Reference; doi:10.4018/978-1-60960-509-4.ch013

Ramachandran, S., Mundada, R., Bhattacharjee, A., Murthy, C., & Sharma, R. (2011). Classifying host anomalies: Using ontology in information security monitoring. In R. Santanam, M. Sethumadhavan, & M. Virendra (Eds.), *Cyber security, cyber crime and cyber forensics: Applications and perspectives* (pp. 70–86). Hershey, PA: Information Science Reference; doi:10.4018/978-1-60960-123-2.ch006

Ramamurthy, B. (2014). Securing business IT on the cloud. In S. Srinivasan (Ed.), *Security, trust, and regulatory aspects of cloud computing in business environments* (pp. 115–125). Hershey, PA: Information Science Reference; doi:10.4018/978-1-4666-5788-5.ch006

Raspotnig, C., & Opdahl, A. L. (2012). Improving security and safety modelling with failure sequence diagrams. [IJSSE]. *International Journal of Secure Software Engineering, 3*(1), 20–36. doi:10.4018/jsse.2012010102

Reddy, A., & Prasad, G. V. (2012). Consumer perceptions on security, privacy, and trust on e-portals. [IJOM]. *International Journal of Online Marketing, 2*(2), 10–24. doi:10.4018/ijom.2012040102

Richet, J. (2013). From young hackers to crackers. [IJTHI]. *International Journal of Technology and Human Interaction, 9*(3), 53–62. doi:10.4018/jthi.2013070104

Rjaibi, N., Rabai, L. B., Ben Aissa, A., & Mili, A. (2013). Mean failure cost as a measurable value and evidence of cybersecurity: E-learning case study. [IJSSE]. *International Journal of Secure Software Engineering, 4*(3), 64–81. doi:10.4018/jsse.2013070104

Roberts, L. D. (2012). Cyber identity theft. In *Cyber crime: Concepts, methodologies, tools and applications* (pp. 21–36). Hershey, PA: Information Science Reference; doi:10.4018/978-1-61350-323-2.ch103

Rodríguez, J., Fernández-Medina, E., Piattini, M., & Mellado, D. (2011). A security requirements engineering tool for domain engineering in software product lines. In N. Milanovic (Ed.), *Non-functional properties in service oriented architecture: Requirements, models and methods* (pp. 73–92). Hershey, PA: Information Science Reference; doi:10.4018/978-1-60566-794-2.ch004

Roldan, M., & Rea, A. (2011). Individual privacy and security in virtual worlds. In A. Rea (Ed.), *Security in virtual worlds, 3D webs, and immersive environments: Models for development, interaction, and management* (pp. 1–19). Hershey, PA: Information Science Reference; doi:10.4018/978-1-61520-891-3.ch001

Rowe, N. C., Garfinkel, S. L., Beverly, R., & Yannakogeorgos, P. (2011). Challenges in monitoring cyberarms compliance. [IJCWT]. *International Journal of Cyber Warfare & Terrorism, 1*(2), 35–48. doi:10.4018/ijcwt.2011040104

Rwabutaza, A., Yang, M., & Bourbakis, N. (2012). A comparative survey on cryptology-based methodologies. [IJISP]. *International Journal of Information Security and Privacy, 6*(3), 1–37. doi:10.4018/jisp.2012070101

Sadkhan, S. B., & Abbas, N. A. (2014). Privacy and security of wireless communication networks. In J. Rodrigues, K. Lin, & J. Lloret (Eds.), *Mobile networks and cloud computing convergence for progressive services and applications* (pp. 58–78). Hershey, PA: Information Science Reference; doi:10.4018/978-1-4666-4781-7.ch004

Saedy, M., & Mojtahed, V. (2011). Machine-to-machine communications and security solution in cellular systems. [IJITN]. *International Journal of Interdisciplinary Telecommunications and Networking, 3*(2), 66–75. doi:10.4018/jitn.2011040105

San Nicolas-Rocca, T., & Olfman, L. (2013). End user security training for identification and access management. [JOEUC]. *Journal of Organizational and End User Computing, 25*(4), 75–103. doi:10.4018/joeuc.2013100104

Satoh, F., Nakamura, Y., Mukhi, N. K., Tatsubori, M., & Ono, K. (2011). Model-driven approach for end-to-end SOA security configurations. In N. Milanovic (Ed.), *Non-functional properties in service oriented architecture: Requirements, models and methods* (pp. 268–298). Hershey, PA: Information Science Reference; doi:10.4018/978-1-60566-794-2.ch012

Saucez, D., Iannone, L., & Bonaventure, O. (2014). The map-and-encap locator/identifier separation paradigm: A security analysis. In M. Boucadair & D. Binet (Eds.), *Solutions for sustaining scalability in internet growth* (pp. 148–163). Hershey, PA: Information Science Reference; doi:10.4018/978-1-4666-4305-5.ch008

Schell, B. H., & Holt, T. J. (2012). A profile of the demographics, psychological predispositions, and social/behavioral patterns of computer hacker insiders and outsiders. In *Cyber crime: Concepts, methodologies, tools and applications* (pp. 1461–1484). Hershey, PA: Information Science Reference; doi:10.4018/978-1-61350-323-2.ch705

Schmidt, H. (2011). Threat and risk-driven security requirements engineering. [IJMCMC]. *International Journal of Mobile Computing and Multimedia Communications, 3*(1), 35–50. doi:10.4018/jmcmc.2011010103

Schmidt, H., Hatebur, D., & Heisel, M. (2011). A pattern-based method to develop secure software. In H. Mouratidis (Ed.), *Software engineering for secure systems: Industrial and research perspectives* (pp. 32–74). Hershey, PA: Information Science Reference; doi:10.4018/978-1-61520-837-1.ch003

Seale, R. O., & Hargiss, K. M. (2011). A proposed architecture for autonomous mobile agent intrusion prevention and malware defense in heterogeneous networks. [IJSITA]. *International Journal of Strategic Information Technology and Applications, 2*(4), 44–54. doi:10.4018/jsita.2011100104

Sen, J. (2013). Security and privacy challenges in cognitive wireless sensor networks. In N. Meghanathan & Y. Reddy (Eds.), *Cognitive radio technology applications for wireless and mobile ad hoc networks* (pp. 194–232). Hershey, PA: Information Science Reference; doi:10.4018/978-1-4666-4221-8.ch011

Sen, J. (2014). Security and privacy issues in cloud computing. In A. Ruiz-Martinez, R. Marin-Lopez, & F. Pereniguez-Garcia (Eds.), *Architectures and protocols for secure information technology infrastructures* (pp. 1–45). Hershey, PA: Information Science Reference; doi:10.4018/978-1-4666-4514-1.ch001

Sengupta, A., & Mazumdar, C. (2011). A markup language for the specification of information security governance requirements. [IJISP]. *International Journal of Information Security and Privacy, 5*(2), 33–53. doi:10.4018/jisp.2011040103

Shaqrah, A. A. (2011). The influence of internet security on e-business competence in Jordan: An empirical analysis. In *Global business: Concepts, methodologies, tools and applications* (pp. 1071–1086). Hershey, PA: Business Science Reference; doi:10.4018/978-1-60960-587-2.ch413

Shareef, M. A., & Kumar, V. (2012). Prevent/control identity theft: Impact on trust and consumers' purchase intention in B2C EC. [IRMJ]. *Information Resources Management Journal, 25*(3), 30–60. doi:10.4018/irmj.2012070102

Sharma, K., & Singh, A. (2011). Biometric security in the e-world. In H. Nemati & L. Yang (Eds.), *Applied cryptography for cyber security and defense: Information encryption and cyphering* (pp. 289–337). Hershey, PA: Information Science Reference; doi:10.4018/978-1-61520-783-1.ch013

Sharma, R. K. (2014). Physical layer security and its applications: A survey. In D. Rawat, B. Bista, & G. Yan (Eds.), *Security, Privacy, Trust, and Resource Management in Mobile and Wireless Communications* (pp. 29–60). Hershey, PA: Information Science Reference; doi:10.4018/978-1-4666-4691-9.ch003

Shaw, R., Keh, H., & Huang, N. (2011). Information security awareness on-line materials design with knowledge maps. [IJDET]. *International Journal of Distance Education Technologies, 9*(4), 41–56. doi:10.4018/jdet.2011100104

Shebanow, A., Perez, R., & Howard, C. (2012). The effect of firewall testing types on cloud security policies. [IJSITA]. *International Journal of Strategic Information Technology and Applications, 3*(3), 60–68. doi:10.4018/jsita.2012070105

Shen, Y., Li, Y., Wu, L., Liu, S., & Wen, Q. (2014). Data protection in the cloud era. In Y. Shen, Y. Li, L. Wu, S. Liu, & Q. Wen (Eds.), *Enabling the new era of cloud computing: Data security, transfer, and management* (pp. 132–154). Hershey, PA: Information Science Reference; doi:10.4018/978-1-4666-4801-2.ch007

Shen, Y., Li, Y., Wu, L., Liu, S., & Wen, Q. (2014). Enterprise security monitoring with the fusion center model. In Y. Shen, Y. Li, L. Wu, S. Liu, & Q. Wen (Eds.), *Enabling the new era of cloud computing: Data security, transfer, and management* (pp. 116–131). Hershey, PA: Information Science Reference; doi:10.4018/978-1-4666-4801-2.ch006

Shore, M. (2011). Cyber security and anti-social networking. In *Virtual communities: Concepts, methodologies, tools and applications* (pp. 1286–1297). Hershey, PA: Information Science Reference; doi:10.4018/978-1-60960-100-3.ch412

Siddiqi, J., Alqatawna, J., & Btoush, M. H. (2011). Do insecure systems increase global digital divide? In *Global business: Concepts, methodologies, tools and applications* (pp. 2102–2111). Hershey, PA: Business Science Reference; doi:10.4018/978-1-60960-587-2.ch717

Simpson, J. J., Simpson, M. J., Endicott-Popovsky, B., & Popovsky, V. (2012). Secure software education: A contextual model-based approach. In K. Khan (Ed.), *Security-aware systems applications and software development methods* (pp. 286–312). Hershey, PA: Information Science Reference; doi:10.4018/978-1-4666-1580-9.ch016

Singh, S. (2012). Security threats and issues with MANET. In K. Lakhtaria (Ed.), *Technological advancements and applications in mobile ad-hoc networks: Research trends* (pp. 247–263). Hershey, PA: Information Science Reference; doi:10.4018/978-1-4666-0321-9.ch015

Sockel, H., & Falk, L. K. (2012). Online privacy, vulnerabilities, and threats: A manager's perspective. In *Cyber crime: Concepts, methodologies, tools and applications* (pp. 101–123). Hershey, PA: Information Science Reference; doi:10.4018/978-1-61350-323-2.ch108

Spruit, M., & de Bruijn, W. (2012). CITS: The cost of IT security framework. [IJISP]. *International Journal of Information Security and Privacy*, 6(4), 94–116. doi:10.4018/jisp.2012100105

Srinivasan, C., Lakshmy, K., & Sethumadhavan, M. (2011). Complexity measures of cryptographically secure boolean functions. In R. Santanam, M. Sethumadhavan, & M. Virendra (Eds.), *Cyber security, cyber crime and cyber forensics: Applications and perspectives* (pp. 220–230). Hershey, PA: Information Science Reference; doi:10.4018/978-1-60960-123-2.ch015

Srivatsa, M., Agrawal, D., & McDonald, A. D. (2012). Security across disparate management domains in coalition MANETs. In *Wireless technologies: Concepts, methodologies, tools and applications* (pp. 1494–1518). Hershey, PA: Information Science Reference; doi:10.4018/978-1-61350-101-6.ch521

Stojanovic, M. D., Acimovic-Raspopovic, V. S., & Rakas, S. B. (2013). Security management issues for open source ERP in the NGN environment. In *Enterprise resource planning: Concepts, methodologies, tools, and applications* (pp. 789–804). Hershey, PA: Business Science Reference; doi:10.4018/978-1-4666-4153-2.ch046

Stoll, M., & Breu, R. (2012). Information security governance and standard based management systems. In M. Gupta, J. Walp, & R. Sharman (Eds.), *Strategic and practical approaches for information security governance: Technologies and applied solutions* (pp. 261–282). Hershey, PA: Information Science Reference; doi:10.4018/978-1-4666-0197-0.ch015

Sundaresan, M., & Boopathy, D. (2014). Different perspectives of cloud security. In S. Srinivasan (Ed.), *Security, trust, and regulatory aspects of cloud computing in business environments* (pp. 73–90). Hershey, PA: Information Science Reference; doi:10.4018/978-1-4666-5788-5.ch004

Takabi, H., Joshi, J. B., & Ahn, G. (2013). Security and privacy in cloud computing: Towards a comprehensive framework. In X. Yang & L. Liu (Eds.), *Principles, methodologies, and service-oriented approaches for cloud computing* (pp. 164–184). Hershey, PA: Business Science Reference; doi:10.4018/978-1-4666-2854-0.ch007

Takabi, H., Zargar, S. T., & Joshi, J. B. (2014). Mobile cloud computing and its security and privacy challenges. In D. Rawat, B. Bista, & G. Yan (Eds.), *Security, privacy, trust, and resource management in mobile and wireless communications* (pp. 384–407). Hershey, PA: Information Science Reference; doi:10.4018/978-1-4666-4691-9.ch016

Takemura, T. (2014). Unethical information security behavior and organizational commitment. In T. Tsiakis, T. Kargidis, & P. Katsaros (Eds.), *Approaches and processes for managing the economics of information systems* (pp. 181–198). Hershey, PA: Business Science Reference; doi:10.4018/978-1-4666-4983-5.ch011

Talib, S., Clarke, N. L., & Furnell, S. M. (2011). Establishing a personalized information security culture. [IJMCMC]. *International Journal of Mobile Computing and Multimedia Communications*, *3*(1), 63–79. doi:10.4018/jmcmc.2011010105

Talukder, A. K. (2011). Securing next generation internet services. In R. Santanam, M. Sethumadhavan, & M. Virendra (Eds.), *Cyber security, cyber crime and cyber forensics: Applications and perspectives* (pp. 87–105). Hershey, PA: Information Science Reference; doi:10.4018/978-1-60960-123-2.ch007

Tchepnda, C., Moustafa, H., Labiod, H., & Bourdon, G. (2011). Vehicular networks security: Attacks, requirements, challenges and current contributions. In K. Curran (Ed.), *Ubiquitous developments in ambient computing and intelligence: Human-centered applications* (pp. 43–55). Hershey, PA: Information Science Reference; doi:10.4018/978-1-60960-549-0.ch004

Tereshchenko, N. (2012). US foreign policy challenges of non-state actors' cyber terrorism against critical infrastructure. [IJCWT]. *International Journal of Cyber Warfare & Terrorism*, *2*(4), 28–48. doi:10.4018/ijcwt.2012100103

Thurimella, R., & Baird, L. C. (2011). Network security. In H. Nemati & L. Yang (Eds.), *Applied cryptography for cyber security and defense: Information encryption and cyphering* (pp. 1–31). Hershey, PA: Information Science Reference; doi:10.4018/978-1-61520-783-1.ch001

Thurimella, R., & Mitchell, W. (2011). Cloak and dagger: Man-in-the-middle and other insidious attacks. In H. Nemati (Ed.), *Security and privacy assurance in advancing technologies: New developments* (pp. 252–270). Hershey, PA: Information Science Reference; doi:10.4018/978-1-60960-200-0.ch016

Tiwari, S., Singh, A., Singh, R. S., & Singh, S. K. (2013). Internet security using biometrics. In *IT policy and ethics: Concepts, methodologies, tools, and applications* (pp. 1680–1707). Hershey, PA: Information Science Reference; doi:10.4018/978-1-4666-2919-6.ch074

Tomaiuolo, M. (2012). Trust enforcing and trust building, different technologies and visions. [IJCWT]. *International Journal of Cyber Warfare & Terrorism*, *2*(4), 49–66. doi:10.4018/ijcwt.2012100104

Tomaiuolo, M. (2014). Trust management and delegation for the administration of web services. In I. Portela & F. Almeida (Eds.), *Organizational, legal, and technological dimensions of information system administration* (pp. 18–37). Hershey, PA: Information Science Reference; doi:10.4018/978-1-4666-4526-4.ch002

Touhafi, A., Braeken, A., Cornetta, G., Mentens, N., & Steenhaut, K. (2011). Secure techniques for remote reconfiguration of wireless embedded systems. In M. Cruz-Cunha & F. Moreira (Eds.), *Handbook of research on mobility and computing: Evolving technologies and ubiquitous impacts* (pp. 930–951). Hershey, PA: Information Science Reference; doi:10.4018/978-1-60960-042-6.ch058

Traore, I., & Woungang, I. (2013). Software security engineering – Part I: Security requirements and risk analysis. In K. Buragga & N. Zaman (Eds.), *Software development techniques for constructive information systems design* (pp. 221–255). Hershey, PA: Information Science Reference; doi:10.4018/978-1-4666-3679-8.ch012

Tripathi, M., Gaur, M., & Laxmi, V. (2014). Security challenges in wireless sensor network. In D. Rawat, B. Bista, & G. Yan (Eds.), *Security, privacy, trust, and resource management in mobile and wireless communications* (pp. 334–359). Hershey, PA: Information Science Reference; doi:10.4018/978-1-4666-4691-9.ch014

Trösterer, S., Beck, E., Dalpiaz, F., Paja, E., Giorgini, P., & Tscheligi, M. (2012). Formative user-centered evaluation of security modeling: Results from a case study. [IJSSE]. *International Journal of Secure Software Engineering*, 3(1), 1–19. doi:10.4018/jsse.2012010101

Tsiakis, T. (2013). The role of information security and cryptography in digital democracy: (Human) rights and freedom. In C. Akrivopoulou & N. Garipidis (Eds.), *Digital democracy and the impact of technology on governance and politics: New globalized practices* (pp. 158–174). Hershey, PA: Information Science Reference; doi:10.4018/978-1-4666-3637-8.ch009

Tsiakis, T., Kargidis, T., & Chatzipoulidis, A. (2013). IT security governance in e-banking. In D. Mellado, L. Enrique Sánchez, E. Fernández-Medina, & M. Piattini (Eds.), *IT security governance innovations: Theory and research* (pp. 13–46). Hershey, PA: Information Science Reference; doi:10.4018/978-1-4666-2083-4.ch002

Turgeman-Goldschmidt, O. (2011). Between hackers and white-collar offenders. In T. Holt & B. Schell (Eds.), *Corporate hacking and technology-driven crime: Social dynamics and implications* (pp. 18–37). Hershey, PA: Information Science Reference; doi:10.4018/978-1-61692-805-6.ch002

Tvrdíková, M. (2012). Information system integrated security. In M. Gupta, J. Walp, & R. Sharman (Eds.), *Strategic and practical approaches for information security governance: Technologies and applied solutions* (pp. 158–169). Hershey, PA: Information Science Reference; doi:10.4018/978-1-4666-0197-0.ch009

Uffen, J., & Breitner, M. H. (2013). Management of technical security measures: An empirical examination of personality traits and behavioral intentions. [IJSODIT]. *International Journal of Social and Organizational Dynamics in IT*, 3(1), 14–31. doi:10.4018/ijsodit.2013010102

Vance, A., & Siponen, M. T. (2012). IS security policy violations: A rational choice perspective. [JOEUC]. *Journal of Organizational and End User Computing*, 24(1), 21–41. doi:10.4018/joeuc.2012010102

Veltsos, C. (2011). Mitigating the blended threat: Protecting data and educating users. In D. Kar & M. Syed (Eds.), *Network security, administration and management: Advancing technology and practice* (pp. 20–37). Hershey, PA: Information Science Reference; doi:10.4018/978-1-60960-777-7.ch002

Venkataraman, R., Pushpalatha, M., & Rao, T. R. (2014). Trust management and modeling techniques in wireless communications. In D. Rawat, B. Bista, & G. Yan (Eds.), *Security, privacy, trust, and resource management in mobile and wireless communications* (pp. 278–294). Hershey, PA: Information Science Reference; doi:10.4018/978-1-4666-4691-9.ch012

Venkataraman, R., & Rao, T. R. (2012). Security issues and models in mobile ad hoc networks. In K. Lakhtaria (Ed.), *Technological advancements and applications in mobile ad-hoc networks: Research trends* (pp. 219–227). Hershey, PA: Information Science Reference; doi:10.4018/978-1-4666-0321-9.ch013

Viney, D. (2011). Future trends in digital security. In D. Kerr, J. Gammack, & K. Bryant (Eds.), *Digital business security development: Management technologies* (pp. 173–190). Hershey, PA: Business Science Reference; doi:10.4018/978-1-60566-806-2.ch009

Vinod, P., Laxmi, V., & Gaur, M. (2011). Metamorphic malware analysis and detection methods. In R. Santanam, M. Sethumadhavan, & M. Virendra (Eds.), *Cyber security, cyber crime and cyber forensics: Applications and perspectives* (pp. 178–202). Hershey, PA: Information Science Reference; doi:10.4018/978-1-60960-123-2.ch013

von Solms, R., & Warren, M. (2011). Towards the human information security firewall. [IJCWT]. *International Journal of Cyber Warfare & Terrorism, 1*(2), 10–17. doi:10.4018/ijcwt.2011040102

Wall, D. S. (2011). Micro-frauds: Virtual robberies, stings and scams in the information age. In T. Holt & B. Schell (Eds.), *Corporate hacking and technology-driven crime: Social dynamics and implications* (pp. 68–86). Hershey, PA: Information Science Reference; doi:10.4018/978-1-61692-805-6.ch004

Wang, H., Zhao, J. L., & Chen, G. (2012). Managing data security in e-markets through relationship driven access control. [JDM]. *Journal of Database Management, 23*(2), 1–21. doi:10.4018/jdm.2012040101

Warren, M., & Leitch, S. (2011). Protection of Australia in the cyber age. [IJCWT]. *International Journal of Cyber Warfare & Terrorism, 1*(1), 35–40. doi:10.4018/ijcwt.2011010104

Weber, S. G., & Gustiené, P. (2013). Crafting requirements for mobile and pervasive emergency response based on privacy and security by design principles. [IJISCRAM]. *International Journal of Information Systems for Crisis Response and Management, 5*(2), 1–18. doi:10.4018/jis-crm.2013040101

Wei, J., Lin, B., & Loho-Noya, M. (2013). Development of an e-healthcare information security risk assessment method. [JDM]. *Journal of Database Management, 24*(1), 36–57. doi:10.4018/jdm.2013010103

Weippl, E. R., & Riedl, B. (2012). Security, trust, and privacy on mobile devices and multimedia applications. In *Cyber crime: Concepts, methodologies, tools and applications* (pp. 228–244). Hershey, PA: Information Science Reference; doi:10.4018/978-1-61350-323-2.ch202

White, G., & Long, J. (2012). Global information security factors. In H. Nemati (Ed.), *Optimizing information security and advancing privacy assurance: New technologies* (pp. 163–174). Hershey, PA: Information Science Reference; doi:10.4018/978-1-4666-0026-3.ch009

White, S. C., Sedigh, S., & Hurson, A. R. (2013). Security concepts for cloud computing. In X. Yang & L. Liu (Eds.), *Principles, methodologies, and service-oriented approaches for cloud computing* (pp. 116–142). Hershey, PA: Business Science Reference; doi:10.4018/978-1-4666-2854-0.ch005

Whyte, B., & Harrison, J. (2011). State of practice in secure software: Experts' views on best ways ahead. In H. Mouratidis (Ed.), *Software engineering for secure systems: Industrial and research perspectives* (pp. 1–14). Hershey, PA: Information Science Reference; doi:10.4018/978-1-61520-837-1.ch001

Wu, Y., & Saunders, C. S. (2011). Governing information security: Governance domains and decision rights allocation patterns. [IRMJ]. *Information Resources Management Journal, 24*(1), 28–45. doi:10.4018/irmj.2011010103

Yadav, S. B. (2011). SEACON: An integrated approach to the analysis and design of secure enterprise architecture–based computer networks. In H. Nemati (Ed.), *Pervasive information security and privacy developments: Trends and advancements* (pp. 309–331). Hershey, PA: Information Science Reference; doi:10.4018/978-1-61692-000-5.ch020

Yadav, S. B. (2012). A six-view perspective framework for system security: Issues, risks, and requirements. In H. Nemati (Ed.), *Optimizing information security and advancing privacy assurance: New technologies* (pp. 58–90). Hershey, PA: Information Science Reference; doi:10.4018/978-1-4666-0026-3.ch004

Yamany, H. F., Allison, D. S., & Capretz, M. A. (2013). Developing proactive security dimensions for SOA. In *IT policy and ethics: Concepts, methodologies, tools, and applications* (pp. 900–922). Hershey, PA: Information Science Reference; doi:10.4018/978-1-4666-2919-6.ch041

Yan, G., Rawat, D. B., Bista, B. B., & Chen, L. (2014). Location security in vehicular wireless networks. In D. Rawat, B. Bista, & G. Yan (Eds.), *Security, privacy, trust, and resource management in mobile and wireless communications* (pp. 108–133). Hershey, PA: Information Science Reference; doi:10.4018/978-1-4666-4691-9.ch006

Yaokumah, W. (2013). Evaluating the effectiveness of information security governance practices in developing nations: A case of Ghana. [IJITBAG]. *International Journal of IT/Business Alignment and Governance, 4*(1), 27–43. doi:10.4018/jitbag.2013010103

Yates, D., & Harris, A. (2011). International ethical attitudes and behaviors: Implications for organizational information security policy. In M. Dark (Ed.), *Information assurance and security ethics in complex systems: Interdisciplinary perspectives* (pp. 55–80). Hershey, PA: Information Science Reference; doi:10.4018/978-1-61692-245-0.ch004

Yau, S. S., Yin, Y., & An, H. (2011). An adaptive approach to optimizing tradeoff between service performance and security in service-based systems. [IJWSR]. *International Journal of Web Services Research, 8*(2), 74–91. doi:10.4018/jwsr.2011040104

Zadig, S. M., & Tejay, G. (2012). Emerging cybercrime trends: Legal, ethical, and practical issues. In A. Dudley, J. Braman, & G. Vincenti (Eds.), *Investigating cyber law and cyber ethics: Issues, impacts and practices* (pp. 37–56). Hershey, PA: Information Science Reference; doi:10.4018/978-1-61350-132-0.ch003

Zafar, H., Ko, M., & Osei-Bryson, K. (2012). Financial impact of information security breaches on breached firms and their non-breached competitors. [IRMJ]. *Information Resources Management Journal, 25*(1), 21–37. doi:10.4018/irmj.2012010102

Zapata, B. C., & Alemán, J. L. (2013). Security risks in cloud computing: An analysis of the main vulnerabilities. In D. Rosado, D. Mellado, E. Fernandez-Medina, & M. Piattini (Eds.), *Security engineering for cloud computing: Approaches and tools* (pp. 55–71). Hershey, PA: Information Science Reference; doi:10.4018/978-1-4666-2125-1.ch004

Zboril, F., Horacek, J., Drahansky, M., & Hanacek, P. (2012). Security in wireless sensor networks with mobile codes. In M. Gupta, J. Walp, & R. Sharman (Eds.), *Threats, countermeasures, and advances in applied information security* (pp. 411–425). Hershey, PA: Information Science Reference; doi:10.4018/978-1-4666-0978-5.ch021

Zhang, J. (2012). Trust management for VANETs: Challenges, desired properties and future directions. [IJDST]. *International Journal of Distributed Systems and Technologies*, *3*(1), 48–62. doi:10.4018/jdst.2012010104

Zhang, Y., He, L., Shu, L., Hara, T., & Nishio, S. (2012). Security issues on outlier detection and countermeasure for distributed hierarchical wireless sensor networks. In A. Pathan, M. Pathan, & H. Lee (Eds.), *Advancements in distributed computing and internet technologies: Trends and issues* (pp. 182–210). Hershey, PA: Information Science Publishing; doi:10.4018/978-1-61350-110-8.ch009

Zheng, X., & Oleshchuk, V. (2012). Security enhancement of peer-to-peer session initiation. In M. Gupta, J. Walp, & R. Sharman (Eds.), *Threats, countermeasures, and advances in applied information security* (pp. 281–308). Hershey, PA: Information Science Reference; doi:10.4018/978-1-4666-0978-5.ch015

Zineddine, M. (2012). Is your automated healthcare information secure? In M. Watfa (Ed.), *E-healthcare systems and wireless communications: Current and future challenges* (pp. 128–142). Hershey, PA: Medical Information Science Reference; doi:10.4018/978-1-61350-123-8.ch006

Compilation of References

2012 Best Mobile Security Software Comparisons and Reviews. (2012). Retrieved April 17, 2012, from Top Ten Reviews: http://mobile-security-software-review.toptenreviews.com/

2012. Norton, C. C. R. (2012, January 1). Retreived May 3, 2014, from http://now-static.norton.com/now/en/pu/images/Promotions/2012/cybercrimeReport/2012_Norton_Cybercrime_Report_Master_FINAL_050912.pdf

Abassi, R., & Guemara El Fatmi, S. (2012a). Towards a Generic Trust Management Model. In *Proceedings of the 19th International Conference on Telecommunication, ICT 2012*, Jounieh, Lebanon.

Abassi, R., & Guemara El Fatmi, S. (2012b). A Trust based Delegation Scheme for Ad Hoc Networks. In *Proceedings of the 7th International Conference on Risks and Security of Internet and Systems CRISIS 2012*, Cork, Ireland.

Abbasi, A., & Chen, H. (2005). Applying authorship analysis to extremist-group web forum messages. IEEE Intelligent Systems, 20(5), 67–75.

Abbasi, A., & Chen, H. (2006). Visualizing authorship for identification. In *Intelligence and Security Informatics* (pp. 60–71). Springer Berlin Heidelberg.

Abdalkrim, G. M. (2013). The impact of strategic planning activities on private sector organizations performance in Sudan: An empirical research. *International Journal of Business and Management*, 8(10). doi:10.5539/ijbm.v8n10p134

Accardi, K. (2009). Is violating an internet service provider's terms of service an example of computer fraud and abuse: An analytical look at the computer fraud and abuse act, lori drew's conviction and cyberbullying. *W.St. UL Rev.*, 37, 67.

Adams, A., & Sasse, M. A. (1999). Users are not the enemy. *Communications of the ACM*, 42(12), 40–46. doi:10.1145/322796.322806

Adams, N., Stiles, R., Zimdars, A., Timmons, R., Leung, J., Stachnick, G., & Mehrotra, S. et al. (2013). Consequence analysis of complex events on critical U.S. infrastructure. *Communications of the ACM*, 56(6), 83–91. doi:10.1145/2461256.2461276 PMID:25284821

Adolphi, B., & Langweg, H. (2012). Security Add-Ons for Mobile Platforms. In A. Jøsang & B. Carlsson (Eds.), *Secure IT Systems* (Vol. 7617, pp. 17–30). Springer Berlin Heidelberg. doi:10.1007/978-3-642-34210-3_2

Africa, A. (2014). The reality of cybercrime in Africa. Informational. *Alert Africa*. Accessed April 28. http://alertafrica.com/

Ahmad, N., Amer, T. N., Qutaifan, F., & Alhilali, A. (2013). Technology adoption model and a road map to successful implementation of ITIL. *Journal of Enterprise Information Management*, 26(5), 553–576. doi:10.1108/JEIM-07-2013-0041

Akerlof, G. A. (1970). The market for" lemons": Quality uncertainty and the market mechanism. *The Quarterly Journal of Economics*, 84(3), 488–500. doi:10.2307/1879431

Akiva, N., & Koppel, M. (2012, August). *Identifying Distinct Components of a Multi-author Document* (pp. 205–209). EISIC.

Al Bawaba. (2009, Jul 13). Rise in cyber crime, cyber terrorism and cyber espionage tied heavily to data-stealing malware. Retrieved from thefreelibrary.com/Rise+in+Cyber+Crime,+Cyber+Terrorism+and+Cyber+Espionage+Tied...-a0203518026

Alazab, A., Alazab, M., Abawajy, J., & Hobbs, M. (2011). *Web application protection against SQL injection attack.* Paper presented at the 7th International Conference on Information Technology and Applications.

Alazab, M., & Batten, L. (2012). Synchronized-blocking mode, Technical report.

Alazab, M., Monsamy, V., Batten, L., Lantz, P., & Tian, R. (2012). *Analysis of Malicious and Benign Android Applications.* Paper presented at the International Conference on Distributed Computing Systems Workshops (ICDCSW), 2012 32nd. doi:10.1109/ICDCSW.2012.13

Alazab, M., Venkataraman, S., & Watters, P. (2010, 19-20 July 2010). *Towards Understanding Malware Behaviour by the Extraction of API Calls.* Paper presented at the Cybercrime and Trustworthy Computing Workshop (CTC), 2010 Second.

Alazab, M., Venkatraman, S., Watters, P., & Alazab, M. (2011). *Zero-day malware detection based on supervised learning algorithms of API call signatures.* Paper presented at the Ninth Australasian Data Mining Conference: AusDM 2011, Ballarat, Australia.

Alazab, M. (2014). *Analysis on Smartphone Devices for Detection and Prevention of Malware. (Doctor of Philosophy).* Deakin University, Deakin University.

Alazab, M., & Venkatraman, S. (2013). Detecting malicious behaviour using supervised learning algorithms of the function calls. *International Journal of Electronic Security and Digital Forensics, 5*(2), 90–109. doi:10.1504/IJESDF.2013.055047

Alazab, M., Venkatraman, S., Watters, P., Alazab, M., & Alazab, A. (2012). Cybercrime: The Case of Obfuscated Malware. In C. Georgiadis, H. Jahankhani, E. Pimenidis, R. Bashroush, & A. Al-Nemrat (Eds.), *Global Security, Safety and Sustainability & e-Democracy* (Vol. 99, pp. 204–211). Springer Berlin Heidelberg. doi:10.1007/978-3-642-33448-1_28

Al-Busaidi, K. A. (2009). The impact of learning management system characteristics and user characteristics on the acceptance of e-learning. *International Journal of Global Management Studies, 1*(2), 75–91.

Alseadoon, I., Chan, T., Foo, E., & Gonzales Nieto, J. (2012, January). Who is more susceptible to phishing emails? A Saudi Arabian study. In *Proceedings of the 23rd Australasian Conference on Information Systems 2012* (pp. 1-11). ACIS.

Al-Shurman, M., Yoo, S., & Park, S. (2004). Black Hole Attack in Mobile Ad Hoc Networks. In *the 42nd Annual Southeast Regional Conference. 2004.* Huntsville, AB: ACM. doi:10.1145/986537.986560

Andersen, D. G. (2003). Mayday: Distributed Filtering for Internet Services. In *4th USENIX Symposium on Internet Technologies and Systems (USITS). 2003.* Seattle, Washington.

Anderson, J. M., & Evans, K. S. (2013). A new way of evaluating cybersecurity to reduce risk. *Public Management, 42*(3), 50–53.

Anderson, T., Roscoe, T., & Wetherall, D. (2004). Preventing Internet Denial-of-Service with Capabilities. *Computer Communication Review, 34*(1), 39–44. doi:10.1145/972374.972382

Anti-Phishing Working Group. (2007). *Phishing Activity Trends Report.* Retrieved December 2014, from docs.apwg.org/reports/apwg_report_dec_2007.pdf

Argamon, S., Koppel, M., Pennebaker, J. W., & Schler, J. (2009). Automatically profiling the author of an anonymous text. *Communications of the ACM, 52*(2), 119–123.

Argamon, S., & Levitan, S. (2005, June). Measuring the usefulness of function words for authorship attribution. In *Proceedings of the Joint Conference of the Association for Computers and the Humanities and the Association for Literary and Linguistic Computing.*

Arijita, B., Sarmistha, N., & Chandreyee, C. (2012). Reputation based trust management system for MANET. *3rd International Conference on Emerging Applications of Information Technology*, pp.376-381.

Asokan, N., & Ginzboorg, P. (2000). Key Agreement in Ad-hoc networks. *Computer Communications, 23*(17), 1627–1637. doi:10.1016/S0140-3664(00)00249-8

Atkinson, R. (2006). Spaces of discipline and control: The compounded citizenship of social renting. *Housing, Urban Governance and Anti-Social Behaviour: Perspectives. Policy & Practice*, 99–116.

Avaya Data Network Solutions. (2014). Technology products. *Avaya Data Network Solutions*. Accessed April 28. http://www.avaya.com/usa/products/networking

Ayers, R., Brothers, S., & Jansen, W. (2013). Guidelines on Mobile Device Forensics (Draft). *NIST Special Publication, 800*, 101.

Babu, K., Franklin, A., & Murthy, S. (2008). On the Prevention of Collusion Attack in OLSR-based mobile ad hoc networks. In *Proceedings of the International Conference of Networks*, pp 1-6.

Backes, M., Gerling, S., & von Styp-Rekowsky, P. (2011). *A Local Cross-Site Scripting Attack against Android Phones*. Retrieved April 4, 2015, from https://www.infsec.cs.uni-saarland.de/projects/android-vuln/android_xss.pdf

Baker, L. D. (2009). President Obama's chilling cybersecurity challenge. *Public Management, 38*(1), 90–92.

Baker, S. A. (2012). From the criminal crowd to the "mediated crowd": The impact of social media on the 2011 english riots. *Safer Communities, 11*(1), 40–49. doi:10.1108/17578041211200100

Ballagas, R., Rohs, M., Sheridan, J. G., & Borchers, J. (2004, September). BYOD: Bring your own device. In *Proceedings of the Workshop on Ubiquitous Display Environments, Ubicomp* (Vol. 2004*)*.

Bandura, A. (1986). The explanatory and predictive scope of self-efficacy theory. *Journal of Clinical and Social Psychology, 4*(3), 359–373. doi:10.1521/jscp.1986.4.3.359

Barbir, A., Murphy, S., & Yang, Y. (2004). *Generic Threats to Routing Protocols 2004, IETF Internet draft.* Available at: http://www.ietf.org/internet-drafts/draft-ietfrpsec-routing-threats-07.txt. Last accessed: 29/09/14.

Barrera, D., & Van Oorschot, P. (2011). Secure Software Installation on Smartphones. *IEEE Security and Privacy, 9*(3), 42–48. doi:10.1109/MSP.2010.202

Barrios, R. (2013). A Multi-Level Approach to Intrusion Detection and Insider Threat. *Journal of Information Security., 4*(1), 54–65. doi:10.4236/jis.2013.41007

Bayer, U., Kirda, E., & Kruegel, C. (2010). *Improving the efficiency of dynamic malware analysis.* Paper presented at the In proceedings of the 2010 ACM Symposium on Applied Computing, Sierre, Switzerland. doi:10.1145/1774088.1774484

Becher, M., Freiling, F., & Leider, B. (2007, June). On the effort to create smartphone worms in Windows Mobile. *Proceedings of the 2007 IEEE workshop on Information Assurance.* United States Military Academy. West Point, NY. Retrieved from http://pi1.informatik.uni-mannheim.de/filepool/publications/on-the-effort-to-create-smartphone-worms-in-windows-mobile.pdf

Bellovin, S. M., & Merrit, M. (1992). Encrypted Key Exchange: *Password-Based Protocols Secure Against Dictionary Attacks. IEEE Symposium on Research in Security and Privacy.*

Ben Ghrobel-Talbi, M., Cuppens, F., Cuppens-Boulahia, N., & Bouhoula, A. (2007). Managing Delegation in Access Control Models. 15th International Conference on Advanced Computing & Communication (AD'COM 2007), Guwahati, India, pp. 744-751. doi:10.1109/ADCOM.2007.105

Bencsáth, B., & Vajda, I. (2004). Protection Against DDoS Attacks Based On Traffic Level Measurements. In *International Symposium on Collaborative Technologies and Systems.* 2004. San Diego, CA.

Benkler, Y. (2011). Free Irresponsible Press: Wikileaks and the Battle over the Soul of the Networked Fourth Estate. *Harvard Civil Rights-Civil Liberties Law Review, 46*, 311.

Berghel, H. (2003). The discipline of Internet forensics. *Communications of the ACM, 46*(8), 15. doi:10.1145/859670.859687

Bhatia, T. K., & Ritchie, W. C. (2004). Bilingualism in the Global Media and Advertising. In T. K. Bhatia & W. C. Ritchie (Eds.), *The Handbook of Bilingualism* (pp. 513–546). Oxford: Blackwell Publishing Ltd.

Bhatia, T. K., & Ritchie, W. C. (2013). Multilingualism and Forensic Linguistics. In *The Handbook of Bilingualism and Multilingualism* (pp. 671–701). Malden, Oxford: Blackwell Publishing Ltd.

Bhattacharya, D. (2008) *Leardership styles and information security in small businesses: An empirical investigation* (Doctoral dissertation, University of Phoenix). Retrieved from www.phoenix.edu/apololibrary

Bhavani, A. B. (2013). Cross-site Scripting Attacks on Android WebView. *arXiv preprint arXiv:1304.7451.*

Bhrommalee, P. (2012). Students' attitudes toward e-learning: A case study in a Thai university. *Clute Institute International Conference*, pp. 567–577.

Bhuasiri, W., Xaymoungkhoun, O., Zo, H., Rho, J. J., & Ciganek, A. P. (2012). Critical success factors for e-learning in developing countries: A comparative analysis between ICT experts and faculty. *Computers & Education, 58*(2), 843–855. doi:10.1016/j.compedu.2011.10.010

Binkley, J., & Trost, W. (2001). Authenticated Ad-hoc Routing at the Link Layer for Mobile Systems. *Wireless Networks, 7*(2), 139–145. doi:10.1023/A:1016633521987

Bishop, J. (2012b). Tackling internet abuse in great britain: Towards a framework for classifying severities of 'flame trolling'. *The 11th International Conference on Security and Management (SAM'12)*, Las Vegas, NV.

Bishop, J. (2013d). Internet trolling and other cyberlaw issues in the UK and the international arena. In D. H. Goldhush, K. Ossian, T. F. Claypoole, J. K. Sherwood, D. Schnapp, C. Bal & J. Bishop (Eds.), Understanding developments in cyberspace law (2013th ed., pp. 109-120). Eagan, MI: West Publishing Co.

Bishop, J. (2014a). 'U r bias love:' Using 'bleasure' and 'motif' as forensic linguistic means to annotate twitter and newsblog comments for the purpose of multimedia forensics. *The 11th International Conference on Web Based Communities and Social Media*, Lisbon, PT.

Bishop, J. (2014f). Using the legal concepts of 'forensic linguistics,' 'bleasure' and 'motif' to enhance multimedia forensics. *The 13th International Conference on Security and Management (SAM'14)*, Las Vegas, NV.

Bishop, J. (In Press). Digital teens and the 'antisocial Network': Prevalence of troublesome online youth groups and internet trolling in great Britain. *International Journal of E-Politics*, Carrabis, A. B., & Haimovitch, S. D. (2011). Cyberbullying: Adaptation from the old school sandlot to the 21st century world wide web-the court system and technology law's race to keep pace. *J. Tech. L. & Pol'Y, 16*, 143.

Bishop, J. (2008). Increasing capital revenue in social networking communities: Building social and economic relationships through avatars and characters. In C. Romm-Livermore & K. Setzekorn (Eds.), *Social networking communities and eDating services: Concepts and implications* (pp. 60–77). Hershey, PA: IGI Global.

Bishop, J. (2010). Tough on data misuse, tough on the causes of data misuse: A review of new labour's approach to information security and regulating the misuse of digital information (1997–2010). *International Review of Law Computers & Technology, 24*(3), 299–303. doi:10.1080/13600869.2010.522336

Bishop, J. (2011a). All's WELL that ends WELL: A comparative analysis of the constitutional and administrative frameworks of cyberspace and the united kingdom. In A. Dudley-Sponaugle & J. Braman (Eds.), *Investigating cyber law and cyber ethics: Issues, impacts and practices* (). Hershey, PA: IGI Global.

Bishop, J. (2011b). *The equatrics of intergenerational knowledge transformation in techno-cultures: Towards a model for enhancing information management in virtual worlds. (Unpublished MScEcon)*. Aberystwyth, UK: Aberystwyth University.

Bishop, J. (2011c). The role of the prefrontal cortex in social orientation construction: A pilot study. *The British Psychological Society's Sustainable Well-being Conference*, Wrexham, GB.

Bishop, J. (2012a). Scope and limitations in the government of wales act 2006 for tackling internet abuses in the form of 'Flame trolling'. *Statute Law Review*, *33*(2), 207–216. doi:10.1093/slr/hms016

Bishop, J. (2012c). Taming the chatroom bob: The role of brain-computer interfaces that manipulate prefrontal cortex optimization for increasing participation of victims of traumatic sex and other abuse online. *Proceedings of the 13th International Conference on Bioinformatics and Computational Biology (BIOCOMP'12)*, Las Vegas, NV.

Bishop, J. (2013a). The art of trolling law enforcement: A review and model for implementing 'flame trolling' legislation enacted in great britain (1981–2012). *International Review of Law Computers & Technology*, *27*(3), 301–318. doi:10.1080/13600869.2013.796706

Bishop, J. (2013b). The effect of deindividuation of the internet troller on criminal procedure implementation: An interview with a hater. *International Journal of Cyber Criminology*, *7*(1), 28–48.

Bishop, J. (2013c). Increasing capital revenue in social networking communities: Building social and economic relationships through avatars and characters. In J. Bishop (Ed.), *Examining the concepts, issues, and implications of internet trolling* (pp. 44–61). Hershey, PA: IGI Global. doi:10.4018/978-1-4666-2803-8.ch005

Bishop, J. (2014b). 'YouTube if you want to, the lady's not for blogging': Using 'bleasures' and 'motifs' to support multimedia forensic analyses of harassment by social media. *Oxford Cyber Harassment Research Symposium*, Oxford, GB.

Bishop, J. (2014c). Internet trolling and the 2011 UK riots: The need for a dualist reform of the constitutional, administrative and security frameworks in great britain. *European Journal of Law Reform*, *16*(1), 154–167.

Bishop, J. (2014d). Representations of 'trolls' in mass media communication: A review of media-texts and moral panics relating to 'internet trolling'. *International Journal of Web Based Communities*, *10*(1), 7–24. doi:10.1504/IJWBC.2014.058384

Bishop, J. (2014e). Trolling is not just a art. it is an science: The role of automated affective content screening in regulating digital media and reducing risk of trauma. In M. M. Cruz-Cunha & I. M. Portela (Eds.), *Handbook of research on digital crime, cyberspace security, and information assurance* (pp. 424–435). Hershey, PA: IGI Global.

Black Box Corp. (2003). *Network Security, A White Paper. 2003*. Available at: http://www.blackbox.com/Tech_Support/White-Papers/Network-Security2.pdf

Blackboard Inc. (2014). A learning management system that brings your vision to life. *Blackboard*. Retrieved from http://www.blackboard.com/platforms/learn/overview.aspx

Black, E. L. (2011). Selecting a web content management system for an academic library website. *Information Technology & Libraries*, *30*(4), 185–189.

Blaze, Ioannis & Keromytis. (2002). Trust Management for IPsec. *ACM Transactions on Information and System Security*, *5*(2).

Blommaert, J. (2010). *The Sociolinguistics of Globalization*. Cambridge: Cambridge University Press. doi:10.1017/CBO9780511845307

Blum, J., & Eskandarian, A. (2004). The Threat of Intelligent Collisions. *IT Professional*, *6*(1), 24–29. doi:10.1109/MITP.2004.1265539

Boehle, S. (2007). Is open source right for you? *Training (New York, N.Y.)*, *44*(7), 36.

Boodaei, M. (2011, January). *Mobile Users Three Times More Vulnerable to Phishing Attacks*. Trusteer. Retrieved January 2015, from http://www.trusteer.com/blog/mobile-users-three-times-more-vulnerable-phishing-attacks

Booker, L. B. (2008). Finding identity group "fingerprints" in documents. In *Computational Forensics* (pp. 113–121). Springer Berlin Heidelberg.

Bortinik, S. (2013, January). *Why Do Phishing Attacks Work Better On Mobile Phones*? Retrieved January 2015, from http://www.welivesecurity.com/2011/01/20/why-do-phishing-attacks-work-better-on-mobile-phones/

Bose, A. (2008). *Propagation, detection and containment of mobile malware*. (Doctoral dissertation, University of Michigan). Retrieved from www.phoenix.edu/apololibrary

Brack, J. (2012). *Maximizing millenials in the workplace*. (Master's thesis). University of North Carolina.

Braunlich, C., & Looney, M. Center for Education Reform (2002). Charter schools 2002: Results from CER's Annual Survey of America's Charter Schools. Washington, DC.

Brck. (2014). Technology. *Brck*. Accessed April 23. http://www.brck.com/specifications/

Brechbuhl, H., Bruce, R., Dynes, S., & Johnson, E. (2010, January). Protecting Critical Information Infrastructure: Developing Cybersecurity Policy. *Information Technology for Development, 16*(1), 83–91. doi:10.1002/itdj.20096

Brennan, M. R., & Greenstadt, R. (2009, April). *Practical Attacks Against Authorship Recognition Techniques*. IAAI.

Bronk, C., Monk, C., & Villasenor, J. (2012). The Dark Side of Cyber Finance. *Survival, 54*(2), 129–142. doi:10.1080/00396338.2012.672794

Brostoff, S., & Sasse, M. A. (2001, September). Safe and sound: a safety-critical approach to security. In *Proceedings of the 2001 workshop on New security paradigms* (pp. 41-50). ACM., 2002. doi:10.1145/508171.508178

Brown, B. (2009). *Beyond Downadup: Security expert worries about smart phone, TinyURL threats: Malware writers just waiting for financial incentive to strike, F-Secure exec warns*. Retrieved from http://business.highbeam.com/409220/article-1G1-214585913/beyond-downadup-security-expert-worries-smart-phone

Buchegger & Boudec. (2002). Performance analysis of the confidant protocol (cooperation of nodes: Fairness in dynamic ad-hoc networks). In *Proceedings of MOBIHOC'02*.

Bullock, J., Haddow, G., Coppola, D., & Yeletaysi, S. (2009). *Introduction to homeland security: Principles of all-hazards response* (3rd ed.). Burlington, MA: Elsevier Inc.

Bureau, D. n. (2012). Android malware threatens 2013. *Android malware threatens 2013*. Retrieved Dec.28, 2012, from http://www.dqweek.com/dq-week/report/154801/android-malware-threats-2013

Burley, L. D., Eisenberg, J., & Goodman, E. S. (2014). Would cybersecurity professionalization help address the cybersecurity crisis? *Communications of the ACM, 57*(2), 24–27. doi:10.1145/2556936

Burnette, E. (2009). *Hello, Android: introducing Google's mobile development platform*. Pragmatic Bookshelf.

Burns, J. (2008). *Developing secure mobile applications for android*.

Burns, L., Bradley, E., & Weiner, B. (2011). *Shortell and Kaluzny's Healthcare Management: Organization Design and Behavior*. New York: Cengage Learning.

Burrows, J. (2002). 'Delta': A measure of stylistic difference and a guide to likely authorship. *Literary and Linguistic Computing, 17*(3), 267–287.

Butler, C. (1985). Article. *Statistics in Linguistics, 9*, 112–113.

California Assembly Bill No. 1950, (2004). Cal. Civ. Code § 1798.82

Cambridge Advanced Learner's Dictionary. (n.d.). Retrieved June, 2014 http://dictionary.cambridge.org/

Caminero, A. C., Hernández, R. R., Ros, S. S., & Tobarra, L. l. (2013). Robles.-Gómez, A. A., & Pastor, R. R. (2013). Comparison of LMSs: Which is the most suitable LMS for my needs? *International Journal of Emerging Technologies In Learning, 8*, 829–836. doi:10.3991/ijet.v8iS2.2758

Canalys. (2011, October 04). *Mobile Security Investment to Climb 44% Each Year Through 2015*. Retrieved April 22, 2012, from Canalys: http://www.canalys.com/newsroom/mobile-security-investment-climb-44-each-year-through-2015

Capkun, S., Buttyan, L., & Hubaux, J. P. (2003). Self Organized Public-Key Management for Mobile Ad Hoc Networks. *IEEE Transactions on Mobile Computing, 2*(1), 52–64. doi:10.1109/TMC.2003.1195151

Carcary, M. (2013). IT risk management: A capability maturity model perspective. *Electronic Journal of Information Systems Evaluation, 16*(1).

Care, M. (2003). *Authorship Attribution: a Comparison of Three Methods.* (Doctoral dissertation). Universidade de Sheffield.

Carin, L., Cybenko, G., & Hughes, J. (2008). Cybersecurity strategies: The QuERIES methology. *IEEE Computer Society, 41*(8), 20–26. doi:10.1109/MC.2008.295

Carroll, M. (2006). "Information Security: Examining and managing the Insider Threat", *Proceedings of the 3rd annual conference on Information security curriculum development*, pp. 156-158. 2006. doi:10.1145/1231047.1231082

CCEVS. (2008). National Security Agency, Common Criteria Evaluation and Validation Scheme. *Common criteria evaluation and validation scheme -- organization, management, and concept of operations (Version 2.0).* Retrieved from National Information Assurance Partnership: http://www.niap-ccevs.org/policy/ccevs/scheme-pub-1.pdf

CERT. (1998). *Smurf Attack CERT Annual Report.* Available at CERT: http://www.cert.org/advisories/CA-1998-01.html. Last accessed: 29/09/14.

Cert. (2009). *"Common Sense Guide to Prevention and Detection of Insider Threat".* Retrieved from http://www.ncix.gov/issues/ithreat/csg-v3.pdf on Dec 3rd, 2011

Chabrow, E, (2011, October 11) Women, Minorities Scarce in IT Security Field: Profession Does Not Mirror Rest of American Workforce. Government Information Security.

Chagarlamudi, M., Panda, B., & Hu, Y. (2009). *"Insider Threat in Database Systems: Preventing Malicious Users. Activities in Databases.* In *Proceedings of the 2009 Sixth International Conference on Information Technology: New Generation*, Las Vegas, pp. 1616-1620, 2009. doi:10.1109/ITNG.2009.67

Champod, C., & Evett, I. W. (1999). A. P. A. Broeders (1999) "Some observations on the use of probability scales in forensic identification. *International Journal of Speech Language and the Law, 6*(June), 228–241.

Chang, G., Tan, C., Li, G., & Zhu, C. (2010). Developing mobile applications on the Android platform. In *Mobile multimedia processing* (pp. 264–286). Springer Berlin Heidelberg. doi:10.1007/978-3-642-12349-8_15

Charles, C. T. (2005). *Security Review of the Light-Weight Access Point Protocol. 2005.* IETF CAPWAP Working Group.

Charleston County School District. (2014). *About Us.* Retrieved from http://www.ccsdschools.com/About_Us/

Chaski, C. E. (1997). Who wrote it? Steps toward a Science of Authorship Identification. *National Institute of Justice Journal, 233,* 15–22.

Chebyshev, V., & Unuchek, R. (2014). Mobile Malware Evolution. *securelist.* Retrieved Apr. 10, 2015, from http://securelist.com/analysis/kaspersky-security-bulletin/58335/mobile-malware-evolution-2013/

Chen, D., Deng, J., & Varshney, P. K. (2003). Protecting wireless networks against a denial of service attack based on virtual jamming, in MOBICOM -Proceedings of the Ninth Annual International Conference on Mobile Computing and Networking, ACM, 2003.

Cheng, Y.-M. (2011). Antecedents and consequences of e-learning acceptance. *Information Systems Journal, 21*(3), 269–299. doi:10.1111/j.1365-2575.2010.00356.x

Chen, L., Franklin, J., & Regenscheid, A. (2012). Guidelines on Hardware-Rooted Security in Mobile Devices (Draft). *NIST Special Publication, 800,* 164.

Chen, X., Ye, Y., Williams, G., & Xu, X. (2007). A survey of open source data mining systems. In *Emerging Technologies in Knowledge Discovery and Data Mining* (pp. 3–14). Springer Berlin Heidelberg. doi:10.1007/978-3-540-77018-3_2

Chuchuen, C., & Chanvarasuth, P. (2010). The Relationships Between Phishing Techniques And The User Personality Model. *ICLT 2010 - 2nd International Conference on Logistics and Transport*, Queenstown NZ.

Cisco. (2014). Technology products. *Cisco.* Accessed April 23. http://palop.comstor.com/content/vendors/cisco

Clarke, J. (Ed.). (2012). *SQL injection attacks and defense.* Elsevier.

CNCCS. N. C. S. A. (2013). *Smartphone Malware: report pandasecurity.* Retrieved http://press.pandasecurity.com/usa/wp-content/uploads/2011/06/CNCCS-Smartphone-Malware-Full-Report-Translated-06-7-11-FINAL.pdf

Community, B. (2014, March, 24). *Ties Between Malware Software and privacy,* Retrieved from http://www.bizcommunity.com/Article/196/542/111169.htm

Compeau, D. R., & Higgins, C. A. (1995). Computer self-efficacy: Development of a measure and initial test. *Management Information Systems Quarterly, 19*(2), 189–211. doi:10.2307/249688

Conde, M. A., Garcia, F., Rodriguez-Conde, M. J., Alier, M., & Garcia-Halgodo, A. (2014). Perceived openness of Learning Management Systems by students and teachers in education and technology courses. *Computers in Human Behavior, 31,* 517–526. doi:10.1016/j.chb.2013.05.023

Connell, R. (2013). Content Management Systems: Trends in Academic Libraries. *Information Technology & Libraries, 32*(2), 42–55. doi:10.6017/ital.v32i2.4632

ConstU.S.. art. IV (1787).

ConstU.S.. Pmbl(1787).

Conti, M., Gregori, E., & Maselli, G. (2003). Towards Reliable Forwarding for Ad Hoc Networks. In Personal Wireless Communications, IFIP-TC6 8th International Conference, PWC 2003. Venice, Italy: Springer. p. 790--804. doi:10.1007/978-3-540-39867-7_71

Convery, S., Miller, D., & Sundaralingam, S. (2003). *Cisco SAFE: Wireless LAN Security in Depth 2003.* CISCO Whitepaper.

Cordasco, J., & Wetzel, S. (2008). Cryptographic versus trust-based methods for MANET routing security. *Electronic Notes in Theoretical Computer Science, 197*(2), 131–140. doi:10.1016/j.entcs.2007.12.022

Cornerstone On Demand. (2014). Learning management. *Learning Cloud.* Retrieved from http://www.cornerstoneondemand.com/global-business/talent-management/learning-management-cloud

Couldry, N., Markham, T., & Livingstone, S. (2005). *Media consumption and the future of public connection.* London, UK: London School of Economics and Political Science.

Coulthard, M. (1994). On the use of corpora in the analysis of forensic texts. *Forensic Linguistics, 1*(1), 27–43.

Coulthard, M., Grant, T., & Kredens, K. (2010). Forensic Linguistics. In B. Johnstone, R. Wodak, & P. Kerswill (Eds.), *The SAGE Handbook of Sociolinguistics* (pp. 529–544).

Crampton, J., & Khambham-mettu, H. (2008). Delegation in Role-Based Access Control. *International Journal of Information Security, 7*(2), 123–136. doi:10.1007/s10207-007-0044-8

Cranor, L. F., Egelman, S., Hong, J. I., & Zhang, Y. (2007, December). Phinding Phish: An Evaluation of Anti-Phishing Toolbars. In NDSS.

Crystal, D. (2001). *Language and the Internet. New York.* Cambridge: Cambridge University Press. doi:10.1017/CBO9781139164771

Csikszentmihalyi, M. (1990). *Flow: The psychology of optimal experience.* New York: Harper & Row.

Cyber, B. (2013, November, 11). *"Dexter Malware" A New Threat in Kenya Banking,* Retrieved from http://bitcyber.wordpress.com/2013/11/11/dexternalware/

Cyber-Intelligence Sharing and Protection Act, (2013). H.R. 3523, 112th Congress (2011-2012), (2012), H.R. 624,113th Congress (2013-2014)

Cybersecurity Act of 2012, (2012). S. 2105, 112th Congress (2011-2012).

Cybersecurity bill wins key Senate vote, upi.com. (2012). Retrieved June 14, 2014 from http://www.upi.com/Top_News/US/2012/07/26/Cybersecurity-bill-wins-key-Senate-vote/UPI-57801343345113/

Cybersecurity Framework . (2014). Retrieved June 14, 2014 from http://www.dhs.gov/publication/eo-13636-improving-ci-cybersecurity

Cybersecurity . (2014). Retrieved June 14, 2014 from http://www.phe.gov/Preparedness/planning/cip/Pages/eo13636.aspx

Dadak, R. (2011). Quashing the beast. *Solicitor's Journal, 155*(36), 9.

Davison, J. (2011). Literacy and social class. *Debates in English Teaching,,* 169.

Dawson, M. (2012). Cyber Security and Mobile Threats: The Need for Antivirus Applications for Smart Phones more. *JISTP, 5*(14), 40-60.

Dawson, M. E., Crespo, M., & Brewster, S. (2013). DoD cyber technology policies to secure automated information systems. *International Journal of Business Continuity and Risk Management, 4*(1), 1–22. doi:10.1504/IJBCRM.2013.053089

Dawson, M., Al Saeed, I., Wright, J., & Onyegbula, F. (2014). Open Source Software to Enhance the STEM Learning Environment. In V. Wang (Ed.), *Handbook of Research on Education and Technology in a Changing Society* (pp. 569–580). Hershey, PA: Information Science Reference; doi:10.4018/978-1-4666-6046-5.ch042

Dawson, M., Omar, M., & Abramson, J. (2015). Understanding the Methods behind Cyber Terrorism. In M. Khosrow-Pour (Ed.), *Encyclopedia of Information Science and Technology* (3rd ed., pp. 1539–1549). Hershey, PA: Information Science Reference; doi:10.4018/978-1-4666-5888-2.ch147

Dawson, M., Omar, M., Abramson, J., & Bessette, D. (2014). The Future of National and International Security on the Internet. In A. Kayem & C. Meinel (Eds.), *Information Security in Diverse Computing Environments* (pp. 149–178). Hershey, PA: Information Science Reference; doi:10.4018/978-1-4666-6158-5.ch009

De Angelis, G. (2005). Interlanguage Transfer of Function Words. *Language Learning, 55*(3), 379–414. doi:10.1111/j.0023-8333.2005.00310.x

De Vel, O., Anderson, A., Corney, M., & Mohay, G. (2001). Mining e-mail content for author identification forensics. *SIGMOD Record, 30*(4), 55–64.

Delong, D. (2004). *Lost Knowledge: Confronting the Threat of an Aging Workforce.* London: Oxford University Press. doi:10.1093/acprof:oso/9780195170979.001.0001

Demirkan, H., Cheng, H., & Bandyopadhyay, S. (2010). Coordination strategies in an SaaS supply chain. *Journal of Management Information Systems, 26*(4), 119–143. doi:10.2753/MIS0742-1222260405

Denning, D. E. (2012). Stuxnet: What has changed? *Future Internet, 4*(3), 672–687. doi:10.3390/fi4030672

Department of Health and Human Services. (2014). *HHS Activities to Enhance.* Author.

Department of Homeland Security. (2014). *Section 10(a) and 10(b) Report on the United States Coast Guard (USCG) and Maritime Critical Infrastructure Cybersecurity Standards, Section 10(b) Report on the Department of Homeland Security's Chemical Facility Anti-Terrorism Standards (CFATS)Section 10(b) Report on the Transportation Security Administration's (TSA's) Approach to Voluntary Industry Adoption of the NIST.* Author.

Deperlioglu, O., Sarpkaya, Y., & Ergun, E. (2011). Development of a relational database for Learning Management Systems. *Turkish Online Journal of Educational Technology - TOJET, 10*(4), 107-120.

Desilver, D. (2013, August 21). Black unemployment rate is consistently twice that of whites. Washington DC: The Pew Research Center.

Desmedt, Y., & Frankel, Y. (1990). Threshold Cryptosystem. Advances in Cryptology Crypto 89 G. Brassard Ed., Springer Verlag, pp 307-15, August. doi:10.1007/0-387-34805-0_28

Desnos, A. (2012). *Android: Static Analysis Using Similarity Distance.* Paper presented at the International Conference on System Science (HICSS), 2012 45th Hawaii.

Deterding, S., Sicart, M., Nacke, L., O'Hara, K., & Dixon, D. (2011). Gamification: Using game-design elements in non-gaming contexts. Paper presented at the *Proceedings of the 2011 Annual Conference on Human Factors in Computing Systems,* New York, NY. 2425-2428. doi:10.1145/1979742.1979575

Dhamija, R., Tygar, J. D., & Hearst, M. (2006, April). Why phishing works. In *Proceedings of the SIGCHI conference on Human Factors in computing systems* (pp. 581-590). ACM.

Diffie, W., & Hellman, M. (1976). New Directions in Cryptography. *IEEE Transactions on Information Theory, IT-22*(6), 644–654. doi:10.1109/TIT.1976.1055638

Dimitrakos, Matthews, & Bicarregui. (2001). *Towards security and trust management policies on the web.* In ERCIM Workshop 'The Role of Trust in e-Business' in conjunction with IFIP I3E Conference, CLRC Rutherford Appleton Laboratory, Oxfordshire.

Ding, Y., & Petersen, H. (1995). *A new approach for delegation using hierarchical delegation tokens.* University of Technology Chemnitz-Zwickau Department of Computer Science.

Dini, G., Martinelli, F., Saracino, A., & Sgandurra, D. (2012). *MADAM: a Multi-Level Anomaly Detector for Android Malware.* Paper presented at the International Conference on Mathematical Methods, Models and Architectures for Computer Network Security. doi:10.1007/978-3-642-33704-8_21

dos Santos, M. R. (2009). Labor supply, criminal behavior and income redistribution. *Brazilian Review of Econometrics, 29*(2), 5–6.

Downs, J. S., Holbrook, M. B., & Cranor, L. F. (2006, July). Decision strategies and susceptibility to phishing. In *Proceedings of the second symposium on Usable privacy and security* (pp. 79-90). ACM. doi:10.1145/1143120.1143131

Downs, J. S., Holbrook, M., & Cranor, L. F. (2007, October). Behavioral response to phishing risk. In *Proceedings of the anti-phishing working groups 2nd annual eCrime researchers summit* (pp. 37-44). ACM. doi:10.1145/1299015.1299019

Doyle, A. C. (1892). *The Adventures of Sherlock Holmes.* New York: Harper and Brothers.

Drucker, P. F. (1992). *Managing for the future: The 1990s and beyond.* New York, NY: Truman Talley Books/Plume.

Dunham, K. (2008). *Mobile malware attacks and defense.* Syngress.

Eeten, M., & Bauer, J. (2009, December). Emerging Threats to Internet Security: Incentives, Externalities and Policy Implications. *Journal of Contingencies and Crisis Management, 17*(4), 221–232. doi:10.1111/j.1468-5973.2009.00592.x

Egan, M. (2014). *Judge Rules FTC Can Sue Wyndham Over Cyber Security Lapses.* Retrieved June 16, 2014 from http://www.foxbusiness.com/industries/2014/04/08/us-ftc-can-sue-hotel-group-over-poor-data-security-court-rules/

Egele, M., Scholte, T., Kirda, E., & Kruegel, C. (2008). A survey on automated dynamic malware-analysis techniques and tools. *ACM Computing Surveys, 44*(2), 1–42. doi:10.1145/2089125.2089126

El-Din, R. S., Cairns, P., & Clark, J. (2014). Mobile Users' Strategies for Managing Phishing Attacks. *Journal of Management and Strategy, 5*(2), 70. doi:10.5430/jms.v5n2p70

Electronic Communications Privacy Act of 1986, (1988). 18 U.S.C. §§ 2510-2511

Elu, J. U. (2012). Terrorism in Africa and South Asia: Economic or existential good? *Journal of Developing Areas, 46*(1), 345–358. doi:10.1353/jda.2012.0008

Enck, W., Octeau, D., McDaniel, P., & Chaudhuri, S. (2011, August). A Study of Android Application Security. In USENIX security symposium (Vol. 2, p. 2).

Enck, W., Ongtang, M., & McDaniel, P. D. (2009). Understanding Android Security. *IEEE Security and Privacy, 7*(1), 50–57. doi:10.1109/MSP.2009.26

Ertaul, L., Singhal, S., & Saldamli, G. (2010). Security challenges in cloud computing. In Security and Management (pp. 36-42).

ESET. (2013). *Trends for 2013 Astounding growth of mobile malware.* Retrieved Jan. 15, 2013, from http://go.eset.com/us/resources/white-papers/Trends_for_2013_preview.pdf

Espinoza, C. (2010, March). *Managers Key to Retaining Millennials.* Talent Management.

Estival, D., Hutchinson, B., Gaustad, T., Pham, S. B., Radford, W., & Nsw, S. (2007). Author Profiling for English Emails, 263–272.

Exec. Order No. 13636, (2013). 78 FR 11737, 11737-11744

Farringdon, J. M. (2004). *How to be a Literary Detective: Authorship Attribution: A brief introduction to cusum analysis.* Available online at http://members.aol.com/qsums/QsumIntroduction.html

Father, H. (2004). Hooking Windows API-Technics of hooking API functions on Windows. *CodeBreakers J, 1*(2).

Fatskunk. (2013). *The Challenge of Smarthone Malware.* Retrieved Jan.05, 2013, from http://www.fatskunk.com/what-is-mobile-malware

Favell, A. (Ed.). (2011, November 2). *96 Percent of Smartphones and Tablets Lack Necessary Security Software. Why It Matters to Your Business - A Lot.* Retrieved April 22, 2012, from MobiThinking: http://mobithinking.com/blog/mobile-security-business-implications

Federal Trade Commission Act, (1914). 15 USC §§ 41-58

Fedler, R., Schutte, J., & Kulicke, M. (2013). *On the effectiveness of malware protection on android an evaluation of android antivirus app.* Technical Report by Fraunhofer AISEC. Retrieved Apr.30, 2013, from http://www.aisec.fraunhofer.de/en/about-us.html

Felt, A. P., Finifter, M., Chin, E., Hanna, S., & Wagner, D. (2011, October). A survey of mobile malware in the wild. In *Proceedings of the 1st ACM workshop on Security and privacy in smartphones and mobile devices* (pp. 3-14). ACM. doi:10.1145/2046614.2046618

Ferguson, P., & Senie, D. (2000). *Network Ingress Filtering: Defeating Denial of Service Attacks Which Employ IP Source Address Spoofing.* IETF. Available on http://www.rfc-archive.org/getrfc.php?rfc=2827

Ferraro, M. F. (2014). "Groundbreaking" or broken? An analysis of sec cybersecurity disclosure guidance, its effectiveness, and implications. *Albany Law Review*, *77*(2), 297–347.

Field, S., & Jones, L. (2011). Death in the workplace: Who pays the price? *Colorado Lawyer*, *32*(6), 166–173.

Finch, A., Burrell, D., & Luna, B. (2009). *An Analysis of the Growth, Emergence, and Development of Leaders and Leadership Philosophies of Charter Schools in the United States.* The John Shepherd Journal of Practical Leadership.

Finn, C., Manno, B., & Vanourek, G. (2000). *Charter schools in action.* Princeton, N.J.: Princeton University Press.

Fletcher, T., Richardson, H. W. K., Carlisle, M. C., & Hamilton, J. A. (2005). Jr. Simulation Experimentation with Secure Overlay Services. In *Summer Computer Simulation Conference. 2005.* Philadelphia, PA.

Fossi, M., Egan, G., Haley, K., Johnson, E., Mack, T., Adams, T., . . . McKinney, D. (2011). Symantec internet security. *threat report trends for 2010, 16*, 20.

Foster, D. (2001). *On the Trail of Anonymous.* New York: Henry Holt & Company.

Franke, D., Elsemann, C., Kowalewski, S., & Weise, C. (2011, October). Reverse engineering of mobile application lifecycles. In *Reverse Engineering (WCRE), 2011 18th Working Conference on* (pp. 283-292). IEEE. doi:10.1109/WCRE.2011.42

Franklin, B., & Glascock, C. (1996, October). *The relationship between grade configuration and student performance in rural schools.* (ERIC document ED 403083). Paper presented at the Annual Conference of the National Rural Education Association, San Antonio, Texas.

FTC Accepts Final Settlement with Twitter for Failure to Safeguard Personal Information. (2014). Retrieved June 16, 2014 from http://www.ftc.gov/news-events/press-releases/2011/03/ftc-accepts-final-settlement-twitter-failure-safeguard-personal

Fung, G. (2003, October). The disputed Federalist Papers: SVM feature selection via concave minimization. In *Proceedings of the 2003 Conference on Diversity in Computing* (pp. 42-46). ACM.

Gamon, M. (2004, August). Linguistic correlates of style: authorship classification with deep linguistic analysis features. In *Proceedings of the 20th international conference on Computational Linguistics* (p. 611). Association for Computational Linguistics.

Garcia, G. F., & Garcia, M. (1996, November). Charter schools—Another top-down innovation. *Educational Researcher*, *25*, 34–36.

Gardner, D. (1998). Newest HTML spec folds in benefits of DHTML. *InfoWorld*, *20*(1), 47.

Gartner. (2015). Gartner Says Smartphone Sales Surpassed One Billion Units in 2014. *Newsroom.* Retrieved Apr. 10, 2015, from http://www.gartner.com/newsroom/id/2996817

Gasser, M., Goldstein, A., Kaufman, C., & Lampson, B. (1989). The Digital distributed system security architecture. In *Proceedings of the National Computer Security Conference*, pp. 305-319, 1989.

Geier, E. (2013). Four ways to make Internet Explorer more secure. *PC World*, *31*(9), 189–191.

Gephi. (2013). *The Open Graph Viz Platform*. Retrieved Jan. 09, 2013, from http://gephi.org/

Geske, T. G., Davis, D., & Hingle, P. (1997). Charter schools: A viable public school choice option? *Economics of Education Review, 16*(1), 15–23. doi:10.1016/S0272-7757(96)00039-8

Ginter, A. (2013). Securing industrial control systems. *Chemical Engineering (Albany, N.Y.), 120*(7), 30–35.

Glenn, M. (2008). The future of higher education: How technology will shape learning. In D. D'Agostino (Ed.), Economist Intelligence Unit Report. New York, NY: The New Media Consortium; Retrieved from http://graphics.eiu.com/upload/The%20Future%20of%20Universities.pdf

Goldberg, J. C. P. (2011). Does the world still need united states tort law? or did it ever?: Tort in three dimensions. *Pepp.L.Rev., 38*, 321–597.

Goldfarb, R., Wasserman, E., Cole, D., Carter, H., Blanton, T., Mills, J., & Siegel, B. (2015). *After Snowden: Privacy, Secrecy, and Security in the Information Age*. Macmillan.

Goodman, J. (2002). *Extended comment on language trees and zipping*. arXiv preprint cond-mat/0202383.

Goodman, S., & Harris, A. (2010). The coming African tsunami of information insecurity. *Communications of the ACM, 53*(12), 24–27. doi:10.1145/1859204.1859215

Google. (2012). *ProGuard*. Retrieved Jul. 17, 2012, from http://developer.android.com/tools/help/proguard.html

Google. (2013). *Get the Android SDK*. Retrieved Jan. 10, 2013, from http://developer.android.com/sdk/index.html

Google. (2014). *Google Play*. Retrieved Jan. 29, 2014, from https://play.google.com/

Görling, S. (2006, October). The myth of user education. In *Virus Bulletin Conference* (Vol. 11, p. 13).

Goth, G. (2009). U.S. Unveils Cybersecurity Plan. *Government Policy, 52*(8), 23.

Goyal, E., & Purohit, S. (2009). Study of using learning management system in a management course. *SIES Journal of Management, 6*(2), 11–20.

Grace, M., Zhou, W., Jiang, X., & Sadeghi, A.-R. (2012). Unsafe Exposure Analysis of Mobile In-App Advertisements. *Association for Computing Machinery - Security and Privacy in Wireless and Mobile Networks, 5*, 101-112. doi:10.1145/2185448.2185464

Grace, M., Zhou, Y., Zhang, Q., Zou, S., & Jiang, X. (2012). *RiskRanker: scalable and accurate zero-day android malware detection*. Paper presented at the 10th international conference on Mobile systems, applications, and services, Low Wood Bay, Lake District, UK. doi:10.1145/2307636.2307663

Graf, K. (2005). *Addressing Challenges in Application Security*. Watchfire White Paper. Retrieved from http://www.watchfire.com

Grafii, K., Mogre, P. S., Hollick, M., & Steimetz, R. (2007). Detection of Colluding Misbehaving Nodes in Mobile Ad hoc and Wireless Mesh Networks. In *Proceedings of IEEE Globecom*, pp. 5097-5101. doi:10.1109/GLOCOM.2007.966

Graham, N., Hirst, G., & Marthi, B. (2005). Segmenting documents by stylistic character. *Natural Language Engineering, 11*(4), 397–415.

Graham, P. (1995). *Mary Parker Follett: prophet of management - a Celebration of Writings from the 1920s*. Boston, Mass: Harvard Business School Press.

Gramm–Leach–Bliley Act of 1999, (2000). 15 U.S.C. §§ 6801-6809; 6821-6827

Grandison, T. (2003). *Trust Management for Internet Applications*. (PhD thesis). Imperial College London, London, UK.

Grant, T., Kredens, K., & Perkins, R. (2010). Identifying an Author's Native Language Phase 2 + Finding and training the bilingual language expert. Birmingham.

Grant, T. (2008). Approaching questions in forensic authorship analysis. In J. Gibbons & M. T. Turell (Eds.), *Dimensions of Forensic Linguistics* (pp. 215–229). Philadelphia, PA: John Benjamins Publishing Company. doi:10.1075/aals.5.15gra

Grant, T. (2010). Text Messaging Forensics: Txt 4n6: Idiolect free authorship analysis? In M. Coulthard & A. Johnson (Eds.), *The Routledge Handbook of World Englishes* (pp. 508–522). London, New York: Routledge. doi:10.4324/9780203855607.ch33

Gray, A., Sallis, P., & MacDonell, S. (1997). *Software forensics: Extending authorship analysis techniques to computer programs.*

Grayston, K., & Herdan, G. (1959). The authorship of the Pastorals in the light of statistical linguistics. *New Testament Studies*, *6*(1), 1–15.

Green, D. (2014). Insider threats and employee deviance: Developing an updated typology of deviant workplace behaviors. *Issues in Information Systems*, *15*(II), 185–189.

Greene, J., Forster, G., & Winters, M. (2003). *Apples to apples: An evaluation of charter schools serving general student populations.* (Education Working Paper 1). New York, N.Y.: Manhattan Institute for Policy Research.

Greenleaf, R. (2012). *The Servant as Leader*. Seattle, WA: Amazon Digital Services.

Greitzer, F.L., Moore, A.P., Cappelli, D.M., Andrews, D.H., Carroll, L.A., & Hull, T.D. (2011). Combating Insider Threats. *IEEE Security & Privacy, 6*(1), 45-60.

Griffith, S. J. (2002). Deal protection provisions in the last period of play. *Fordham Law Review*, *71*, 1899.

Griffiths, S. (2011). The retreat of the state: Conservative 'modernisation' and the public services. *Public Policy Research*, *18*(1), 23–29. doi:10.1111/j.1744-540X.2011.00637.x

GSMA. (2013). Sub-Saharan Africa mobile economy 2013. Retrieved from *GSMA*. http://www.gsmamobileeconomyafrica.com/Sub-Saharan%20Africa_ME_ExecSummary_English_2013.pdf

Haan, P. D. (1998). A review of 'analysing for authorship'. *Forensic Linguistics*, *5*, 69–76.

Haigh, J. T., Harp, S. A., O'Brien, R. C., Payne, C. N., Gohde, J., & Maraist, J. (2009) Adventium Labs., Minneapolis, MN. "*Trapping Malicious Insiders in the SPDR Web*". *Proceedings of the 42nd Hawaii International Conference on System Sciences – 2009.*

Halbronn, C., & Sigwald, J. (2010). iPhone security model & vulnerabilities. In Proceedings of Hack in the box sec-conference. Kuala Lumpur, Malaysia.

Halevi, T., Lewis, J., & Memon, N. (2013). Phishing, Personality Traits and Facebook. *arXiv preprint arXiv:1301.7643*.

Halleck, T. (2014). We Spend More Time On Smartphones Than Traditional PCs. *International Business Times*. Retrieved Apr. 10, 2015, from http://www.ibtimes.com/we-spend-more-time-smartphones-traditional-pcs-nielsen-1557807

Halliday, M. A. K., McIntosh, A., & Strevens, P. (1965). *The linguistic sciences and language teaching* (pp. 5–6). Longmans.

Halvani, O., Steinebach, M., & Zimmermann, R. (2013). *Authorship Verification via k-Nearest Neighbor Estimation.*

Halzack, S. (2014, March 5). Evidence that the D.C. area really is a hotbed for cybersecurity jobs. Capital Business

Hamilton Research. (2011, Jan. 17). *Submarine cables reach 4.4% of Africa's population, terrestrial fibre networks reach 31%*. Author. Retrieved from http://www.africabandwidthmaps.com/?p=1735

Hancock, L., & Mooney, G. (2013). "Welfare ghettos" and the "Broken society": Territorial stigmatization in the contemporary UK. *Housing. Theory and Society*, *30*(1), 46–64.

Han, K.-S., Kim, I.-K., & Im, E. (2012). Malware Classification Methods Using API Sequence Characteristics. In KimK. J.AhnS. J. (Eds.), *Proceedings of the International Conference on IT Convergence and Security 2011* (Vol. 120, pp. 613-626). Springer Netherlands. doi:10.1007/978-94-007-2911-7_60

Hankey, S., & Clunaigh, D. Ó. (2013). Rethinking Risk and Security of Human Rights Defenders in the Digital Age. *Journal of Human Rights Practice*, *5*(3), 535–547. doi:10.1093/jhuman/hut023

Harknett, R., & Stever, J. (2011). In N. Roberts (Ed.), *The New Policy World of Cybersecurity* (pp. 455–460). Public Administration Review.

Harper College. (2014). *Sub Saharan African countries.* Accessed September 30. http://www.harpercollege.edu/mhealy/mapquiz/ssa/ssacoufr.htm

Harris, S., & Meyers, M. (2002). *CISSP.* McGraw-Hill/Osborne.

Hassan, F. I. H., & Chaurasia, M. A. (2012). N-Gram Based Text Author Verification. *International Proceedings of Computer Science & Information Technology, 36.*

Hassel, B., and Herdman, P. (2000, April). *Charter school accountability: A guide to issues and options for charter authorizers.* Charlotte, N.C.: Public Impact.

Health Insurance Portability and Accountability Act of 1996, (2000). 42 U.S.C. §§1320d-1320d-9

Health Insurance Portability and Accountability Act of 1996, Privacy and Security Rule, (2003). 45 C.F.R. §§ 164.102-164.534

Henderson, A. M. (2009). High-tech words do hurt: A modern makeover expands missouri's harassment law to include electronic communications. *Missouri Law Review, 74,* 379.

Hersberger, J. (2003). Are the economically poor information poor? does the digital divide affect the homeless and access to information? *Canadian Journal of Information and Library Science, 27*(3), 45–64.

Hersman, E. (2014). *Erik Hersman CEO at BRCK.* Social Media. *Linkedin.* Accessed April 23. http://ke.linkedin.com/in/erikhersman

Herzberg, A., & Gbara, A. (2004). *Trustbar: Protecting (even naive) web users from spoofing and phishing attacks.*

Hidalgo, B. (2011). *Behavior-based malware detection system for the Android platform.* (Master's project). Linkoping University, Linkoping, Sweden.

Hill, P., Lake, R., & Celio, M. B. (2002). *Charter schools and accountability in public education.* Washington, D.C.: The Brookings Institution.

Hill, P., Lake, R., Celio, M. B., Campbell, C., Herdman, P., & Bulkley, K. (2001). *A study of charter school accountability.* Washington, D.C.: U.S. Department of Education, Office of Educational Research and Improvement.

Hilse, L. (2013). *Threat-Assessment: Bitcoin: Danger to the United States' National Security and her Economic & Commercial Interests.* Lars Hilse.

Hoang, X. D., Hu, J., & Bertok, P. (2009). A program-based anomaly intrusion detection scheme using multiple detection engines and fuzzy inference. *Journal of Network and Computer Applications, 32*(6), 1219–1228. doi:10.1016/j.jnca.2009.05.004

Homeland Security Act of 2002, (2006). 6 U.S.C. §§ 101-613 Federal Information Security Management Act of 2002, (2006). 44 U.S.C. §§ 3541-3549

Hommel, W. (2010). Security and privacy management for learning management systems. In Y. Kats (Ed.), *Learning management system technologies and software solutions for online teaching: Tools and applications* (pp. 37–56). Hershey, PA: IGI Global; doi:10.4018/978-1-61520-853-1.ch003

Hoog, A., & Strzempka, K. (2011). iPhone and iOS Forensics: Investigation, Analysis and Mobile Security for Apple iPhone, iPad and iOS Devices. Elsevier.

Hoog, A. (2011). *Android forensics: investigation, analysis and mobile security for Google Android.* Elsevier.

Hoover, D. L. (2001). Statistical stylistics and authorship attribution: An empirical investigation. *Literary and Linguistic Computing, 16*(4), 421–444.

Houvardas, J., & Stamatatos, E. (2006). N-gram feature selection for authorship identification. In Artificial Intelligence: Methodology, Systems, and Applications (pp. 77-86). Springer Berlin Heidelberg.

How To Spot Spoof (fake) eBay+PayPal Phishing Emails. (n.d.). Retrieved December 2014, from http://www.ebay.co.uk/gds/how-to-spot-spoof-fake-ebay-paypal-phishing-emails/10000000001711994/g.htmls

Howcroft, D. (1999). The hyperbolic age of information: An empirical study of internet usage. *Information Communication and Society, 2*(3), 277–299. doi:10.1080/136911899359592

Hu, Y.-C., Perrig, A., & Johnson, D. B. (2003). Rushing Attacks and Defense in Wireless Ad Hoc Network Routing Protocols. In 2nd ACM Wireless Security (WiSe'03). 2003. pp. 30-40. doi:10.1145/941311.941317

Huawei. (2014). Technology products. *Huawei*. Accessed April 23. http://enterprise.huawei.com/en/products/index.htm

Hubaux, J. P., Gross, T., Boudec, J. Y., & Vetterli, M. (2001, January). Toward self-organized mobile ad hoc networks: The terminodes project. *IEEE Communications Magazine, 39*(1), 118–124. doi:10.1109/35.894385

Hubbard, E. H. H. (1996). Errors in Court: A Forensic Application of Error Analysis. In H. Kniffka, S. Blackwell, & M. Coulthard (Eds.), *Recent Developments in Forensic Linguistics* (pp. 123–140). Frankfurt Am Main: Peter Lang GmbH.

Humphries, J. W. & Carlisle, M.C. (2002). Introduction to Cryptography. *ACM Journal of Educational Resources in Computing, 2*(3), 2.

Hunston, S. (2002). *Corpora in Applied Linguistics*. Cambridge: Cambridge University Press. doi:10.1017/CBO9781139524773

Hustad, E., & Arntzen, A. (2013). Facilitating Teaching and Learning Capabilities in Social Learning Management Systems: Challenges, Issues, and Implications for Design. *Journal of Integrated Design & Process Science, 17*(1), 17–35. doi:10.3233/jid-2013-0003

Iacob, J. L. N. M. (2013). Information security management in e-learning. *Knowledge Horizons, 5*(2).

i-Com. (2014). Interactive Communication. Mobile Cellular Router. *I-com Interactive Communication Managed Service*. Accessed April 23. http://www.icom.co.bw/icom_cat_desc.php?cid=17

Iglesias, J., Angelov, P., Ledezma, A., & Sanchis, A. (2012). Creating evolving user behavior profiles automatically. *IEEE Transactions on Knowledge and Data Engineering, 24*(5), 854–867. doi:10.1109/TKDE.2011.17

Informa Telecoms and Media. (2009). Informa Telecoms & Media report. Technical Report, London.

Insider Threat Study. (2005). Retrieved on Dec 2nd, 2011 from www.secretservice.gov/ntac/its_report_050516.pdf

International Telecommunication Union. ITU-T Recommendation X.509. (2000). Retrieved June 2014, http://www.itu.int/ITU-T/recommendations/rec.aspx?rec=11735&lang=en

Ioannidis, J., & Bellovin, S. M. (2002). Implementing Pushback: Router-Based Defense Against DDoS Attacks. In *Network and Distributed System Security Symposium*. 2002. San Diego, CA. pp.79-86.

Iqbal, F., Khan, L. A., Fung, B., & Debbabi, M. (2010, March). E-mail authorship verification for forensic investigation. In *Proceedings of the 2010 ACM Symposium on Applied Computing* (pp. 1591-1598). ACM.

IT News Africa. (2012, August 21). *Top ten largest telecoms companies in Africa*. Retrieved from http://www.itnewsafrica.com/2012/08/top-ten-largest-telecoms-companies-in-africa/

Iwamoto, K., & Wasaki, K. (2012). *Malware classification based on extracted API sequences using static analysis*. Paper presented at the Asian Internet Engineeering Conference, Bangkok, Thailand. doi:10.1145/2402599.2402604

Iyer, R., Dabrowski, P., Nakka, N., & Kalbarczyck, Z. (2008). *Pre-configurable Tamper-resistant Hardware Support Against Insider Threats: The Tested ILLIAC Approach. Insider Attack and Cyber Security* (pp. 133–152). Springer.

Jabbour, G., & Menasce, D. A. (2009). *The Insider Threat Security Architecture: A Framework for an Integrated, Inseparable, and Uninterrupted Self-Protection Mechanism.International Conference on Computational Science and Engineering*.

Jacquet, P., Muhlethaler, P., & Qayyum, A. (1998). *Optimized Link State Routing Protocol*. Internet Draft. Retrieved from June 7, 2014 https://tools.ietf.org/html/draft-ietf-manet-olsrv2-19

Jagatic, T. N., Johnson, N. A., Jakobsson, M., & Menczer, F. (2007). Social phishing. *Communications of the ACM, 50*(10), 94-100.-100, October 2007.

Jakobsson, M. (2011). *Why Mobile Security is not Like Traditional Security*.

Jakobsson, M. (2007). The human factor in phishing. *Privacy & Security of Consumer Information, 7*, 1–19.

Jakobsson, M., & Myers, S. (Eds.). (2006). *Phishing and countermeasures: understanding the increasing problem of electronic identity theft*. John Wiley & Sons. doi:10.1002/0470086106

Jaleh. (2011). *Jamigen's Iranian Affairs Blog Site*. Retrieved July 19, 2011, from http://jamigen.com/index.htm

Jamak, A., Savatić, A., & Can, M. (2012). Principal component analysis for authorship attribution. *Business Systems Research*, *3*(2), 49–56.

James, S., & Michael, R. (2008). Insider Threats to Information Systems. *SAIS (2008) Proceedings*. Retrieved from http://aisel.aisnet.org/sais2008/26

Janczewski, L., & Colarik, A. (2007). *Cyber Warfare and Cyber Terrorism*. Hershey, PA: IGI Global; doi:10.4018/978-1-59140-991-5

Jane, H. (2003). The role of shared values and vision in creating professional learning communities. *National Association of Secondary School Principals. NASSP Bulletin*, *87*(637), 21–34. doi:10.1177/019263650308763703

Jansen, W., & Karygiannis, A. T. (1999). *SP 800-19. Mobile Agent Security*. Gaithersburg, MD: National Institute of Standards & Technology.

Jansen, W., & Scarfone, K. (2008). Guidelines on cell phone and PDA security. *NIST Special Publication*, *800*, 124.

Jeannine, L. F. (2002). Organizational structures and perceived cultures of community-charter schools in Ohio. *Phi Delta Kappan*, *83*(7), 525–531. doi:10.1177/003172170208300712

Jeffrey, R. H., Thomas, T. H., Heath, B., & Natalie, L.-P. (2005). The influence of founder type on charter school structures and operations. *American Journal of Education*, *111*(4), 487–588. doi:10.1086/431181

Jensen, T. (2013). Riots, restraint and the new cultural politics of wanting. *Sociological Research Online*, *18*(4), 7. doi:10.5153/sro.3158

Jiang, X. (2012). *An Evaluation of the Application ("App") Verification Service in Android 4.2* Technical Report. Retrieved from http://www.cs.ncsu.edu/faculty/jiang/appverify/

Johari, R., & Sharma, P. (2012, May). A survey on web application vulnerabilities (SQLIA, XSS) exploitation and security engine for SQL injection. In *Communication Systems and Network Technologies (CSNT), 2012 International Conference on* (pp. 453-458). IEEE.

Johnson, D. B., & Maltz, D. A. (1996). In T. Imielinski & H. Korth (Eds.), *Dynamic source routing in ad hoc wireless networks, in mobile Computing* (pp. 153–181). Kluwer Academic Publishers.

Jouini, M., Aissa, A. B., Rabai, L. B. A., & Mili, A. (2012). Towards quantitative measures of information security: A cloud computing case study. *International Journal of Cyber-Security and Digital Forensics*, *1*(3), 248–262.

Juola, P. (2006). Authorship attribution. Foundations and Trends in information *Retrieval, 1*(3), 233-334.

Just, M., Kranakis, E., & Wan, T. (2003). Resisting Malicious Packet Dropping in Wireless Ad Hoc Networks. In ADHOCNOW'03. 2003. Montreal, Canada. doi:10.1007/978-3-540-39611-6_14

Kadam, Y. (2011). Security Issues in Cloud Computing A Transparent View. *International Journal of Computer Science Emerging Technology*, *2*(5), 316–322.

Kallbekken, S., & Sælen, H. (2011). Public acceptance for environmental taxes: Self-interest, environmental and distributional concerns. Energy Policy, Kim, A. J. (2011). Do you know the score on gamification? The Gamification Summit 2010, San Francisco, CA.

Kamvar, S. & Garcia-Molina. (2003).EigenRep: Reputation Management in P2P Networks. Proceedings of the Twelfth International World Wide Web Conference, Budapest.

Kaner, S., & Lind, L. (1996). *Facilitator's Guide to Participatory Decision-making*. Gabriola Island, BC, Canada: New Society Publishers.

Kannhavong, B., Nakayama, H., & Jamalipour, A. (2006). A Collusion Attack against OLSR-based Mobile Ad Hoc Networks. In Proceedings of IEEE GLOBECOM Conference. doi:10.1109/GLOCOM.2006.262

Kaplan, J., Sharma, S., & Weinberg, A. (2011). Cybersecurity: A Senior Executive's Guide. *The McKinsey Quarterly*, 4.

Karygiannis, T., & Owens, L. (2002). Wireless Network Security 802.11 Bluetooth and Handheld Devices, National Institute of Standards and Technology Special Publication, 800-48, Nov 2002, Available at: http://csrc.nist.gov/publications/nistpubs/800-48/NIST_SP_800-48.pdf

Kaspersky. (2012). Android Under Attack: Malware Levels for Google's OS Rise Threefold in Q2 2012. *Kaspersky.* Retrieved Jan.04, 2013, from http://www.kaspersky.com/about/news/press/2012/Android_Under_Attack__Malware_Levels_for_Googles_OS_Rise_Threefold_in_Q2_2012

Kaspersky. (2013). *File Anti-Virus.* Retrieved Apr. 30, 2013, from http://support.kaspersky.com/learning/courses/kl_102.98/chapter2.2/section1

Katz, J. (2002). Efficient Cryptographic Protocols Preventing "Man-in-the-Middle" Attacks. 2002, PhD Dissertation, Columbia University.

Katzan, H. Jr, & Dowling, W. A. (2010). Software-as-A-service economics. *The Review of Business Information Systems, 14*(1), 27–37.

Kaufman, C., Perlman, R., & Speciner, M. (2002). Network Security Private Communication in a Public World. 2002: Prentice Hall PTR. p. 752.

Keromytis, A. D., & Rubenstein, D. (2002). SOS: Secure Overlay Services. In ACM SIGCOMM'02. 2002. Pittsburgh, PA.

Kešelj, V., Peng, F., Cercone, N., & Thomas, C. (2003, August). N-gram-based author profiles for authorship attribution. In *Proceedings of the conference pacific association for computational linguistics, PACLING* (Vol. 3, pp. 255-264).

Ketari, L., & Khanum, M. A. (2012). A Review of Malicious Code Detection Techniques for Mobile Devices. *International Journal of Computer Theory and Engineering, 4*(2).

Khmelev, D. V., & Teahan, W. J. (2003, July). A repetition based measure for verification of text collections and for text categorization. In *Proceedings of the 26th annual international ACM SIGIR conference on Research and development in informaion retrieval* (pp. 104-110). ACM.

Kim, H. S., & Sundar, S. S. (2011). Using interface cues in online health community boards to change impressions and encourage user contribution. Paper presented at the *Proceedings of the 2011 Annual Conference on Human Factors in Computing Systems*, 599-608. doi:10.1145/1978942.1979028

Kirlappos, I., & Sasse, M. A. (2012). Security Education against Phishing: A Modest Proposal for a Major Rethink. *IEEE Security and Privacy Magazine, 10*(2), 24–32. doi:10.1109/MSP.2011.179

Kjell, B., Woods, W., & Frieder, O. (1994). Discrimination of authorship using visualization. *Information Processing & Management, 30*(1), 141–150.

Kniffka, H. (1996). On Forensic Linguistic "Differential Diagnosis.". In H. Kniffka, S. Blackwell, & M. Coulthard (Eds.), *Recent Developments in Forensic Linguistics* (pp. 75–122). Frankfurt Am Main: Peter Lang GmbH.

Kodeswaran, P., Nandakumar, V., Kapoor, S., Kamaraju, P., Joshi, A., & Mukherjea, S. (2012, July). Securing enterprise data on smartphones using run time information flow control. In *Mobile Data Management (MDM), 2012 IEEE 13th International Conference on* (pp. 300-305). IEEE. doi:10.1109/MDM.2012.50

Kong, J., Zerfos, P., Luo, H., Lu, S., & Zhang, L. (2001). Providing Robust and Ubiquitous Security Support for Mobile Adhoc Networks, in Ninth International Conference on Network Protocols (ICNP), 2001, pp. 251–260, also available at http://citeseer.nj.nec.com/kong01providing.html

Koppel, M., Schler, J., & Zigdon, K. (2005). Determining an author's native language by mining a text for errors. In *Proceedings of the eleventh ACM SIGKDD international conference on Knowledge discovery in data mining - KDD '05* (pp. 624–628). New York: ACM Press. doi:10.1145/1081870.1081947

Koppel, M., & Schler, J. (2004, July). Authorship verification as a one-class classification problem. In *Proceedings of the twenty-first international conference on Machine learning* (p. 62). ACM.

Koppel, M., Schler, J., & Bonchek-Dokow, E. (2007). Measuring Differentiability: Unmasking Pseudonymous Authors. *Journal of Machine Learning Research, 8*(6).

Kowalski, E.F., Cappelli, D.M., & Moore, A.P. (2008). *Insider Threat Study: Illicit Cyber Activity in the Information Technology and Telecommunications Sector.* Joint SEI and U.S. Secret Service Report, January 2008.

Kreitner, R., & Kinicki, A. (2007). *Organizational Behavior* (7th ed.). New York, New York: McGraw-Hill.

Kshetri, N. (2010). Diffusion and effects of cyber-crime in developing economies. *Third World Quarterly, 31*(7), 1057–1079. doi:10.1080/01436597.2010.518752

Kuman, D., & Morarjee, K. (2014). Insider data theft detection using decoy and user behavior profile. International Journal of Research in Computer Applications and Robotics. 2(2), 51-55.

Kumar, G., & Chelikani, A. (2011). Analysis of security issues in cloud based e-learning.

Kumaraguru, P., Sheng, S., Acquisti, A., Cranor, L. F., & Hong, J. (2010). Teaching Johnny not to fall for phish. *ACM Transactions on Internet Technology, 10*(2), 7. doi:10.1145/1754393.1754396

Kyung Kim, T., & Suk Seo, H. (2008). *A Trust Model using Fuzzy Logic in Wireless Sensor Network.* World Academy of Science, Engineering and Technology.

Labov, W. (1984). Field Methods of the Project on Linguistic Change and Variation. In J. Baugh & J. Sherzer (Eds.), *Language in Use: Reading in Sociolinguistics* (pp. 29–53).

Lakshminarayanan, K., Adkins, D., Perrig, A., & Stoica, I. (2003). Taming IP Packet Flooding Attacks. In *2nd ACM Workshop on Hot Topics in Networks.* 2003. Cambridge, MA: ACM Press pp. 45-50.

Lane, L. M. (2009). Insidious pedagogy. How course management systems impact technology. *First Monday Peer-Reviewed Online Journal.* Retrieved from http://firstmonday.org/ojs/index.php/fm/article/view/2530/2303

Lango, J. (2014). Toward software - defined SLAs. *Communications of the ACM, 57*(1), 54–60. doi:10.1145/2541883.2541894

Lantz, P. (2011). *An Android Application Sandbox for Dynamic Analysis.* (Master's Thesis at Department of Electrical and Information Technology), Lund University, Sweden.

Lardinois, F. (2012), *U.S. House passes controversial CISPA cybersecurity bill 248 To 168.* Retrieved June 14, 2014 from http://techcrunch.com/2012/04/26/u-s-house-passes-cispa-248-to-168/

Latitude Learning, L. L. C. (2014). Our clients love our LMS. *Latitude Learning.* Retrieved from http://www.latitudelearning.com

Lawson, L. (2005). Session Hijacking Packet Analysis. 2005, SecurityDocs.com Report.

Layton, R., Watters, P., & Dazeley, R. (2012, October). Unsupervised authorship analysis of phishing webpages. In Communications and Information Technologies (ISCIT), 2012 International Symposium on (pp. 1104-1109). IEEE.

Lazos, L., Poovendran, R., Meadows, C., Syverson, P., & Chang, L. W. (2005) Preventing Wormhole Attacks on Wireless Ad Hoc Networks: A Graph Theoretic Approach. In *IEEE Wireless Communications and Networking Conference.* 2005. pp. 1193-1199. doi:10.1109/WCNC.2005.1424678

Leighton, A., Keenan, M., & McAnulty, U. (2013). 'In all fairness...?' Housing policy and welfare reform.

Leiwo, J., Aura, T., & Nikander, P. (2000). Towards Network Denial Of Service Resistant Protocols. In 15th International Information Security Conference 2000. Beijing, China. pp. 301-310. doi:10.1007/978-0-387-35515-3_31

Leonard, R. A. (2005). Forensic Linguistics. *The International Journal of the Humanities, 3,* 65–70.

Leung, C., Harris, R., & Rampton, B. (1997). The Idealised Native Speaker, Reified Ethnicities, and Classroom Realities. *TESOL Quarterly, 31*(3), 543–560. http://www.ncbi.nlm.nih.gov/pubmed/21344620 doi:10.2307/3587837

Levijoki, S. (2000). Authentication, Authorization and Accounting in Ad-hoc networks Department of Computer Science Helsinki University of Technology 26th of May 2000 http://www.hut.fi/~slevijok/aaa.htm

Levy, Y., Ramim, M. M., & Hackney, R. A. (2013). Assessing ethical severity of e-Learning systems security attacks. *Journal of Computer Information Systems, 53*(3), 75–84.

Lewis, J. A. (2002). *Assessing the risks of cyber terrorism, cyber war and other cyber threats.* Center for Strategic & International Studies.

Lewis, K. D., & Lewis, J. E. (2010). Web single sign-on authentication using SAML. [IJCSI]. *International Journal of Computer Science Issues, 7*(4).

Li, J., Gu, D., & Luo, Y. (2012, June). Android malware forensics: reconstruction of malicious events. In *Distributed Computing Systems Workshops (ICDCSW), 2012 32nd International Conference on* (pp. 552-558). IEEE. doi:10.1109/ICDCSW.2012.33

Li, J., Sung, M., Xu, J., & Li, L. E. (2004). Large-Scale IP Traceback in High-Speed Internet: Practical Techniques and Theoretical Foundation. In IEEE Symposium on Security and Privacy 2004. Oakland, California, USA. 115.

Library of Congress. (2014). *List of Sub-Saharan African countries. Africana Collections.* Accessed April 23. http://www.loc.gov/rr/amed/guide/afr-countrylist.html

Lim, J., Stratopoulos, C. T., & Wirjanto, S. T. (2013). Sustainability of a firm's reputation for information technology capability: The role of senior IT executives. *Journal of Management Information Systems, 30*(1), 57–96. doi:10.2753/MIS0742-1222300102

Lindenberg, S. (2014). Finding the right LMS fit. *T+D, 68*(4), 28.

Li-ping, D. I. N. G. (2012). Analysis the Security of Android. *Netinfo Security, 3*, 011.

Lockefeer, L. (2010). *Encrypted SMS, an analysis of the theoretical necessities and implementation possibilities.* Retrieved from http://www.cs.ru.nl

Love, S. (2005). *Understanding mobile human-computer interaction.* Oxford, UK: Butterworth-Heinemann.

Lowe, K. M. (2014). How to make the SaaS decision. *Chief Learning Officer, 13*(2), 38–47.

LRN. (n.d.). *About LRN.* Retrieved from http://dotlrn.org/about/

Luo, H., Kong, J., Zerfos, P., Lu, S., & Zhang, L. (2000). *Self Securing Ad-hoc Wireless Networks. IEEE Symposium on Computers and Communications (ISCC'02).*

Luo, T., Hao, H., Du, W., Wang, Y., & Yin, H. (2011, December). Attacks on WebView in the Android system. In *Proceedings of the 27th Annual Computer Security Applications Conference* (pp. 343-352). ACM. doi:10.1145/2076732.2076781

Lu, T., Zheng, K., Fu, R., Liu, Y., Wu, B., & Guo, S. (2012). A Danger Theory Based Mobile Virus Detection Model and Its Application in Inhibiting Virus. *Journal of Networks, 7*(8), 1227–1232. doi:10.4304/jnw.7.8.1227-1232

Luther, W. J., & Olson, J. (2013). *Bitcoin is Memory.* Available at SSRN 2275730.

Lyncaster, L., & Stillman, D. (2010). *The M-Factor: How the Millennial Generation Is Rocking the Workplace.* Los Angeles, CA: Harper Collins.

Lynch, A. (2008). *ROI on generation Y employees.* Bottom Line Conversations, LLC. Retrieved from http://www.knoxvillechamber.com/pdf/workforce/ROIonGenYWhitePaper.pdf

Macharia, J. (2014). Internet access is no longer a luxury. *Africa Renewal.* Retrieved from http://www.un.org/africarenewal/magazine/april-2014/internet access-no-longer-luxury.

MacWillson, A. (2011, May 9). *Rethinking Cybersecurity in a Mobile World.* Retrieved March 9, 2012, from Security Week: Internet and Enterprise Security News, Insights & Analysis: http://www.securityweek.com/rethinking-cybersecurity-mobile-world

Madigan, D., Genkin, A., Lewis, D. D., Argamon, S., Fradkin, D., & Ye, L. (2005, June). Author identification on the large scale. In *Proc. of the Meeting of the Classification Society of North America.*

Ma, J., Li, Y., & Teng, G. (2014). CWAAP: An Authorship Attribution Forensic Platform for Chinese Web Information. *Journal of Software, 9*(1), 11–19.

Malone, E. (1787). *A Dissertation on the three parts of King Henry VI., tending to shew that those plays were not written originally by Shakspeare.* Gale Ecco, Print Editions.

Mangiuc, D. M. (2010). Modelul "software as a service" si posibilele sale aplicatii în domeniul auditului financial. *Audit Financiar, 8*(8), 29-39. Retrieved from http://search.proquest.com/docview/729259251?accountid=62746

Marbury v. Madison, (1803). 5 U.S. 137

Marmol, F. G., & Perez, G. M. (2009). Security threats scenarios in trust and reputation models for distributed systems. *Computers & Security*, *28*(7), 545–556. doi:10.1016/j.cose.2009.05.005

Marrone, M., Gacenga, F., Cater-Steel, A., & Kolbe, L. (2014). IT service management: A cross-national study of ITIL adoption. *Communications of the Association for Information Systems*, *34*, 865–892.

Martins, L. L., & Kellermanns, F. (2004). A model of business school students' acceptance of a web-based course management system. *Academy of Management Learning & Education*, *3*(1), 7–26. doi:10.5465/AMLE.2004.12436815

Marti, S., Giuli, T., Lai, K., & Baker, M. (2000). Mitigating Routing Misbehaviour in Mobile Ad-hoc Networks. In *Proceedings of the ACM International Conference on Mobile Computing and Networking MobiCom*.

Marwan, O., & Dawson, M. E., Jr. (2013). *Research in progress- defending android smartphones from malware attacks*. Paper presented at the 2012 Third International Conference on Advanced Computing & Communication Technologies, Gymkhana Club, HUDA Sector 4, Rohtak. Retrieved from http://jpinfotech.org/wp-content/plugins/infotech/file/upload/pdf/559Research-in-Progress--Defending-Android-Smartphones-from-Malware-Attacks-pdf.pdf

Mathews, Sudarsan, Kannan, & Karthik. (2012). A Secure and Energy Enhanced Protocol for Routing in Mobile Ad-Hoc Networks. *International Journal of Scientific & Engineering Research*, *3*(11).

Maxwell, J. (2011). *The 5 levels of leadership*. New York, NY: Hachette Book Group.

McDaniel, A. E. (2013). Securing the information and communications technology global supply chain from exploitation: Developing a strategy for education, training, and awareness. *Issues in Informing Science & Information Technology*, *10*, 313–324.

McGrath, M. (2009, October). How to Motivate Millennials. *Talent Management Magazine*.

McGregor, D. (1960). *The Human side of Enterprise*. New York: McGraw Hill.

McMahon, B, Miles, S. & Bennett, N. (2011, June). *Managing the Millennials*. Talent Management.

Mendenhall, T. C. (1887). The characteristic curves of composition. *Polar Science*, *11*, 237–246.

Michiardi & Molva. (2002). CORE: a collaborative reputation mechanism to enforce node cooperation in mobile ad hoc networks. In *Proceedings of the Communication and Multimedia Security Conference*.

Micro, T. (2013). *Mobile security*. Retrieved December 2014, from apac.trendmicro.com

Miller, K. W., Voas, J., & Hurlburt, G. F. (2012). BYOD: security and privacy considerations. *It Professional*, *14*(5), 0053-55.

Millie, A. (2011). Big society, small government: The british coalition government and tackling anti-social behaviour. *Crime Prevention and Community Safety*, *13*(4), 284–287. doi:10.1057/cpcs.2011.17

Mills, E. (2011). *Android hole could be used to disable antivirus apps*. Retrieved Jan.09, 2013, from http://news.cnet.com/8301-27080_3-20115108-245/android-hole-could-be-used-to-disable-antivirus-apps/

Mimoso, M. (2013). *New Dexter point-of-sale malware campaigns discovered*. Retrieved from the Internet at.

Min, S. (2004). A Study on the Security of NTRUSign Digital Signature Scheme. 2004, Master Thesis in Information and Communications University, Korea.

Mirkovic, J., Prier, G., & Reiher, P. (2002). Attacking DDoS at the Source In the 10th IEEE International Conference on Network Protocols. 2002: IEEE Computer Society. pp. 312-321.

Misra, A., & Dubey, A. (2013). *Android security: attacks and defenses*. CRC Press. doi:10.1201/b14672

Mohebzada, J. G., El Zarka, A., Bhojani, A. H., & Darwish, A. (2012, March). Phishing in a university community: Two large scale phishing experiments. In *Innovations in Information Technology (IIT), 2012 International Conference: Abu Dhabi* (pp. 249-254). IEEE.

Molva, R., & Michiardi, P. (2002). Security in Ad Hoc Networks. In Personal Wireless Communications, IFIP-TC6 8th International Conference. 2002. Venice, Italy: Springer. pp. 756-775. doi:10.1007/978-3-540-39867-7_69

Monarch Media Inc. (2010). The open-source LMS. *Open-Source Learning Management Systems: Sakai and Moodle.*

Moodle. (2014). Decision FAQ. *Documentation.* Retrieved from http://docs.moodle.org/27/en/index.php?search=cms&title=Special%3ASearch

Moody, G., Galletta, D., Walker, J., & Dunn, B. (2011). Which Phish Get Caught? An Exploratory Study of Individual Susceptibility to Phishing.*Proceedings of the International Conference on Information Systems, ICIS 2011*, Shanghai, China.

Mosteller, F., & Wallace, D. (1964). *Inference and disputed authorship: The Federalist.*

Muir, J. (2003). Decoding mobile device security. *Computerworld*, 14.

Mulliner, C., & Miller, C. (2009). Injecting SMS messages into smartphones for security analysis. *Proceedings of the 3rd USENIX Workshop on Offensive Technologies Montreal, Canada.* Retrieved from www.usenix.org

Munro, K. (2012). Deconstructing Flame: The limitations of traditional defences. *Computer Fraud & Security*, *2012*(10), 8–11. doi:10.1016/S1361-3723(12)70102-1

Murphy, S. D. (2002). Terrorism and the Concept of Armed Attack in Article 51 of the UN Charter. *Harvard International Law Journal*, *43*, 41.

Myers, M. A. (1982). Common law in action: The prosecution of felonies and misdemeanors*. *Sociological Inquiry*, *52*(1), 1–15. doi:10.1111/j.1475-682X.1982.tb01235.x PMID:11618150

Nakamoto, S. (2008). Bitcoin: A peer-to-peer electronic cash system. *Consulted, 1*(2012), 28.

Nakashima, E. (2013). US Target of Massive Cyber-Espionage Campaign. *Washington Post.*

Nash, J. F. (1950). Equilibrium points in n-person games. *Proceedings of the National Academy of Sciences of the United States of America*, *38*(1), 48–49. doi:10.1073/pnas.36.1.48 PMID:16588946

Nasinar, M. A., & Rasheed, A. A. (2014). Dynamic security technique for content management repository system. *International Journal of Research in Advent Technology*, *2*(1), 10–15.

Nathan, J. (1996). *Charter schools: Creating hope and opportunity for American education.* San Francisco: Jossey-Bass Publishers.

National Institute of Standards and Technology (NIST). (2014). *Framework for Improving Critical Infrastructure Cybersecurity.* United States of America.

Ndubueze, P., Mazindu, I., Emmanuel, U., & Okoye, U. (2013). Cyber crime victimization among internet active Nigerians: An analysis of socio-demographic correlates. *International Journal of Criminal Justice Sciences.*, *8*(2), 225–234.

Nelson, B., Berman, P., Ericson, J., Kamprath, N., Perry, R., Silverman, D., & Solomon, D. (2000). *The state of charter schools 2000: Fourth-year report.* Washington, D.C.: U.S. Department of Education, Office of Educational Research and Improvement.

Neumann, P. G. (1997). Identity-related misuse. *Communications of the ACM*, *40*(7), 112–112. doi:10.1145/256175.256196

Nguyan, D., Zhao, L., Uisawang, P., & Platt, J. (2000). Security Routing Analysis For Mobile Ad-hoc Networks. Interdisciplinary Telecommunications Program of Colorado University, Spring 2000.

Nichols, R. K., & Lekkas, P. C. (2002). Wireless Security: Models, Threats, and Solutions 1ed. 2002: McGraw-Hill Professional. pp. 657.

Notice of Breach of Security Act, (2003). Cal. Civ. Code § 1798.29

Nwabueze, C., & Ekwughe, V. (2014). Nigerian newspapers' coverage of the effect of Boko Haram activities on the environment. *Journal of African Media Studies.*, *6*(1), 71–89. doi:10.1386/jams.6.1.71_1

Oh, H. S., Kim, B. J., Choi, H. K., & Moon, S. M. (2012, October). Evaluation of Android Dalvik virtual machine. In *Proceedings of the 10th International Workshop on Java Technologies for Real-time and Embedded Systems* (pp. 115-124). ACM. doi:10.1145/2388936.2388956

Olsson, J. (2004). *Forensic Linguistics. An Introduction to Language, Crime and the Law*. London, New York: Continuum.

Omar, A., Alijani, D., & Mason, R. (2011). Information technology disaster recovery plan: Case Study. *Academy of Strategic Management Journal*, *10*(2), 127–141.

O'Neill, B. (1995). Weak models, nil hypotheses, and decorative statistics. *The Journal of Conflict Resolution*, *39*(4), 731–748. doi:10.1177/0022002795039004007

Ontang, M., McLaughlin, S., Enck, W., & McDaniel, P. (2009). *Semantically rich application-centric security in Android*. Retrieved from Proceedings of teh 25th Annual Computer Security Applciations Conference (ACSAC '09): http://dl.acm.org

Owasp, T. (2010). *The Ten Most Critical Web Application Security Risks*. Retrieved April 4, 2015, from https://www.owasp.org

Oxford Dictionaries on-line. (n.d.). Retrieved December 2014, from http://oxforddictionaries.com/

Paganini, P. (2012). Cyber security landscape in Africa. *Security Affairs*. Retrieved from http://securityaffairs.co/wordpress/9746/security/cyber-security-landscape-in-africa.html

Pal, A. K. (2014). Application of digital rights management in library. *DESIDOC Journal of Library & Information Technology*, *34*(1), 11–15. doi:10.14429/djlit.34.5490

Palmer, L. B., and Gau, R. (2003, June). *Charter school authorizing: Are states making the grade*? Washington, D.C.: Thomas B. Fordham Institute.

Papadimitratos, P., & Haas, Z. J. (2002). Secure Routing for Mobile Ad-hoc Networks. In *Proceedings of the SCS Communication Networks and Distributed Systems Modelling and Simulations Conference (CNDS 2002)*, San Antonio, TX, January 27-31, 2002.

Parrish, J. L. Jr, Bailey, J. L., & Courtney, J. F. (2009). *A Personality Based Model for Determining Susceptibility to Phishing Attacks*. Little Rock: University of Arkansas.

Pastor, R., Hernandez, R., Ros, S., Robles-Gomez, A., Caminero, A. C., & Castro, M. (2011). A video-message evaluation tool integrated in the unedited e-learning platform. *Proceedings of the 41st ASEE/IEEE Frontiers in Education Conference (FIE)*, Rapid City, SD, F3C-1 – F3C-6.

Patrikakis, C., Masikos, M., & Zouraraki, O. (2004). Distributed Denial of Service Attacks. *The Internet Protocol J.*, *7*(4), 13–35.

Pattinson, M., Jerram, C., Parsons, K., McCormac, A., & Butavicius, M. (2012). Why do some people manage phishing e-mails better than others? *Information Management & Computer Security*, *20*(1), 18–28. doi:10.1108/09685221211219173

Peng, F., Schuurmans, D., & Wang, S. (2004). Augmenting naive Bayes classifiers with statistical language models. *Information Retrieval*, *7*(3-4), 317–345.

Penrose, J. (2007, July). Tracking Employee Engagement. *Talent Management Magazine*.

Perkins & Royer. (1999). Ad-hoc On-Demand Distance Vector Routing. In *Proceedings of the Second IEEE Workshop on Mobile Computer Systems and Applications*. doi:10.1109/INFOCOM.2006.154

Perkins, R. C. (2012). *Linguistic Identifiers of L1 Persian speakers writing in English. NLID for Authorship Analysis* Unpublished doctoral dissertation. Aston University, Birmingham, U.K.

Perkins, R., & Grant, T. (2013). Forensic linguistics. In Encyclopedia of Forensic Sciences. doi:10.1016/B978-0-12-382165-2.00030-1

Perloth, N. (2013). Researchers Find 25 Countries Using Surveillance Software. *New York Times*, Bits blog. 10 December. Retrieved from http://bits.blogs.nytimes.com/2013/03/13/researchers-find-25-countries-using-surveillance-software

Pestian, J., Nasrallah, H., Matykiewicz, P., Bennett, A., & Leenaars, A. (2010). Suicide Note Classification Using Natural Language Processing: A Content Analysis. *Biomedical informatics insights*, *2010*(3), 19-28.

Phillips, W. (2011). LOLing at tragedy: Facebook trolls, memorial pages and resistance to grief online. *First Monday, 16*(12). doi:10.5210/fm.v16i12.3168

Phishing Scams. (n.d.). Retrieved March 2014, from http://www.onguardonline.gov

Picciotto, S. (2007). Constructing compliance: Game playing, tax law, and the regulatory state. *Law & Policy, 29*(1), 11–30. doi:10.1111/j.1467-9930.2007.00243.x

Pickering, S., McCulloch, J., & Wright-Neville, D. (2008). Counter-terrorism policing: Towards social cohesion. *Crime, Law, and Social Change, 50*(1-2), 91–109. doi:10.1007/s10611-008-9119-3

Pickett, J. P. (2000). *The American Heritage dictionary of the English language* (4th ed.). Boston: Houghton Mifflin Company.

Ponemon Institute. (2012). *Third Annual Benchmark Study on Patient Privacy & Data Security.* Portland, Oregon: Ponemon Institute.

Prescott, A. (1998). Writing about rebellion: Using the records of the peasants' revolt of 1381. Paper presented at the *History Workshop Journal, 1998*(45) 1-28. doi:10.1093/hwj/1998.45.1

Probst, C., Hunker, J., Gollmann, D., & Bishop, M. (2010). "Insider Threats in Cyber Security" (Advances in Information Security) (pp 20-30). New York: Springer. doi:10.1007/978-1-4419-7133-3

Probst, C., Hunker, J., Gollmann, D., & Bishop, M. (2010). Aspects of Insider Threats. *Advances in Information Security, 49*(10), 1–15.

Protecting You against Phishing. (n.d.). Retrieved March 2013, from http://www.vodafone.co.uk/about-this-site/our-privacy-policy/protecting-our-customers/phishing

Pusey, P., & Sadera, W. A. (2012). Cyberethics, cybersafety, and cybersecurity: Preservice teacher knowledge, preparedness, and the need for teacher education to make a difference. *Journal of Digital Learning in Teacher Education, 28*(2).

Quinche, F. (2011). Cyber-harcèlement. jeunes et violences" virtuelles. *Jeunes Et Médias-Les Cahiers Francophones De L'Éducation Aux Médias-N° 1, 1*, 143.

Quinlan, J. R. (1993). *C4. 5: programs for machine learning* (Vol. 1). Morgan Kaufmann.

Qureshi, Min & Kouvatsos. (2011). Countering the collusion attack with a multidimentionnal decentralized trust and reputation model in disconnected MANETs. Journal of Multimedia Tools and Applications, Springer.

Rabahi, Y., Mujica-V, V. E., & Sisalem, D. (2005), A Reputation-Based Trust Mechanism for Ad hoc Networks. In *ISCC '05: Proceedings of the 10th IEEE Symposium on Computers and Communications (ISCC'05)*, pages 37–42, Washington, DC, USA doi:10.1109/ISCC.2005.17

Rabin, T. (1998). A Simplified Approach to Threshold and Proactive RSA. In. Lecture Notes in Computer Science: Vol. 1462. *Advances in Cryptology – Crypto 98 Proceedings* (pp. 89–104). Springer-Verlag. doi:10.1007/BFb0055722

Radvilavicius, L., Marozas, L., & Cenys, A. (2012). Overview of Real-Time Antivirus Scanning Engines. *Journal of Engineering Science and Technology Review, 5*(1), 63–71.

Rafique, K. (2002). *A Survey of Mobile Ad Hoc Networks. ELEN 695, Presented to Dr. Campbell.* Available at: http://www.columbia.edu/itc/ee/e6951/2002spring/Projects/CVN/report13.pdf

Rahman, A., & Gburzynski, P. (2006). *Hidden Problems with the Hidden Node Problem.* Available at: http://citeseerx.ist.psu.edu/viewdoc/download?doi=10.1.1.61.365&rep=rep1&type=pdf

Ramaswamy, S., Fu, H., Sreekantaradhya, M., Dixon, J., & Nygard, K. (2003). Prevention of Cooperative Black Hole Attack in Wireless Ad Hoc Networks. In International Conference on Wireless Networks 2003. 2003. pp.570-575.

Rampton, M. B. H. (1990). Displacing the "native speaker": Expertise, affiliation, and inheritance. *ELT Journal, 44*(2), 97–101. http://eltj.oupjournals.org/cgi/doi/10.1093/elt/44.2.97 doi:10.1093/elt/44.2.97

Randazzo, M. R., Keeney, M., Kowalski, E., Cappelli, D., & Moore, A. (2005). *Insider Threat Study: Illicit Cyber Activity in the Banking and Finance Sector.* U.S. Secret Service and CERT Coordination Center: Software Engineering Institute.

Rao, L. (2011, December 13). *Lookout's 2012 Mobile Security Threat Predictions: SMS Fraud, Botnets And Malvertising*. Retrieved April 22, 2012, from Tech Crunch: http://techcrunch.com/2011/12/13/lookouts-2012-mobile-security-threat-predictions-sms-fraud-botnets-and-malvertising/

Rash, W. (2004). *Latest skulls Trojan foretells risky smartphone future*. Retrieved from www.eweek.com

Rathi, A. (2013). *Android Malware will Increase in 2013*. Retrieved Jan.15, 2013, from http://newamazingtech. blogspot.com.au/p/about-us.html

Ravi, C., & Manoharan, R. (2012). Malware Detection using Windows API Sequence and Machine Learning. *International Journal of Computers and Applications*, *43*(17), 12–16. doi:10.5120/6194-8715

Red Bank Regional High School. (2013). *Red Bank Regional High School Profile 2013*, Retrieved from http://www.rbrhs.org/Services/Guidance/Profile.pdf

Reed, A., & Smith, G. (2004). Omission to act can amount to an assault or battery. *Journal of Criminal Law*, *68*(6), 459–465. doi:10.1350/jcla.68.6.459.54142

Reid, F., & Harrigan, M. (2013). *An analysis of anonymity in the bitcoin system* (pp. 197–223). Springer New York. doi:10.1007/978-1-4614-4139-7_10

Reisinger, D. (2014). 10 Ways to protect yourself from the zero-day IE exploit. *Eweek, 1*.

Reisinger, D. (2014). Target's massive data breach: 10 things you need to know. eWeek. 1/13/2014, p. 8.

Renchler, R. (2002). *School organization: Grade span Trends and issues (ERIC document ED 472994)*. Washington, D.C.: Office of Educational Research and Improvement.

Rhodes-Ousley, M. (2013). *Information Security*. Washington, DC: McGraw Hill.

Richard, B., & Ron, Z. (2005). Student achievement in charter schools: A complex picture. *Journal of Policy Analysis and Management*, *24*(2), 351–371. doi:10.1002/pam.20093

Roberts, J. (2011). *Beyond Learning by Doing: Theoretical Currents in Experiential Education*. London: Routledge.

Ross, A. (2008). Why legislate for sustainable development? an examination of sustainable development provisions in UK and scottish statutes. *Journal of Environmental Law*, *20*(1), 35–68. doi:10.1093/jel/eqm019

Royer, E., & Toh, C. (1999). A Review of Current Routing Protocols for Ad Hoc Mobile Wireless Networks. *IEEE Personal Communications*, *6*(2), 46–55. doi:10.1109/98.760423

Roy, R., Tomar, D., & Singh, N. (2010). An Approach to Understand the End User Behaviour through Log Analysis. *International Journal of Computers and Applications*, *5*(Issue.11), 27–34. doi:10.5120/953-1330

RPP International and University of Minnesota. (1997). *A study of charter schools: First-year report*. Washington, D.C.: U.S. Department of Education, Office of Educational Research and Improvement.

Ruggiero, P. a. (2011). *Cyber Threats to Mobile Phones*. Pittsburgh: United States Computer Emergency Readiness Team.

Rygl, J. (2013, January). *Determining Authorship of Anonymous Texts*. PhD thesis proposal, Masaryk University, (pp.2-3).

Rygl, J., & Horák, A. (2011). *A Framework for Authorship Identification in the Internet Environment*.

Saba Software, Inc. (2014). LMS. *Learn@work*. Retrieved from http://www.saba.com/us/lms/

Sabater, & Sierra. (2002). Reputation and social network analysis in multi-agent systems. First International Joint Conference on Autonomous Agents and Multi-Agent Systems, Bologna, Italy

Sachan & Mohan Khilar. (2011). Securing AODV Routing Protocol in MANET Based on Cryptographic Authentication Mechanism. *International Journal of Network Security & Its Applications*, *3*(5).

Salya, A., & Ravi, M. (2013). Survey on defense against insider misuse attacks in the cloud. *International Journal of Advanced Computing*, *5*(1), 20-25.

Sandra, H. (2002). Children with special needs and school choice: Five stories. *Preventing School Failure*, *46*(2), 75–78. doi:10.1080/10459880209603350

Sans. (2000). *Egress Filtering v 0.2. 2000, SANS*. Available at: http://www.sans.org/y2k/egress.htm

Sanyal, S., & Gupta, S. (2010). "New Frontiers of Network Security: The Threat Within," *Second Vaagdevi International Conference on Information Technology for Real World Problems*, 2010. pp.63-66 doi:10.1109/VCON.2010.19

Sarker, S., & Wells, J. D. (2003). Understanding mobile handheld device use and adoption. *Communications of the ACM*, *46*(12), 35–40. doi:10.1145/953460.953484

Savage, S., Wetherall, D., Karlin, A., & Anderson, T. (2000). Practical Network Support for IP Traceback. In the 2000 ACM SIGCOMM Conference. 2000. Stockholm, Sweden. pp. 295-306.

Schiller, J. H. (Ed.). (2003). *Mobile communications*. Pearson Education.

Schmidt, A. D., Schmidt, H. G., Clausen, J., Yuksel, K. A., Kiraz, O., Camtepe, A., & Albayrak, S. (2008). *Enhancing security of linux-based android devices*. Paper presented at the 15th International Linux Kongress. Lehmann.

Schmidt, A.-D., Bye, R., Schmidt, H.-G., Clausen, J., & Kiraz, O. (2009). *Static analysis of executables for collaborative malware detecion on Android*. Retrieved from www.dai-labor.de

Schnackenberg, D., Djahandari, K., & Sterne, D. (2000). Infrastructure for Intrusion Detection and Response. In DARPA Information Survivability Conference and Exposition. 2000. pp. 1003-1011.

Schuller, J. (2003). *Understanding Wireless LAN Technology and Its Security Risks*. Available at GIAC: http://www.giac.org/practical/GSEC/Julie_Schuller_GSEC.pdf

Schwartz, M. J. (2011). Zeus Banking Trojan Hits Android Phones. *informationweek*. Retrieved Apr. 29, 2013, from http://www.informationweek.com/security/mobile/zeus-banking-trojan-hits-android-phones/231001685

Schwingenschlögl, C., & Horn, M.-P. (2002). Building Blocks for Secure Communication in Ad-hoc Networks. In *Proceedings of the 4th European Wireless (EW'02) Florence*, Italy.

Sebastiani, F. (2002). Machine learning in automated text categorization.[CSUR]. *ACM Computing Surveys*, *34*(1), 1–47.

Secure Mail Anti-Phishing. (n.d.). Retrieved December 2014, from http://www.hsbc.com/1/2/online-security/phishing

Security Cartoon. (2013). Retrieved February 2103, from http://Securitycartoon.com

Security For The Post-PC Era. Mobile Security. (2013). Retrieved March 2103, from http://www.Lookout.com

Selinker, L. (1972). Interlanguage. *IRAL*, *10*(1-4), 209–231. doi:10.1515/iral.1972.10.1-4.209

Senge, P. (1990). *The Fifth Discipline: The Art and Practice of the Learning Organization*. New York: Doubleday.

Shabtai, A., Fledel, Y., Kanonov, U., Elovici, Y., Dolev, S., & Glezer, C. (2010, March/April). Android: A comprehensive security assessment. *IEEE Security and Privacy*, *8*(2), 35–44. doi:10.1109/MSP.2010.2

Shaw, E. (2009). The consumer and new labour: The consumer as king? *The Consumer in Public Services: Choice, Values and Difference,*, 19.

Sheng, S., Magnien, B., Kumaraguru, P., Acquisti, A., Cranor, L. F., Hong, J., & Nunge, E. (2007, July). Antiphishing phil: the design and evaluation of a game that teaches people not to fall for phish. In *Proceedings of the 3rd symposium on Usable privacy and security* (pp. 88-99). ACM. doi:10.1145/1280680.1280692

Shih-Yao, D., & Sy-Yen, K. (2007). *MAPMon: A Host-Based Malware Detection Tool*. Paper presented at the International Symposium on Dependable Computing, 2007. PRDC 2007. 13th Pacific Rim

Shoffner, M., Owen, P., Mostafa, J., Lamm, B., Wang, X., Schmitt, C., & Ahalt, S. C. (2013). The secure medical research workspace: An IT Infrastructure to enable secure research on clinical data. *CTS Clinical & Translational Science*, *6*(3), 222–225. doi:10.1111/cts.12060 PMID:23751029

Shoup, V. (2000). Practical Threshold Signatures. In. Lecture Notes in Computer Science: Vol. 1807. *Advances in Cryptology-Eurocrypt 2000 proceedings* (pp. 207–221). Springer Verlag. doi:10.1007/3-540-45539-6_15

Shuy, R. (2001). Forensic Lingusitics. In M. Aronoff & J. Rees-Miller (Eds.), The Handbook of Linguistics (Kindle., pp. 683–691). Oxford & Malden: Blackwell Publishing Ltd.

Silva, R. S., & Laboreiro, G. (2011). Automatic Authorship Analysis of Micro-Blogging Messages. *ReCALL*, 161–168.

Simpson, E. H. (1949). Measurement of diversity. *Nature*.

Singh, S. (2012). *Malware target on Android OS set to increase in 2013*. Retrieved Jan.15, 2013, from http://articles.economictimes.indiatimes.com/2012-12-25/news/35999218_1_malware-android-os-flash-drives

Sinha, R., Machado, F., & Sellman, C. (2010). Don't think twice, it's all right: Music piracy and pricing in a DRM-free environment. *Journal of Marketing*, *74*(2), 40–54. doi:10.1509/jmkg.74.2.40

Six, J. (2011). *Application Security for the Android Platform: Processes, Permissions, and Other Safeguards*. O'Reilly Media, Inc.

Solo, A. M. G., & Bishop, J. (2011). The new field of network politics. Paper presented at the *The 2011 International Conference on E-Learning, E-Business, Enterprise Information Systems & E-Government (EEE'11)*, Las Vegas, NV. 442-444.

Solo, A. M. G., & Bishop, J. (2014). Conceptualizing network politics following the arab spring. In A. M. G. Solo (Ed.), *Handbook of research on political activism in the information age* (pp. 231–238). Hershey, PA: IGI Global. doi:10.4018/978-1-4666-6066-3.ch014

Sophos. (2012). *Fixing Sophos AutoUpdate after required files were deleted or moved by Sophos Anti-Virus due to a false positive*. Retrieved Jan. 05, 2013, from http://www.sophos.com/en-us/support/knowledgebase/118323.aspx

Srikwan, S., & Jakobsson, M. (2008). Using cartoons to teach internet security. *Cryptologia*, *32*(2), 137–154. doi:10.1080/01611190701743724

Staffeld, M. (2013). Terrorism, instability, and democracy in Asia and Africa. *Air & Space Power Journal*, *27*(2), 178–180.

Stajano, F., & Anderson, R. (1999). The Resurrecting Duckling: Security Issues for Ad-Hoc Wireless networks. In *Proceedings of the 7th International Workshop on Security Protocols*.

Stamatatos, E. (2009). A survey of modern authorship attribution methods. *Journal of the American Society for Information Science and Technology*, *60*(3), 538–556.

Stamatatos, E., Fakotakis, N., & Kokkinakis, G. (1999, June). Automatic authorship attribution. In *Proceedings of the ninth conference on European chapter of the Association for Computational Linguistics* (pp. 158-164). Association for Computational Linguistics.

Stannard, J. E. (2010). Sticks, stones and words: Emotional harm and the english criminal law. *Journal of Criminal Law*, *74*(6), 533–556. doi:10.1350/jcla.2010.74.6.668

Starmer, K. (2013). *Guidelines on prosecuting cases involving communications sent via social media*. London, GB: Crown Prosecution Service.

State of California Department of Justice Office of the Attorney General. (2013). *Getting smart about smartphones, tips for parents*. Retrieved June 14, 2014 from http://oag.ca.gov/privacy/facts/online-privacy/smartphones-parents

Stoica, I., Adkins, D., Zhuang, S., Shenker, S., & Surana, S. (2002). Internet Indirection Infrastructure. In ACM SIGCOMM Conference 2002. Pittsburgh, PA, USA. pp.73-88.

Stubblefield, A., Ioannidis, J., & Rubin, A. D. (2002). Using the Fluhrer, Mantin, and Shamir attack to break WEP. In Symposium on Network and Distributed System Security. 2002. Also available at http://www.isoc.org/isoc/conferences/ndss/02/proceedings/papers/stubbl.pdf. Last accessed: 29/09/14

Stubbs, M. (1996). *Text and Corpus Analysis*. Oxford: Blackwell Publishing Ltd.

Sun, S. T., Boshmaf, Y., Hawkey, K., & Beznosov, K. (2010, September). A billion keys, but few locks: the crisis of web single sign-on. *Proceedings of the 2010 Workshop on New Security Paradigms*, Concord, MA, 61-72. doi:10.1145/1900546.1900556

Sun, Y. L., Han, Z., Yu, W., & Liu, K. J. R. (2006). A Trust Evaluation Framework in Distributed Networks: Vulnerability Analysis and Defense against Attacks. [Spain.]. *IEEE INFOCOM, 2006*, 1–13.

Svajcer, V. (2014). Sophos Mobile Security Threat Report. *Sophos Mobile Security Threat Report*. Retrieved Apr. 10, 2015

Symantec, Inc. (2011, April 5). Retrieved April 17, 2012, from Symantec Report Finds Cyber Threats Skyrocket in Volume and Sophistication: http://www.symantec.com/about/news/release/article.jsp?prid=20110404_03

Tamarkin, E. (2014). South Africa must pay more attention to cybercrime. Retrieved from http://www.issafrica.org/iss-today/south-africa-must-pay-more-attention-to-cybercrime

Taylor, F. W. (1911). The Principles of Scientific Management. *Fundaments of Scientific Management*. New York: Harper and Brothers. US government Printing Office. (2013, January 25).[US Government Printing Office.]. *Federal Register*, 78(17).

Tella, A. (2011). Reliability and factor analysis of a blackboard course management system success: A scale development and validation in an educational context. *Journal of Information Technology Education*, 10, 1055–1080.

Teng, G. F., Lai, M. S., Ma, J. B., & Li, Y. (2004, August). E-mail authorship mining based on SVM for computer forensic. In *Proceedings of 2004 International Conference on Machine Learning and Cybernetics, 2004*. (Vol. 2, pp. 1204-1207). IEEE.

Tentena, P. (2014). Cyber crime on the increase in Africa. Retrieved from http://www.busiweek.com/index1.php?Ctp=2&pI=868&pLv=3&srI=69&spI=221&cI=11

Teresa, M.T., & Coulthard, M. (2011, September). Forensic Plagiarism Detection and Authorship Attribution: on the linguists' achievements and the challenges for computerized analysis. *CLEF 2011 - PAN'5 2011 Lab Forensic Linguistics Panel*, 19-22.

Tesfay, W. B., Booth, T., & Andersson, K. (2012, June). Reputation Based Security Model for Android Applications. In *Trust, Security and Privacy in Computing and Communications (TrustCom), 2012 IEEE 11th International Conference on* (pp. 896-901). IEEE. doi:10.1109/TrustCom.2012.236

Thawte. (2014). Cybercrime is a 'national crisis' in South Africa 2014.Business News. *Thawte*. Accessed April 23. https://www.thawte.com/about/news/?story=450371

The International Herald Tribune. (2010). From the International Herald Tribune - 100, 75, 50 Years Ago - NYTimes.com. *International Herald Tribune*. Retrieved December 04, 2012, from http://www.nytimes.com/2010/01/25/opinion/25iht-oldjan25.html?_r=1

The White House. (2014). *Assessing Cybersecurity Regulations*. Retrieved June 14, 2014 from http://m.whitehouse.gov/blog/2014/05/22/assessing-cybersecurity-regulations

Thomason, S. (2001). *Language Contact: An Introduction*. Baltimore: Georgetown University Press. doi:10.1016/B0-08-043076-7/03032-1

Thuente, D., & Acharya, M. (2006). Intelligent jamming in wireless networks with applications to 802.11b and other networks, in *Proceedings of the 25th IEEE Communications Society Military Communications Conference (MILCOM)*, October 2006.

Tian, R. (2011). *An Integrated Malware Detection and Classification System*. PhD Thesis at Deakin University. Melbourne, Australia.

Torgerson, M. and Leeuwen, B.V., (2001). Routing Data in Wireless Ad-hoc Networks. Sandia laboratories report SAND2001-3119 October 2001.

Traynor, P., Ahamad, M., Alperovitch, D., Conti, G., & Davis, J. (2012). *Emerging Cyber Threats Report 2012*. Atlanta: Georgia Tech Information Security Center.

Trend Micro. (2009, August 17). *Smartphone Users: Not Smart Enough About Security*. Retrieved April 17, 2012, from Trend Micro: http://newsroom.trendmicro.com/index.php?s=43&news_item=738&type=archived&year=2009

Trendmicro. (2012). *Adding Android and Mac OS X Malware to the APT Toolbox.* Trend Micro Incorporated Research Paper. Retrieved from http://www.trendmicro.com/cloud-content/us/pdfs/security-intelligence/white-papers/wp_adding-android-and-mac-osx-malware-to-the-apt-toolbox.pdf

Tsanas, A., Little, M. A., McSharry, P. E., Spielman, J., & Ramig, L. O. (2012). Novel Speech Signal Processing Algorithms for High-Accuracy Classification of Parkinson's Disease. *Biomedical Engineering. IEEE Transactions on, 59*(5), 1264–1271. doi:10.1109/TBME.2012.2183367

Tsur, O., & Rappoport, A. (2007). Using Classifier Features for Studying the Effect of Native Language on the Choice of Written Second Language Words. In P. Buttery, A. Villavicencio, & A. Korhonen (Eds.), *Cognitive Aspects of Computational Language Acquisition* (pp. 9–17). Madison: Omnipress. doi:10.3115/1629795.1629797

Tull, C. (2002). *WAP 2.0 Development.* Que Publishing.

U.S. Const. amend. IV (1791).

U.S. Const. art. I, § 8, cl. 1 (1787).

U.S. Const. art. I, § 8, cl. 3 (1787).

U.S. Const. art. III, §§ 1-2 (1787).

U.S. Department of Education. (2000). *Evaluation of the public charter schools program: Year one evaluation report.* Washington, D.C.: Office of the Under Secretary, Planning and Evaluation Service, Elementary and Secondary Program Division.

U.S. Environmental Protection Agency. (2014). *Section 10(b) report on the environmental protection agency's water and wastewater critical infrastructure cybersecurity preparedness.* Retrieved June 14, 2014 from http://water.epa.gov/infrastructure/watersecurity/upload/EO_13696_10-b-_EPA_response.pdf

Ullah, A., Lai, R., & Majoribanks, T. (2013). A proposed model for business sustainability based on business and information technology. *Journal of Software, 8*(11), 2796–2806. doi:10.4304/jsw.8.11.2796-2806

Unal, Z., & Unal, A. (2011). Evaluating and comparing the usability of web-based course management systems. *Journal of Information Technology Education, 10*, 1019–1038.

United States Computer Emergency Readiness Team. (2010, April 15). Cyber Threats to Mobile Devices. (TIP - 10-105-01), 1-16.

University of Delaware. (2014, July 17). University to host US Cyber Challenge summer camp, competition. UD Daily. Retrieved from http://www.udel.edu/udaily/2015/jul/cyber-camp-071714.html

University of Exeter, School of Psychology. (2012). The psychology of scams: Provoking and Committing Errors Of Judgment. Devon, UK

Updegrove, A. (2009). How we'll get the job done: An interview with NIST's Dr. George W. Arnold. Standards Today, 8(3), 32-39.

Van Halteren, H. (2004, July). Linguistic profiling for author recognition and verification. In *Proceedings of the 42nd Annual Meeting on Association for Computational Linguistics* (p. 199). Association for Computational Linguistics.

Vapnik, V. (2000). *The nature of statistical learning theory.* Springer.

Venkatraman, L., & Agrawal, D. P. (2001). An Optimized Inter-Router Authentication Scheme for Ad-hoc networks. In *Proceedings of the 13th International Conference on Wireless Communications*, pp. 129-1, Calgary, Canada.

Vennon, T. (2010). *Android malware.* Retrieved from http://threatcenter.smobilesystems.com/

Venugopal, D., & Hu, G. (2008). Efficient signature based malware detection on mobile devices. *Mobile Information Systems, 4*(1), 33–49. doi:10.1155/2008/712353

Vigna, G., Gwalani, S., Srinivasan, K., Elizabeth, M., Royer, B., & Kemmerer, R. (2004). An Intrusion Detection Tool for AODV-based Ad hoc Wireless Networks. in *20th Annual Computer Security Applications Conference (ACSAC'04).* 2004: IEEE Computer Society pp. 16-27. doi:10.1109/CSAC.2004.6

Vis, F. (2013). Twitter as a reporting tool for breaking news: Journalists tweeting the 2011 UK riots. *Digital Journalism, 1*(1), 27–47. doi:10.1080/21670811.2012.741316

Vishwanath, A., Herath, T., Chen, R., Wang, J., & Rao, H. R. (2011). Why do people get phished? Testing individual differences in phishing vulnerability within an integrated, information processing model. *Decision Support Systems*, *51*(3), 576–586. doi:10.1016/j.dss.2011.03.002

Vogten, H., & Koper, R. (2014). Towards a new generation of Learning Management Systems. Paper presented at the Proceedings of the 6th International Conference on Computer Supported Education, Barcelona, Spain, 514-519.

Voznak, M., & Safarik, J. (2012). DoS attacks targeting SIP server and improvements of robustness. *International Journal of Mathematics and Computers in Simulation*, *6*(1), 177–184.

Waks, L. (2007). The concept of fundamental educational change. *Educational Theory*, *57*(3), 277–295. doi:10.1111/j.1741-5446.2007.00257.x

Walter, T., Hourizi, R., Moncur, W., & Pitsillides, S. (2011). Does the internet change how we die and mourn? an overview. *Omega*, *64*(4), 12. PMID:22530294

Wang, X., Feng, D., Lai, X. and H. Yu (2004). Collisions for Hash Functions MD4, MD5, HAVAL-128 and RIPEMD. 2004, Cryptology ePrint Archive.

Wang, H. C., & Chiu, Y. F. (2011). Assessing E-Learning 2.0 System Success. *Computers & Education*, *57*(2), 1790–1800. doi:10.1016/j.compedu.2011.03.009

Ward, M. (2014). Africa's digital revolution: Full speed ahead. *World Policy Blog*. Retrieved from http://www.worldpolicy.org/blog/2014/03/04/africas-digital-revolution-full-speed-ahead

Warkentin & Willison. (2009). "*Motivations for Employee Computer Crime: Understanding and Addressing Workplace Disgruntlement through the Application of Organizational Justice*". Retrieved on Dec 3rd, 2011, from http://scholar.googleusercontent.comscholar?q=cache:B4zLaLcU80QJ:scholar.google.com/+Warkentin+Willison,+2009+insider+threats&hl=en&as_sdt=0,44

Washington, Jesse (2011, October 23). STEM Education And Jobs: Declining Numbers Of Blacks Seen In Math, Science. *The Huffington Post*.

Wayne, K. H. (2003). An analysis of enabling and mindful school structures: Some theoretical, research and practical considerations. *Journal of Educational Administration*, *41*(1), 87–109. doi:10.1108/09578230310457457

Wei, X., Gomez, L., Neamtiu, I., & Faloutsos, M. (2012, April). Malicious android applications in the enterprise: What do they do and how do we fix it? In *Data Engineering Workshops (ICDEW), 2012 IEEE 28th International Conference on* (pp. 251-254). IEEE.

Weimerskirch, A., & Thonet, G. (2001). A Distributed Lightweight Authentication Model for Ad-hoc Networks. In the Proceedings of the 4th International Conference on Information Security and Cryptology (ICICS 2001) December 6-7 2001 Korea.

Weinreich, U. (1953). *Languages in contact*. The Hague: Mouton & Co.

Weirich, D., & Sasse, M. A. (2001, September). Pretty good persuasion: a first step towards effective password security in the real world. In *Proceedings of the 2001 workshop on New security paradigms* (pp. 137-143). ACM. doi:10.1145/508171.508195

Welch, D., & Lathrop, S. (2003, June). Wireless security threat taxonomy. In *Information Assurance Workshop* (pp. 76-83). IEEE.

Whalen, D. T., & Bell, G. (2014). The cybersecurity challenge. *NACD Directorship*, *40*(3), 75.

Whittaker, Z. (2012). *Sophos antivirus detects own update as false positive malware*. Retrieved Jan.05, 2013, from http://www.zdnet.com/sophos-antivirus-detects-own-update-as-false-positive-malware-7000004565/

Williams, K. (2007). Litigation against english NHS ambulance services and the rule in kent v. griffiths. *Medical Law Review*, *15*(2), 153–175. doi:10.1093/medlaw/fwm001 PMID:17517759

Winford, D. (2003). *An Introduction to Contact Linguistics*. Oxford: Wiley-Blackwell.

Witte, J. (2012) Author identification techniques, *Charter college, 4*:13-14.

Wolfe, D., & Logan, R. (2009). Public law and the provision of healthcare. *Judicial Review, 14*(2), 210-223. Retrieved from http://libezproxy.open.ac.uk/login?url=http://search.ebscohost.com/login.aspx?direct=true&db=a9h&AN=44834301&site=eds-live&scope=site

Wong, L. (2005). *Potential Bluetooth vulnerabilities in smartphones*. Retrieved from http://citeseerx.ist.psu.edu

Wong, S. J., Dras, M., & Johnson, M. (2011). Exploring Adaptor Grammars for Native Language Identification, (July), 699–709.

Wood, A. D., & Stankovic, J. A. (2002). Denial of Service in Sensor Networks. *Computer, 35*(10), 54–62. doi:10.1109/MC.2002.1039518

Workman, M. (2008). Wisecrackers: A Theory-Grounded Investigation of Phishing and Pretext Social Engineering Threats to Information Security. *Journal of the American Society for Information Science and Technology, 59*(4), 662–674. doi:10.1002/asi.20779

Wright, J., Dawson, M. E. Jr, & Omar, M. (2012). Cyber Security and Mobile Threats: The Need For Antivirus Applications For Smart Phones. *Journal of Information Systems Technology and Planning, 5*(14), 40–60.

Wright, R., Chakraborty, S., Basoglu, A., & Marett, K. (2010). Where did they go right? Understanding the deception in phishing communications. *Group Decision and Negotiation, 19*(4), 391–416. doi:10.1007/s10726-009-9167-9

Wu, M., Miller, R. C., & Garfinkel, S. L. (2006, April). Do security toolbars actually prevent phishing attacks?*InProceedings of the SIGCHI conference on Human Factors in computing systems* (pp. 601-610). ACM. doi:10.1145/1124772.1124863

Xianyong, M., & Yangmin, L. (2012, 6-8 June 2012). *A novel verifiable threshold signature scheme based on bilinear pairing in mobile Ad Hoc Network*. Paper presented at the International Conference on Information and Automation (ICIA), Shenyang.

Xie, L., Zhang, X., Chaugule, A., Jaeger, T., & Zhu, S. (2009). *Designing system-level defenses against cellphone malware*. Retrieved from www.cse.psu.edu

Xu, W., Wade, T., Yanyong, Z., & Timothy, W. (2005). The Feasibility of Launching and Detecting Jamming Attacks in Wireless Networks. In 6th ACM International Symposium on Mobile Ad Hoc Networking and Computing 2005. Urbana-Champaign, IL, USA: ACM Press pp. 46-57.

Yaar, A., Perrig, A., & Song, D. (2004). SIFF: A Stateless Internet Flow Filter to Mitigate DDoS Flooding Attacks. In the IEEE Security and Privacy Symposium. 2004. Philadelphia, Pennsylvania, USA ACM Press New York, NY, USA pp. 241-252. doi:10.1109/SECPRI.2004.1301320

Yan, L. K., & Yin, H. (2012). *DroidScope: Seamlessly Reconstructing the OS and Dalvik Semantic Views for Dynamic Android Malware Analysis*. Paper presented at the 21st USENIX Conference on Security Symposium.

Yang, Y., & Pedersen, J. O. (1997, July). A comparative study on feature selection in text categorization. In ICML (Vol. 97, pp. 412-420).

Yang, M., Kiang, M., Chen, H., & Li, Y. (2012). Artificial immune system for illicit content identification in social media. *Journal of the American Society for Information Science and Technology, 63*(2), 256–269.

Yang, S., & Wang, Y. (2011). System Dynamics Based Insider Threats Modeling. *International Journal of Network Security & Its Applications, 3*(3), 1–13. doi:10.5121/ijnsa.2011.3301

Yau, S. S., Wang, Y., & Karim, F. (2002). Development of Situation-Aware Application Software for Ubiquitous Computing Environment. In 26th International Computer Software and Applications Conference on Prolonging Software Life: Development and Redevelopment 2002: IEEE Computer Society. pp. 233-238. doi:10.1109/CMPSAC.2002.1044557

Yerima, S. Y., Sezer, S., McWilliams, G., & Muttik, I. (2013). *A New Android Malware Detection Approach Using Bayesian Classification*. Paper presented at the IEEE 27th International Conference on Advanced Information Networking and Applications (AINA), Barcelona. doi:10.1109/AINA.2013.88

Ye, Z. E., Smith, S., & Anthony, D. (2005). Trusted paths for browsers.[TISSEC]. *ACM Transactions on Information and System Security, 8*(2), 153–186. doi:10.1145/1065545.1065546

Yi, P., Dai, Z., Zhong, Y., & Zhang, S. (2005). Resisting Flooding Attacks in Ad Hoc Networks. In Proceedings of the International Conference on Information Technology: Coding and Computing (ITCC'05) 0-7695-2315-3/05, IEEE, 2005.

Ying, L., Dinglong, H., Haiyi, Z., & Rau, P. (2007). *Users' Perception of Mobile Information Security*. Hacker Journals White Papers.

Yin, L., Lien, N., & Werner, J. M. (2009). Learning in virtual groups: Identifying key aspects of a course management system affecting teamwork in an it training course. *Information Technology, Learning and Performance Journal, 25*(2), 30–41.

Yukl, G. (1994). *Leadership in organizations*. Upper Saddle River, NJ: Prentice Hall.

ZDNet. (2010). *Google fixes android root-access flaw*. Retrieved from ZDNet: www.zdnetasia.com

Zhang, Y., & Lee, W. (2000). Intrusion detection in wireless ad-hoc networks, The 6th Annual International Conference on Mobile Computing and Networking, pp. 275–283, 2000.

Zhang, Y., Hong, J. I., & Cranor, L. F. (2007, May). Cantina: a content-based approach to detecting phishing web sites. In *Proceedings of the 16th international conference on World Wide Web* (pp. 639-648). ACM. doi:10.1145/1242572.1242659

Zhao, Y. (2007). *Effective authorship attribution in large document collections*. PhD thesis, School of Computer Science and Information Technology, RMIT University, Melbourne, Aus content analysis. Biomedical informatics insights 2010.3 (2010): 19.

Zhao, M., Zhang, T., Ge, F., & Yuan, Z. (2012). RobotDroid: A Lightweight Malware Detection Framework On Smartphones. *Journal of Networks, 7*(4), 715–722. doi:10.4304/jnw.7.4.715-722

Zhao, Y., & Zobel, J. (2005). Effective and scalable authorship attribution using function words. In *Information Retrieval Technology* (pp. 174–189). Springer Berlin Heidelberg.

Zheng, R., Li, J., Chen, H., & Huang, Z. (2006). A framework for authorship identification of online messages: Writing-style features and classification techniques. *Journal of the American Society for Information Science and Technology, 57*(3), 378–393.

Zhou, Y., & Jiang, X. (2011). *An Analysis of the Anserver-Bot Trojan*. Retrieved Jan.10, 2013, from http://www.csc.ncsu.edu/faculty/jiang/pubs/AnserverBot_Analysis.pdf

Zhou, Y., & Jiang, X. (2012). *Dissecting Android Malware: Characterization and Evolution*. Paper presented at the Security and Privacy (SP), 2012 IEEE Symposium on. doi:10.1109/SP.2012.16

Zhou, L., & Haas, Z. J. (1999). *Securing Ad-hoc Networks. IEEE Networks, Special Issues on Network Security* (pp. 24–30). November/December.

Zhou, L., Schneider, F. B., & Renesse, R. V. (2002). COCA: A Secure Distributed On-line Certification Authority. *ACM Transactions on Computer Systems, 20*(4), 329–368. doi:10.1145/571637.571638

Zolkos, R., & Kenealy, B. (2014). Target tested by huge holiday data breach. *Business Insurance, 48*(1).

Zonouz, S., Houmansadr, A., Berthier, R., Borisov, N., & Sanders, W. (2013). Secloud: A cloud-based comprehensive and lightweight security solution for smartphones. *Computers & Security, 37*(0), 215–227. doi:10.1016/j.cose.2013.02.002

About the Contributors

Maurice Dawson serves as an Assistant Professor of Information Systems at University of Missouri-St. Louis, Visiting Assistant Professor (Honorary) of Industrial and Systems Engineering at The University of Tennessee Space Institute, and Fulbright. Dawson is recognized as an Information Assurance System Architect and Engineer by the U.S. Department of Defense. Research focus area is cyber security, systems security engineering, open source software (OSS), mobile security, and engineering management.

Marwan Omar serves as a full time faculty member of computer science and IT at Nawroz University, Duhok, Iraq. Omar is recognized for his information security expertise and knowledge and holds a security + certification from Comptia. Research interests are: cyber security, mobile security, open source software, and cloud computing.

* * *

Ryma Abassi has obtained a PhD degree in ICT from the Higher School of Communication of Tunis (Sup'Com) in March 2010. She obtained a master degree in Telecommunication from Sup'Com in December 2005 as well as an engineer diploma from the National Institute of Applied Science and Technology of Tunis (INSAT) in February 2004. Since September 2010, Dr Abassi is an assistant professor in the Higher Institute of Technological Studies in Communication of Tunis where she is responsible of several courses for the network security option. Dr Abassi's actual research interests include security policies modeling, validation, verification and test, XACML, XML updates, trust management, etc. Dr Abassi has published several papers in international journals and conferences.

Moutaz Alazab is an assistant professor at Isra University, department of information technology. He studied computer engineering from Al-Balqa Applied University in 2009 with thesis title "Designing and Implementing an Intelligent Wireless-Enabled Robot Car", and has a PhD in computer security from Deakin University, Australia in 2014. His PhD thesis entitled "Analysis on Smartphone Devices for Detection and Prevention of Malware" focused on cyber security including smartphone devices, data mining, cloud computing, big data and software systems. After getting his PhD, he was employed as an associate professor in Jordan, working in projects dealing with cyber-crime and a lecturer. He now teaches, Introduction to Computing, Computer Skills, Network Security, Computer Crime and Digital Forensic, Computer Architecture, Data Mining and Compilers and Translators. In 2012, he was in visiting the Stratsec/UniSA Winter School which take place in Adelaide. He worked as a System and Network administrator in Jordan and at the University of Ballarat, Australia. His research interests include mobile malware, computer malware, host and network intrusion detection system, mobile digital forensic, reverse engineer and mobile ad-hoc network. He has published research papers in different well-known international conferences and journals. He is regularly invited to give keynote and talks at different international conferences, research institutes and universities around the world.

Lukas Aron is a PhD student at Brno University of Technology Faculty of Information Technology. His research is about mobile security and he has been interested in the area of security for a few years. He is working on his privacy protection on mobile devices thesis.

Dustin Bessette is a doctoral candidate at the National Graduate School of Quality Management, located in Falmouth, MA. Academically, he is involved in scholarly research including publications in informatics, security, quality management, marketing and advertising, education, and career development. He currently has over 45 peer reviewed publications in scholarly journals, conference proceedings, and three published book chapters with three in review. Dustin is also a park ranger for Oregon Parks & Recreation Department, based at Fort Stevens State park and an adjunct faculty member at Post University.

Jonathan Bishop is an information technology executive, researcher and writer. He is the founder of the companies that form part of the Crocels Community Media Group, and founded the Centre for Research into Online Communities and E-Learning Systems in 2005 from which the group is named. Jonathan's research generally falls within human-computer interaction, and he has numerous publications in this area, such as on Internet trolling, gamification, Classroom 2.0, and multimedia forensics. In addition to his BSc(Hons) in Multimedia Studies and various postgraduate degrees, including in law, economics and computing, Jonathan has served in local government as a councillor and school governor, as well as having contested numerous elections. He is also a fellow of numerous learned bodies, including BCS - The Chartered Institute for IT, the Royal Anthropological Institute, and the Royal Society of Arts. Jonathan has won prizes for his literary skills and been a finalist in national and local competitions for his environmental, community and equality work, which often form part of action research studies. In his spare time Jonathan enjoys listening to music, swimming and chess.

Kim L. Brown-Jackson, ABD, MBS, CQIA, DTM, CTC has over 18 years of leadership expertise in quality, training, program, project, and curriculum management. Previously she was the director for product development in a financial management division for a training company. She has also been a learning and human capital strategist and project manager. Brown-Jackson holds certifications in Kirkpatrick Four Levels Evaluation, quality improvement (CQIA) and greenbelt experience, advanced instructional design/development, leadership, performance management, and diversity. Academically, Brown-Jackson is a doctoral student and adjunct faculty for The National Graduate School – Quality Management. She holds a MSc. in Biomedical Sciences with additional coursework towards a Ph.D. and holds a MBA certificate. She holds a B.A. in Biological Sciences from Clemson University, cluster minor in Business Administration and language emphasis- Japanese. Brown-Jackson received a National Science Foundation Fellowship. She holds an A.S. in Biotechnology and Forensic Science from Massachusetts Bay Community College (joint ventures at Boston University/University of Massachusetts). Brown-Jackson has prior experience as a scientist, corporate trainer, business/financial analyst, information consultant; human/ financial resources. Kim L. Brown-Jackson was featured in the April 2013 edition of American Society of Quality, Quality Progress Journal as the Who's Who in Q. She has co-published in the Journal of Applied

Learning Technologies and Cancer Research. Brown-Jackson has co-authored and/or virtually presented at over 18 academic conferences proceedings, contributed to academic book chapters, and co-written journal articles, in the USA and in Madrid, Barcelona, and Valencia, Spain. View publications on researchgate.net and academia.edu. She served as peer reviewer for Academy of Management Annual Meeting, Academic Business World and the International Conference on Learning and Administration in Higher Education, Informing Science + International Journal of Doctoral Studies, + IT Education Conferences, and Journal of Educational Research and Reviews for Scienceweb Publishing.

Darrell Norman Burrell is currently a faculty member and the academic site director for the Florida Institute of Technology's Fort Lee Virginia satellite campus at the US Army Logistics University where the university offers specialized graduate degrees for military officers and has done so since 1973. He is a certified executive and career coach. Dr. Burrell is a certified diversity specialist. Dr. Burrell is an alumnus of the Presidential Management Fellows Program (PMF). He was competitively selected as a Presidential Management Fellow in 2006 through a rigorous application process from a pool of over 7,100 applicants. Through the PMF, Dr. Burrell was appointed to serve as a government training and development executive with the US Nuclear Regulatory Commission, which regulates the commercial and academic uses of nuclear power in the United States. At the US Nuclear Regulatory Commission, he developed leadership programs for scientists and engineers in junior and senior supervisory roles. He has over 18 years of human resources management experience in academia, government, and private industry. Dr Burrell received a doctoral degree in Health Education with majors in Environmental Public Health and Executive Leadership Coaching from A.T. Still University in 2010. He has graduate degrees (2) in Human Resources Management/Development and Organizational Management in Health Care Leadership from National Louis University. He has a 4th graduate degree in Sales and Marketing Management from Prescott College. He also has a graduate degree in Higher Education Administration from the Graduate School of Education and Human Development at The George Washington University. He has over 13 years of college teaching experience with several universities including the George Mason University, The University of Virginia, Averett University in VA, Marylhurst University in OR, Webster University in DC, and the University of Liverpool in the UK. Dr. Burrell has over 70 publications and over 45 peer reviewed conference presentations.

Sharon L. Burton serves as the Director of Publishing Initiatives at American Meridian University. In support of academic excellence, she is published in over 25 conference proceedings. Two books are published under her name, *Quality Customer Service; Rekindling the Art of Service to Customers,* and *Diversity: Just What Is It And Why Does It Keep Changing?* She has had four journal articles accepted for publishing, and five textbook chapters. Dr. Burton's writings are in the areas of Andragogy (adult learning), Quality Systems Management, Diversity and Inclusion, Quality Customer Service, Training and Development, and CyberSecurity. Publications are registered with scholar.google.com, researchgate. net, and academia.edu. Dr. Burton is an advocate for the rights of the people. She is a mentor and an adviser. She guides leaders of all levels to achieve their individual bests.

Paul Cairns is a Reader in Human-Computer Interaction at the Universityof York. He has a long-standing interest in human-computer interaction and has focused particularly on the study of human error. He was formerly at UCL where,with Anna Cox, he produced the first book on Research Methods for Human-Computer Interaction.

John Clark, Professor of Critical Systems, MA Maths (Oxon), MSc Applies Statistics (Oxon), PhD in Computer Science (York). Deputy Head of Department (Responsible for Research) Computer Science Department, University of York (2009-2015)..

Aikyna Finch is a university dean and professor. She holds a Doctorate in Management and 2 M.B.A.s from Colorado Technical University, a MSM in Marketing from Strayer University and a Bachelor of Science degree from the School of Engineering of Tennessee State University. Dr. Finch has published several articles in the areas of Business and Education.

Ronnie S. Kurlander, Assistant Vice President of Global Technology Services at T. Rowe Price.

Jane LeClair is the Chief Operating Officer of the National Cybersecurity Institute (NCI) at Excelsior College in Washington, D.C., whose mission is to serve as an academic and research center dedicated to increasing the knowledge of the cybersecurity discipline. Dr. LeClair served as Dean of the School of Business and Technology at Excelsior College in Albany, NY prior to assuming her current position. She has extensive managerial experience in the energy industry and is a consultant with the International Atomic Energy Agency. Her new book 'Protecting Our Future: Educating a Cybersecurity Workforce' was published in December 2013.

Brian Leonard, J.D., LL.M., serves as an Assistant Professor of Business Law. He holds a Bachelor's of Business Administration (B.B.A.) in Accounting from Tennessee State University, a Juris Doctor (J.D.) from the Cumberland School of Law of Samford University, and a Master of Laws (LL.M.) in Taxation Law from the University of Alabama School of Law. He passed the bar in Alabama, North Carolina, and Tennessee. He practiced law for several years first in private practice and then as a local government attorney. His area of research is employment, labor, and civil rights law. His research has been published in the Journal of Employment and Labor Law. His research was also published in the book: Technology, Innovation, and Enterprise Transformation, (Wadhwa and Harper, 2014, by IGI-Global).

Shanel Lu is an operational support professional for a financial banking institution. She executes organizational goals that sustain operational excellence through change management and workforce strategy. Lu's latest project is spearheading the research and development of custom-built in-house workforce staffing endeavors. This effort includes analyzing workforce balancing and allocation, and then consulting with senior operational leaders to strategize their workforce. Academically, Lu is a Doctoral student earning a Doctorate of Business Administration (DBA) in Quality Management from National Graduate School in Falmouth, MA. She plans to use her academic and practical experiences to support public service efforts through community outreach programs. She recognizes that quality is vital in all industries and desires to center her career on quality initiatives that will optimize more efficient processes operations. Lu believes strongly in community outreach. She is an active member of the American Asian Government Executive Network, AAGEN. Lu supports the vision and mission to uplift the community through academic and professional excellence. As a facilitator and secretary of AAGEN's Annual Leadership Workshop and Banquet, she manages weekly stakeholder meetings that ensure quality execution and delivery of service. Lu's most passionate service is mentorship and coaching. She believes that villages are created to uplift and provide pathways for future generations of emerging scholars and leaders.

Rondalynne McClintock, leveraging organizational learning, training development, electronic learning, distance education, and mobile learning to serve as an education delivery team member. Offer 19 years' experience in organizational education, adult learning, and curriculum development as part of conducting employee training, distance learning and internal consulting. With a unique combination of business, technology, leadership, and research skills, provide a well-rounded approach to teaching and training adults at all levels. Encourage and support the open exchange of ideas to keep students engaged, motivated, and committed to the learning process. Excellent ability to learn new technologies quickly. Cognizant of PCI compliance and personal information management security guidelines and principals. Ph.D. in Information Systems expected May 2016, Claremont Graduate University. Certified Leadership Trainer.

Ivan Mugabi is a lawyer by professional background with three degrees in law. Namely is a Bachelor's Degree in law LLB (Hons.), a master's degree in International Commercial law (LLM International Commercial law), a master's degree in Human Rights law (LLM Human Rights law). I must admit that my enthusiasm for research stretched from my second year of the law school, when I embarked on a legal internship with a Law Chamber with senior Advocates. This exposed me to research skills and I gained in depth knowledge of both the substantive and procedural aspects more especially from the context of the administrative law perspective. I also embraced a research project towards the climax of my first Master's degree at the University of South Wales. Perhaps it is fair to admit that this undertaking was of course challenging but also a changing experience that improved my knowledge and experience of law through involvement with Crocels under the auspices of my long term colleague Jonathan Bishop to whom I am highly indebted for his relentless efforts and unwavering inspiration in this regard. This piece of writing shall in various ways contribute to the epistemological and ontological discourses. Particularly illuminating narratives of how the criminal and civil laws could interact with the virtual or online world in our contemporary World at national, regional and international settings.

Marwan Omar serves as a full time faculty member of computer science and IT at Nawroz University, Duhok, Iraq. Omar is recognized for his information security expertise and knowledge and holds a security + certification from Comptia. Research interests are: cyber security, mobile security, open source software, and cloud computing.

Ria Perkins is a research and teaching associate at the Centre for Forensic Linguistics, Aston University, Birmingham UK. Her research has focused predominantly on native language identification and the linguistics of persuasion. Her research interests include; interlanguage, authorship analysis, computer mediated communication, persuasion, sociolinguistics, and the application of forensic linguistics to intelligence investigations. She also consults as a forensic linguist.

Rasha Salah El-Din is an assistant lecturer at Computer Science department, Sadat Academy for Management Sciences. She is currently pursing a PhD degree from University of York, UK. Her research investigates humans' vulnerability to phishing attacks and the ethics of conducting phishing experiments. Her scholarly interests range around the ethical and legal challenges that face vulnerability researchers in general and phishing researchers in particular. Ms Salah El-Din comes from an advanced academic and analytical background with more than 9 years teaching experience in academia. She has also worked in Telecommunications industry for four years, an experience that helped shaping her research directions where she got inspired by the mobile technology and had her Masters in mobile communications. Her thesis was the first among Egyptian Universities to tackle the topic of Wireless Application Protocol that was relatively new at that time.

Arif Sari, born October 21 1986 in Nicosia (Northern Cyprus), is a full time instructor of the department of Management Information Systems at the European University of Lefke, North Cyprus. He received his BS degree - in Computer Information Systems and MBA degree - (2008 and 2010) at European University of Lefke, and Ph.D. degree (2013) in Management Information Systems at The American University. He is an IEEE, ACM, and IEICE Member since Sept. 2012 and has published various papers, book chapters, participated in variety of conferences in the fields of Network Security, Network Simulation, Computer Applications, Mobile Networks, Information Communication Technologies, Mobile Network Security and Mobile Security Systems. His research interests include Network Security, Mobile and Wireless Networks, Network Simulations, Security and Cryptography and Radio Frequency Identification Systems. He is reviewer of many international journals and refereed conferences.

Janet Simmons is the President and CEO of Innovative Global Security Solutions, LLC. (IGSS), a Cybersecurity and Information Technology, and Telecommunication company. She retired from the United States Army as a Military Intelligence Officer after 20 years of service, culminating her service as the Battalion Commander of 3,500 Soldiers of the Headquarters Battalion, Fort Belvoir, Virginia. She is a recipient of the 25 Influential Women in Business Award; Maryland Top 100 Women Award; 50 Women of Power Award; and numerous other civilian awards to include the Presidential Service Award and military awards to include the Army's Legion of Merit and Parachutist Badge. Lady Janet is a graduate of South Carolina State University (B.S. in Criminal Justice); Central Michigan University (M.S. in Administration); and is currently pursuing her Doctor of Business Administration from The National Graduate School of Quality Management. She is involved in several non-profit organizations, where she focuses on coaching and mentoring teen girls.

Randall Sylvertooth is a career industry cybersecurity subject matter expert (SME), and is currently working as a contractor for the U.S. Government in various management and leadership capacities. Mr. Sylvertooth is serving academia in many ways; he is currently contributing as an adjunct professor and advisor for the University of Virginia's School of Continuing and Professional Studies (SCPS), Cyber Security Management Program and as an assistant professor teaching at The University of Maryland University College (UMUC) Cybersecurity Program. Mr. Sylvertooth holds two Masters degrees, one in The Management of Information Technology from the University of Virginia's McIntire School of Commerce and the second Master's degree in Information Security and Insurance (Cybersecurity) from George Mason University's Volgenau School of Engineering. Mr. Sylvertooth is currently working on his Doctorate of Science degree at Capitol Technology University (formerly Capitol College). Mr. Sylvertooth is currently serving as a National Cybersecurity Institute Fellow.

Clishia Taylor, President of American Health Care Professionals (AHCP) and Global Health Awards/Access (GHA). Editor in chief of Health Care Pulse Ezine a 21st century health care magazine. She lives in the Washington DC area and is a author of Implementing Wellness Programs in Faith Based Communties. She serves on many White House initiatives and is a USA lobbyists for both the House and Senate. A graduate from College of New Rochelle with a BSN, University of Connecticut MBA and Assemblies of God Theological Seminary with a doctoral in Health Care Ministries.

Sabu Thampi is an Associate Professor at Indian Institute of Information Technology and Management - Kerala (IIITM-K), Technopark Campus, Trivandrum, Kerala State, India. He is the group leader of intelligence and security informatics research group at IIITM-K. He has completed Ph.D in Computer Engineering from National Institute of Technology Karnataka. Sabu has several years of teaching and research experience in various institutions in India. His research interests include network security, terrorism informatics, bio-inspired computing, authorship analysis, clustering in very large databases, image forensics, video surveillance, cloud security, secure information sharing, secure localization, distributed computing etc.... He has authored and edited few books published by reputed international publishers and published papers in academic journals and international and national proceedings. Sabu has served as Guest Editor for special issues in few international journals and program committee member for many international conferences and workshops. He has co-chaired several international workshops and conferences. He is the founder of International Conference on Advances in Computing, Communications and Informatics (ICACCI). He is serving as reviewer and editorial board member of few international journals. Sabu is the founding Editor-in-Chief of two journals - International Journal of Trust Management in Computing and Communications (IJTMCC) and International Journal of Humanitarian Technology (IJHT), Inder Science Publishers, UK. Sabu is a Senior Member of Institute of Electrical and Electronics Engineers(IEEE) and member of IEEE Communications Society, IEEE CIS, IEEE SMCS, ACM, ISTE etc... Currently, he is the Chairman of ACM Trivandrum Chapter. He was honored with the ASDF Award for Best Computer Science Faculty in 2012.

Darryl Williams is currently a PhD student in Finance at Walden University with several years of professional experience as a financial advisor, researcher, business owner, in addition to consulting. His academic exposure as a college instructor in business administration has helped students and professionals become financially disciplined and well versed in social economic matters. As licensed professional, he speaks at public functions, seminars, and workshops.

Jorja Wright is an MBA graduate at Nathan M. Bisk College of Business at Florida Institute of Technology, concentrating on healthcare management. She earned her Bachelor's degree in Biology from University of Alabama-Huntsville in 2011. For the past two years, Ms. Wright has published various peer-reviewed articles and conference proceedings on cybersecurity, information technology (IT), health IT, and healthcare management. Additionally, she is a member of National Society of Leadership and Success, Intellectbase International Consortium, Alabama Academy of Sciences, American Telemedicine Association, and a Huntsville Hospital Volunteer. Her research interest aims to understand how diversity and inclusion in healthcare leadership can positively improve patient care.

Index

Information Resources Management Association

Become an IRMA Member

Members of the **Information Resources Management Association (IRMA)** understand the importance of community within their field of study. The Information Resources Management Association is an ideal venue through which professionals, students, and academicians can convene and share the latest industry innovations and scholarly research that is changing the field of information science and technology. Become a member today and enjoy the benefits of membership as well as the opportunity to collaborate and network with fellow experts in the field.

IRMA Membership Benefits:

- **One FREE Journal Subscription**

- **30% Off Additional Journal Subscriptions**

- **20% Off Book Purchases**

- Updates on the latest events and research on Information Resources Management through the IRMA-L listserv.

- Updates on new open access and downloadable content added to Research IRM.

- A copy of the Information Technology Management Newsletter twice a year.

- A certificate of membership.

IRMA Membership $195

Scan code to visit irma-international.org and begin by selecting your free journal subscription.

Membership is good for one full year.

Printed in the United States
By Bookmasters